3/23/93

Information Retrieval

Data Structures
& Algorithms

Edited by

William B. Frakes
Software Engineering Guild

Ricardo Baeza-Yates
University of Chile

 Prentice Hall, Englewood Cliffs, New Jersey 07632

Library of Congress Cataloging-in-Publication Data

Information retrieval : data structures and algorithms / edited by
  William B. Frakes, Ricardo Baeza-Yates.
    p.   cm.
  Includes bibliographical references and index.
  ISBN 0-13-463837-9
  1. Data structures (Computer science).   2. Computer algorithms.
  I. Frakes, William B. (William Bruce), 1952–   II. Baeza-Yates,
  R. (Ricardo)
  QA76.9.D351543   1992
  005—dc20

92-8197
CIP

Editorial production		**Copy editor:** *Karen Verde*	
and interior design: *bookworks*		**Editor-in-Chief:** *Bernard Goodwin*	
Acquisitions editor: *Greg Doench*		**Prepress buyer:** *Mary McCartney*	
Managing editor: *Sophie Papanikolaou*		**Manufacturing buyer:** *Susan Brunke*	
Cover designer: *Bruce Kenselaar*		**Indexer:** *Word Finders*	

Cover art credited to: Piet Mondrian. Composition in Brown and Gray. (1913–14). Oil on canvas.
$33\frac{3}{4} \times 29\frac{3}{4}$". Collection, the Museum of Modern Art, New York. Purchase.
Photograph © 1993 The Museum of Modern Art, New York.

© 1992 by Prentice Hall
A division of Simon & Schuster
Englewood Cliffs, New Jersey 07632

The publisher offers discounts on this book when ordered in bulk quantities. For more information write:
  Special Sales/College Marketing
  Prentice Hall
  College Technical and Reference Division
  Englewood Cliffs, New Jersey 07632

Printed in the United States of America

10 9 8 7 6 5 4 3 2 1

ISBN   0-13-463837-9

Prentice-Hall International (UK) Limited, *London*
Prentice-Hall of Australia Pty. Limited, *Sydney*
Prentice-Hall Canada, Inc., *Toronto*
Prentice-Hall Hispanoamericana S.A., *Mexico*
Prentice-Hall of India Private Limited, *New Delhi*
Prentice-Hall of Japan, Inc., *Tokyo*
Simon & Schuster Asia Pte. Ltd., *Singapore*
Editora Prentice-Hall do Brasil, Ltda., *Rio de Janeiro*

Contents

Foreword

Udi Manber

Department of Computer Science, University of Arizona

In the not-so-long ago past, information retrieval meant going to the town's library and asking the librarian for help. The librarian usually knew all the books in his possession, and could give one a definite, although often negative, answer. As the number of books grew—and with them the number of libraries and librarians—it became impossible for one person or any group of persons to possess so much information. Tools for information retrieval had to be devised. The most important of these tools is the *index*—a collection of terms with pointers to places where information about them can be found. The terms can be subject matters, author names, call numbers, etc., but the structure of the index is essentially the same. Indexes are usually placed at the end of a book, or in another form, implemented as card catalogs in a library. The Sumerian literary catalogue, of c. 2000 B.C., is probably the first list of books ever written. Book indexes had appeared in a primitive form in the 16th century, and by the 18th century some were similar to today's indexes. Given the incredible technology advances in the last 200 years, it is quite surprising that today, for the vast majority of people, an index, or a hierarchy of indexes, is still the only available tool for information retrieval! Furthermore, at least from my experience, many book indexes are not of high quality. Writing a good index is still more a matter of experience and art than a precise science.

Why do most people still use 18th century technology today? It is not because there are no other methods or no new technology. I believe that the main reason is simple: Indexes work. They are extremely simple and effective to use for small to medium-size data. As President Reagan was fond of saying "if it ain't broke, don't fix it." We read books in essentially the same way we did in the 18th century, we walk the same way (most people don't use small wheels, for example, for walking, although it is technologically feasible), and some people argue that we teach our students in the same way. There is a great comfort in not having to learn something new to perform an old task. However, with the information explosion just upon us, "it" is about to be broken. We not only have an immensely greater amount of information from which to retrieve, we also have much more complicated needs. Faster computers, larger capacity high-speed data storage devices, and higher bandwidth networks will all come along, but they will not be enough. We will need better techniques for storing, accessing, querying, and manipulating information.

It is doubtful that in our lifetime most people will read books, say, from a notebook computer, that people will have rockets attached to their backs, or that teaching will take a radical new form (I dare not even venture what form), but it is likely that information will be retrieved in many new ways, but many more people, and on a grander scale.

I exaggerated, of course, when I said that we are still using ancient technology for information retrieval. The basic concept of indexes—searching by keywords—may be the same, but the implementation is a world apart from the Sumerian clay tablets. And information retrieval of today, aided by computers, is not limited to search by keywords. Numerous techniques have been developed in the last 30 years, many of which are described in this book. There are efficient data structures to store indexes, sophisticated query algorithms to search quickly, data compression methods, and special hardware, to name just a few areas of extraordinary advances. Considerable progress has been made for even seemingly elementary problems, such as how to find a given pattern in a large text with or without preprocessing the text. Although most people do not yet enjoy the power of computerized search, and those who do cry for better and more powerful methods, we expect major changes in the next 10 years or even sooner. The wonderful mix of issues presented in this collection, from theory to practice, from software to hardware, is sure to be of great help to anyone with interest in information retrieval.

An editorial in the Australian Library Journal in 1974 states that "the history of cataloging is exceptional in that it is endlessly repetitive. Each generation rethinks and reformulates the same basic problems, reframing them in new contexts and restating them in new terminology." The history of computerized cataloging is still too young to be in a cycle, and the problems it faces may be old in origin but new in scale and complexity. Information retrieval, as is evident from this book, has grown into a broad area of study. I dare to predict that it will prosper. Oliver Wendell Holmes wrote in 1872 that "It is the province of knowledge to speak and it is the privilege of wisdom to listen." Maybe, just maybe, we will also be able to say in the future that it is the province of knowledge to write and it is the privilege of wisdom to query.

Preface

Text is the primary way that human knowledge is stored, and after speech, the primary way it is transmitted. Techniques for storing and searching for textual documents are nearly as old as written language itself. Computing, however, has changed the ways text is stored, searched, and retrieved. In traditional library indexing, for example, documents could only be accessed by a small number of index terms such as title, author, and a few subject headings. With automated systems, the number of indexing terms that can be used for an item is virtually limitless.

The subfield of computer science that deals with the automated storage and retrieval of documents is called information retrieval (IR). Automated IR systems were originally developed to help manage the huge scientific literature that has developed since the 1940s, and this is still the most common use of IR systems. IR systems are in widespread use in university, corporate, and public libraries. IR techniques have also been found useful, however, in such disparate areas as office automation and software engineering. Indeed, any field that relies on documents to do its work could potentially benefit from IR techniques.

IR shares concerns with many other computer subdisciplines, such as artificial intelligence, multimedia systems, parallel computing, and human factors. Yet, in our observation, IR is not widely known in the computer science community. It is often confused with DBMS—a field with which it shares concerns and yet from which it is distinct. We hope that this book will make IR techniques more widely known and used.

Data structures and algorithms are fundamental to computer science. Yet, despite a large IR literature, the basic data structures and algorithms of IR have never been collected in a book. This is the need that we are attempting to fill. In discussing IR data structures and algorithms, we attempt to be evaluative as well as descriptive. We discuss relevant empirical studies that have compared the algorithms and data structures, and some of the most important algorithms are presented in detail, including implementations in C.

Our primary audience is software engineers building systems with text processing components. Students of computer science, information science, library science, and other disciplines who are interested in text retrieval technology should also find the book useful. Finally, we hope that information retrieval researchers will use the book as a basis for future research.

Bill Frakes
Ricardo Baeza-Yates

ACKNOWLEDGEMENTS

Many people improved this book with their reviews. The authors of the chapters did considerable reviewing of each others' work. Other reviewers include Jim Kirby, Jim O'Connor, Fred Hills, Gloria Hasslacher, and Ruben Prieto-Diaz. All of them have our thanks. Special thanks to Chris Fox, who tested The Code on the disk that accompanies the book; to Steve Wartik for his patient unravelling of many Latex puzzles; and to Donna Harman for her helpful suggestions.

1

Introduction to Information Storage and Retrieval Systems

W. B. Frakes

Software Engineering Guild
Sterling, VA 22170

Abstract

This chapter introduces and defines basic IR concepts, and presents a domain model of IR systems that describes their similarities and differences. The domain model is used to introduce and relate the chapters that follow. The relationship of IR systems to other information systems is discussed, as is the evaluation of IR systems.

1.1 INTRODUCTION

Automated information retrieval (IR) systems were originally developed to help manage the huge scientific literature that has developed since the 1940s. Many university, corporate, and public libraries now use IR systems to provide access to books, journals, and other documents. Commercial IR systems offer databases containing millions of documents in myriad subject areas. Dictionary and encyclopedia databases are now widely available for PCs. IR has been found useful in such disparate areas as office automation and software engineering. Indeed, any discipline that relies on documents to do its work could potentially use and benefit from IR.

This book is about the data structures and algorithms needed to build IR systems. An IR system matches user *queries*—formal statements of information needs—to documents stored in a database. A document is a data object, usually textual, though it may also contain other types of data such as photographs, graphs, and so on. Often, the documents themselves are not stored directly in the IR system, but are represented in the system by document surrogates. This chapter, for example, is a document and could be stored in its entirety in an IR database. One might instead, however, choose to create a document surrogate for it consisting of the title, author, and abstract. This is typically done for efficiency, that is, to reduce the size of the database and searching time. Document surrogates are also called documents, and in the rest of the book we will use *document* to denote both documents and document surrogates.

An IR system must support certain basic operations. There must be a way to enter documents into a database, change the documents, and delete them. There must also be some way to search for documents, and present them to a user. As the following chapters illustrate, IR systems vary greatly in the ways they accomplish these tasks. In the next section, the similarities and differences among IR systems are discussed.

1.2 A DOMAIN ANALYSIS OF IR SYSTEMS

This book contains many data structures, algorithms, and techniques. In order to find, understand, and use them effectively, it is necessary to have a conceptual framework for them. Domain analysis—systems analysis for multiple related systems—described in Prieto-Diaz and Arrango (1991), is a method for developing such a framework. Via domain analysis, one attempts to discover and record the similarities and differences among related systems.

The first steps in domain analysis are to identify important concepts and vocabulary in the domain, define them, and organize them with a faceted classification. Table 1.1 is a faceted classification for IR systems, containing important IR concepts and vocabulary. The first row of the table specifies the facets—that is, the attributes that IR systems share. Facets represent the parts of IR systems that will tend to be constant from system to system. For example, all IR systems must have a database structure—they vary in the database structures they have; some have inverted file structures, some have flat file structures, and so on.

A given IR system can be classified by the facets and facet values, called terms, that it has. For example, the CATALOG system (Frakes 1984) discussed in Chapter 8 can be classified as shown in Table 1.2.

Terms within a facet are not mutually exclusive, and more than one term from a facet can be used for a given system. Some decisions constrain others. If one

Table 1.1 Faceted Classification of IR Systems
(numbers in parentheses indicate chapters)

Conceptual Model	File Structure	Query Operations	Term Operations	Document Operations	Hardware
Boolean(1)	Flat File(10)	Feedback(11)	Stem(8)	Parse(3,7)	vonNeumann(1)
Extended Boolean(15)	Inverted File(3)	Parse(3,7)	Weight(14)	Display	Parallel(18)
Probabilistic(14)	Signature(4)	Boolean(12)	Thesaurus(9)	Cluster(16)	IR Specific(17)
String Search(10)	Pat Trees(5)	Cluster(16)	Stoplist(7)	Rank(14)	Optical Disk(6)
Vector Space(14)	Graphs(1)		Truncation(10)	Sort(1)	Mag. Disk(1)
	Hashing(13)			Field Mask(1)	
				Assign IDs(3)	

Table 1.2 Facets and Terms for CATALOG IR System

Facets	Terms
File Structure	Inverted file
Query Operations	Parse, Boolean
Term Operations	Stem, Stoplist, Truncation
Hardware	von Neumann, Mag. Disk
Document Operations	parse, display, sort, field mask, assign IDs
Conceptual Model	Boolean

chooses a Boolean conceptual model, for example, then one must choose a parse method for queries.

Viewed another way, each facet is a design decision point in developing the architecture for an IR system. The system designer must choose, for each facet, from the alternative terms for that facet. We will now discuss the facets and their terms in greater detail.

1.2.1 Conceptual Models of IR

The most general facet in the previous classification scheme is *conceptual model*. An IR conceptual model is a general approach to IR systems. Several taxonomies for IR conceptual models have been proposed. Faloutsos (1985) gives three basic approaches: text pattern search, inverted file search, and signature search. Belkin and Croft (1987) categorize IR conceptual models differently. They divide retrieval techniques first into exact match and inexact match. The exact match category contains text pattern search and Boolean search techniques. The inexact match category contains such techniques as probabilistic, vector space, and clustering, among others. The problem with these taxonomies is that the categories are not mutually exclusive, and a single system may contain aspects of many of them.

Almost all of the IR systems fielded today are either Boolean IR systems or text pattern search systems. Text pattern search queries are strings or regular expressions. Text pattern systems are more common for searching small collections, such as personal collections of files. The grep family of tools, described in Earhart (1986), in the UNIX environment is a well-known example of text pattern searchers. Data structures and algorithms for text pattern searching are discussed in Chapter 10.

Almost all of the IR systems for searching large document collections are Boolean systems. In a Boolean IR system, documents are represented by sets of keywords, usually stored in an inverted file. An inverted file is a list of keywords and identifiers of the documents in which they occur. Boolean list operations are discussed in Chapter 12. Boolean queries are keywords connected with Boolean logical operators (AND, OR, NOT). While Boolean systems have been criticized (see Belkin and Croft [1987] for a summary), improving their retrieval effectiveness has been difficult. Some extensions to the Boolean model that may improve IR performance are discussed in Chapter 15.

Researchers have also tried to improve IR performance by using information about the statistical distribution of terms, that is the frequencies with which terms occur in documents, document collections, or subsets of document collections such as documents considered relevant to a query. Term distributions are exploited within the context of some statistical model such as the vector space model, the probabilistic model, or the clustering model. These are discussed in Belkin and Croft (1987). Using these probabilistic models and information about term distributions, it is possible to assign a probability of relevance to each document in a retrieved set allowing retrieved documents to be ranked in order of probable relevance. Ranking is useful because of the large document sets that are often retrieved. Ranking algorithms using the vector space model and the probabilistic model are discussed in Chapter 14. Ranking algorithms that use information about previous searches to modify queries are discussed in Chapter 11 on relevance feedback.

In addition to the ranking algorithms discussed in Chapter 14, it is possible to group (cluster) documents based on the terms that they contain and to retrieve from these groups using a ranking methodology. Methods for clustering documents and retrieving from these clusters are discussed in Chapter 16.

1.2.2 File Structures

A fundamental decision in the design of IR systems is which type of file structure to use for the underlying document database. As can be seen in Table 1.1, the file structures used in IR systems are flat files, inverted files, signature files, PAT trees, and graphs. Though it is possible to keep file structures in main memory, in practice IR databases are usually stored on disk because of their size.

Using a flat file approach, one or more documents are stored in a file, usually as ASCII or EBCDIC text. Flat file searching (Chapter 10) is usually done via pattern matching. On UNIX, for example, one can store a document collection one per file in a UNIX directory, and search it using pattern searching tools such as grep (Earhart 1986) or awk (Aho, Kernighan, and Weinberger 1988).

An inverted file (Chapter 3) is a kind of indexed file. The structure of an inverted file entry is usually keyword, document-ID, field-ID. A keyword is an indexing term that describes the document, document-ID is a unique identifier for a document, and field-ID is a unique name that indicates from which field in the document the keyword came. Some systems also include information about the paragraph and sentence location where the term occurs. Searching is done by looking up query terms in the inverted file.

Signature files (Chapter 4) contain signatures—bit patterns—that represent documents. There are various ways of constructing signatures. Using one common signature method, for example, documents are split into logical blocks each containing a fixed number of distinct significant, that is, non-stoplist (see below), words. Each word in the block is hashed to give a signature—a bit pattern with some of the bits set to 1. The signatures of each word in a block are OR'ed together to create a block signature. The block signatures are then concatenated to produce the document signature. Searching is done by comparing the signatures of queries with document signatures.

PAT trees (Chapter 5) are Patricia trees constructed over all *sistrings* in a text. If a document collection is viewed as a sequentially numbered array of characters, a sistring is a subsequence of characters from the array starting at a given point and extending an arbitrary distance to the right. A Patricia tree is a digital tree where the individual bits of the keys are used to decide branching.

Graphs, or networks, are ordered collections of nodes connected by arcs. They can be used to represent documents in various ways. For example, a kind of graph called a semantic net can be used to represent the semantic relationships in text often lost in the indexing systems above. Although interesting, graph-based techniques for IR are impractical now because of the amount of manual effort that would be needed to represent a large document collection in this form. Since graph-based approaches are currently impractical, we have not covered them in detail in this book.

1.2.3 Query Operations

Queries are formal statements of information needs put to the IR system by users. The operations on queries are obviously a function of the type of query, and the capabilities of the IR system. One common query operation is parsing (Chapters 3 and 7), that is breaking the query into its constituent elements. Boolean queries, for example, must be parsed into their constituent terms and operators. The set of document identifiers associated with each query term is retrieved, and the sets are then combined according to the Boolean operators (Chapter 12).

In feedback (Chapter 11), information from previous searches is used to modify queries. For example, terms from relevant documents found by a query may be added to the query, and terms from nonrelevant documents deleted. There is some evidence that feedback can significantly improve IR performance.

1.2.4 Term Operations

Operations on terms in an IR system include stemming (Chapter 8), truncation (Chapter 10), weighting (Chapter 14), and stoplist (Chapter 7) and thesaurus (Chapter 9) operations. Stemming is the automated conflation (fusing or combining) of related words, usually by reducing the words to a common root form. Truncation is manual conflation of terms by using wildcard characters in the word, so that the truncated term will match multiple words. For example, a searcher interested in finding documents about truncation might enter the term "truncat?" which would match terms such as truncate, truncated, and truncation. Another way of conflating related terms is with a thesaurus which lists synonymous terms, and sometimes the relationships among them. A stoplist is a list of words considered to have no indexing value, used to eliminate potential indexing terms. Each potential indexing term is checked against the stoplist and eliminated if found there.

In term weighting, indexing or query terms are assigned numerical values usually based on information about the statistical distribution of terms, that is, the frequencies with which terms occur in documents, document collections, or subsets of document collections such as documents considered relevant to a query.

1.2.5 Document Operations

Documents are the primary objects in IR systems and there are many operations for them. In many types of IR systems, documents added to a database must be given unique identifiers, parsed into their constituent fields, and those fields broken into field identifiers and terms. Once in the database, one sometimes wishes to mask off certain fields for searching and display. For example, the searcher may wish to search only the title and abstract fields of documents for a given query, or may wish to see only the title and author of retrieved documents. One may also wish to sort retrieved documents by some field, for example by author. There are many sorting algorithms and because of the generality of the subject we have not covered it in this book. A good description of sorting algorithms in C can be found in Sedgewick (1990). Display operations include printing the documents, and displaying them on a CRT.

Using information about term distributions, it is possible to assign a probability of relevance to each document in a retrieved set, allowing retrieved documents to be ranked in order of probable relevance (Chapter 14). Term distribution information can also be used to cluster similar documents in a document space (Chapter 16).

Another important document operation is display. The user interface of an IR system, as with any other type of information system, is critical to its successful usage. Since user interface algorithms and data structures are not IR specific, we have not covered them in detail here.

1.2.6 Hardware for IR

Hardware affects the design of IR systems because it determines, in part, the operating speed of an IR system—a crucial factor in interactive information systems—and the amounts and types of information that can be stored practically in an IR system. Most IR systems in use today are implemented on von Neumann machines—general purpose computers with a single processor. Most of the discussion of IR techniques in this book assumes a von Neumann machine as an implementation platform. The computing speeds of these machines have improved enormously over the years, yet there are still IR applications for which they may be too slow. In response to this problem, some researchers have examined alternative hardware for implementing IR systems. There are two approaches—parallel computers and IR specific hardware.

Chapter 18 discusses implementation of an IR system on the Connection machine—a massively parallel computer with 64,000 processors. Chapter 17 discusses IR specific hardware—machines designed specifically to handle IR operations. IR specific hardware has been developed both for text scanning and for common operations like Boolean set combination.

Along with the need for greater speed has come the need for storage media capable of compactly holding the huge document databases that have proliferated. Optical storage technology, capable of holding gigabytes of information on a single disk, has met this need. Chapter 6 discusses data structures and algorithms that allow optical disk technology to be successfully exploited for IR.

1.2.7 Functional View of Paradigm IR System

Figure 1.1 shows the activities associated with a common type of Boolean IR system, chosen because it represents the operational standard for IR systems.

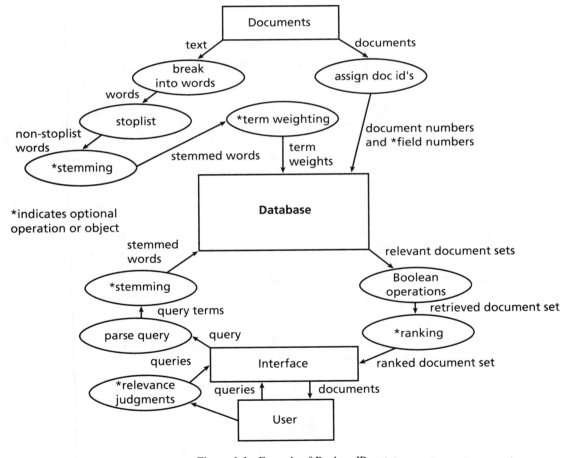

Figure 1.1 Example of Boolean IR system

When building the database, documents are taken one by one, and their text is broken into words. The words from the documents are compared against a stoplist—a list of words thought to have no indexing value. Words from the document not found in the stoplist may next be stemmed. Words may then also be counted, since the frequency of words in documents and in the database as a whole are often used for ranking retrieved documents. Finally, the words and associated information such as the documents, fields within the documents, and counts are put into the database. The database then might consist of pairs of document identifiers and keywords as follows.

```
keyword1 - document1-Field_2
keyword2 - document1-Field_2,5
keyword2 - document3-Field_1,2
keyword3 - document3-Field_3,4
                .
                .
                .
keyword-n - document-n-Field_i,j
```

Such a structure is called an *inverted file*. In an IR system, each document must have a unique identifier, and its fields, if field operations are supported, must have unique field names.

To search the database, a user enters a query consisting of a set of keywords connected by Boolean operators (AND, OR, NOT). The query is parsed into its constituent terms and Boolean operators. These terms are then looked up in the inverted file and the list of document identifiers corresponding to them are combined according to the specified Boolean operators. If frequency information has been kept, the retrieved set may be ranked in order of probable relevance. The result of the search is then presented to the user. In some systems, the user makes judgments about the relevance of the retrieved documents, and this information is used to modify the query automatically by adding terms from relevant documents and deleting terms from nonrelevant documents. Systems such as this give remarkably good retrieval performance given their simplicity, but their performance is far from perfect. Many techniques to improve them have been proposed.

One such technique aims to establish a connection between morphologically related terms. Stemming (Chapter 8) is a technique for conflating term variants so that the semantic closeness of words like "engineer," "engineered," and "engineering" will be recognized in searching. Another way to relate terms is via thesauri, or synonym lists, as discussed in Chapter 9.

1.3 IR AND OTHER TYPES OF INFORMATION SYSTEMS

How do IR systems relate to different types of information systems such as database management systems (DBMS), and artificial intelligence (AI) systems? Table 1.3 summarizes some of the similarities and differences.

Table 1.3 IR, DBMS, AI Comparison

	Data Object	Primary Operation	Database Size
IR	document	retrieval (probabilistic)	small to very large
DBMS (relational)	table	retrieval (deterministic)	small to very large
AI	logical statements	inference	usually small

One difference between IR, DBMS, and AI systems is the amount of usable structure in their data objects. Documents, being primarily text, in general have less usable structure than the tables of data used by relational DBMS, and structures such as frames and semantic nets used by AI systems. It is possible, of course, to analyze a document manually and store information about its syntax and semantics in a DBMS or an AI system. The barriers for doing this to a large collection of documents are practical rather than theoretical. The work involved in doing knowledge engineering on a set of say 50,000 documents would be enormous. Researchers have devoted much effort to constructing hybrid systems using IR, DBMS, AI, and other techniques; see, for example, Tong (1989). The hope is to eventually develop practical systems that combine IR, DBMS, and AI.

Another distinguishing feature of IR systems is that retrieval is probabilistic. That is, one cannot be certain that a retrieved document will meet the information need of the user. In a typical search in an IR system, some relevant documents will be missed and some nonrelevant documents will be retrieved. This may be contrasted with retrieval from, for example, a DBMS where retrieval is deterministic. In a DBMS, queries consist of attribute-value pairs that either match, or do not match, records in the database.

One feature of IR systems shared with many DBMS is that their databases are often very large—sometimes in the gigabyte range. Book library systems, for example, may contain several million records. Commercial on-line retrieval services such as Dialog and BRS provide databases of many gigabytes. The need to search such large collections in real time places severe demands on the systems used to search them. Selection of the best data structures and algorithms to build such systems is often critical.

Another feature that IR systems share with DBMS is database volatility. A typical large IR application, such as a book library system or commercial document retrieval service, will change constantly as documents are added, changed, and deleted. This constrains the kinds of data structures and algorithms that can be used for IR.

In summary, a typical IR system must meet the following functional and nonfunctional requirements. It must allow a user to add, delete, and change documents in the database. It must provide a way for users to search for documents by entering queries, and examine the retrieved documents. It must accommodate databases in the megabyte to gigabyte range, and retrieve relevant documents in response to queries interactively—often within 1 to 10 seconds.

1.4 IR SYSTEM EVALUATION

IR systems can be evaluated in terms of many criteria including execution efficiency, storage efficiency, retrieval effectiveness, and the features they offer a user. The relative importance of these factors must be decided by the designers of the system, and the selection of appropriate data structures and algorithms for implementation will depend on these decisions.

Execution efficiency is measured by the time it takes a system, or part of a system, to perform a computation. This can be measured in C based systems by using profiling tools such as prof (Earhart 1986) on UNIX. Execution efficiency has always been a major concern of IR systems since most of them are interactive, and a long retrieval time will interfere with the usefulness of the system. The nonfunctional requirements of IR systems usually specify maximum acceptable times for searching, and for database maintenance operations such as adding and deleting documents.

Storage efficiency is measured by the number of bytes needed to store data. Space overhead, a common measure of storage efficiency, is the ratio of the size of the index files plus the size of the document files over the size of the document files. Space overhead ratios of from 1.5 to 3 are typical for IR systems based on inverted files.

Most IR experimentation has focused on retrieval effectiveness—usually based on document *relevance judgments*. This has been a problem since relevance judgments are subjective and unreliable. That is, different judges will assign different relevance values to a document retrieved in response to a given query. The seriousness of the problem is the subject of debate, with many IR researchers arguing that the relevance judgment reliability problem is not sufficient to invalidate the experiments that use relevance judgments. A detailed discussion of the issues involved in IR experimentation can be found in Salton and McGill (1983) and Sparck-Jones (1981).

Many measures of retrieval effectiveness have been proposed. The most commonly used are *recall* and *precision*. Recall is the ratio of relevant documents retrieved for a given query over the number of relevant documents for that query in the database. Except for small test collections, this denominator is generally unknown and must be estimated by sampling or some other method. Precision is the ratio of the number of relevant documents retrieved over the total number of documents retrieved. Both recall and precision take on values between 0 and 1.

Since one often wishes to compare IR performance in terms of both recall and precision, methods for evaluating them simultaneously have been developed. One method involves the use of recall-precision graphs—bivariate plots where one axis is recall and the other precision. Figure 1.2 shows an example of such a plot. Recall-precision plots show that recall and precision are inversely related. That is, when

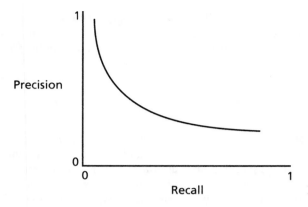

Figure 1.2 Recall-precision graph

precision goes up, recall typically goes down and vice-versa. Such plots can be done for individual queries, or averaged over queries as described in Salton and McGill (1983), and van Rijsbergen (1979).

A combined measure of recall and precision, E, has been developed by van Rijsbergen (1979). The evaluation measure E is defined as:

$$E = 1 - \frac{(1 + b^2)\,P\,R}{b^2\,P + R}$$

where P = precision, R = recall, and b is a measure of the relative importance, to a user, of recall and precision. Experimenters choose values of E that they hope will reflect the recall and precision interests of the typical user. For example, b levels of .5, indicating that a user was twice as interested in precision as recall, and 2, indicating that a user was twice as interested in recall as precision, might be used.

IR experiments often use test collections which consist of a document database and a set of queries for the data base for which relevance judgments are available. The number of documents in test collections has tended to be small, typically a few hundred to a few thousand documents. Test collections are available on an optical disk (Fox 1990). Table 1.4 summarizes the test collections on this disk.

Table 1.4 IR Test Collections

Collection	Subject	Documents	Queries
ADI	Information Science	82	35
CACM	Computer Science	3200	64
CISI	Library Science	1460	76
CRAN	Aeronautics	1400	225
LISA	Library Science	6004	35
MED	Medicine	1033	30
NLM	Medicine	3078	155
NPL	Electrical Engineering	11429	100
TIME	General Articles	423	83

IR experiments using such small collections have been criticized as not being realistic. Since real IR databases typically contain much larger collections of documents, the generalizability of experiments using small test collections has been questioned.

1.5 SUMMARY

This chapter introduced and defined basic IR concepts, and presented a domain model of IR systems that describes their similarities and differences. A typical IR system must meet the following functional and nonfunctional requirements. It must allow a user to add, delete, and change documents in the database. It must provide a way for users to search for documents by entering queries, and examine the retrieved documents. An IR system will typically need to support large databases, some in the megabyte to gigabyte range, and retrieve relevant documents in response to queries interactively—often within 1 to 10 seconds. We have summarized the various approaches, elaborated in subsequent chapters, taken by IR systems in providing these services. Evaluation techniques for IR systems were also briefly surveyed. The next chapter is an introduction to data structures and algorithms.

REFERENCES

AHO, A., B. KERNIGHAN, and P. WEINBERGER. 1988. *The AWK Programming Language*. Reading, Mass.: Addison-Wesley.

BELKIN N. J., and W. B. CROFT. 1987. "Retrieval Techniques," in *Annual Review of Information Science and Technology,* ed. M. Williams. New York: Elsevier Science Publishers, 109–145.

EARHART, S. 1986. *The UNIX Programming Language,* vol. 1. New York: Holt, Rinehart, and Winston.

FALOUTSOS, C. 1985. "Access Methods for Text," *Computing Surveys*, 17(1), 49–74.

FOX, E., ed. 1990. Virginia Disk One, Blacksburg: Virginia Polytechnic Institute and State University.

FRAKES, W. B. 1984. "Term Conflation for Information Retrieval," in *Research and Development in Information Retrieval,* ed. C. S. van Rijsbergen. Cambridge: Cambridge University Press.

PRIETO–DIAZ, R., and G. ARANGO. 1991. *Domain Analysis: Acquisition of Reusable Information for Software Construction.* New York: IEEE Press.

SALTON, G., and M. MCGILL 1983. *An Introduction to Modern Information Retrieval.* New York: McGraw-Hill.

SEDGEWICK, R. 1990. *Algorithms in C.* Reading, Mass.: Addison-Wesley.

SPARCK-JONES, K. 1981. *Information Retrieval Experiment.* London: Butterworths.

TONG, R, ed. 1989. Special Issue on Knowledge Based Techniques for Information Retrieval, *International Journal of Intelligent Systems*, 4(3).

VAN RIJSBERGEN, C. J. 1979. *Information Retrieval.* London: Butterworths.

2

Introduction to Data Structures and Algorithms Related to Information Retrieval

Ricardo A. Baeza-Yates

Depto. de Ciencias de la Computación
Universidad de Chile
Casilla 2777, Santiago, Chile

Abstract

In this chapter we review the main concepts and data structures used in information retrieval, and we classify information retrieval related algorithms.

2.1 INTRODUCTION

Infomation retrieval (IR) is a multidisciplinary field. In this chapter we study data structures and algorithms used in the implementation of IR systems. In this sense, many contributions from theoretical computer science have practical and regular use in IR systems.

The first section covers some basic concepts: strings, regular expressions, and finite automata. In section 2.3 we have a look at the three classical foundations of structuring data in IR: search trees, hashing, and digital trees. We give the main performance measures of each structure and the associated trade-offs. In section 2.4 we attempt to classify IR algorithms based on their actions. We distinguish three main classes of algorithms and give examples of their use. These are retrieval, indexing, and filtering algorithms.

The presentation level is introductory, and assumes some programming knowledge as well as some theoretical computer science background. We do not include code because it is given in most standard textbooks. For good C or Pascal code we suggest the Handbook of Algorithms and Data Structures of Gonnet and Baeza-Yates (1991).

2.2 BASIC CONCEPTS

We start by reviewing basic concepts related with text: strings, regular expressions (as a general query language), and finite automata (as the basic text processing machine). Strings appear everywhere, and the simplest model of text is a single long string. Regular expressions provide a powerful query language, such that word searching or Boolean expressions are particular cases of it. Finite automata are used for string searching (either by software or hardware), and in different ways of text filtering and processing.

2.2.1 Strings

We use Σ to denote the *alphabet* (a set of symbols). We say that the alphabet is *finite* if there exists a bound in the size of the alphabet, denoted by $|\Sigma|$. Otherwise, if we do not know a priori a bound in the alphabet size, we say that the alphabet is *arbitrary*. A *string* over an alphabet Σ is a finite length sequence of symbols from Σ. The *empty string* (ϵ) is the string with no symbols. If x and y are strings, xy denotes the *concatenation* of x and y. If $\omega = xyz$ is a string, then x is a *prefix*, and z a *suffix* of ω. The *length* of a string x ($|x|$) is the number of symbols of x. Any contiguous sequence of letters y from a string ω is called a *substring*. If the letters do not have to be contiguous, we say that y is a *subsequence*.

2.2.2 Similarity between Strings

When manipulating strings, we need to know how similar are a pair of strings. For this purpose, several *similarity measures* have been defined. Each similarity model is defined by a distance function d, such that for any strings s_1, s_2, and s_3, satisfies the following properties:

$$d(s_1, s_1) = 0, \qquad d(s_1, s_2) \geq 0, \qquad d(s_1, s_3) \leq d(s_1, s_2) + d(s_2, s_3)$$

The two main distance functions are as follows:

- The **Hamming distance** is defined over strings of the same length. The function d is defined as the number of symbols in the same position that are different (number of mismatches). For example, $d(text, that) = 2$.
- The **edit distance** is defined as the minimal number of symbols that is necessary to insert, delete, or substitute to transform a string s_1 to s_2. Clearly, $d(s_1, s_2) \geq |length(s_1) - length(s_2)|$. For example, $d(text, tax) = 2$.

2.2.3 Regular Expressions

We use the usual definition of regular expressions (RE for short) defined by the operations of concatenation, union ($+$) and star or Kleene closure (*) (Hopcroft and

Ullman (1979). A *language* over an alphabet Σ is a set of strings over Σ. Let L_1 and L_2 be two languages. The language $\{xy \mid x \in L_1 \text{ and } y \in L_2\}$ is called the *concatenation* of L_1 and L_2 and is denoted by $L_1 L_2$. If L is a language, we define $L^0 = \{\epsilon\}$ and $L^i = LL^{i-1}$ for $i \geq 1$. The *star or Kleene closure* of L, L^*, is the language $\cup_{i=0}^{\infty} L^i$. The *plus or positive closure* is defined by $L^+ = LL^*$.

We use $L(r)$ to represent the *set of strings* in the language denoted by the regular expression r. The *regular expressions* over Σ and the languages that they denote (*regular sets* or *regular languages*) are defined recursively as follows:

- $\emptyset$ is a regular expression and denotes the empty set.
- ϵ (empty string) is a regular expression and denotes the set $\{\epsilon\}$.
- For each symbol a in Σ, a is a regular expression and denotes the set $\{a\}$.
- If p and q are regular expressions, then $p + q$ (union), pq (concatenation), and p^* (star) are regular expressions that denote $L(p) \cup L(q)$, $L(p)L(q)$, and $L(p)^*$, respectively.

To avoid unnecessary parentheses we adopt the convention that the star operator has the highest precedence, then concatenation, then union. All operators are left associative.

We also use:

- Σ to denote any symbol from Σ (when the ambiguity is clearly resolvable by context).
- $r?$ to denote zero or one occurrence of r (that is, $r? = \epsilon + r$).
- $[a_1 .. a_m]$ to denote a *range* of symbols from Σ. For this we need an *order* in Σ.
- $r^{\leq k}$ to denote $\Sigma_{i=0}^{k} r^i$ (finite closure).

Examples:

All the examples given here arise from the Oxford English Dictionary:

1. All citations to an author with prefix Scot followed by at most 80 arbitrary characters then by works beginning with the prefix Kenilw or Discov:

$$<A>\text{Scot } \Sigma^{\leq 80} <W>(\text{Kenilw} + \text{Discov})$$

   where $<>$ are characters in the OED text that denote tags (A for author, W for work).

2. All "bl" tags (lemma in bold) containing a single word consisting of lowercase alphabetical only:

$$<bl>[a..z]^*</bl>$$

3. All first citations accredited to Shakespeare between 1610–11:

$$<EQ>(<LQ>)?<Q><D>161(0+1)</D> \qquad <A>\text{Shak}$$

   where EQ stands for the earliest quotation tag, LQ for quotation label, Q for the quotation itself, and D for date.

4. All references to author W. Scott:

$$<A>((Sirb)?\ W)?b\ \text{Scott}\ b?</A>$$

where b denotes a literal space.

We use regular languages as our query domain, and regular languages can be represented by regular expressions. Sometimes, we restrict the query to a subset of regular languages. For example, when searching in plain text, we have the exact string matching problem, where we only allow single strings as valid queries.

2.2.4 Finite Automata

A finite automaton is a mathematical model of a system. The automaton can be in any one of a finite number of states and is driven from state to state by a sequence of discrete inputs. Figure 2.1 depicts an automaton reading its input from a tape.

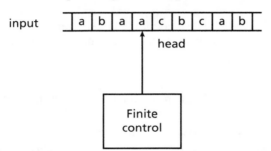

Figure 2.1   A finite automaton

Formally, a *finite automaton* (FA) is defined by a 5-tuple $(Q, \Sigma, \delta, q_0, F)$ (see Hopcroft and Ullman [1979]), where

- Q is a finite set of *states,*
- Σ is a finite *input alphabet,*
- $q_0 \in Q$ is the *initial* state,
- $F \subseteq Q$ is the set of *final* states, and
- δ is the (partial) *transition function* mapping $Q \times (\Sigma + \{\epsilon\})$ to zero or more elements of Q. That is, $\delta(q, a)$ describes the next state(s), for each state q and input symbol a; or is undefined.

A finite automaton starts in state q_0 reading the input symbols from a tape. In one move, the FA in state q and reading symbol a enters state(s) $\delta(q, a)$, and moves the reading head one position to the right. If $\delta(q, a) \in F$, we say that the FA has accepted the string written on its input tape up to the last symbol read. If $\delta(q, a)$ has an unique value for every q and a, we say that the FA is *deterministic* (DFA); otherwise we say that it is *nondeterministic* (NFA).

The languages accepted by finite automata (either DFAs or NFAs) are regular languages. In other words, there exists a FA that accepts $L(r)$ for any regular expression r; and given a DFA or NFA, we can express the language that it recognizes as a RE. There is a simple algorithm that, given a regular expression r, constructs a NFA that accepts $L(r)$ in $O(|r|)$ time and space. There are also algorithms to convert a NFA to a NFA without ϵ transitions ($O(|r|^2)$ states) and to a DFA ($0(2^{|r|})$ states in the worst case).

Figure 2.2 shows the DFA that searches an occurrence of the fourth query of the previous section in a text. The double circled state is the final state of the DFA. All the transitions are shown with the exception of

- the transition from every state (with the exception of states 2 and 3) to state 1 upon reading a $<$, and
- the default transition from all the states to state 0 when there is no transition defined for the read symbol.

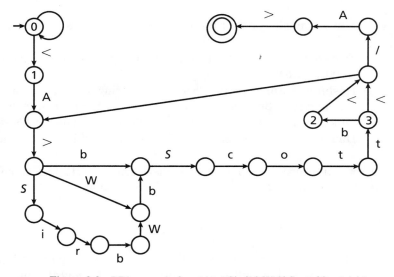

Figure 2.2 DFA example for $<A>((Sir\ b)?\ W)?b\ Scott\ b?\ </A>$.

A DFA is called *minimal* if it has the minimum possible number of states. There exists an $O(|\Sigma|n \log n)$ algorithm to minimize a DFA with n states.

A finite automaton is called *partial* if the δ function is not defined for all possible symbols of Σ for each state. In that case, there is an implicit *error* state belonging to F for every undefined transition.

DFA will be used in this book as searching machines. Usually, the searching time depends on how the transitions are implemented. If the alphabet is known and finite, using a table we have constant time per transition and thus $O(n)$ searching time. If the alphabet is not known in advance, we can use an ordered table in each state. In this case, the searching time is $O(n \log m)$. Another possibility would be to use a hashing table in each state, achieving constant time per transition on average.

2.3 DATA STRUCTURES

In this section we cover three basic data structures used to organize data: search trees, digital trees, and hashing. They are used not only for storing text in secondary memory, but also as components in searching algorithms (especially digital trees). We do not describe arrays, because they are a well-known structure that can be used to implement static search tables, bit vectors for set manipulation, suffix arrays (Chapter 5), and so on.

These three data structures differ on how a search is performed. Trees define a lexicographical order over the data. However, in search trees, we use the complete value of a key to direct the search, while in digital trees, the digital (symbol) decomposition is used to direct the search. On the other hand, hashing "randomizes" the data order, being able to search faster on average, with the disadvantage that scanning in sequential order is not possible (for example, range searches are expensive).

Some examples of their use in subsequent chapters of this book are:

- **Search trees:** for optical disk files (Chapter 6), prefix B-trees (Chapter 3), stoplists (Chapter 7).
- **Hashing:** hashing itself (Chapter 13), string searching (Chapter 10), associated retrieval, Boolean operations (Chapters 12 and 15), optical disk file structures (Chapter 6), signature files (Chapter 4), stoplists (Chapter 7).
- **Digital trees:** string searching (Chapter 10), suffix trees (Chapter 5).

We refer the reader to Gonnet and Baeza-Yates (1991) for search and update algorithms related to the data structures of this section.

2.3.1 Search Trees

The most well-known search tree is the binary search tree. Each internal node contains a key, and the left subtree stores all keys smaller that the parent key, while the right subtree stores all keys larger than the parent key. Binary search trees are adequate for main memory. However, for secondary memory, multiway search trees are better, because internal nodes are bigger. In particular, we describe a special class of balanced multiway search trees called B-tree.

A B-tree of order m is defined as follows:

- The root has between 2 and $2m$ keys, while all other internal nodes have between m and $2m$ keys.
- If k_i is the i-th key of a given internal node, then all keys in the $i - 1$-th child are smaller than k_i, while all the keys in the i-th child are bigger.
- All leaves are at the same depth.

Usually, a B-tree is used as an index, and all the associated data are stored in the leaves or *buckets*. This structure is called B$^+$-tree. An example of a B$^+$-tree of order 2 is shown in Figure 2.3, using bucket size 4.

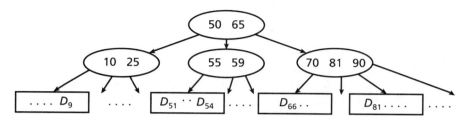

Figure 2.3 A B$^+$-tree example (D_i denotes the primary key i, plus its associated data).

B-trees are mainly used as a primary key access method for large databases in secondary memory. To search a given key, we go down the tree choosing the appropriate branch at each step. The number of disk accesses is equal to the height of the tree.

Updates are done bottom-up. To insert a new record, we search the insertion point. If there is not enough space in the corresponding leaf, we split it, and we promote a key to the previous level. The algorithm is applied recursively, up to the root, if necessary. In that case, the height of the tree increases by one. Splits provides a minimal storage utilization of 50 percent. Therefore, the height of the tree is at most $\log_{m+1}(n/b) + 2$ where n is the number of keys, and b is the number of records that can be stored in a leaf. Deletions are handled in a similar fashion, by merging nodes. On average, the expected storage utilization is $\ln 2 \approx .69$ (Yao 1979; Baeza-Yates 1989).

To improve storage utilization, several overflow techniques exist. Some of them are:

- B*-trees: in case of overflow, we first see if neighboring nodes have space. In that case, a subset of the keys is shifted, avoiding a split. With this technique, 66 percent minimal storage utilization is provided. The main disadvantage is that updates are more expensive (Bayer and McCreight 1972; Knuth 1973).
- Partial expansions: buckets of different sizes are used. If an overflow occurs, a bucket is expanded (if possible), or split. Using two bucket sizes of relative ratio 2/3, 66 percent minimal and 81 percent average storage utilization is achieved (Lomet 1987; Baeza-Yates and Larson 1989). This technique does not deteriorate update time.
- Adaptive splits: two bucket sizes of relative ratios 1/2 are used. However, splits are not symmetric (balanced), and they depend on the insertion point. This technique achieves 77 percent average storage utilization and is robust against nonuniform distributions (low variance) (Baeza-Yates 1990).

A special kind of B-trees, Prefix B-trees (Bayer and Unterauer 1977), supports efficiently variable length keys, as is the case with words. This kind of B-tree is discussed in detail in Chapter 3.

2.3.2 Hashing

A *hashing function* $h(x)$ maps a key x to an integer in a given range (for example, 0 to $m - 1$). Hashing functions are designed to produce values uniformly distributed in the given range. For a good discussion about choosing hashing functions, see Ullman (1972), Knuth (1973), and Knott (1975). The hashing value is also called a *signature*.

A hashing function is used to map a set of keys to slots in a *hashing table*. If the hashing function gives the same slot for two different keys, we say that we have a *collision*. Hashing techniques mainly differ in how collisions are handled. There are two classes of collision resolution schemas: *open addressing* and *overflow addressing*.

In open addressing (Peterson 1957), the collided key is "rehashed" into the table, by computing a new index value. The most used technique in this class is *double hashing*, which uses a second hashing function (Bell and Kaman 1970; Guibas and Szemeredi 1978). The main limitation of this technique is that when the table becomes full, some kind of reorganization must be done. Figure 2.4 shows a hashing table of size 13, and the insertion of a key using the hashing function $h(x) = x \bmod 13$ (this is only an example, and we do not recommend using this hashing function!).

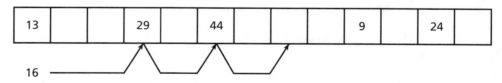

Figure 2.4   Insertion of a new key using double hashing.

In overflow addressing (Williams 1959; Knuth 1973), the collided key is stored in an overflow area, such that all key values with the same hashing value are linked together. The main problem of this schema is that a search may degenerate to a linear search.

Searches follow the insertion path until the given key is found, or not (unsuccessful case). The average search time is constant, for nonfull tables.

Because hashing "randomizes" the location of keys, a sequential scan in lexicographical order is not possible. Thus, ordered scanning or range searches are very expensive. More details on hashing can be found in Chapter 13.

Hashing schemes have also been used for secondary memory. The main difference is that tables have to grow dynamically as the number of keys increases. The main techniques are *extendible hashing* which uses hashing on two levels: a directory and a bucket level (Fagin et al. 1979), and linear hashing which uses an overflow area, and grows in a predetermined way (Litwin 1980; Larson 1980; Larson and Kajla 1984). For the case of textual databases, a special technique called *signature files* (Faloutsos 1987) is used most frequently. This technique is covered in detail in Chapter 4 of this book.

To improve search time on B-trees, and to allow range searches in hashing schemes, several hybrid methods have been devised. Between them, we have to mention the *bounded disorder* method (Litwin and Lomet 1987), where B$^+$-tree buckets are organized as hashing tables.

2.3.3 Digital Trees

Efficient prefix searching can be done using indices. One of the best indices for prefix searching is a binary digital tree or binary trie constructed from a set of substrings of the text. This data structure is used in several algorithms.

Tries are recursive tree structures that use the digital decomposition of strings to represent a set of strings and to direct the searching. Tries were invented by de la Briandais (1959) and the name was suggested by Fredkin (1960), from information re*trie*val. If the alphabet is ordered, we have a lexicographically ordered tree. The root of the trie uses the first character, the children of the root use the second character, and so on. If the remaining subtrie contains only one string, that string's identity is stored in an external node.

Figure 2.5 shows a binary trie (binary alphabet) for the string "01100100010111 . . . " after inserting all the substrings that start from positions 1 through 8. (In this case, the substring's identity is represented by its starting position in the text.)

The *height* of a trie is the number of nodes in the longest path from the root to an external node. The length of any path from the root to an external node is bounded by the height of the trie. On average, the height of a trie is logarithmic for any square-integrable probability distribution (Devroye 1982). For a random uniform distribution (Regnier 1981), we have

$$\mathcal{H}(n) = 2 \log_2(n) + o(\log_2(n))$$

for a binary trie containing n strings.

The average number of internal nodes inspected during a (un)successful search in a binary trie with n strings is $\log_2 n + O(1)$. The average number of internal nodes is $\frac{n}{\ln 2} + O(n)$ (Knuth 1973).

A *Patricia tree* (Morrison 1968) is a trie with the additional constraint that single-descendant nodes are eliminated. This name is an acronym for "Practical Algorithm To Retrieve Information Coded In Alphanumerical." A counter is kept in each node to indicate which is the next bit to inspect. Figure 2.6 shows the Patricia tree corresponding to the binary trie in Figure 2.5.

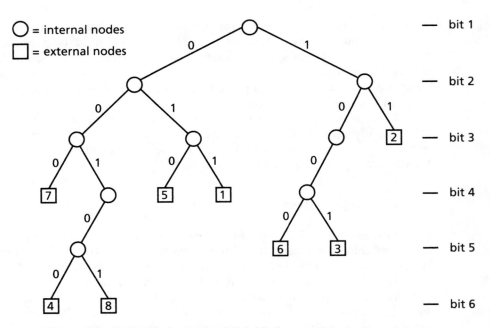

Figure 2.5 Binary trie (external node label indicates position in the text) for the first eight suffixes in "01100100010111 . . .".

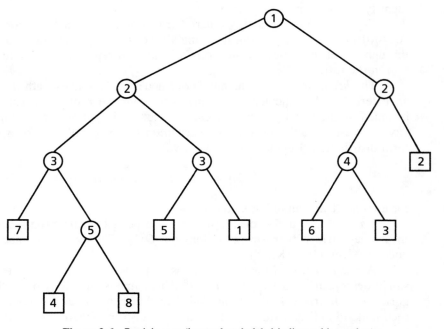

Figure 2.6 Patricia tree (internal node label indicates bit number).

For *n* strings, such an index has *n* external nodes (the *n* positions of the text) and $n - 1$ internal nodes. Each internal node consists of a pair of pointers plus some counters. Thus, the space required is $O(n)$.

It is possible to build the index in $O(n\mathcal{H}(n))$ time, where $\mathcal{H}(n)$ denotes the height of the tree. As for tries, the expected height of a Patricia tree is logarithmic (and at most the height of the binary trie). The expected height of a Patricia tree is $\log_2 n + o(\log_2 n)$ (Pittel 1986).

A trie built using the substrings (suffixes) of a string is also called *suffix tree* (McCreight [1976] or Aho et al. [1974]). A variation of these are called position trees (Weiner 1973). Similarly, a Patricia tree is called a *compact suffix tree*.

2.4 ALGORITHMS

It is hard to classify IR algorithms, and to draw a line between each type of application. However, we can identify three main types of algorithms, which are described below.

There are other algorithms used in IR that do not fall within our description, for example, user interface algorithms. The reason that they cannot be considered as IR algorithms is because they are inherent to any computer application.

2.4.1 Retrieval Algorithms

The main class of algorithms in IR is retrieval algorithms, that is, to extract information from a textual database. We can distinguish two types of retrieval algorithms, according to how much extra memory we need:

- Sequential scanning of the text: extra memory is in the worst case a function of the query size, and not of the database size. On the other hand, the running time is at least proportional to the size of the text, for example, string searching (Chapter 10).
- Indexed text: an "index" of the text is available, and can be used to speed up the search. The index size is usually proportional to the database size, and the search time is sublinear on the size of the text, for example, inverted files (Chapter 3) and signature files (Chapter 4).

Formally, we can describe a generic searching problem as follows: Given a string *t* (the text), a regular expression *q* (the query), and information (optionally) obtained by preprocessing the pattern and/or the text, the problem consists of finding whether $t \in \Sigma^* q \Sigma^*$ (*q* for short) and obtaining some or all of the following information:

1. The location where an occurrence (or specifically the first, the longest, etc.) of *q* exists. Formally, if $t \in \Sigma^* q \Sigma^*$, find a position $m \geq 0$ such that

$t \in \Sigma^m q \Sigma^*$. For example, the first occurrence is defined as the least m that fulfills this condition.

2. The number of occurrences of the pattern in the text. Formally, the number of all possible values of m in the previous category.

3. All the locations where the pattern occurs (the set of all possible values of m).

In general, the complexities of these problems are different.

We assume that ϵ is not a member of $L(q)$. If it is, the answer is trivial. Note that string matching is a particular case where q is a string. Algorithms to solve this problem are discussed in Chapter 10.

The efficiency of retrieval algorithms is very important, because we expect them to solve on-line queries with a short answer time. This need has triggered the implementation of retrieval algorithms in many different ways: by hardware, by parallel machines, and so on. These cases are explained in detail in Chapter 17 (algorithms by hardware) and Chapter 18 (parallel algorithms).

2.4.2 Filtering Algorithms

This class of algorithms is such that the text is the input and a processed or filtered version of the text is the output. This is a typical transformation in IR, for example to reduce the size of a text, and/or standardize it to simplify searching.

The most common filtering/processing operations are:

- Common words removed using a list of stopwords. This operation is discussed in Chapter 7.
- Uppercase letters transformed to lowercase letters.
- Special symbols removed and sequences of multiple spaces reduced to one space.
- Numbers and dates transformed to a standard format (Gonnet 1987).
- Spelling variants transformed using Soundex-like methods (Knuth 1973).
- Word stemming (removing suffixes and/or prefixes). This is the topic of Chapter 8.
- Automatic keyword extraction.
- Word ranking.

Unfortunately, these filtering operations may also have some disadvantages. Any query, before consulting the database, must be filtered as is the text; and, it is not possible to search for common words, special symbols, or uppercase letters, nor to distinguish text fragments that have been mapped to the same internal form.

2.4.3 Indexing Algorithms

The usual meaning of indexing is to build a data structure that will allow quick searching of the text, as we mentioned previously. There are many classes of indices, based on different retrieval approaches. For example, we have inverted files (Chapter 3), signature files (Chapter 4), tries (Chapter 5), and so on, as we have seen in the previous section. Almost all type of indices are based on some kind of tree or hashing. Perhaps the main exceptions are clustered data structures (this kind of indexing is called *clustering*), which is covered in Chapter 16, and the Direct Acyclic Word Graph (DAWG) of the text, which represents all possible subwords of the text using a linear amount of space (Blumer et al. 1985), and is based on finite automata theory.

Usually, before indexing, the text is filtered. Figure 2.7 shows the complete process for the text.

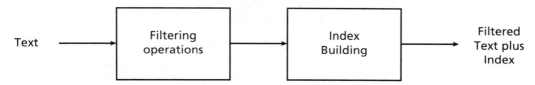

Figure 2.7   Text preprocessing

The preprocessing time needed to build the index is amortized by using it in searches. For example, if building the index requires $O(n \log n)$ time, we would expect to query the database at least $O(n)$ times to amortize the preprocessing cost. In that case, we add $O(\log n)$ preprocessing time to the total query time (that may also be logarithmic).

Many special indices, and their building algorithms (some of them in parallel machines), are covered in this book.

REFERENCES

AHO, A., J. HOPCROFT, and J. ULLMAN. 1974. *The Design and Analysis of Computer Algorithms*. Reading, Mass.: Addison-Wesley.

BAEZA-YATES, R. 1989. "Expected Behaviour of B$^+$-Trees under Random Insertions." *Acta Informatica*, 26(5), 439–72. Also as Research Report CS-86-67, University of Waterloo, 1986.

BAEZA-YATES, R. 1990. "An Adaptive Overflow Technique for the B-tree," in *Extending Data Base Technology Conference (EDBT 90)*, eds. F. Bancilhon, C. Thanos and D. Tsichritzis, pp. 16–28, Venice. Springer Verlag Lecture Notes in Computer Science 416.

BAEZA-YATES, R., and P.-A. LARSON. 1989. "Performance of B$^+$-trees with Partial Expansions." *IEEE Trans. on Knowledge and Data Engineering*, 1, 248–57. Also as Research Report CS-87-04, Dept. of Computer Science, University of Waterloo, 1987.

BAYER, R., and E. MCCREIGHT. 1972. "Organization and Maintenance of Large Ordered Indexes." *Acta Informatica*, 1(3), 173–89.

BAYER, R., and K. UNTERAUER. 1977. "Prefix B-trees." *ACM TODS*, 2(1), 11–26.

BELL, J., and C. KAMAN. 1970. "The Linear Quotient Hash Code." *CACM*, 13(11), 675–77.

BLUMER, A., J. BLUMER, D. HAUSSLER, A. EHRENFEUCHT, M. CHEN, and J. SEIFERAS. 1985. "The Smallest Automaton Recognizing the Subwords of a Text." *Theoretical Computer Science*, 40, 31–55.

DE LA BRIANDAIS, R. 1959. "File Searching Using Variable Length Keys, in *AFIPS Western JCC*, pp. 295–98, San Francisco, Calif.

DEVROYE, L. 1982. "A Note on the Average Depth of Tries." *Computing*, 28, 367–71.

FAGIN, R., J. NIEVERGELT, N. PIPPENGER, and H. STRONG. 1979. "Extendible Hashing—a Fast Access Method for Dynamic Files. *ACM TODS*, 4(3), 315–44.

FALOUTSOS, C. 1987. Signature Files: An Integrated Access Method for Text and Attributes, Suitable for Optical Disk Storage." Technical Report CS-TR-1867, University of Maryland.

FREDKIN, E. 1960. "Trie Memory." *CACM*, 3, 490–99.

GONNET, G. 1987. "Extracting Information from a Text Database: An Example with Dates and Numerical Data," in *Third Annual Conference of the UW Centre for the New Oxford English Dictionary*, pp. 85–89, Waterloo, Canada.

GONNET, G. and R. BAEZA-YATES. 1991. *Handbook of Algorithms and Data Structures—In Pascal and C*. (2nd ed.). Wokingham, U.K.: Addison-Wesley.

GUIBAS, L., and E. SZEMEREDI. 1978. "The Analysis of Double Hashing." *JCSS*, 16(2), 226–74.

HOPCROFT, J., and J. ULLMAN. 1979. *Introduction to Automata Theory*. Reading, Mass.: Addison-Wesley.

KNOTT, G. D. 1975. "Hashing Functions." *Computer Journal*, 18(3), 265–78.

KNUTH, D. 1973. *The Art of Computer Programming: Sorting and Searching*, vol. 3. Reading, Mass.: Addison-Wesley.

LARSON, P.-A. 1980. "Linear Hashing with Partial Expansions," in *VLDB*, vol. 6, pp. 224–32, Montreal.

LARSON, P.-A., and A. KAJLA. 1984. "File Organization: Implementation of a Method Guaranteeing Retrieval in One Access." *CACM*, 27(7), 670–77.

LITWIN, W. 1980. "Linear Hashing: A New Tool for File and Table Addressing," in *VLDB*, vol. 6, pp. 212–23, Montreal.

LITWIN, W., and LOMET, D. 1987. "A New Method for Fast Data Searches with Keys. *IEEE Software*, 4(2), 16–24.

LOMET, D. 1987. "Partial Expansions for File Organizations with an Index. *ACM TODS*, 12: 65–84. Also as tech report, Wang Institute, TR-86-06, 1986.

MCCREIGHT, E. 1976. "A Space-Economical Suffix Tree Construction Algorithm." *JACM*, 23, 262–72.

MORRISON, D. 1968. "PATRICIA-Practical Algorithm to Retrieve Information Coded in Alphanumeric." *JACM,* 15, 514–34.

PETERSON, W. 1957. "Addressing for Random-Access Storage. *IBM J Res. Development,* 1(4), 130–46.

PITTEL, B. 1986. "Paths in a Random Digital Tree: Limiting Distributions." *Adv. Appl. Prob.,* 18, 139–55.

REGNIER, M. 1981. "On the Average Height of Trees in Digital Search and Dynamic Hashing." *Inf. Proc. Letters,* 13, 64–66.

ULLMAN, J. 1972. "A Note on the Efficiency of Hashing Functions." *JACM,* 19(3), 569–75.

WEINER, P. 1973. "Linear Pattern Matching Algorithm," in *FOCS,* vol. 14, pp. 1–11.

WILLIAMS, F. 1959. "Handling Identifiers as Internal Symbols in Language Processors." *CACM,* 2(6), 21–24.

YAO, A. 1979. "The Complexity of Pattern Matching for a Random String." *SIAM J. Computing,* 8, 368–87.

3

Inverted Files

Donna Harman

*National Institute
of Standards and Technology
Gaithersburg, MD 20899*

Edward Fox

*Virginia Polytechnic Institute
and State University
Department of Computer Science
Blacksburg, VA 24061-0106*

R. Baeza-Yates

*Depto. de Ciencias de la Computación
Universidad de Chile
Casilla 2777, Santiago, Chile*

W. Lee

*Virginia Polytechnic Institute
and State University
Department of Computer Science
Blacksburg, VA 24061-0106*

Abstract

This chapter presents a survey of the various structures (techniques) that can be used in building inverted files, and gives the details for producing an inverted file using sorted arrays. The chapter ends with two modifications to this basic method that are effective for large data collections.

3.1 INTRODUCTION

Three of the most commonly used file structures for information retrieval can be classified as lexicographical indices (indices that are sorted), clustered file structures, and indices based on hashing. One type of lexicographical index, the inverted file, is presented in this chapter, with a second type of lexicographical index, the Patricia (PAT) tree, discussed in Chapter 5. Clustered file structures are covered in Chapter 16, and indices based on hashing are covered in Chapter 13 and Chapter 4 (signature files).

The concept of the inverted file type of index is as follows. Assume a set of documents. Each document is assigned a list of keywords or attributes, with optional relevance weights associated with each keyword (attribute). An inverted file is then the sorted list (or index) of keywords (attributes), with each keyword having links to the documents containing that keyword (see Figure 3.1). This is the kind of index found in most commercial library systems. The use of an inverted file improves search efficiency by several orders of magnitude, a necessity for very large text files. The penalty paid for this efficiency is the need to store a data structure that ranges from 10 percent to 100 percent or more of the size of the text itself, and a need to update that index as the data set changes.

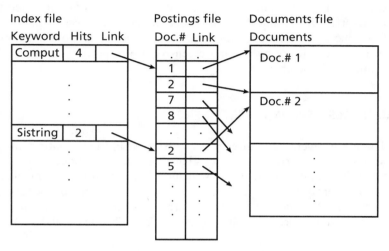

Figure 3.1 An inverted file implemented using a sorted array

Usually there are some restrictions imposed on these indices and consequently on later searches. Examples of these restrictions are:

- a controlled vocabulary which is the collection of keywords that will be indexed. Words in the text that are not in the vocabulary will not be indexed, and hence are not searchable.
- a list of stopwords (articles, prepositions, etc.) that for reasons of volume or precision and recall will not be included in the index, and hence are not searchable.
- a set of rules that decide the beginning of a word or a piece of text that is indexable. These rules deal with the treatment of spaces, punctuation marks, or some standard prefixes, and may have signficant impact on what terms are indexed.
- a list of character sequences to be indexed (or not indexed). In large text databases, not all character sequences are indexed; for example, character sequences consisting of all numerics are often not indexed.

It should be noted that the restrictions that determine what is to be indexed are critical to later search effectiveness and therefore these rules should be carefully constructed and evaluated. This problem is further discussed in Chapter 7.

A search in an inverted file is the composition of two searching algorithms; a search for a keyword (attribute), which returns an index, and then a possible search on that index for a particular attribute value. The result of a search on an inverted file is a set of records (or pointers to records).

This Chapter is organized as follows. The next section presents a survey of the various implementation structures for inverted files. The third section covers the complete implementation of an algorithm for building an inverted file that is stored as a sorted array, and the fourth section shows two variations on this implementation, one that uses no sorting (and hence needs little working storage) and one that increases efficiency by making extensive use of primary memory. The final section summarizes the chapter.

3.2 STRUCTURES USED IN INVERTED FILES

There are several structures that can be used in implementing inverted files: sorted arrays, B-trees, tries, and various hashing structures, or combinations of these structures. The first three of these structures are sorted (lexicographically) indices, and can efficiently support range queries, such as all documents having keywords that start with "comput." Only these three structures will be further discussed in this chapter. (For more on hashing methods, see Chapters 4 and 13.)

3.2.1 The Sorted Array

An inverted file implemented as a sorted array structure stores the list of keywords in a sorted array, including the number of documents associated with each keyword and a link to the documents containing that keyword. This array is commonly searched using a standard binary search, although large secondary-storage-based systems will often adapt the array (and its search) to the characteristics of their secondary storage.

The main disadvantage of this approach is that updating the index (for example appending a new keyword) is expensive. On the other hand, sorted arrays are easy to implement and are reasonably fast. (For this reason, the details of creating a sorted array inverted file are given in section 3.3.)

3.2.2 B-trees

Another implementation structure for an inverted file is a B-tree. More details of B-trees can be found in Chapter 2, and also in a recent paper (Cutting and Pedersen 1990) on efficient inverted files for dynamic data (data that is heavily updated). A special case of the B-tree, the prefix B-tree, uses prefixes of words as primary keys in a B-tree index (Bayer and Unterauer 1977) and is particularly suitable for storage of textual indices. Each internal node has a variable number of keys.

Each key is the shortest word (in length) that distinguishes the keys stored in the next level. The key does not need to be a prefix of an actual term in the index. The last level or leaf level stores the keywords themselves, along with their associated data (see Figure 3.2). Because the internal node keys and their lengths depend on the set of keywords, the order (size) of each node of the prefix B-tree is variable. Updates are done similarly to those for a B-tree to maintain a balanced tree. The prefix B-tree method breaks down if there are many words with the same (long) prefix. In this case, common prefixes should be further divided to avoid wasting space.

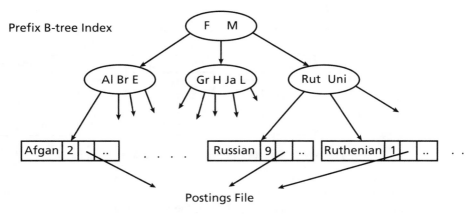

Figure 3.2 A prefix B-tree

Compared with sorted arrays, B-trees use more space. However, updates are much easier and the search time is generally faster, especially if secondary storage is used for the inverted file (instead of memory). The implementation of inverted files using B-trees is more complex than using sorted arrays, and therefore readers are referred to Knuth (1973) and Cutting and Pedersen (1990) for details of implementation of B-trees, and to Bayer and Unterauer (1977) for details of implementation of prefix B-trees.

3.2.3 Tries

Inverted files can also be implemented using a trie structure (see Chapter 2 for more on tries). This structure uses the digital decomposition of the set of keywords to represent those keywords. A special trie structure, the Patricia (PAT) tree, is especially useful in information retrieval and is described in detail in Chapter 5. An additional source for tested and optimized code for B-trees and tries is Gonnet and Baeza-Yates (1991).

3.3 BUILDING AN INVERTED FILE USING A SORTED ARRAY

The production of sorted array inverted files can be divided into two or three sequential steps as shown in Figure 3.3. First, the input text must be parsed into a list of words along with their location in the text. This is usually the most time consuming and storage consuming operation in indexing. Second, this list must then be inverted, from a list of terms in location order to a list of terms ordered for use in searching (sorted into alphabetical order, with a list of all locations attached to each term). An optional third step is the postprocessing of these inverted files, such as for adding term weights, or for reorganizing or compressing the files.

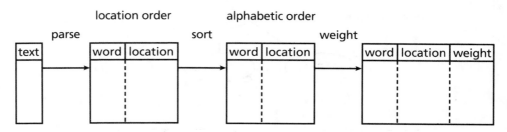

Figure 3.3 Overall schematic of sorted array inverted file creation

Creating the initial word list requires several different operations. First, the individual words must be recognized from the text. Each word is then checked against a stoplist of common words, and if it can be considered a noncommon word, may be passed through a stemming algorithm. The resultant stem is then recorded in the word-within-location list. The parsing operation and the use of a stoplist are described in Chapter 7, and the stemming operation is described in Chapter 8.

The word list resulting from the parsing operation (typically stored as a disk file) is then inverted. This is usually done by sorting on the word (or stem), with duplicates retained (see Figure 3.4). Even with the use of high-speed sorting utilities, however, this sort can be time consuming for large data sets (on the order of n log n). One way to handle this problem is to break the data sets into smaller pieces, process each piece, and then correctly merge the results. Methods that do not use sorting are given in section 3.4.1. After sorting, the duplicates are merged to produce within-document frequency statistics. (A system not using within-document frequencies can just sort with duplicates removed.) Note that although only record numbers are shown as locations in Figure 3.4, typically inverted files store field locations and possibly even word location. These additional locations are needed for field and proximity searching in Boolean operations and cause higher inverted file storage overhead than if only record location was needed. Inverted files for ranking retrieval systems (see Chapter 14) usually store only record locations and term weights or frequencies.

term	recno		term	recno		term	recno	freq
pap	1		ab	2		ab	2	1
report	1		being	2		being	2	1
novel	1		charact	2		charact	2	1
technique	1		human	2		human	2	1
literat	1		index	1		index	1	1
result	1		literat	1		literat	1	1
technique	1		novel	1		novel	1	1
index			pap	1		pap	1	1
.			report	1		report	1	1
.			report	2		report	2	1
report	2		result	1		result	1	1
charact	2		technique	1		technique	1	2
human	2		technique	1				
being	2		.			.		
ab	2		.			.		
.			.			.		
.			.			.		
.			.			.		

sort → remove duplicates →

Figure 3.4 Inversion of word list

Although an inverted file could be used directly by the search routine, it is usually processed into an improved final format. This format is based on the search methods and the (optional) weighting methods used. A common search technique is to use a binary search routine on the file to locate the query words. This implies that the file to be searched should be as short as possible, and for this reason the single file shown containing the terms, locations, and (possibly) frequencies is usually split into two pieces. The first piece is the dictionary containing the term, statistics about that term such as number of postings, and a pointer to the location of the postings file for that term. The second piece is the postings file itself, which contains the record numbers (plus other necessary location information) and the (optional) weights for all occurrences of the term. In this manner, the dictionary used in the binary search has only one "line" per unique term. Figure 3.5 illustrates the conceptual form of the necessary files; the actual form depends on the details of the search routine and on the hardware being used. Work using large data sets (Harman and Candela 1990) showed that for a file of 2,653 records, there were 5,123 unique terms with an average of 14 postings/term and a maximum of over 2,000 postings for a term. A larger data set of 38,304 records had dictionaries on the order of 250,000 lines (250,000 unique terms, including some numbers) and an average of 88 postings per record. From these numbers it is clear that efficient storage structures for both the binary search and the reading of the postings are critical.

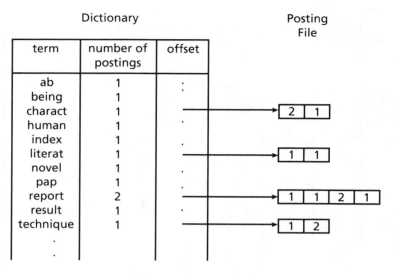

Figure 3.5 Dictionary and postings file from the last example

3.4 MODIFICATIONS TO THE BASIC TECHNIQUE

Two different techniques are presented as improvements on the basic inverted file creation discussed in section 3.3. The first technique is for working with very large data sets using secondary storage. The second technique uses multiple memory loads for inverting files.

3.4.1 Producing an Inverted File for Large Data Sets without Sorting

Indexing large data sets using the basic inverted file method presents several problems. Most computers cannot sort the very large disk files needed to hold the initial word list within a reasonable time frame, and do not have the amount of storage necessary to hold a sorted and unsorted version of that word list, plus the intermediate files involved in the internal sort. Whereas the data set could be broken into smaller pieces for processing, and the resulting files properly merged, the following technique may be considerably faster. For small data sets, this technique carries a significant overhead and therefore should not be used. (For another approach to sorting large amounts of data, see Chapter 5.)

The new indexing method (Harman and Candela 1990) is a two-step process that does not need the middle sorting step. The first step produces the initial inverted file, and the second step adds the term weights to that file and reorganizes the file for maximum efficiency (see Figure 3.6).

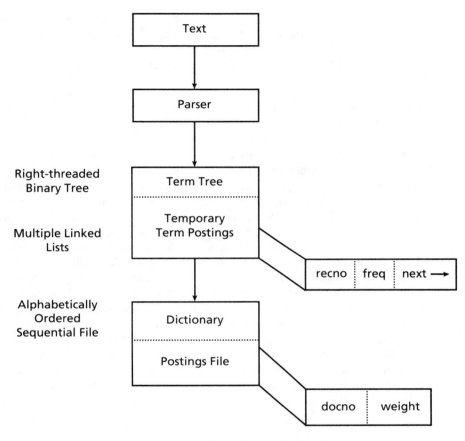

Figure 3.6 Flowchart of new indexing method

The creation of the initial inverted file avoids the use of an explicit sort by using a right-threaded binary tree (Knuth 1973). The data contained in each binary tree node is the current number of term postings and the storage location of the postings list for that term. As each term is identified by the text parsing program, it is looked up in the binary tree, and either is added to the tree, along with related data, or causes tree data to be updated. The postings are stored as multiple linked lists, one variable length linked list for each term, with the lists stored in one large file. Each element in the linked postings file consists of a record number (the location of a given term), the term frequency in that record, and a pointer to the next element in the linked list for that given term. By storing the postings in a single file, no storage is wasted, and the files are easily accessed by following the links. As the location of both the head and tail of each linked list is stored in the binary tree, the entire list does not need to be read for each addition, but only once for use in creating the final postings file (step two).

Note that both the binary tree and the linked postings list are capable of further growth. This is important in indexing large data sets where data is usually processed from multiple separate files over a short period of time. The use of the binary tree and linked postings list could be considered as an updatable inverted file. Although these structures are not as efficient to search, this method could be used for creating and storing supplemental indices for use between updates to the primary index. However, see the earlier discussion of B-trees for better ways of producing updatable inverted files.

The binary tree and linked postings lists are saved for use by the term weighting routine (step two). This routine walks the binary tree and the linked postings list to create an alphabetical term list (dictionary) and a sequentially stored postings file. To do this, each term is consecutively read from the binary tree (this automatically puts the list in alphabetical order), along with its related data. A new sequentially stored postings file is allocated, with two elements per posting. The linked postings list is then traversed, with the frequencies being used to calculate the term weights (if desired). The last step writes the record numbers and corresponding term weights to the newly created sequential postings file. These sequentially stored postings files could not be created in step one because the number of postings is unknown at that point in processing, and input order is text order, not inverted file order. The final index files therefore consist of the same dictionary and sequential postings file as for the basic inverted file described in section 3.3.

Table 3.1 gives some statistics showing the differences between an older indexing scheme and the new indexing schemes. The old indexing scheme refers to the indexing method discussed in section 3.3 in which records are parsed into a list of words within record locations, the list is inverted by sorting, and finally the term weights are added.

Table 3.1 Indexing Statistics

Text Size (megabytes)	Indexing Time (hours)		Working Storage (megabytes)		Index Storage (megabytes)	
	old	new	old	new	old	new
1.6	0.25	0.50	4.0	0.7	0.4	0.4
50	8	10.5	132	6	4	4
359	—	137	—	70	52	52
806	—	313	—	163	112	112

Note that the size of the final index is small, only 8 percent of the input text size for the 50 megabyte database, and around 14 percent of the input text size for the larger databases. The small size of the final index is caused by storing only the record identification number as location. As this index was built for a ranking retrieval system (see Chapter 14), each posting contains both a record id number and the term's weight in that record. This size remains constant when using the new indexing method as the format of the final indexing files is unchanged. The working storage (the storage needed to build the index) for the new indexing method is not much larger than the size of the final index itself, and substantially smaller than the size of the input text. However, the amount of working storage needed by the older indexing method would have been approximately 933 megabytes for the 359 megabyte database, and over 2 gigabytes for the 806 megabyte database, an amount of storage beyond the capacity of many environments. The new method takes more time for the very small (1.6 megabyte) database because of its additional processing overhead. As the size of the database increases, however, the processing time has an n log n relationship to the size of the database. The older method contains a sort (not optimal) which is n log n (best case) to n squared (worst case), making processing of the very large databases likely to have taken longer using this method.

3.4.2 A Fast Inversion Algorithm

The second technique to produce a sorted array inverted file is a fast inversion algorithm called FAST-INV (Copyright © Edward A. Fox, Whay C. Lee, Virginia Tech). This technique takes advantage of two principles: the large primary memories available on today's computers and the inherent order of the input data. The following summary of this technique is adapted from a technical report by Fox and Lee (1991).

The first principle is important since personal computers with more than 1 megabyte of primary memory are common, and mainframes may have more than 100 megabytes of memory. Even if databases are on the order of 1 gigabyte, if they can be split into memory loads that can be rapidly processed and then combined, the overall cost will be minimized.

The second principle is crucial since with large files it is very expensive to use polynomial or even n log n sorting algorithms. These costs are further compounded if memory is not used, since then the cost is for disk operations.

The FAST-INV algorithm follows these two principles, using primary memory in a close to optimal fashion, and processing the data in three passes. The overall scheme can be seen in Figure 3.7.

The input to FAST-INV is a document vector file containing the concept vectors for each document in the collection to be indexed. A sample document vector file can be seen in Figure 3.8. The document numbers appear in the left-hand column and the concept numbers of the words in each document appear in the right-hand column. This is similar to the initial word list shown in Figure 3.4 for the basic method, except that the words are represented by concept numbers, one concept number for each unique word in the collection (i.e., 250,000 unique words implies 250,000 unique concept numbers). Note however that the document vector file is in sorted order, so that concept numbers are sorted within document numbers, and document numbers are sorted within collection. This is necessary for FAST-INV to work correctly.

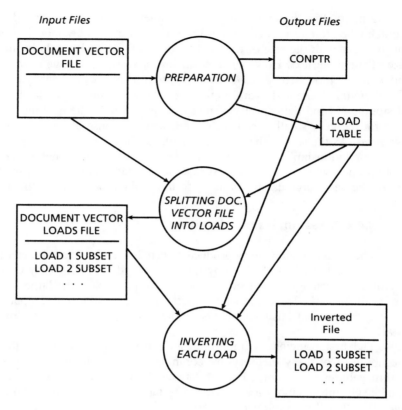

Figure 3.7 Overall scheme of FAST-INV

DOC	CON.
1	3
1	5
1	12
1	14
2	1
2	3
2	4
2	11
2	12
3	2
3	4
3	5

Figure 3.8 Sample document vector

Preparation

In order to better explain the FAST-INV algorithm, some definitions are needed.

HCN = highest concept number in dictionary
L = number of document/concept (or concept/document) pairs in the collection
M = available primary memory size, in bytes

In the first pass, the entire document vector file can be read and two new files produced: a file of concept postings/pointers (CONPTR) and a load table. It is assumed that M >> HCN, so these two files can be built in primary memory. However, it is assumed that M < L, so several primary memory loads will be needed to process the document data. Because entries in the document vector file will already be grouped by concept number, with those concepts in ascending order, it is appropriate to see if this data can be somehow transformed beforehand into j parts such that:

L / j < M, so that each part will fit into primary memory

HCN / j concepts, approximately, are associated with each part

This allows each of the j parts to be read into primary memory, inverted there, and the output to be simply appended to the (partially built) final inverted file.

Specifically, preparation involves the following:

1. Allocate an array, con_entries_cnt, of size HCN, initialized to zero.
2. For each <doc#,con#> entry in the document vector file: increment con_entries_cnt[con#].
3. Use the just constructed con_entries_cnt to create a disk version of CONPTR.
4. Initialize the load table.
5. For each <con#,count> pair obtained from con_entries_cnt: if there is no room for documents with this concept to fit in the current load, then create an entry in the load table and initialize the next load entry; otherwise update information for the current load table entry.

After one pass through the input, the CONPTR file has been built and the load table needed in later steps of the algorithm has been constructed. Note that the test for room in a given load enforces the constraint that data for a load will fit into available memory. Specifically:

Let LL = length of current load (i.e., number of concept/weight pairs)
S = spread of concept numbers in the current load (i.e., end concept - start concept + 1)

8 bytes = space needed for each concept/weight pair

4 bytes = space needed for each concept to store count of postings for it

Then the constraint that must be met for another concept to be added to the current load is

$$8 * LL + 4 * S < M$$

Splitting document vector file

The load table indicates the range of concepts that should be processed for each primary memory load. There are two approaches to handling the multiplicity of loads. One approach, which is currently used, is to make a pass through the document vector file to obtain the input for each load. This has the advantage of not requiring additional storage space (though that can be obviated through the use of magnetic tapes), but has the disadvantage of requiring expensive disk I/O.

The second approach is to build a new copy of the document vector collection, with the desired separation into loads. This can easily be done using the load table, since sizes of each load are known, in one pass through the input. As each document vector is read, it is separated into parts for each range of concepts in the load table, and those parts are appended to the end of the corresponding section of the output document collection file. With I/O buffering, the expense of this operation is proportional to the size of the files, and essentially costs the same as copying the file.

Inverting each load

When a load is to be processed, the appropriate section of the CONPTR file is needed. An output array of size equal to the input document vector file subset is needed. As each document vector is processed, the offset (previously recorded in CONPTR) for a given concept is used to place the corresponding document/weight entry, and then that offset is incremented. Thus, the CONPTR data allows the input to be directly mapped to the output, without any sorting. At the end of the input load the newly constructed output is appended to the inverted file.

An example

Figure 3.9 illustrates the FAST-INV processing using sample data. The document vector input files are read through once to produce the concept postings/pointers file (stored on disk as CONPTR) and the load table. Three loads will be needed, for concepts in ranges 1-4, 5-11, and 12-14. There are 10 distinct concepts, and HCN is 14.

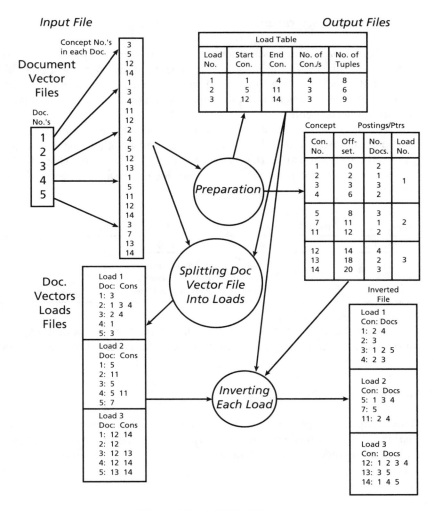

Figure 3.9 A FAST-INV example

The second phase of processing uses the load table to split the input document vector files and create the document vector loads files. There are three parts, corresponding to the three loads. It can be seen that the document vectors in each load are shortened since only those concepts in the allowable range for the load are included.

The final phase of processing involves inverting each part of the document vectors loads file, using primary memory, and appending the result to the inverted file. The appropriate section of the CONPTR file is used so that inversion is simply a copying of data to the correct place, rather than a sort.

Performance results

Based on the discussion above, it can be seen that FAST-INV is a linear algorithm in the size of the input file, L. The input disk files must be read three times, and written twice (using the second splitting scheme). Processing in primary memory is limited to scans through the input, with appropriate (inexpensive) computation required on each entry.

Thus, it should be obvious that FAST-INV should perform well in comparison to other inversion methods, such as those used in other systems such as SIRE and SMART. To demonstrate this fact, a variety of tests were made. Table 3.2 summarizes the results for indexing the 12,684 document/8.68 megabyte INSPEC collection.

Table 3.2 Real Time Requirements (min.)[:sec.] for SIRE, SMART

Method	Comments	Indexing	Inversion
SIRE	Dictionary built during inversion	35	72
SMART	Dictionary built during indexing	49	11
FAST-INV	Dictionary built during indexing	49	1:14

More details of these results, including the various loading experiments made during testing, can be found in the full technical report (Fox and Lee 1991).

3.5 SUMMARY

This Chapter has presented a survey of inverted file structures and detailed the actual building of a basic sorted array type of inverted file. Two modifications that are effective for indexing large data collections were also presented.

REFERENCES

BAYER, R., and K. UNTERAUER. 1977. "Prefix B-Trees." *ACM Transactions on Database Systems,* 2(1), 11–26.

CUTTING, D., and J. PEDERSEN. 1990. "Optimizations for Dynamic Inverted Index Maintenance." Paper presented at the 13th International Conference on Research and Development in Information Retrieval. Brussels, Belgium.

FOX, E. A., and W. C. LEE. 1991. "FAST-INV: A Fast Algorithm for Building Large Inverted Files." Technical Report TR-91-10, VPI&SU Department of Computer Science, March, 1991. Blacksburg, Va. 24061-0106.

GONNET, G. H., and R. BAEZA-YATES. 1991. *Handbook of Algorithms and Data Structures* (2nd ed.). Reading, Mass.: Addison-Wesley.

HARMAN, D., and G. CANDELA. 1990. "Retrieving Records from a Gigabyte of Text on a Minicomputer using Statistical Ranking." *Journal of the American Society for Information Science,* 41(8), 581–89.

KNUTH, DONALD E. 1973. *The Art of Computer Programming.* Reading, Mass.: Addison-Wesley.

4

Signature Files

Christos Faloutsos

*University of Maryland, College Park
and UMIACS*

Abstract

This chapter presents a survey and discussion on signature-based text retrieval methods. It describes the main idea behind the signature approach and its advantages over other text retrieval methods, it provides a classification of the signature methods that have appeared in the literature, it describes the main representatives of each class, together with the relative advantages and drawbacks, and it gives a list of applications as well as commercial or university prototypes that use the signature approach.

4.1 INTRODUCTION

Text retrieval methods have attracted much interest recently (Christodoulakis et al. 1986; Gonnet 1982; Gonnet and Tompa 1987; Stanfill and Kahle 1986; Tsichritzis and Christodoulakis 1983). There are numerous applications involving storage and retrieval of textual data:

- Electronic office filing (Tsichritzis and Christodoulakis 1983; Christodoulakis et al. 1986).
- Computerized libraries. For example, the U.S. Library of Congress has been pursuing the "Optical Disk Pilot Program" (Price 1984; Nofel 1986), where the goal is to digitize the documents and store them on an optical disk. A similar project is carried out at the National Library of Medicine (Thoma et al. 1985).
- Automated law (Hollaar 1979) and patent offices (Hollaar et al. 1983). The U.S. Patent and Trademark Office has been examining electronic storage and retrieval of the recent patents on a system of 200 optical disks.
- Electronic storage and retrieval of articles from newspapers and magazines.
- Consumers' databases, which contain descriptions of products in natural language.
- Electronic encyclopedias (Ewing et al. 1986; Gonnet and Tompa 1987).
- Indexing of software components to enhance reusabililty (Standish 1984).

- Searching databases with descriptions of DNA molecules (Lipman and Pearson 1985).
- Searching image databases, where the images are manually annotated (Christodoulakis et al. 1986). A similar approach could be used to search a database with animations, if scripted animation is used (Lewis 1989).

The main operational characteristics of all the above applications are the following two:

- Text databases are traditionally large.
- Text databases have archival nature: there are insertions in them, but almost never deletions and updates.

Test retrieval methods form the following large classes (Faloutsos 1985): Full text scanning, inversion, and signature files, on which we shall focus next.

Signature files are based on the idea of the inexact filter: They provide a quick test, which discards many of the nonqualifying items. The qualifying items definitely pass the test; some additional items ("false hits" or "false drops") may also pass it accidentally. The signature file approach works as follows: The documents are stored sequentially in the "text file." Their "signatures" (hash-coded bit patterns) are stored in the "signature file." When a query arrives, the signature file is scanned and many nonqualifying documents are discarded. The rest are either checked (so that the "false drops" are discarded) or they are returned to the user as they are.

A brief, qualitative comparison of the signature-based methods versus their competitors is as follows: The signature-based methods are much faster than full text scanning (1 or 2 orders of magnitude faster, depending on the individual method). Compared to inversion, they require a modest space overhead (typically $\approx 10-15\%$ [Christodoulakis and Faloutsos 1984], as opposed to $50-300\%$ that inversion requires [Haskin 1981]); moreover, they can handle insertions more easily than inversion, because they need "append-only" operations—no reorganization or rewriting of any portion of the signatures. Methods requiring "append-only" insertions have the following advantages: (a) increased concurrency during insertions (the readers may continue consulting the old portion of index structure, while an insertion takes place) (b) these methods work well on Write-Once-Read-Many (WORM) optical disks, which constitute an excellent archival medium (Fujitani 1984; Christodoulakis 1987).

On the other hand, signature files may be slow for large databases, precisely because their response time is linear on the number of items N in the database. Thus, signature files have been used in the following environments:

1. PC-based, medium size db
2. WORMs
3. parallel machines
4. distributed text db

This chapter is organized as follows: In section 4.2 we present the basic concepts in signature files and superimposed coding. In section 4.3 we discuss methods based on compression. In section 4.4 we discuss methods based on vertical partitioning of the signature file. In section 4.5 we discuss methods that use both vertical partitioning and compression. In section 4.6 we present methods that are based on horizontal partitioning of the signature file. In section 4.7 we give the conclusions.

4.2 BASIC CONCEPTS

Signature files typically use superimposed coding (Moders 1949) to create the signature of a document. A brief description of the method follows; more details are in Faloutsos (1985). For performance reasons, which will be explained later, each document is divided into "logical blocks," that is, pieces of text that contain a constant number D of distinct, noncommon words. (To improve the space overhead, a stoplist of common words is maintainted.) Each such word yields a "word signature," which is a bit pattern of size F, with m bits set to "1", while the rest are "0" (see Figure 4.1). F and m are design parameters. The word signatures are OR'ed together to form the block signature. Block signatures are concatenated, to form the document signature. The m bit positions to be set to "1" by each word are decided by hash functions. Searching for a word is handled by creating the signature of the word and by examining each block signature for "1"'s in those bit positions that the signature of the search word has a "1".

Word	Signature
free	001 000 110 010
text	000 010 101 001
block signature	001 010 111 011

Figure 4.1 Illustration of the superimposed coding method. It is assumed that each logical block consists of $D=2$ words only. The signature size F is 12 bits, $m=4$ bits per word.

In order to allow searching for parts of words, the following method has been suggested (Faloutsos and Christodoulakis 1984): Each word is divided into successive, overlapping triplets (e.g., "fr", "fre", "ree", "ee" for the word "free"). Each such triplet is hashed to a bit position by applying a hashing function on a numerical encoding of the triplet, for example, considering the triplet as a base-26 number. In the case of a word that has l triplets, with $l > m$, the word is allowed to set l (nondistinct) bits. If $l < m$, the additional bits are set using a random number generator, initialized with a numerical encoding of the word.

An important concept in signature files is the false drop probability F_d. Intuitively, it gives the probability that the signature test will fail, creating a "false alarm" (or "false hit" or "false drop"). Notice that the signature test never gives a false dismissal.

DEFINITION: False drop probability, F_d, is the probability that a block signature seems to qualify, *given that the block does not actually qualify*. Expressed mathematically:

$$F_d = \text{Prob}\{\text{signature qualifies/block does not}\}$$

The signature file is an $F \times N$ binary matrix. Previous analysis showed that, for a given value of F, the value of m that minimizes the false drop probability is such that each row of the matrix contains "1"'s with probability 50 percent. Under such an optimal design, we have (Stiassny 1960):

$$F_d = 2^{-m}$$

$$F \ln 2 = mD$$

This is the reason that documents have to be divided into logical blocks: Without logical blocks, a long document would have a signature full of "1"'s, and it would always create a false drop. To avoid unnecessary complications, for the rest of the discussion we assume that all the *documents span exactly one logical block*.

Table 4.1. Symbols and definitions

Symbol	Definition
F	signature size in bits
m	number of bits per word
D	number of distinct noncommon words per document
F_d	false drop probability

The most straightforward way to store the signature matrix is to store the rows sequentially. For the rest of this work, the above method will be called **SSF**, for Sequential Signature File. Figure 4.2 illustrates the file structure used: In addition to the text file and the signature file, we need the so-called "pointer file," with pointers to the beginnings of the logical blocks (or, alternatively, to the beginning of the documents).

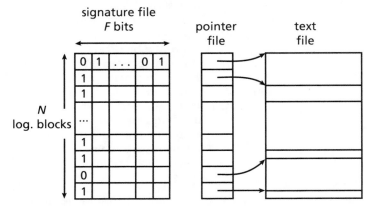

Figure 4.2 File structure for SSF

Although SSF has been used as is, it may be slow for large databases. Many methods have been suggested, trying to improve the response time of SSF, trading off space or insertion simplicity for speed. The main ideas behind all these methods are the following:

1. **Compression:** If the signature matrix is deliberately sparse, it can be compressed.
2. **Vertical partitioning:** Storing the signature matrix columnwise improves the response time on the expense of insertion time.
3. **Horizontal partitioning:** Grouping similar signatures together and/or providing an index on the signature matrix may result in better-than-linear search.

The methods we shall examine form the classes shown in Figure 4.3. For each of these classes we shall describe the main idea, the main representatives, and the available performance results, discussing mainly

- the storage overhead,
- the response time on single word queries,
- the performance on insertion, as well as whether the insertion maintains the "append-only" property.

```
Sequential storage of the signature matrix
        without compression
                sequential signature files (SSF)
        with compression
                bit-block compression (BC)
                variable bit-block compression (VBC)
Vertical partitioning
        without compression
                bit-sliced signature files (BSSF, B'SSF))
                frame sliced (FSSF)
                generalized frame-sliced (GFSSF)
        with compression
                compressed bit slices (CBS)
                doubly compressed bit slices (DCBS)
                no-false-drop method (NFD)
Horizontal partitioning
        data independent partitioning
                Gustafson's method
                partitioned signature files
        data dependent partitioning
                2-level signature files
                S-trees
```

Figure 4.3 Classification of the signature-based methods

4.3 COMPRESSION

In this section we examine a family of methods suggested in Faloutsos and Christodoulakis (1987). These methods create sparse document signatures on purpose, and then compress them before storing them sequentially. Analysis in that paper showed that, whenever compression is applied, the best value for m is 1. Also, it was shown that the resulting methods achieve better false drop probability than SSF for the same space overhead.

The idea in these methods is that we use a (large) bit vector of B bits and we hash each word into one (or perhaps more, say n) bit position(s), which are set to "1" (see Figure 4.4). The resulting bit vector will be sparse and therefore it can be compressed.

data	0000 0000 0000 0010 0000
base	0000 0001 0000 0000 0000
management	0000 1000 0000 0000 0000
system	0000 0000 0000 0000 1000
block	
signature	0000 1001 0000 0010 1000

Figure 4.4 Illustration of the compression-based methods. With $B = 20$ and $n = 1$ bit per word, the resulting bit vector is sparse and can be compressed.

The spacewise best compression method is based on run-length encoding (McIlroy 1982), using the approach of "infinite Huffman codes" (Golomb 1966; Gallager and van Voorhis 1975). However, searching becomes slow. To determine whether a bit is "1" in the sparse vector, the encoded lengths of all the preceding intervals (runs) have to be decoded and summed (see Figure 4.5).

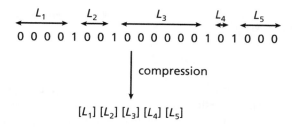

$$[L_1]\ [L_2]\ [L_3]\ [L_4]\ [L_5]$$

Figure 4.5 Compression using run-length encoding. The notation $[x]$ stands for the encoded value of number x

4.3.1 Bit-block Compression (BC)

This method accelerates the search by sacrificing some space, compared to the run-length encoding technique. The compression method is based on bit-blocks, and was called BC (for bit-Block Compression). To speed up the searching, the sparse vector is divided into groups of consecutive bits (bit-blocks); each bit-block is encoded individually. The size of the bit-blocks is chosen according to Eq. (A2.2) in Faloutsos and Christodoulakis (1987) to achieve good compression. For each bit-block we create a signature, which is of variable length and consists of at most three parts (see Figure 4.6):

Part I. It is one bit long and it indicates whether there are any "1"s in the bit-block (1) or the bit-block is empty (0). In the latter case, the bit-block signature stops here.

Part II. It indicates the number s of "1"s in the bit-block. It consists of $s-1$ "1"s and a terminating zero. This is not the optimal way to record the number of "1"s. However this representation is simple and it seems to give results close to the optimal. [See Eq. (4.1.4, 4.1.5) in Faloutsos and Christodoulakis (1987)].

Part III. It contains the offsets of the "1"s from the beginning of the bit-block ($1\,gb$ bits for each "1", where b is the bit-block size).

	b				
	$<->$				
sparse vector	0000	1001	0000	0010	1000
Part I	0	1	0	1	1
Part II		10		0	0
Part III		0011		10	00

Figure 4.6 Illustration of the BC method with bit-block size $b = 4$.

Figure 4.6 illustrates how the BC method compresses the sparse vector of Figure 4.4. Figure 4.7 illustrates the way to store parts of a document signature: the first parts of all the bit-block signatures are stored consecutively, then the second parts, and so on.

0 1 0 1 1 | 10 0 0 | 00 11 10 00

Figure 4.7 BC method—Storing the signature by concatenating the parts. Vertical lines indicate the part boundaries.

4.3.2 Variable Bit-block Compression (VBC)

The BC method was slightly modified to become insensitive to changes in the number of words D per block. This is desirable because the need to split messages in logical blocks is eliminated, thus simplifying the resolution of complex queries: There is no need to "remember" whether some of the terms of the query have appeared in one of the previous logical blocks of the message under inspection.

The idea is to use a different value for the bit-block size b_{opt} for each message, according to the number W of bits set to "1" in the sparse vector. The size of the sparse vector B is the same for all messages. Analysis in Faloutsos and Christodoulakis (1987) shows how to choose the optimal size b of the bit-blocks for a document with W (distinct) words; arithmetic examples in the same paper indicate the advantages of the modified method.

This method was called VBC (for Variable bit-Block Compression). Figure 4.8 illustrates an example layout of the signatures in the VBC method. The upper row corresponds to a small message with small W, while the lower row to a message with large W. Thus, the upper row has a larger value of b_{opt}, fewer bit-blocks, shorter Part I (the size of Part I is the number of bit-blocks), shorter Part II (its size is W) and fewer but larger offsets in Part III (the size of each offset is log b_{opt} bits).

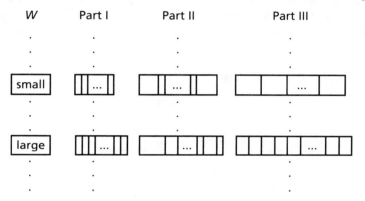

Figure 4.8 An example layout of the message signatures in the VBC method.

4.3.3 Performance

With respect to space overhead, the two methods (BC and VBC) require less space than SSF for the same false drop probability. Their response time is slightly less than SSF, due to the decreased I/0 requirements. The required main-memory operations are more complicated (decompression, etc.), but they are probably not the bottleneck. VBC achieves significant savings even on main-memory operations. With respect to insertions, the two methods are almost as easy as the SSF; they require a few additional CPU cycles to do the compression.

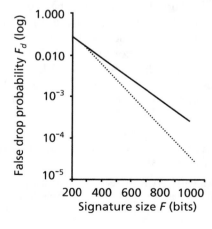

Figure 4.9 Comparison of F_d of BC (dotted line) against SSF (solid line), as a function of the space overhead O_v. Analytical results, from Faloutsos and Christodoulakis (1987).

As shown in Figure 4.9, the BC method achieves ≈50 percent savings in false drops for documents with $D = 40$ vocabulary words each.

4.4 VERTICAL PARTITIONING

The idea behind the vertical partitioning is to avoid bringing useless portions of the document signature in main memory; this can be achieved by storing the signature file in a bit-sliced form (Roberts 1979; Faloutsos and Chan 1988) or in a "frame-sliced" form (Lin and Faloutsos 1988).

4.4.1 Bit-Sliced Signature Files (BSSF)

The bit-sliced design is illustrated in Figure 4.10.

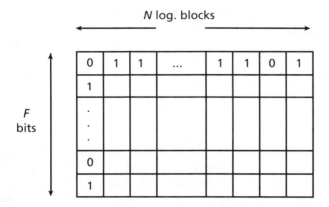

Figure 4.10 Transposed bit matrix

To allow insertions, we propose using F different files, one per each bit position, which will be referred to as "bit-files." The method will be called **BSSF,** for "Bit-Sliced Signature Files." Figure 4.11 illustrates the proposed file structure.

Searching for a single word requires the retrieval of m bit vectors (instead of all of the F bit vectors) which are subsequently ANDed together. The resulting bit vector has N bits, with "1"'s at the positions of the qualifying logical blocks.

An insertion of a new logical block requires F disk accesses, one for each bit-file, but **no rewriting!** Thus, the proposed method is applicable on WORM optical disks. As mentioned in the introduction, commercial optical disks do not allow a

The following data are taken from product specification:

Micropolis, $5\frac{1}{4}$" Winchester, 1350 Series Seek time (avg) = 28 ms; Latency time (avg) = 8.33 ms; Transfer rate = 10 Mbits/sec; Sector size = 512 bytes.

Alcatel Thompson Gigadisk GM 1001 (WORM) Seek time within +/− 100 tracks = 35 ms; Seek time beyond current band = 200 ms; Latency (avg) = 27 ms; Transfer rate = 3.83 Mbits/sec; Sector size = 1K bytes.

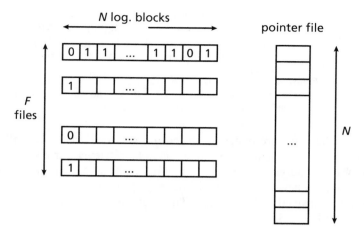

Figure 4.11 File structure for Bit-Sliced Signature Files. The text file is omitted.

single bit to be written; thus, we have to use a magnetic disk, that will hold the last page of each file; when they become full, we will dump them on the optical disk. The size of each bit file can be predicted (Faloutsos and Chan 1988) and the appropriate space can be preallocated on the disk.

4.4.2 B'SSF, a Faster Version of BSSF

The traditional design of BSSF suggests chosing the optimal value for m to be such that the document signatures contain "1"s by 50 percent. A typical value of m is of the order of 10 (Christodoulakis and Faloutsos 1984). This implies 10 random disk accesses on a single word query. In Lin and Faloutsos (1988) it is suggested to use a smaller than optimal value of m; thus, the number of random disk accesses decreases. The drawback is that, in order to maintain the same false drop probability, the document signatures have to be longer.

4.4.3 Frame-Sliced Signature File

The idea behind this method (Lin and Faloutsos 1988) is to force each word to hash into bit positions that are close to each other in the document signature. Then, these bit files are stored together and can be retrieved with few random disk accesses. The main motivation for this organization is that random disk accesses are more expensive than sequential ones, since they involve movement of the disk arm.

More specifically, the method works as follows: The document signature (F bits long) is divided into k frames of s consecutive bits each. For each word in the document, one of the k frames will be chosen by a hash function; using another hash function, the word sets m bits (not necessarily distinct) in that frame. F, k, s, m are design parameters. Figure 4.12 gives an example for this method.

Word	Signature
free	000000 110010
text	010110 000000
doc. signature	010110 110010

Figure 4.12 $D = 2$ words. $F=12$, $s=6$, $k=2$, $m=3$. The word *free* is hashed into the second frame and sets 3 bits there. The word *text* is hashed into the first frame and also sets 3 bits there.

The signature matrix is stored framewise. Each frame will be kept in consecutive disk blocks. Only one frame has to be retrieved for a single word query, that is, only one random disk access is required. At most, n frames have to be scanned for an n word query. Insertion will be much faster than BSSF since we need only access k frames instead of F bit-slices. This method will be referred to as Frame-Sliced Signature file (**FSSF**).

4.4.4 The Generalized Frame-Sliced Signature File (GFSSF)

In FSSF, each word selects only one frame and sets m bit positions in that frame. A more general approach is to select n distinct frames and set m bits (not necessarily distinct) in each frame to generate the word signature. The document signature is the OR-ing of all the word signatures of all the words in that document. This method is called Generalized Frame-Sliced Signature File (GFSSF; Lin and Faloutsos 1988).

Notice that BSSF, B'SSF, FSSF, and SSF are actually special cases of GFSSF:

- When $k = F$, $n = m$, it reduces to the BSSF or B'SSF method.
- When $n = 1$, it reduces to the FSSF method.
- When $k = 1$, $n = 1$, it becomes the SSF method (the document signature is broken down to one frame only).

4.4.5 Performance

Since GFSSF is a generalized model, we expect that a careful choice of the parameters will give a method that is better (whatever the criterion is) than any of its special cases. Analysis in the above paper gives formulas for the false drop probability and the expected response time for GFSSF and the rest of the methods. Figure 4.13 plots the theoretically expected performance of GFSSF, BSSF, B'SSF, and FSSF. Notice that GFSSF is faster than BSSF, B'SSF, and FSSF, which are all its special cases. It is assumed that the transfer time for a page

$$T_{trans} = 1 \text{ msec}$$

and the combined seek and latency time T_{seek} is

$$T_{seek} = 40 \text{ msec}$$

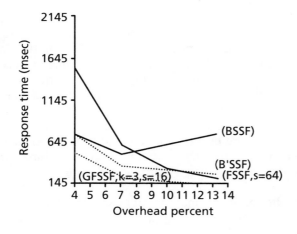

Figure 4.13 Response time vs. space overhead: a comparison between BSSF, B'SSF, FSSF and GFSSF. Analytical results on a 2.8Mb database.

The text file was 2.8Mb long, with average document size ≈ 1 Kb. Each document contained $D = 58$ distinct noncommon words.

The experiments were conducted on a SUN 3/50 with a local disk, when the load was light; the system was implemented in C, under UNIX. The experiments on the 2.8Mb database showed good agreement between the theoretical and experimental values for the false drop probability. The maximum relative error was 16 percent. The average response time ("real time") was 420 ms for FSSF with $s = 63$, $m = 8$, $O_v = 18$ percent, and 480 ms for GFSSF with $s = 15$, $n = 3$, $m = 3$, and $O_v = 18$ percent.

4.5 VERTICAL PARTITIONING AND COMPRESSION

The idea in all the methods in this class (Faloutsos and Chan 1988) is to create a very sparse signature matrix, to store it in a bit-sliced form, and compress each bit slice by storing the position of the "1"s in the slice. The methods in this class are closely related to inversion with a hash table.

4.5.1 Compressed Bit Slices (CBS)

Although the bit-sliced method is much faster than SSF on retrieval, there may be room for two improvements:

1. On searching, each search word requires the retrieval of m bit files, exactly because each word signature has m bits set to "1". The search time could be improved if m was forced to be "1".
2. The insertion of a logical block requires too many disk accesses (namely, F, which is typically $600-1,000$).

If we force $m = 1$, then F has to be increased, in order to maintain the same false drop probability (see the formulas in Faloutsos and Chan [1988]. For the next three methods, we shall use S to denote the size of a signature, to highlight the similarity of these methods to inversion using hash tables. The corresponding bit matrix and bit files will be sparse and they can be compressed. Figure 4.14 illustrate a sparse bit matrix. The easiest way to compress each bit file is to store the positions of the "1"'s. However, the size of each bit file is unpredictable now, subject to statistical variations. Therefore, we store them in buckets of size B_p, which is a design parameter. As a bit file grows, more buckets are allocated to it on demand. These buckets are linked together with pointers. Obviously, we also need a directory (hash table) with S pointers, one for each bit slice. Notice the following:

1. There is no need to split documents into logical blocks any more.
2. The pointer file can be eliminated. Instead of storing the position of each "1" in a (compressed) bit file, we can store a pointer to the document in the text file.

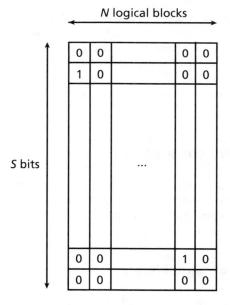

Figure 4.14 Sparse bit matrix

Thus, the compressed bit files will contain pointers to the appropriate documents (or logical blocks). The set of all the compressed bit files will be called "level 1" or "postings file," to agree with the terminology of inverted files (Salton and McGill 1983).

The postings file consists of postings buckets, of size B_p bytes (B_p is a design parameter). Each such bucket contains pointers to the documents in the text file, as well as an extra pointer, to point to an overflow postings bucket, if necessary.

Figure 4.15 illustrates the proposed file structure, and gives an example, assuming that the word "base" hashes to the 30-th position (h("base") = 30), and that it appears in the document starting at the 1145-th byte of the text file.

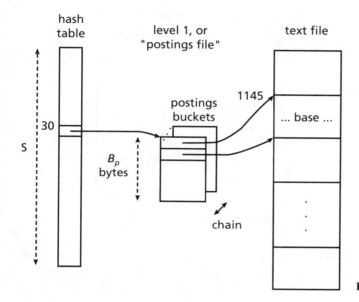

Figure 4.15 Illustration of CBS

Searching is done by hashing a word to obtain the postings bucket address. This bucket, as well as its overflow buckets, will be retrieved, to obtain the pointers to the relevant documents. To reduce the false drops, the hash table should be sparse. The method is similar to hashing. The differences are the following:

a. The directory (hash table) is sparse; Traditional hashing schemes require loads of 80–90 percent.

b. The actual word is stored nowhere. Since the hash table is sparse, there will be few collisions. Thus, we save space and maintain a simple file structure.

4.5.2 Doubly Compressed Bit Slices (DCBS)

The motivation behind this method is to try to compress the sparse directory of CBS. The file structure we propose consists of a hash table, an intermediate file, a postings file and the text file as in Figure 4.16. The method is similar to CBS. It uses a hashing function $h_1()$, which returns values in the range $(0,(S-1))$ and determines the slot in the directory. The difference is that DCBS makes an effort to distinguish among synonyms, by using a second hashing function $h_2()$, which returns

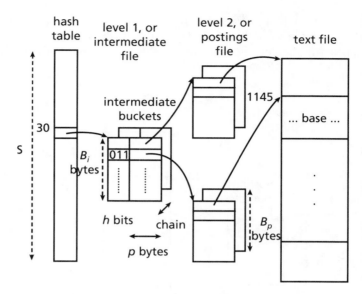

Figure 4.16 Illustration of DCBS

bit strings that are h bits long. These hash codes are stored in the "intermediate file," which consists of buckets of B_i bytes (design parameter). Each such bucket contains records of the form (*hashcode, ptr*). The pointer *ptr* is the head of a linked list of postings buckets.

Figure 4.16 illustrates an example, where the word "base" appears in the document that starts at the 1145-th byte of the text file. The example also assumes that $h = 3$ bits, $h_1(\text{"base"}) = 30$, and $h_2(\text{"base"}) = (011)_2$.

Searching for the word "base" is handled as follows:

Step 1 $h_1(\text{"base"}) = 30$: The 30-th pointer of the directory will be followed. The corresponding chain of intermediate buckets will be examined.

Step 2 $h_2(\text{"base"}) = (011)_2$: The records in the above intermediate buckets will be examined. If a matching hash code is found (at most one will exist!), the corresponding pointer is followed, to retrieve the chain of postings buckets.

Step 3 The pointers of the above postings buckets will be followed, to retrieve the qualifying (actually or falsely) documents.

Insertion is omitted for brevity.

4.5.3 No False Drops Method (NFD)

This method avoids false drops completely, without storing the actual words in the index. The idea is to modify the intermediate file of the DCBS, and store a pointer to the word in the text file. Specifically, each record of the intermediate file will have the format (*hashcode, ptr, ptr–to–word*), where *ptr–to–word* is a pointer to the word in the text file. See Figure 4.17 for an illustration.

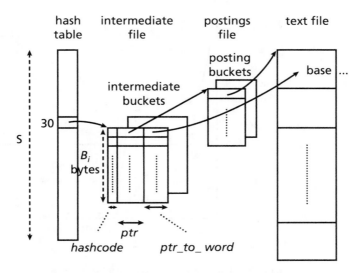

Figure 4.17 Illustration of NFD

This way each word can be completely distinguished from its synonyms, using only *h* bits for the hash code and *p* (=4 bytes, usually) for the *ptr–to–word*. The advantages of storing *ptr–to–word* instead of storing the actual word are two: (1) space is saved (a word from the dictionary is ≈8 characters long (Peterson 1980), and (2) the records of the intermediate file have fixed length. Thus, there is no need for a word delimiter and there is no danger for a word to cross bucket boundaries.

Searching is done in a similar way with DCBS. The only difference is that, whenever a matching hash code is found in Step 2, the corresponding *ptr–to–word* is followed, to avoid synonyms completely.

4.5.4 Performance

In Faloutsos and Chan (1988), an analytical model is developed for the performance of each of the above methods. Experiments on the 2.8Mb database showed that the model is accurate. Figure 4.18 plots the theoretical performance of the methods (search time as a function of the overhead).

The final conclusion is that these methods are fast, requiring few disk accesses, they introduce 20–25 percent space overhead, and they still require append-only operations on insertion.

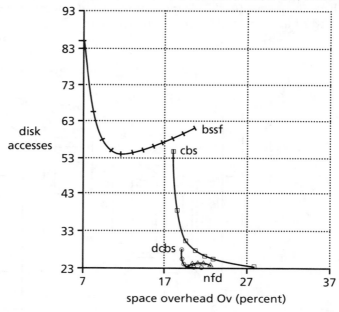

disk accesses on suc. search vs. Ov, for BSSF, CBS, DCBS, and NFD

Figure 4.18 Total disk accesses on successful search versus space overhead. Analytical results for the 2.8 Mb database, with $p = 3$ bytes per pointer. Squares correspond to the CBS method, circles to DCBS, and triangles to NFD.

4.6 HORIZONTAL PARTITIONING

The motivation behind all these methods is to avoid the sequential scanning of the signature file (or its bit-slices), in order to achieve better than $O(N)$ search time. Thus, they group the signatures into sets, partitioning the signature matrix horizontally. The grouping criterion can be decided beforehand, in the form of a hashing function $h(S)$, where S is a document signature (data independent case). Alternatively, the groups can be determined on the fly, using a hierarchical structure (e.g. a B-tree—data dependent case).

4.6.1 Data Independent Case

Gustafson's method

The earliest approach was proposed by Gustafson (1971). Suppose that we have records with, say six attributes each. For example, records can be documents and attributes can be keywords describing the document. Consider a hashing function h that hashes a keyword w to a number $h(w)$ in the range 0–15. The signature of a keyword is a string of 16 bits, all of which are zero except for the bit at position $h(w)$. The record signature is created by superimposing the corresponding keyword

Signature Files   Chap. 4

signatures. If $k < 6$ bits are set in a record signature, additional $6 - k$ bits are set by some random method. Thus, there are $comb(16,6) = 8{,}008$ possible distinct record signatures (where $C(m,n)$ denotes the combinations of m choose n items). Using a hash table with 8,008 slots, we can map each record signature to one such slot as follows: Let $p_1 < p_2 < \cdots < p_6$ the positions where the "1"s occur in the record signature. Then the function

$$C(p_1, 1) + C(p_2, 2) + \cdots + C(p_6, 6)$$

maps each distinct record signature to a number in the range $0{-}8{,}007$. The interesting point of the method is that the extent of the search decreases quickly (almost exponentially) with the number of terms in the (conjunctive) query. Single word queries touch $C(15, 5) = 3{,}003$ slots of the hash table, two-word queries touch $C(14, 4) = 1{,}001$ slots, and so on.

Although elegant, Gustafson's method suffers from some practical problems:

1. Its performance deteriorates as the file grows.

2. If the number of keywords per document is large, then either we must have a huge hash table or usual queries (involving 3–4 keywords) will touch a large portion of the database.

3. Queries other than conjunctive ones are handled with difficulty.

Partitioned signature files

Lee and Leng (1989) proposed a family of methods that can be applied for longer documents. They suggested using a portion of a document signature as a signature key to partition the signature file. For example, we can choose the first 20 bits of a signature as its key and all signatures with the same key will be grouped into a so-called "module." When a query signature arrives, we will first examine its signature key and look for the corresponding modules, then scan all the signatures within those modules that have been selected. They report 15 to 85 percent speedups over SSF, depending on the number of bits being specified in the query signature.

4.6.2 Data Dependent Case

Two-level signature files

Sacks-Davis and his colleagues (1983, 1987) suggested using two levels of signatures. Their documents are bibliographic records of variable length. The first level of signatures consists of document signatures that are stored sequentially, as in the SSF method. The second level consists of "block signatures"; each such signature corresponds to one block (group) of bibliographic records, and is created by superimposing the signatures of all the words in this block, ignoring the record boundaries. The second level is stored in a bit-sliced form. Each level has its own hashing functions that map words to bit positions.

Searching is performed by scanning the block signatures first, and then concentrating on these portions of the first-level signature file that seem promising.

Analysis on a database with $N \approx 10^6$ records (with 128 bytes per record on the average) reported response times as low as 0.3 seconds for single word queries, when 1 record matched the query. The BSSF method required $\approx 1-5$ seconds for the same situation.

A subtle problem arises when multiterm conjunctive queries are asked, (e.g., "data *and* retrieval"): A block may result in an unsuccessful block match, because it may contain the desired terms, but not within the same record. The authors propose a variety of clever ways to minimize these block matches.

S-tree

Deppisch (1986) proposed a B-tree like structure to facilitate fast access to the records (which are signatures) in a signature file. The leaf of an S-tree consists of k "similar" (i.e., with small Hamming distance) document signatures along with the document identifiers. The OR-ing or these k document signatures forms the "key" of an entry in an upper level node, which serves as a directory for the leaves. Recursively we construct directories on lower level directories until we reach the root. The S-tree is kept balanced in a similar manner as a B-trees: when a leaf node overflows it is split in two groups of "similar" signatures; the father node is changed appropriately to reflect the new situation. Splits may propagate upward until reaching the root.

The method requires small space overhead; the response time on queries is difficult to estimate analytically. The insertion requires a few disk accesses (proportional to the height of the tree at worst), but the append-only property is lost. Another problem is that higher level nodes may contain keys that have many 1's and thus become useless.

4.7 DISCUSSION

Signature files provide a space-time trade-off between full text scanning, which is slow but requires no overheads, and inversion, which is fast but requires expensive insertions and needs significant space overhead. Thus, signature-based methods have been applied in the following environments:

1. Medium-size databases. "Hyperties" (Lee et al. 1988), a hypertext package that is commercially available on IBM PCs, uses the SSF method, due to its simplicity, low space overhead, and satisfactory search time (3–10 seconds, for queries with low selectivities) on databases of ≈ 200 Kb (after compression). Thanks to the low overhead, the whole package (software, data, and indices) fits in floppy diskettes. Another commercial product (Kimbrell 1988) is also reported to use signature files for text retrieval.

2. Databases with low query frequencies. In this case, it is not worth building and maintaining a B-tree inverted index; signature files provide a low-cost alternative, that avoids scanning the full text. This situation is probably true for message files in Office Automation; several prototype systems use the signature approach, like the Office Filing Project (Tsichritzis et al. 1983) at the University of Toronto, MINOS (Christodoulakis et al. 1986) at the University of Waterloo, the MULTOS project (Croft and Savino 1988) funded by the ESPRIT project of the European Community.

3. Due to the append-only insertion, signature-based methods can be used on WORM optical disks.

4. Due to the linear searching, signature files can easily benefit from parallelism. Stanfill and Kahle (1986) used signature files on the Connection Machine (Hillis 1985). Keeping the whole signature file in core, they can provide fast responses against databases that are ≈ 10 times larger than the available main memory storage.

5. In distributed environments. In this case, keeping copies of signature files of all the sites can save remote-logins, for a modest space overhead.

6. Chang and Schek (1989) recommend signature files as a simple and flexible access method for records and "long fields" (=text and complex objects) in IBM's STAR-BUST extensible DBMS.

REFERENCES

CHANG, W. W. and H. J. SCHEK. 1989. "A Signature Access Method for the Starbust Database System." *Proc. VLDB Conference*, pp. 145–53. Amsterdam, Netherlands, Aug. 22–25.

CHRISTODOULAKIS, S. 1987. "Analysis of Retrieval Performance for Records and Objects Using Optical Disk Technology," *ACM TODS,* 12(2), 137–69.

CHRISTODOULAKIS, S., and C. FALOUTSOS. 1984. "Design Considerations for a Message File Server." *IEEE Trans. on Software Engineering*, SE-10 (2), 201–10.

CHRISTODOULAKIS, S., F. HO, and M. THEODORIDOU. 1986. "The Multimedia Object Presentation Manager in MINOS: A Symmetric Approach." *Proc. ACM SIGMOD.*

CHRISTODOULAKIS, S., M. THEODORIDOU, F. HO, M. PAPA, and A. PATHRIA. 1986. "Multimedia Document Presentation, Information Extraction and Document Formation in MINOS: A Model and a System." *ACM TOOIS*, 4 (4).

CROFT, W. B, and P. SAVINO. 1988. "Implementing Ranking Strategies Using Text Signatures." *ACM Trans. on Office Informations Systems (TOOIS)*, 6 (1), 42–62.

DEPPISCH, U. 1986. "S-tree: A Dynamic Balanced Signature Index for Office Retrieval." *Proc. of ACM "Research and Development in Information Retrieval,"* pp. 77–87, Pisa, Italy, Sept. 8–10.

EWING, J., S. MEHRABANZAD, S. SHECK, D. OSTROFF, and B. SHNEIDERMAN. 1986. "An Experimental Comparison of a Mouse and Arrow-jump Keys for an Interactive Encyclopedia." *Int. Journal of Man-Machine Studies*, 24, (1) 29–45.

FALOUTSOS, C. 1985. "Access Methods for Text." *ACM Computing Surveys*, 17 (1), 49–74.

FALOUTSOS, C., and R. CHAN. 1988. "Fast Text Access Methods for Optical and Large Magnetic Disks: Designs and Performance Comparison." *Proc. 14th International Conf. on VLDB*, pp. 280–93, Long Beach, Calif. August.

FALOUTSOS, C., and S. CHRISTODOULAKIS. 1984. "Signature Files: An Access Method for Documents and its Analytical Performance Evaluation." *ACM Trans. on Office Information Systems*, 2 (4), 267–88.

FALOUTSOS, C., and S. CHRISTODOULAKIS. 1987. "Description and Performance Analysis of Signature File Methods." *ACM TOOIS*, 5 (3), 237–57.

FUJITANI, L. 1984. "Laser Optical Disk: The Coming Revolution in On-Line Storage." *CACM*, 27 (6), 546–54.

GALLAGER, R. G., and D. C. VAN VOORHIS. 1975. "Optimal Source Codes for Geometrically Distributed Integer Alphabets." *IEEE Trans. on Information Theory*, IT-21, 228–30.

GOLOMB, S. W. 1966. "Run Length Encodings." *IEEE Trans. on Information Theory*, IT-12, 399–401.

GONNET, G. H. 1982. "Unstructured Data Bases," Tech Report CS-82-09, University of Waterloo.

GONNET, G. H., and F. W. TOMPA. 1987. "Mind Your Grammar: A New Approach to Modelling Text." *Proc. of the Thirteenth Int. Conf. on Very Large Data Bases*, pp. 339–346, Brighton, England, September 1–4.

GUSTAFSON, R. A. 1971. "Elements of the Randomized Combinatorial File Structure." *ACM SIGIR, Proc. of the Symposium on Information Storage and Retrieval*, pp. 163–74, University of Maryland. April.

HASKIN, R. L. 1981. "Special-Purpose Processors for Text Retrieval." *Database Engineering*, 4 (1), 16–29.

HILLIS, D. 1985. *The Connection Machine*. Cambridge, Mass.: MIT Press.

HOLLAAR, L. A. 1979. "Text Retrieval Computers." *IEEE Computer Magazine*, 12 (3), 40–50.

HOLLAAR, L. A., K. F. SMITH, W. H. CHOW, P. A. EMRATH, and R. L. HASKIN. 1983. "Architecture and Operation of a Large, Full-Text Information-Retrieval System," in *Advanced Database Machine Architecture*, D. K. Hsiao, ed. pp. 256–99. Englewood Cliffs, N.J.: Prentice Hall.

KIMBRELL, R. E. 1988. "Searching for Text? Send an N-gram!" *Byte*, 13 (5) 297–312.

LEE, D. L., and C.-W. LENG. 1989. "Partitioned Signature File: Designs and Performance Evaluation." *ACM Trans. on Information Systems (TOIS)*, 7 (2), 158–80.

LEE, R., C. FALOUTSOS, C. PLAISANT, and B. SHNEIDERMAN. 1988. "Incorporating String Search in a Hypertext System: User Interface and Physical Design Issues." Dept. of Computer Science, University of Maryland, College Park. Working paper.

LEWIS, E. P. 1989. "Animated Images for a Multimedia Database." Master's Thesis, Dept. of Computer Science, University of Maryland.

LIN, Z., and C. FALOUTSOS. 1988. "Frame Sliced Signature Files," CS-TR-2146 and UMI-ACS-TR-88-88, Dept. of Computer Science, University of Maryland.

LIPMAN, D. J., and W. R. PEARSON. 1985. "Rapid and Sensitive Protein Similarity Searches." *Science*, 227, 1435–41, American Association for the Advancement of Science, March 22.

McILROY, M. D. 1982. "Development of a Spelling List." *IEEE Trans. on Communications,* COM-30, (1), 91–99.

MOOERS, C. 1949. "Application of Random Codes to the Gathering of Statistical Information." Bulletin 31, Zator Co., Cambridge, Mass. Based on M.S. thesis, MIT, January 1948.

NOFEL, P. J. 1986. "40 Million Hits on Optical Disk." *Modern Office Technology*, 84–88. March.

PETERSON, J. L. 1980. "Computer Programs for Detecting and Correcting Spelling Errors." *CACM*, 23 (12), 676–87.

PRICE, J. 1984. "The Optical Disk Pilot Project At the Library of Congress." *Videodisc and Optical Disk*, 4 (6), 424–32.

ROBERTS, C. S. 1979. "Partial-Match Retrieval via the Method of Superimposed Codes." *Proc. IEEE*, 67 (12), 1624–42.

SACKS-DAVIS, R., A. KENT, and K. RAMAMOHANARAO. 1987. "Multikey Access Methods Based on Superimposed Coding Techniques" *ACM Trans. on Database Systems (TODS)*, 12 (4), 655–96.

SACKS-DAVIS, R., and K. RAMAMOHANARAO. 1983. "A Two Level Superimposed Coding Scheme for Partial Match Retrieval." *Information Systems*, 8 (4), 273–80.

SALTON, G., and M. J. McGILL. 1983. *Introduction to Modern Information Retrieval.* New York: McGraw-Hill.

STANDISH, T. A. 1984. "An Essay on Software Reuse." *IEEE Trans. on Software Engineering,* SE-10 (5), 494–97.

STANFILL, C., and B. KAHLE. 1986. "Parallel Free-Text Search on the Connection Machine System." *CACM*, 29 (12), 1229–39.

STIASSNY, S., 1960. "Mathematical Analysis of Various Superimposed Coding Methods." *American Documentation*, 11 (2), 155–69.

THOMA, G. R., S. SUTHASINEKUL, F. A. WALKER, J. COOKSON, and M. RASHIDIAN. 1985. "A Prototype System for the Electronic Storage and Retrieval of Document Images." *ACM TOOIS*, 3 (3).

TSICHRITZIS, D., and S. CHRISTODOULAKIS. 1983. "Message Files." *ACM Trans. on Office Information Systems*, 1 (1), 88–98.

TSICHRITZIS, D., S. CHRISTODOULAKIS, P. ECONOMOPOULOS, C. FALOUTSOS, A. LEE, D. LEE, J. VANDENBROEK, and C. WOO. 1983. "A Multimedia Office Filing System." *Proc. 9th International Conference on VLDB*, Florence, Italy, October–November.

5

New Indices for Text: PAT Trees and PAT Arrays

Gaston H. Gonnet
Dept. of Computer Science
ETH, Zurich, Switzerland

Ricardo A. Baeza-Yates
Depto. de Ciencias de la Computación
Universidad de Chile
Casilla 2777,
Santiago, Chile

Tim Snider
Centre for the New OED and Text Research
University of Waterloo
Waterloo, Ontario
Canada N2L 3G1

Abstract

We survey new indices for text, with emphasis on PAT arrays (also called suffix arrays). A PAT array is an index based on a new model of text that does not use the concept of word and does not need to know the structure of the text.

5.1 INTRODUCTION

Text searching methods may be classified as lexicographical indices (indices that are sorted), clustering techniques, and indices based on hashing. In this chapter we discuss two new lexicographical indices for text, called PAT trees and PAT arrays. Our aim is to build an index for the text of size similar to or smaller than the text.

Briefly, the traditional model of text used in information retrieval is that of a *set of documents*. Each document is assigned a list of *keywords* (attributes), with optional relevance *weights* associated to each keyword. This model is oriented to library applications, which it serves quite well. For more general applications, it has some problems, namely:

- A basic structure is assumed (documents and words). This may be reasonable for many applications, but not for others.

- Keywords must be extracted from the text (this is called "indexing"). This task is not trivial and error prone, whether it is done by a person, or automatically by a computer.
- Queries are restricted to keywords.

For some indices, instead of indexing a set of keywords, all words except for those deemed to be too common (called *stopwords*) are indexed.

We prefer a different model. We see the text as one long *string*. Each position in the text corresponds to a semi-infinite string (*sistring*), the string that starts at that position and extends arbitrarily far to the right, or to the end of the text. It is not difficult to see that any two strings not at the same position are different. The main advantages of this model are:

- No structure of the text is needed, although if there is one, it can be used.
- No keywords are used. The queries are based on *prefixes* of sistrings, that is, on any substring of the text.

This model is simpler and does not restrict the query domain. Furthermore, almost any searching structure can be used to support this view of text.

In the traditional text model, each document is considered a database record, and each keyword a value or a secondary key. Because the number of keywords is variable, common database techniques are not useful in this context. Typical database queries are on equality or on ranges. They seldom consider "approximate text searching."

This paper describes PAT trees and PAT arrays. PAT arrays are an efficient implementation of PAT trees, and support a query language more powerful than do traditional structures based on keywords and Boolean operations. PAT arrays were independently discovered by Gonnet (1987) and Manber and Myers (1990). Gonnet used them for the implementation of a fast text searching system, PAT™ (Gonnet 1987; Fawcett 1989), used with the *Oxford English Dictionary* (*OED*). Manber and Myers' motivation was searching in large genetic databases. We will explain how to build and how to search PAT arrays.

5.2 THE PAT TREE STRUCTURE

The PAT tree is a data structure that allows very efficient searching with preprocessing. This section describes the PAT data structure, how to do some text searches and algorithms to build two of its possible implementations. This structure was originally described by Gonnet in the paper "Unstructured Data Bases" by Gonnet (1983). In 1985 it was implemented and later used in conjunction with the computerization of the *Oxford English Dictionary*. The name of the implementation, the PAT™ system, has become well known in its own right, as a software package for very fast string searching.

5.2.1 Semi-infinite Strings

In what follows, we will use a very simple model of text. Our text, or text database, will consist of a single (possibly very long) array of characters, numbered sequentially from one onward. Whether the text is already presented as such, or whether it can be viewed as such is not relevant. To apply our algorithms it is sufficient to be able to view the entire text as an array of characters.

A semi-infinite string is a subsequence of characters from this array, taken from a given starting point but going on as necessary to the right. In case the semi-infinite string (sistring) is used beyond the end of the actual text, special null characters will be considered to be added at its end, these characters being different than any other in the text. The name semi-infinite is taken from the analogy with geometry where we have semi-infinite lines, lines with one origin, but infinite in one direction. Sistrings are uniquely identified by the position where they start, and for a given, fixed text, this is simply given by an integer.

Example:

```
Text            Once upon a time, in a far away land ...

sistring 1      Once upon a time ...
sistring 2      nce upon a time ...
sistring 8      on a time, in a ...
sistring 11     a time, in a far ...
sistring 22     a far away land ...
```

Sistrings can be defined formally as an abstract data type and as such present a very useful and important model of text. For the purpose of this section, the most important operation on sistrings is the lexicographical comparison of sistrings and will be the only one defined. This comparison is the one resulting from comparing two sistrings' contents (not their positions). Note that unless we are comparing a sistring to itself, the comparison of two sistrings cannot yield equal. (If the sistrings are not the same, sooner or later, by inspecting enough characters, we will have to find a character where they differ, even if we have to start comparing the fictitious null characters at the end of the text).

For example, the above sistrings will compare as follows:

$$22 < 11 < 2 < 8 < 1$$

Of the first 22 sistrings (using ASCII ordering) the lowest sistring is "a far away. . ." and the highest is "upon a time. . . ."

5.2.2 PAT Tree

A PAT tree is a Patricia tree (Morrison 1968; Knuth 1973; Flajolet and Sedgewick 1986; and Gonnet 1988) constructed over all the possible sistrings of a text. A Patricia tree is a digital tree where the individual bits of the keys are used to decide on the branching. A zero bit will cause a branch to the left subtree, a one bit will cause a branch to the right subtree. Hence Patricia trees are binary digital trees. In addition, Patricia trees have in each internal node an indication of which bit of the query is to be used for branching. This may be given by an absolute bit position, or by a count of the number of bits to *skip*. This allows internal nodes with single descendants to be eliminated, and thus all internal nodes of the tree produce a useful branching, that is, both subtrees are non-null. Patricia trees are very similar to compact suffix trees or compact position trees (Aho et al. 1974).

Patricia trees store key values at external nodes; the internal nodes have no key information, just the skip counter and the pointers to the subtrees. The external nodes in a PAT tree are sistrings, that is, integer displacements. For a text of size n, there are n external nodes in the PAT tree and $n - 1$ internal nodes. This makes the tree $O(n)$ in size, with a relatively small asymptotic constant. Later we will want to store some additional information (the size of the subtree and which is the taller subtree) with each internal node, but this information will always be of a constant size.

Figure 5.1 shows an example of a PAT tree over a sequence of bits (normally it would be over a sequence of characters), just for the purpose of making the example easier to understand. In this example, we show the Patricia tree for the text "01100100010111..." after the first 8 sistrings have been inserted. External nodes are indicated by squares, and they contain a reference to a sistring, and internal nodes are indicated by a circle and contain a displacement. In this case we have used, in each internal node, the total displacement of the bit to be inspected, rather than the skip value.

Notice that to reach the external node for the query 00101 we first inspect bit 1 (it is a zero, we go left) then bit 2 (it is zero, we go left), then bit 3 (it is a one, we go right), and then bit 5 (it is a one, we go right). Because we may skip the inspec-

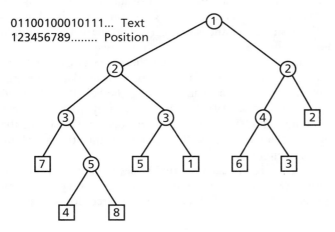

01100100010111... Text
123456789........ Position

Figure 5.1 PAT tree when the sistrings 1 through 8 have been inserted

tion of some bits (in this case bit 4), once we reach our desired node we have to make one final comparison with one of the sistrings stored in an external node of the current subtree, to ensure that all the skipped bits coincide. If they do not coincide, then the key is not in the tree.

5.2.3 Indexing Points

So far we have assumed that every position in the text is indexed, that is, the Patricia tree has n external nodes, one for each position in the text. For some types of search this is desirable, but in some other cases not all points are necessary or even desirable to index. For example, if we are interested in word and phrase searches, then only those sistrings that are at the beginning of words (about 20% of the total for common English text) are necessary. The decision of how many sistrings to include in the tree is application dependent, and will be a trade-off between size of the index and search requirements.

5.3 ALGORITHMS ON THE PAT TREE

In this section we will describe some of the algorithms for text searching when we have a PAT tree of our text.

5.3.1 Prefix Searching

Notice that every subtree of the PAT tree has all the sistrings with a given prefix, by construction. Then prefix searching in a PAT tree consists of searching the prefix in the tree up to the point where we exhaust the prefix or up to the point where we reach an external node. At this point we need to verify whether we could have skipped bits. This is done with a single comparison of any of the sistrings in the subtree (considering an external node as a subtree of size one). If this comparison is successful, then all the sistrings in the subtree (which share the common prefix) are the answer; otherwise there are no sistrings in the answer.

It is important to notice that the search ends when the prefix is exhausted or when we reach an external node and at that point all the answer is available (regardless of its size) in a single subtree. For random Patricia trees, the height is $O(\log n)$ (Pittel 1985; Apostolico and Szpankowski 1987) and consequently with PAT trees we can do arbitrary prefix searching in $O(\log n)$ time, independent of the size of the answer. In practice, the length of the query is less than $O(\log n)$, thus the searching time is proportional to the query length.

By keeping the size of each subtree in each internal node, we can trivially find the size of any matched subtree. (Knowing the size of the answer is very appealing for information retrieval purposes.) Figure 5.2 shows the search for the prefix "10100" and its answer.

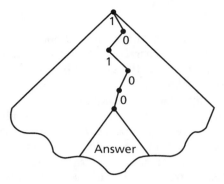

Figure 5.2 Prefix searching.

5.3.2 Proximity Searching

We define a proximity search as finding all places where a string s_1 is at most a fixed (given by the user) number of characters away from another string s_2. The simplest algorithm for this type of query is to search for s_1 and s_2. Then, sort by position the smaller of the two answers. Finally, we traverse the unsorted answer set, searching every position in the sorted set, and checking if the distance between positions (and order, if we always want s_1 before s_2) satisfies the proximity condition. If m_1 and m_2 ($m_1 < m_2$) are the respective answer set sizes, this algorithm requires $(m_1 + m_2) \log m_1$ time. This is not very appealing if m_1 or m_2 are $O(n)$. For the latter case (when one of the strings s_1 or s_2 is small), better solutions based on PAT arrays have been devised by Manber and Baeza-Yates (1991).

5.3.3 Range Searching

Searching for all the strings within a certain range of values (lexicographical range) can be done equally efficiently. More precisely, range searching is defined as searching for all strings that lexicographically compare between two given strings. For example, the range "abc" . . "acc" will contain strings like "abracadabra," "acacia," "aboriginal," but not "abacus" or "acrimonious."

To do range searching on a PAT tree, we search each end of the defining intervals and then collect all the subtrees between (and including) them. It should be noticed that only $O(height)$ subtrees will be in the answer even in the worst case (the worst case is $2\ height - 1$) and hence only $O(\log n)$ time is necessary in total. As before, we can return the answer and the size of the answer in time $O(\log n)$ independent of the actual size of the answer.

5.3.4 Longest Repetition Searching

The longest repetition of a text is defined as the match between two different positions of a text where this match is the longest (the most number of characters) in the entire text. For a given text, the longest repetition will be given by the tallest internal node in the PAT tree, that is, the tallest internal node gives a pair of sistrings that match for the greatest number of characters. In this case, tallest means not only the shape of the tree but has to consider the skipped bits also. For a given text, the longest repetition can be found while building the tree and it is a constant, that is, will not change unless we change the tree (that is, the text).

It is also interesting and possible to search for the longest repetition not just for the entire tree/text, but for a subtree. This means searching for the longest repetition among all the strings that share a common prefix. This can be done in $O(height)$ time by keeping one bit of information at each internal node, which will indicate on which side we have the tallest subtree. By keeping such a bit, we can find one of the longest repetitions starting with an arbitrary prefix in $O(\log n)$ time. If we want to search for all of the longest repetitions, we need two bits per internal node (to indicate equal heights as well) and the search becomes logarithmic in height and linear in the number of matches.

5.3.5 "Most Significant" or "Most Frequent" Searching

This type of search has great practical interest, but is slightly difficult to describe. By "most significant" or "most frequent" we mean the most frequently occurring strings within the text database. For example, finding the "most frequent" trigram is finding a sequence of three letters that appears most often within our text.

In terms of the PAT tree, and for the example of the trigrams, the number of occurrences of a trigram is given by the size of the subtree at a distance 3 characters from the root. So finding the most frequent trigram is equivalent to finding the largest subtree at a distance 3 characters from the root. This can be achieved by a simple traversal of the PAT tree which is at most $O(n/average\ size\ of\ answer)$ but is usually much faster.

Searching for "most common" word is slightly more difficult but uses a similar algorithm. A word could be defined as any sequence of characters delimited by a blank space. This type of search will also require a traversal, but in this case the traversal is only done in a subtree (the subtree of all sistrings starting with a space) and does not have a constant depth; it traverses the tree to the places where each second blank appears.

We may also apply this algorithm within any arbitrary subtree. This is equivalent to finding the most frequently occurring trigram, word, and the like, that follows some given prefix.

In all cases, finding the most frequent string with a certain property requires a subtree selection and then a tree traversal which is at most $O(n/k)$ but typically much smaller. Here, k is the average size of each group of strings of the given property. Techniques similar to alpha-beta pruning can be used to improve this search.

5.3.6 Regular Expression Searching

The main steps of the algorithm due by Baeza-Yates and Gonnet (1989) are:

a. Convert the regular expression passed as a query into a minimized deterministic finite automation (DFA), which may take exponential space/time with respect to the query size but is independent of the size of the text (Hopcroft and Ullman 1979).

b. Next eliminate outgoing transitions from final states (see justification in step (e). This may induce further minimization.

c. Convert character DFAs into binary DFAs using any suitable binary encoding of the input alphabet; each state will then have at most two outgoing transitions, one labeled 0 and one labeled 1.

d. Simulate the binary DFA on the binary digital trie from all sistrings of text using the same binary encoding as in step b. That is, associate the root of the tree with the initial state, and, for any internal node associated with state i, associate its left descendant with state j if $i \rightarrow j$ for a bit 0, and associate its right descendant with state k if $i \rightarrow k$ for a 1 (see Figure 5.3).

e. For every node of the index associated with a final state, accept the whole subtree and halt the search in that subtree. (For this reason, we do not need outgoing transitions in final states).

f. On reaching an external node, run the remainder of the automaton on the single string determined by this external node.

Automaton   Tree

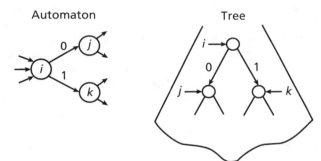

Figure 5.3 Simulating the automaton on a binary digital tree

For random text, it is possible to prove that for any regular expression, the average searching time is sublinear (because of step e), and of the form:

$$O(\log^m(n)\, n^\alpha)$$

where $\alpha < 1$, and $m \geq 0$ (integer) depend on the incidence matrix of the simulated DFA (that is, they depend on the regular expression). For details, see Baeza-Yates and Gonnet (1989).

5.4 BUILDING PAT TREES AS PATRICIA TREES

The implementation of PAT trees using conventional Patricia trees is the obvious one, except for some implementation details which cannot be overlooked as they would increase the size of the index or its accessing time quite dramatically. Since this type of index is typically built over very large text databases, and the size of the index tree is linear in the size of the text, an economic implementation is mandatory.

It is easy to see that the internal nodes will be between 3 and 4 words in size. Each external node could be one word and consequently we are taking between $4n$ and $5n$ words for the index, or about $18n$ chars for indexing n characters, most likely unacceptable from the practical point of view.

Second, the organization for the tree should be such that we can gain from the reading of large records (external files will use physical records which are certainly larger than one internal node).

The main ideas to solve (or alleviate) both problems are

a. bucketing of external nodes, and
b. mapping the tree onto the disk using supernodes.

Collecting more than one external node is called bucketing and is an old idea in data processing. A bucket replaces any subtree with size less than a certain constant (say b) and hence saves up to $b - 1$ internal nodes. The external nodes inside a bucket do not have any structure associated with them, and any search that has to be done in the bucket has to be done on all the members of the bucket. This increases the number of comparisons for each search, in the worst case by b. On the other hand, and assuming a random distribution of keys, buckets save a significant number of internal nodes. In general, it is not possible to have all buckets full, and on average the number of keys per bucket is $b \ln 2$. Hence, instead of $n - 1$ internal nodes, we have about $(n/b\ln2)$ internal nodes for random strings.

This means that the overhead of the internal nodes, which are the largest part of the index, can be cut down by a factor of $b\ln2$. We have then a very simple trade-off between time (a factor of b) and space (a factor of $b\ln2$).

Organizing the tree in super-nodes has advantages from the point of view of the number of accesses as well as in space. The main idea is simple: we allocate as much as possible of the tree in a disk page as long as we preserve a unique entry point for every page. De facto, every disk page has a single entry point, contains as much of the tree as possible, and terminates either in external nodes or in pointers to other disk pages (notice that we need to access disk pages only, as each disk page has a single entry point). The pointers in internal nodes will address either a disk page or another node inside the same page, and consequently can be substantially smaller (typically about half a word is enough). This further reduces the storage cost of internal nodes.

Unfortunately, not all disk pages will be 100 percent full. A bottom-up greedy construction guarantees at least 50 percent occupation. Actual experiments indicate an occupation close to 80 percent.

With these constraints, disk pages will contain on the order of 1,000 internal/ external nodes. This means that on the average, each disk page will contain about 10 steps of a root-to-leaf path, or in other words that the total number of accesses is a tenth of the height of the tree. Since it is very easy to keep the root page of the tree in memory, this means that a typical prefix search can be accomplished with 2-3 disk accesses to read the index (about 30 to 40 tree levels) and one additional final access to verify the skipped bits (buckets may require additional reading of strings). This implementation is the most efficient in terms of disk accesses for this type of search.

5.5 PAT TREES REPRESENTED AS ARRAYS

The previous implementation has a parameter, the external node bucket size, b. When a search reaches a bucket, we have to scan all the external nodes in the bucket to determine which if any satisfy the search. If the bucket is too large, these costs become prohibitive.

However, if the external nodes in the bucket are kept in the same relative order as they would be in the tree, then we do not need to do a sequential search, we could do an indirect binary search (i.e., compare the sistrings referred to by the external node) to find the nodes that satisfy the search. Consequently, the cost of searching a bucket becomes $2 \log b - 1$ instead of b.

Although this is not significant for small buckets, it is a crucial observation that allows us to develop another implementation of PAT trees. This is simply to let the bucket grow well beyond normal bucket sizes, including the option of letting it be equal to n, that is, the whole index degenerates into a single array of external nodes ordered lexicographically by sistrings. With some additions, this idea was independently discovered by Manber and Myers (1990), who called the structures suffix arrays.

There is a straightforward argument that shows that these arrays contain most of the information we had in the Patricia tree at the cost of a factor of $\log_2 n$. The argument simply says that for any interval in the array which contains all the external nodes that would be in a subtree, in $\log_2 n$ comparisons in the worst case we can divide the interval according to the next bit which is different. The sizes of the subtrees are trivially obtained from the limits of any portion of the array, so the only information that is missing is the longest-repetition bit, which is not possible to represent without an additional structure. Any operation on a Patricia tree can be simulated in $O(\log n)$ accesses. Figure 5.4 shows this structure.

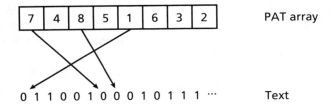

PAT array

Text

Figure 5.4 A PAT array.

5.5.1 Searching PAT Trees as Arrays

It turns out that it is not necessary to simulate the Patricia tree for prefix and range searching, and we obtain an algorithm which is $O(\log n)$ instead of $O(\log^2 n)$ for these operations. Actually, prefix searching and range searching become more uniform. Both can be implemented by doing an indirect binary search over the array with the results of the comparisons being less than, equal (or included in the case of range searching), and greater than. In this way, the searching takes at most $2 \log_2 n - 1$ comparisons and $4 \log_2 n$ disk accesses (in the worst case).

The "most frequent" searching can also be improved, but its discussion becomes too technical and falls outside the scope of this section. The same can be said about "longest repetition" which requires additional supporting data structures. For regular expression searching, the time increases by a $O(\log n)$ factor. Details about proximity searching are given by Manber and Baeza-Yates (1991).

In summary, prefix searching and range searching can be done in time $O(\log_2 n)$ with a storage cost that is exactly one word (a sistring pointer) per index point (sistring). This represents a significant economy in space at the cost of a modest deterioration in access time.

5.5.2 Building PAT Trees as Arrays

A historical note is worth entering at this point. Most of the research on this structure was done within the Centre for the New Oxford English Dictionary at the University of Waterloo, which was in charge of researching and implementing different aspects of the computerization of the *OED* from 1985. Hence, there was considerable interest in indexing the *OED* to provide fast searching of its 600Mb of text. A standard building of a Patricia tree in any of its forms would have required about $n \times \log_2(n) \times t$ hours, where n is the number of index points and t is the time for a random access to disk. As it turned out, the dictionary had about $n = 119,000,000$ and our computer systems would give us about 30 random accesses per second. That is, $119,000,000 \times 27/30 \times 60 \times 60 = 29,750$ hours or about 3.4 years. That is, we would still be building the index for the *OED*, *2nd ed.*

Even if we were using an algorithm that used a single random access per entry point (a very minimal requirement!), the total disk time would be $119,000,000/30 \times 60 \times 60 \times 24 = 45.9$ days. Still not acceptable in practical terms. It is clear from these numbers that we have to investigate algorithms that do not do random access to the text, but work based on different principles.

Clearly we need better algorithms than the "optimal" algorithm here. We would like to acknowledge this indirect contribution by the *OED*, as without this real test case, we would never have realized how difficult the problem was and how much more work had to be done to solve it in a reasonable time. To conclude this note, we would say that we continue to research for better building algorithms although we can presently build the index for the *OED* during a weekend.

This subsection will be divided in two. First we will present the building operations, which can be done efficiently, and second, two of the most prominent algorithms for large index building.

Building PAT arrays in memory

If a portion of the text is small enough to fit in main memory together with its PAT array, then this process can be done very efficiently as it is equivalent to string sorting. Note that here we are talking about main memory; if paging is used to simulate a larger memory, the random access patterns over the text will certainly cause severe memory thrashing.

Quicksort is an appropriate algorithm for this building phase since it has an almost sequential pattern of access over the sorted file. For maximal results we can put all of the index array on external storage and apply external quicksort (see Gonnet and Baeza-Yates, section 4.4.5 [1984]) indirectly over the text. In this case it is possible to build an index for any text which together with the program can fit in main memory. With today's memory sizes, this is not a case to ignore. This is the algorithm of choice for small files and also as a building block for other algorithms.

Merging small against large PAT arrays

A second case that can be solved efficiently is the case of merging two indices (to produce a single one) when the text plus twice the index of one of them fits in main memory. This algorithm is not trivial and deserves a short explanation. The text of the small file together with a PAT array for the small file (of size n_1) plus an integer array of size $n_1 + 1$ are kept in main memory. The integer array is used to count how many sistrings of the big file fall between each pair of index points in the small file (see Figure 5.5). To do this counting, the large file is read sequentially and each sistring is searched in the PAT array of the small file until it is located between a pair of points in the index. The corresponding counter is incremented. This step will require $O(n_2 \log n_1)$ comparisons and $O(n_2)$ characters to be read sequentially. Once the counting is finished, the merging takes place by reading the PAT array of the large file and inserting the PAT array of the small file guided by the counts (see

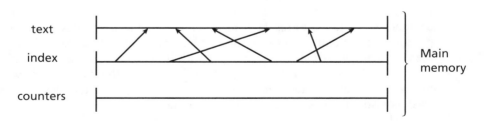

Figure 5.5 Small index in main memory

Figure 5.6). This will require a sequential reading of $n_1 + n_2$ words. In total, this algorithm performs a linear amount of sequential input and output and $O(n_2 \log n_1)$ internal work, and its behavior is not only acceptable but exceptionally good.

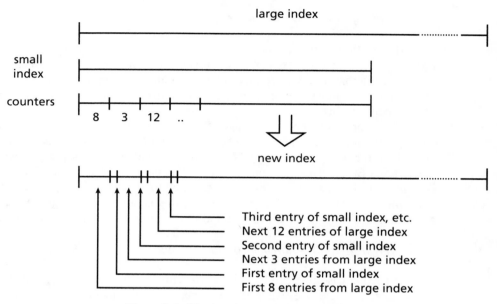

Figure 5.6 Merging the small and the large index

Given these simple and efficient building blocks we can design a general index building algorithm. First we split the text file into pieces, the first piece being as large as possible to build an index in main memory. The remaining pieces are as large as possible to allow merging via the previous algorithm (small against large). Then we build indices for all these parts and merge each part.

An improvement may be made by noticing that index points at the front of the text will be merged many times into new points being added at the end. We take advantage of this by constructing partial indices on blocks of text one half the size of memory. These indices may be merged with each other, the entire merge taking place in memory. The merged index is not created at this point, since it would fill memory and could not be merged with any further index. As before, a vector of counters is kept, indicating how many entries of the first index fall between each pair of adjacent entries in the second. When the nth block of text is being indexed, the $n - 1$ previous indices are merged with it. The counters are accumulated with each merge. When all of the merges have been done, the counters are written to a file. When all of the blocks have been indexed and merged, the files of counters are used as instructions to merge all the partial indices.

The number of parts is $O(n/m)$ where m is the total amount of available memory, and overall the algorithm requires $O(n^2/m)$ sequential access and $O(n^2 \log n/m)$ time. Given the sizes of present day memories and the differences of accessing time for random versus sequential access, the above quadratic algorithm would beat a linear algorithm even for databases like the *Oxford English Dictionary*!

An interesting property of the last version of the algorithm is that each of the merges of partial indices is independent. Therefore, all of the $O((n/m)^2)$ merges may be run in parallel on separate processors. After all merges are complete, the counters for each partial index must be accumulated and the final index merge may be done.

Another practical advantage of this algorithm is that the final index merge is done without reference to the text. Thus, at the time that the final merge is being done, the text may be removed from the system and reloaded after removal of the partial indices. In situations where the text, the final index, and the sum of partial indices may each be one or more gigabytes, this is an important consideration.

5.5.3 Delayed Reading Paradigm

The fact that comparing sistrings through random access to disk is so expensive is a consequence of two phenomena. First, the reading itself requires some (relatively slow) physical movement. Second, the amount of text actually used is a small fraction of the text made available by an I/O operation.

Here we will describe a programming technique that tries to alleviate the above problem without altering the underlying algorithms. The technique is simply to suspend execution of the program every time a random input is required, store these requests in a request pool, and when convenient/necessary satisfy all requests in the best ordering possible.

This technique works on algorithms that do not block on a particular I/O request but could continue with other branches of execution with a sufficiently high degree of parallelism. More explicitly, we have the following modules:

a. the index building program
b. a list of blocked requests
c. a list of satisfied requests

The c list is processed in a certain order. This ordering is given inversely by the likelihood of a request to generate more requests: the requests likely to generate fewer requests are processed first. Whenever the c list is exhausted or the available memory for requests is exhausted, then the b list is sorted for the best I/O performance and all the I/O is performed.

5.5.4 Merging Large Files

We have seen an algorithm for merging a large file against a small file, small meaning that it fits, with its index, in memory. We may also need to merge two or more large indices. We can do this by reading the text associated with each key and comparing. If we have n keys and m files, and use a heap to organize the current keys for each file being merged, this gives us $O(n \log m)$ comparisons. More importantly, it gives us n random disk accesses to fetch key values from the text. If n is 100,000,000 and we can do 50 random disk accesses per second, then this approach will take 2,000,000 seconds or about 23 days to merge the files. A second problem inherent with sistrings is that we do not know how many characters will be necessary to compare the keys. This will be addressed later.

An improvement can be made by reducing the number of random disk accesses and increasing the amount of sequential disk I/O. The sistring pointers in the PAT array are ordered lexicographically according to the text that they reference and so will be more or less randomly ordered by location in the text. Thus, processing them sequentially one at a time necessitates random access to the text. However, if we can read a sufficiently large block of pointers at one time and indirectly sort them by location in the text, then we can read a large number of keys from the text in a sequential pass. The larger the number of keys read in a sequential pass, the greater the improvement in performance. The greatest improvement is achieved when the entire memory is allocated to this key reading for each merge file in turn. The keys are then written out to temporary disk space. These keys are then merged by making a sequential pass over all the temporary files.

Thus, there are two constraints affecting this algorithm: the size of memory and the amount of temporary disk space available. They must be balanced by the relationship

$$memory \times number\ of\ files = temporary\ disk\ space$$

We must also consider how many characters are necessary for each comparison. This will be dependent on the text being indexed. In the case of the *OED*, the longest comparison necessary was 600 characters. Clearly it is wasteful to read (and write) 600 characters for each key being put in a temporary file. In fact, we used 48 characters as a number that allowed about 97 percent of all comparisons to be resolved, and others were flagged as unresolved in the final index and fixed in a later pass. With 48 characters per key it was possible to read 600,000 keys into a 32Mb memory. For a 600Mb text, this means that on average we are reading 1 key per kilobyte, so we can use sequential I/O. Each reading of the file needs between 30 and 45 minutes and for 120,000,000 index points it takes 200 passes, or approximately 150 hours. Thus, for building an index for the *OED*, this algorithm is not as effective as the large against small indexing described earlier.

However, this algorithm will work for the general case of merging indices, whether they are existing large indices for separate text files, being merged to allow simultaneous searching, or whether they are partial indices for a large text file, each constructed in memory and being merged to produce a final index. In the latter case, there are some further improvements that can be made.

Since partial indices were constructed in memory, we know that the entire text fits in memory. When we are reading keys, the entire text may be loaded into memory. Keys may then be written out to fill all available temporary disk space, without the constraint that the keys to be written must fit in memory.

Another improvement in this situation can be made by noticing that lexico-graphically adjacent keys will have common prefixes for some length. We can use "stemming" to reduce the data written out for each key, increasing the number of keys that can be merged in each pass.

5.6 SUMMARY

We finish by comparing PAT arrays with two other kind of indices: signature files and inverted files.

Signature files use hashing techniques to produce an index being between 10 percent and 20 percent of the text size. The storage overhead is small; however, there are two problems. First, the search time on the index is linear, which is a drawback for large texts. Second, we may find some answers that do not match the query, and some kind of filtering must be done (time proportional to the size of the enlarged answer). Typically, false matches are not frequent, but they do occur.

On the other hand, inverted files need a storage overhead varying from 30 percent to 100 percent (depending on the data structure and the use of stopwords). The search time for word searches is logarithmic. Similar performance can be achieved by PAT arrays. The big plus of PAT arrays is their potential use in other kind of searches, that are either difficult or very inefficient over inverted files. That is the case with searching for phrases (especially those containing frequently occurring words), regular expression searching, approximate string searching, longest repetitions, most frequent searching, and so on. Moreover, the full use of this kind of index is still an open problem.

REFERENCES

AHO, A., HOPCROFT, J., and J. ULLMAN. 1974. *The Design and Analysis of Computer Algorithms*. Reading, Mass.: Addison-Wesley.

APOSTOLICO, A., and W. SZPANKOWSKI. 1987. "Self-alignments in Words and their Applications." Technical Report CSD-TR-732, Department of Computer Science, Purdue University, West Lafayette, Ind. 47907.

BAEZA-YATES, R., and G. GONNET. 1989. "Efficient Text Searching of Regular Expressions," in *ICALP'89, Lecture Notes in Computer Science 372*, eds. G. Ausiello, M. Dezani-Ciancaglini, and S. Ronchi Della Rocca. pp. 46–62, Stresa, Italy: Springer-Verlag. Also as UW Centre for the New OED Report, OED-89-01, University of Waterloo, April, 1989.

FAWCETT, H. 1989. *A Text Searching System: PAT 3.3, User's Guide*. Centre for the New Oxford English Dictionary, University of Waterloo.

FLAJOLET, P. and R. SEDGEWICK. 1986. "Digital Search Trees Revisited." *SIAM J Computing*, 15; 748–67.

GONNET, G. 1983. "Unstructured Data Bases or Very Efficient Text Searching," in *ACM PODS*, vol. 2, pp. 117–24, Atlanta, Ga.

GONNET, G. 1984. *Handbook of Algorithms and Data Structures*. London: Addison-Wesley.

GONNET, G. 1987. "PAT 3.1: An Efficient Text Searching System, User's Manual." UW Centre for the New OED, University of Waterloo.

GONNET, G. 1988. "Efficient Searching of Text and Pictures (extended abstract)." Technical Report OED-88-02, Centre for the New OED., University of Waterloo.

HOPCROFT, J., and J. ULLMAN. 1979. *Introduction to Automata Theory*. Reading, Mass.: Addison-Wesley.

KNUTH, D. 1973. *The Art of Computer Programming: Sorting and Searching,* vol. 3. Reading, Mass.: Addison-Wesley.

MANBER, U., and R. BAEZA-YATES. 1991. "An Algorithm for String Matching with a Sequence of Don't Cares." *Information Processing Letters,* 37; 133–36.

MANBER, U., and G. MYERS. 1990. "Suffix Arrays: A New Method for On-line String Searches," in *1st ACM-SIAM Symposium on Discrete Algorithms,* pp. 319–27, San Francisco.

MORRISON, D. 1968. "PATRICIA-Practical Algorithm to Retrieve Information Coded in Alphanumeric." *JACM,* 15; 514–34.

PITTEL, B. 1985. "Asymptotical Growth of a Class of Random Trees." *The Annals of Probability,* 13; 414–27.

6

File Organizations
for Optical Disks

Daniel Alexander Ford   **Stavros Christodoulakis**
Department of Computer Science
University of Waterloo
Waterloo, Ontario
Canada

Abstract

Optical disk technology is a new and promising secondary storage technology. Optical disks have immense capacities and very fast retrieval performance; they are also rugged and have very long storage lifetimes. These characteristics are making them a serious threat to the traditional dominance of magnetic disks. It is important to understand and study this young and significant technology and to design retrieval structures that best utilize its characteristics.

This chapter first presents a tutorial on optical disk technology and a discussion of important technical issues of file system design for optical disks, many of which are quite subtle. It then proceeds to discuss six file systems that have been developed for optical disks, including the *Write-Once B-Tree* of Easton (1986), the *Time Split B-Tree* of Lomet and Salzberg (1989), the *Compact Disk File System* of Garfinkel (1986), the *Optical File Cabinet* of Gait (1988), *Buffered Hashing* of Christodoulakis and Ford (1989a), and *BIM trees* of Christodoulakis and Ford (1989b).

6.1 INTRODUCTION

In this section we discuss file structures for optical disks. We first present an overview of optical disk technology, explaining where it came from and how it works. We then discuss some technical issues affecting the implementation of file structures on some common forms of optical disk technology. Later, we discuss in detail a variety of different structures that have been developed.

6.2 OVERVIEW OF OPTICAL DISK TECHNOLOGY

The foundation for all current optical disk technology was formed in the late 1960s and early 1970s by early video disk research. In mid-1971, N. V. Philips began conducting experiments in recording video signals on a flat glass plate using a spiral track of optically detectable depressions. This system was refined until it could store

30 minutes of color video and sound, and was called Video Long Play (VLP); it was first demonstrated on September 5, 1972. At about this time, other companies also began research efforts, including M.C.A., 3-M, Thomson-CSF, KODAK and Harris, among others.

The development of small inexpensive semiconductor laser diodes in 1975 stimulated development further, and the use of plastic disk platters which were cheaper and more easily replicated than glass platters was pioneered. Eventually, the technological base for the development of the optical disks in use today was emerged from the research efforts in the fields of optics, disk material technology, tracking and focus control servo system and lasers.

Features and benefits

Optical disks have many features and benefits that make them a useful storage medium. In general, their immense capacity, fast random access, and long storage life are major advantages. Other advantages are their portability and durability. Disks usually come encased in a protective cassette that can be easily carried. They are not subject to wear or head crashes as there is no physical contact between the disk and the access mechanism. The recording surface itself is not exposed, but rather, is protected by the plastic substrate that forms the disk platter. Optical disks, including erasable optical disks which employ a magneto-optic process for data registration, are also completely unaffected by magnetic fields.

The integrity of data stored on optical disks is also impressive. The process by which data is recorded on a Write-Once Read Many (WORM) disk surface causes an irreversible physical change. There is no chance of accidental erasure and overwrites are usually prevented by the drive or by driver software. Erasable optical disks cannot prevent accidental or malicious data destruction, but are still more durable then magnetic media. CD-ROM (Compact Disk Read Only Memory) disks are physically pressed out of plastic and so cannot be written to, or erased. Further, since there is no physical contact between an optical disk platter and the access mechanism, the disk is not subject to wear with use (the head of a Winchester type magnetic disk actually rides on the lubricated disk surface before it reaches flying speed). Small scratches and dust on the disk surface do not affect stored data as they are far enough away from the recording surface to be out of the optical system's focal plane. Data is also not subject to destruction from external magnetic fields and does not require periodic rewriting as is the case for magnetic media. The expected lifetime of an optical disk is not really known for certain (they have not been around long enough), but accelerated aging tests place it at least ten years and possibly as high as thirty. In contrast, the lifetime of magnetic tape is between two years to ten years, depending how it is handled and stored.

Optical disks also have the advantage of being removable. WORM and erasable disks are encased in a sturdy protective cassette when not in the drive and can be easily and safely transported, as can CD-ROM disks, which are designed to endure unrestrained consumer use.

There are few disadvantages inherent to optical disk technology. In fact, some characteristics that might be considered undesirable are actually advantages in certain applications. The unerasability of WORM type optical disks, for instance, make them the storage medium of choice for archival type applications. Some records such as transaction logs, banking records, and school transcripts are never legitimately altered, so some systems that maintain these types of records use WORM disks to ensure this.

Technical description

Optical disks are typically available in two different access configurations, either mounted in a single disk drive or as a set of disks in a "jukebox." In the single drive arrangement, disks are mounted manually be inserting the disk (and its protective cassette for WORM and erasable) into a slot on the front of the drive. For WORM disks, the platter is actually released and the cassette withdrawn; to remove the disk, the process is reversed. In the jukebox arrangement, the disks are stored in groups of several tens or even hundreds, representing many gigabytes of storage. They are selected and mounted mechanically in a manner similar to that used in audio disk jukeboxes. The time needed to switch a disk is about 5 to 20 seconds. For both types of configurations, the drive, disks, associated access mechanisms, and optics are the same.

When mounted, the disk is clamped to a spindle that protrudes through a large hole in its center. The access mechanism is usually a sled that slides along a guide path beneath the rotating disk platter. The sled contains the laser and associated optics. Note that only one side of the disk surface can be accessed when the disk is mounted. To access the other side, the disk must be physically removed, turned over, and remounted. CD-ROM disks are single sided and cannot be accessed if improperly mounted.

Electrical interfacing to the disk drives is usually done via standard interfaces such as the Small Computer Serial Interface (SCSI), the Enhanced Small Device Interface (ESDI), or more commonly for small personal computers through a direct bus interface.

There are three common sizes and storage capacities of optical disks available. The 305.5 millimeter (12 inch) platter is the most widely used for WORM disks and has a capacity of roughly 1 gigabyte per disk side. WORM disks are also available in 203 millimeter (8 inch, 750 megabytes) and 130 millimeter (5.25 inch, 200 megabytes) sizes. Erasable disks are available in 130 millimeter (5.25 inch, 600 megabytes) and, depending on the manufacturer, 86, 87, 88, or 89 millimeter (3.5 inch, 80 megabytes) sizes. The CD-ROM disk platters are standardized at 130 millimeters. The exact capacity of a disk will depend on the recording format employed (discussed later); some formats will increase the values stated above.

The way in which a disk platter is constructed varies with the type of optical disk. WORM disks usually use a construction know as the "air sandwich." This fabrication technique joins two transparent 1.5 millimeter thick platter halves together leaving a small "clean room" air gap sandwiched between them where the recording surfaces reside. The two halves both support and protect the recording surfaces while allowing light from the laser to reach them. The final disk platter is about 3 to 4 millimeters thick. Erasable disks are fabricated in a similar manner.

CD-ROM disks are single sided and are essentially a smaller version of one of the platter halves used for WORM disks. Data is permanently registered on a CD-ROM disk when it is fabricated by a pressing process. After pressing, the disk is given a thin coating of aluminum to make it reflective and is then sealed.

Materials and registration techniques for WORM disks

A single-sided optical disk platter, which is one side of an "air sandwich," consists of a thin film of Tellurium alloy (10–50 nanometers) that forms the active recording surface, and a supporting plastic substrate, usually poly(vinyl chloride) or poly(methyl methacrylate).

The disk is formed using an injection molding process. This is done under clean room conditions as the high storage densities of optical disks makes them particularly sensitive to contaminants like dust. It is during the molding process that the disk is pregrooved and sometimes also preformatted with address and synchronization information. These steps are important as they define the positions of tracks and identify individual sectors on what would otherwise be a featureless surface.

Data is recorded on the disk by a series of optically detectable changes to its surface. Small changes in reflectivity called "pits" are thermally induced in the active layer through the application of energy from a laser. The unaltered spaces between pits are called "lands." It takes 50–100 nanoseconds of 10 milliwatts of incident power focused on a 1 micron diameter spot to form the pit. Spacing between adjacent tracks of pits and lands is 1.6 microns.

There are several methods by which the applied energy can form pits in the active layer. Of these, the techniques called *Ablation* and *Vesicular* are favored.

With the Ablation technique, surface tension causes the thin film to pull away from the spot heated by the laser, leaving a hole in the surface. Sometimes, a layer of aluminum is deposited beneath the tellurium film to act as a mirror to be exposed when the hole is formed. With the *Vesicular* technique, a bubble is formed in the recording surface when vapor resulting from the heating process is trapped under the film. The bubble forms a bump that tends to disperse the light hitting it (making the pit darker).

Materials and registration techniques for erasable disks

Erasable optical disks are physically much like WORM disks. The main difference between the two is in the coating used on the recording surface. There are two types of erasable optical disk: *Phase-Change* and *Magneto-Optic*.

Erasable optical disks that employ phase-change technology rely on coatings for the recording surface consisting of thin films of tellurium or selenium. These coatings have the ability to exist in two different optically detectable states, *amorphous* and *crystalline,* and will switch between the two when heated to two different temperatures. If a spot on the recording surface is heated to a low temperature with a laser with 8 milliwatts of power, the spot will crystallize. If it is heated to a higher temperature with a laser with 18 milliwatts of power, the spot will melt and when it cools will *revitrify* to the amorphous state.

To register data on the recording surface, the power of the laser scanning the disk is simply modulated between 8 and 18 milliwatts. If a crystallized spot is scanned with 8 milliwatts of power, it will remain crystallized, if it is scanned with 18 milliwatts of power it will switch to the amorphous state. Similarly, if an amorphous spot is scanned with 18 milliwatts of power, it will remain in the amorphous state, and if it is scanned with 8 milliwatts of power it will switch to the crystallized state.

Reading data from the disk is simply a matter of scanning the surface with a low power laser (1 milliwatt) and detecting the changes in reflectivity that exist on the recording surface.

Erasable optical disks that employ magneto-optic technology store data on the disk magnetically, but read and write it optically. The coating used on the recording surface is a rare-earth transition-metal alloy such as terbium iron cobalt, terbium iron, or gadolinium terbium iron. It has the property of allowing the polarity of its magnetization to be changed when it is heated to a certain temperature (150° C).

Recording data is a two-stage process requiring two passes of the disk head over a sector. The first pass serves to erase the contents of the sector. This is done by first placing a magnetic field with north-pole down in the vicinity of the spot upon which the laser focuses. As the sector is scanned, this spot will quickly heat to 150° C and then immediately cool. As it does, domains of north-pole down are recorded throughout the sector; a north-pole down domain represents a 0 bit. Once the sector has been erased by the first pass, data can be written by the second.

When the sector is scanned a second time, the applied magnetic field is reversed. By modulating the power of the laser, selected portions of the sector can be heated to the required temperature and have their magnetizations reversed to north-pole up; a north-pole up domain represents a 1 bit. The remaining unheated portions of the sector retain their north-pole down magnetization.

Recorded data is read from the disk in a single pass. Reading relies on a physical effect known as the *Kerr magneto-optic effect*, which was discovered by Kerr (1877) and which causes light passing through a magentic field to become elliptically polarized. This effect allows the magnetization of a spot or domain of the disk surface to be detected optically. To read a disk sector, it is scanned with the laser in a lower power mode (1 milliwatt) than used for writing (8 milliwatts). If the magnetization of a domain being scanned is north-pole-up, the polarization of the light reflected from the surface will be rotated clockwise, if north-pole-down, counterclockwise. The sequence of polarity changes is detected and interpreted to produce a bit stream.

Sec. 6.2   Overview of Optical Disk Technology

The main stumbling block in the development of erasable magneto-optic disk technology was the chemical instability of the coating caused by its repeated heating and cooling during the write-erase cycle. This instability limited the number of cycles that could occur and was caused by the high temperature (600° C) required to change the magnetization of a domain. The development of newer coatings that require lower temperatures (150° C) solved this problem. Current erasable magneto-optic disks now allow some ten million or more write-erase cycles.

There are performance differences between the two types of erasable technologies. The Kerr effect only causes about a 1 percent change in the polarization of the reflected light. This requires more optics and associated hardware in the disk head of a magneto-optic disk drive to detect such a small change. The reflectivity difference between the two states of phase-change type erasable optical disks is relatively large and much easier to detect so the disk head can be much simpler. The net result is that the seek performance of a magneto-optic disk drive will generally be poorer than that of a phase-change drive because of its more massive disk head.

Optics

The optical assemblies found in all types of optical disk drives are similar in nature and resemble those of a medium power microscope. The task of the assembly is to focus a beam of coherent light from a semiconductor laser on to a 1 micron size spot and provide a return path for reflected light to reach a photodetector. This is a difficult feat to accomplish as the requirements for economical mass production of disks and drives imply a certain degree of flexibility in their precision. As such, it cannot be guaranteed that the disk platter will be perfectly flat or round, or that the hole for the drive's spindle will be perfectly centered. These imperfections can cause the outer edge of the disk to move up and down as much as 1 millimeter and the disk itself side-to-side as much as 60 micrometers (37 tracks) as it rotates several times a second. These motions cause the position of a track to vary with time in three dimensions and require the optical assemblies to be much more than a simple arrangement of lenses.

To follow the moving track, the objective lens is encased in a voice-coil like arrangement that allows it to be moved up and down to adjust its focus and from side to side to allow it to follow the wandering track. This radial flexibility gives most optical disk drives the ability to quickly access more than one track on the disk from a single position of the access mechanism, simply by adjusting the position of the objective lens. This viewing capability is usually limited to a *window* of some 10 to 20 tracks on either side of the current position of the access mechanism.

Lasers and light paths

The light source in an optical disk drive is a Gallium Arsenide (GaAlAs) laser diode with a wavelength of about 800 nanometers (.8 microns). The first experimental drives employed gas lasers (HeNe) which have a shorter wavelength and allowed higher storage densities and data transfer rates, but they were later abandoned in favor of the longer wavelength semiconductor laser diodes, which are cheaper and small enough to be mounted in the optical assembly. Laser diodes also have the advantage of being modulated electrically, eliminating the need for the expensive external acoustooptic or electrooptic modulator required by the gas lasers.

The recording density is limited by the wavelength of the laser because the wavelength determines the size of the smallest feature that can be resolved on the disk surface. The shorter the wavelength, the smaller the feature and hence, the higher the possible recording density.

The light path in the optical assembly consists of a collimating lens, a polarizing beam splitter, a quarter-wave plate, and an objective lens. The collimating lens takes the highly divergent light from the diode and forms a straight directed beam. This beam passes unchanged through the beam splitter and on to the quarter-wave plate that rotates its polarization by 90 degrees (a quarter of a wave). The altered beam then enters the objective lens that focuses it on the disk surface to the required 1 micron size spot.

On the return path, light reflected from the disk surface passes back through the objective lens and on again through the quarter-wave plate where its polarization is given another 90 degree twist. Now 180 degrees out of phase, the returning beam is not passed by the beam splitter but is instead reflected perpendicularly toward the photodetector.

Recording formats

While optical disks as a family share similar optical assemblies, disk fabrication materials and techniques, they can differ considerably in their recording formats. There are four different formats now in current use. The most common are the *Constant Angular Velocity* (CAV) and the *Constant Linear Velocity* (CLV) formats. The other two are modified versions of the above called, appropriately enough, *Modified Constant Angular Velocity* (MCAV) and *Modified Constant Linear Velocity* (MCLV; also called *Quantized Linear Velocity*—QLV).

In the CAV format, the sequences of pits and lands are usually arranged into equal capacity concentric tracks and the disk drive rotates the disk at a constant rate (angular velocity). This causes the length of both the pits and the lands to become elongated as their position moves away from the center of the disk because the outer surface of the disk platter passes beneath the optical assembly at a faster linear rate than does the inner surface. This elongation causes the storage density on the surface of a CAV format WORM disk to be less at the outer edge of the disk than at the center.

In the CLV format, the sequence of pits and lands forms a single spiral track and the rate at which the disk platter rotates is adjusted by the drive to match the position of the optical assembly. The disk rotates faster when accessing the inner surface and slower when accessing the outer surface. This adjustment ensures that the disk surface passes beneath the assembly and its optics at a constant rate (linear velocity). Adjusting the rotation rate prevents the pits and lands from becoming elongated and results in a constant storage density across the surface of the disk.

The two formats, CAV and CLV, have complimentary advantages and disadvantages. As stated above, CLV disks have a greater storage capacity than CAV disks, but they also tend to have slower seek times. This is a consequence of the extra time required to accelerate the disk to the rotation rate that matches the new position of the access mechanism. So while a CAV disk may store less data than a CLV disk, accesses to that data are slightly faster.

The Modified CAV and Modified CLV formats each combine features of the CAV and CLV formats in an attempt to obtain greater storage capacities and seek times. A disk employing the MCAV format rotates at a constant rate and also has a nearly constant storage density across its surface. Its concentric tracks are divided into equal track capacity bands. Each band has one more sector in each of its tracks than the next innermost band that it surrounds. A clocking scheme adjusts to the varying linear rates at which pits and lands pass beneath the optical assembly. The MCLV scheme is similar except that the disk platter rotates at a different rate for each band.

All the formats are available for WORM disks. Erasable disks are available in the CAV and MCAV formats. CD-ROM disks are standardized and use only the CLV format.

6.3 FILE SYSTEMS

Virtually all of the research into file systems for optical disks has concentrated on WORM and CD-ROM optical disks. These are the oldest forms of optical disk technology and the types with the most differences from magnetic disks. Commercially available erasable optical disks are a relatively recent phenomenon and are close enough in capabilities to magnetic disks that conventional file systems can usually be adapted. Thus, we concentrate our discussion on file systems developed for WORM and CD-ROM optical disks. But, before we proceed we first present a short discussion on some technical issues affecting the implementation of file structures on optical disks.

6.3.1 Technical Issues for File Systems

Optical disk technology is similar enough to magnetic disk technology that the same types of file structures that are used on magnetic disks can usually be used in some form on optical disks. There are, however, some differences that can make some choices better than others.

For example, conventional pointer linked file structures (e.g., B-trees) are a poor choice for WORM optical disks. The reason for this is that each modification of the file usually requires some of the pointers linking the file structure together to change; rebalancing a B-tree after an insert or delete is a good example. Since storage space cannot be reclaimed on a WORM optical disk, changing the value of a pointer requires the new value to be stored in a new disk sector, consuming space. Thus, in the course of normal file maintenance operations, extra storage space is consumed.

This type of problem is present when linked lists or trees are used (as is true for B-trees). If an element or node is modified, then it must be stored on the disk in a new position and all pointers to the position of the old version of the node must be updated to point to the position of the new version. Changing those pointers in turn changes their positions on the disk requiring any pointers to their old positions to be changed as well. This means that if an element of a list is modified, all elements between it and the head of the list must be duplicated. The same is true for trees: if a node is modified, all nodes on the path up to, and including, the root, must be duplicated.

This is not the only problem with using pointer linked structures on WORM optical disks; the *direction* that the pointers point is also of considerable consequence. A *forward pointer* is one that points from an older disk sector (written before) to a younger disk sector (written after), and a *backward pointer* points from a younger sector to an older sector. It is a characteristic of WORM optical disks that it is not possible to detect a bad disk sector before the sector has been written; thus, if a forward pointer is stored on the disk, there is a chance that the sector is points to may subsequently turn out to be unusable, making the forward pointer invalid. Sector substitution schemes that might deal with this problem can be envisioned, but a better solution is to simply avoid the problem where possible by using backward pointers. Backward pointers do not have this problem as they always point to valid sectors.

Preallocation of disk space on a WORM disk can also lead to problems. Most disk drives are unable to differentiate between reading a blank sector and reading a defective sector (i.e., they both are unreadable). Thus, if space has been reserved on a disk, it will be impossible to detect the difference between the beginning of preallocated (and blank) space on the disk and a previously written sector that is now unreadable (possibly because of a media defect, dirt, or scratches). This inability will render unreliable any organization that depends on preallocated space on a WORM disk.

A further aspect of WORM optical disk technology to consider when designing file structures is the granularity of data registration. On a WORM disk the smallest unit of data storage is the disk sector which has a typical capacity of 1 kilobyte. It is not possible to write a portion of a disk sector at one time and then another portion of the same sector later. A sector may be written once, and only once, and can never be updated. This restriction comes from the error correction code added to the data when the disk sector is written. If a sector is modified after its initial write, its contents would become inconsistent with the error correction code and the drive would either correct the "error" without comment or report a bad sector. With the inability to update the contents of a disk sector, there is a danger of wasting the storage capacity of the disk through sector fragmentation.

Not all of the characteristics of optical disks lead to problems for the implementations of file structures. On CD-ROM disks, for example, since the data never changes some optimizations are possible. Also, the spiral track found on CLV format disks lends itself nicely to hash file organizations by allowing hash buckets of arbitrary size to be created, allowing bucket overflow to be eliminated.

6.3.2 Write-Once B-Tree

The Write-Once B-Tree (WOBT) of Easton (1986) is a variation of a B-tree organization developed for WORM disks. The difference between the two structures is the manner in which the contents of the tree's nodes are maintained.

In a conventional B-tree, when a node is modified, its previous value or state is discarded in favor of the new value. This practice recycles storage space, but is not desirable in all situations. For some applications the ability to access any previous state of the tree is a distinct advantage; the WOBT allows this.

The WOBT manages the contents of the tree nodes in a manner that preserves all versions of a node throughout the life of the tree. This is accomplished by not overwriting nodes when they change, but instead appending new time-stamped entries to the node. The most current state of the tree is represented by the latest version of each entry (including pointers) in a node.

When a node is split in a WOBT, only those entries that are valid at the current time are copied into the new version of the node. The old version is retained intact. Deletions are handled by inserting a deletion marking record that explicitly identifies the record to be deleted and its deletion time.

The diagram in Figure 6.1 illustrates a WOBT with three nodes containing the records C, D, F, G, and H. The diagram shows the root node labeled 1 and two children, nodes 2 and 3. The root has an extra entry used to link different versions of the root node together. Being the first root of the tree, node 1 has a NULL (0) pointer for this entry. The rest of the entries in the root point to the children of the root. The first data entry indicates that C is the highest record in node 2, and F the highest in node 3.

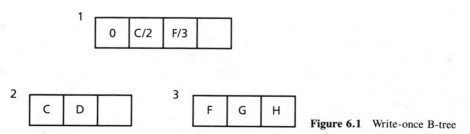

Figure 6.1 Write-once B-tree

When a record A is added to the tree, it is simply appended to node 2 in the space available for it, and an entry is propagated up to the parent of node 2, the root. This is illustrated in Figure 6.2.

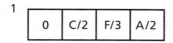

Figure 6.2 Write-once B-tree after insertion of "A"

The root now contains two entries which point to node 2. When we access the tree with respect to the current time, we use only the most recent values of the record/pointer pairs, in this case A/2 and F/3, which are found by a sequential search of the node. If we access the tree with respect to a time before the insertion of A, we find the record/pointer pairs C/2 and F/3. The record A in node 2 would not be found in that search because its later time-stamp would disqualify it.

When we insert a further record "J" into the tree, we must split both node 3 and the root node 1. The result is illustrated in Figure 6.3. When we split node 3 we end up with two new nodes 4 and 5. When node 1 is "split" in this case, we can make room in the new node by not including the data/pointer pair C/2 which is now obsolete. This results in one new node, node 6. The extra entry in the new root node now points back to the old root, node 1, so that accesses with respect to a previous time are still possible. Node 3 is no longer in the current version of the tree, but can still be accessed as part of the old version of the tree (prior to the insertion of "J") through the old root.

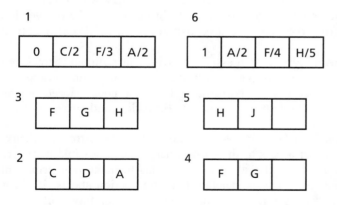

Figure 6.3 Write-once B-tree after insertion of "J"

Features to note about the WOBT are that search times will be slower than for a conventional B-tree as extra time will be required for a sequential search of each node to determine the current values of the data/pointer pairs. The WOBT also has problems with sector fragmentation since all modifications of the tree are stored as they are made directly on the WORM disk. It is also not particularly efficient with frequent updates to a single record, since each update must be stored on the disk in at least one disk sector.

However, despite these drawbacks, the WOBT is a robust (using backward pointers only) and elegant solution to the problem of efficiently implementing a multiway tree on an indelible storage device.

6.3.3 Time-Split B-Tree

The *Time-Split B-tree* (TSBT) of Lomet and Salzberg (1989) is an enhancement of the Write-once B-tree that eliminates some of its problems while adding to its utility. The basic structure and operation of the TSBT are identical to that of the WOBT. The difference between the two is that the TSBT distributes the contents of the tree over both a magentic disk and a WORM optical disk, and employs a slightly different approach to node splitting that reduces redundancy.

Combining magnetic and optical storage technologies allows their individual strengths to complement each other. This is an idea also employed in the buffered hashing organization of Christodoulakis and Ford (1989a). Write-once optical disks have a very low cost per stored bit and, as well, ensure that data cannot be accidently or maliciously deleted. Magnetic disks offer faster access and allow modifications to stored data without consuming storage space. A TSBT employs a magnetic disk to store the current changeable contents of the tree and the write-once disk to store the unchangeable historical contents.

The migration of the historical contents of the TSBT to the write-once disk is a consequence of node splitting. The TSBT divides node splits into two types: *Time Splits* and *Key Splits*. A time split occurs when a node is full of many historical (i.e., not in the current version of the tree) entries. A time split makes a new version of the node that omits the historical versions of records. In the TSBT, the old version of the node is removed from the magnetic disk and stored on the WORM optical disks.

A key split is the normal type of split associated with conventional B-trees and occurs when a node is full and most of the records are current (in a conventional B-tree, the records are always current). The result is two new nodes stored on the magnetic disk, each with roughly half of the records (historical and current) of the original node.

The advantages of the Time-split B-tree over the Write-once B-tree are many. The magnetic disk allows faster access to the current data than is possible if it were stored on an optical disk alone. It also allows transactions to make nonpermanent entries before they commit; these can be deleted if the transaction aborts. Records can also be updated without consuming disk space. Lower sector fragmentation is also a result, since buffering on the magnetic disk tends to reduce fragmentation by buffering many small changes into one larger change.

The splitting policy of a TSBT can be skewed to favor different objectives. If the total amount of storage space consumed is a concern, then key space splits should be favored as time splits tend to increase redundancy in the database. If the size of the current version of the B-tree (i.e., the part of the tree being stored on the magnetic disk) is a concern, then time splits should be favored as they free occupied space on the magnetic disk.

When implementing the TSBT, care must be taken to recognize that the size of the tree is limited not by the capacity of the optical disk, but by the capacity of the magnetic disk, as it stores all of the current contents of the tree. If the magnetic disk is full, the amount of remaining storage space on the optical disk will be irrelevant.

6.3.4 Compact Disk File System

The *Compact Disk File System* (CDFS) of Garfinkel (1986) is a system independent hierarchical file system for WORM optical disks. The goals of the CDFS are to be completely transportable across a variety of modern operating systems, to make efficient use of storage space, and to have a relatively high retrieval performance.

Unlike the write-once and time-split B-trees, the CDFS does not provide a structure for the organization of records, but rather a structure for the organization of groups of complete files. The application for which it is primarily intended is to organize files that experience few modifications, such as those belonging to a source code archive. The smallest unit of registration in the CDFS organization is the file.

The basic unit of organization in the CDFS is called a "transaction." A transaction results from the process of writing a complete group of files on the optical disk. All the files in a transaction group are placed on the disk immediately adjacent to the position of the previous transaction. Each individual file is stored contiguously. At the end of a transaction, an updated *directory list* for the entire file system is stored along with an "End of Transaction" (EOT) record. The EOT record contains a link to the EOT record of the previous transaction allowing access to historical versions of the organization (a dummy EOT record is stored at the start of an empty disk). The last transaction on the disk is the starting point for all accesses and the directory list it contains represents the current version of the file hierarchy.

The CDFS contains three types of "files": *regular files, directories,* and *links.* Each file is given a unique sequence number for the file system and a version number. If a file is updated by writing a new copy of it at some later time, the new copy retains the sequence number, but receives a new version number.

Each stored file entry consists of two parts, a file header and a file body. The header, which is invisible to a user, stores a large amount of explicit information about the file. This is an attempt by the CDFS to span the entire space of file characteristics that any given operating system might record or require. For example, the file header contains the name of the owner of the file; on some systems (e.g., UNIX) this information must be derived by consulting a system database. This explicit information allows the contents of a single disk employing a CDFS to appear to be a native file system on more than one operating system (with appropriate drivers for each system).

A directory is a special type of file that contains entries identifying other files known as *members*. These entries include pointers to the disk positions of the members and other information such as file sizes and modification times. This extra information is redundant since it is also stored in the file header, but it serves to improve the performance of directory list operations by eliminating the seeks required to access each member.

A link entry is simply a pointer to a file or a directory and allows a file to be a member of more than one directory.

The directory list stored at the end of the files in the transaction is an optimization to reduce seeks. It is a list of the positions of all current directories and subdirectories in the hierarchical file system. Using the directory list improves performance by reducing the seeks needed to traverse the file directory tree.

The diagram in Figure 6.4 illustrates how an instance of a CDFS is stored in a series of disk sectors. The example is for two transactions for a CDFS consisting of three files. The second transaction is used to store a second expanded version of the second file in the file system. The arrows in the diagram represent the pointers which link the various constituents of the CDFS together. For example, (backward) pointers exist between the EOT records, between each EOT record and its directory

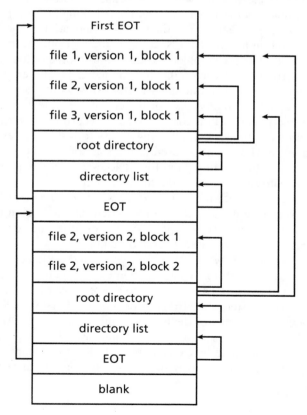

Figure 6.4 State of compact disk file system after two transactions

list, between the directory list and the directories (in this case just one, the root), and between the root and the three files.

The CDFS is an efficient means of organizing an archive of a hierarchical file system. Its main drawback is that it does not allow efficient updates to files. Any change to a single file requires the entire file to be rewritten along with a new copy of the directory list. Extra information could be added to the file header to allow files to be stored noncontiguously. This would allow portions of the file to be changed while other parts remained intact.

The robustness of the CDFS inherent in the degree of redundancy found in the organization, coupled with the access it allows to all previous versions of a file, makes it ideal for use in storing file archives.

Being relatively system independent, the CDFS is also an excellent organization for data interchange. It would be possible, for example, to copy a complete UNIX file system to an optical disk employing the CDFS and then transport it to an appropriate VMS installation and access the archived UNIX file system as if it were a native VMS file system.

6.3.5 The Optical File Cabinet

The Optical File Cabinet (OFC) of Gait (1988) is another file system for WORM optical disks. Its goals are quite different from those of the CDFS described previously. Its main objective is to use a WORM disk to simulate an erasable file system such as that found on a magnetic disk, and appear to an operating system just as if it was any other magnetic disk file system. It does this by creating a logical disk block space which can be accessed and modified at random on a block-by-block basis through a conventional file system interface.

The mapping between the logical and physical blocks is provided by a structure called the *File System Tree* (FST) which resides on the WORM optical disk, (see Figure 6.5). To translate between logical and physical blocks, the logical block

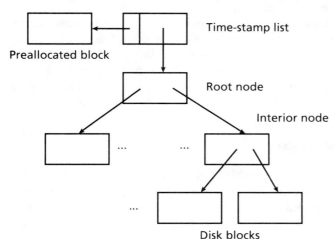

Preallocated block
Time-stamp list
Root node
Interior node
Disk blocks

Figure 6.5 File system tree (FST) for optical file cabinet

number is used to find a path through the FST to a leaf; the leaves of the tree are the physical disk blocks of the WORM optical disk.

Both the interior nodes and the leaves of the tree are buffered in main memory. The buffers are periodically flushed (e.g., every 5 minutes) and written on the optical disk in a process called *checkpointing*. Each flush results in a new version of the FST residing on the WORM disk. The roots of each of the different versions of the FST are pointed to by members of a list also residing on the optical disk called the *time-stamp list*. The current version of the FST is found by traversing the time-stamp list to find its last element.

The time-stamp list is implemented by a "continuation list." A continuation list consists of a series of disk blocks linked together via *forward pointers*. The pointer in the last element of a continuation list contains a pointer to a preallocated but empty disk block. The end of the list is detected when an attempt to read the next disk block in the list fails. In the OFC, it is assumed that the reason for the failure is because the preallocated (and empty) sector was read.

The use of forward pointers by the Optical File Cabinet file system seems to be a major flaw. As discussed previously, forward pointers are unreliable on WORM optical disks. It would also appear that if any of the disk sectors in which the time-stamp list is stored were ever damaged (e.g., by a permanent scratch or temporary dirt), the entire organization would be crippled. The system would interpret the bad sector read as the end of the time-stamp list and access historical contents of the file system rather than the current contents. At the next checkpoint time it would attempt to write to the damaged sector and find itself in a dead end. Even if none of the current sectors of the time-stamp list are damaged, the list could still encounter a preallocated sector that is damaged (e.g., media defect). An error such as this would require the entire time-stamp list to be copied and a scheme for identifying and locating alternate time stamp lists on the disk.

The utility of the Optical File Cabinet file system is also difficult to establish. As a replacement for magnetic disks it is an expensive substitute, as the write-once disks eventually fill up and must be replaced.

The most appropriate application seems to be in fault-tolerant systems that require their entire file systems to be permanently checkpointed at frequent intervals.

For systems with less demanding requirements the Write-once B-tree or the Time-split B-tree implemented for specific files might be more appropriate. The same is true for the archiving of copies of specific files (e.g., source code), where an organization such as the Compact Disk File System would be a better choice.

6.3.6 Buffered Hashing (Bhash)

Buffered Hashing (Bhash) of Christodoulakis and Ford (1989a) is a Hash file organization for WORM optical disks which employs a rewritable buffer to obtain performance improvements and reductions in storage space consumption. The buffer helps to reduce sector fragmentation, but its main purpose is to group many small changes to the file (record insertions) into one larger insertion. This is important because preallocating space for a hash bucket, as is done on magnetic disks, is not really a viable option for a WORM disk. This is because it is difficult to distinguish between a preallocated empty disk sector and an occupied but damaged sector; both are read as bad sectors.

Since successive insertions are unlikely to be to the same hash bucket, it is likely that the contents of a hash bucket will be stored in different (unpredictable) spots spread around the disk. By having a larger insertion, the degree to which the contents of a bucket are spread around the disk as a function of the number of record insertions is reduced. This, in turn, will reduce the number of seeks required to retrieve the contents of a hash bucket.

The rewritable buffer employed can be either main memory or a magnetic disk. As records are added to the file, they are first stored in the buffer and linked into a list of other records that belong to their hash bucket. When the buffer is full, the largest group of records belonging to a single hash bucket are removed (flushed) from the buffer and stored as a contiguous unit on the WORM optical disk. This group is linked to a list on the optical disk of other such groups that were flushed previously and that belong to the same bucket. The space in the buffer freed by the flush is then reused to store more records belonging to any hash bucket.

The length of the list (number of different groups) on the WORM disk will determine the number of seeks required to complete the retrieval of a bucket. If adding a new group to the list would make the length exceed some retrieval performance limit on the number of seeks required to access a bucket, the groups of the list are merged together to form a single larger contiguous group. This group is stored on the WORM disk as well, and is used in subsequent retrievals of the bucket. The new bucket group also becomes the first member of a new group list, to which subsequent bucket flushes will be appended. When the length of that list exceeds the limit, it too will be merged.

Deleted records are either removed from the buffer if they have not yet been flushed at the time of the deletion, or are marked as deleted by storing a deletion record in the bucket.

Because pointers to all previous groups on the disk are available and can be stored on a magnetic disk (such as the one being used for the buffer), access to all previous versions of the database is possible.

The parameters of the organization can be adjusted to obtain either fast retrieval performance at the expense of high storage space consumption or low disk space consumption at the expense of slower retrieval performance. Retrieval performance is affected primarily by the length limits placed on the group lists. If high performance is desired, the allowed length of the lists will be very short, resulting in many merges and increased storage consumption. If low storage consumption is required, the allowed length of the lists will be quite long, resulting in very infrequent merges but more seeks.

The size of the buffer and the number of buckets also plays a role in determining the performance of the organization. If the buffer is large, it will obviously require less flushing and hence fewer merges will occur and less space will be consumed. If the number of buckets is very large, then we can expect that the size of a group flushed from the buffer will be small, so flushes will occur more often, this will consume more space since it will increase the number of merges and in turn the number of redundantly stored records.

The Bhash file organization is a good method for implementing a hash file organization on a WORM optical disk. It can be tuned by an implementor to make efficient use of storage space or to meet strict retrieval performance demands. It also can function as a roll-back database, giving access to all previous versions of each record ever stored in the hash file.

6.3.7 Balanced Implicit Multiway Trees (BIM Trees)

The static nature of data stored on a CD-ROM optical disk allows conventional B-tree structures to be fine tuned to produce a completely balanced multiway tree that does not require storage space for pointers. Such a tree is called a *Balanced Implicit Multiway Tree* or a *BIM tree*, as presented in Christodoulakis and Ford (1989b). Because all the data to be stored on a CD-ROM disk is available at the time the disk is created, it is possible to preconstruct a perfectly balanced multitree for the data. And given that the size of all nodes of the tree and their layout is known, no pointers need to be stored since it is easy to compute the position on the disk for a given node in the tree.

When constructing a BIM tree, it is possible to choose node sizes and layouts that will improve the expected retrieval performance for accesses from the tree. If the node size is chosen such that a parent node and all of its children can fill within the viewing window of the objective lens of the disk drive, it will be possible to eliminate the seek required to traverse the link between the parent and one of its children. For example, with the root buffered in main memory and each of the second level nodes stored with all of their children within the viewing window of the objective lens, only a single seek, to the second level, would be required to retrieve any record within a three-level BIM tree.

6.3.8 Hashing for CD-ROM and CLV Format Optical Disks

The spiral track that is characteristic of Constant Linear Velocity (CLV) format optical disks such as CD-ROM is ideal for implementing hashing file organizations and can guarantee single seek access as discussed in Christodoulakis and Ford (1989b).

The biggest complication in a hashing organization, and the biggest source of performance degradation, is the resolution of hash bucket overflows. Buckets overflow because they are usually associated with a physical division on the storage device that has a finite capacity, either a track or a cylinder. The spiral track, which can be read continuously for the entire capacity of CLV format disks, allows hash buckets to be as large or as small as is necessary to store their contents. With a spiral track there is no need to impose an arbitrary physical limit (up to the capacity of the disk) on a bucket. This is particularly true for CD-ROM disks on which the data never changes.

On such disks, hash buckets can be laid out along the spiral track one after another. To determine the position of each bucket, a small *bucket position translation table* recording the beginning position of each bucket can be used. With the translation table in main memory, the contents of a bucket can be accessed with a single seek. This last feature is particularly attractive for optical disks, as they have relatively slow seek times.

REFERENCES

CHRISTODOULAKIS, S., and D. A. FORD. 1989a, June. *Retrieval Performance Versus Disc Space Utilization on WORM Optical Discs*. Paper presented at the annual meeting of the Special Interest Group for the Management of Data of the Association of Computing Machinery (ACM SIGMOD'89), Portland, Oregon, 306–14.

CHRISTODOULAKIS, S., and D. A. FORD. 1989b, June. *File Organizations and Access Methods for CLV Optical Disks*. Paper presented at the annual meeting of the Special Interest Group for Information Retrieval of the Association of Computing Machinery (ACM SIGIR'89), Cambridge, Massachusetts.

EASTON, M. C. 1986. "Key-Sequence Data Sets on Indelible Storage." *IBM Journal of Research and Development*, 30(3), 230–41.

GAIT, J. 1988. "The Optical File Cabinet: A Random-Access File System for Write-Once Optical Disks." *Computer*, 21(6), 11–22.

GARFINKEL, S. L. 1986. "A File System For Write-Once Media." *Technical Report MIT Media Lab*, September.

KERR, J. 1877. "On the Rotation of the Plane of Polarization by Reflection from the Pole of a Magnet. *Philosophical Magazine*, 3, 321–43.

LOMET, D., and B. SALZBERG 1989, June. *Access Method for Multiversion Data*. Paper presented at the annual meeting of the Special Interest Group for the Management of Data of the Association of Computing Machinery (ACM SIGMOD'89), Portland, Oregon, 315–24.

7

Lexical Analysis and Stoplists

Christopher Fox

AT&T Bell Laboratories
Holmdel, NJ 07733

Abstract

Lexical analysis is a fundamental operation in both query processing and automatic indexing, and filtering stoplist words is an important step in the automatic indexing process. This chapter presents basic algorithms and data structures for lexical analysis, and shows how stoplist word removal can be efficiently incorporated into lexical analysis.

7.1 INTRODUCTION

Lexical analysis is the process of converting an input stream of characters into a stream of words or tokens. *Tokens* are groups of characters with collective significance. Lexical analysis is the first stage of automatic indexing, and of query processing. *Automatic indexing* is the process of algorithmically examining information items to generate lists of index terms. The lexical analysis phase produces candidate index terms that may be further processed, and eventually added to indexes (see Chapter 1 for an outline of this process). *Query processing* is the activity of analyzing a query and comparing it to indexes to find relevant items. Lexical analysis of a query produces tokens that are parsed and turned into an internal representation suitable for comparison with indexes.

In automatic indexing, candidate index terms are often checked to see whether they are in a *stoplist*, or *negative dictionary*. Stoplist words are known to make poor index terms, and they are immediately removed from further consideration as index terms when they are identified.

This chapter discusses the design and implementation of lexical analyzers and stoplists for information retrieval. These topics go well together because, as we will see, one of the most efficient ways to implement stoplists is to incorporate them into a lexical analyzer.

7.2 LEXICAL ANALYSIS

7.2.1 Lexical Analysis for Automatic Indexing

The first decision that must be made in designing a lexical analyzer for an automatic indexing system is: *What counts as a word or token in the indexing scheme?* At first, this may seem an easy question, and there are some easy answers to it—for example, terms consisting entirely of letters should be tokens. Problems soon arise, however. Consider the following:

- Digits—Most numbers do not make good index terms, so often digits are not included as tokens. However, certain numbers in some kinds of databases may be important (for example, case numbers in a legal database). Also, digits are often included in words that should be index terms, especially in databases containing technical documents. For example, a database about vitamins would contain important tokens like "B6" and "B12." One partial (and easy) solution to the last problem is to allow tokens to include digits, but not to begin with a digit.

- Hyphens—Another difficult decision is whether to break hyphenated words into their constituents, or to keep them as a single token. Breaking hyphenated terms apart helps with inconsistent usage (e.g., "state-of-the-art" and "state of the art" are treated identically), but loses the specificity of a hyphenated phrase. Also, dashes are often used in place of ems, and to mark a single word broken into syllables at the end of a line. Treating dashes used in these ways as hyphens does not work. On the other hand, hyphens are often part of a name, such as "Jean-Claude," "F-16," or "MS-DOS."

- Other Punctuation—Like the dash, other punctuation marks are often used as parts of terms. For example, periods are commonly used as parts of file names in computer systems (e.g., "COMMAND.COM" in DOS), or as parts of section numbers; slashes may appear as part of a name (e.g., "OS/2"). If numbers are regarded as legitimate index terms, then numbers containing commas and decimal points may need to be recognized. The underscore character is often used in terms in programming languages (e.g., "max_size" is an identifier in Ada, C, Prolog, and other languages).

- Case—The case of letters is usually not significant in index terms, and typically lexical analyzers for information retrieval systems convert all characters to either upper or lower case. Again, however, case may be important in some situations. For example, case distinctions are important in some programming languages, so an information retrieval system for source code may need to preserve case distinctions in generating index terms.

There is no technical difficulty in solving any of these problems, but information system designers must think about them carefully when setting lexical analysis policy. Recognizing numbers as tokens adds many terms with poor discrimination value to an index, but may be a good policy if exhaustive searching is important. Breaking up hyphenated terms increases recall but decreases precision, and may be inappropriate in some fields (like an author field). Preserving case distinctions enhances precision but decreases recall.

Commercial information systems differ somewhat in their lexical analysis policies, but are alike in usually taking a conservative (recall enhancing) approach. For example, Chemical Abstracts Service, ORBIT Search Service, and Mead Data Central's LEXIS/NEXIS all recognize numbers and words containing digits as index terms, and all are case insensitive. None has special provisions for most punctuation marks in most indexed fields. However, Chemical Abstracts Service keeps hyphenated words as single tokens, while the ORBIT Search Service and LEXIS/NEXIS break them apart (if they occur in title or abstract fields).

The example we use to illustrate our discussion is simple so it can be explained easily, and because the simplest solution often turns out to be best. Modifications to it based on the considerations discussed above are easy to make. In the example, any nonempty string of letters and digits, not beginning with a digit, is regarded as a token. All letters are converted to lower case. All punctuation, spacing, and control characters are treated as token delimiters.

7.2.2 Lexical Analysis for Query Processing

Designing a lexical analyzer for query processing is like designing one for automatic indexing. It also depends on the design of the lexical analyzer for automatic indexing: since query search terms must match index terms, the same tokens must be distinguished by the query lexical analyzer as by the indexing lexical analyzer. In addition, however, the query lexical analyzer must usually distinguish operators (like the Boolean operators, stemming or truncating operators, and weighting function operators), and grouping indicators (like parentheses and brackets). A lexical analyzer for queries should also process certain characters, like control characters and disallowed punctuation characters, differently from one for automatic indexing. Such characters are best treated as delimiters in automatic indexing, but in query processing, they indicate an error. Hence, a query lexical analyzer should flag illegal characters as unrecognized tokens.

The example query lexical analyzer presented below recognizes left and right parentheses (as grouping indicators), ampersand, bar, and caret (as Boolean operators), and any alphanumeric string beginning with a letter (as search terms). Spacing characters are treated as delimiters, and other characters are returned as unrecognized tokens. All uppercase characters are converted to lowercase.

7.2.3 The Cost of Lexical Analysis

Lexical analysis is expensive because it requires examination of every input character, while later stages of automatic indexing and query processing do not. Although no studies of the cost of lexical analysis in information retrieval systems have been done, lexical analysis has been shown to account for as much as 50 percent of the computational expense of compilation (Wait 1986). Thus, it is important for lexical analyzers, particularly for automatic indexing, to be as efficient as possible.

7.2.4 Implementing a Lexical Analyzer

Lexical analysis for information retrieval systems is the same as lexical analysis for other text processing systems; in particular, it is the same as lexical analysis for program translators. This problem has been studied thoroughly, so we ought to adopt the solutions in the program translation literature (Aho, Sethi, and Ullman 1986). There are three ways to implement a lexical analyzer:

- Use a *lexical analyzer generator*, like the UNIX tool lex (Lesk 1975), to generate a lexical analyzer automatically;
- Write a lexical analyzer by hand ad hoc; or
- Write a lexical analyzer by hand as a finite state machine.

The first approach, using a lexical analyzer generator, is best when the lexical analyzer is complicated; if the lexical analyzer is simple, it is usually easier to implement it by hand. In our discussion of stoplists below, we present a special purpose lexical analyzer generator for automatic indexing that produces efficient lexical analyzers that filter stoplist words. Consequently, we defer further discussion of this alternative.

The second alternative is the worst. An ad hoc algorithm, written just for the problem at hand in whatever way the programmer can think to do it, is likely to contain subtle errors. Furthermore, finite state machine algorithms are extremely fast, so ad hoc algorithms are likely to be less efficient.

The third approach is the one we present in this section. We assume some knowledge of *finite state machines* (also called *finite automata*), and their use in program translation systems. Readers unfamiliar with these topics can consult Hopcroft and Ullman (1979), and Aho, Sethi, and Ullman (1986). Our example is an implementation of a query lexical analyzer as described above.

The easiest way to begin a finite state machine implementation is to draw a transition diagram for the target machine. A transition diagram for a machine recognizing tokens for our example query lexical analyzer is pictured in Figure 7.1.

In this diagram, characters fall into ten classes: space characters, letters, digits, the left and right parentheses, ampersand, bar, caret, the end of string character, and all other characters. The first step in implementing this finite state machine is to build a mechanism for classifying characters. The easiest and fastest way to do this is to preload an array with the character classes for the character set. Assuming the ASCII character set, such an array would contain 128 elements with the character classes for the corresponding ASCII characters. If such an array is called

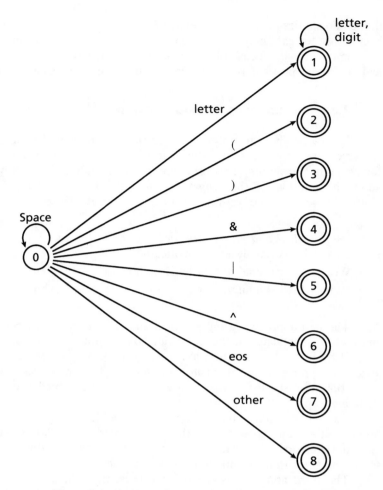

Figure 7.1 Transition diagram for a query lexical analyzer

char_class, for example, then the character class for character 'c' is simply char_class[c]. The character classes themselves form a distinct data type best declared as an enumeration in C. Figure 7.2 contains C declarations for a character class type and array. (Note that the end of file character requires special treatment in C because it is not part of ASCII).

The same technique is used for fast case conversion. In Figure 7.2, an array of 128 characters called convert_case is preloaded with the printing characters, with lowercase characters substituted for uppercase characters. Nonprinting character positions will not be used, and are set to 0.

Lexical Analysis and Stoplists   Chap. 7

```
/************** Character Classification ****************/
/* Tokenizing requires that ASCII be broken into character */
/* classes distinguished for tokenizing. White space       */
/* characters separate tokens. Digits and letters make up  */
/* the body of search terms. Parentheses group sub-        */
/* expressions. The ampersand, bar, and caret are          */
/* operator symbols.                                       */

typedef enum {

        WHITE_CH,              /* whitespace characters */
        DIGIT_CH,              /* the digits */
        LETTER_CH,             /* upper and lower case */
        LFT_PAREN_CH,          /* the "(" character */
        RGT_PAREN_CH,          /* the ")" character */
        AMPERSAND_CH,          /* the "&" character */
        BAR_CH,                /* the "|" character */
        CARET_CH,              /* the "^" character */
        EOS_CH,                /* the end of string character */
        OTHER_CH,              /* catch-all for everything else */

        } CharClassType;

static CharClassType char_class[128] = {
    /* ^@ */ EOS_CH,        /* ^A */ OTHER_CH,     /* ^B */ OTHER_CH,
    /* ^C */ OTHER_CH,      /* ^D */ OTHER_CH,     /* ^E */ OTHER_CH,
    /* ^F */ OTHER_CH,      /* ^G */ OTHER_CH,     /* ^H */ WHITE_CH,
    /* ^I */ WHITE_CH,      /* ^J */ WHITE_CH,     /* ^K */ WHITE_CH,
    /* ^L */ WHITE_CH,      /* ^M */ WHITE_CH,     /* ^N */ OTHER_CH,
    /* ^O */ OTHER_CH,      /* ^P */ OTHER_CH,     /* ^Q */ OTHER_CH,
    /* ^R */ OTHER_CH,      /* ^S */ OTHER_CH,     /* ^T */ OTHER_CH,
    /* ^U */ OTHER_CH,      /* ^V */ OTHER_CH,     /* ^W */ OTHER_CH,
    /* ^X */ OTHER_CH,      /* ^Y */ OTHER_CH,     /* ^Z */ OTHER_CH,
    /* ^[ */ OTHER_CH,      /* ^\ */ OTHER_CH,     /* ^] */ OTHER_CH,
    /* ^^ */ OTHER_CH,      /* ^_ */ OTHER_CH,     /*    */ WHITE_CH,
    /* ! */ OTHER_CH,       /* " */ OTHER_CH,      /* # */ OTHER_CH,
    /* $ */ OTHER_CH,       /* % */ OTHER_CH,      /* & */ AMPERSAND_CH,
    /* ' */ OTHER_CH,       /* ( */ LFT_PAREN_CH,  /* ) */ RGT_PAREN_CH,
    /* * */ OTHER_CH,       /* + */ OTHER_CH,      /* , */ OTHER_CH,
    /* - */ OTHER_CH,       /* . */ OTHER_CH,      /* / */ OTHER_CH,
    /* 0 */ DIGIT_CH,       /* 1 */ DIGIT_CH,      /* 2 */ DIGIT_CH,
    /* 3 */ DIGIT_CH,       /* 4 */ DIGIT_CH,      /* 5 */ DIGIT_CH,
    /* 6 */ DIGIT_CH,       /* 7 */ DIGIT_CH,      /* 8 */ DIGIT_CH,
    /* 9 */ DIGIT_CH,       /* : */ OTHER_CH,      /* ; */ OTHER_CH,
    /* < */ OTHER_CH,       /* = */ OTHER_CH,      /* > */ OTHER_CH,
```

Figure 7.2 Declarations for a simple query lexical analyzer

```
/*  ?  */  OTHER_CH,     /*  @  */  OTHER_CH,     /*  A  */  LETTER_CH,
/*  B  */  LETTER_CH,    /*  C  */  LETTER_CH,    /*  D  */  LETTER_CH,
/*  E  */  LETTER_CH,    /*  F  */  LETTER_CH,    /*  G  */  LETTER_CH,
/*  H  */  LETTER_CH,    /*  I  */  LETTER_CH,    /*  J  */  LETTER_CH,
/*  K  */  LETTER_CH,    /*  L  */  LETTER_CH,    /*  M  */  LETTER_CH,
/*  N  */  LETTER_CH,    /*  O  */  LETTER_CH,    /*  P  */  LETTER_CH,
/*  Q  */  LETTER_CH,    /*  R  */  LETTER_CH,    /*  S  */  LETTER_CH,
/*  T  */  LETTER_CH,    /*  U  */  LETTER_CH,    /*  V  */  LETTER_CH,
/*  W  */  LETTER_CH,    /*  X  */  LETTER_CH,    /*  Y  */  LETTER_CH,
/*  Z  */  LETTER_CH,    /*  [  */  OTHER_CH,     /*  \  */  OTHER_CH,
/*  ]  */  OTHER_CH,     /*  ^  */  CARET_CH,     /*  _  */  OTHER_CH,
/*  `  */  OTHER_CH,     /*  a  */  LETTER_CH,    /*  b  */  LETTER_CH,
/*  c  */  LETTER_CH,    /*  d  */  LETTER_CH,    /*  e  */  LETTER_CH,
/*  f  */  LETTER_CH,    /*  g  */  LETTER_CH,    /*  h  */  LETTER_CH,
/*  i  */  LETTER_CH,    /*  j  */  LETTER_CH,    /*  k  */  LETTER_CH,
/*  l  */  LETTER_CH,    /*  m  */  LETTER_CH,    /*  n  */  LETTER_CH,
/*  o  */  LETTER_CH,    /*  p  */  LETTER_CH,    /*  q  */  LETTER_CH,
/*  r  */  LETTER_CH,    /*  s  */  LETTER_CH,    /*  t  */  LETTER_CH,
/*  u  */  LETTER_CH,    /*  v  */  LETTER_CH,    /*  w  */  LETTER_CH,
/*  x  */  LETTER_CH,    /*  y  */  LETTER_CH,    /*  z  */  LETTER_CH,
/*  {  */  OTHER_CH,     /*  |  */  BAR_CH,       /*  }  */  OTHER_CH,
/*  ~  */  OTHER_CH,     /*  ^? */  OTHER_CH,                              };

/*************  Character Case Conversion  *************/
/* Term text must be accumulated in a single case. This    */
/* array is used to convert letter case but otherwise      */
/* preserve characters.                                    */

static char convert_case[128] = {
/*  ^@ */   0,    /*  ^A */   0,    /*  ^B */   0,    /*  ^C */   0,
/*  ^D */   0,    /*  ^E */   0,    /*  ^F */   0,    /*  ^G */   0,
/*  ^H */   0,    /*  ^I */   0,    /*  ^J */   0,    /*  ^K */   0,
/*  ^L */   0,    /*  ^M */   0,    /*  ^N */   0,    /*  ^O */   0,
/*  ^P */   0,    /*  ^Q */   0,    /*  ^R */   0,    /*  ^S */   0,
/*  ^T */   0,    /*  ^U */   0,    /*  ^V */   0,    /*  ^W */   0,
/*  ^X */   0,    /*  ^Y */   0,    /*  ^Z */   0,    /*  ^[ */   0,
/*  ^\ */   0,    /*  ^] */   0,    /*  ^^ */   0,    /*  ^_ */   0,
/*     */  ' ',   /*  !  */  '!',   /*  "  */  '"',   /*  #  */  '#',
/*  $  */  '$',   /*  %  */  '%',   /*  &  */  '&',   /*  '  */  '\'',
/*  (  */  '(',   /*  )  */  ')',   /*  *  */  '*',   /*  +  */  '+',
/*  ,  */  ',',   /*  -  */  '-',   /*  .  */  '.',   /*  /  */  '/',
/*  0  */  '0',   /*  1  */  '1',   /*  2  */  '2',   /*  3  */  '3',
/*  4  */  '4',   /*  5  */  '5',   /*  6  */  '6',   /*  7  */  '7',
/*  8  */  '8',   /*  9  */  '9',   /*  :  */  ':',   /*  ;  */  ';',
/*  <  */  '<',   /*  =  */  '=',   /*  >  */  '>',   /*  ?  */  '?',
/*  @  */  '@',   /*  A  */  'a',   /*  B  */  'b',   /*  C  */  'c',
/*  D  */  'd',   /*  E  */  'e',   /*  F  */  'f',   /*  G  */  'g',
```

Figure 7.2 (*cont.*)

```
/*  H */  'h',   /*  I */  'i',   /*  J */  'j',   /*  K */  'k',
/*  L */  'l',   /*  M */  'm',   /*  N */  'n',   /*  O */  'o',
/*  P */  'p',   /*  Q */  'q',   /*  R */  'r',   /*  S */  's',
/*  T */  't',   /*  U */  'u',   /*  V */  'v',   /*  W */  'w',
/*  X */  'x',   /*  Y */  'y',   /*  Z */  'z',   /*  [ */  '[',
/*  \ */  '\\',  /*  ] */  ']',   /*  ^ */  '^',   /*  _ */  '_',
/*  ` */  '`',   /*  a */  'a',   /*  b */  'b',   /*  c */  'c',
/*  d */  'd',   /*  e */  'e',   /*  f */  'f',   /*  g */  'g',
/*  h */  'h',   /*  i */  'i',   /*  j */  'j',   /*  k */  'k',
/*  l */  'l',   /*  m */  'm',   /*  n */  'n',   /*  o */  'o',
/*  p */  'p',   /*  q */  'q',   /*  r */  'r',   /*  s */  's',
/*  t */  't',   /*  u */  'u',   /*  v */  'v',   /*  w */  'w',
/*  x */  'x',   /*  y */  'y',   /*  z */  'z',   /*  { */  '{',
/*  | */  '|',   /*  } */  '}',   /*  ~ */  '~',   /* ^? */   0,  };


/********************  Tokenizing  ********************/
/* The lexer distinguishes terms, parentheses, the and, or */
/* and not operators, the unrecognized token, and the end  */
/* of the input.                                           */

typedef enum {

        TERM_TOKEN      = 1,    /* a search term */
        LFT_PAREN_TOKEN = 2,    /* left parenthesis */
        RGT_PAREN_TOKEN = 3,    /* right parenthesis */
        AND_TOKEN       = 4,    /* set intersection connective */
        OR_TOKEN        = 5,    /* set union connective */
        NOT_TOKEN       = 6,    /* set difference connective */
        END_TOKEN       = 7,    /* end of the query */
        NO_TOKEN        = 8,    /* the token is not recognized */

    } TokenType;
```

Figure 7.2 (*cont.*)

There also needs to be a type for tokens. An enumeration type is best for this as well. This type will have an element for each of the tokens: term, left parenthesis, right parenthesis, ampersand, bar, caret, end of string, and the unrecognized token. Processing is simplified by matching the values of the enumeration type to the final states of the finite state machine. The declaration of the token type also appears in Figure 7.2.

The code for the finite state machine must keep track of the current state, and have a way of changing from state to state on input. A state change is called a *transition*. Transition information can be encoded in tables, or in flow of control. When there are many states and transitions, a tabular encoding is preferable; in our example, a flow of control encoding is probably clearest. Our example implementation reads characters from an input stream supplied as a parameter. The routine returns the next token from the input each time it is called. If the token is a term, the text of the term (in lowercase) is written to a term buffer supplied as a parameter. Our example code appears in Figure 7.3.

```
/*FN********************************************************************

        GetToken( stream )

    Returns: void

    Purpose: Get the next token from an input stream

    Plan:       Part 1: Run a state machine on the input
                Part 2: Coerce the final state to return the token type

    Notes:      Run a finite state machine on an input stream, collecting
                the text of the token if it is a term. The transition table
                for this DFA is the following (negative states are final):

                State | White Letter (     )     &   |    ^   EOS Digit Other
                ──────────────────────────────────────────────────────────────
                  0   |   0     1    -2   -3   -4  -5   -6   -7   -8    -8
                  1   |  -1     1    -1   -1   -1  -1   -1   -1    1    -1

                See the token type above to see what is recognized in the
                various final states.
**/

static TokenType
GetToken( stream, term )
    FILE *stream;     /* in: where to grab input characters */
    char *term;       /* out: the token text if the token is a term */
    {
    int next_ch;  /* from the input stream */
    int state;    /* of the tokenizer DFA */
    int i;        /* for scanning through the term buffer */

                /* Part 1: Run a state machine on the input */
    state = 0;
    i = 0;
    while ( 0 <= state )
        {
        if ( EOF == (next_ch = getc(stream)) ) next_ch = '\0';
        term[i++] = convert_case[next_ch];
        switch( state )
```

Figure 7.3 Code for a simple query lexical analyzer

```
    {
    case 0 :
        switch( char_class[next_ch] )
            {
            case WHITE_CH :        i = 0; break;
            case LETTER_CH :       state =  1; break;
            case LFT_PAREN_CH :    state = -2; break;
            case RGT_PAREN_CH :    state = -3; break;
            case AMPERSAND_CH :    state = -4; break;
            case BAR_CH :          state = -5; break;
            case CARET_CH :        state = -6; break;
            case EOS_CH :          state = -7; break;
            case DIGIT_CH :        state = -8; break;
            case OTHER_CH :        state = -8; break;
            default :              state = -8; break;
            }
        break;

    case 1 :
        if (    (DIGIT_CH != char_class[next_ch])
            && (LETTER_CH != char_class[next_ch]) )
            {
            ungetc( next_ch, stream );
            term[i-1] = '\0';
            state = -1;
            }
        break;

    default : state = -8; break;
        }
    }

        /* Part 2: Coerce the final state to return the type token */
return( (TokenType)(-state) );

} /* GetToken */
```

Figure 7.3 (*cont.*)

The algorithm begins in state 0. As each input character is consumed, a switch on the state determines the transition. Input is consumed until a final state (indicated by a negative state number) is reached. When recognizing a term, the algorithm keeps reading until some character other than a letter or a digit is found. Since this character may be part of another token, it must be pushed back on the input stream. The final state is translated to a token type value by changing its sign and coercing it to the correct type (this was the point of matching the token type values to the final machine states).

```
/*FN*************************************************************************

        main( argc, argv )

    Returns: int -- 0 on success, 1 on failure

    Purpose: Program main function

    Plan:       Part 1: Open a file named on the command line
                Part 2: List all the tokens found in the file
                Part 3: Close the file and return

    Notes:     This program simply lists the tokens found in a single file
               named on the command line.
**/

int
main(argc, argv)
    int argc;        /* in: how many arguments */
    char *argv[];    /* in: text of the arguments */
    {
    TokenType token;   /* next token in the input stream */
    char term[128];    /* the term recognized */
    FILE *stream;      /* where to read the data from */

    if ( (2 != argc) || !(stream = fopen(argv[1],"r")) ) exit(1);

    do
        switch( token = GetToken(stream,term) )
            {
            case TERM_TOKEN :        (void)printf( "term: %s\n", term ); break;
            case LFT_PAREN_TOKEN :   (void)printf( "left parenthesis\n" ); break;
            case RGT_PAREN_TOKEN :   (void)printf( "right parenthesis\n" ); break;
            case AND_TOKEN :         (void)printf( "and operator\n" ); break;
            case OR_TOKEN :          (void)printf( "or operator\n" ); break;
            case NOT_TOKEN :         (void)printf( "not operator\n" ); break;
            case END_TOKEN :         (void)printf( "end of string\n" ); break;
            case NO_TOKEN :          (void)printf( "no token\n" ); break;
            default :                (void)printf( "bad data\n" ); break;
            }
    while ( END_TOKEN != token );

    fclose( stream );

    } /* main */
```

Figure 7.4   Test program for a query lexical analyzer

Figure 7.4 contains a small main program to demonstrate the use of this lexical analyzer. The program reads characters from a file named on the command line, and writes out a description of the token stream that it finds. In real use, the tokens returned by the lexical analyzer would be processed by a query parser, which would also probably call retrieval and display routines.

The code above, augmented with the appropriate include files, is a complete and efficient implementation of our simple lexical analyzer for queries. When tested, this code tokenized at about a third the speed that the computer could read characters—about as fast as can be expected. An even simpler lexical analyzer for automatic indexing can be constructed in the same way, and it will be just as fast.

7.3 STOPLISTS

It has been recognized since the earliest days of information retrieval (Luhn 1957) that many of the most frequently occurring words in English (like "the," "of," "and," "to," etc.) are worthless as index terms. A search using one of these terms is likely to retrieve almost every item in a database regardless of its relevance, so their discrimination value is low (Salton and McGill 1983; van Rijsbergen 1975). Furthermore, these words make up a large fraction of the text of most documents: the ten most frequently occurring words in English typically account for 20 to 30 percent of the tokens in a document (Francis and Kucera 1982). Eliminating such words from consideration early in automatic indexing speeds processing, saves huge amounts of space in indexes, and does not damage retrieval effectiveness. A list of words filtered out during automatic indexing because they make poor index terms is called a *stoplist* or a *negative dictionary*.

One way to improve information retrieval system performance, then, is to eliminate stopwords during automatic indexing. As with lexical analysis, however, it is not clear which words should be included in a stoplist. Traditionally, stoplists are supposed to have included the most frequently occurring words. However, some frequently occurring words are too important as index terms. For example, included among the 200 most frequently occurring words in general literature in English are "time," "war," "home," "life," "water," and "world." On the other hand, specialized databases will contain many words useless as index terms that are not frequent in general English. For example, a computer literature database probably need not use index terms like "computer," "program," "source," "machine," and "language."

As with lexical analysis in general, stoplist policy will depend on the database and features of the users and the indexing process. Commercial information systems tend to take a very conservative approach, with few stopwords. For example, the ORBIT Search Service has only eight stopwords: "and," "an," "by," "from," "of," "the," and "with." Larger stoplists are usually advisable. An oft-cited example of a stoplist of 250 words appears in van Rijsbergen (1975). Figure 7.5 contains a stoplist of 425 words derived from the Brown corpus (Francis and Kucera 1982) of

a	about	above	across	after
again	against	all	almost	alone
along	already	also	although	always
among	an	and	another	any
anybody	anyone	anything	anywhere	are
area	areas	around	as	ask
asked	asking	asks	at	away
b	back	backed	backing	backs
be	because	became	become	becomes
been	before	began	behind	being
beings	best	better	between	big
both	but	by	c	came
can	cannot	case	cases	certain
certainly	clear	clearly	come	could
d	did	differ	different	differently
do	does	done	down	downed
downing	downs	during	e	each
early	either	end	ended	ending
ends	enough	even	evenly	ever
every	everybody	everyone	everything	everywhere
f	face	faces	fact	facts
far	felt	few	find	finds
first	for	four	from	full
fully	further	furthered	furthering	furthers
g	gave	general	generally	get
gets	give	given	gives	go
going	good	goods	got	great
greater	greatest	group	grouped	grouping
groups	h	had	has	have
having	he	her	herself	here
high	higher	highest	him	himself
his	how	however	i	if
important	in	interest	interested	interesting
interests	into	is	it	its
itself	j	just	k	keep
keeps	kind	knew	know	known
knows	l	large	largely	last
later	latest	least	less	let
lets	like	likely	long	longer
longest	m	made	make	making
man	many	may	me	member
members	men	might	more	most
mostly	mr	mrs	much	must

Figure 7.5 A stoplist for general text

my	myself	n	necessary	need
needed	needing	needs	never	new
newer	newest	next	no	non
not	nobody	noone	nothing	now
nowhere	number	numbered	numbering	numbers
o	of	off	often	old
older	oldest	on	once	one
only	open	opened	opening	opens
or	order	ordered	ordering	orders
other	others	our	out	over
p	part	parted	parting	parts
per	perhaps	place	places	point
pointed	pointing	points	possible	present
presented	presenting	presents	problem	problems
put	puts	q	quite	r
rather	really	right	room	rooms
s	said	same	saw	say
says	second	seconds	see	seem
seemed	seeming	seems	sees	several
shall	she	should	show	showed
showing	shows	side	sides	since
small	smaller	smallest	so	some
somebody	someone	something	somewhere	state
states	still	such	sure	t
take	taken	than	that	the
their	them	then	there	therefore
these	they	thing	things	think
thinks	this	those	though	thought
thoughts	three	through	thus	to
today	together	too	took	toward
turn	turned	turning	turns	two
u	under	until	up	upon
us	use	uses	used	v
very	w	want	wanted	wanting
wants	was	way	ways	we
well	wells	went	were	what
when	where	whether	which	while
who	whole	whose	why	will
with	within	without	work	worked
working	works	would	x	y
year	years	yet	you	young
younger	youngest	your	yours	z

Figure 7.5 (*cont.*)

1,014,000 words drawn from a broad range of literature in English. Fox (1990) discusses the derivation of (a slightly shorter version of) this list, which is specially constructed to be used with the lexical analysis generator described below.

7.3.1 Implementing Stoplists

There are two ways to filter stoplist words from an input token stream: (a) examine lexical analyzer output and remove any stopwords, or (b) remove stopwords as part of lexical analysis.

The first approach, filtering stopwords from lexical analyzer output, makes the stoplist problem into a standard list searching problem: every token must be looked up in the stoplist, and removed from further analysis if found. The usual solutions to this problem are adequate, including binary search trees, binary search of an array, and hashing (Tremblay and Sorenson, 1984, Chapter 13). Undoubtedly the fastest solution is hashing.

When hashing is used to search a stoplist, the list must first be inserted into a hash table. Each token is then hashed into the table. If the resulting location is empty, the token is not a stopword, and is passed on; otherwise, comparisons must be made to determine whether the hashed value really matches the entries at that hash table location. If not, then the token is passed on; if so, the token is a stopword, and is eliminated from the token stream. This strategy is fast, but is slowed by the need to re-examine each character in a token to generate its hash value, and by the need to resolve collisions.

The hashing strategy can be improved by incorporating computation of hash values into the character-by-character processing of lexical analysis. The output of the lexical analysis phase is then a hash value as well as a token, with a small increase in the cost of lexical analysis. Some improvement can also be realized by generating a perfect hashing function for the stoplist (a *perfect hashing function* for a set of keys hashes the keys with no collisions—see Chapter 13). This minimizes the overhead of collision resolution, but has no effect on the number of collisions, which is sure to be large unless the hash table is enormous.

Although hashing is an excellent approach, probably the best implementation of stoplists is the second strategy: remove stoplist words as part of the lexical analysis process. Since lexical analysis must be done anyway, and recognizing even a large stoplist can be done at almost no extra cost during lexical analysis, this approach is extremely efficient. Furthermore, lexical analyzers that filter stoplists can be generated automatically, which is easier and less error-prone than writing stopword filters by hand.

The rest of this chapter presents a lexical analyzer generator for automatic indexing. The lexical analyzer generator accepts an arbitrary list of stopwords. It should be clear from the code presented here how to elaborate the generator, or the driver program, to fit other needs.

7.3.2 A Lexical Analyzer Generator

The heart of the lexical analyzer generator is its algorithm for producing a finite state machine. The algorithm presented here is based on methods of generating minimum state deterministic finite automata (DFAs) using derivatives of regular expressions (Aho and Ullman 1975) adapted for lists of strings. (A DFA is *minimum state* if it has a few states as possible.) This algorithm is similar to one described by Aho and Corasick (1975) for string searching.

During machine generation, the algorithm labels each state with the set of strings the machine would accept if that state were the initial state. It is easy to examine these state labels to determine: (a) the transition out of each state, (b) the target state for each transition, and (c) the states that are final states. For example, suppose a state is labeled with the set of strings {*a, an, and, in, into, to*}. This state must have transitions on *a*, *i*, and *t*. The transition on *a* must go to a state labeled with the set {*n, nd, λ*}, the transition on *i* to a state labeled {*n, nto*}, and the transition on *t* to a state labeled {*o*}. A state label L labeling a target state for a transition on symbol *a* is called a *derivative label L with transition a*. A state is made a final state if and only if its label contains the empty string.

An algorithm for generating a minimum state DFA using this labeling mechanism is presented in Figure 7.6. An example of a fully constructed machine appears in Figure 7.7.

```
create an initial state q₀ and label it with the input set L₀;
place q₀ in a state queue Q;
while Q is not empty do:
    {
    remove state qᵢ from Q;
    generate the derivative state labels from the label Lᵢ for qᵢ;
    for each derivative state label Lⱼ with transition a:
        {
        if no state qⱼ labelled Lⱼ exists, create qⱼ and put it in Q;
        create an arc labelled a from qᵢ to qⱼ;
        }
    }
make all states whose label contains λ final states.
```

Figure 7.6 Algorithm for generating a finite state machine

A C language implementation for this algorithm for generating a finite state machine appears in Figure 7.8. This algorithm relies on simple routines for allocating memory and manipulating lists of strings not listed to save space.

Several techniques are used to speed up the algorithm and to save space. State labels are hashed to produce a signature for faster label searching. Labels are also kept in a binary search tree by hash signature. To save space in the transition table, which is very sparse, transitions are kept in a short list that is searched whenever a

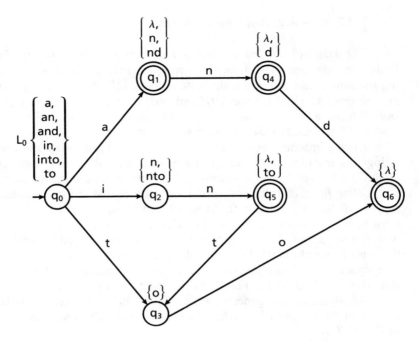

Figure 7.7 An example of a generated finite state machine

```
#define DEAD_STATE              -1    /* used to block a DFA */
#define TABLE_INCREMENT         256   /* used to grow tables */

    /*********************** Hashing ************************  /
    /* Sets of suffixes labeling states during the DFA construction */
    /* are hashed to speed searching. The hashing function uses an  */
    /* entire integer variable range as its hash table size; in an  */
    /* effort to get a good spread through this range, hash values  */
    /* start big, and are incremented by a lot with every new word  */
    /* in the list. The collision rate is low using this method.    */

#define HASH_START                  5775863
#define HASH_INCREMENT              38873647

    /************** State Label Binary Search Tree ***************/
    /* During DFA construction, all states must be searched by      */
    /* their labels to make sure that the minimum number of states  */
    /* are used. This operation is sped up by hashing the labels    */
    /* to a signature value, then storing the signatures and labels */
    /* in a binary search tree. The tree is destroyed once the DFA  */
    /* is fully constructed.                                        */
```

Figure 7.8 Code for DFA generation

```
typedef struct TreeNode {
        StrList label;              /* state label used as search key    */
        unsigned signature;         /* hashed label to speed searching   */
        int state;                  /* whose label is representd by node */
        struct TreeNode *left;      /* left binary search subtree        */
        struct TreeNode *right;     /* right binary search subtree       */
        } SearchTreeNode, *SearchTree;


/******************** DFA State Table ********************  /
/* The state table is an array of structures holding a state    */
/* label, a count of the arcs out of the state, a pointer into  */
/* the arc table for these arcs, and a final state flag. The    */
/* label field is used only during machine construction.        */

typedef struct {
        StrList label;              /* for this state – used during build */
        int num_arcs;               /* for this state in the arc table    */
        int arc_offset;             /* for finding arcs in the arc table  */
        short is_final;             /* TRUE iff this is a final state      */
        } StateTableEntry, *StateTable;


/********************* DFA Arc Table **********************/
/* The arc table lists all transitions for all states in a DFA  */
/* in compacted form. Each state's transitions are offset from  */
/* the start of the table, then listed in arc label order.      */
/* Transitions are found by a linear search of the sub–section  */
/* of the table for a given state.                              */

typedef struct {
        char label;                 /* character label on an out–arrow   */
        int target;                 /* the target state for the out–arrow */
        } ArcTableEntry, *ArcTable;


******************** DFA Structure ********************  /
/* A DFA is represented as a pointer to a structure holding the */
/* machine's state and transition tables, and bookkeeping       */
/* counters. The tables are arrays whose space is malloc'd,      */
/* then realloc'd if more space is required. Once a machine is   */
/* constructed, the table space is realloc'd one last time to    */
/* fit the needs of the machine exactly.                         */

typedef struct {
        int num_states;             /* in the DFA (and state table)      */
        int max_states;             /* now allocated in the state table  */
        int num_arcs;               /* in the arc table for this machine */
```

Figure 7.8 (*cont.*)

```
        int max_arcs;              /* now allocated in the arc table     */
        StateTable state_table;    /* the compacted DFA state table      */
        ArcTable arc_table;        /* the compacted DFA transition table */
        SearchTree tree;           /* storing state labels used in build */
        } DFAStruct, *DFA;
```

```
/*FN*************************************************************************

        DestroyTree( tree )

    Returns: void

    Purpose: Destroy a binary search tree created during machine construction

    Plan:      Part 1: Return right away of there is no tree
               Part 2: Deallocate the subtrees
               Part 3: Deallocate the root

    Notes:   None.
**/

static void
DestroyTree( tree )
    SearchTree tree;     /* in: search tree destroyed */
    {
                /* Part 1: Return right away of there is no tree */
    if ( NULL == tree ) return;

                    /* Part 2: Deallocate the subtrees */
    if ( NULL != tree->left )  DestroyTree( tree->left );
    if ( NULL != tree->right ) DestroyTree( tree->right );

                    /* Part 3: Deallocate the root */
    tree->left = tree->right = NULL;
    (void)free( (char *)tree );

    } /* DestroyTree */

/*FN*************************************************************************

        GetState( machine, label, signature )

    Returns: int -- state with the given label

    Purpose: Search a machine and return the state with a given state label
```

Figure 7.8 (*cont.*)

Plan: Part 1: Search the tree for the requested state
           Part 2: If not found, add the label to the tree
           Part 3: Return the state number

Notes: This machine always returns a state with the given label
           because if the machine does not have a state with the given
           label, then one is created.
**/


```
static int
GetState( machine, label, signature )
   DFA machine;            /* in: DFA whose state labels are searched; */
   StrList label;          /* in: state label searched for */
   unsigned signature;     /* in: signature of the label requested */
   {
   SearchTree *ptr;           /* pointer to a search tree link field */
   SearchTree new_node;       /* for a newly added search tree node */

              /* Part 1: Search the tree for the requested state */
   ptr = &(machine->tree);
   while ( (NULL != *ptr) && (   (signature != (*ptr)->signature)
                              || !StrListEqual(label, (*ptr)->label)) )
      ptr = (signature <= (*ptr)->signature) ? &(*ptr)->left : &(*ptr)->right;

              /* Part 2: If not found, add the label to the tree */
   if ( NULL == *ptr )
      {
         /* create a new node and fill in its fields */
      new_node = (SearchTree)GetMemory( NULL, sizeof(SearchTreeNode) );
      new-node->signature = signature;
      new_node->label = (StrList)label;
      new_node->state = machine->num_states;
      new_node->left = new_node->right = NULL;


         /* allocate more states if needed, set up the new state */
      if ( machine->num_states == machine->max_states )
         {
         machine->max_states += TABLE_INCREMENT;
         machine->state_table =
            (StateTable)GetMemory( machine-state_table,
                                   machine-max_states*sizeof(StateTableEntry));
         }
      machine->state_table[machine-num_states].label = (StrList)label;
      machine->num_states++;
```

Figure 7.8   (*cont.*)

```
              /* hook the new node into the binary search tree */
        *ptr = new_node;
        }
    else
        StrListDestroy( label );

                    /* Part 3: Return the state number */
    return( (*ptr)->state );

    } /* GetState */

/*FN****************************************************************************

        AddArc( machine, state, arc_label, state_label, state_signature )

    Returns: void

    Purpose: Add an arc between two states in a DFA

    Plan:      Part 1: Search for the target state among existing states
               Part 2: Make sure the arc table is big enough
               Part 3: Add the new arc

    Notes:     None.
**/

static void
AddArc( machine, state, arc_label, state_label, state_signature )
    DFA machine;                   /* in/out: machine with an arc added */
    int state;                     /* in: with an out arc added */
    char arc_label;                /* in: label on the new arc */
    StrList state_label;           /* in: label on the target state */
    unsigned state_signature;  /* in: label hash signature to speed searching */
    {
    register int target;    /* destination state for the new arc */

        /* Part 1: Search for the target state among existing states */
    StrListSort( 0, state_label );
    target = GetState( machine, state_label, state_signature );

                /* Part 2: Make sure the arc table is big enough */
    if ( machine->num_arcs == machine->max_arcs )
        {
        machine->max_arcs += TABLE_INCREMENT;
        machine->arc_table =
            (ArcTable)GetMemory( machine->arc_table,
```

Figure 7.8 (*cont.*)

```
                        machine->max_arcs * sizeof(ArcTableEntry) );
    }

                        /* Part 3: Add the new arc */
    machine->arc_table[machine->num_arcs].label = arc_label;
    machine->arc_table[machine->num_arcs].target = target;
    machine->num_arcs++;
    machine->state_table[state].num_arcs++;

    } /* AddArc */


/*FN**************************************************************************

        BuildDFA( words )

    Returns: DFA -- newly created finite state machine

    Purpose: Build a DFA to recognize a list of words

    Plan:       Part 1: Allocate space and initialize variables
                Part 2: Make and label the DFA start state
                Part 3: Main loop - build the state and arc tables
                Part 4: Deallocate the binary search tree and the state labels
                Part 5: Reallocate the tables to squish them down
                Part 6: Return the newly constructed DFA

    Notes:      None.
**/

DFA
BuildDFA( words )
    StrList words;   /* in: that the machine is built to recognize */
    {
    DFA machine;                    /* local for easier access to machine */
    register int state;             /* current state's state number */
    char arc_label;                 /* for the current arc when adding arcs */
    char *string;                   /* element in a set of state labels */
    char ch;                        /* the first character in a new string */
    StrList current_label;          /* set of strings labeling a state */
    StrList target_label;           /* labeling the arc target state */
    unsigned target_signature;      /* hashed label for binary search tree */
    register int i;                 /* for looping through strings */

                /* Part 1: Allocate space and initialize variables */
    machine = (DFA)GetMemory( NULL, sizeof(DFAStruct) );
```

Figure 7.8 (*cont.*)

```
machine->max_states = TABLE_INCREMENT;
machine->state_table =
    (StateTable)GetMemory(NULL, machine->max_states*sizeof(StateTableEntry));
machine->num_states = 0;

machine->max_arcs = TABLE_INCREMENT;
machine->arc_table =
    (ArcTable)GetMemory( NULL, machine->max_arcs * sizeof(ArcTableEntry) );
machine->num_arcs = 0;

machine->tree = NULL;

            /* Part 2: Make and label the DFA start state */
StrListUnique( 0, words );               /* sort and unique the list */
machine->state_table[0].label = words;
machine->num_states = 1;

        /* Part 3: Main loop - build the state and arc tables */
for ( state = 0; state < machine->num_states; state++ )
  {
        /* The current state has nothing but a label, so */
        /* the first order of business is to set up some */
        /* of its other major fields                     */
    machine->state_table[state].is_final = FALSE;
    machine->state_table[state].arc_offset = machine->num_arcs;
    machine->state_table[state].num_arcs = 0;

        /* Add arcs to the arc table for the current state */
        /* based on the state's derived set.  Also set the */
        /* state's final flag if the empty string is found */
        /* in the suffix list                              */
    current_label = machine->state_table[state].label;
    target_label = StrListCreate();
    target_signature = HASH_START;
    arc_label = EOS;
    for ( i = 0; i < StrListSize(current_label); i++ )
      {
        /* get the next string in the label and lop it */
        string = StrListPeek( current_label, i );
        ch = *string++;

        /* the empty string means mark this state as final */
        if ( EOS == ch )
          { machine->state_table[state].is_final = TRUE; continue; }
```

Figure 7.8 (*cont.*)

```
              /* make sure we have a legitimate arc_label */
        if ( EOS == arc_label ) arc_label = ch;

              /* if the first character is new, then we must */
              /* add an arc for the previous first character */
        if ( ch != arc_label )
            {
            AddArc(machine, state, arc_label, target_label, target_signature);
            target_label = StrListCreate();
            target_signature = HASH_START;
            arc_label = ch;
            }

              /* add the current suffix to the target state label */
        StrListAppend( target_label, string );
        target_signature += (*string + 1) * HASH_INCREMENT;
        while ( *string ) target_signature += *string++;
        }

              /* On loop exit we have not added an arc for the */
              /* last bunch of suffixes, so we must do so, as  */
              /* long as the last set of suffixes is not empty */
              /* (which happens when the current state label    */
              /* is the singleton set of the empty string).    */
    if ( 0 < StrListSize(target_label) )
        AddArc( machine, state, arc_label, target_label, target_signature );
    }

  /* Part 4: Deallocate the binary search tree and the state labels */
  DestroyTree( machine->tree ); machine->tree = NULL;
  for ( i = 0; i < machine->num_states; i++ )
      {
      StrListDestroy( machine->state_table[i].label );
      machine->state_table[i].label = NULL;
      }

              /* Part 5: Reallocate the tables to squish them down */
  machine->state_table = (StateTable)GetMemory( machine->state_table,
                              machine->num_states * sizeof(StateTableEntry) );
  machine->arc_table = (ArcTable)GetMemory( machine->arc_table,
                              machine->num_arcs * sizeof(ArcTableEntry) );

                /* Part 6: Return the newly constructed DFA */
  return( machine );

  } /* BuildDFA */
```

Figure 7.8 *(cont.)*

transition for a given state is needed. These lists usually have no more than three or four items, so searching them is still reasonably fast. Once the machine is constructed, all the space used for the state labels is deallocated, so the only data structures of any size that remain are the state table and the compressed transition table. When a transition for a symbol is not found in the transition table, a default transition to a special dead state is used. When a machine blocks in the dead state, it does not recognize its input.

After a finite state machine is constructed, it is easy to generate a simple driver program that uses it to process input. Figure 7.9 contains an example of such a driver program. This program assumes the existence of a character class array like the one in Figure 7.2, except that it has only three character classes: one for digits, one for letters, and one for everything else (called delimiters). It also assumes there is a character case conversion array like the one in Figure 7.2. The driver takes a machine constructed using the code in Figure 7.7, and uses it to filter all stopwords, returning only legitimate index terms. It filters numbers, but accepts terms containing digits. It also converts the case of index terms.

```
/*FN***********************************************************************

        GetTerm( stream, machine, size, output )

    Returns: char * -- NULL if stream is exhausted, otherwise output buffer

    Purpose: Get the next token from an input stream, filtering stop words

    Plan:    Part 1: Return NULL immediately if there is no input
             Part 2: Initialize the local variables
             Part 3: Main Loop: Put an unfiltered word into the output buffer
             Part 4: Return the output buffer

    Notes:   This routine runs the DFA provided as the machine parameter,
             and collects the text of any term in the output buffer. If
             a stop word is recognized in this process, it is skipped.
             Care is also taken to be sure not to overrun the output buffer.
**/

char *
GetTerm( stream, machine, size, output )
    FILE *stream;        /* in: source of input characters */
    DFA machine;         /* in: finite state machine driving process */
    int size;            /* in: bytes in the output buffer */
    char *output;        /* in/out: where the next token in placed */
    {
    char *outptr;            /* for scanning through the output buffer */
    int ch;                  /* current character during input scan */
    register int state;      /* current state during DFA execution */
```

Figure 7.9 An example of DFA driver program

```
        /* Part 1: Return NULL immediately if there is no input */
if ( EOF == (ch = getc(stream)) ) return( NULL );

            /* Part 2: Initialize the local variables */
outptr = output;

  /* Part 3: Main Loop: Put an unfiltered word into the output buffer */
do
  {
    /* scan past any leading delimiters */
  while ( (EOF != ch ) &&
          ((DELIM_CH == char_class[ch]) ||
           (DIGIT_CH == char_class[ch])) ) ch = getc( stream );

    /* start the machine in its start state */
  state = 0;

    /* copy input to output until reaching a delimiter, and also */
    /* run the DFA on the input to watch for filtered words    */
  while ( (EOF != ch) && (DELIM_CH != char_class[ch]) )
    {
    if ( outptr == (output+size-1) ) { outptr = output; state = 0; }
    *outptr++ = convert_case[ch];

    if ( DEAD_STATE != state )
      {
      register int i;     /* for scanning through arc labels */
      int arc_start;      /* where the arc label list starts */
      int arc_end;        /* where the arc label list ends */

      arc_start = machine->state_table[state].arc_offset;
      arc_end = arc_start + machine->state_table[state].num_arcs;

      for ( i = arc_start; i < arc_end; i++ )
        if ( convert_case[ch] == machine->arc_table[i].label )
          { state = machine->arc_table[i].target; break; }

      if ( i == arc_end ) state = DEAD_STATE;
      }

    ch = getc( stream );
    }

    /* start from scratch if a stop word is recognized */
  if ( (DEAD_STATE != state) && machine->state_table[state].is_final )
    outptr = output;
```

Figure 7.9 (*cont.*)

```
                    /* terminate the output buffer */
        *outptr = EOS;
        }
    while ( (EOF != ch) && !*output );


                        /* Part 4: Return the output buffer */
        return( output );

    } /* GetTerm */
```

Figure 7.9 *(cont.)*

Once the finite state machine blocks in the dead state, the string is not recognized. The driver program takes advantage of this fact by not running the finite state machine once it enters the dead state.

A lexical analyzer generator program can use these components in several ways. A lexical analyzer can be generated at indexing time, or ahead of time and stored in a file. The input can be read from a stream, as in the example driver program, or from another input source. A lexical analyzer data structure can be defined, and different stoplists and lexical analysis rules used in each one, then different analyzers can be run on different sorts of data. All these alternatives are easy to implement once the basic finite state machine generator and driver generator programs are in place.

As an illustration, Figure 7.10 contains the main function for a program that reads a stoplist from a file, builds a finite state machine using the function from Figure 7.8, then uses the driver function from Figure 7.9 to generate and print all the terms in an input file, filtering out the words in the stoplist.

```
/*FN***************************************************************************


    main( argc, argv )

Returns:  int -- 0 on success, 1 on failure

Purpose:  Program main function

Plan:     Part 1: Read the stop list from the stop words file
          Part 2: Create a DFA from a stop list
          Part 3: Open the input file and list its terms
          Part 4: Close the input file and return

Notes:    This program reads a stop list from a file called "words.std,"
          and uses it in generating the terms in a file named on the
          command line.
**/
```

Figure 7.10 Main function for a term generator program

```
int
main( argc, argv )
    int argc;       /* in: how many arguments */
    char *argv[]; /* in: text of the arguments */
    {
    char term[128];   /* for the next term found */
    FILE *stream;     /* where to read characters from */
    StrList words;    /* the stop list filtered */
    DFA machine;      /* build from the stop list */

                /* Part 1: Read the stop list from the stop words file */
    words = StrListCreate();
    StrListAppendFile( words, "words.std" );

                /* Part 2: Create a DFA from a stop list */
    machine = BuildDFA( words );

                /* Part 3: Open the input file and list its terms */
    if ( !(stream = fopen(argv[1],"r")) ) exit(1);
    while ( NULL != GetTerm(stream,machine,128,term) )
        (void)printf( "%s/n", term );

                /* Part 4: Close the input file and return */
    (void)fclose( stream );
    return(0);

    } /* main */
```

Figure 7.10 (*cont.*)

Lexical analyzers built using the method outlined here can be constructed quickly, and are small and fast. For example, the finite state machine generated by the code in Figure 7.8 for the stoplist of 425 words in Figure 7.5 has only 318 states and 555 arcs. The program in Figure 7.10 built this finite state machine from scratch, then used it to lexically analyze the text from this chapter in under 1 second on a Sun SparcStation 1.

7.4 SUMMARY

Lexical analysis must be done in automatic indexing and in query processing. Important decisions about the lexical form of indexing and query terms, and of query operators and grouping indicators, must be made in the design phase based on characteristics of databases and uses of the target system. Once this is done, it is a simple matter to apply techniques from program translation to the problem of lexical analysis. Finite state machine based lexical analyzers can be built quickly and reliably by hand or with a lexical analyzer generator.

Problems in the selection of stoplist words for automatic indexing are similar to those encountered in designing lexical analyzers, and likewise depend on the characteristics of the database and the system. Removing stoplist words during automatic indexing can be treated like a search problem, or can be incorporated into the lexical analysis process. Although hashing can be used to solve the searching problem very efficiently, it is probably best to incorporate stoplist processing into lexical analysis. Since stoplists may be large, automatic generation of lexical analyzers is the preferred approach in this case.

REFERENCES

AHO, A., and M. CORASICK. 1975. "Efficient String Matching: An Aid to Bibliographic Search." *Communications of the ACM*, 18(6), 333–40.

AHO, A., R. SETHI, and J. ULLMAN. 1986. *Compilers: Principles, Techniques, and Tools.* New York: Addison-Wesley.

FOX, C. 1990. "A Stop List for General Text." *SIGIR Forum*, 24(1-2), 19–35.

FRANCIS, W., and H. KUCERA. 1982. *Frequency Analysis of English Usage.* New York: Houghton Mifflin.

HOPCROFT, J., and J. ULLMAN. 1979. *Introduction to Automata Theory, Languages, and Computation.* New York: Addison-Wesley.

LESK, M. 1975. *Lex-A Lexical Analyzer Generator.* Murray Hill, N.J.: AT&T Bell Laboratories.

LUHN, H. P. 1957. "A Statistical Approach to Mechanized Encoding and Searching of Literary Information. *IBM Journal of Research and Development,* 1(4).

SALTON, G., and M. MCGILL. 1983. *Modern Information Retrieval.* New York: McGraw-Hill.

TREMBLAY, J. P., and P. SORENSON. 1984. *An Introduction to Data Structures with Applications, Second Edition.* New York: McGraw-Hill.

VAN RIJSBERGEN, C. J. 1975. *Information Retrieval.* London: Butterworths.

WAIT, W. 1986. "The Cost of Lexical Analysis." *Software Practice and Experience,* 16(5), 473–88.

8

Stemming Algorithms

W. B. Frakes

Software Engineering Guild
Sterling, VA 22170

Abstract

This chapter describes stemming algorithms—programs that relate morphologically similar indexing and search terms. Stemming is used to improve retrieval effectiveness and to reduce the size of indexing files. Several approaches to stemming are described—table lookup, affix removal, successor variety, and n-gram. Empirical studies of stemming are summarized. The Porter stemmer is described in detail, and a full implementation in C is presented.

8.1 INTRODUCTION

One technique for improving IR performance is to provide searchers with ways of finding morphological variants of search terms. If, for example, a searcher enters the term *stemming* as part of a query, it is likely that he or she will also be interested in such variants as *stemmed* and *stem*. We use the term *conflation,* meaning the act of fusing or combining, as the general term for the process of matching morphological term variants. Conflation can be either manual—using some kind of regular expressions—or automatic, via programs called *stemmers*. Stemming is also used in IR to reduce the size of index files. Since a single stem typically corresponds to several full terms, by storing stems instead of terms, compression factors of over 50 percent can be achieved.

As can be seen in Figure 1.2 in Chapter 1, terms can be stemmed at indexing time or at search time. The advantage of stemming at indexing time is efficiency and index file compression—since index terms are already stemmed, this operation requires no resources at search time, and the index file will be compressed as described above. The disadvantage of indexing time stemming is that information about the full terms will be lost, or additional storage will be required to store both the stemmed and unstemmed forms.

Figure 8.1 shows a taxonomy for stemming algorithms. There are four automatic approaches. Affix removal algorithms remove suffixes and/or prefixes from terms leaving a *stem*. These algorithms sometimes also transform the resultant stem. The name stemmer derives from this method, which is the most common. Successor

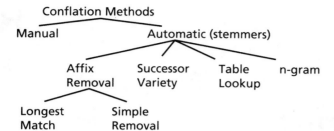

Figure 8.1 Conflation methods

variety stemmers use the frequencies of letter sequences in a body of text as the basis of stemming. The n-gram method conflates terms based on the number of digrams or n-grams they share. Terms and their corresponding stems can also be stored in a table. Stemming is then done via lookups in the table. These methods are described below.

There are several criteria for judging stemmers: correctness, retrieval effectiveness, and compression performance. There are two ways stemming can be incorrect—overstemming and understemming. When a term is overstemmed, too much of it is removed. Overstemming can cause unrelated terms to be conflated. The effect on IR performance is retrieval of nonrelevant documents. Understemming is the removal of too little of a term. Understemming will prevent related terms from being conflated. The effect of understemming on IR performance is that relevant documents will not be retrieved. Stemmers can also be judged on their retrieval effectiveness—usually measured with recall and precision as defined in Chapter 1, and on their speed, size, and so on. Finally, they can be rated on their compression performance. Stemmers for IR are not usually judged on the basis of linguistic correctness, though the stems they produce are usually very similar to root morphemes, as described below.

8.1.1 Example of Stemmer Use in Searching

To illustrate how a stemmer is used in searching, consider the following example from the CATALOG system (Frakes 1984, 1986). In CATALOG, terms are stemmed at search time rather than at indexing time. CATALOG prompts for queries with the string "Look for:". At the prompt, the user types in one or more terms of interest. For example:

```
Look for: system users
```

will cause CATALOG to attempt to find documents about system users. CATALOG takes each term in the query, and tries to determine which other terms in the database might have the same stem. If any possibly related terms are found, CATALOG presents them to the user for selection. In the case of the query term "users," for example, CATALOG might respond as follows:

Stemming Algorithms   Chap. 8

```
                Search Term: users

                Term            Occurrences

            1.  user                15
            2.  users                1
            3.  used                 3
            4.  using                2

            Which terms (0 = none, CR = all):
```

The user selects the terms he or she wants by entering their numbers.

This method of using a stemmer in a search session provides a naive system user with the advantages of term conflation while requiring little knowledge of the system or of searching techniques. It also allows experienced searchers to focus their attention on other search problems. Since stemming may not always be appropriate, the stemmer can be turned off by the user. Having a user select the terms from the set found by the stemmer also reduces the likelihood of false matches.

8.2 TYPES OF STEMMING ALGORITHMS

There are several approaches to stemming. One way to do stemming is to store a table of all index terms and their stems. For example:

Term	Stem
engineering	engineer
engineered	engineer
engineer	engineer

Terms from queries and indexes could then be stemmed via table lookup. Using a B-tree or hash table, such lookups would be very fast.

There are problems with this approach. The first is that there is no such data for English. Even if there were, many terms found in databases would not be represented, since they are domain dependent that is, not standard English. For these terms, some other stemming method would be required. Another problem is the storage overhead for such a table, though trading size for time is sometimes warranted. Storing precomputed data, as opposed to computing the data values on the fly, is useful when the computations are frequent and/or expensive. Bentley (1982), for example, reports cases such as chess computations where storing precomputed results gives significant performance improvements.

8.2.1 Successor Variety

Successor variety stemmers (Hafer and Weiss 1974) are based on work in structural linguistics which attempted to determine word and morpheme boundaries based on the distribution of phonemes in a large body of utterances. The stemming method based on this work uses letters in place of phonemes, and a body of text in place of phonemically transcribed utterances.

Hafer and Weiss formally defined the technique as follows:

> Let α be a word of length n; α_i is a length i prefix of α. Let D be the corpus of words. $D_{\alpha i}$ is defined as the subset of D containing those terms whose first i letters match α_i exactly. The successor variety of α_i, denoted S_{α_i}, is then defined as the number of distinct letters that occupy the i+1st position of words in $D_{\alpha i}$. A test word of length n has n successor varieties $S_{\alpha_i}, S_{\alpha_2}, \ldots, S_{\alpha_n}$. (p. 372)

In less formal terms, the successor variety of a string is the number of different characters that follow it in words in some body of text. Consider a body of text consisting of the following words, for example.

able, axle, accident, ape, about.

To determine the successor varieties for "apple," for example, the following process would be used. The first letter of apple is "a." "a" is followed in the text body by four characters: "b," "x," "c," and "p." Thus, the successor variety of "a" is four. The next successor variety for apple would be one, since only "e" follows "ap" in the text body, and so on.

When this process is carried out using a large body of text (Hafer and Weiss report 2,000 terms to be a stable number), the successor variety of substrings of a term will decrease as more characters are added until a segment boundary is reached. At this point, the successor variety will sharply increase. This information is used to identify stems.

Once the successor varieties for a given word have been derived, this information must be used to segment the word. Hafer and Weiss discuss four ways of doing this.

1. Using the *cutoff method*, some cutoff value is selected for successor varieties and a boundary is identified whenever the cutoff value is reached. The problem with this method is how to select the cutoff value—if it is too small, incorrect cuts will be made; if too large, correct cuts will be missed.

2. With the *peak and plateau method*, a segment break is made after a character whose successor variety exceeds that of the character immediately preceding it and the character immediately following it. This method removes the need for the cutoff value to be selected.

3. In the *complete word method* method, a break is made after a segment if the segment is a complete word in the corpus.

4. The *entropy method* takes advantage of the distribution of successor variety letters. The method works as follows. Let $|D_{\alpha i}|$ be the number of words in a text body beginning with the i length sequence of letters α. Let $|D_{\alpha ij}|$ be the number of words in $D_{\alpha i}$ with the successor j. The probability that a member of $D_{\alpha i}$ has the successor j is given by $\dfrac{|D_{\alpha ij}|}{|D_{\alpha i}|}$. The entropy of $|D_{\alpha i}|$ is

$$H_{\alpha i} = \sum_{p=1}^{26} - \frac{|D_{\alpha ij}|}{|D_{\alpha i}|} \cdot \log_2 \frac{|D_{\alpha ij}|}{|D_{\alpha i}|}$$

Using this equation, a set of entropy measures can be determined for a word. A set of entropy measures for predecessors can also be defined similarly. A cutoff value is selected, and a boundary is identified whenever the cutoff value is reached.

Hafer and Weiss experimentally evaluated the various segmentation methods using two criteria: (1) the number of correct segment cuts divided by the total number of cuts, and (2) the number of correct segment cuts divided by the total number of true boundaries. They found that none of the methods performed perfectly, but that techniques that combined certain of the methods did best.

To illustrate the use of successor variety stemming, consider the example below where the task is to determine the stem of the word READABLE.

```
Test Word:  READABLE
Corpus:     ABLE, APE, BEATABLE, FIXABLE, READ, READABLE
            READING, READS, RED, ROPE, RIPE.
```

Prefix	Successor Variety	Letters
R	3	E,I,0
RE	2	A,D
REA	1	D
READ	3	A,I,S
READA	1	B
READAB	1	L
READABL	1	E
READABLE	1	BLANK

Using the complete word segmentation method, the test word "READABLE" will be segmented into "READ" and "ABLE," since READ appears as a word in the corpus. The peak and plateau method would give the same result.

After a word has been segmented, the segment to be used as the stem must be selected. Hafer and Weiss used the following rule:

```
if(first segment occurs in <= 12 words in corpus)
            first segment is stem
      else(second segment is stem)
```

The check on the number of occurrences is based on the observation that if a segment occurs in more than 12 words in the corpus, it is probably a prefix. The authors report that because of the infrequency of multiple prefixes in English, no segment beyond the second is ever selected as the stem. Using this rule in the example above, READ would be selected as the stem of READABLE.

In summary, the successor variety stemming process has three parts: (1) determine the successor varieties for a word, (2) use this information to segment the word using one of the methods above, and (3) select one of the segments as the stem. The aim of Hafer and Weiss was to develop a stemmer that required little or no human processing. They point out that while affix removal stemmers work well, they require human preparation of suffix lists and removal rules. Their stemmer requires no such preparation. The retrieval effectiveness of the Hafer and Weiss stemmer is discussed below.

8.2.2 n-gram stemmers

Adamson and Boreham (1974) reported a method of conflating terms called the shared digram method. A digram is a pair of consecutive letters. Since trigrams, or n-grams could be used, we have called it the n-gram method. Though we call this a "stemming method," this is a bit confusing since no stem is produced.

In this approach, association measures are calculated between pairs of terms based on shared unique digrams. For example, the terms statistics and statistical can be broken into digrams as follows.

```
statistics => st ta at ti is st ti ic cs
unique digrams = at cs ic is st ta ti

statistical => st ta at ti is st ti ic ca al
unique digrams = al at ca ic is st ta ti
```

Thus, "statistics" has nine digrams, seven of which are unique, and "statistical" has ten digrams, eight of which are unique. The two words share six unique digrams: at, ic, is, st, ta, ti.

Once the unique digrams for the word pair have been identified and counted, a similarity measure based on them is computed. The similarity measure used was Dice's coefficient, which is defined as

$$S = \frac{2C}{A + B}$$

where A is the number of unique digrams in the first word, B the number of unique digrams in the second, and C the number of unique digrams shared by A and B. For the example above, Dice's coefficient would equal $(2 \times 6)/(7 + 8) = .80$. Such similarity measures are determined for all pairs of terms in the database, forming a similarity matrix. Since Dice's coefficient is symmetric ($S_{ij} = S_{ji}$), a lower triangular similarity matrix can be used as in the example below.

	$word_1$	$word_2$	$word_3 \ldots word_{n-1}$	
$word_1$				
$word_2$	S_{21}			
$word_3$	S_{31}	S_{32}		
.				
.				
$word_n$	S_{n1}	S_{n2}	S_{n3}	$S_{n(n-1)}$

Once such a similarity matrix is available, terms are clustered using a single link clustering method as described in Chapter 16. The algorithm for calculating a digram similarity matrix follows.

```
/* calculate similarity matrix for words based on digrams */
#define MAXGRAMS 50   /* maximum n-grams for a word */
#define GRAMSIZE 2    /* size of the n-gram */

void
digram_smatrix(wordlist, word_list_length, smatrix)
char *wordlist[]; /* list of sorted unique words */
int word_list_length;      /* length of wordlist */
double *smatrix[];

{

int i, j;    /* loop counters */
int uniq_in_word1; /* number of unique digrams in word 1 */
int uniq_in_word2; /* number of unique digrams in word 2 */
int common_uniq;   /* number of unique digrams shared by words 1 and 2 */
char uniq_digrams_1[MAXGRAMS][GRAMSIZE]; /* array of digrams */
char uniq_digrams_2[MAXGRAMS][GRAMSIZE]; /* array of digrams */
int unique_digrams(); /* function to calculate # of unique digrams in word */
int common_digrams(); /* function to calculate # of shared unique digrams */

for ( i=0; i< word_list_length; ++i)

  for (j=i+1; j < word_list_length ;++j) {
```

```
/* find unique digrams for first word in pair */
uniq_in_word1 = unique_digrams(wordlist[i], uniq_digrams_1);
/* find unique digrams for second word in pair */
uniq_in_word2 = unique_digrams(wordlist[j], uniq_digrams_2);
/* find number of common unique digrams */
common_uniq = common_digrams(uniq_digrams_1, uniq_digrams_2);
/* calculate similarity value and store in similarity matrix */
smatrix[i][j] = (2*common_uniq)/(uniq_in_word1+uniq_in_word2);

    } /* end for */

} /* end digram_smatrix */
```

When they used their method on a sample of words from *Chemical Titles,* Adamson and Boreham found that most pairwise similarity measures were 0. Thus, the similarity matrix will be sparse, and techniques for handling sparse matrices will be appropriate. Using a cutoff similarity value of .6, they found ten of the eleven clusters formed were correct. More significantly, in hardly any cases did the method form false associations. The authors also report using this method successfully to cluster document titles.

8.2.3 Affix Removal Stemmers

Affix removal algorithms remove suffixes and/or prefixes from terms leaving a *stem*. These algorithms sometimes also transform the resultant stem. A simple example of an affix removal stemmer is one that removes the plurals from terms. A set of rules for such a stemmer is as follows (Harman 1991).

```
If a word ends in "ies" but not "eies" or "aies"
        Then "ies" -> "y"
If a word ends in "es" but not "aes", "ees", or "oes"
        then "es" -> "e"
If a word ends in "s", but not "us" or "ss"
        then "s" -> NULL
```

In this algorithm only the first applicable rule is used.

Most stemmers currently in use are iterative longest match stemmers, a kind of affix removal stemmer first developed by Lovins (1968). An iterative longest match stemmer removes the longest possible string of characters from a word according to a set of rules. This process is repeated until no more characters can be removed. Even after all characters have been removed, stems may not be correctly conflated. The word "skies," for example, may have been reduced to the stem "ski" which will not match "sky." There are two techniques to handle this—recoding or partial matching.

Recoding is a context sensitive transformation of the form AxC -> AyC where A and C specify the context of the transformation, x is the input string, and y is the transformed string. We might, for example, specify that if a stem ends in an "i" following a "k," then i -> y. In partial matching, only the n initial characters of stems are used in comparing them. Using this approach, we might say that two stems are equivalent if they agree in all but their last characters.

In addition to Lovins, iterative longest match stemmers have been reported by Salton (1968), Dawson (1974), Porter (1980), and Paice (1990). As discussed below, the Porter algorithm is more compact than Lovins, Salton, and Dawson, and seems, on the basis of experimentation, to give retrieval performance comparable to the larger algorithms. The Paice stemmer is also compact, but since experimental data was not available for the Paice algorithm, we chose the Porter algorithm as the example of this type of stemmer.

The Porter algorithm consists of a set of condition/action rules. The conditions fall into three classes: conditions on the stem, conditions on the suffix, and conditions on the rules.

There are several types of stem conditions.

1. The *measure,* denoted m, of a stem is based on its alternate vowel-consonant sequences. Vowels are a, e, i, o, u, and y if preceded by a consonant. Consonants are all letters that are not vowels. Let C stand for a sequence of consonants, and V for a sequence of vowels. The measure m, then, is defined as

$$[C](VC)^m[V]$$

The superscript m in the equation, which is the measure, indicates the number of VC sequences. Square brackets indicate an optional occurrence. Some examples of measures for terms follows.

Measure	Examples
m=0	TR, EE, TREE, Y, BY
m=1	TROUBLE, OATS, TREES, IVY
m=2	TROUBLES, PRIVATE, OATEN

2. $* < X >$ —the stem ends with a given letter X
3. $*v*$—the stem contains a vowel
4. $*d$—the stem ends in a double consonant
5. $*o$—the stem ends with a consonant-vowel-consonant, sequence, where the final consonant is not w, x, or y.

Suffix conditions take the form: (current_suffix $==$ pattern). Rule conditions take the form: (rule was used).

Actions are rewrite rules of the form:

```
old_suffix -> new_suffix
```

The rules are divided into steps. The rules in a step are examined in sequence, and only one rule from a step can apply. The longest possible suffix is always removed because of the ordering of the rules within a step. The algorithm is as follows.

```
{
        step1a(word);
        step1b(stem);
        if (the second or third rule of step 1b was used)
                step1b1(stem);
        step1c(stem);
        step2(stem);
        step3(stem);
        step4(stem);
        step5a(stem);
        step5b(stem);
}
```

The rules for the steps of the stemmer are as follows.

Step 1a Rules

Conditions	Suffix	Replacement	Examples
NULL	sses	ss	caresses -> caress
NULL	ies	i	ponies -> poni
			ties -> tie
NULL	ss	ss	carress -> carress
NULL	s	NULL	cats -> cat

Step 1b Rules

Conditions	Suffix	Replacement	Examples
(m>0)	eed	ee	feed -> feed
			agreed -> agree
(*v*)	ed	NULL	plastered -> plaster
			bled -> bled
(*v*)	ing	NULL	motoring -> motor
			sing -> sing

Step 1b1 Rules

Conditions	Suffix	Replacement	Examples
NULL	at	ate	conflat(ed) -> conflate
NULL	bl	ble	troubl(ing) -> trouble
NULL	iz	ize	siz(ed) -> size
(*d and not (*\<L> or *\<S> or *\<Z>))	NULL	single letter	hopp(ing) -> hop
			tann(ed) -> tan
			fall(ing) -> fall
			hiss(ing) -> hiss
			fizz(ed) -> fizz
(m=1 and *o)	NULL	e	fail(ing) -> fail
			fil(ing) -> file

Step 1c Rules

Conditions	Suffix	Replacement	Examples
(*v*)	y	i	happy -> happi
			sky -> sky

Step 2 Rules

Conditions	Suffix	Replacement	Examples
(m>0)	ational	ate	relational -> relate
(m>0)	tional	tion	conditional -> condition
			rational -> rational
(m>0)	enci	ence	valenci -> valence
(m>0)	anci	ance	hesitanci -> hesitance
(m>0)	izer	ize	digitizer -> digitize
(m>0)	abli	able	conformabli -> conformable
(m>0)	alli	al	radicalli -> radical
(m>0)	entli	ent	differentli -> different
(m>0)	eli	e	vileli -> vile
(m>0)	ousli	ous	analogousli -> analogous
(m>0)	ization	ize	vietnamization -> vietnamize
(m>0)	ation	ate	predication -> predicate
(m>0)	ator	ate	operator -> operate
(m>0)	alism	al	feudalism -> feudal
(m>0)	iveness	ive	decisiveness -> decisive
(m>0)	fulness	ful	hopefulness -> hopeful
(m>0)	ousness	ous	callousness -> callous
(m>0)	aliti	al	formaliti -> formal
(m>0)	iviti	ive	sensitiviti -> sensitive
(m>0)	biliti	ble	sensibiliti -> sensible

Step 3 Rules

Conditions	Suffix	Replacement	Examples
(m>0)	icate	ic	triplicate -> triplic
(m>0)	ative	NULL	formative -> form
(m>0)	alize	al	formalize -> formal
(m>0)	iciti	ic	electriciti -> electric
(m>0)	ical	ic	electrical -> electric
(m>0)	ful	NULL	hopeful -> hope
(m>0)	ness	NULL	goodness -> good

Step 4 Rules

Conditions	Suffix	Replacement	Examples
(m>1)	al	NULL	revival -> reviv
(m>1)	ance	NULL	allowance -> allow
(m>1)	ence	NULL	inference -> infer
(m>1)	er	NULL	airliner -> airlin
(m>1)	ic	NULL	gyroscopic -> gyroscop
(m>1)	able	NULL	adjustable -> adjust
(m>1)	ible	NULL	defensible -> defens
(m>1)	ant	NULL	irritant -> irrit
(m>1)	ement	NULL	replacement -> replac
(m>1)	ment	NULL	adjustment -> adjust
(m>1)	ent	NULL	dependent -> depend
(m>1 and (*<S> or *<T>))	ion	NULL	adoption->adopt
(m>1)	ou	NULL	homologou->homolog
(m>1)	ism	NULL	communism->commun
(m>1)	ate	NULL	activate->activ
(m>1)	iti	NULL	angulariti->angular
(m>1)	ous	NULL	homologous ->homolog
(m>1)	ive	NULL	effective->effect
(m>1)	ize	NULL	bowdlerize->bowdler

Step 5a Rules

Conditions	Suffix	Replacement	Examples
(m>1)	e	NULL	probate -> probat rate- > rate
(m=1 and not *o)	e	NULL	cease- > ceas

Step 5b Rules

Conditions	Suffix	Replacement	Examples
(m>1 and *d and *<L>)	NULL	single letter	controll -> control roll -> roll

A full implementation of this stemmer, in C, is in the appendix to this chapter.

8.3 EXPERIMENTAL EVALUATIONS OF STEMMING

There have been many experimental evaluations of stemmers. Salton (1968) examined the relative retrieval performance of fully stemmed terms against terms with only the suffix "s" removed. The stemmer used was an iterative longest match stemmer of the type described above, employing about 200 endings. Three document collections were used in these studies: the IRE-3 collection consisting of 780 computer science abstracts and 34 search requests, the ADI collection consisting of 82 papers and 35 search requests, and the Cranfield-1 collection consisting of 200 aerodynamics abstracts and 42 search requests.

Differences between the two conflation methods, fully stemmed and "s" stemmed, were calculated on 14 dependent variables for each query: rank recall, log precision, normalized recall, normalized precision, and precision for ten recall levels. As Salton points out, these measures are probably intercorrelated, and since the inferential tests used require independence of the dependent variables, the results reported must be viewed with caution. This data was analyzed using both related group t tests and sign tests. Both of these statistical methods yielded significant results at the .05 probability level, but since none of the t values are reported, precluding their use in an estimate of effect size, and since sufficient data is provided for the estimate of effect size from the sign tests, the latter will be discussed here. (The effect size is the percentage of the variance of the independent variable accounted for by the dependent variables.) The effect size for a sign test is the difference between the obtained proportion (that is, the number of cases favoring a given method over the number of all cases where a difference was detected), and the expected proportion if there is no difference between means (that is, .50*).

For the IRE-3 collection, 476 differences were used for the sign test (the 14 dependent variables measures × 34 queries). Of these, 272 pairs favored full stemming, 132 pairs favored suffix "s" stemming, and in 72 cases neither method was favored. Thus, the effect size for the IRE-3 collection is 272/(272+132) − .50 = .175. In the test of ADI collection, 254 cases were found to favor full stemming, 107 cases favored suffix "s" stemming, and 129 cases favored neither. The effect size for this collection is .20. The results for the Cranfield-1 collection are opposite those for IRE-3 and ADI. For Cranfield-1, 134 cases favored full stemming, 371 favored the suffix "s" stemming, and 183 favored neither. The effect size for this collection is .235.

The most striking feature of these experiments is the discrepancy between the results for the IRE-3 and ADI collections, and the results for the Cranfield-1 collection. Salton offers the plausible explanation that the discrepancy is due to the highly technical and homogenous nature of the Cranfield vocabulary. He states:

> To be able to differentiate between the various document abstracts, it is . . . important to maintain finer distinctions for the Cranfield case than for ADI and IRE, and these

---

* The effect size for a sign test can only take on values in the range 0 to .5.

finer distinctions are lost when several different words are combined into a unique class through the suffix cutoff process. (p. 330)

One of Salton's assertions about these experiments seems ill founded in light of the effect sizes calculated above. He states that, "For none of the collections (ADI, IRE-3, Cranfield-1) is the improvement of one method over the other really dramatic, so that in practice, either procedure might reasonably be used" (p. 330). It seems much more reasonable, given the differences observed between the methods, to conclude that conflation may have a significant effect on retrieval performance, but that the effect may depend on the vocabulary involved. It may be, however, that Salton's remarks are based on unreported t-test data which may have indicated small effect sizes. The sign test is insensitive to the magnitude of differences, and thus a large effect might be found using a sign test, while a small effect was found using a t-test.

Hafer and Weiss (1974) tested their stemmer against other stemming methods using the ADI collection, and the Carolina Population Center (CPC) Collection consisting of 75 documents and five queries. Comparisons were made on the basis of recall-precision plots. No statistical testing was reported. For the ADI collection, the Hafer and Weiss stemmer outperformed the SMART stemmer. The authors also determined "each family derived from a common stem . . . by hand." (p. 380). The method and criteria used are not reported. In a test using the CRC collection, the Hafer and Weiss stemmer performed equally to the manually derived stems. All methods of stemming outperformed full terms for both test collections.

Van Rijsbergen et al. (1980) tested their stemmer (Porter 1980) against the stemmer described by Dawson (1974) using the Cranfield-1 test collection. Both of these stemmers are of the longest match type, though the Dawson stemmer is more complex. They report that the performance of their stemmer was slightly better across ten paired recall-precision levels, but that the observed differences are probably not meaningful. No statistical results of any kind are reported.

Katzer et al. (1982) examined the performance of stemmed title-abstract terms against six other document representations: unstemmed title-abstract terms, unstemmed abstract terms, unstemmed title terms, descriptors, identifiers, and descriptors and identifiers combined. The stemmer used was a simple suffix removal stemmer employing 20 endings.

The database consisted of approximately 12,000 documents from Computer and Control Abstracts. Seven experienced searchers were used in the study, with each searcher searching different representations for each query. Relevance judgments on a scale of 1–4 (highly relevant to nonrelevant) were obtained from the users who requested the searches.

The dependent variable measures used were recall and precision for highly relevant documents, and recall and precision for all documents. On no dependent variable did stemmed terms perform less well than other representations, and in some cases they performed significantly better than descriptors, and on all document recall, stemming did significantly better than both descriptors and title terms. The effect sizes, calculated here on the basis of reported data, were .26 for highly relevant, and .22 and .20 for all relevant. The results of this study must be viewed with some caution because for a given query, different searchers searched different representations. This means that observed differences between representations may to some degree have been caused by searcher-representation interactions.

Lennon et al. (1981) examined the performance of various stemmers both in terms of retrieval effectiveness and inverted file compression. For the retrieval comparisons, the Cranfield-1400 collection was used. This collection contains 1,396 documents, and also 225 queries. The titles of documents and the queries were matched, and the documents ranked in order of decreasing match value. A cutoff was then applied to specify a given number of the highest ranked documents. This procedure was done for each of the methods used, that is, eight stemming methods, and nonstemmed terms.

The evaluation measure was E, as defined in Chapter 1. The various methods were evaluated at b levels of .5 (indicating that a user was twice as interested in precision as recall), and 2 (indicating that a user was twice as interested in recall as precision). These levels of b were not chosen by users, but were set by the experimenters.

The eight stemmers used in this study were: the Lovins stemmer, the Porter stemmer, the RADCOL stemmer, a suffix frequency stemmer based on the RADCOL project, a stemmer developed by INSPEC, the Hafer and Weiss stemmer, a trigram stemmer, and a stemmer based on the frequency of word endings in a corpus. As stated above, unstemmed terms were also used.

Thus, the two questions that this study addressed concerned (1) the relative effectiveness of stemming versus nonstemming, and (2) the relative performance of the various stemmers examined. In terms of the first question, only the Hafer and Weiss stemmer did worse than unstemmed terms at the two levels of b. At the b = .5 level, the INSPEC, Lovins, Porter, trigram, and both frequency stemmers all did better than unstemmed terms, and at the b = 2 level, all but Hafer and Weiss did better than unstemmed terms.

This information was derived from a table of means reported for the two b levels. As for the second question, though Lennon et al. (1981) report that, "a few of the differences between algorithms were statistically significant at the .05 probability level of significance in the precision oriented searches" (p. 182), they fail to report any test statistics or effect sizes, or even identify which pairs of methods were significantly different. They conclude that

> Despite the very different means by which the various algorithms have been developed, there is relatively little difference in terms of the dictionary compression and retrieval performance obtained from their use; in particular, simple, fully automated methods perform as well as procedures which involve a large degree of manual involvement in their development. (p. 183)

This assertion seems to be contradicted by the significant differences found between algorithms. However, the paucity of reported data in this study makes an independent evaluation of the results extremely difficult.

Frakes (1982) did two studies of stemming. The first tested the hypothesis that the closeness of stems to root morphemes will predict improved retrieval effectiveness. Fifty-three search queries were solicited from users and searched by four professional searchers under four representations: title, abstract, descriptors, and identifiers. The experiments were done using a database of approximately 12,000 document representations from six months of psychological abstracts. The retrieval system used was DIATOM (Waldstein 1981), a DIALOG simulator. In addition to most of the features of DIALOG, DIATOM allows stemmed searching using Lovins' (1968) algorithm, and permits search histories to be trapped and saved into files. As is the case with almost all IR systems, DIATOM allows only right and internal truncation; thus, the experiments did not address prefix removal.

User need statements were solicited from members of the Syracuse University academic community and other institutions. Each user need statement was searched by four experienced searchers under four different representations (abstract, title, identifiers, and descriptors). Each searcher did a different search for each representation. In addition, some user statements were searched using a stemmed title-abstract representation. This study made use of only title and abstract searches, since searches of these fields were most likely to need conflation, together with stemmed searches. However, relevant documents retrieved under all representations were used in the calculation of recall measures.

The hypothesis for the first experiment, based on linguistic theory, was that terms truncated on the right at the root morpheme boundary will perform better than terms truncated on the right at other points. To test this hypothesis, searches based on 34 user need statements were analyzed using multiple regression, and the non-parametric Spearman's test for correlation. The independent variables were positive and negative deviations of truncation points from root boundaries, where deviation was measured in characters. Root morphemes were determined by applying a set of generation rules to searcher supplied full-term equivalents of truncated terms, and checking the results against the linguistic intuitions of two judges.

The dependent variables were E measures (see Chapter 1) at three trade-off values : $b = .5$ (precision twice as important as recall), $b = 1$ (precision equals recall in importance), $b = 2$ (recall twice as important as precision). The data analysis showed that searchers truncated at or near the root morpheme boundaries. The mean number of characters that terms truncated by searchers varied from root boundaries in a positive direction was .825 with a standard deviation of .429. Deviations in a negative direction were even smaller with a mean of .035 and a standard deviation of .089. The tests of correlation revealed no significant relationship between the small deviations of stems from root boundaries, and retrieval effectiveness.

The purpose of the second experiment was to determine if conflation can be automated with no loss of retrieval effectiveness. Smith (1979), in an extensive survey of artificial intelligence techniques for information retrieval, stated that "the application of truncation to content terms cannot be done automatically to duplicate the use of truncation by intermediaries because any single rule [used by the conflation algorithm] has numerous exceptions" (p. 223). However, no empirical test of the relative effectiveness of automatic and manual conflation had been made. The hypothesis adopted for the second experiment was that stemming will perform as well or better than manual conflation.

To test this hypothesis, searches based on 25 user need statements were analyzed. The primary independent variable was conflation method—with the levels automatic (stemming) and manual. The blocking variable was queries, and searchers was included as an additional independent variable to increase statistical power. Data was derived by re-executing each search with stemmed terms in place of the manually conflated terms in the original searches. The dependent variables were E measures at the three trade-off levels as described above. No significant difference was found between manual and automatic conflation, indicating that conflation can be automated with no significant loss in retrieval performance.

Walker and Jones (1987) did a thorough review and study of stemming algorithms. They used Porter's stemming algorithm in the study. The database used was an on-line book catalog (called RCL) in a library. One of their findings was that since weak stemming, defined as step 1 of the Porter algorithm, gave less compression, stemming weakness could be defined by the amount of compression. They also found that stemming significantly increases recall, and that weak stemming does not significantly decrease precision, but strong stemming does. They recommend that weak stemming be used automatically, with strong stemming reserved for those cases where weak stemming finds no documents. Another finding was that the number of searches per session was about the same for weak and strong stemming.

Harman (1991) used three stemmers—Porter, Lovins, and S removal—on three databases—Cranfield 1400, Medlars, and CACM—and found that none of them significantly improved retrieval effectiveness in a ranking IR system called IRX. The dependent variable measure was again E, at b levels of .5, 1.0, and 2.0. Attempts to improve stemming performance by reweighting stemmed terms, and by stemming only shorter queries, failed in this study.

8.3.1 Stemming Studies: Conclusion

Table 8.1 summarizes the various studies of stemming for improving retrieval effectiveness.

These studies must be viewed with caution. The failure of some of the authors to report test statistics, especially effect sizes, make interpretation difficult. Since some of the studies used sample sizes as small as 5 (Hafer and Weiss), their validity is questionable. Given these cautions, we offer the following conclusions.

- Stemming can affect retrieval performance, but the studies are equivocal. Where effects have been found, the majority have been positive, with the

Table 8.1 Stemming Retrieval Effectiveness Studies Summary

Study	Question	Test Collection	Dependent Vars	Results
Salton	Full stemmer vs. suffix s stemmer	IRE-3 ADI Cranfield-1	14 DV's	Full $>$ s Full $>$ s s $>$ Full
Hafer and Weiss	HW stemmer vs. SMART stemmer	ADI	recall(R), precision (P)	HW $>$ SMART
	HW stemmer vs. manual stemming	CRC		HW $=$ Manual
	stemmed vs. unstemmed	ADI CRC		Stemmed $>$ Unstemmed
VanRijsbergen et al.	Porter vs. Dawson stemmer	Cranfield-1	R,P	Porter $=$ Dawson
Katzer et al.	stemmed vs. unstemmed	CCA 12,000	R,P(highest) R,P(all)	stemmed $=$ unstemmed
	stemmed vs. other reps.			stemmed $>$ title, descriptors
Lennon et al.	stemmed vs. unstemmed	Cranfield-1400	E(.5,2)	stemmed $>$ unstemmed $>$ HW stemmer
	stemmer comparison			stemmers $=$
Frakes	closeness of stem to root morpheme improves IR performance	Psychabs	E(.5,1,2)	No improvement
	truncation vs. stemming			truncation $=$ stemming
Walker and Jones	stemmed vs. unstemmed	PCL	R	stemmed $>$ unstemmed
	weak stemmed vs. unstemmed	PCL	P	weak stemmed $=$ unstemmed
	strong stemmed vs. unstemmed	PCL	P	strong stemmed $<$ unstemmed
Harman	stemmed vs. unstemmed	Cranfield-1400 Medlars CACM	E(.5,1,2)	stemmed $=$ unstemmed " " " "

Hafer and Weiss stemmer in the study by Lennon et al., and the effect of the strong stemmer in the Walker and Jones study, being the exceptions. Otherwise there is no evidence that stemming will degrade retrieval effectiveness.

- Stemming is as effective as manual conflation.
- Salton's results indicate that the effect of stemming is dependent on the nature of the vocabulary used. A specific and homogeneous vocabulary may exhibit different conflation properties than will other types of vocabularies.
- There also appears to be little difference between the retrieval effectiveness of different full stemmers, with the exception of the Hafer and Weiss stemmer, which gave poorer performance in the Lennon et al. study.

8.4 STEMMING TO COMPRESS INVERTED FILES

Since a stem is usually shorter than the words to which it corresponds, storing stems instead of full words can decrease the size of index files. Lennon et al. (1981), for example, report the following compression percentages for various stemmers and databases. For example, the indexing file for the Cranfield collection was 32.1 percent smaller after it was stemmed using the INSPEC stemmer.

Index Compression Percentages from Stemming

Stemmer	Cranfield	National Physical Laboratory	INSPEC	Brown Corpus
INSPEC	32.1	40.7	40.5	47.5
Lovins	30.9	39.2	39.5	45.8
RADCOL	32.1	41.8	41.8	49.1
Porter	26.2	34.6	33.8	38.8
Frequency	30.7	39.9	40.1	50.5

It is obvious from this table that the savings in storage using stemming can be substantial.

Harman (1991) reports that for a database of 1.6 megabytes of source text, the index was reduced 20 percent, from .47 megabytes to .38 megabytes, using the Lovins stemmer. For larger databases, however, reductions are smaller. For a database of 50 megabytes, the index was reduced from 6.7 to 5.8 megabytes—a savings of 13.5 percent. She points out, however, that for real world databases that contain numbers, misspellings, proper names, and the like, the compression factors are not nearly so large.

Compression rates increase for affix removal stemmers as the number of suffixes increases, as the following table, also from the Lennon et al. study, shows.

Compression vs. Suffix Set Size: NPL Database								
Number of Suffixes	100	200	300	400	500	600	700	800
Compression	28.2	33.7	35.9	37.3	38.9	40.1	41.0	41.6

8.5 SUMMARY

Stemmers are used to conflate terms to improve retrieval effectiveness and/or to reduce the size of indexing files. Stemming will, in general, increase recall at the cost of decreased precision. Studies of the effects of stemming on retrieval effectiveness are equivocal, but in general stemming has either no effect, or a positive effect, on retrieval performance where the measures used include both recall and precision. Stemming can have a marked effect on the size of indexing files, sometimes decreasing the size of the files as much as 50 percent.

Several approaches to stemming were described—table lookup, affix removal, successor variety, and n-gram. The Porter stemmer was described in detail, and a full implementation of it, in C, is presented in the appendix to this chapter. In the next chapter, the thesaurus approach to conflating semantically related words is discussed.

REFERENCES

ADAMSON, G., and J. BOREHAM. 1974. "The Use of an Association Measure Based on Character Structure to Identify Semantically Related Pairs of Words and Document Titles," *Information Storage and Retrieval*, 10, 253–60.

BENTLEY, J. 1982. *Writing Efficient Programs*. Englewood Cliffs, N.J.: Prentice Hall.

DAWSON, J. 1974. "Suffix Removal and Word Conflation." *ALLC Bulletin*, Michelmas, 33–46.

FRAKES, W. B. 1982. *Term Conflation for Information Retrieval*, Doctoral Dissertation, Syracuse University.

FRAKES, W. B. 1984. "Term Conflation for Information Retrieval" in *Research and Development in Information Retrieval*, ed. C. van Rijsbergen. New York: Cambridge University Press.

FRAKES, W. B. 1986. "LATTIS: A Corporate Library and Information System for the UNIX Environment," *Proceedings of the National Online Meeting*, Medford, N.J.: Learned Information Inc., 137–42.

HAFER, M., and S. WEISS. 1974. "Word Segmentation by Letter Successor Varieties," *Information Storage and Retrieval*, 10, 371–85.

HARMAN, D. 1991. "How Effective is Suffixing?" *Journal of the American Society for Information Science*, 42(1), 7–15.

KATZER, J., M. MCGILL, J. TESSIER, W. FRAKES, and P. DAS GUPTA. 1982. "A Study of the Overlaps among Document Representations," *Information Technology: Research and Development*, 1, 261–73.

LENNON, M., D. PIERCE, B. TARRY, and P. WILLETT. 1981. "An Evaluation of Some Conflation Algorithms for Information Retrieval." *Journal of Information Science* 3, 177–83.

LOVINS, J. B. 1968. "Development of a Stemming Algorithm." *Mechanical Translation and Computational Linguistics,* 11(1–2), 22–31.

PAICE, C. 1990. "Another Stemmer," *ACM SIGIR Forum,* 24(3), 56–61.

PORTER, M. F. 1980. "An Algorithm for Suffix Stripping." *Program,* 14(3), 130–37.

SALTON, G. 1968. *Automatic Information Organization and Retrieval.* New York: McGraw-Hill.

SMITH, L. C. 1979. *Selected Artificial Intelligence Techniques in Information Retrieval.* Doctoral Dissertation, Syracuse University.

VAN RIJSBERGEN, C. J., S. E. ROBERTSON, and M. F. PORTER. 1980. *New Models in Probabilistic Information Retrieval.* Cambridge: British Library Research and Development Report no. 5587.

WALKER, S., and R. JONES. 1987. "Improving Subject Retrieval in Online Catalogues." British Library Research Paper no. 24, vol. 1.

WALDSTEIN, R. 1981. "Diatom: A Dialog Simulator." *Online,* 5, 68–72.

APPENDIX

```
/******************************   stem.c   **********************************



   Version:    1.1

   Purpose:    Implementation of the Porter stemming algorithm.

   Provenance: Written by C. Fox, 1990.

   Notes:      This program is a rewrite of earlier versions by B. Frakes and
S. Cox
**/

/*********************   Standard Include Files   ***********************/


#include <stdio.h>
#include <string.h>
#include <ctype.h>
```

```
/******************** Private Function Declarations ********************/


static int WordSize( /* word */ );
static int ContainsVowel( /* word */ );
static int EndsWithCVC( /* word */ );
static int AddAnE( /* word */ );
static int RemoveAnE( /* word */ );
static int ReplaceEnd( /* word, rule */ );


/***************** Private Defines and Data Structures *****************/

#define FALSE                    0
#define TRUE                     1
#define EOS                      '\0'

#define IsVowel(c)           ('a'==(c)||'e'==(c)||'i'==(c)||'o'==(c)||'u'==(c))


typedef struct {
          int id;                /* returned if rule fired */
          char *old_end;         /* suffix replaced */
          char *new_end;         /* suffix replacement */
          int old_offset;        /* from end of word to start of suffix */
          int new_offset;        /* from beginning to end of new suffix */
          int min_root_size;     /* min root word size for replacement */
          int (*condition)();    /* the replacement test function */
          } RuleList;

static char LAMBDA[1] = " ";     /* the constant empty string */
static char *end;                /* pointer to the end of the word */

static RuleList step1a_rules[] =
          {
            101,   "sses",      "ss",      3,   1,  -1,   NULL,
            102,   "ies",       "i",       2,   0,  -1,   NULL,
            103,   "ss",        "ss",      1,   1,  -1,   NULL,
            104,   "s",         LAMBDA,    0,  -1,  -1,   NULL,
            000,   NULL,        NULL,      0,   0,   0,   NULL,
          };

static RuleList step1b_rules[] =
          {
            105,   "eed",       "ee",      2,   1,   0,   NULL,
            106,   "ed",        LAMBDA,    1,  -1,  -1,   ContainsVowel,
            107,   "ing",       LAMBDA,    2,  -1,  -1,   ContainsVowel,
            000,   NULL,        NULL,      0,   0,   0,   NULL,
          };
```

```
static RuleList step1b1_rules[] =
        {
        108,    "at",       "ate",    1,  2,  −1,   NULL,
        109,    "bl",       "ble",    1,  2,  −1,   NULL,
        110,    "iz",       "ize",    1,  2,  −1,   NULL,
        111,    "bb",       "b",      1,  0,  −1,   NULL,
        112,    "dd",       "d",      1,  0,  −1,   NULL,
        113,    "ff",       "f",      1,  0,  −1,   NULL,
        114,    "gg",       "g",      1,  0,  −1,   NULL,
        115,    "mm",       "m",      1,  0,  −1,   NULL,
        116,    "nn",       "n",      1,  0,  −1,   NULL,
        117,    "pp",       "p",      1,  0,  −1,   NULL,
        118,    "rr",       "r",      1,  0,  −1,   NULL,
        119,    "tt",       "t",      1,  0,  −1,   NULL,
        120,    "ww",       "w",      1,  0,  −1,   NULL,
        121,    "xx",       "x",      1,  0,  −1,   NULL,
        122,    LAMBDA,     "e",      −1, 0,  −1,   AddAnE,
        000,    NULL,       NULL,     0,  0,  0,    NULL,
        };

static RuleList step1c_rules[] =
        {
        123,    "y",        "i",      0,  0,  −1,   ContainsVowel,
        000,    NULL,       NULL,     0,  0,  0,    NULL,
        };

static RuleList step2_rules[] =
        {
        203,    "ational",  "ate",    6,  2,  0,    NULL,
        204,    "tional",   "tion",   5,  3,  0,    NULL,
        205,    "enci",     "ence",   3,  3,  0,    NULL,
        206,    "anci",     "ance",   3,  3,  0,    NULL,
        207,    "izer",     "ize",    3,  2,  0,    NULL,
        208,    "abli",     "able",   3,  3,  0,    NULL,
        209,    "alli",     "al",     3,  1,  0,    NULL,
        210,    "entli",    "ent",    4,  2,  0,    NULL,
        211,    "eli",      "e",      2,  0,  0,    NULL,
        213,    "ousli",    "ous",    4,  2,  0,    NULL,
        214,    "ization",  "ize",    6,  2,  0,    NULL,
        215,    "ation",    "ate",    4,  2,  0,    NULL,
        216,    "ator",     "ate",    3,  2,  0,    NULL,
        217,    "alism",    "al",     4,  1,  0,    NULL,
        218,    "iveness",  "ive",    6,  2,  0,    NULL,
        219,    "fulnes",   "ful",    5,  2,  0,    NULL,
        220,    "ousness",  "ous",    6,  2,  0,    NULL,
        221,    "aliti",    "al",     4,  1,  0,    NULL,
        222,    "iviti",    "ive",    4,  2,  0,    NULL,
        223,    "biliti",   "ble",    5,  2,  0,    NULL,
        000,    NULL,       NULL,     0,  0,  0,    NULL,
        };
```

```
static RuleList step3_rules[] =
        {
        301,    "icate",    "ic",     4,   1,   0,   NULL,
        302,    "ative",    LAMBDA,   4,  -1,   0,   NULL,
        303,    "alize",    "al",     4,   1,   0,   NULL,
        304,    "iciti",    "ic",     4,   1,   0,   NULL,
        305,    "ical",     "ic",     3,   1,   0,   NULL,
        308,    "ful",      LAMBDA,   2,  -1,   0,   NULL,
        309,    "ness",     LAMBDA,   3,  -1,   0,   NULL,
        000,    NULL,       NULL,     0,   0,   0,   NULL,
        };

static RuleList step4_rules[] =
        {
        401,    "al",       LAMBDA,   1,  -1,   1,   NULL,
        402,    "ance",     LAMBDA,   3,  -1,   1,   NULL,
        403,    "ence",     LAMBDA,   3,  -1,   1,   NULL,
        405,    "er",       LAMBDA,   1,  -1,   1,   NULL,
        406,    "ic",       LAMBDA,   1,  -1,   1,   NULL,
        407,    "able",     LAMBDA,   3,  -1,   1,   NULL,
        408,    "ible",     LAMBDA,   3,  -1,   1,   NULL,
        409,    "ant",      LAMBDA,   2,  -1,   1,   NULL,
        410,    "ement",    LAMBDA,   4,  -1,   1,   NULL,
        411,    "ment",     LAMBDA,   3,  -1,   1,   NULL,
        412,    "ent",      LAMBDA,   2,  -1,   1,   NULL,
        423,    "sion",     "s",      3,   0,   1,   NULL,
        424,    "tion",     "t",      3,   0,   1,   NULL,
        415,    "ou",       LAMBDA,   1,  -1,   1,   NULL,
        416,    "ism",      LAMBDA,   2,  -1,   1,   NULL,
        417,    "ate",      LAMBDA,   2,  -1,   1,   NULL,
        418,    "iti",      LAMBDA,   2,  -1,   1,   NULL,
        419,    "ous",      LAMBDA,   2,  -1,   1,   NULL,
        420,    "ive",      LAMBDA,   2,  -1,   1,   NULL,
        421,    "ize",      LAMBDA,   2,  -1,   1,   NULL,
        000,    NULL,       NULL,     0,   0,   0,   NULL,
        };

static RuleList step5a_rules[] =
        {
        501,    "e",        LAMBDA,   0,  -1,   1,   NULL,
        502,    "e",        LAMBDA,   0,  -1,  -1,   RemoveAnE,
        000,    NULL,       NULL,     0,   0,   0,   NULL,
        };

static RuleList step5b_rules[] =
        {
        503,    "ll",       "l",      1,   0,   1,   NULL,
        000,    NULL,       NULL,     0,   0,   0,   NULL,
        };
```

```
/*****************************************************************************/

/********************  Private Function Declarations   *********************/


/*FN*************************************************************************

        WordSize( word )

   Returns:  int — a weird WordSize of word size in adjusted syllables

   Purpose:  Count syllables in a special way:  count the number
             vowel-consonant pairs in a word, disregarding initial
             consonants and final vowels.  The letter "y" counts as a
             consonant at the beginning of a word and when it has a vowel
             in front of it; otherwise (when it follows a consonant) it
             is treated as a vowel.  For example, the WordSize of "cat"
             is 1, of "any" is 1, of "amount" is 2, of "anything" is 3.

   Plan:     Run a DFA to compute the word size


   Notes:    The easiest and fastest way to compute this funny measure is
             with a finite state machine.  The initial state 0 checks
             the first letter.  If it is a vowel, then the machine changes
             to state 1, which is the "last letter was a vowel" state.
             If the first letter is a consonant or y, then it changes
             to state 2, the "last letter was a consonant state".  In
             state 1, a y is treated as a consonant (since it follows
             a vowel), but in state 2, y is treated as a vowel (since
             it follows a consonant.  The result counter is incremented
             on the transition from state 1 to state 2, since this
             transition only occurs after a vowel-consonant pair, which
             is what we are counting.
**/

static int
WordSize( word )
    register char *word;     /* in: word having its WordSize taken */
    {
    register int result;    /* WordSize of the word */
    register int state;     /* current state in machine */

    result = 0;
    state = 0;

                /* Run a DFA to computer the word size */
    while ( EOS != *word )
```

```
        {
      switch ( state )
          {
        case 0:  state = (IsVowel(*word)) ? 1 : 2;
                 break;
        case 1:  state = (IsVowel(*word)) ? 1 : 2;
                 if ( 2 == state ) result++;
                 break;
        case 2:  state = (IsVowel(*word) || ('y' == *word)) ? 1 : 2;
                 break;
          }
      word++;
      }

  return( result );

  } /* WordSize */
```

```
/*FN*********************************************************************

        ContainsVowel( word )
```

Returns: int -- TRUE (1) if the word parameter contains a vowel,
         FALSE (0) otherwise.

Purpose: Some of the rewrite rules apply only to a root containing
         a vowel, where a vowel is one of "aeiou" or y with a
         consonant in front of it.

Plan: Obviously, under the definition of a vowel, a word contains
         a vowel iff either its first letter is one of "aeiou", or
         any of its other letters are "aeiouy". The plan is to
         test this condition.

Notes: None
```
**/
```

```
static int
ContainsVowel( word )
   register char *word;    /* in: buffer with word checked */
   {

   if ( EOS == *word )
      return( FALSE );
   else
      return( IsVowel(*word) || (NULL != strpbrk(word+1,"aeiouy")) );


   } /* ContainsVowel */
```

```
/*FN****************************************************************************

        EndsWithCVC( word )

    Returns:  int -- TRUE (1) if the current word ends with a
              consonant-vowel-consonant combination, and the second
              consonant is not w, x, or y, FALSE (0) otherwise.


    Purpose:  Some of the rewrite rules apply only to a root with
              this characteristic.

    Plan:     Look at the last three characters.

    Notes:    None
**/

static int
EndsWithCVC( word )
    register char *word;    /* in: buffer with the word checked */
    {
    int length;            /* for finding the last three characters */

    if ( (length = strlen(word)) < 2 )
        return( FALSE );
    else
        {
        end = word + length - 1;
        return(    (NULL == strchr("aeiouwxy", *end--))    /* consonant */
                && (NULL != strchr("aeiouy",   *end--))    /* vowel */
                && (NULL == strchr("aeiou",    *end  )) );  /* consonant */
        }

    } /* EndsWithCVC */

/*FN****************************************************************************

        AddAnE( word )

    Returns:  int -- TRUE (1) if the current word meets special conditions
              for adding an e.

    Purpose:  Rule 122 applies only to a root with this characteristic.

    Plan:     Check for size of 1 and a consonant-vowel-consonant ending.

    Notes:    None
**/
```

```
static int
AddAnE ( word )
   register char *word;
   {

   return ( (1 == WordSize(word)) && EndsWithCVC(word) );

   } /* AddAnE */
```

/*FN***

        RemoveAnE (word)

   Returns: int -- TRUE (1) if the current word meets special conditions
             for removing an e.

   Purpose: Rule 502 applies only to a root with this characteristic.

   Plan: Check for size of 1 and no consonant-vowel-consonant ending.

   Notes: None
**/

```
static int
RemoveAnE ( word )
   register char *word;
   {

   return ( (1 == WordSize(word)) && !EndsWithCVC(word) );
   } /* RemoveAnE */
```

/*FN***

        ReplaceEnd (word, rule)

   Returns: int -- the id for the rule fired, 0 is none is fired

   Purpose: Apply a set of rules to replace the suffix of a word

   Plan: Loop through the rule set until a match meeting all conditions
             is found. If a rule fires, return its id, otherwise return 0.
             Connditions on the length of the root are checked as part of this
             function's processing because this check is so often made.

   Notes: This is the main routine driving the stemmer. It goes through
             a set of suffix replacement rules looking for a match on the
             current suffix. When it finds one, if the root of the word

```
            is long enough, and it meets whatever other conditions are
            required, then the suffix is replaced, and the function returns.
**/

static int
ReplaceEnd( word, rule )
    register char *word;      /* in/out: buffer with the stemmed word */
    RuleList *rule;           /* in: data structure with replacement rules */
    {
    register char *ending;    /* set to start of possible stemmed suffix */
    char tmp_ch;              /* save replaced character when testing */

    while  ( 0 != rule->id )
        {
        ending = end - rule->old_offset;
        if  ( word = ending )
            if  ( 0 == strcmp(ending,rule->old_end) )
                {
                tmp_ch = *ending;
                *ending = EOS;
                if  ( rule->min_root_size < WordSize(word) )
                    if  ( !rule->condition || (*rule->condition)(word) )
                        {
                        (void)strcat( word, rule->new_end );
                        end = ending + rule->new_offset;
                        break;
                        }
                *ending = tmp_ch;
                }
        rule++;
        }

    return( rule->id );

    } /* ReplaceEnd */

/*****************************************************************************/

/********************   Public Function Declarations   *********************/

/*FN*************************************************************************

        Stem( word )

    Returns: int -- FALSE (0) if the word contains non-alphabetic characters
             and hence is not stemmed, TRUE (1) otherwise
```

```
            Purpose: Stem a word

            Plan:    Part 1: Check to ensure the word is all alphabetic
                     Part 2: Run through the Porter algorithm
                     Part 3: Return an indication of successful stemming

            Notes:   This function implements the Porter stemming algorithm, with
                     a few additions here and there.  See:

                         Porter, M.F., "An Algorithm For Suffix Stripping,"
                         Program 14 (3), July 1980, pp. 130-137.

                     Porter's algorithm is an ad hoc set of rewrite rules with
                     various conditions on rule firing.  The terminology of
                     "step 1a" and so on, is taken directly from Porter's
                     article, which unfortunately gives almost no justification
                     for the various steps.  Thus this function more or less
                     faithfully refects the opaque presentation in the article.
                     Changes from the article amount to a few additions to the
                     rewrite rules;  these are marked in the RuleList data
                     structures with comments.
**/

int
Stem( word )
    register char *word;    /* in/out: the word stemmed */
    {
    int rule;      /* which rule is fired in replacing an end */

            /* Part 1: Check to ensure the word is all alphabetic */
    for ( end = word; *end != EOS; end++ )
        if ( !isalpha(*end) ) return( FALSE );
    end--;

                    /*  Part 2: Run through the Porter algorithm */
    ReplaceEnd( word, step1a_rules );
    rule = ReplaceEnd( word, step1b_rules );
    if ( (106 == rule) || (107 == rule) )
        ReplaceEnd( word, step1b1_rules );
    ReplaceEnd( word, step1c_rules );

    ReplaceEnd( word, step2_rules );

    ReplaceEnd( word, step3_rules );

    ReplaceEnd( word, step4_rules );

    ReplaceEnd( word, step5a_rules );
    ReplaceEnd( word, step5b_rules );

            /* Part 3: Return an indication of successful stemming */
    return( TRUE );

    } /* Stem */
```

9

Thesaurus Construction

Padmini Srinivasan

University of Iowa

Abstract

Thesauri are valuable structures for Information Retrieval systems. A thesaurus provides a precise and controlled vocabulary which serves to coordinate document indexing and document retrieval. In both indexing and retrieval, a thesaurus may be used to select the most appropriate terms. Additionally, the thesaurus can assist the searcher in reformulating search strategies if required. This chapter first examines the important features of thesauri. This should allow the reader to differentiate between thesauri. Next, a brief overview of the manual thesaurus construction process is given. Two major approaches for automatic thesaurus construction have been selected for detailed examination. The first is on thesaurus construction from collections of documents, and the second, on thesaurus construction by merging existing thesauri. These two methods were selected since they rely on statistical techniques alone and are also significantly different from each other. Programs written in C language accompany the discussion of these approaches.

9.1 INTRODUCTION

Roget's thesaurus is very different from the average thesaurus associated with Information Retrieval (IR) systems accessing machine readable document databases. The former is designed to assist the writer in creatively selecting vocabulary. In IR systems, used to retrieve potentially relevant documents from large collections, the thesaurus serves to coordinate the basic processes of indexing and document retrieval. (The term document is used here generically and may refer to books, articles, magazines, letters, memoranda, and also software.) In indexing, a succinct representation of the document is derived, while retrieval refers to the search process by which relevant items are identified. The IR thesaurus typically contains a list of terms, where a term is either a single word or a phrase, along with the relationships between them. It provides a common, precise, and controlled vocabulary which assists in coordinating indexing and retrieval. Given this objective, it is clear that thesauri are designed for specific subject areas and are therefore domain dependent.

Figure 9.1 displays a short extract from an alphabetical listing of thesaurus terms and their relationships in the INSPEC thesaurus. This thesaurus is designed for the INSPEC domain, which covers physics, electrical engineering, electronics, as well as computers and control. The thesaurus is logically organized as a set of hierarchies. In addition to this hierarchical arrangement, the printed INSPEC thesaurus also includes an alphabetical listing of thesaural terms. Each hierarchy is built from a root term representing a high-level concept in the domain. In Figure 9.1, "computer-aided instruction" is a part of the hierarchy whose root note or top term

```
cesium
        USE caesium


computer-aided instruction
        see also education
        UF   teaching machines
        BT   educational computing
        TT   computer applications
        RT   education
             teaching
        CC   C7810C
        FC   c7810Cf
```

Figure 9.1 A short extract from the 1979 INSPEC thesaurus

(TT) is "computer applications." The "see also" link leads to cross-referenced thesaural terms. NT suggests a more specific thesaural term; similarly, BT provides a more general thesaural term. RT signifies a related term and this relationship includes a variety of links such as part-whole and object-property. UF is utilized to indicate the chosen form from a set of alternatives. In the above example, "computer-aided instruction" is used for the alternative "teaching machines." The converse of UF is USE, which takes the user from a form that is not part of the vocabulary to a valid alternative. The example shows that "caesium" is the preferred form over "cesium." CC and FC are from the INSPEC classification scheme and indicate the subject area in which the term is used.

A carefully designed thesaurus can be of great value. The indexer is typically instructed to select the most appropriate thesaural entries for representing the document. In searching, the user can employ the thesaurus to design the most appropriate search strategy. If the search does not retrieve enough documents, the thesaurus can be used to expand the query by following the various links between terms. Similarly, if the search retrieves too many items, the thesaurus can suggest more specific search vocabulary. In this way the thesaurus can be valuable for reformulating search strategies. It is quite common to provide on-line thesauri, which simplifies the query reformulation process. In addition, such query modifications can also be more system initiated than user initiated. However, this obviously requires rather complex algorithms since the system has to know not only how to reformulate the query but also when to do so.

There exists a vast literature on the principles, methodologies, and problems involved in thesaurus construction. However, only a small portion is devoted to the "automatic" construction of thesauri. This mirrors the current state of art, marked by an abundance of manually generated thesauri. In fact, there is even much skepticism over the possibility of fully automating this procedure. This is because manual thesauri are highly complex structures which exhibit a variety of relationships including hierarchical, nonhierarchical, equivalent, and associative ones. The automatic detection of such relationships continues to be challenging. But, the reader can be assured that some automatic methodologies have emerged over the last few decades. As in most other subfields of IR, these methods are strongly motivated by statistics. In contrast, manual thesaurus construction is a highly conceptual and knowledge-intensive task and therefore also extremely labor intensive. Consequently, the search for alternative automatic methods is definitely of value.

The rest of this chapter is organized into six sections. The next, section 9.2, describes features of thesauri. Section 9.3 introduces the different approaches for automatic thesaurus construction following a brief description of manual thesaurus construction. Sections 9.4 and 9.5 focus on two major approaches for automatic thesaurus construction. The three C programs included with this chapter are described briefly in section 9.6. The last section presents the conclusions.

9.2 FEATURES OF THESAURI

Some important features of thesauri will be highlighted here. For a more detailed discussion, please consult Aitchison and Gilchrist (1972). The objective is for the reader to be able to compare thesauri. In general, the discussion applies to both manually and automatically generated thesauri. However, differences between the two are also identified where appropriate.

9.2.1 Coordination Level

Coordination refers to the construction of phrases from individual terms. Two distinct coordination options are recognized in thesauri: precoordination and postcoordination. A precoordinated thesaurus is one that can contain phrases. Consequently, phrases are available for indexing and retrieval. A postcoordinated thesaurus does not allow phrases. Instead, phrases are constructed while searching. The choice between the two options is difficult. The advantage in precoordination is that the vocabulary is very precise, thus reducing ambiguity in indexing and in searching. Also, commonly accepted phrases become part of the vocabulary. However, the disadvantage is that the searcher has to be aware of the phrase construction rules employed. Thesauri can adopt an intermediate level of coordination by allowing both phrases and single words. This is typical of manually constructed thesauri. However, even within this group there is significant variability in terms of coordination level. Some thesauri may emphasize two or three word phrases, while others may emphasize even larger sized phrases. Therefore, it is insufficient to state that two thesauri are similar simply because they follow precoordination. The level of coordination is important as well. It should be recognized that the higher the level of coordination, the greater the precision of the vocabulary but the larger the vocabulary size. It also implies an increase in the number of relationships to be encoded. Therefore, the thesaurus becomes more complex. The advantage in postcoordination is that the user need not worry about the exact ordering of the words in a phrase. Phrase combinations can be created as and when appropriate during searching. The disadvantage is that search precision may fall, as illustrated by the following well known example, from Salton and McGill (1983): the distinction between phrases such as "Venetian blind" and "blind Venetian" may be lost. A more likely example is "library school" and "school library." The problem is that unless search strategies are designed carefully, irrelevant items may also be retrieved. Precoordination is more common in manually constructed thesauri. Automatic phrase construction is still quite difficult and therefore automatic thesaurus construction usually implies postcoordination. Section 9.4 includes a procedure for automatic phrase construction.

9.2.2 Term Relationships

Term relationships are the most important aspect of thesauri since the vocabulary connections they provide are most valuable for retrieval. Many kinds of relationships are expressed in a manual thesaurus. These are semantic in nature and reflect the underlying conceptual interactions between terms. We do not provide an exhaustive discussion or listing of term relationships here. Instead, we only try to illustrate the variety of relationships that exist. Aitchison and Gilchrist (1972) specify three categories of term relationships: (1) equivalence relationships, (2) hierarchical relationships, and (3) nonhierarchical relationships. The example in Figure 9.1 illustrates all three categories. Equivalence relations include both synonymy and quasi-synonymy. Synonyms can arise because of trade names, popular and local usage, superseded terms, and the like. Quasi-synonyms are terms which for the purpose of retrieval can be regarded as synonymous, for example, "genetics" and "heredity," which have significant overlap in meaning. Also, the terms "harshness" and "tenderness," which represent different viewpoints of the same property continuum. A typical example of a hierarchical relation is genus–species, such as "dog" and "german shepherd." Nonhierarchical relationships also identify conceptually related terms. There are many examples including: thing—part such as "bus" and "seat"; thing—attribute such as "rose" and "fragance."

Wang, Vandendorpe, and Evens (1985) provide an alternative classification of term relationships consisting of: (1) parts—wholes, (2) collocation relations, (3) paradigmatic relations, (4) taxonomy and synonymy, and (5) antonymy relations. Parts and wholes include examples such as set—element; count—mass. Collocation relates words that frequently co-occur in the same phrase or sentence. Paradigmatic relations relate words that have the same semantic core like "moon" and "lunar" and are somewhat similar to Aitchison and Gilchrist's quasi-synonymy relationship. Taxonomy and synonymy are self-explanatory and refer to the classical relations between terms. It should be noted that the relative value of these relationships for retrieval is not clear. However, some work has been done in this direction as in Fox (1981) and Fox et al. (1988). Moreover, at least some of these semantic relationships are commonly included in manual thesauri. Identifying these relationships requires knowledge of the domain for which the thesaurus is being designed. Most if not all of these semantic relationships are difficult to identify by automatic methods, especially by algorithms that exploit only the statistical relationships between terms as exhibited in document collections. However, it should be clear that these statistical associations are only as good as their ability to reflect the more interesting and important semantic associations between terms.

9.2.3 Number of Entries for Each Term

It is in general preferable to have a single entry for each thesaurus term. However, this is seldom achieved due to the presence of homographs—words with multiple meanings. Also, the semantics of each instance of a homograph can only be contextually deciphered. Therefore, it is more realistic to have a unique representation or entry for each meaning of a homograph. This also allows each homograph entry to be associated with its own set of relations. The problem is that multiple term entries add a degree of complexity in using the thesaurus—especially if it is to be used automatically. Typically the user has to select between alternative meanings. In a manually constructed thesaurus such as INSPEC, this problem is resolved by the use of parenthetical qualifiers, as in the pair of homographs, bonds (chemical) and bonds (adhesive). However, this is hard to achieve automatically.

9.2.4 Specificity of Vocabulary

Specificity of the thesaurus vocabulary is a function of the precision associated with the component terms. A highly specific vocabulary is able to express the subject in great depth and detail. This promotes precision in retrieval. The concomitant disadvantage is that the size of the vocabulary grows since a large number of terms are required to cover the concepts in the domain. Also, specific terms tend to change (i.e., evolve) more rapidly than general terms. Therefore, such vocabularies tend to require more regular maintenance. Further, as discussed previously, high specificity implies a high coordination level which in turn implies that the user has to be more concerned with the rules for phrase construction.

9.2.5 Control on Term Frequency of Class Members

This has relevance mainly for statistical thesaurus construction methods which work by partitioning the vocabulary into a set of classes where each class contains a collection of equivalent terms. Salton and McGill (1983, 77–78) have stated that in order to maintain a good match between documents and queries, it is necessary to ensure that terms included in the same thesaurus class have roughly equal frequencies. Further, the total frequency in each class should also be roughly similar. (Appropriate frequency counts for this include: the number of term occurrences in the document collection; the number of documents in the collection in which the term appears at least once). These constraints are imposed to ensure that the probability of a match between a query and a document is the same across classes. In other words, terms within the same class should be equally specific, and the specificity across classes should also be the same.

9.2.6 Normalization of Vocabulary

Normalization of vocabulary terms is given considerable emphasis in manual thesauri. There are extensive rules which guide the form of the thesaural entries. A simple rule is that terms should be in noun form. A second rule is that noun phrases should avoid prepositions unless they are commonly known. Also, a limited number of adjectives should be used. There are other rules to direct issues such as the singularity of terms, the ordering of terms within phrases, spelling, capitalization, transliteration, abbreviations, initials, acronyms, and punctuation. In other words, manual thesauri are designed using a significant set of constraints and rules regarding the structure of individual terms. The advantage in normalizing the vocabulary is that variant forms are mapped into base expressions, thereby bringing consistency to the vocabulary. As a result, the user does not have to worry about variant forms of a term. The obvious disadvantage is that, in order to be used effectively, the user has to be well aware of the normalization rules used. This is certainly nontrivial and often viewed as a major hurdle during searching (Frost 1987). In contrast, normalization rules in automatic thesaurus construction are simpler, seldom involving more than stoplist filters and stemming. (These are discussed in more detail later.) However, this feature can be regarded both as a weakness and a strength.

These different features of thesauri have been presented so that the reader is aware of some of the current differences between manual and automatic thesaurus construction methods. All features are not equally important and they should be weighed according to the application for which the thesaurus is being designed. This section also gives an idea of where further research is required. Given the growing abundance of large-sized document databases, it is indeed important to be challenged by the gaps between manual and automatic thesauri.

9.3 THESAURUS CONSTRUCTION

9.3.1 Manual Thesaurus Construction

The process of manually constructing a thesaurus is both an art and a science. We present here only a brief overview of this complex process. First, one has to define the boundaries of the subject area. (In automatic construction, this step is simple, since the boundaries are taken to be those defined by the area covered by the document database.) Boundary definition includes identifying central subject areas and peripheral ones since it is unlikely that all topics included are of equal importance. Once this is completed, the domain is generally partitioned into divisions or subareas. Once the domain, with its subareas, has been sufficiently defined, the desired characteristics of the thesaurus have to be identified. Since manual thesauri are more complex structurally than automatic ones, as the previous section has shown, there are more decisions to be made.

Now, the collection of terms for each subarea may begin. A variety of sources may be used for this including indexes, encyclopedias, handbooks, textbooks, journal titles and abstracts, catalogues, as well as any existing and relevant thesauri or vocabulary systems. Subject experts and potential users of the thesaurus should also be included in this step. After the initial vocabulary has been identified, each term is analyzed for its related vocabulary including synonyms, broader and narrower terms, and sometimes also definitions and scope notes. These terms and their relationships are then organized into structures such as hierarchies, possibly within each subarea. The process of organizing the vocabulary may reveal gaps which can lead to the addition of terms; identify the need for new levels in the hierarchies; bring together synonyms that were not previously recognized; suggest new relationships between terms; and reduce the vocabulary size. Once the initial organization has been completed, the entire thesaurus will have to be reviewed (and refined) to check for consistency such as in phrase form and word form. Special problems arise in incorporating terms from existing thesauri which may for instance have different formats and construction rules. At this stage the hierarchically structured thesaurus has to be "inverted" to produce an alphabetical arrangement of entries—a more effective arrangement for use. Typically both the alphabetical and hierarchical arrangements are provided in a thesaurus. Following this, the manually generated thesaurus is ready to be tested by subject experts and edited to incorporate their suggestions.

The above informal description is very sketchy. It is a long process that involves a group of individuals and a variety of resources. Once the thesaurus has been designed and implemented for use within a retrieval system, the next problem is that it needs to be maintained in order to ensure its continued viability and effectiveness. That is, the thesaurus should reflect any changes in the terminology of the area. The problem is that since the older documents are still within the system, the updated thesaurus must also retain the older information. Updates are typically slow and again involve several individuals who regularly review and suggest new and modified vocabulary terms as well as relationships. Therefore, typically a thesaurus evolves with time and slowly responds to changes in the terminology of the subject.

9.3.2 Automatic Thesaurus Construction

In selecting automatic thesaurus construction approaches for discussion here, the criteria used are that they should be quite different from each other in addition to being interesting. Also, they should use purely statistical techniques. (The alternative is to use linguistic methods.) Consequently, the two major approaches selected here have not necessarily received equal attention in the literature. The first approach, on designing thesauri from document collections, is a standard one. The second, on merging existing thesauri, is better known using manual methods. Programs included with this chapter are based on these two major approaches. We also discuss a third automatic approach which is quite novel and interesting, although it is based on tools from expert systems and does not use statistical methods. In this approach, thesauri are built using information obtained from users. We first present a brief overview of each approach and then provide detailed descriptions.

9.3.3 From a Collection of Document Items

Here the idea is to use a collection of documents as the source for thesaurus construction. This assumes that a representative body of text is available. The idea is to apply statistical procedures to identify important terms as well as their significant relationships. It is reiterated here that the central thesis in applying statistical methods is to use computationally simpler methods to identify the more important semantic knowledge for thesauri. It is semantic knowledge that is used by both indexer and searcher. Until more direct methods are known, statistical methods will continue to be used. Work by Soergel (1974) is relevant to this point since it includes an interesting discussion on the various semantic interpretations of significant statistical associations between words. The first two programs, select.c and hierarchy.c, included with this chapter are based on this approach of designing a thesaurus from a collection of documents.

9.3.4 By Merging Existing Thesauri

This second approach is appropriate when two or more thesauri for a given subject exist that need to be merged into a single unit. If a new database can indeed be served by merging two or more existing thesauri, then a merger perhaps is likely to be more efficient than producing the thesaurus from scratch. This approach has been discussed at some length in Forsyth and Rada (1986). The challenge is that the merger should not violate the integrity of any component thesaurus. Rada has experimented with augmenting the MeSH thesaurus with selected terms from SNOMED (Forsyth and Rada 1986, 216). MeSH stands for Medical Subject Headings and is the thesaurus used in MEDLINE, a medical document retrieval system, constructed and maintained by the National Library of Medicine. It provides a sophisticated controlled vocabulary for indexing and accessing medical documents. SNOMED, which stands for Systematized Nomenclature of Medicine, is a detailed thesaurus developed by the College of American Pathologists for use in hospital records. MeSH terms are used to describe documents, while SNOMED terms are for describing patients. Ideally, a patient can be completely described by choosing one or more terms from each of several categories in SNOMED. Both MeSH and SNOMED follow a hierarchical structure. Rada's focus in his experiments has been on developing suitable algorithms for merging related but separate thesauri such as MeSH and SNOMED and also in evaluating the end products. The third program (merge.c) included here implements two different merging algorithms adapted from Rada's work.

9.3.5 User Generated Thesaurus

In this third alternative, the idea is that users of IR systems are aware of and use many term relationships in their search strategies long before these find their way into thesauri. The objective is to capture this knowledge from the user's search. This is the basis of TEGEN—the thesaurus generating system designed by Guntzer et al. (1988). They propose TEGEN as a viable alternative technique for automatic thesaurus construction. The procedure involves examining the types of Boolean operators used between search terms, the type of query modification performed by the user, and so on. User feedback is included to resolve any ambiguities and uncertainties. Feedback is also required to select the specific type of relationship between two terms once it has been decided that the terms are indeed related. Therefore, their approach requires considerable interaction with the user population. TEGEN is designed using production rules which perform a detailed analysis of the user's search pattern. Given that this approach utilizes mainly expert system methodologies, no representative program is included here.

9.4 THESAURUS CONSTRUCTION FROM TEXTS

The overall process may be divided into three stages: (1) Construction of vocabulary: This involves normalization and selection of terms. It also includes phrase construction depending on the coordination level desired. (2) Similarity computations between terms: This step identifies the significant statistical associations between terms. (3) Organization of vocabulary: Here the selected vocabulary is organized, generally into a hierarchy, on the basis of the associations computed in step 2. The first program select.c implements procedures for stages 1 and 2. Program hierarchy.c implements one method for organizing the vocabulary in the third stage.

9.4.1 Construction of Vocabulary

The objective here is to identify the most informative terms (words and phrases) for the thesaurus vocabulary from document collections. The first step is to identify an appropriate document collection. The only loosely stated criteria is that the collection should be sizable and representative of the subject area. The next step is to determine the required specificity for the thesaurus. If high specificity is needed, then the emphasis will be on identifying precise phrases; otherwise, more general terms can be sought. Terms can be selected from titles, abstracts, or even the full text of the documents if available. This initial set of vocabulary terms is now ready for normalization. The simplest and most common normalization procedure is to eliminate very trivial words such as prepositions and conjunctions. For this, an appropriate stoplist of trivial words needs to be constructed. The article by Fox (1989–1990) on the construction of stoplists may be useful here. The next standard normalization procedure is to stem the vocabulary. Stemming reduces each word into its root form. For example, the terms "information," "informing," and "informed" could all be stemmed into the same root "inform." The chapter in this book on stemming algorithms may be consulted for this. The resulting pool of stems is now ready to be analyzed statistically with two objectives: first, to select the most interesting stems as discussed in the following section, and second, to create interesting phrases for a higher coordination level as discussed in the section on phrase construction.

Stem evaluation and selection

There are a number of methods for statistically evaluating the worth of a term. The ones we discuss here are: (1) selection of terms based on frequency of occurrence, (2) selection of terms based on Discrimination Value, (3) selection of terms based on the Poisson model. Program select.c, includes routines for all three methods, which are described briefly below.

Selection by Frequency of Occurence: This is one of the oldest methods and is based on Luhn's work, which has been extensively discussed in the literature; see for example, Salton and McGill (1983). The basic idea is that each term may be placed in one of three different frequency categories with respect to a collection of documents: high, medium, and low frequency. Terms in the mid-frequency range are the best for indexing and searching. Terms in the low-frequency range have minimal impact on retrieval, while high-frequency terms are too general and negatively impact search precision. Salton recommends creating term classes for the low-frequency terms; however, it is not evident how to do this automatically. High-frequency terms are generally coordinated into phrases to make them more specific (see the later section on phrase construction for this). Threshold frequencies are generally not fixed and therefore user specified. Program select.c includes a routine for this selection method. Threshold frequencies are specified by the user via the global variables LOW_THRESHOLD and HIGH_THRESHOLD.

Selection by Discrimination Value (DV): *DV* measures the degree to which a term is able to discriminate or distinguish between the documents of the collection as described by Salton and Yang (1973). The more discriminating a term, the higher its value as an index term. The overall procedure is to compute the average inter-document similarity in the collection, using some appropriate similarity function. Next, the term k being evaluated is removed from the indexing vocabulary and the same average similarity is recomputed. The discrimination value (DV) for the term is then computed as:

$$DV(k) = (\text{Average similarity without } k) - (\text{Average similarity with } k)$$

Good discriminators are those that decrease the average similarity by their presence, that is, those for which DV is positive. Poor discriminators have negative DV, while neutral discriminators have no effect on average similarity. Terms that are positive discriminators can be included in the vocabulary and the rest rejected.

Program select.c includes a routine called dv-all which computes DV for all terms with respect to a collection. In the program, average similarity with all terms intact is referred to as the baseline. The algorithm used is a straightforward one using the method of centroids. In this method the average interdocument similarity is computed by first calculating the average document vector or centroid vector for the collection. This is performed by a routine called centroid. Next, the similarity between every document and this centroid is calculated. This generates the total similarity in the collection, which can then be used to calculate the average similarity. For large collections of documents, a more efficient algorithm such as that based on the cover coefficient concept may be tried as suggested by Can and Ozkarahan (1987). However, this is not done here.

Selection by the Poisson Method: This is based on the work by Bookstein and Swanson (1974), Harter (1975), and Srinivasan (1990) on the family of Poisson models. The Poisson distribution is a discrete random distribution that can be used to model a variety of random phenomena including the number of typographical errors in a page of writing and the number of red cars on a highway per hour. In all the research that has been performed on the family of Poisson models, the one significant result is that trivial words have a single Poisson distribution, while the distribution of nontrivial words deviates significantly from that of a Poisson distribution. This result is used here to select nontrivial words as thesaurus terms.

The get-Poisson-dist routine in the select.c program prints out the distributions in a collection for all terms in the inverted file. Two distributions are produced for each term: the actual distribution and the one expected under the assumption of a single Poisson model. These distributions will have to be compared using the chi-square test to identify any significant differences. The reader is referred to Harter (1975) for information on these chi-square comparisons. Terms whose distributions deviate significantly are selected to be in the vocabulary. The rest may be discarded.

Phrase construction

This step may be used to build phrases if desired. As mentioned before, this decision is influenced by the coordination level selected. Also, phrase construction can be performed to decrease the frequency of high-frequency terms and thereby increase their value for retrieval. Two methods are described below. Program select.c includes routines for the first method. Given insufficient details for the second method, it is not implemented here. However, since it is an interesting approach, we include a sketchy algorithm.

Salton and McGill Procedure: This is the standard one proposed in Salton and McGill (1983, 133–34) and adapted by Rada in Forsyth and Rada (1986, 200). Their procedure is a statistical alternative to syntactic and/or semantic methods for identifying and constructing phrases. Basically, a couple of general criteria are used. First, the component words of a phrase should occur frequently in a common context, such as the same sentence. More stringent contextual criteria are possible, such as the words should also appear within some specified distance. The second general requirement is that the component words should represent broad concepts, and their frequency of occurrence should be sufficiently high. These criteria motivate their algorithm, which is described below.

1. Compute pairwise co-occurrence for high-frequency words. (Any suitable contextual constraint such as the ones above may be applied in selecting pairs of terms.)

2. If this co-occurrence is lower than a threshold, then do not consider the pair any further.

3. For pairs that qualify, compute the cohesion value. Two formulas for computing cohesion are given below. Both ti and tj represent terms, and size-factor is related to the size of the thesaurus vocabulary.

```
COHESION (ti, tj) =
co-occurrence-frequency/sqrt(frequency(ti) * frequency(tj))
                                            (Rada, page 200)
COHESION (ti, tj) =
    size-factor * (co-occurrence-frequency/(total-frequency(ti) *
            total-frequency(tj))) (Salton and McGill, 85)
```

4. If cohesion is above a second threshold, retain the phrase as a valid vocabulary phrase.

We do not include a program for this complete algorithm. However, the routine cohesion in select.c is an implementation of the Rada formula.

Choueka Procedure: The second phrase construction method is based on the work by Choueka (1988). He proposes a rather interesting and novel approach for identifying collocational expressions by which he refers to phrases whose meaning cannot be derived in a simple way from that of the component words, for example, "artificial intelligence." The algorithm proposed is statistical and combinatorial and requires a large collection (at least a million items) of documents to be effective. The author has been quite successful in identifying meaningful phrases and is apparently extending the algorithm. Unfortunately, some critical details are missing from their paper. Therefore, we do not include an implementation of their approach. However, a sketchy procedure is included since the overall process looks rather interesting.

1. Select the range of length allowed for each collocational expression. Example: two to six words.
2. Build a list of all potential expressions from the collection with the prescribed length that have a minimum frequency (again, a preset value).
3. Delete sequences that begin or end with a trivial word. The trivial words include prepositions, pronouns, articles, conjunctions, and so on.
4. Delete expressions that contain high-frequency nontrivial words.
5. Given an expression such as a b c d, evaluate any potential subexpressions such as a b c and b c d for relevance. Discard any that are not sufficiently relevant. (It is not clear from the paper how relevance is decided, but perhaps it is also based on frequency.)
6. Try to merge smaller expressions into larger and more meaningful ones. For example, a b c d and b c d may merge to form a b c d. (Again, the exact criteria for allowing a merger are not given.)

The main difference between this procedure and the previous one is that this one considers phrases that have more than two words. It is of course possible to extend the previous procedure to include phrases with more than two words. However, computing cohesion is likely to be more challenging than simply applying the formula recursively over larger sized phrases. Choueka's procedure also allows phrases to be substituted by longer and more general phrases as in step 6. However, the criteria used for allowing this should be carefully formulated.

9.4.2 Similarity Computation

Once the appropriate thesaurus vocabulary has been identified, and phrases have been designed if necessary, the next step is to determine the statistical similarity between pairs of terms. There are a number of similarity measures available in the literature. An extensive study has been done on the comparison of different similarity measures (McGill et al. 1979). Select.c includes two similarity routines:

1. Cosine: which computes the number of documents associated with both terms divided by the square root of the product of the number of documents associated with the first term and the number of documents associated with the second.
2. Dice: which computes the number of documents associated with both terms divided by the sum of the number of documents associated with one term and the number associated with the other.

Either measure can be used to assess the similarity or association between terms in a document collection. The algorithms implemented in the program select.c can be made more accurate by including only those instances in each numerator wherein the two terms co-occur in the same sentence and within some specified distance (that is, in a unit smaller than the entire document), as suggested in Salton and McGill (1983) and Soergel (1974). This makes the criteria for similarity more stringent.

9.4.3 Vocabulary Organization

Once the statistical term similarities have been computed, the last step is to impose some structure on the vocabulary which usually means a hierarchical arrangement of term classes. For this, any appropriate clustering program can be used. A standard clustering algorithm generally accepts all pairwise similarity values corresponding to a collection of objects and uses these similarity values to partition the objects into clusters or classes such that objects within a cluster are more similar than objects in different clusters. Some clustering algorithms can also generate hierarchies. It should be noted there are major differences between available clustering algorithms, and the selection should be made after carefully studying their characteristics.

Given the chapter in this book on clustering, such programs are not included here. Instead, we include the implementation of an alternative simple procedure to organize the vocabulary which is described in Forsyth and Rada (1986, 200–01). This algorithm implemented in hierarchy.c is quite different from the standard clustering algorithms and is based on the following assumptions: (1) high-frequency words have broad meaning, while low-frequency words have narrow meaning; and (2) if the density functions of two terms, p and q (of varying frequencies) have the same shape, then the two words have similar meaning. As a consequence of these two assumptions, if p is the term with the higher frequency, then q becomes a child of p. These two assumptions motivate their entire procedure as outlined below. Besides illustrating the procedure, hierarchy.c also includes appropriate data structures for storing thesauri organized as hierarchies.

1. Identify a set of frequency ranges.
2. Group the vocabulary terms into different classes based on their frequencies and the ranges selected in step 1. There will be one term class for each frequency range.
3. The highest frequency class is assigned level 0, the next, level 1 and so on.
4. Parent–child links are determined between adjacent levels as follows. For each term t in level i, compute similarity between t and every term in level i-1. Term t becomes the child of the most similar term in level i-1. If more than one term in level i-1 qualifies for this, then each becomes a parent of t. In other words, a term is allowed to have multiple parents.
5. After all terms in level i have been linked to level i-1 terms, check level i-1 terms and identify those that have no children. Propagate such terms to level i by creating an identical "dummy" term as its child.
6. Perform steps 4 and 5 for each level starting with level 1.

9.5 MERGING EXISTING THESAURI

The third program, merge.c, is designed to merge different hierarchies. This is useful when different thesauri (perhaps with different perspectives) are available for the same subject, or when a new subject is being synthesized from existing ones. The algorithm for the program has been adapted from Chapter 14 of Forsyth and Rada (1986) in which experiments in augmenting MeSH and SNOMED have been described. Two different merging algorithms have been implemented. The first, called simple-merge, links hierarchies wherever they have terms in common. The second, called complex-merge, adopts a more interesting criteria. It links terms from different hierarchies if they are similar enough. Here, similarity is computed as a function of the number of parent and child terms in common. Also, sufficiency is decided based on a preset user specified threshold.

9.6 BRIEF DESCRIPTION OF C PROGRAMS INCLUDED

Three programs are included at the end of this chapter. The first can be used to select terms and to construct phrases; the second generates (or reads) and stores hierarchies. The third program merges different hierarchies.

9.6.1 Program Select.c

This program contains a variety of routines for the various selection criteria used in designing the thesaurus vocabulary (see Appendix 9.A). It requires two input files: a direct file and an inverted file. Both contain the same information, but arranged differently. The direct file is a listing of document numbers corresponding to the database of interest. Each document number is associated with a set of term and term-weight pairs. A document may be associated with all its component terms or perhaps only a select few. The term-weight represents the strength of association between the document and the term. This term-weight may be assigned manually, or for example be some function of the term's frequency of occurrence in the document. The file is arranged such that the rows pertaining to the same document are grouped together. The inverted file is a listing of terms. Here each term is linked to its associated document numbers and the term-weights. The interpretation of term-weights should be the same in both input files. In fact, the two files should contain identical information. The inverted index is arranged such that rows corresponding to a term are grouped together. In both files, document numbers are represented by integers; the terms are character strings and the weights are decimal numbers. One or more spaces may be used to distinguish between the three. Figure 9.2 below shows a brief extract of both files.

```
2 math 2.0                    mellitus 1 1.0
2 logic 1.0                   logic 2 1.0
1 diabetes 2.0                diabetes 1 2.0
1 mellitus 1.0                math 2 2.0
3 math 1.0                    math 3 1.0

    Direct file extract        Inverted file extract
```

Figure 9.2 Short extracts from both input files

Besides these two files, an output file must also be specified. The user will have to specify four global variables. The first two are MAXWORD: specifying the maximum number of characters in a term; and MAXWDF: specifying the expected maximum frequency of occurrence for a term within a document. The other two parameters are: LOW-THRESHOLD AND HIGH-THRESHOLD, which are used when partitioning the terms by frequency of occurrence in the collection into HIGH, MEDIUM, and LOW frequency classes.

9.6.2 Program Hierarchy.c

This program can perform two major and separate functions (see Appendix 9.B). First, if given the hierarchical relationships between a set of terms, it records these relationships in its internal inverted file structure. This can then be used for other purposes. Second, it is also capable of generating the hierarchical structure automatically using Rada's algorithm. For this, the input required is the inverted file, which has the same structure as in Figure 9.2. The second input file is a link file, which is a sequence of rows representing link information. A row consists of a parent term followed by any number of spaces and then a child term. This file is used if the link information is simply provided to the program. For this the user will have to set two parameters: MAXWORD, which specifies the maximum size for a term, and NUMBER-OF-LEVELS, which constrains the size of the generated hierarchy.

9.6.3 Program merge.c

This program contains routines to perform the two types of merging functions described (see Appendix 9.C). Four input files are required here: an inverted file and a link file for each thesaurus hierarchy. Their formats are as described before. Two parameters will have to be set: MAXWORD described before and THRESHOLD which specifies the minimum similarity for use in the complex merge routine.

9.7 CONCLUSION

This chapter began with an introduction to thesauri and a general description of thesaural features. Two major automatic thesaurus construction methods have been detailed. A few related issues pertinent to thesauri have not been considered here: evaluation of thesauri, maintenance of thesauri, and how to automate the usage of thesauri. The focus has been on the central issue, which is the construction of thesauri. However, these secondary issues will certainly be important in any realistic situation.

REFERENCES

AITCHISON, J., and A. GILCHRIST. 1972. *Thesaurus Construction—A Practical Manual.* London: ASLIB.

BOOKSTEIN, A., and D. R. SWANSON. 1974. "Probabilistic Models for Automatic Indexing." *J. American Society for Information Science*, 25(5), 312–18.

CAN, F., and E. OZKARAHAN. 1985. *Concepts of the Cover-Coefficient-Based Clustering Methodology.* Paper presented at the Eighth International Conference on Research and Development in Information Retrieval. Association for Computing Machinery, 204–11.

CHOUEKA, Y. 1988. *Looking for Needles in a Haystack OR Locating Interesting Collocational*

Expressions in Large Textual Databases. Paper presented at the Conference on User-Oriented Content-Based Text and Image Handling, MIT, Cambridge, Mass. 609–23.

FORSYTH, R., and R. RADA. 1986. *Machine Learning—Applications in Expert Systems and Information Retrieval.* West Sussex, England: Ellis Horwood Series in Artificial Intelligence.

FOX, E. A. 1981. "Lexical Relations: Enhancing Effectiveness of Information Retrieval Systems." *SIGIR Newsletter, 15*(3).

FOX, E. A., J. T. NUTTER, T. AHLSWERE, M. EVENS, and J. MARKOWITZ. 1988. *Building A Large Thesaurus for Information Retrieval.* Paper presented at the Second Conference on Applied Natural Language Processing. Association for Computational Linguistics, 101–08.

FOX, C. FALL 1989/Winter 1990. "A Stop List for General Text." *SIGIR Forum, 21*(1–2), 19–35.

FROST, C. O. 1987. "Subject Searching in an Online Catalog." *Information Technology and Libraries, 6,* 60–63.

GUNTZER, U., G. JUTTNER, G. SEEGMULLER, and F. SARRE. 1988. *Automatic Thesaurus Construction by Machine Learning from Retrieval Sessions.* Paper presented at the Conference on User-Oriented Content-Based Text and Image Handling, MIT, Cambridge, Mass., 588–96.

HARTER, S. P. 1975. "A Probabilistic Approach to Automatic Keyword Indexing. Parts I and II." *J. American Society for Information Science, 26,* 197–206 and 280–89.

McGILL, M. et al. 1979. *An Evaluation of Factors Affecting Document Ranking by Information Retrieval Systems.* Project report. Syracuse, New York: Syracuse University School of Information Studies.

SALTON, G., and M. McGILL. 1983. *Introduction to Modern Information Retrieval.* New York: McGraw-Hill.

SALTON, G., and C. S. YANG. 1973. "On the Specification of Term Values in Automatic Indexing." *Journal of Documentation, 29*(4), 351–72.

SOERGEL, D. 1974. "Automatic and Semi-Automatic Methods as an Aid in the Construction of Indexing Languages and Thesauri." *Intern. Classif.* 1(1), 34–39.

SRINIVASAN, P. 1990. "A Comparison of Two-Poisson, Inverse Document Frequency and Discrimination Value Models of Document Representation." *Information Processing and Management*, 26(2) 269–78.

WANG, Y-C., J. VANDENDORPE, and M. EVENS. 1985. "Relationship Thesauri in Information Retrieval." *J. American Society of Information Science*, 15–27.

APPENDIX

```
/*

    PROGRAM NAME: hierarky.c

    PURPOSE:  This program will generate a hierarchy in two ways.

              1)  It can simply read the parent-child links from an input fifile and
                  store the links in the inverted file structure,
         OR
              2)  It can use the Rada algorithm which splits up words
                  into different frequency groups and then builds links
                  between them.

    INPUT FILES REQUIRED:  (Depends on the option selected).
```

```
                    Option 1:   requires inverted file and link file.
                    Option 2:   requires inverted file.

                    1)   inverted file: sequences of

                         term          document number     weight.

                         (multiple entries for any term should be grouped together)

                    2)   links file: sequences of

                         parent term        child term

        NOTES:      Filters such as stop lists and stemmers should be used
                    before running this program.

     PARAMETERS TO BE SET BY USER:

                    1)   MAXWORD:   identifies the maximum size of a term
                    2)   NUMBER_OF_LEVELS:  specifies the desired number of levels
                         in the thesaurus hierarchy to be generated, used by the
                         Rada algorithm

COMMAND LINE:   (INPUT & OUTPUT FILES ARE SPECIFIED INTERACTIVELY)

        hierarky


    *****************************************************************************/
    #include <stdio.h>
    #include <string.h>
    #include <math.h>
    #define MAXWORD 20                   /* maximum size of a term               */
    #define NUMBER_OF_LEVELS 10          /* # of levels desired in the thesaurus */

    struct doclist {                     /* sequences of document # and weight pairs */
      int doc;                           /* document number                      */
      float weight                       /* term weight in document              */
      struct doclist *nextdoc;           /* ptr. to next doclist record          */
    } doclistfile;

    struct parentlist {
      char term[MAXWORD];                /* parent term                          */
      struct invert *parent;             /* ptr. to parent term in inverted file */
      struct parentlist *nextparent;     /* ptr. to next parentlist record       */
    } parentfile;

    struct childlist {
      char term[MAXWORD];                /* child term                           */
      struct invert *child;              /* ptr. to child term in inverted file  */

      struct childlist *nextchild;       /* ptr. to next childlist record        */
    } childfile;

    struct invert {                      /* inverted file                        */
      char term[MAXWORD];                /* term                                 */
      struct doclist *doc;               /* sequences of document # and weight   */
      struct parentlist *parents;        /* ptr. to parent terms                 */
      struct childlist *children;        /* ptr. to child terms                  */
      int level;                         /* thesaurus level based on term frequency*/
      struct invert *nextterm;           /* ptr. to next invert record           */
    } invfile;
```

Chap. 9   Appendix

```
struct invert *startinv;        /* ptr. to first record in inverted file  */
struct invert *lastinv;         /* ptr. to last record in inverted file   */
struct doclist *lastdoc;        /* ptr. to last document in doclist        */


static char currentterm[MAXWORD]; /* tracks current term in inverted file   */
static int Number_of_docs;       /* total # of documents which is computed */

static struct invert *get_mem_invert();          /* these 4 functions will obtain    */
static struct doclist *get_mem_doclist();        /* memory for records.  The type of */
static struct parentlist *get_mem_parentlist();/* is indicated by the name of      */
static struct childlist *get_mem_childlist();   /* the function                     */

static FILE *input;              /* inverted file                  */
static FILE *input1;             /* link file                      */
static FILE *output;             /* holds any output               */

static
float cohesion(),                /* compute cohesion between two terms   */
      total_wdf(),               /* compute total frequency of term in dbse. */
      get_freq_range();
static
void  read_invfile(),            /* read in the inverted file            */
      read_links(),              /* read in the links file               */
      add_link(),                /* called within read_links()           */
      pr_invert(),               /* print the inverted file              */
      add_invert(),              /* called within read_invfile()         */
      write_levels(),            /* initialize the levels information    */
      generate_Rada_hierarchy(), /* generate the Rada hierarchy          */
      get_term_data();           /* get basic information about terms    */

struct invert *find_term();      /* searches for term in inverted file and */
                                 /* returns its address.                 */

int main(argc)
int argc;
{

char ch, fname[128];
startinv = NULL; lastinv = NULL; lastdoc = NULL;
currentterm[0] = '\0'; Number_of_docs = 0;

if (argc > 1)
   {
   (void) printf("There is an error in the command line\n");
   (void) printf("Correct usage is:\n");
   (void) printf("hierarchy\n");
   exit(1);
   }

(void) printf("\nMake a selection\n");
(void) printf("To simply read links from a link file enter 1\n");
(void) printf("To use Rada's algorithm to generate links enter 2\n");
(void) printf("To quit enter 3\n");
(void) printf("Enter selection: ");

ch=getchar();

switch(ch)
   {
   case '1':
       (void) printf("\nEnter name of inverted file: ");
       (void) scanf("%s", fname);
```

```
          if ((input=fopen(fname,"r"))==NULL) {
            (void) printf("cannot open file %s\n",fname);
            exit(1);
          }
          (void) printf("Enter name of link file: ");
          (void) scanf("%s",fname);
          if ((input1=fopen(fname,"r"))==NULL) {
            (void) printf("cannot open file %s\n",fname);
            exit(1);
          }
          (void) printf("Enter name of output file: ");
          (void) scanf("%s",fname);
          if ((output=fopen(fname,"w"))==NULL) {
            (void) printf("cannot open file %s\n",fname);
            exit(1);
          }
          read_invfile();
          (void) fprintf(output,"\nINVERTED FILE\n\n");
          pr_invert();
          read_links();
          (void) fprintf(output,"\nINVERTED FILE WITH LINK INFORMATION\n\n");
          pr_invert();
          (void) fclose(input);  (void) fclose(input1);  (void) fclose(output);
          break;
    case '2':
        (void) printf("\nEnter name of inverted file: ");
        (void) scanf("%s",fname);
        if ((input=fopen(fname,"r"))==NULL) {
          (void) printf("cannot open file %s\n",fname);
          exit(1);
        }
        (void) printf("Enter name of output file: ");
        (void) scanf("%s",fname);
        if ((output=fopen(fname,"w"))==NULL) {
          (void) printf("cannot open file %s\n",fname);
          exit(1);
        }
              read_invfile();
              (void) fprintf(output,"\nINVERTED FILE\n\n");
              pr_invert();
              generate_Rada_hierarchy();
              (void) fprintf(output,"\nINVERTED FILE AFTER GENERATING RADA HIERARCHY\n\n");
              pr_invert();
              (void) fclose(input);  (void) fclose(output);
              break;
        case '3':
              exit(0);
    }

    return(0);

    }


    /****************************************************************************

        read_invfile()

        Returns:  void

        Purpose:  Read in the inverted file entries from the disk file

    **/
```

```
static void read_invfile()
{
int docid;                 /* holds current document number         */
char temp[MAXWORD];        /* holds current term                    */
float weight;              /* holds current term weight             */
struct doclist *p;         /* structure to store doc#-weight pair   */

(void) fscanf(input,"%s%d%f",temp,&docid,&weight);  /* read next line */
while (strlen(temp) > 0)
      /* while its found a legitimate term     */
{
if (!strncmp(currentterm,temp,MAXWORD)) {
    /* if this term has previously been entered in inverted file then   */
    /* only need to attach a doclist record to the same entry           */
    p = get_mem_doclist();       /* get memory for doclist record       */
    p->doc = docid;              /* assign document number     */
    p->weight = weight;          /* assign term weight         */
    p->nextdoc = NULL;
    if (lastdoc) lastdoc->nextdoc = p;   /* connect p to the doclist chain */
               for this term if it already exists              */
    lastdoc = p;     /* set this global variable                */
}
else add_invert(docid,temp,weight);
      /* else term is a brand new term & need to make a new inverted file entry */
temp[0] = '\0';
(void) fscanf(input,"%s%d%f",temp,&docid,&weight);  /* read next line   */
}
}

/*****************************************************************************

      add_invert(docid,temp,weight)

      Returns:  void

      Purpose:  Start a new entry in the inverted file.  It is called in the
                read_invfile function when a new term is read from the input
                file.

**/

static void add_invert(docid,temp,weight)
int docid;                              /* in: document number      */
char temp[MAXWORD];                     /* in: new index term       */
float weight;                           /* in: index term weight    */
{
struct invert *p;                       /* p will get attached to inverted file  */

p = get_mem_invert();                   /* get memory for p         */
(void) strncpy(p->term,temp,MAXWORD);   /* copy over the term       */
p->parents = NULL;                      /* to begin this term has no parent terms*/
p->children = NULL;                     /* also no child terms      */

p->doc = get_mem_doclist();             /* start a doclist structure */
p->doc->doc = docid;                    /* assign document number    */
p->doc->weight = weight;                /* assign term weight        */
p->doc->nextdoc = NULL;
p->nextterm = NULL;
if (startinv == NULL) startinv = p;
    /* if this is the first entry in inverted file, then update global variable  */
if (lastinv) lastinv->nextterm = p; /* update ptr. to last inverted file record */
lastinv = p;
lastdoc = p->doc;                       /* update ptr. to last document*/
```

```
          (void) strncpy (currentterm, temp, MAXWORD) ; /* update global variable current term */
          }                                       /* to the new term just added           */
```

/**

     read_links ()

     Returns: void

     Purpose: Read parent-child link information from a file and record
     links in the inverted record structure

**/

```
static void read_links ()
{
char parent[MAXWORD],        /* tracks parent term        */
     child[MAXWORD];         /* tracks child term         */

(void) fscanf (input1, "%s%s", parent, child) ;  /* read input line     */
while (strlen (parent) > 0)
     /* while a legitimate parent has been found    */
{
add_link (parent, child) ;  /* this function will add the appropriate links in   */
                            /* the inverted file                                 */
child[0] = '\0'; parent[0] = '\0';  /* now throw out the old parent & child  */
(void) fscanf (input1, "%s%s", parent, child) ;   /* read next input line      */
}
}
```

/**

     add_link (parent, child)

     Returns: void.

     Purpose: Used within read_links. Basically, for each parent-child
               link specified, it adds the appropriate link information into
               the inverted file.

     Notes: If a term in the link file is not in the inverted file then
               the program will give a suitable message and exit.

**/

```
static void add_link (parent, child)
char parent[MAXWORD],                      /* in: holds the parent term        */
     child[MAXWORD];                       /* in: holds the child term         */
{
struct invert *p,                /* holds add. of parent term in inv. file    */
              *q;                /* holds add. of child term in inv. file     */
struct parentlist *new_parent; /* structure used to store parent info.       */
struct childlist *new_child;   /* structure used to store child info.        */

p = find_term (parent) ;              /* find address of parent term          */
if (!p) { printf ("\nPlease check the input files. \n") ;
          printf ("\nParent term %s is not in the inverted file\n", parent) ;
          exit (0) ; }
q = find_term (child) ;               /* find address of child term           */
if (!q) { printf ("\nPlease check the input files. Output may be incorrect. \n") ;
          printf ("\nChild term %s is not in the inverted file\n", child) ;
          exit (0) ; }
```

```
/* first add parent links for given child */

new_parent = get_mem_parentlist();          /* get memory for parentlist record*/
(void) strncpy(new_parent->term,parent,MAXWORD);     /* copy over parent term*/
new_parent->parent = p;       /* store address of parent term in inverted file*/
if (q->parents == NULL) {      /* i.e. no parents listed for given child yet */
    q->parents = new_parent;                      /* first parent link made */
    new_parent->nextparent = NULL;
}
else {                    /* at least 1 parent already listed for given child */
    new_parent->nextparent = q->parents;/* attach newparent to front of list */
    q->parents = new_parent;
}

/* next add child links for given parent */

new_child = get_mem_childlist();             /* get memory for childlist record */
(void) strncpy(new_child->term,child,MAXWORD);      /* copy over child term  */
new_child->child = q;         /* store address of child term in inverted file */
if (p->children == NULL) {         /* no children listed for given parent yet */
    p->children = new_child;                       /* first child link made */
    new_child->nextchild = NULL;
}
else {                   /* at least 1 child already listed for given parent */
    new_child->nextchild = p->children; /* attach newchild to front of list  */
    p->children = new_child;
}
}

/****************************************************************************

    pr_invert()

    Returns:  void

    Purpose:  Print the inverted file.  It prints each term, its
    associated document numbers, term-weights and parent child terms.

**/

static void pr_invert()
{
struct invert *inv_addr;         /* tracks address of current inv. file record  */
struct doclist *doc_addr;        /* tracks address of current doclist record    */
struct parentlist *parent_addr;/* tracks address of current parentlist record */
struct childlist *child_addr;  /* tracks address of current childlist record  */

inv_addr = startinv;                            /* begin at top of inverted file*/
while (inv_addr) {                     /* while a legitimate term.... */
  (void) fprintf(output,"TERM: %s\nPARENT TERMS: ",inv_addr->term);
  parent_addr = inv_addr->parents;              /* find addr. of first parent  */
  while (parent_addr) {                          /* printing all parents        */
     (void) fprintf(output,"%s ",parent_addr->term);
     parent_addr = parent_addr->nextparent;     /*loop through remaining parents*/
  }
  (void) fprintf(output,"\nCHILD TERMS: ");
  child_addr = inv_addr->children;               /* find addr. of first child   */
  while (child_addr) {                           /* printing all children       */
     (void) fprintf(output,"%s ",child_addr->term);
     child_addr = child_addr->nextchild;         /*loop through remaining children */
  }
  (void) fprintf(output,"\n\n");
```

```
    (void) fprintf(output,"                    DOCUMENT NUMBER              TERM
    doc_addr = inv_addr->doc;                  /* find addr. of first associated doc.*/
    while (doc_addr) {                          /* print all docs. and term weights*/
       (void) fprintf(output,"                  %-30d ",doc_addr->doc);
       (void) fprintf(output,"%-10.5f\n",doc_addr->weight);
       doc_addr = doc_addr->nextdoc;            /* loop through remaining documents*/
    }
    (void) fprintf(output,"\n");
    inv_addr = inv_addr->nextterm;              /*  go to next inverted file entry */
  }
}


/****************************************************************************

     total_wdf(term)

     Returns:  float

     Purpose:  Compute total within document frequency for specified term
               in the database
**/

static float total_wdf(term)
char term[MAXWORD];                    /* in: term for which total_wdf is required */
{
struct invert *term_addr;              /* add. of above term in inverted file     */
struct doclist *doc_ad;                /* tracks add. of associated doclist record */
float totalwdf;                        /* tracks total wdf                         */

totalwdf = 0.0;
term_addr = find_term(term);           /* obtain address of the term in inv. file  */
if (term_addr) {                       /* if term was found                        */
  doc_ad = term_addr->doc;             /* find address of associated doclist record*/
  while (doc_ad) {
    totalwdf = totalwdf + doc_ad-weight;  /* loop through doclist records to      */
    doc_ad = doc_ad-nextdoc;              /* compute the total weight             */
  }}
else (void) fprintf(output,"Term %s is not in the inverted file.  Could lead to
problems\n",term);
return(totalwdf);
}


/****************************************************************************

    get_freq_range(minimum,maximum)

    Returns:  float

    Purpose:  Compute the difference between the maximum total term frequency
              and the minimum total term frequency observed in the inverted file.
**/

static float get_freq_range(minimum, maximum)
float *minimum,                  /* out: returns minimum totalwdf      */
      *maximum;                  /* out: returns maximum totalwdf      */
{
struct invert *inv_addr;
float freq, max, min;

inv_addr = startinv;     /* begin at top of inverted file        */
/* initialize min and max to equal frequency of 1st term in file */
if (inv_addr) {
  freq = total_wdf(inv_addr->term);
```

```
    min = freq; max = freq;
    inv_addr = inv_addr->nextterm; /* go to next term in inv. file */
}
while (inv_addr) {
/* while a legitimate term compare with max and min.            */
   freq = total_wdf(inv_addr->term);
   if (freq < max) max = freq;
   if (freq > min) min = freq;
   inv_addr = inv_addr->nextterm; /* go to next term in inv. file */
}
*minimum = min;  *maximum = max;
return(max - min); /* returning the difference */
}


/****************************************************************************

     write_levels()

     Returns:  void

     Purpose:  Write the level numbers for each term into the inverted file
               depending on the total wdf of the term in the database and
               the user selected parameter NUMBER_OF_LEVELS.
               The level numbers are marked 0, 1, 2, ... etc.  Level 0
               refers to the highest frequency class, level 1 the next
               frequency class etc.

**/

static void write_levels()
{
int    i,               /* counter through the different levels     */
       number;          /* holds NUMBER_OF_LEVELS                   */
float  freq,            /* holds frequency of term in database      */
       range,           /* holds diff. between highest & lowest freqs.*/
       current_low,     /* tracks lower frequency of current level  */
       current_high;    /* tracks higher frequency of current level */
float  high,            /* highest term frequency in database       */
       low;             /* lowest term frequency in database        */
struct invert *inv_addr;    /* tracks current inverted file record  */

/* range holds the difference between highest & lowest totalwdf in dbse.  */
range = get_freq_range(&low,&high);

number = NUMBER_OF_LEVELS;  /* user specified global parameter          */

inv_addr = startinv;        /* start with the first term in inverted file */
while(inv_addr) {           /* while a legitimate term was found         */
  freq = total_wdf(inv_addr->term);
  current_low = low;
  for (i=(number-1); i>=0; i--) {
    if (i==0) current_high = high; else current_high = current_low + (range/number);
    /* if the term's frequency is within this narrow range, then level = i*/
    if ((freq >= current_low) && (freq <= current_high)) {
       inv_addr->level = i;
       break;
    }
    current_low = current_high; /* loop through the frequency levels     */
  }  /* ending for loop */
  inv_addr = inv_addr->nextterm;  /* loop through other inv. file terms   */
}

}
```

```
/***********************************************************************

        generate_Rada_hierarchy()

        Returns:  void

        Purpose:  Create the levelptrs data structure and generate the hierarchy
                  according to Rada's algorithm

**/

static void generate_Rada_hierarchy()
{
struct termlist {
  struct invert *term;       /* pointer to term in inverted file      */
  int mark;                  /* equals 1 if term is propagated else 0  */
  struct termlist *nextterm; /* pointer to next termlist record       */
} termlistfile, *p, *q, *r;

/* levelptrs is an array of pointers.  Each slot points to the start of
   the chain of termlist records for that level  */

struct termlist *levelptrs[NUMBER_OF_LEVELS];

int i;
struct invert *inv_addr;    /* tracks current term in inverted file    */
float coh, max_cohesion;

write_levels();  /* this routine computes and writes the level number for each */
                 /* term in the inverted file                                  */
for (i=0; i < NUMBER_OF_LEVELS; i++) levelptrs[i] = NULL;  /* intializing the array*/

/* now create the termlist chain for each level  */

inv_addr = startinv;                   /* start with first term in inverted file */
while (inv_addr) {                      /* while there is a term there            */
  p = (struct termlist *)malloc(sizeof(termlistfile)); /* get memory for termlist */
  if (!p) {
     (void) fprintf(output,"\nout of memory\n");
     exit(1);
  }
  p-term = inv_addr;                    /* assign the address of term in inverted file*/
  p-mark = 0;                           /* initially term not linked */

  /* Note: this term has been assigned to a frequency level already.  Now, if this */
  /* is the first term read for this level then set the appropriate levelptrs entry*/
  /* to point to this term    */
  if (levelptrs[inv_addr->level] == NULL) {
     levelptrs[inv_addr->level] = p;
     p->nextterm = NULL;
  }
  else {   /* now this is not the first term encountered for this level, so simply  */
         /* attach it to the front of the chain                                   */
     p->nextterm = levelptrs[inv_addr->level];
     levelptrs[inv_addr->level] = p;
  }
  inv_addr = inv_addr->nextterm;                       /* process next inverted file term */

} /* end while */

/* start with each level and compute max-cohesion with previous level */

for (i=1; i < NUMBER_OF_LEVELS; i++) {
   p = levelptrs[i];
```

```
    while (p) {
      max_cohesion = 0.0;
      q = levelptrs[i-1];                    /* q set to the previous level's first term */
      while (q) {          /* as long as there are terms in this previous level ... */
         coh = cohesion(p->term->term, q->term->term);
         if (coh > max_cohesion) max_cohesion = coh;
         q = q->nextterm;
      }
      /* max_cohesion for terms in p has been computed */

      /*  adding parent-child links and marking parents as propagated */

      q = levelptrs[i-1];
      while (q && max_cohesion  0.0) {
         coh = cohesion(p->term->term, q->term->term);
         if (coh == max_cohesion) {          /* this ensures multiple links possible */
            add_link(q->term->term, p->term->term);   /* routine adds the actual link */
            q-mark = 1;                     /* to show that parent term has been linked */
         }
         q = q->nextterm;
      } /* end while(q) */
      p = p->nextterm;                          /* go to next term in level i */
      max_cohesion = 0.0;
    }  /* end while(p) */

    /* checking all terms in level[i-1] to make sure they have propagated */

    q = levelptrs[i-1];
    while (q) {
      if (q->mark == 0) {                          /* i.e. term has no child in next level */
         q->mark = 1;
         r = (struct termlist *)malloc(sizeof(termlistfile));
         if (!r) { (void) fprintf(output,"\nout of memory\n");
            exit(2);
         }
         r->term = q->term;  r->mark = 0; /* making a copy of term as its dummy child */
         r->nextterm = levelptrs[i];   /* inserting r at beginning of level i chain */
         levelptrs[i] = r;
      }
    q = q->nextterm;
    }
    }  /* for */
}

/*****************************************************************************

        cohesion(term1, term2)

        Returns:  void

        Purpose:  Compute the cohesion between two terms

**/

static float cohesion(term1, term2)
char   term1[MAXWORD],     /* in: the two terms which are being        */
       term2[MAXWORD];     /* in: compared to determine cohesion       */
{
float l1,                 /* holds # of documents associated with term 1  */
      l2,                 /* holds # of documents associated with term 2  */
      common;             /* holds # of documents in common               */

get_term_data(term1, term2, &l1, &l2, &common);
return(common/(sqrt(l1 * l2)));
}

/*****************************************************************************
```

```
        get_term_data(term1,term2,l1,l2,common)

    Returns:   void

    Purpose:   Given two terms, it determines the number of documents in
               each and in common between them.

**/

static void get_term_data(term1,term2,l1,l2,common)
char    term1[MAXWORD],         /* in: term 1                              */
        term2[MAXWORD];         /* in: term 2                              */
float *l1,                      /* out: # of documents associated with term 1 */
      *l2,                      /* out: # of documents associated with term 2 */
      *common;                  /* out: # of documents associated with both   */
{
struct invert *p, *q;           /* holds addresses of both terms in inv. file */
struct doclist *doc_ad1, *doc_ad2; /* tracks addresses of doclists records  */
int     count1,                 /* # of documents associated with term 1   */
        count2,                 /* # of documents associated with term 2   */
        com;                    /* # of documents in common                */

p = find_term(term1);  q = find_term(term2);     /* find addresses of terms */
doc_ad1 = p->doc;                         /* start with doclist record for term1*/

count1 = 0;  count2 = 0;  com = 0;      /* initialize */

/* first get length for document 1 and number of common terms */

while (doc_ad1) {
  count1 = count1 +1;
  doc_ad2 = q->doc;
  /* for each doc. of term1 loop through all docs. of term2           */
  while (doc_ad2) {
    if (doc_ad1->doc == doc_ad2->doc) {      /* if they are the same doc. #   */
      com = com +1;
      break;
    }

    doc_ad2 = doc_ad2->nextdoc;
  }
  doc_ad1 = doc_ad1->nextdoc;
}

/* now get length of document 2 */

doc_ad2 = q->doc;
while (doc_ad2) {
  count2 = count2 + 1;
  doc_ad2 = doc_ad2->nextdoc;
}
*l1 = count1;  *l2 = count2;  *common = com;
}


/***************************************************************************

    *find_term(term)

    Returns:   address of a struct invert record

    Purpose:   Search for a specified term in the inverted file and
               return address of the corresponding inverted file record.
```

```
**/
static struct invert *find_term(term)
char term[MAXWORD];            /* in: term to be located in inverted file    */
{
struct invert *inv_addr;      /* tracks addr. of current rec. in inv, file */

inv_addr = startinv;                           /* begin at top on inv. file */
while(inv_addr) {
  if (!strcmp(term,inv_addr-term)) return(inv_addr);
  inv_addr = inv_addr-nextterm;
}
(void) fprintf(output,"Term %s not found\n",term);
return(NULL);
}

/***************************************************************************

     *get_mem_invert()

     Returns:   address of a struct invert record

     Purpose:   dynamically obtain enough memory to store 1 invert record.

**/

static struct invert *get_mem_invert()
{
struct invert *record;

record = (struct invert *)malloc(sizeof(invfile));
if (!record) {
    (void) fprintf(output,"\nout of memory\n");
    return(NULL);
}
return(record);
}

/***************************************************************************

     *get_mem_doclist()

     Returns:   address of a struct doclist record

     Purpose:   dynamically obtain enough memory to store 1 doclist record.

**/

static struct doclist *get_mem_doclist()
{
struct doclist *record;

record = (struct doclist *)malloc(sizeof(doclistfile));
if (!record) {
    (void) fprintf(output,"\nout of memory\n");
    return(NULL);
}
return(record);
}

/***************************************************************************

     *get_mem_parentlist()

     Returns:   address of a struct parentlist record
```

Purpose: dynamically obtain enough memory to store i parentlist record

```
**/

static struct parentlist *get_mem_parentlist()
{
struct parentlist *record;

record = (struct parentlist *)malloc(sizeof(parentfile));
if (!record) {
    (void) fprintf(output,"\nout of memory\n");
    return(NULL);
}
return(record);
}


/****************************************************************************

    *get_mem_childlist()

    Returns:  address of a struct childlist record

    Purpose:  dynamically obtain enough memory to store 1 childlist record

**/

static struct childlist *get_mem_childlist()
{
struct childlist *record;

record = (struct childlist *)malloc(sizeof(childfile));
if (!record) {
    (void) fprintf(output,"\nout of memory\n");
    return(NULL);
}
return(record);
}

/*
    PROGRAM NAME:  select.c

    PURPOSE:    1) Compute Discrimination Value of terms,
                2) Compute Poisson Distributions for terms,
                3) Parition terms by their total within document frequencies,
                4) Compute cohesion between pairs of terms,
                5) Compute Dice's coefficient of similarity between two terms.

    INPUT FILES REQUIRED:

                1) a direct file, sequences of:

                    document#    term    weight

                    (multiple entries for any document should be grouped together )

                2) an inverted file, sequences of

                    term    document#    weight

                    (multiple entries for any term should be grouped together)
```

```
        NOTES:     Filters such as stop lists and stemmers should be used before
                   before running this program.

        PARAMETERS TO BE SET BY USER:

                1) MAXWORD — maximum size of a term
                2) MAXWDF  — maximum value expected for the within document
                            frequency for a term in the collecgtion.
                3) LOW_THRESHOLD — threshold for LOW and MID frequency ranges
                4) HIGH_THRESHOLD — threshold for MID and HIGH frequency ranges

        COMMAND LINE:

                select direct_file inverted_file output_file

**************************************************************************/
#include <stdio.h>
#include <string.h>
#include <math.h>
#define MAXWORD 20          /* maximum size of a term              */
#define MAXWDF 30           /* maximum WDF for a word in a database    */
#define LOW_THRESHOLD 2.0
#define HIGH_THRESHOLD 4.0

struct termlist {           /* sequences of term and weight pairs      */
  char term[MAXWORD];       /* term                                 */
  float weight;             /* term weight in document              */
  struct termlist *nextterm;/* ptr. to next termlist record         */
} termlistfile;

struct doclist {            /* sequences of document # and weight pairs*/
  int doc;                  /* document number                      */
  float weight;             /* term weight in document              */
  struct doclist *nextdoc;  /* ptr. to next doclist record          */
} doclistfile;

struct direct {             /* direct file: document to list of terms  */
  int docnum;               /* document #                           */
  struct termlist *terms;   /* sequences of term and weight pairs       */
  struct direct *next;      /* ptr. to next direct record           */
} directfile;

struct invert {             /* inverted file: term to list of documnts */
  char term[MAXWORD];       /* term                                 */
  struct doclist *doc;      /* sequences of document # and weight pairs*/
  struct invert *next;      /* ptr. to next invert record           */
} invfile;

static struct invert *startinv;    /* ptr. to first record in inverted file  */
static struct invert *lastinv;     /* ptr. to last record in inverted file   */
static struct doclist *lastdoc;    /* ptr. to last document in doclist       */
static struct direct *startdir;    /* ptr. to first record in direct file    */
static struct direct *lastdir;     /* ptr. to last record in direct file     */
static struct termlist *lastterm;  /* ptr. to last term in termlist          */
static struct direct *start_centroid; /* ptr. to centroid record             */

static FILE *input;                /* direct file                          */
static FILE *input1;               /* inverted file                        */
static FILE *output;               /* file to hold all output              */

static int currentdoc;             /* tracks current document in direct file */
static char currentterm[MAXWORD];  /* tracks current term in inverted file   */
static int Number_of_docs;         /* total # of documents which is computed */
```

```c
          static
          float av_doc_similarity(),      /* compute average doc. similarity in dbse. */
                factorial(),              /* compute factorial of a number            */
                cosine(),                 /* compute cosine between two terms         */
                dice(),                   /* compute dice beteen two terms            */
                total_wdf(),              /* compute total frequency of term in dbse. */
                cohesion();               /* compute cohesion between two terms       */
          static
          void initialize(),              /* initialize files and global variables    */
                read_directfile(),        /* read in the direct file                  */
                add_direct(),             /* called within read_directfile()          */
                pr_direct(),              /* print the direct file                    */
                read_invfile(),           /* read in the inverted file                */
                add_invert(),             /* called within read_invfile()             */
                pr_invert(),              /* print the inverted file                  */
                centroid(),               /* compute the document centroid for dbse.  */
                pr_centroid(),            /* print the document centroid              */
                get_Poisson_dist(),       /* compute Poisson distributions for terms  */
                Partition_terms(),        /* partition terms by frequency             */
                dv_all(),                 /* compute discrimination value of terms    */
                get_doc_data(),            /* get basic info. about documents         */
                get_term_data();           /* get basic info. about terms             */

     static struct direct *get_mem_direct();      /* these 4 get_mem functions are */
     static struct invert *get_mem_invert();      /* used to obtain memory for a   */
     static struct doclist *get_mem_doclist();    /* record. The record type is    */

     static struct termlist *get_mem_termlist(); /* obvious from the name          */

     struct invert *find_term();             /* searches for term in inverted file*/
                                             /* and returns its address           */
     int main(argc,argv)
     int argc;
     char *argv[];
     {

     char ch, word1[MAXWORD], word2[MAXWORD];

     if (argc!=4)
        {
        (void) printf("There is an error in the command line\n");
        (void) printf("Correct usage is\n");
        (void) printf("select direct_file inverted_file output_file\n");
        exit(1);
        }

     initialize(argv);
     (void) fprintf(output,"\nREADING IN DIRECT FILE\n");
     read_directfile();
     (void) fprintf(output,"\nPRINTING DIRECT FILE\n\n");
     pr_direct();
     (void) fprintf(output,"\nNUMBER OF DOCUMENTS IS: %d\n\n",Number_of_docs);
     (void) fprintf(output,"\nREADING IN INVERTED FILE\n");
     read_invfile();
     (void) fprintf(output,"\nPRINTING INVERTED FILE\n");
     pr_invert();

     (void) printf("\nPlease make a selection\n\n");
     (void) printf("To compute DV for all terms enter 1\n");
     (void) printf("To compute Poisson distributions enter 2\n");
     (void) printf("To partition terms by frequency enter 3\n");
     (void) printf("To compute cohesion between two terms (for phrase construction) enter 4\n");
```

```
(void) printf ("To compute Dice's coefficient between two terms enter 5\n");
(void) printf ("To quit enter 6\n\n");
(void) printf ("Enter your choice: ");
ch = getchar ();
   switch (ch)
       {
       case '1':
           centroid ();
           (void) fprintf (output, "\nCENTROID\n\n");
           pr_centroid ();
           (void) fprintf (output, "\nDISCRIMINATION VALUES FOR ALL TERMS\n\n");
           dv_all ();
           break;
       case '2':
           (void) fprintf (output, "\nACTUAL AND POISSON DISTRIBUTIONS OF WITHIN DOCUMENT
           FREQUENCIES FOR ALL TERMS\n\n");
           (void) fprintf (output, "WDF = Within Document Frequency & #docs = Number of
           documents\n\n");
           get_Poisson_dist ();
           break;
       case '3':
           (void) printf ("Make sure that the threshold parameters are set correctly in
           the programm\n");
           (void) fprintf (output, "\nPARTITIONING THE TERMS INTO LOW, MEDIUM, HIGH
           FREQUENCY CLASSES\n\n");
           Partition_terms ();
           break;
       case '4':
           (void) printf ("enter first word: ");
           (void) scanf ("%s", word1);
           if (find_term (word1) == NULL) {
               printf ("sorry, %s is not in the inverted file\n", word1);
               break;
           }
           (void) printf ("enter second word: ");
           (void) scanf ("%s", word2);
           if (find_term (word2) == NULL) {
               printf ("sorry, %s is not in the inverted file\n", word2);
               break;
           }
           (void) fprintf (output, "Cohesion between %s and %s is %f\n", word1, word2,
           cohesion (word1, word2));
           break;
       case '5':
           (void) printf ("enter first word: ");
           (void) scanf ("%s", word1);
           if (find_term (word1) == NULL) {
               printf ("sorry, %s is not in the inverted file\n", word1);
               break;
           }

           (void) printf ("enter second word: ");
           (void) scanf ("%s", word2);
           if (find_term (word2) == NULL) {
               printf ("sorry, %s is not in the inverted file\n", word2);
               break;
           }
           (void) fprintf (output, "Dice's coefficient between %s and %s is %f\n", word1,
           word2, dice (word1, word2));
           break;
       case '6':
           exit (0);
```

```
              default:
                  (void) printf ("no selection made\n");
              }

     (void) fclose (input1);  (void) fclose (input);  (void) fclose (output);
     return (0);

     }
     /*****************************************************************************

         initialize (argv)

         Returns:  void

         Purpose:  Open all required files and initialize global variables
     **/

     static void initialize (argv)
     char *argv[];    /* in: holds the three parameters input at the command line */
     {
     if (( input = fopen (argv[1], "r")) == NULL ) {
        (void) printf ("couldn't open file %s\n", argv[1]);
        exit (1); /* input direct file */}
     if (( input1 = fopen (argv[2], "r")) == NULL ) {
        (void) printf ("couldn't open file %s\n", argv[2]);
        exit (1); /* input inverted file */}
     if (( output = fopen (argv[3], "w")) == NULL) {
        (void) printf ("couldn't open file %s for output\n", argv[3]);
        exit (1); /* output file */
     }
     /* set initial values of global variables */
     startinv = NULL; lastinv = NULL;  lastdoc = NULL;
     startdir = NULL;  lastdir = NULL;  lastterm = NULL;
     start_centroid = NULL;
     currentdoc = 0;    currentterm[0] = '\0';  Number_of_docs = 0;
     }

     /*****************************************************************************/
     /*

         read_directfile ()

         Returns:  void

         Purpose:  Read in the direct file entries from the 1st input file

     **/

     static void read_directfile ()
     {
     int docid;             /* holds the current document number     */
     char temp[MAXWORD];    /* holds the current term                */
     float weight;          /* holds the current term weight         */
     struct termlist *p;    /* structure to store the term—weight pair */

     (void) fscanf (input, "%d%s%f", &docid, temp, &weight); /* read the next line */
     while (docid > 0)
           /* while its found a legitimate document number          */
     {

     if (docid == currentdoc) {
           /* if this document number has previously been entered in direct file */
           /* then only need to attach a termlist record to the same entry     */
        p = get_mem_termlist ();   /* get memory for a termlist record */
```

```
        (void) strncpy(p-term,temp,MAXWORD);   /* copy the new word over */
        p->weight = weight;              /* assign the new weight over */
        p->nextterm = NULL;
        if (lastterm) lastterm->nextterm = p; /* connect p to the termlist */
                                chain for this document */
        lastterm = p;     /* set this global variable */
    }
    else {  /* else docid represents a new document */
      Number_of_docs = Number_of_docs +1;  /* increment global variable */
      add_direct(docid,temp,weight); /* starts a brand new entry in */
/* the direct file               */
    }
    docid = 0;
    (void) fscanf(input,"%d%s%f",&docid,temp,&weight);
    }
}
/****************************************************************************/

    add_direct(docid,temp,weight)

    Returns:   void

    Purpose:   Start a new entry in the direct file.  It is called in
               the read_directfile function when a new document number is
               read from the input file.
**/
static void add_direct(docid,temp,weight)
int docid;                /* in: new document number            */
char temp[MAXWORD];       /* in: index term                     */
float weight;             /* in: index term weight              */
{
struct direct *p;         /* structure p will be attached to direct file */

p = get_mem_direct();     /* get memory for p */
p->docnum = docid;        /* assign the document number */
p->terms = get_mem_termlist();  /* get memory for termlist structure */
(void) strncpy(p->terms->term,temp,MAXWORD); /* assign index term to it   */
p->terms->weight = weight;          /* assign term weight to it   */
p->terms->nextterm = NULL;          /* current end of termlist */
p->next = NULL;                     /* current end of direct file   */
if (startdir == NULL) startdir = p; /* if this is the very first document */
    then global variable pointing to start of direct file should be updated */
if (lastdir) lastdir->next = p;  /* update pointer to last direct file rec. */
lastdir = p;
lastterm = p->terms;  /* update pointer to last term */
currentdoc = docid;   /* update the global variable currentdoc to the */
                    /* document number just added              */
}

/****************************************************************************/
    pr_direct()

    Returns:   void

    Purpose:   Print the direct file.  It prints sequences of
               document#  term  weight.

**/

static void pr_direct()
{
struct direct *dir_addr;    /* tracks address of current direct file record */
struct termlist *term_addr; /* tracks address of current termlist record   */
```

194   Thesaurus Construction   Chap. 9

```c
  dir_addr = startdir;  /* start with beginning of direct file       */
  while (dir_addr) { /* check for legitimate direct file record       */
    (void) fprintf(output,"DOCUMENT NUMBER: %d \n",dir_addr-docnum);
    (void) fprintf(output,"                          TERM              TERM WEIGHT\n");
    term_addr = dir_addr-terms; /* get addr. of first term            */
    while (term_addr) {  /* loop through all the terms                */
       (void) fprintf(output,"                          %-30s ",term_addr-term);
       (void) fprintf(output,"%-10.3f \n",term_addr-weight);
       term_addr = term_addr-nextterm;  /* go to next term for the doc. */
    }
    (void) fprintf(output,"\n");
    dir_addr = dir_addr-next;   /* go to next direct file record       */
  }
}
/***************************************************************************
```

     read_invfile()

     Returns: void

     Purpose: Read in the inverted file entries from 2nd input file

```
**/

static void read_invfile()
{
int docid;              /* holds currenct document number            */
char temp[MAXWORD];  /* holds current term                           */
float weight;           /* holds current term weight                 */
struct doclist *p;   /* structure to store doc#-weight pair          */

(void) fscanf(input1,"%s%d%f",temp,&docid,&weight); /* read next line   */
while (strlen(temp) > 0)
       /* while its found a legitimate term                          */
{
if (!strncmp(currentterm,temp,MAXWORD)) {
    /* if this term has previously been entered in inverted file     */
    /* then only need to attach a doclist record to same term entry  */
    p = get_mem_doclist();  /* get memory for doclist record         */
    p->doc = docid;         /* assign document number */
    p->weight = weight;  /* assign weight          */
    p->nextdoc = NULL;
    if (lastdoc) lastdoc->nextdoc = p; /* connect p to the doclist   */
                      chain for this term  */

    lastdoc = p;  /* set this global variable   */
}
else add_invert(docid,temp,weight);
  /* else term is a brand new term & need to make a new inverted file entry */
temp[0] = '\0';
(void) fscanf(input1,"%s%d%f",temp,&docid,&weight); /* read next line */
}
}
/***************************************************************************
```

     add_invert(docid,temp,weight);

     Returns: void

     Purpose: Start a new entry in the inverted file. It is called in the
               read_invfile function when a new term is read from the
               input file

```
**/

static void add_invert(docid,temp,weight)
int docid;                      /* in: document number     */
char temp[MAXWORD];             /* in: new index term      */
float weight;                   /* in: index term weight   */
{
struct invert *p;               /* structure p will be attached to inverted file */

p = get_mem_invert();           /* get memory for p */
(void) strncpy(p->term,temp,MAXWORD); /* copy over the term  */
p->doc = get_mem_doclist();     /* start a doclist structure */
p->doc->doc = docid;            /* assign document number    */
p->doc->weight = weight;        /* assign term weight        */
p->doc->nextdoc = NULL;
p->next = NULL;
if (startinv == NULL) startinv = p;
  /* if this is the first entry in inverted file, then update global var. */
if (lastinv) lastinv->next = p; /* update ptr. to last inverted file record */
lastinv = p;
lastdoc = p->doc; /* update ptr. to last document */
(void) strncpy(currentterm,temp,MAXWORD); /* update global var. currentterm to the */
                                /* new term just entered           */
}
/*****************************************************************************

    pr_invert()

    Returns:  void

    Purpose:  Print the inverted file.  It prints sequences of
              term  document#  weight.

**/

static void pr_invert()
{
struct invert *inv_addr; /* tracks address of current inverted file record */
struct doclist *doc_addr; /* tracks address of current doclist record     */

inv_addr = startinv;   /* start with beginning of inverted file */
while (inv_addr) {     /* check for legitimate inverted file record */
  (void) fprintf(output,"TERM: %s\n",inv_addr->term);
  (void) fprintf(output,"                        DOCUMENT NUMBER        TERM WEIGHT\n");
  doc_addr = inv_addr->doc; /* get addr. of first document */

  while (doc_addr) { /*loop through all the associated doc.#s and weights*/
     (void) fprintf(output,"                  %-30d ",doc_addr->doc);
     (void) fprintf(output,"%-10.5f\n",doc_addr->weight);
     doc_addr = doc_addr->nextdoc; /* get addr. of next document */
  }
  (void) fprintf(output,"\n");
  inv_addr = inv_addr->next; /* go to next inverted file record */
}
}
/*****************************************************************************

    centroid()

    Returns:  void

    Purpose:  Compute and return the centroid for the documents of
              the database.
```

Centroid is stored as a direct file record. Document
number given to it is Number_of_docs + 1. The centroid is
computed by determining for each index term in the inverted
file, its average weight in the database. These average
weights are then stored in the direct file entry for the
centroid. (Note that these average weights are not used
anywhere, but could be used in computing DV for terms).

```
**/

static void centroid()
{
struct invert *inv_addr;    /* tracks address of current inverted file record */
struct doclist *doc_addr;   /* tracks address of current doclist record      */
float  total_weight,        /* tracks total weight for each term             */
       av_term_weight;      /* holds average term weight for each term       */
struct termlist *q,         /* structure used to create centroid entry in
                               the direct file                               */
       *lastterm;           /* tracks the last term in the centroid          */

start_centroid = get_mem_direct();  /* centroid stored as direct file record  */
start_centroid->docnum = Number_of_docs +1;  /* assign its pseudo doc.#       */
start_centroid->next = NULL;    /* end of direct file chain                   */
lastterm = NULL;
inv_addr = startinv;   /* begin at top of inverted file  */
while (inv_addr) {   /* while there is a legitimate inv. file record... */
  doc_addr = inv_addr->doc;  /* get address of first document  */
  total_weight = 0.0;   /* start with a 0 total weight for this term */
  while (doc_addr) {  /* if this is a legitimate doc. addr. */
    total_weight = total_weight + doc_addr->weight;
        /* update total weight for term */
    doc_addr = doc_addr->nextdoc;   /* loop through all docs. for the term */
  }
  av_term_weight = total_weight/Number_of_docs;
        /* calculating average term wt. */
  q = get_mem_termlist();
  (void) strncpy(q->term, inv_addr->term, MAXWORD);
  q->weight = av_term_weight;
  q->nextterm = NULL;
  if (lastterm == NULL) start_centroid->terms = q;
     /* if this is the first term entry for the centroid */
     else lastterm->nextterm = q;
     /* else connect this term to the centroid's termlist chain */
  lastterm = q;
  inv_addr = inv_addr->next; /* go on to the next inverted file entry */
}
}


/****************************************************************************

     pr_centroid()

     Returns:  void

     Purpose:  Print the centroid from the direct file

**/

static void pr_centroid()
{
struct termlist *term_addr;   /* tracks address of current termlist record */

/* note the centroid is given a document number = Number_of_docs + 1 */
/* therefore it may be treated as a special kind of document vector   */
if (start_centroid) {
```

```
                /* if there is a centroid */
        (void) fprintf(output,"——————————————————————————————————————————\n");
        (void) fprintf(output,"TERM                                WEIGHT \n");
        (void) fprintf(output,"——————————————————————————————————————————\n");
        term_addr = start_centroid->terms; /* get first term address */
        while (term_addr) { /* printing out term and weight pairs */
            (void) fprintf(output,"%-30s ",term_addr->term);
            (void) fprintf(output,"%-10.5f\n",term_addr->weight);
            term_addr = term_addr->nextterm; /* loop through all terms */
        }
        (void) fprintf(output,"\n");
    }
}
/**************************************************************************

        get_Poisson_dist()

    Returns:  void

    Purpose:  Get the Poisson distribution data for any term

    Notes:    This function has two parts:
              PART I:  Determine the actual within doc. freq. distribution
              PART II: Determine the distribution anticipated under the
                       single Poisson model.
              It is assumed that the within document frequency of a term
              is stored as the term weight in the inverted file.

**/
static void get_Poisson_dist()
{
struct invert *inv_addr;    /* tracks address of current inverted file record */
struct doclist *doc_ad;     /* tracks address of current doclist record       */
float dist[MAXWDF][2];      /* store for each term                            */
                            /* column 1 = within document frequency (wdf)     */
                            /* column 2 = document frequency                  */
int i,                      /* counter to add information to the dist array   */
    j,                      /* counter to loop through dist array             */
    found,                  /* flag used to match wdf in dist array           */
    numdocs,                /* counter to track # of docs. with the same wdf  */
    docs_with_term;         /* tracks the number of documents having the term */
float first,                /* these five local variables are                 */

      second,               /* used to determine expected distribution        */
      result,
      exponent,
      lambda;               /* single Poisson parameter                       */

inv_addr = startinv; /* start at the beginning of the inverted file */

/* PART I:  For each term determine the number of documents in the
collection that have a particular wdf */
while (inv_addr) {  /* check for legitimate inv. file record */
  docs_with_term = 0;
  doc_ad = inv_addr->doc;  /* get the first doc. address    */
  i = 0;  /* used to check if this is the very first entry in dist */
  while (doc_ad) {
    if (i == 0) { /* if first entry in dist */
        dist[i][0] = doc_ad->weight;  dist[i][1] = 1;
            /* assign wdf and doc. frequency = 1 to first row in dist */
        i++;
        docs_with_term++;
    }
```

```
          else {   /* dist already has other entries, hence look for
                    any previous entries for the same wdf value    */
             found = 0;
             for (j=0;j < i;j++) { /* loop through dist  */
                if (dist[j][0] == doc_ad->weight) { /* if found the same wdf */
                    dist[j][1] = dist[j][1] + 1;   /* add 1 to the doc. frequency */
                    found = 1;
                    docs_with_term++;
                }
             }  /* ending for */
             if (found == 0) { /* if not found the same wdf in dist */
                 /* start new row in dist */
               dist[i][0] = doc_ad->weight;   dist[i][1] = 1;
               i++;
               docs_with_term++;
             }
          }  /* ending else */
       doc_ad = doc_ad->nextdoc;/* loop through other documents for same term */
       }  /* ending while */
    /* ending if */

    /* now print out actual distribution information for this term  */
    (void) fprintf(output,"\nTerm = %s\n",inv_addr->term);
    (void) fprintf(output,"\nActual Distribution:  ");
    (void) fprintf(output,"          WDF                #docs\n");
    (void) fprintf(output,"                            0                %d\n",Number_
    of_docs->docs_with_term);
    for (j=0;j < i;j++)
      (void) fprintf(output,"                            %-16.0f %-6.0f\n",dist[j][0]
    ,dist[j][1]);


    /* PART II:  */
    /* computing lambda - the only single Poisson parameter  */

    (void) fprintf(output,"\nExpected Distribution:  ");
    (void) fprintf(output,"          WDF              #docs\n");
    /* call the function total_wdf to compute the total frequency of the term */
    lambda = (total_wdf(inv_addr->term))/Number_of_docs;
    first = exp(-lambda);
    numdocs = -1; j = -1;
    /* computing document frequency for each within document frequency value */
    while (numdocs != 0) {
       j = j + 1;
       exponent = j; /* type conversion necessary for pow function */
       if (j == 0) result = first * Number_of_docs;
        else {
          second = pow(lambda,exponent);
          result = (((first * second)/factorial(j)) * Number_of_docs);
       }

       if ((result - floor(result))  0.5) numdocs = floor(result);
          else numdocs = ceil(result);
       (void) fprintf (output,"                              %-16d %-6d\n",j,numdocs);
    }
    inv_addr = inv_addr->next; /* continue with the next inverted file term */
    } /* end while */
}

/******************************************************************************

    factorial(n)

    Returns:  float
```

```
        Purpose:    Return the factorial of a number.   Used in get_poisson_dist
**/

static float factorial(n)
int n;    /* in:  compute factorial for this parameter */
{
float answer; /* holds the result */

if (n==1) return(1.0);
answer = factorial(n-1)*n;
return(answer);
}

/*****************************************************************************

    total_wdf(term)

    Returns:   float

    Purpose:   Compute total frequency in the database for a specified
               term using the inverted file.

    Notes:     It is assumed that the appropriate term frequency is stored
               as the term weight in the inverted file.  This routine can
               also be used to filter out the low and high frequency terms.
               The resulting mid frequency terms can be used as input to
               the program which generates hierarchies.

**/

static float total_wdf(term)
char term[MAXWORD];    /* in: term for which total frequency is to be found */
{
struct invert *inv_addr;    /* tracks current inverted file record */
struct doclist *doc_addr;   /* tracks current doclist record    */
float total;                /* tracks the total frequency       */

total = 0.0;  /* initial value */
/* function find_term will find out where the term is in the inverted file */
inv_addr = find_term(term);
if (inv_addr) { /* if this term was found in the inverted file */
  doc_addr = inv_addr->doc; /* get first associated document address  */
  while (doc_addr) { /* update the total frequency */
    total = total + doc_addr->weight;
    doc_addr = doc_addr->nextdoc;  /* loop through other associated docs. */
  }
}
return(total);
}
/*****************************************************************************

    Partition_terms()

    Returns:   void

    Purpose:   Assign each term in the inverted file to one class:
               HIGH, MEDIUM or LOW frequency depending upon its total
               frequency in the collection.  This function utilizes
               two parameters defined at the top of the program:
               LOW_THRESHOLD and HIGH_THRESHOLD, which should be set
               by the user.
```

```c
**/

static void Partition_terms()
{
struct invert *inv_addr;   /* tracks address of current inverted file record */
float total;               /* holds total frequency of each term           */

inv_addr = startinv; /* start at the beginning of the inverted file */
(void) fprintf(output,"\nTerm - Total Frequency - Frequency Class\n\n");

while (inv_addr) {    /* if a legitimate address */
 /* compute total frequency for term in collection */
 total = total_wdf(inv_addr->term);
 (void) fprintf(output,"\n%s - %f -",inv_addr->term,total);
 if (total < LOW_THRESHOLD) (void) fprintf(output," LOW\n");
    else if (total > HIGH_THRESHOLD) (void) fprintf(output," HIGH\n");
        else (void) fprintf(output," MEDIUM\n");
inv_addr = inv_addr->next; /* continue with next inverted file entry */
}
}


/****************************************************************************

    cohesion(term1,term2)

    Returns:  float

    Purpose:  Compute the cohesion between two terms

**/

static float cohesion(term1,term2)
char term1[MAXWORD],   /* in: the two terms which are being  */
     term2[MAXWORD];   /* in: compared to determine cohesion */
{
float l1,              /* holds # of documents associated with term1 */
      l2,              /* holds # of documents associated with term2 */
      common;          /* holds # of documents in common             */

get_term_data(term1,term2,&l1,&l2,&common);
return(common/(sqrt(l1 * l2)));
}


/****************************************************************************

    dv_all()

    Returns:  void

    Purpose:  Compute Discrimination Value (DV) for all terms in the
              database

    Notes:    Similarity between two documents as calculated here is a
              function of the number of terms in common and the number
              of terms in each.  Term weights are not involved

**/

static void dv_all()
{
struct invert *inv_addr;       /* tracks address of current inv. file record */
float DV,                      /* holds computed DV                          */
      baseline;                /* holds baseline similarity                  */
```

```
    /* first compute baseline similarity */

    baseline = av_doc_similarity("-");  /* the dummy term '-' is used for this */
    (void) fprintf(output,"—————————————————————————————————————————————————\n");

    (void) fprintf(output,"TERM                              DV\n");
    (void) fprintf(output,"—————————————————————————————————————————————————\n");

    inv_addr = startinv;  /* begin at top of inverted file */
    while (inv_addr) {  /* if legitimate inverted file record */
      DV = av_doc_similarity(inv_addr->term) - baseline;
      (void) fprintf(output,"%-30s %-10.5f \n",inv_addr->term,DV);
      inv_addr = inv_addr->next;  /* go to next inverted file record */
    }
}


/**************************************************************************

     av_doc_similarity(term)

     Returns:  float

     Purpose:  Compute average similarity between each document
               and the centroid of the database.  The word specified in
               term is ignored during computations.

**/

static float av_doc_similarity(term)
char term[MAXWORD];              /* in: term is ignored during computations */
{
struct direct *dir_addr;      /* tracks current direct file record      */
float dl1,                    /* holds # of terms in document           */
      dl2,                    /* holds # of terms in centroid           */
      common,                 /* holds # of terms in common between them */
      total_sim;              /* holds total similarity between them     */

total_sim = 0.0;
dir_addr = startdir; /* begin with first direct file record */
while (dir_addr) {
  /* get_doc_data returns #of terms in each document and #of terms in common */
  get_doc_data(dir_addr,start_centroid,&dl1,&dl2,&common,term);
  total_sim = total_sim + cosine(dl1,dl2,common);
  dir_addr = dir_addr->next;  /* go to next direct file record */
}
return(total_sim/Number_of_docs);
}


/**************************************************************************

     dice(term1,term2)

     Returns:  float

     Purpose:  Returns Dice's coefficient of similarity between
               any two documents

**/

static float dice(term1,term2)
char term1[MAXWORD],            /* in: the two terms that are being compared */
     term2[MAXWORD];            /* in:                                       */
{
float l1, l2, common;
```

```
get_term_data(term1, term2, &l1, &l2, &common);

if (l1 == 0 || l2 == 0) return(0.0);
return(common/(l1 + l2));
}
```

/***

    cosine(l1, l2, common)

    Returns: float

    Purpose: Returns cosine similarity between two documents

**/

```
static float cosine(l1, l2, common)
float l1,                   /* in: # of terms associated with document 1 */
      l2,                   /* in: # of terms associated with document 2 */
      common;               /* in: # of terms in common between them     */
{
float temp;

if (l1 == 0 || l2 == 0) return(0.0);
temp = sqrt(l1 * l2);
return(common/temp);
}
```
/***

    get_doc_data(p, q, l1, l2, common, index)

    Returns: void

    Purpose: Given two document numbers, it determines the number of
    of index terms in each and in common. It will exclude the index
    term (specified as the last parameter) from consideration. Used
    in av_doc_similarity for DV calculations.

**/

```
static void get_doc_data(p, q, l1, l2, common, index)
char index[MAXWORD];        /* in: term to be excluded from computations */
struct direct *p, *q;       /* in: addresses of two documents numbers    */
float *l1, *l2;             /* out: number of terms in each document     */
float *common;              /* out: number of terms in common            */
{
struct termlist *term_addr1, /* holds address of first docs. termlist  */
                *term_addr2; /* holds address of second docs. termlist */
int count1,                 /* number of terms in first doc.           */
    count2,                 /* number of terms in second doc.          */
    com;                    /* number of terms in common               */

term_addr1 = p->terms;
count1 = 0;   count2 = 0;   com = 0;
/* first find out number of terms in document 1 & # of common terms */
while (term_addr1) {
  if (strncmp(term_addr1->term, index, MAXWORD)) count1 = count1 + 1;
     /* if its not the term to exclude */
  term_addr2 = q->terms;
  while (term_addr2) {
    if (!strncmp(term_addr1-term, term_addr2-term, MAXWORD)) {
        /* if the two terms are the same */
```

```
            if (strncmp(term_addr1-term,index,MAXWORD)) com = com + 1;
              /* if they do not match the term to exclude */
            break;
      }
      term_addr2 = term_addr2-nextterm;
    }
    term_addr1 = term_addr1-nextterm;
  }

  /* now find out number of terms in document 2 */
  term_addr2 = q->terms;
  while (term_addr2) {
    if (strncmp(term_addr2->term,index,MAXWORD)) count2 = count2 + 1;
    term_addr2 = term_addr2-nextterm;
  }
  *l1 = count1;   *l2 = count2;   *common = com;
}

/*****************************************************************************

    get_term_data(term1,term2,l1,l2,common)

    Returns:   void

    Purpose:   Get info regarding number of documents in common
               between any two terms.

**/

static void get_term_data(term1,term2,l1,l2,common)
char    term1[MAXWORD],      /* in: term 1 to be compared with        */
        term2[MAXWORD];      /* in: term 2                            */
float   *l1,                 /* out: # of documents associated with 1st term */
        *l2,                 /* out: # of documents associated with 2nd term */
        *common;             /* out: # of documents in common between them   */
{
struct invert *p,           /* holds address of first term in inverted file  */
              *q;           /* holds address of second term in inv. file     */
struct doclist *doc_ad1,    /* tracks doclist for first term                 */
               *doc_ad2;    /* tracks doclist for second term                *
int count1,                 /* holds # of documents associated with 1st term */
    count2,                 /* holds # of documents associated with 2nd term */
    com;                    /* holds # of documents common between them      */

/* find addresses of both terms in the inverted file */
p = find_term(term1);   q = find_term(term2);
doc_ad1 = p-doc; /* obtain 1st terms doclist address */
count1 = 0;   count2 = 0;   com = 0;

/* first get # of documents indexed by term 1 & # of docs. in common */
while (doc_ad1) {
  count1 = count1 +1;
  doc_ad2 = q->doc;
  while (doc_ad2) {
    if (doc_ad1->doc == doc_ad2->doc) {
      /* if the document numbers are the same  */
      com = com +1;
      break;
    }
    doc_ad2 = doc_ad2->nextdoc;
  }
  doc_ad1 = doc_ad1->nextdoc;
}
```

```
/* now get # of documents indexed by term 2 */
doc_ad2 = q->doc;
while (doc_ad2) {
  count2 = count2 + 1;
  doc_ad2 = doc_ad2->nextdoc;
}
*l1 = count1;   *l2 = count2;   *common = com;
}


/***************************************************************************

      *find_term(term)

      Returns:   address of a struct invert record

      Purpose:   search for a specified term in the inverted file &
                 return address of the record
**/
struct invert *find_term(term)
char term[MAXWORD];              /* in: term to be located in inverted file   */
{
struct invert *inv_addr;         /* tracks addr. of current rec. in inv. file */
inv_addr = startinv;             /* begin at top of inv. file                 */

while(inv_addr) {
  if (!strcmp(term,inv_addr->term)) {return(inv_addr);}
  inv_addr = inv_addr->next;
}
(void) fprintf(output,"Findterm routine:   Term %s not found\n",term);
return(NULL);
}


/***************************************************************************

      *get_mem_direct()

      Returns:   address of a struct direct record

      Purpose:   dynamically obtain enough memory to store 1 direct record
**/
static struct direct *get_mem_direct()
{
struct direct *record;

record = (struct direct *)malloc(sizeof(directfile));
if (!record) {
    (void) fprintf(output,"\nout of memory\n");
    exit(0);
}
return(record);
}


/***************************************************************************

      *get_mem_termlist()

      Returns:   address of a struct termlist record

      Purpose:   dynamically obtain enough memory to store one termlist record
```

```
**/
static struct termlist *get_mem_termlist()
{
struct termlist *record;

record = (struct termlist *)malloc(sizeof(termlistfile));
if (!record) {
    (void) fprintf(output,"\nout of memory\n");
    exit(0);
}
return(record);
}

/*****************************************************************************

    *get_mem_invert()

    Returns:   address of a struct invert record

    Purpose:   dynamically obtain enough memory to store one inverted
               file record

**/

static struct invert *get_mem_invert()
{
struct invert *record;

record = (struct invert *)malloc(sizeof(invfile));
if (!record) {
    (void) fprintf(output,"\nout of memory\n");
    exit(0);
}
return(record);
}

/*****************************************************************************

    *get_mem_doclist()

    Returns:   address of a struct doclist record

    Purpose:   dynamically obtain enough memory to store one doclist
               record

**/

static struct doclist *get_mem_doclist()
{
struct doclist *record;

record = (struct doclist *)malloc(sizeof(doclistfile));
if (!record) {
    (void) (void) fprintf(output,"\nout of memory\n");
    exit(0);
}
return(record);

/*
```

```
PROGRAM NAME:   merge.c

PURPOSE:    This program is used to merge two separate hierarchies.
            The program first reads each inverted file.  It then reads in the
            corresponding link file which gives parent-child links to build
            the hierarchy.  It can then perform two different types of mergers:

            1)  Simple merge in which a point of connection between the two
                thesauri is made wherever they have terms in common.

            2)  Complex merge in which any two terms are connected if they
                have sufficiently (above a specified threshold) similar
                sets of parent and child terms.

    INPUT FILES REQUIRED:

                1)   inverted file for 1st hierarchy

                2)   links file for 1st hierarchy

                3)   inverted file for 2nd hierarchy

                4)   links file for 2nd hierarchy

            An inverted file consists of sequences of

                term         document number         weight

                    (multiple entries for any term should be grouped together)

            A link file consists of sequences of

                parent term             child term

    PARAMETERS TO BE SET BY USER:

                1) MAXWORD:  which specifies the maximum size of a term
                2) THRESHOLD:  which specifies the minimum similarity level
                   for use in complex merge.

    COMMAND LINE:

        merge inverted_file_1 link_file_1 inverted_file_2 link_file_2 output_file


*************************************************************************/

#include <stdio.h>
#include <string.h>
#include <math.h>
#define MAXWORD 20              /* maximum size of a term                   */
#define THRESHOLD 0.6           /* similarity threshold for complex_merge   */

struct doclist {               /* sequences of document # and weight       */
  int doc;                     /* document number                          */
  float weight;                /* term weight in document                  */
  struct doclist *nextdoc;     /* ptr. to next doclist record              */
} doclistfile;

struct parentlist {            /* sequences of parent terms                */
  char term[MAXWORD];          /* parent term                              */
  struct invert *parent;       /* ptr. to parent term in inverted file     */
  struct parentlist *nextparent;/* ptr. to next parentlist record          */
} parentfile;
```

```c
struct connections {              /* holds information about connected terms  */
  struct invert *termadd;         /* address of connected term in inverted file */
  struct connections *next_connection /* ptr. to next connections record     */
} connectlist;

struct childlist {                /* sequences of child terms                */
  char term[MAXWORD];             /* child term                              */
  struct invert *child;           /* ptr. to child term in inverted file     */
  struct childlist *nextchild;    /* ptr. to next childlist record           */
} childfile;

struct invert {                   /* inverted file                           */
  char term[MAXWORD];             /* term                                    */
  struct doclist *doc;            /* sequences of document # and weight      */
  struct parentlist *parents;     /* pointer to list of parent terms         */
  struct childlist *children;     /* pointer to list of children terms       */
  struct connections *connect;    /* pointer to connection in other hierarchy */
  struct invert *nextterm;        /* ptr. to next invert record              */
} invfile;

static struct invert *startinv;       /* ptr. to first record in inverted file  */
static struct invert *lastinv;        /* ptr. to last record in inverted file   */
static struct doclist *lastdoc;       /* ptr. to last document in doclist       */
static struct invert *start_inv1;     /* ptr. to the start of 1st inverted file  */
static struct invert *start_inv2;     /* ptr. to the start of 2nd inverted file  */

static FILE *input1;                  /* first inverted file                    */
static FILE *input2;                  /* first link file                        */
static FILE *input3;                  /* second inverted file                   */
static FILE *input4;                  /* second link file                       */
static FILE *output;                  /* holds any outputs                      */

static char currentterm[MAXWORD];     /* tracks current term in inverted file   */
static struct invert *get_mem_invert();          /* these four get_mem functions */
static struct doclist *get_mem_doclist();        /* obtain memory dynamically for */
static struct parentlist *get_mem_parentlist();/* storing different types of    */
static struct childlist *get_mem_childlist();  /* records.                      */
static struct connections *get_mem_connections();

static struct invert *find_term();        /* searches for term in inverted file and */
                                          /* returns address of the term            */
static int compare();

static
void initialize(),                    /* initialize global variables      */
     open_files(),                    /* open files                       */
     read_invfile(),                  /* read in the inverted file        */
     add_invert(),                    /* called within read_invfile()     */
     read_links(),                    /* read in the links information    */
     add_link(),                      /* called within read_links()       */
     pr_invert(),                     /* print the inverted file          */
     simple_merge(),                  /* simple merge between both hierarchies*/
     complex_merge();                 /* complex merge between hierarchies */

int main(argc,argv)
int argc;
char *argv[];
{

char ch;

if (argc!=6)
  {
  (void) printf("There is an error in the command line\n");
```

```
        (void) printf ("Correct usage is: \n") ;
        (void) printf ("merge inverted_file_1 link_file_1 inverted_file_2 link_file_2 output_file\n") ;
        exit (1) ;
        }

   start_inv1 = NULL; start_inv2 = NULL; /* initialize start of both inverted files */

   initialize () ;
   open_files (argv) ;
   (void) fprintf (output, "\nREADING FIRST INVERTED FILE\n") ;
   read_invfile (input1) ;
   start_inv1 = startinv;
   (void) fprintf (output, "\nREADING FIRST LINK FILE\n") ;
   read_links (input2, start_inv1) ;
   (void) fprintf (output, "\nPRINTING FIRST INVERTED FILE\n\n") ;
   pr_invert (start_inv1) ;
   /* re-initialize */
   initialize () ;
   (void) fprintf (output, "\nREADING SECOND INVERTED FILE\n") ;
   read_invfile (input3) ;
   start_inv2 = startinv;
   (void) fprintf (output, "\nREADING SECOND LINK FILE\n") ;
   read_links (input4, start_inv2) ;
   (void) fprintf (output, "\nPRINTING SECOND INVERTED FILE\n\n") ;
   pr_invert (start_inv2) ;

   (void) printf ("Make a selection\n") ;
   (void) printf ("To use the simple_merge algorithm, enter 1\n") ;
   (void) printf ("To use the complex_merge algorithm, enter 2\n") ;
   (void) printf ("\nEnter selection: ") ;

ch = getchar () ;

switch (ch)
   {
   case '1':
       (void) fprintf (output, "\nPERFORMING A SIMPLE MERGE OF THE TWO INVERTED FILES\n") ;
       simple_merge (start_inv1, start_inv2) ;
       (void) fprintf (output, "\nPRINTING FIRST INVERTED FILE AFTER SIMPLE MERGE\n\n") ;
       pr_invert (start_inv1) ;
       (void) fprintf (output, "\nPRINTING SECOND INVERTED FILE AFTER SIMPLE MERGE\n\n") ;
       pr_invert (start_inv2) ;
       break;
   case '2':
       (void) fprintf (output, "\nPERFORMING A COMPLEX MERGE OF THE TWO INVERTED FILES\n") ;
       complex_merge (start_inv1, start_inv2) ;
       (void) fprintf (output, "\nPRINTING FIRST INVERTED FILE AFTER COMPLEX MERGE\n\n") ;
       pr_invert (start_inv1) ;
       (void) fprintf (output, "\nPRINTING SECOND INVERTED FILE AFTER COMPLEX MERGE\n\n") ;
       pr_invert (start_inv2) ;
   }

(void) fclose (input1) ; (void) fclose (input2) ;
(void) fclose (input3) ; (void) fclose (input4) ; (void) fclose (output) ;

return (0) ;

}

/*****************************************************************************

            open_files (argv)
```

```
        Returns:  void

        Purpose:  Open all input & output files

**/

static void open_files(argv)
char *argv[];
{
if (( input1 = fopen(argv[1],"r")) == NULL ) {
   (void) printf("couldn't open file %s\n",argv[1]);
   exit(1); /* inverted file for first thesaurus hierarchy  */
}

if (( input2 = fopen(argv[2],"r")) == NULL ) {
   (void) printf("couldn't open file %s\n",argv[2]);
   exit(1); /* link file for first thesaurus hierarchy */
}

if (( input3 = fopen(argv[3],"r")) == NULL ) {
   (void) printf("couldn't open file %s\n",argv[3]);
   exit(1); /* inverted file for second thesaurus hierarchy  */
}

if (( input4 = fopen(argv[4],"r")) == NULL ) {
   (void) printf("couldn't open file %s\n",argv[4]);
   exit(1); /* link file for second thesaurus hierarchy */
}

if (( output = fopen(argv[5],"w")) == NULL) {
   (void) printf("couldn't open file %s for output \n",argv[5]);
   exit(1); /* output file */
}

}


/******************************************************************************

     initialize()

     Returns:  void

     Purpose:  Initialize global variables

**/

static void initialize()
{
startinv = NULL;              /* start of inverted file      */
lastinv = NULL;               /* end of inverted file        */
lastdoc = NULL;               /* last document considered    */
currentterm[0] = '\0';        /* current term being considered */

}

/******************************************************************************

     read_invfile(input)

     Returns:  void

     Purpose:  Read the inverted file from a disk file

**/
```

```
static void read_invfile(input)
FILE *input;
{
int docid;                        /* holds current document number        */
char temp[MAXWORD];               /* holds current term                   */
float weight;                     /* holds current term weight            */
struct doclist *p;                /* structure to hold document numner-weight pair */

(void) fscanf(input,"%s%d%f",temp,&docid,&weight);   /* read next line    */
while (strlen(temp) > 0)                          /* while a legitimate line */
{
if (!strncmp(currentterm,temp,MAXWORD)) {
/* if temp is the same as current term then simply add next document-weight info*/
    p = get_mem_doclist();
    p->doc = docid;               /* assign doc. number   */
    p->weight = weight;           /* assign doc. weight   */
    p->nextdoc = NULL;
    if (lastdoc) lastdoc->nextdoc = p; /* connect p to doclist chain for this term */
    lastdoc = p;                  /* set this global variable   */
}
else add_invert(docid,temp,weight); /* temp not the same as current term, hence */
temp[0] = '\0';                     /* start a new entry in the inverted file   */
(void) fscanf(input,"%s%d%f",temp,&docid,&weight);       /* read next input line */
}
}


/***************************************************************************

     add_invert(docid,temp,weight)

     Returns:  void

     Purpose:  Called in read_invfile when a new term is being read from the file.
               Starts a new entry in the inverted file.
**/
static void add_invert(docid,temp,weight)
int docid;                              /* in: document number           */
char temp[MAXWORD];                     /* in: new index term            */
float weight;                           /* in: index term weight         */
{
struct invert *p;                       /* structure p will be attached to inv. file */

p = get_mem_invert();                   /* get memory for p              */
(void) strncpy(p->term,temp,MAXWORD);        /* copy over the term       */
p->parents = NULL;                      /* initially term has no parents */
p->children = NULL;                     /* also no children terms        */
p->doc = get_mem_doclist();             /* get memory for a doclist structure */
p->doc->doc = docid;                    /* assign the document number    */
p->doc->weight = weight;                /* assign term weight            */
p->doc->nextdoc = NULL;
p->connect = NULL;                      /* initially this term not connected to any */
                                        /* other in any other hierarchy  */
p->nextterm = NULL;
if (startinv == NULL) startinv = p;  /* if this is the 1st term in inverted file */
if (lastinv) lastinv->nextterm = p;  /* always update lastinv pointer            */
lastinv = p;
lastdoc = p->doc;
(void) strncpy(currentterm,temp,MAXWORD);   /* update the value of currentterm to the  */

                                        /* new term that has just been read        */
}

/***************************************************************************
```

```
        read_links(input,startinv)

        Returns:  void

        Purpose:  Add the link information to the inverted file

**/
static void read_links(input,startinv)
FILE *input;                            /* in:  input file            */
struct invert *startinv;                /* in: start of this inverted file */
{
char parent[MAXWORD],                   /* holds parent term          */
     child[MAXWORD];                    /* holds child term           */

(void) fscanf(input,"%s%s",parent,child);    /* read first input line  */
while (strlen(parent) > 0 && strlen(child) > 0) /* while non-trivial input  */
{

if (!find_term(parent,startinv) || !find_term(child,startinv))
   {
   (void) printf("Please check your input files\n");
   (void) printf("Term %s or term %s is not in inverted file\n",parent,child);
   exit(0);
   }
add_link(parent,child,startinv);        /* this function makes links    */
child[0] = '\0'; parent[0] = '\0';      /* throw out old parent & child info*/
(void) fscanf(input,"%s%s",parent,child);    /* read next line         */
}
}

/*****************************************************************************

        add_link(parent,chile,startinv)

        Returns:  void

        Purpose:  Function is used within read_links

**/
static void add_link(parent,child,startinv)
char    parent[MAXWORD],        /* in:  specify parent term           */
        child[MAXWORD];         /* in:  specify child term            */
struct invert *startinv;        /* in:  specify start of this inv. file */
{
struct invert *p, *q;           /* holds adds. of both terms in inv. file */
struct parentlist *new_parent;  /* structure to hold new parent info.   */
struct childlist *new_child;    /* structure to hold new child info.    */

p = find_term(parent, startinv);            /* find address of parent & child*/
q = find_term(child, startinv);             /* terms in the inverted file  */

/* first add parent links for the given child  */

new_parent = get_mem_parentlist();          /* get memory for parent record */
(void) strncpy(new_parent->term,parent,MAXWORD);        /* copy over parent term   */
new_parent->parent = p;    /* store addr. (in inverted file) of parent term*/
if (q->parents == NULL) {    /* i.e. no parents listed for this child yet */
   q->parents = new_parent;                 /* first parent link made      */
   new_parent->nextparent = NULL;
}
else {                    /* at least 1 parent already listed for given child */
   new_parent->nextparent = q->parents; /* attach new parent in front of list */
```

```
        q->parents = new_parent;
}

/* next add child links for given parent   */

new_child = get_mem_childlist();            /* get memory for child record    */
(void) strncpy(new_child->term, child, MAXWORD);        /* copy over child term    */
new_child->child = q;          /* store addr. (in inverted file) of child term */
if (p->children == NULL) {      /* i.e. no child terms listed for this parent*/
    p->children = new_child;                        /* first child link made     */
    new_child->nextchild = NULL;
}
else {                   /* at least 1 child already exists for given parent */

    new_child->nextchild = p->children; /* attach new child to front of list */
    p->children = new_child;
}
}

/******************************************************************************

    pr_invert(startinv)

    Returns:  void

    Purpose:  Print either inverted file.  Prints each term, its
              associated document numbers, term-weights and parent
              and child terms.
**/

static void pr_invert(startinv)
struct invert *startinv;                /* in: specifies start of inverted file   */
{
struct invert *inv_addr;            /* tracks add. of current inv. file record */
struct doclist *doc_addr;           /* tracks add. of current doclist record   */
struct parentlist *parent_addr;     /* tracks add. of current parentlist record*/
struct childlist *child_addr;       /* tracks add. of current childlist record */
struct connections *connect_term_add; /* tracks connected terms               */

inv_addr = startinv;                            /* begin at top of inv. file       */
while (inv_addr) {                              /* while a legitimate term....     */
  (void) fprintf(output,"TERM: %s\nPARENT TERMS: ",inv_addr->term);
  parent_addr = inv_addr->parents;              /* find addr. of first parent      */
  while (parent_addr) {                         /* printing all parents            */
      (void) fprintf(output,"%s",parent_addr->term);
      parent_addr = parent_addr->nextparent;    /* loop through remaining parents */
      if(parent_addr) (void) fprintf(output,", ");
  }
  (void) fprintf(output,"\nCHILD TERMS: ");
  child_addr = inv_addr->children;              /* find addr. of first child       */
  while (child_addr) {                          /* printing all children           */
      (void) fprintf(output,"%s",child_addr->term);
      child_addr = child_addr->nextchild;       /* loop through remaining childrend */
      if(child_addr) (void) fprintf(output,", ");
  }
  (void) fprintf(output,"\nDOCUMENT NUMBER              TERM WEIGHT\n");
  doc_addr = inv_addr->doc;                     /* find addr. of first associated doc. */
  while (doc_addr) {                            /* printing all documents          */
      (void) fprintf(output,"%-30d ",doc_addr->doc);
      (void) fprintf(output,"%-10.5f\n",doc_addr->weight);
      doc_addr = doc_addr->nextdoc;             /* loop through remaining docs.    */
  }
```

```
/* if the terms is connected then print the term from the other hierarchy */
  (void) fprintf(output,"CONNECTIONS IN OTHER THESAURUS HIERARCHY:\n");
  connect_term_add = inv_addr->connect;
  while (connect_term_add)
    {
    (void) fprintf(output,"   %s",connect_term_add-termadd-term);
    connect_term_add = connect_term_add-next_connection;
    if(connect_term_add) (void) fprintf(output,", ");
    }
  (void) fprintf(output,"\n\n");
  inv_addr = inv_addr->nextterm;                 /* loop to next term in inverted file */
}
}


/****************************************************************************

     simple_merge(startinv1,startinv2)

     Returns:  void

     Purpose:  In this function, two terms in different hierarchies are merged
               if they are identical.

**/
static void simple_merge(startinv1, startinv2)
struct invert *startinv1,          /* in:  specifies start of 1st inv. file */
             *startinv2;           /* in:  specifies start of 2nd inv. file */
{
struct invert *inv_addr1, *inv_addr2;
struct connections *r1, *r2;   /* storage to hold info. about connected terms */

inv_addr1 = startinv1;                  /* start with top of 1st inv. file       */
while(inv_addr1) {          /* looking for this term in the other inv. file   */
  inv_addr2 = find_term(inv_addr1->term, startinv2);
  if (inv_addr2) {                      /* if term was found then update connect */
    r1 = get_mem_connections();
    r1->termadd = inv_addr2;
    r1->next_connection = inv_addr1->connect;
    inv_addr1->connect = r1;
    r2 = get_mem_connections();
    r2->termadd = inv_addr1;
    r2->next_connection = inv_addr2->connect;
    inv_addr2->connect = r2;
  }
  inv_addr1 = inv_addr1->nextterm;
}
}


/****************************************************************************

     complex_merge(startinv1,startinv2)

     Returns:  void

     Purpose:  In this routine any two terms in different hierarchies are merged
               if they have 'similar' parents and children.  Similarity is
               computed and compared to a pre-fixed user specified THRESHOLD

**/
static void complex_merge(startinv1, startinv2)
struct invert *startinv1,          /* in: specifies start of 1st inv. file */
             *startinv2;           /* in: specifies start of 2nd inv. file */
```

```
{
  struct invert *inv1_addr,          /* tracks current term in 1st inv. file  */
                *inv2_addr;          /* tracks current term in 2nd inv. file  */
  struct connections *r1, *r2;       /* tracks connected terms                */
  int compare();

  inv1_addr = startinv1;             /* begin at top of 1st inv. file         */
  while(inv1_addr) {                 /* while addr. legitimate ....           */
    inv2_addr = startinv2;           /* now begin at top of 2nd inv. file     */
    while(inv2_addr) {
      if (compare(inv1_addr,inv2_addr)) {   /* this returns 1 of 2 terms are  */
                                /* similar enough, then connect the two terms */
        r1 = get_mem_connections();
        r1->termadd = inv2_addr;
        r1->next_connection = inv1_addr->connect;
        inv1_addr->connect = r1;
        r2 = get_mem_connections();
        r2->termadd = inv1_addr;
        r2->next_connection = inv2_addr->connect;
        inv2_addr->connect = r2;
      }
      inv2_addr = inv2_addr->nextterm;     /* loop through 2nd inv. file      */
    }
    inv1_addr = inv1_addr->nextterm;       /* loop through 1st inv. file      */
  }
}


/****************************************************************************

        compare(p,q)

        Returns:  int

        Purpose:  Used to compare two terms for more than just equality.
                  A similarity value is computed and if it is greater than a
                  THRESHOLD then 1 is returned, else 0
**/

static int compare(p,q)
struct invert *p, *q;      /* addresses of two terms to be compared       */
{
  struct parentlist *parent1,  /* tracks parentlist of 1st term   */
                    *parent2;  /* tracks parentlist of 2nd term   */
  struct childlist  *child1,   /* tracks childlist of 1st term    */
                    *child2;   /* trakcs childlist of 2nd term    */
  float count1,                /* tracks # of parents + children of 1st term */
        count2,                /* tracks # of parents + children of 2nd term */
        count;                 /* tracks # of common parents + children      */

  count = 0.0; count1 = 0.0; count2 = 0.0;  /* initialize all counts         */

  /* first check # of parents for p-term & the # of common parents */

  parent1 = p->parents;
  while(parent1) {    /* parent of 1st term */
    count1 = count1 + 1.0;
    parent2 = q->parents;
    while(parent2) {          /* loop through parents of second term   */
      if (!strncmp(parent1->term,parent2->term,MAXWORD)) count = count + 1.0;
      parent2 = parent2->nextparent;
    }
```

```
      parent1 = parent1->nextparent;
      }

      /* next compute # of parents for q->term */

      parent2 = q->parents;
      while (parent2) {    /* loop through parents of 2nd term again */
        count2 = count2 + 1.0;
        parent2 = parent2->nextparent;
      }

      /* now check # of children for p-term & the # of common children */

      child1 = p->children;
      while(child1) {    /* loop through children of 1st term      */
        count1 = count1 + 1.0;
        child2 = q->children;
        while(child2) {    /* loop through children of 2nd term      */
          if (!strncmp(child1->term,child2->term,MAXWORD)) count = count + 1.0;
          child2 = child2->nextchild;
        }
      child1 = child1->nextchild;
      }

      /* next compute # of children for q->term */

      child2 = q->children;
      while (child2) {      /* loop through children of 2nd term    */
        count2 = count2 + 1.0;
        child2 = child2->nextchild;
      }

      if (count != 0.0) { /* if there is anything in common at all */
        if ((count/(sqrt(count1 * count2))) = THRESHOLD) {
          /* printf("value is %f\n", (count/(sqrt(count1*count2)))); */
          return(1);
        }
        else return(0);
      }
      return(0);
      }

      /***************************************************************************

           find_term(term,startinv)

           Returns:  address of a struct invert record

           Purpose:  Search for a specified term in the specified inverted file
                     and return address of the corresponding record.  If not
                     found then returns NULL.
      **/
      static struct invert *find_term(term, startinv)
      char term[MAXWORD];        /* in: term to be searched         */
      struct invert *startinv;   /* in:  inverted file to search in */
      {
      struct invert *inv_addr;

      inv_addr = startinv;        /* begin at top of inverted file    */
      while(inv_addr) {
        if (!strcmp(term,inv_addr->term)) return(inv_addr);
        inv_addr = inv_addr-nextterm;
      }
      return(NULL);
      }
```

```
/****************************************************************************

      *get_mem_invert()

    Returns:   address of a struct invert record

    Purpose:   dynamically obtain enough memory to store 1 invert record
**/

static struct invert *get_mem_invert()
{
struct invert *record;

record = (struct invert *)malloc(sizeof(invfile));
if (!record) {
    (void) fprintf(output,"\nout of memory\n");
    return(NULL);
}
return(record);
}


/****************************************************************************

      *get_mem_doclist()

    Returns:   address of a struct doclist record

    Purpose:   dynamically obtain enough memory to store 1 doclist record
**/

static struct doclist *get_mem_doclist()
{
struct doclist *record;

record = (struct doclist *)malloc(sizeof(doclistfile));
if (!record) {
    (void) fprintf(output,"\nout of memory\n");
    return(NULL);
}
return(record);
}


/****************************************************************************

      *get_mem_parentlist()

    Returns:   address of a struct parentlist record

    Purpose:   dynamically obtain enough memory to store 1 parentlist record.
**/

static struct parentlist *get_mem_parentlist()
{
struct parentlist *record;

record = (struct parentlist *)malloc(sizeof(parentfile));
if (!record) {
    (void) fprintf(output,"\nout of memory\n");
    return(NULL);
}
return(record);
}
```

```
/****************************************************************************

     *get_mem_childlst()

     Returns:   address of a struct childlist record

     Purpose:   dynamically obtain enough memory to store 1 childlist record.

**/

static struct childlist *get_mem_childlist()
{
struct childlist *record;

record = (struct childlist *)malloc(sizeof(childfile));
if (!record) {
     (void) fprintf(output,"\nout of memory\n");
     return(NULL);
}
return(record);
}


/****************************************************************************

     *get_mem_connections()

     Returns:   address of a struct connections record

     Purpose:   dynamically obtain enough memory to store 1 connections record.

**/

static struct connections *get_mem_connections()
{
struct connections *record;

record = (struct connections *)malloc(sizeof(connectlist));
if (!record) {
  (void) fprintf(output,"\nout of memory\n");
  return(NULL);
}
return(record);
}
```

10

String Searching Algorithms

Ricardo A. Baeza-Yates

Department of Computer Science
University of Chile
Casilla 2777, Santiago
Chile

Abstract

We survey several algorithms for searching a string in a text. We include theoretical and empirical results, as well as the actual code of each algorithm. An extensive bibliography is also included.

10.1 INTRODUCTION

String searching is an important component of many problems, including text editing, data retrieval, and symbol manipulation. Despite the use of indices for searching large amounts of text, string searching may help in an information retrieval system. For example, it may be used for filtering of potential matches or for searching retrieval terms that will be highlighted in the output.

The string searching or string matching problem consists of finding all occurrences (or the first occurrence) of a pattern in a text, where the pattern and the text are strings over some alphabet. We are interested in reporting all the occurrences. It is well known that to search for a pattern of length m in a text of length n (where $n > m$) the search time is $O(n)$ in the worst case (for fixed m). Moreover, in the worst case, at least $n - m + 1$ characters must be inspected. This result is due to Rivest (1977). However, for different algorithms the constant in the linear term can be very different. For example, in the worst case, the constant multiple in the naive algorithm is m, whereas for the Knuth-Morris-Pratt (1977) algorithm it is two.

We present the most important algorithms for string matching: the naive or brute force algorithm, the Knuth-Morris-Pratt (1977) algorithm, different variants of the Boyer-Moore (1977) algorithm, the Shift-or algorithm from Baeza-Yates and Gonnet (1989), and the Karp-Rabin (1987) algorithm, which is probabilistic. Experimental results for random text and one sample of English text are included. We also survey the main theoretical results for each algorithm.

Although we only cover string searching, references for related problems are given. We use the C programming language described by Kernighan and Ritchie (1978) to present our algorithms.

10.2 PRELIMINARIES

We use the following notation:

- n: the length of the text
- m: the length of the pattern (string)
- c: the size of the alphabet Σ
- $\overline{C}_n$: the expected number of comparisons performed by an algorithm while searching the pattern in a text of length n

Theoretical results are given for the worst case number of comparisons, and the average number of comparisons between a character in the text and a character in the pattern (text pattern comparisons) when finding all occurrences of the pattern in the text, where the average is taken uniformly with respect to strings of length n over a given finite alphabet.

Quoting Knuth et al. (1977). "It might be argued that the average case taken over random strings is of little interest, since a user rarely searches for a random string. However, this model is a reasonable approximation when we consider those pieces of text that do not contain the pattern, and the algorithm obviously must compare every character of the text in those places where the pattern does occur." Our experimental results show that this is the case.

The emperical data, for almost all algorithms, consists of results for two types of text: random text and English text. The two cost functions we measured were the number of comparisons performed between a character in the text and a character in the pattern, and the execution time. To determine the number of comparisons, 100 runs were performed. The execution time was measured while searching 1,000 patterns. In each case, patterns of lengths 2 to 20 were considered.

In the case of random text, the text was of length 40,000, and both the text and the pattern were chosen uniformly and randomly from an alphabet of size c. Alphabets of size $c = 4$ (DNA bases) and $c = 30$ (approximately the number of lowercase English letters) were considered.

For the case of English text we used a document of approximately 48,000 characters, with the patterns chosen at random from words inside the text in such a way that a pattern was always a prefix of a word (typical searches). The alphabet used was the set of lowercase letters, some digits, and punctuation symbols, giving

32 characters. Unsuccessful searches were not considered, because we expect unsuccessful searches to be faster than successful searches (fewer comparisons on average). The results for English text are not statistically significant because only one text sample was used. However, they show the correlation of searching patterns extracted from the same text, and we expect that other English text samples will give similar results. Our experimental results agree with those presented by Davies and Bowsher (1986) and Smit (1982).

We define a *random string* of length ℓ as a string built as the concatenation of ℓ characters chosen independently and uniformly from Σ. That is, the probability of two characters being equal is $1/c$. Our random text model is similar to the one used in Knuth et al. (1977) and Schaback (1988).

For example, the probability of finding a match between a random text of length m and a random pattern of length m is

$$Prob\{match\} = \frac{1}{c^m}$$

The expected number of matches of a random pattern of length m in a random text of length n is

$$E[matches] = \begin{cases} \dfrac{n-m+1}{c^m}, & \text{if } n \geq m; \\ 0 & \text{otherwise} \end{cases}$$

10.3 THE NAIVE ALGORITHM

The naive, or brute force, algorithm is the simplest string matching method. The idea consists of trying to match any substring of length m in the text with the pattern (see Figure 10.1).

```
naivesearch( text, n, pat, m )  /* Search pat[1..m] in text[1..n] */
char text[], pat[];
int n, m;
{
    int i, j, k, lim;

    lim = n-m+1;
    for( i = 1; i<= lim; i++ )   /* Search */
    {
        k = i;
        for( j=1; j<=m && text[k] == pat[j]; j++ ) k++;
        if( j > m ) Report_match_at_position( i-j+1 );
    }
}
```

Figure 10.1 The naive or brute force string matching algorithm

The expected number of text pattern comparisons performed by the naive or brute force algorithm when searching with a pattern of length m in a text of length n ($n \geq m$) is given by Baeza-Yates (1989c) as

$$\overline{C}_n = \frac{c}{c-1}\left(1 - \frac{1}{c^m}\right)(n - m + 1) + O(1)$$

This is drastically different from the worst case mn.

10.4 THE KNUTH-MORRIS-PRATT ALGORITHM

The classic Knuth, Morris, and Pratt (1977) algorithm, discovered in 1970, is the first algorithm for which the constant factor in the linear term, in the worst case, does not depend on the length of the pattern. It is based on preprocessing the pattern in time $O(m)$. In fact, the expected number of comparisons performed by this algorithm (search time only) is bounded by

$$n + O(1) \leq \overline{C}_n \leq 2n + O(1)$$

The basic idea behind this algorithm is that each time a mismatch is detected, the "false start" consists of characters that we have already examined. We can take advantage of this information instead of repeating comparisons with the known characters. Moreover, it is always possible to arrange the algorithm so that the pointer in the text is never decremented. To accomplish this, the pattern is preprocessed to obtain a table that gives the next position in the pattern to be processed after a mismatch. The exact definition of this table (called *next* in Knuth et al. [1977]) is

$$next[j] = \max\{i \,|\, (pattern[k] = pattern[j - i + k] \text{ for } k = 1, \ldots, i - 1)$$

$$\text{and } pattern[i] \neq pattern[j]\}$$

for $j = 1, \ldots, m$. In other words, we consider the maximal matching prefix of the pattern such that the next character in the pattern is *different* from the character of the pattern that caused the mismatch. This algorithm is presented in Figure 10.2.

Example 1 The next table for the pattern *abracadabra* is

```
        a b r a c a d a b r a
next[j] 0 1 1 0 2 0 2 0 1 1 0 5
```

When the value in the next table is zero, we have to advance one position in the text and start comparing again from the beginning of the pattern. The last value of the next table (five) is used to continue the search after a match has been found.

In the worst case, the number of comparisons is $2n + O(m)$. Further explanation of how to preprocess the pattern in time $O(m)$ to obtain this table can be found in the original paper or in Sedgewick (1983; see Figure 10.3).

```
kmpsearch( text, n, pat, m )  /* Search pat[1..m] in text[1..n] */
char text[], pat[];
int n, m;
{
    int j, k, resume;
    int next[MAX_PATTERN_SIZE];

    pat[m+1] = CHARACTER_NOT_IN_THE_TEXT;
    initnext( pat, m+1, next );  /* Preprocess pattern */
    resume = next[m+1];
    j = k = 1;
    do {                                /* Search */
        if ( j==0 || text[k]==pat[j] )
        {
            k++; j++;
        }
        else j = next[j];
        if ( j > m )
        {
            Report_match_at_position( k-m );
            j = resume;
        }
    } while( k <= n );
pat[m+1] = END_OF_STRING;
}
```

Figure 10.2 The Knuth-Morris-Pratt algorithm

```
initnext( pat, m, next )  /* Preprocess pattern of length m */
char pat[];
int m, next[];
{
    int i, j;

    i = 1; j = next[1] = 0;
    do
    {
        if ( j == 0 || pat[i] == pat[j] )
        {
            i++; j++;
            if ( pat[i] != pat[j] ) next[i] = j;
            else                    next[i] = next[j];
        }
        else j = next[j];
    }
    while( i <= m ) ;
}
```

Figure 10.3 Pattern preprocessing in the Knuth-Morris-Pratt algorithm

An algorithm for searching a set of strings, similar to the KMP algorithm, was developed by Aho and Corasick (1975). However the space used and the preprocessing time to search for one string is improved in the KMP algorithm. Variations that compute the *next* table "on the fly" are presented by Barth (1981) and Takaoka (1986). Variations for the Aho and Corasick algorithm are presented by Bailey and Dromey (1980) and Meyer (1985).

10.5 THE BOYER-MOORE ALGORITHM

Also in 1977, the other classic algorithm was published by Boyer and Moore (1977). Their main idea is to search from right to left in the pattern. With this scheme, searching is faster than average.

The Boyer-Moore (BM) algorithm positions the pattern over the leftmost characters in the text and attempts to match it from right to left. If no mismatch occurs, then the pattern has been found. Otherwise, the algorithm computes a shift; that is, an amount by which the pattern is moved to the right before a new matching attempt is undertaken.

The shift can be computed using two heuristics: the match heuristic and the occurrence heuristic. The *match* heuristic is obtained by noting that when the pattern is moved to the right, it must

1. match *all* the characters previously matched, and
2. bring a *different* character to the position in the text that caused the mismatch.

The last condition is mentioned in the Boyer-Moore paper (1977), but was introduced into the algorithm by Knuth et al. (1977). Following the later reference, we call the original shift table dd, and the improved version $\widehat{dd}$. The formal definitions are

$$\widehat{dd}[j] = \min\{s + m - j \mid s \geq 1 \text{ and}$$
$$((s \geq i \text{ or } pattern[i - s] = pattern[i]) \text{ for } j < i \leq m)\},$$

for $j = 1, \ldots, m$; and

$$\widehat{dd}[j] = \min\{s + m - j \mid s \geq 1 \text{ and } (s \geq j \text{ or } pattern[j - s] \neq pattern[j]) \text{ and}$$
$$((s \geq i \text{ or } pattern[i - s] = pattern[i]) \text{ for } j < i \leq m)\}.$$

Example 2 The $\widehat{dd}$ table for the pattern *abracadabra* is

	a	b	r	a	c	a	d	a	b	r	a
ddhat[j]	17	16	15	14	13	12	11	13	12	4	1

The *occurrence* hueristic is obtained by noting that we must align the position in the text that caused the mismatch with the first character of the pattern that matches it. Formally calling this table d, we have

$$d[x] = \min\{s \mid s = m \text{ or } (0 \le s < m \text{ and } pattern[m - s] = x)\}$$

for every symbol x in the alphabet. See Figure 10.4 for the code to compute both tables (i.e., $\widehat{dd}$ and d) from the pattern.

```
bmsearch( text, n, pat, m )   /* Search pat[1..m] in text[1..n] */
char text[], pat[];
int n, m;
{
    int k, j, skip;
    int dd[MAX_PATTERN_SIZE], d[MAX_ALPHABET_SIZE];

    initd( pat, m, d );   /* Preprocess the pattern */
    initdd( pat, m, dd );
    k = m; skip = dd[1] + 1;
    while( k <= n )      /* Search */
    {
        j = m;
        while( j>0 && text[k] == pat[j] )
        {
            j--; k--;
        }
        if( j == 0 )
        {
            Report_match_at_position( k+1 );
            k += skip;
        }
        else k += max( d[text[k]], dd[j] );
    }
}
```

Figure 10.4 The Boyer-Moore algorithm

Example 3 The d table for the pattern *abracadabra* is

```
d['a'] = 0    d['b'] = 2    d['c'] = 6    d['d'] = 4    d['r'] = 1
```

and the value for any other character is 11.

Both shifts can be precomputed based solely on the pattern and the alphabet. Hence, the space needed is $m + c + O(1)$. Given these two shift functions, the algorithm chooses the larger one. The same shift strategy can be applied after a match. In Knuth et al. (1977) the preprocessing of the pattern is shown to be linear in the size of the pattern, as it is for the KMP algorithm. However, their algorithm is incorrect. The corrected version can be found in Rytter's paper (1980; see Figure 10.5).

```
initd( pat, m, d ) /* Preprocess pattern of length m : d table */
char pat[];
int m, d[];
{
    int k;

    for( k=0;  k = MAX_ALPHABET_SIZE;  k++ )  d[k] = m;
    for( k=1;  k<=m;  k++ )  d[pat[k]] = m-k;
}
initdd( pat, m, dd ) /* Preprocess pattern of length m : dd hat table */
char pat[];
int m, dd[];
{
    int j, k, t, t1, q, q1;
    int f[MAX_PATTERN_SIZE+1];

    for( k=1;  k<=m;  k++ )  dd[k] = 2*m-k;
    for( j=m, t=m+1;  j > 0;  j--, t-- )      /* setup the dd hat table */
    {
        f[j] = t;
        while( t <= m && pat[j] != pat[t] )
        {
            dd[t] = min( dd[t], m-j );
            t = f[t];
        }
    }
    q = t;  t = m + 1 - q;  q1 = 1;  /* Rytter's correction */
    for( j=1, t1=0;  j <= t;  t1++, j++ )
    {
        f[j] = t1;
        while( t1 >= 1 && pat[j] != pat[t1] )  t1 = f[t1];
    }
    while( q < m )
    {
        for( k=q1;  k<=q;  k++ )  dd[k] = min( dd[k], m+q-k );
        q1 = q + 1;  q = q + t - f[t];  t = f[t];
    }
}
```

Figure 10.5 Preprocessing of the pattern in the Boyer-Moore algorithm

Knuth et al. (1977) have shown that, in the worst case, the number of comparisons is $O(n + rm)$, where r is the total number of matches. Hence, this algorithm can be as bad as the naive algorithm when we have many matches, namely, $\Omega(n)$ matches. A simpler alternative proof can be found in a paper by Guibas and Odlyzko (1980). In the best case $C_n = n/m$. Our simulation results agree well with the emprical and theoretical results in the original Boyer-Moore paper (1977). Some experiments in a distributed environment are presented by Moller-Nielsen and Straunstrup (1984). A variant of the BM algorithm when m is similar to n is given by Iyengar and Alia (1980). Boyer-Moore type algorithms to search a set of strings are presented by Commentz-Walter (1979) and Baeza-Yates and Regnier (1990).

To improve the worst case, Galil (1979) modifies the algorithm so that it remembers how many overlapping characters it can have between two successive matches. That is, we compute the length, ℓ, of the longest proper prefix that is also a suffix of the pattern. Then, instead of going from m to 1 in the comparison loop, the algorithm goes from m to k, where $k = \ell - 1$ if the last event was a match, or $k = 1$ otherwise. For example, $\ell = 3$ for the pattern *ababa*. This algorithm is truly linear, with a worst case of $O(n + m)$ comparisons. Recently, Cole (1991) proved that the exact worst case is $3n + O(m)$ comparisons. However, according to empirical results, as expected, it only improves the average case for small alphabets, at the cost of using more instructions. Recently, Apostolico and Giancarco (1986) improved this algorithm to a worst case of $2n - m + 1$ comparisons.

10.5.1 The Simplified Boyer-Moore Algorithm

A simplified version of the Boyer-Moore algorithm (simplified-Boyer-Moore, or SBM, algorithm) is obtained by using only the occurrence heuristic. The main reason behind this simplification is that, in practice, patterns are not periodic. Also, the extra space needed decreases from $O(m + c)$ to $O(c)$. That is, the space depends only on the size of the alphabet (almost always fixed) and not on the length of the pattern (variable). For the same reason, it does not make sense to write a simplified version that uses Galil's improvement because we need $O(m)$ space to compute the length of the overlapping characters. Of course, the worst case is now $O(mn)$, but it will be faster on the average.

10.5.2 The Boyer-Moore-Horspool Algorithm

Horspool (1980) presented a simplification of the Boyer-Moore algorithm, and based on empirical results showed that this simpler version is as good as the original Boyer-Moore algorithm. Moreover, the same results show that for almost all pattern lengths this algorithm is better than algorithms that use a hardware instruction to find the occurrence of a designated character.

Horspool noted that when we know that the pattern either matches or does not, any of the characters from the text can be used to address the heuristic table. Based on this, Horspool (1980) improved the SBM algorithm by addressing the occurrence table with the character in the text corresponding to the last character of the pattern. We call this algorithm the Boyer-Moore-Horspool, or BMH, algorithm.

To avoid a comparison when the value in the table is zero (the last character of the pattern), we define the initial value of the entry in the occurrence table, corresponding to the last character in the pattern, as m, and then we compute the occurrence heuristic table for only the first $m - 1$ characters of the pattern. Formally

$$d[x] = \min\{s \mid s = m \text{ or } (1 \leq s < m \text{ and } pattern[m - s] = x)\}$$

Example 4 The *d* table for the pattern *abracadabra* is

```
d['a'] = 3   d['b'] = 2   d['c'] = 6   d['d'] = 4   d['r'] = 1
```

and the value for any other character is 11.

The code for an efficient version of the Boyer-Moore-Horspool algorithm is extremely simple and is presented in Figure 10.6 where MAX_ALPHABET_SIZE is the size of the alphabet. In this algorithm, the order of the comparisons is not relevant, as noted by Baeza-Yates (1989c) and Sunday (1990). Thus, the algorithm compares the pattern from left to right. This algorithm also includes the idea of using the character of the text that corresponds to position *m* + 1 of the pattern, a modification due to Sunday (1990). Further improvements are due to Hume and Sunday (1990).

```
bmhsearch( text, n, pat, m )   /* Search pat[1..m] in text[1..n] */
char text[], pat[];
int n, m;
{
    int d[MAX_ALPHABET_SIZE], i, j, k, lim;

    for( k=0; k<MAX_ALPHABET_SIZE; k++ ) d[k] = m+1; /* Preprocessing */
    for( k=1; k<=m; k++ ) d[pat[k]] = m+1-k;
    pat[m+1] = CHARACTER_NOT_IN_THE_TEXT; /* To avoid having code      */
                                          /* for special case n-k+1=m */
    lim = n-m+1;
    for( k=1; k <= lim; k += d[text[k+m]] ) /* Searching */
    {
        i=k;
        for( j=1; text[i] == pat[j]; j++ ) i++;
        if ( j == m+1 ) Report_match_at_position( k );
    }
    /* restore pat[m+1] if necessary */
}
```

Figure 10.6 The Boyer-Moore-Horspool-Sunday algorithm

Based on empirical and theoretical analysis, the BMH algorithm is simpler and faster than the SBM algorithm, and is as good as the BM algorithm for alphabets of size at least 10. Also, it is not difficult to prove that the expected shift is larger for the BMH algorithm. Improvements to the BMH algorithm for searching in English text are discussed by Baeza-Yates (1989b, 1989a) and Sunday (1990). A hybrid algorithm that combines the BMH and KMP algorithms is proposed by Baeza-Yates (1989c).

Figure 10.7 shows, for the algorithms studied up to this point, the expected number of comparisons per character for random text with $c = 4$. The codes used

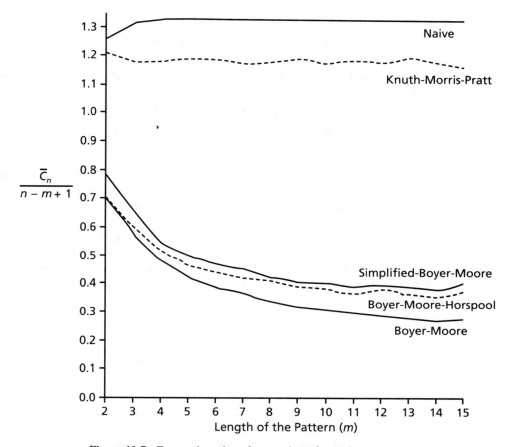

Figure 10.7 Expected number of comparisons for random text ($c = 4$)

are the ones given in this chapter, except that the Knuth-Morris-Pratt algorithm was implemented as suggested by their authors. (The version given here is slower but simpler.)

10.6 THE SHIFT-OR ALGORITHM

The main idea is to represent the state of the search as a number, and is due to Baeza-Yates and Gonnet (1989). Each search step costs a small number of arithmetic and logical operations, provided that the numbers are large enough to represent all possible states of the search. Hence, for small patterns we have an $O(n)$ time algorithm using $O(|\Sigma|)$ extra space and $O(m + |\Sigma|)$ preprocessing time, where Σ denotes the alphabet.

The main properties of the shift-or algorithm are:

- Simplicity: the preprocessing and the search are very simple, and only bitwise logical operations, shifts, and additions are used.
- Real time: the time delay to process one text character is bounded by a constant.
- No buffering: the text does not need to be stored.

It is worth noting that the KMP algorithm is not a real time algorithm, and the BM algorithm needs to buffer the text. All these properties indicate that this algorithm is suitable for hardware implementation.

This algorithm is based on finite automata theory, as the KMP algorithm, and also exploits the finiteness of the alphabet, as in the BM algorithm.

Instead of trying to represent the global state of the search as previous algorithms do, we use a vector of m different states, where state i tells us the state of the search between the positions $1, \ldots, i$ of the pattern and the positions $(j - i + 1), \ldots, j$ of the text, where j is the current position in the text.

We use one bit to represent each individual state, where the state is 0 if the last i characters have matched, or 1 if not. We can then represent the vector state efficiently as a number in base 2 by

$$state = \sum_{i=0}^{m-1} s_{i+1} 2^i$$

where the s_i are the individual states. We report a match if s_m is 0, or equivalently, if $state < 2^{m-1}$. That match ends at the current position.

To update the state after reading a new character in the text, we must:

- shift the vector state 1 bit to the left to reflect that we have advanced one position in the text. In practice, this sets the initial state of s_1 to be 0 by default.
- update the individual states according to the new character. For this we use a table T that is defined by preprocessing the pattern with one entry per alphabet symbol, and the bitwise operator *or* that, given the old vector state and the table value, gives the new state.

Each search step is then:

$$state = (state \ll 1) \; or \; T[curr \; char]$$

where $\ll$ denotes the shift left operation.

The definition of the table T is

$$T_x = \sum_{i=0}^{m-1} \delta(pat_{i+1} = x) 2^i$$

for every symbol x of the alphabet, where $\delta(C)$ is 0 if the condition C is true, and 1 otherwise. Therefore, we need $m \cdot |\Sigma|$ bits of extra memory, but if the word size is at least m, only $|\Sigma|$ words are needed. We set up the table by preprocessing the pattern before the search. This can be done in $O(\lceil \frac{m}{w} \rceil (m + |\Sigma|))$ time.

Example 5 Let $\{a, b, c, d\}$ be the alphabet, and *ababc* the pattern. The entries for table T (one digit per position in the pattern) are then:

$$T[a] = 11010 \quad T[b] = 10101 \quad T[c] = 01111 \quad T[d] = 11111$$

We finish the example by searching for the first occurrence of *ababc* in the text *abdabababc*. The initial state is 11111.

```
text :    a      b      d      a      b      a      b      a      b      c
T[x] :  11010  10101  11111  11010  10101  11010  10101  11010  10101  01111
state:  11110  11101  11111  11110  11101  11010  10101  11010  10101  01111
```

For example, the state 10101 means that in the current position we have two partial matches to the left, of lengths two and four, respectively. The match at the end of the text is indicated by the value 0 in the leftmost bit of the state of the search.

The complexity of the search time in both the worst and average case is $O(\lceil \frac{m}{w} \rceil n)$, where $\lceil \frac{m}{w} \rceil$ is the time to compute a shift or other simple operation on numbers of m bits using a word size of w bits. In practice, for small patterns (word size 32 or 64 bits), we have $O(n)$ time for the worst and the average case.

Figure 10.8 shows an efficient implementation of this algorithm. The programming is independent of the word size insofar as possible. We use the following

```
sosearch( text, n, pat, m )  /* Search pat[1..m] in text[1..n] */
register char *text;
char pat[];
int n, m;
{
    register char *end;
    register unsigned int state, lim;
    unsigned int T[MAXSYM], i, j;
    char *start;

    if( m > WORD )
        Abort( "Use pat size <= word size" );
    for( i=0; i<MAXSYM; i++ ) T[i] = ~0;              /* Preprocessing */
    for( lim=0, j=1, i=1; i<=m; lim |= j, j <<= B, i++ )
        T[pat[i]] &= ~j;
    lim = ~(lim >>B);
    text++; end = text+n+1;                           /* Search */
    state = ~0;                                       /* Initial state */
    for( start=text; text end; text++ )
    {
        state = (state <<B) | T[*text]; /* Next state */
        if( state < lim ) Report_match_at_position( text-start-m+2 );
    }
}
```

Figure 10.8 Shift-Or algorithm for string matching (simpler version)

symbolic constants:

- MAXSYM: size of the alphabet. For example, 128 for ASCII code.
- WORD: word size in bits (32 in our case).
- B: number of bits per individual state; in this case, one.

The changes needed for a more efficient implementation of the algorithm (that is, scan the text until we see the first character of the pattern) are shown in Figure 10.9. The speed of this version depends on the frequency of the first letter of the pattern in the text. The empirical results for this code are shown in Figures 10.11 and 10.12. Another implementation is possible using the bitwise operator *and* instead of the *or* operation, and complementing the value of T_x for all $x \in \Sigma$.

```
initial = ~0; first = pat[1]; start = text; /* Search */
do {
    state = initial;
    do {
        state = (state << B) | T[*text]; /* Next state */
        if( state < lim ) Report_match_at_position( text-start-m+2 );
        text++;
    } while( state != initial );
    while( text < end && *text != first ) /* Scan */
        text++;
} while( text < end );
```

Figure 10.9 Shift-Or algorithm for string matching
*Based on implementation of Knuth, Morris, and Pratt (1977).

By just changing the definition of table T we can search for patterns such that every pattern position is:

- a set of characters (for example, match a vowel),
- a "don't care" symbol (match any character), or
- the complement of a set of characters.

Furthermore, we can have "don't care" symbols in the text. This idea has been recently extended to string searching with errors and other variants by Wu and Manber (1991).

10.7 THE KARP-RABIN ALGORITHM

A different approach to string searching is to use hashing techniques, as suggested by Harrison (1971). All that is necessary is to compute the signature function of each possible m-character substring in the text and check if it is equal to the signature function of the pattern.

Karp and Rabin (1987) found an easy way to compute these signature functions efficiently for the signature function $h(k) = k \bmod q$, where q is a large prime. Their method is based on computing the signature function for position i given the value for position $i - 1$. The algorithm requires time proportional to $n + m$ in almost all cases, without using extra space. Note that this algorithm finds positions in the text that have the same signature value as the pattern. To ensure that there is a match, we must make a direct comparison of the substring with the pattern. This algorithm is probabilistic, but using a large value for q makes collisions unlikely [the probability of a random collision is $O(1/q)$].

Theoretically, this algorithm may still require mn steps in the worst case, if we check each potential match and have too many matches or collisions. In our empirical results we observed only 3 collisions in 10^7 computations of the signature function, using large alphabets.

The signature function represents a string as a base-d number, where $d = c$ is the number of possible characters. To obtain the signature value of the next position, only a constant number of operations is needed. The code for the case $d = 128$ (ASCII) and $q = 16647133$ for a word size of 32 bits, based in Sedgewick's exposition (1983), is given in Figure 10.10 (D $= \log_2 d$ and Q $= q$). By using a power of

```
rksearch( text, n, pat, m )   /* Search pat[1..m] in text[1..n] */
char text[], pat[];           /* (0  m = n)                     */
int n, m;
{
    int h1, h2, dM, i, j;

    dM = 1;
    for( i=1; i<m; i++ ) dM = (dM << D) % Q; /* Compute the signature  */
    h1 = h2 = 0;                             /* of the pattern and of  */
    for( i=1; i<=m; i++ )                    /* the beginning of the   */
    {                                        /* text                   */
        h1 = ((h1 <<  D) +  pat[i] ) % Q;
        h2 = ((h2 <<  D) +  text[i] ) % Q;
    }
    for( i = 1;  i <= n-m+1;  i++ )   /* Search */
    {
        if( h1 == h2 ) /* Potential match */
        {
            for(j=1; j<=m && text[i-1+j] == pat[j]; j++ ); /* check */
            if( j > m )                                    /* true match */
                Report_match_at_position( i );
        }
        h2 = (h2 + (Q << D) - text[i]*dM ) % Q; /* update the signature */
        h2 = ((h2 << D) + text[i+m] ) % Q;      /* of the text */
    }
}
```

Figure 10.10 The Karp-Rabin algorithm

2 for d $(d \geq c)$, the multiplications by d can be computed as shifts. The prime q is chosen as large as possible, such that $(d + 1)q$ does not cause overflow. We also impose the condition that d is a primitive root mod q. This implies that the signature function has maximal cycle; that is

$$\min_{k}(d^k \equiv 1 \pmod{q}) = q - 1$$

Thus, the period of the signature function is much larger than m for any practical case, as shown in Gonnet and Baeza-Yates (1990).

In practice, this algorithm is slow due to the multiplications and the modulus operations. However, it becomes competitive for long patterns. We can avoid the computation of the modulus function at every step by using implicit modular arithmetic given by the hardware. In other words, we use the maximum value of an integer (determined by the word size) for q. The value of d is selected such that d^k mod 2^r has maximal cycle length (cycle of length 2^{r-2}), for r from 8 to 64, where r is the size, in bits, of a word. For example, an adequate value for d is 31.

With these changes, the evaluation of the signature at every step (see Figure 10.10) is

```
h2 = h2*D - text[j-m]*dM + text[i+m]; /* update the signature value */
```

and overflow is ignored. In this way, we use two multiplications instead of one multiplication and two modulus operations.

10.8 CONCLUSIONS

We have presented the most important string searching algorithms. Figure 10.11 shows the execution time of searching 1000 random patterns in random text for all the algorithms considered, with $c = 30$. Based on the empirical results, it is clear that Horspool's variant is the best known algorithm for almost all pattern lengths and alphabet sizes. Figure 10.12 shows the same empirical results as Figure 10.11, but for English text instead of random text. The results are similar. For the shift-or algorithm, the given results are for the efficient version. The results for the Karp-Rabin algorithm are not included because in all cases the time exceeds 300 seconds.

The main drawback of the Boyer-Moore type algorithms is the preprocessing time and the space required, which depends on the alphabet size and/or the pattern size. For this reason, if the pattern is small (1 to 3 characters long) it is better to use the naive algorithm. If the alphabet size is large, then the Knuth-Morris-Pratt algorithm is a good choice. In all the other cases, in particular for long texts, the Boyer-Moore algorithm is better. Finally, the Horspool version of the Boyer-Moore algorithm is the best algorithm, according to execution time, for almost all pattern lengths.

The shift-or algorithm has a running time similar to the KMP algorithm. However, the main advantage of this algorithm is that we can search for more general

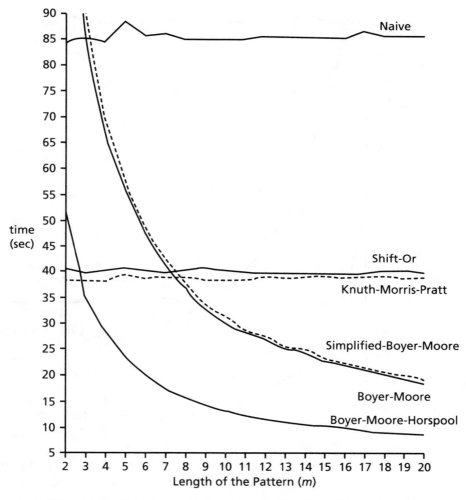

Figure 10.11 Simulation results for all the algorithms in random text ($c = 30$)

patterns ("don't care" symbols, complement of a character, etc.) using exactly the same searching time (see Baeza-Yates and Gonnet [1989]); only the preprocessing is different.

The linear time worst case algorithms presented in previous sections are optimal in the worst case with respect to the number of comparisons (see Rivest [1977]). However, they are not space optimal in the worst case because they use space that depends on the size of the pattern, the size of the alphabet, or both. Galil and Seiferas (1980, 1983) show that it is possible to have linear time worst case algorithms using constant space. (See also Slisenko [1980, 1983].) They also show that

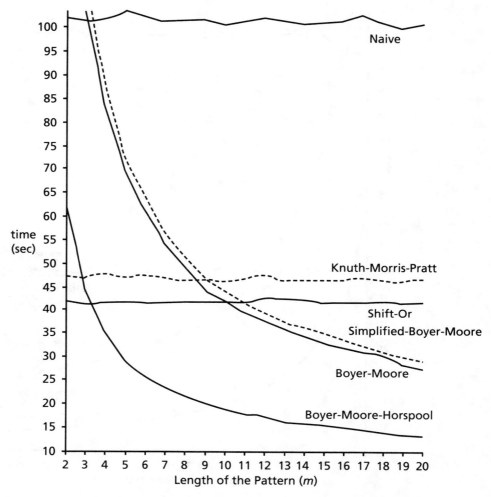

Figure 10.12 Simulation results for all the algorithms in English text

the delay between reading two characters of the text is bounded by a constant, which is interesting for any real time searching algorithms (Galil 1981). Practical algorithms that achieve optimal worst case time and space are presented by Crochemore and Perrin (1988, 1989). Optimal parallel algorithms for string matching are presented by Galil (1985) and by Vishkin (1985). (See also Berkman et al. [1989] and Kedem et al. [1989].)

Many of the algorithms presented may be implemented with hardware (Haskin 1980; Hollaar 1979). For example, Aho and Corasick machines (see Aoe et al. (1985), Cheng and Fu (1987), and Wakabayashi et al. (1985).

If we allow preprocessing of the text, we can search a string in worst case time proportional to its length. This is achieved by using a Patricia tree (Morrison 1968) as an index. This solution needs $O(n)$ extra space and $O(n)$ preprocessing time, where n is the size of the text. See also Weiner (1973), McCreight (1976), Majster and Reiser (1980), and Kemp et al. (1987). For other kinds of indices for text, see Faloutsos (1985), Gonnet (1983), Blumer et al. (1985; 1987). For further references and problems, see Gonnet and Baeza-Yates (1991).

REFERENCES

AHO, A. 1980. "Pattern Matching in Strings," in *Formal Language Theory: Perspectives and Open Problems*, ed. R. Book, pp. 325–47. London: Academic Press.

AHO, A., and M. CORASICK. 1975. "Efficient String Matching: An Aid to Bibliographic Search," *Communications of the ACM*, 18, pp. 333–40.

AOE, J., Y. YAMAMOTO, and R. SHIMADA. 1985. "An Efficient Implementation of Static String Pattern Matching Machines," in *IEEE Int. Conf. on Supercomputing Systems*, vol. 1, pp. 491–98, St. Petersburg, Fla.

APOSTOLICO, A., and R. GIANCARLO. 1986. "The Boyer-Moore-Galil String Searching Strategies Revisited." *SIAM J on Computing*, 15, 98–105.

BAEZA-YATES, R. 1989a. *Efficient Text Searching*. Ph.D. thesis, Dept. of Computer Science, University of Waterloo. Also as Research Report CS-89-17.

BAEZA-YATES, R. 1989b. "Improved String Searching." *Software-Practice and Experience*, 19(3), 257–71.

BAEZA-YATES, R. 1989c. "String Searching Algorithms Revisited," in *Workshop in Algorithms and Data Structures*, F. Dehne, J.-R. Sack, and N. Santoro, eds. pp. 75–96, Ottawa, Canada. Springer Verlag Lecture Notes on Computer Science 382.

BAEZA-YATES, R., and G. GONNET. 1989. "A New Approach to Text Searching," in *Proc. of 12th ACM SIGIR*, pp. 168–75, Cambridge, Mass. (To appear in *Communications of ACM*).

BAEZA-YATES, R., and M. REGNIER. 1990. "Fast Algorithms for Two Dimensional and Multiple Pattern Matching," in *2nd Scandinavian Workshop in Algorithmic Theory, SWAT'90*, R. Karlsson and J. Gilbert. eds. Lecture Notes in Computer Science 447, pp. 332–47, Bergen, Norway: Springer-Verlag.

BAILEY, T., and R. DROMEY. 1980. "Fast String Searching by Finding Subkeys in Subtext." *Inf. Proc. Letters*, 11, 130–33.

BARTH, G. 1981. "An Alternative for the Implementation of Knuth-Morris-Pratt Algorithm." *Inf. Proc. Letters*, 13, 134–37.

BERKMAN, O., D. BRESLAUER, Z. GALIL, B. SCHIEBER, and U. VISHKIN. 1989. "Highly Parellelizable Problems," in *Proc. 20th ACM Symp. on Theory of Computing*, pp. 309–19, Seattle, Washington.

BLUMER, A., J. BLUMER, A. EHRENFEUCHT, D. HAUSSLER, and R. McCONNELL. 1987. "Completed Inverted Files for Efficient Text Retrieval and Analysis". *JACM*, 34, 578–95.

BLUMER, A., J. BLUMER, D. HAUSSLER, A. EHRENFEUCHT, M. CHEN, and J. SEIFERAS. 1985. "The Smallest Automaton Recognizing the Subwords of a Text. *Theoretical Computer Science*, 40, 31–55.

BOYER, R., and S. MOORE. 1977. "A Fast String Searching Algorithm." *CACM*, 20, 762–72.

CHENG, H., and K. FU. 1987. "Vlsi Architectures for String Matching and Pattern Matching." *Pattern Recognition*, 20, 125–41.

COLE, R. 1991. "Tight Bounds on the Complexity of the Boyer-Moore String Matching Algorithm, 2nd Symp. on Discrete Algorithms," pp. 224–33, *SIAM*, San Francisco, Cal.

COMMENTZ-WALTER, B. 1979. "A String Matching Algorithm Fast on the Average," in *ICALP, Lecture Notes in Computer Science* 71, pp. 118–32. Springer-Verlag.

CROCHEMORE, M. 1988. "String Matching with Constraints," in *Mathematical Foundations of Computer Science*, Carlesbad, Czechoslovakia. Lecture Notes in Computer Science 324. Springer-Verlag.

CROCHEMORE, M., and D. PERRIN. 1988. "Pattern Matching in Strings," in *4th Conference on Image Analysis and Processing*, ed. D. Gesu. pp. 67–79. Springer-Verlag.

CROCHEMORE, M., and D. PERRIN. 1989. "Two Way Pattern Matching." Technical Report 98-8, L.I.T.P., University. Paris 7 (submitted for publication).

DAVIES, G., and S. BOWSHER. 1986. "Algorithms for Pattern Matching." *Software–Practice and Experience*, 16, 575–601.

FALOUTSOS, C. 1985. "Access Methods for Text." *ACM C. Surveys*, 17, 49–74.

GALIL, Z. 1979. "On Improving the Worst Case Running Time of the Boyer-Moore String Matching Algorithm. *CACM*, 22, 505–08.

GALIL, Z. 1981. "String Matching in Real Time." *JACM*, 28, 134–49.

GALIL, Z. 1985. "Optimal Parallel Algorithms for String Matching." *Information and Control*, 67, 144–57.

GALIL, Z., and J. SEIFERAS. 1980. "Saving Space in Fast String-Matching." *SIAM J on Computing*, 9, 417–38.

GALIL, Z., and J. SEIFERAS. 1983. "Time-Space-Optimal String Matching." *JCSS*, 26, 280–94.

GONNET, G. 1983. "Unstructured Data Bases or Very Efficient Text Searching," in *ACM PODS*, vol. 2, pp. 117–24, Atlanta, Ga.

GONNET, G., and R. BAEZA-YATES. 1990. "An Analysis of the Karp-Rabin String Matching Algorithm. *Information Processing Letters*, pp. 271–74.

GONNET, G. H., and BAEZA-YATES, R. 1991. "Handbook of Algorithms and Data Structures," 2nd Edition, Addison-Wesley.

GUIBAS, L., and A. ODLYZKO. 1980. "A New Proof of the Linearity of the Boyer-Moore String Searching Algorithm. *SIAM J on Computing*, 9, 672–82.

HARRISON, M. 1971. "Implementation of the Substring Test by Hashing." *CACM*, 14, 777–79.

HASKIN, R. 1980. "Hardware for Searching Very Large Text Databases," in *Workshop Computer Architecture for Non-Numeric Processing*, vol. 5, pp. 49–56, California.

HOLLAAR, L. 1979. "Text Retrieval Computers." *IEEE Computer*, 12, 40–50.

HORSPOOL, R. N. 1980. "Practical Fast Searching in Strings." *Software—Practice and Experience,* 10, 501–06.

HUME, A., and D. M. SUNDAY. 1991. "Fast String Searching." AT&T Bell Labs Computing Science Technical Report No. 156. To appear in Software-Practice and Experience.

IYENGAR, S., and V. ALIA. 1980. "A String Search Algorithm." *Appl. Math. Comput.,* 6, 123–31.

KARP, R., and M. RABIN. 1987. "Efficient Randomized Pattern-Matching Algorithms. *IBM J Res. Development*, 31, 249–60.

KEDEM, Z., G. LANDAU, and K. PALEM. 1989. "Optimal Parallel Suffix-Prefix Matching Algorithm and Applications," in *SPAA'89*, Santa Fe, New Mexico.

KEMP, M., R. BAYER, and U. GUNTZER. 1987. "Time Optimal Left to Right Construction of Position Trees." *Acta Informatica*, 24, 461–74.

KERNIGHAN, B., and D. RITCHIE. 1978. *The C Programming Language.* Englewood Cliffs, N.J.: Prentice Hall.

KNUTH, D., J. MORRIS, and V. PRATT. 1977. "Fast Pattern Matching in Strings." *SIAM J on Computing,* 6, 323–50.

MAJSTER, M., and A. REISER. 1980. "Efficient On-Line Construction and Correction of Position Trees." *SIAM J on Computing,* 9, 785–807.

MCCREIGHT, E. 1976. "A Space-Economical Suffix Tree Construction Algorithm." *JACM*, 23, 262–72.

MEYER, B. 1985. "Incremental String Matching." *Inf. Proc. Letters*, 21, 219–27.

MOLLER-NIELSEN, P., and J. STAUNSTRUP. 1984. "Experiments with a Fast String Searching Algorithm." *Inf. Proc. Letters,* 18, 129–35.

MORRIS, J., and V. PRATT. 1970. "A Linear Pattern Matching Algorithm." Technical Report 40, Computing Center, University of California, Berkeley.

MORRISON, D. 1968. "PATRICIA-Practical Algorithm to Retrieve Information Coded in Alphanumeric." *JACM*, 15, 514–34.

RIVEST, R. 1977. "On the Worst-Case Behavior of String-Searching Algorithms." *SIAM J on Computing,* 6, 669–74.

RYTTER, W. 1980. "A Correct Preprocessing Algorithm for Boyer-Moore String-Searching." *SIAM J on Computing,* 9, 509–12.

SCHABACK, R. 1988. "On the Expected Sublinearity of the Boyer-Moore Algorithm." *SIAM J on Computing*, 17, 548–658.

SEDGEWICK, R. 1983. *Algorithms.* Reading, Mass.: Addison-Wesley.

SLISENKO, A. 1980. "Determination in Real Time of all the Periodicities in a Word." *Sov. Math. Dokl.,* 21, 392–95.

SLISENKO, A. 1983. "Detection of Periodicities and String-Matching in Real Time." *J. Sov. Math.*, 22, 1316–86.

SMIT, G. 1982. "A Comparison of Three String Matching Algorithms." *Software–Practice and Experience*, 12, 57–66.

SUNDAY, D. 1990. "A Very Fast Substring Search Algorithm." *Communications of the ACM*, 33(8), 132–42.

TAKAOKA, T. 1986. "An On-Line Pattern Matching Algorithm." *Inf. Proc. Letters*, 22, 329–30.

VISHKIN, U. 1985. "Optimal Parallel Pattern Matching in Strings." *Information and Control*, 67, 91–113.

WAKABAYASHI, S., T. KIKUNO, and N. YOSHIDA. 1985. "Design of Hardware Algorithms by Recurrence Relations." *Systems and Computers in Japan*, 8, 10–17.

WEINER, P. 1973. "Linear Pattern Matching Algorithm," in *FOCS*, vol. 14, pp. 1–11.

WU, S., and U. MANBER. 1991. "Fast Text Searching With Errors." Technical Report TR-91-11, Department of Computer Science, University of Arizona. To appear in Proceedings of USENIX Winter 1992 Conference, San Francisco, January, 1992.

11

Relevance Feedback and Other Query Modification Techniques

Donna Harman

National Institute of Standards and Technology

Abstract

This chapter presents a survey of relevance feedback techniques that have been used in past research, recommends various query modification approaches for use in different retrieval systems, and gives some guidelines for the efficient design of the relevance feedback component of a retrieval system.

11.1 INTRODUCTION

Even the best of the information retrieval systems have a limited recall; users may retrieve a few relevant documents in response to their queries, but almost never all the relevant documents. In many cases this is not important to users, but in those cases where high recall is critical, users seldom have many ways to retrieve more relevant documents. As a first choice they can "expand" their search by broadening a narrow Boolean query or by looking further down a ranked list of retrieved documents. Often this is wasted effort: a broad Boolean search pulls in too many unrelated documents and the tail of a ranked list of documents contains documents matching mostly less discriminating query terms. The second choice for these users is to modify the original query. Very often, however, this becomes a random operation in that users have already made their best effort at a statement of the problem in the original query and are uncertain as to what modification(s) may be useful.

Users often input queries containing terms that do not match the terms used to index the majority of the relevant documents (either controlled or full text indexing) and almost always some of the unretrieved relevant documents are indexed by a different set of terms than those in the query or in most of the other relevant documents. This problem has long been recognized as a major difficulty in information retrieval systems (Lancaster 1969). More recently, van Rijsbergen (1986) spoke of the limits of providing increasingly better ranked results based solely on the initial query, and indicated a need to modify that query to further increase performance.

The vast majority of research in the area of relevance feedback and automatic query modification has dealt with a ranking model of retrieval systems, although some of this work has been adapted for the Boolean model. This chapter will deal almost exclusively with feedback and query modification based on the ranking model, and readers are referred to a special issue of *Information Processing and Management* (Radecki 1988) for discussion of relevance feedback and query modification in Boolean models. Because relevance feedback is strongly related to ranking, readers unfamiliar with basic ranking models should read Chapter 14 before this chapter.

Two components of relevance feedback have evolved in research. First, extensive work has been done in the reweighting of query terms based on the distribution of these terms in the relevant and nonrelevant documents retrieved in response to those queries. This work forms the basis of the probabilistic model for ranking (see Chapter 14 on Ranking Algorithms for a description of this model). Specifically it has been shown that query terms appearing in relevant documents should have increased term weights for later searching (and conversely terms in nonrelevant documents should have decreased term weights). The details of this reweighting appear later in this chapter. Note that this is a very similar idea to traditional feedback in cybernetics or in biologically based systems such as neural networks.

A second component of relevance feedback or query modification is based on changing the actual terms in the query. Whereas query reweighting will increase the ranks of unretrieved documents that contain the reweighted terms, it provides no help for unretrieved relevant documents containing terms that do not match the original query terms. Various methods of query expansion have been tried and these methods are discussed later in the chapter.

This chapter on relevance feedback is organized as follows. Section 11.2 is a discussion of the research in the area of relevance feedback and query modification, starting with early research in the SMART environment, discussing problems in evaluation, and then reviewing research using the two different components of relevance feedback: the reweighting of query terms and the addition of new query terms. The final part of section 11.2 describes research experiments involving other types of relevance feedback. Section 11.3 reviews the use of relevance feedback and query modification in operational retrieval systems, mostly in experimental prototypes. Section 11.4 contains recommendations for the use of relevance feedback in Boolean systems, in systems based on vector space search models, and in systems based on probabilistic indexing or ad hoc combinations of term-weighting schemes. Section 11.5 presents some thoughts on constructing efficient relevance feedback operations, an area that has received little actual experimental work, and section 11.6 summarizes the chapter.

11.2 RESEARCH IN RELEVANCE FEEDBACK AND QUERY MODIFICATION

11.2.1 Early Research

In their forward-looking paper published in 1960, Maron and Kuhns mentioned query modification, suggesting that terms closely related to the original query terms can be added to the query and thus retrieve more relevant documents. Relevance feedback was the subject of much experimentation in the early SMART system (Salton 1971). In 1965 Rocchio published (republished as Rocchio 1971) some experiments in query modification that combined term reweighting and query expansion. Based on what is now known as the vector space model (for more on the vector space model, see Chapter 14 on Ranking Algorithms), he defined the modified query to be

$$Q_1 = Q_0 + \frac{1}{n_1} \sum_{i=1}^{n_1} R_i - \frac{1}{n_2} \sum_{i=1}^{n_2} S_i$$

where

Q_0 = the vector for the initial query
R_i = the vector for relevant document i
S_i = the vector for nonrelevant document i
n_1 = the number of relevant documents
n_2 = the number of nonrelevant documents

Q_1 therefore is the vector sum of the original query plus the vectors of the relevant and nonrelevant documents. Using this as the basic relation, he suggested possible additional constraints such as extra weighting for the original query, or limits to the amount of feedback from nonrelevant documents. He ran a variation of the basic formula on a very small test collection, constraining the feedback by only allowing terms to be in Q_1 if they either were in Q_0 or occurred in at least half the relevant documents and in more relevant than nonrelevant documents. The results of these experiments were very positive.

In 1969 Ide published a thesis based on a series of experiments extending Rocchio's work, again using the SMART system (Ide 1971). She not only verified the positive results of Rocchio, but developed three particular strategies that seemed to be the most successful. The first was the basic Rocchio formula, minus the normalization for the number of relevant and nonrelevant documents. The second strategy was similar, but allowed only feedback from relevant documents, and the third strategy (Ide dec hi) allowed limited negative feedback from only the highest-ranked nonrelevant document. She found no major significant difference between performance of the three strategies on average, but found that the relevant only strategies worked best for some queries, and other queries did better using negative feedback in addition.

Although the early SMART work was done with small collections, it provided clear evidence of the potential power of this technique. Additionally it defined some of the major problems in the area of evaluation (Hall and Weiderman 1967; Ide 1969). These are discussed in the next section because the evaluation problem has continued to plague feedback research, with the use of inappropriate evaluation procedures often indicating performance gains using feedback that are unrealistic.

11.2.2 Evaluation of Relevance Feedback

Standard evaluation in information retrieval (Salton and McGill 1983) compares recall-precision figures generated from averaging the performance in individual queries and comparing this averaged performance across different retrieval techniques. If this evaluation method is used in a simplistic manner in comparing the results after one iteration of feedback against those using no feedback, the results generally show spectacular improvement. Unfortunately, a significant part of this improvement results from the relevant documents used to reweight the query terms moving to higher ranks (e.g., documents initially ranked at 1, 4, and 8 moving to ranks 1, 2, and 4). Not only is this an unrealistic evaluation because presumably the user has already seen these documents, but it also masks any real improvement in relevant document ranks below those initially shown the user.

There were several more realistic methods of evaluation tried (Salton 1970) but a de facto standard (the residual collection method) has since been used for most research. In this method the initial run is made and the user is shown the top x documents. These documents are then used for relevance feedback purposes. The evaluation of the results compares only the residual collections, that is, the initial run is remade minus the documents previously shown the user and this is compared with the feedback run minus the same documents. This method provides an unbiased and more realistic evaluation of feedback. However, because highly ranked relevant documents have been removed from the residual collection, the recall-precision figures are generally lower than those for standard evaluation methods and cannot be directly compared with performance as measured by the standard evaluation method.

11.2.3 Research in Term Reweighting without Query Expansion

The probabilistic model proposed by Robertson and Sparck Jones (1976) is based on the distribution of query terms in relevant and nonrelevant documents (for more on the probabilistic model, see Chapter 14). They developed a formula for query term-weighting that relies entirely on this distribution.

$$W_{ij} = \log_2 \frac{\dfrac{r}{R - r}}{\dfrac{n - r}{N - n - R + r}}$$

where

W_{ij} = the term weight for term i in query j
r = the number of relevant documents for query j having term i
R = the total number of relevant documents for query j
n = the number of documents in the collection having term i
N = the number of documents in the collection

Note that this weighting method assumes that all relevant documents are known before a query is submitted, a situation not in itself realistic, but suggestive of a method of relevance feedback after some knowledge is gained about relevance (especially for use in SDI services). Robertson and Sparck Jones used this formula to get significantly better retrieval performance for the manually indexed Cranfield 1400 collection, employing an acceptable alternative method of evaluation (the test and control method).

Sparck Jones (1979a) extended this experiment to a larger collection and again showed significant improvements. She also performed an experiment (1979b) to simulate the use of this relevance weighting formula in an operational relevance feedback situation in which a user sees only a few relevant documents in the initial set of retrieved documents, and those few documents are the only ones available to the weighting scheme. These experiments required adding a constant to the above formula to handle situations in which query terms appeared in none of the retrieved relevant documents. The results from this reweighting with only a few relevant documents still showed significant performance improvements over weighting using only the IDF measure (Sparck Jones 1972; see Chapter 14 on Ranking Algorithms for a definition of IDF), indicating that the probabilistic weighting schemes provide a useful method for relevance feedback, especially in the area of term reweighting.

Croft (1983) extended this weighting scheme both by suggesting effective initial search methods (Croft and Harper 1979) using probabilistic indexing and by adapting the weighting using the probabilistic model to handle within-document frequency weights.

Initial search $\qquad W_{ijk} = (C + IDF_i) * f_{ik}$

Feedback $\qquad W_{ijk} = \left(C + \log \dfrac{p_{ij}(1 - q_{ij})}{(1 - p_{ij})q_{ij}} \right) * f_{ik}$

where

W_{ijk} = the term weight for term i in query j and document k
IDF_1 = the IDF weight for term i in the entire collection
p_{ij} = the probability that term i is assigned within the set of relevant documents for query j

$$p_{ij} = \frac{r + 0.5}{R + 1.0} \text{ when } r > 0$$

$$= 0.01 \quad \text{when } r = 0$$

q_{ij} = the probability that term i is assigned within the set of nonrelevant documents for query j

$$q_{ij} = \frac{n - r + 0.5}{N - R + 1.0}$$

r = the number of relevant documents for query j having term i
R = the total number of relevant documents for query j
n = the number of documents in the collection having term i
N = the number of documents in the collection

$$f_{ik} = K + (1 - K) \frac{freq_{ik}}{maxfreq_k}$$

where
$freq_{ik}$ = the frequency of term i in document k
$maxfreq_k$ = the maximum frequency of any term in document k

Two constants, C and K, allow this scheme to be adjusted to handle different types of data. Croft and Harper (1979) found that for the manually indexed Cranfield collection, C needed to dominate the initial search because the mere assignment of an index term to a document implied the importance of that term to that document. For automatically indexed collections, the importance of a term is better measured by the IDF alone, with C set to 0 for the initial search. Croft (1983) found that the best value for K was 0.3 for the automatically indexed Cranfield collection, and 0.5 for the NPL collection, confirming that within-document term frequency plays a much smaller role in the NPL collection with its short documents having few repeating terms. When K is used in the subsequent feedback runs, the optimum value increases to 0.5 for Cranfield and 0.7 for NPL. This could reflect the improved weighting for term importance within an entire collection using the relevance weighting instead of the IDF, requiring a lesser role for within-document frequency weighting.

The results of this new weighting scheme with optimal C and K settings showed improvements in the automatically indexed Cranfield collection of up to 35 percent over weighting using only the term distribution in the initial set of relevant and nonrelevant documents, although this improvement was somewhat less using the NPL collection where documents are shorter.

It is interesting to note the parallel between the best methods of initial searching and the results of adding within-document frequency weighting to the probabilistic weighting. In the initial searching it was shown (see Chapter 14) that it is important in most situations to weight the terms both by a measure of their importance in a collection (such as using the IDF measure) and by a measure of their importance within a given document. Harman (1986) suggested that these two measures are complementary and that combining them provided improvements roughly analogous to adding the improvements found by using each measure separately. Probabilistic weighting affects only the importance of a term within a collection for a given query; the importance of that term within a given document can only be measured by some function of its frequency within that document, and therefore it should be expected that including both weighting components produces the best results.

Other models of probabilistic indexing have been proposed (or re-evaluated) recently; in particular see Fuhr (1989) and Wong and Yao (1990).

11.2.4 Query Expansion without Term Reweighting

If a query has retrieved no relevant documents or if the terms in the query do not match the terms in the relevant documents not yet retrieved, it becomes critical to expand the query. The early SMART experiments both expanded the query and reweighted the query terms by adding the vectors of the relevant and nonrelevant documents. However, it is possible to expand a query without reweighting terms.

Ideally, query expansion should be done using a thesaurus that adds synonyms, broader terms, and other appropriate words. The manually constructed thesaurus needed for this is seldom available, however, and many attempts have been made to automatically create one. Most of these involve term-term associations or clustering techniques. As these techniques are discussed in Chapter 16 on clustering, only the results will be briefly described here.

Lesk (1969) tried several variations of term-term clustering using the SMART system and had little success. The fact that term co-occurrence is used to generate these thesauri implies that most terms entering the thesaurus occur in the same documents as the seed or initial term (especially in small collections), and this causes the same set of documents to be retrieved using these related terms, only with a higher rank. Not only does this cause little overall improvement, but that improvement is only in the precision of the search rather than in increasing recall.

Sparck Jones and Barber (1971) also tried term-term clustering. Again they did not get much improvement and found that it was critical to limit the query expansion to only those terms strongly connected to initial query terms, with no expansion of high-frequency terms, to avoid any degradation in performance. These results were confirmed by Minker, Wilson, and Zimmerman (1972) who found no significant improvement in relevant document retrieval, with degradations in performance often occurring.

Harman (1988) used a variation of term-term association (the nearest neighbor technique) and found similar results, with no improvement and with less degradation when adding only the top connected terms and no high-frequency terms. She suggested that users could "filter" the new query terms, that is, show users a list of suggested additional query terms and ask them to select appropriate ones. In a simulation assuming a perfect user selection, however, the improvements were only 8.7 percent using the automatically indexed Cranfield collection. By comparison, applying a similar user filtering process with a selection of terms from relevant documents provided an improvement of over 16 percent, almost twice that for term-term clustering techniques.

Because the area of automatic thesaurus building is so intuitively appealing, work still continues. Crouch (1988) presented preliminary results of another term-term correlation study, and Guntzer et al. (1989) is currently working on a semi-automatic method to construct a thesaurus based on actual term usage in queries. Two additional promising methods involve the use of highly structured networks. Belew (1989) described a rich connectionist representation which was modified based on retrieval experience, and Dumais (1990) used an elaborate factor analysis method called latent semantic indexing to expand queries.

It is also possible to provide query expansion using terms from the relevant documents without term reweighting. As mentioned earlier, Harman (1988) produced lists of terms from relevant documents using several methods of ranking those terms. These terms were then automatically added to the query. She found significant differences between the ranking methods, with techniques involving a combination of the normalized noise measure (similar to the IDF; see Chapter 14 on Ranking Algorithms) with the total frequency of the term within the set of relevant documents outperforming simple sorts based only on the number of relevant documents containing the term. She also found that adding too many terms from a sorted list decreased performance, with the best performance for the Cranfield collection occurring after adding about 20 terms, and slightly worse performance both for higher than 20 terms and for only 10 terms. As a third part of the experiment, it was shown that using a simulated perfect user selection from the top 20 terms produced a 31 percent improvement over methods with no user selection. Several on-line retrieval systems have also used this approach of showing users sorted term lists (see section 11.3).

11.2.5 Query Expansion with Term Reweighting

The vast amount of relevance feedback and query expansion research has been done using both query expansion and term-reweighting. The early SMART experiments (see section 11.2.1) added term vectors to effectively reweight the query terms and to expand the query. Researchers using probabilistic indexing techniques for reweighting also tried some specific experiments in query expansion.

Harper and van Rijsbergen (1978) used the probabilistic model to reweight query terms, using all relevant document information for weighting, and expanding the query by adding all terms directly connected to a query term by a maximum spanning tree (MST) technique of term-term clustering. Additionally, they developed a new relevance weighting scheme, the EMIM weighting measure (see Harper 1980 for implementation details of EMIM). This weighting scheme better handles the parameter estimation problem seen in the Robertson-Sparck Jones measure (1976) when a query term appears in no retrieved relevant documents, although it is not as theoretically optimal as the Robertson-Sparck Jones measure. The EMIM weighting scheme with query expansion by MST showed significant improvements (using all relevant documents) over the formula used by Robertson and Sparck Jones. Using only 10 or 20 documents for feedback, the EMIM reweighting with expansion still showed significant improvements over the old formula. It should be noted, however, that two effects are compounded in this experiment: reweighting using an improved weighting scheme (EMIM) and query expansion using a MST technique.

Harper's thesis (1980) elaborated on the area of query expansion and reweighting. Using the EMIM relevance weighting scheme, he tried the same MST expansion on the manually indexed Cranfield 1400 collection, a Cranfield 1400 collection with only titles for documents, and the larger UKCIS2 collection. The improvements for query expansion were much less with the Cranfield titles and the UKCIS2 collection than for the manually indexed Cranfield collection, largely because the MST had much shorter documents to use for expansion. In addition to the expansion using the MST, Harper tried expanding queries using a selection of terms from retrieved relevant documents. He selected these terms by ranking a union of all terms in the retrieved relevant documents using the EMIM measure, and then selecting a given number from the top of this list. He found significant performance improvements for the manually indexed Cranfield collection over that using the MST expansion, but no improvement for the UKCIS2 collection.

Performance improvements for query expansion seem to be heavily dependent on the test collection being used. The Cranfield collection, either as manually indexed, or with automatically indexed abstracts, consistently shows performance improvements for query expansion, either using the MST method or expanding by terms from relevant documents. Collections with short documents such as the Cranfield title collection or the UKCIS collection probably do not provide enough terms to make expansion effective. A further example of this effect is shown in Smeaton and van Rijsbergen (1983), where a very extensive number of different query expansion methods showed no improvements when run using the NPL test collection, a collection having documents indexed by only 20 terms apiece on the average.

Wu and Salton (1981) experimented with term relevance weighting (also known as term precision weighting), a method for reweighting using relevance feedback that is very similar to the Robertson-Sparck Jones formula. They tried reweighting and expanding the query by all the terms from relevant documents. They found a 27 percent improvement in average precision for the small (424 document) Cranfield collection using reweighting alone, with an increase up to 32.7 percent when query expansion was added to reweighting. There was more improvement with the Medlars 450 collection, with 35.6 percent improvement for reweighting alone and 61.4 percent for both reweighting and expansion.

A recent paper by Salton and Buckley (1990) compared twelve different feedback procedures, involving two different levels of query expansion, across six different test collections. The standard three-vector feedback methods were used, in addition to other probabilistic feedback methods. Concentrating only on the vector feedback methods, the three they used were as follows.

$$\textit{Ide Regular} \qquad Q_1 = Q_0 + \sum_{i=1}^{n_1} R_i - \sum_{i=1}^{n_2} S_i$$

$$\text{Ide dec-hi} \qquad Q_1 = Q_0 + \sum_{i=1}^{n_1} R_i - S_i$$

$$\text{Standard Rocchio} \qquad Q_1 = Q_0 + \beta \sum_{i=1}^{n_1} \frac{R_i}{n_1} - \gamma \sum_{i=1}^{n_2} \frac{S_i}{n_2}$$

where

Q_0 = the vector for the initial query
R_i = the vector for relevant document i
S_i = the vector for nonrelevant document i
n_1 = the number of relevant documents
n_2 = the number of nonrelevant documents

The basic operational procedure in these three methods is the merging of document vectors and original query vectors. This automatically reweights query terms by adding the weights from the actual occurrence of those query terms in the relevant documents, and subtracting the weights of those terms occurring in the nonrelevant documents. Queries are automatically expanded by adding all the terms not in the original query that are in the relevant documents and nonrelevant documents, using both positive and negative weights based on whether the terms are coming from relevant or nonrelevant documents (no new terms are actually added with negative weights; the contribution of nonrelevant document terms is to modify the weighting of new terms coming from relevant documents). The Ide dec-hi method only uses the top nonrelevant document for feedback, instead of all nonrelevant documents retrieved within the first set shown the user. The Rocchio method both allows adjustment for the relative input of relevant and nonrelevant documents and uses a weighting scheme based on a normalized version of the document weights rather than the actual document weights themselves.

The results favored the Ide dec-hi method for all six collections, although the other methods follow closely behind. Setting $\gamma = 0.25$ and $\beta = 0.75$ for the Rocchio method created the best results, limiting the effects of negative feedback. These results confirm earlier work on the smaller collections by the SMART project in which Ide found no major significant difference between performance of the three strategies on average, but found that the "relevant only" strategies worked best for some queries, and other queries did better using negative feedback in addition.

Two types of document weighting were used in these experiments: a binary weighting and weighting done using the best SMART weighting schemes involving a combination of within-document frequencies of terms and the IDF measure for these terms. It was concluded that using appropriate term weighting for the documents (as opposed to binary weighting schemes) is important for most collections. This agrees with Croft's results (1983) using within-document frequencies in addition to reweighting by term distribution in relevant and nonrelevant documents. They also found differences in performance across test collections and suggested that the types of data to be used in retrieval should be examined in selecting feedback and query expansion mechanisms (see Section 4 on Recommendations for Use of Relevance Feedback).

11.2.6 Other Research in Relevance Feedback

Noreault (1979) tried an entirely different approach to relevance feedback. After users had selected a relevant document(s), he used this (these) document(s) as a "new query," effectively ranking (using the cosine correlation as implemented in the SIRE system) all the documents in the collection against this document(s). The top 30 of these retrieved documents were then added to those initially selected by the original query. He found on average that this added 5.1 new relevant documents per query. This feedback method would work with any type of retrieval system such as Boolean systems, provided some method existed for selecting related documents, as the query itself is not modified during the retrieval process.

Attar and Fraenkel (1981) used an approach based on local feedback only. They produced an ordered list of the terms in all the documents retrieved in a first iteration search, with the list ordered by the frequency of a term in that set and by its "distance" from the initial query. These terms were shown to a user for selection as new query terms or sifted by an automatic procedure for addition to the query. They found that both expert and nonexpert users could correctly select terms from the suggested list, but that their automatic sifting mechanism could not do this well. Note that terms are selected from all retrieved documents, not just relevant ones, so that this technique could be used as a feedback technique for queries retrieving no relevant documents on the first iteration.

Dillon et al. (1983) used a hybrid approach to provide relevance feedback to a Boolean environment. They devised a new query based only on terms from previously retrieved documents, with terms weighted by a formula similar to the term precision formula used by Salton (but with significant differences). The weighted terms were not used, however, to produce a ranked list of retrieved documents, but were used to automatically construct a revised Boolean query. Results suggest that this method can be effective if very careful attention is paid to the construction of the revised Boolean query.

11.3 USE OF RELEVANCE FEEDBACK IN ON-LINE RETRIEVAL SYSTEMS

One of the earliest (and few) applications of relevance feedback in an operational system was by Vernimb (1977) in the European Nuclear Documentation System (ENDS). This system has an automatic procedure based on a user/system dialogue, removing the need for a user to deal with a Boolean retrieval system. The starting position for this approach is at least two relevant documents, either obtained by a manual search, or by any type of search using a Boolean or ranking retrieval system. The ENDS system then automatically constructs a Boolean query using an elaborate procedure based on the co-occurrence of terms in these known relevant documents, and the user is shown a new set of documents for another iteration of relevance judgments and automatic query adjustments. This procedure is further modified by a term-weighting scheme based on the SMART model that allows the list of documents shown the user to be ranked based on occurrences of terms in the set of relevant documents versus the set of nonrelevant documents. The users of this system found it very satisfactory, and some limited experimental results showed that its performance was considerably better than traditional procedures (such as traditional Boolean retrieval).

Another type of man-machine dialogue using relevance feedback was developed by Oddy (1977) in his THOMAS system. Although this system was purely experimental, it was designed to be a prototype system for the end-user and therefore resembles an on-line retrieval system more than a system designed for retrieval experiments. In this system the user inputs a natural language phrase or sentence and the system returns a single reference based on a search in the concept network (a network built by the MEDUSA system at the University of Newcastle for access to MEDLARS records). This reference contains both a list of authors of the reference and a list of index terms associated with that reference. The user is asked to not only judge the relevance of that reference, but to select index terms that are relevant (or optionally insert new index terms). The query is appropriately modified by the system and a new reference is sought. This type of query modification allows users to browse the references and, although it is not as automatic as the ENDS system, it gives a user more explicit control over the browsing process.

The CUPID system (Porter 1982) implemented the probabilistic retrieval model at the University of Cambridge. This system takes a natural language query, returns a ranked list of titles, and asks the user for relevance judgments. These judgments are used for two distinct purposes: (1) to reweight the original query terms using the Robertson-Sparck Jones reweighting formula, and (2) to select a ranked set of terms from the relevant documents to submit to the user for possible addition to the query. This process can be iterated repeatedly until the user has sufficient information. An improved version of CUPID, the MUSCAT system, is currently running at the Scott Polar Research Institute, Cambridge (Porter and Galpin 1988).

Doszkocs's CITE system (1982) was designed as an interface to MEDLINE and was used as an on-line catalog system (Doszkocs 1983). It combined a ranking retrieval method (see Chapter 14 for more on the CITE system) with an effective search strategy for the huge document files and the controlled and full text vocabulary used in MEDLINE. CITE returned a list of ranked references based on a user's natural language query, and asked for relevance judgments from the user. The system used these judgments to display a ranked list of medical subject headings (ranked by a frequency analysis of their use in the retrieved documents). The user then selected terms for adding to the query and the search was repeated.

Cirt, a front end to a standard Boolean retrieval system, uses term-weighting, ranking, and relevance feedback (Robertson et al. 1986). The system accepts lists of terms without Boolean syntax and converts these terms into alternative Boolean searches for searching on the Boolean system. The user is then shown sets of documents, defined by Boolean combinations of terms, in rank order as specified by a special weighting and ranking algorithm (Bovey and Robertson 1984). If relevance judgments are made, feedback takes the form of appropriately reweighting terms to produce different ranked orders of documents.

Relevance feedback plays a crucial role in the Connection Machine retrieval system (Stanfill and Kahle 1986). Here a query is automatically expanded by adding all the terms in the relevant documents, causing very large queries that can take advantage of the speed offered by the massively parallel architecture. This system relies heavily on co-occurrence of terms and therefore needs large numbers of query terms to work effectively.

Two approaches for query expansion produce lists of related terms in ranked order for user selection and addition to the query. The first approach, the Associative Interactive Dictionary on the TOXLINE system (Doszkocs 1978), does a statistical analysis of the terms appearing in relevant documents in comparison to their appearance in all documents, and displays a list of terms ranked on these statistics. The second, the ZOOM facility of ESA-IRS Online search (Ingwersen 1984), generalizes the first approach to deal with a complete set of retrieved documents. It analyzes the frequency of single words, phrases, or codes appearing in the set of documents, and displays these in order of highest frequency of occurrence for user selection.

11.4 RECOMMENDATIONS FOR USE OF RELEVANCE FEEDBACK

11.4.1 Relevance Feedback Methodologies

It should be stated again that relevance feedback and/or query modification are not necessary for many queries, are of marginal use to many users, and may possibly be of marginal use in some operational systems. Often users are only interested in an "answer" to their question (such as a paragraph in an on-line manual), or in a single good bibliographic reference for introduction to a new area of interest. Some users may never be interested in a high-recall search; others may not be willing to spend any extra effort in retrieving more relevant documents or may be unaware of the low recall of their initial search. An experiment by Fox (1987) showed little use of relevance feedback in a student experiment, probably because it was "not explained adequately" and because the nine test queries did not need further modification.

Some situations call for high recall, however. In a test of a large operational full-text retrieval system (Blair and Maron 1985), only about 20 percent of the relevant documents were retrieved, even though the users thought they had retrieved most of the relevant documents (and felt they needed all the relevant documents).

If a decision is made to offer relevance feedback or some type of query expansion technique, then the appropriate method depends on two issues: the type of retrieval system being used for initial searching, and the type of data that is being used. Three basic retrieval systems are being addressed here: Boolean-based systems, systems based on ranking using a vector space model, and systems based on ranking using either an ad hoc combination of term-weighting schemes or using the probabilistic indexing methods. In terms of data characteristics, two characteristics have been found to be important experimentally: the length of the documents (short or not short), and the type of indexing (controlled or full text). Possibly other factors exist, but there is a lack of direct experimentation about these issues.

Feedback in Boolean retrieval systems

If a Boolean retrieval system is being used, two options seem feasible. The most difficult option would be to modify the system to specially handle relevance feedback either by designing frontends to automatically construct modified Boolean queries (such as was done by Dillon, Vernimb, and the Cirt system), or to graft a ranking system onto the Boolean system to handle all but the initial query (such as done by Noreault). Front-end construction or specially modified Boolean systems (see again the special issue of Information Processing and Management, [Radecki 1988]) require major modifications to the entire system and can be difficult to tune. However, they offer the greatest improvement in performance.

The second option would be to produce ranked lists of terms for user selection (such as the ZOOM feature on ERA-IRS [Ingwersen 1984]). This option leaves the Boolean mechanism intact, but improves the query by suggesting alternative terms and by showing the user the term distribution in the retrieved set of documents. The ranking of the list could be done by term frequency within the entire retrieved set (the simplest method) or by more complex methods taking account of term distribution within only the relevant documents (such as Doszkocs's AID system [Doszkocs 1978]). The first method would be useful in helping a user construct a better query by pointing out the term distribution in the entire retrieved document set (relevant and nonrelevant), and the second method would help a user zero in on new terms by narrowing the term list to only those terms in the relevant documents. Note that the effects of the type of data being used for retrieval are minimal for this type of feedback as user selection is providing the term filter rather than automatic term distribution statistics.

Feedback in retrieval systems based on the vector space model

If the retrieval system is based on the vector space model using a cosine correlation as a ranking measure, then the feedback methods developed in the SMART project are appropriate. As discussed earlier, the vector space model automatically combines the two components of feedback, term reweighting and query expansion, making implementation of relevance feedback more straightforward using this method but somewhat less flexible. Experiments showed that the Ide dec-hi method is the best general purpose feedback technique for the vector space model. It uses minimal negative feedback and can be implemented without concern for deciding parameter settings.

$$Ide\ dec\text{-}hi \qquad Q_1 = Q_0 + \sum_{i=1}^{n_1} R_i - S$$

where

Q_0 = the vector for the initial query
R_i = the vector for relevant document i
S = the vector for top nonrelevant document

The use of normalized vector space document weighting is highly recommended for most data rather than binary weighting schemes (see section 14.5 of Chapter 14 for details on these weighting schemes). The only decision to be made using this type of relevance feedback is how much query expansion to allow. Since results suggest that query expansion using all terms from the retrieved relevant documents may be only slightly better than a selection of those terms (Salton and Buckley 1990), it is recommended that only a limited number of terms be added (mainly to improve response time), and that those be chosen based on the criteria presented in that paper. This means that whereas all query terms will be reweighted during query modification, the terms to be added to the query are automatically pulled from a sorted list of new terms taken from relevant documents. These terms are sorted by their total frequency within all retrieved relevant documents, and the number of terms added is the average number of terms in the retrieved relevant documents. A possible alternative to this selection method would be to substitute user selection from the top of the list rather than adding a fixed number of terms.

Feedback in retrieval systems based on other types of statistical ranking

If the retrieval system is based on either the probabilistic indexing model or an ad hoc combination of term-weighting schemes, then the term-weighting and query expansion can be viewed as two separate components of feedback, with no specific relationship.

The term-weighting schemes should be carefully examined to determine the correct method for implementing reweighting based on relevance feedback. As noted earlier, the reweighting schemes only affect the weighting based on the importance of a term within an entire collection (global importance). Term-weighting based on term importance within a given document (local importance, such as those based on normalized within-document frequencies) should not be changed; nor should term-weightings based on document structure or other such considerations. The approach taken by Croft (1983) and described earlier in section 11.2.3 is the recommended model to follow in reweighting methodology, in which he simply replaced the portion of the term-weighting based on global term importance (the IDF in this case) with a revised version of the Robertson-Jones weighting formula.

$$\textit{Initial search} \quad W_{ijk} = (C + IDF_i) * f_{ik}$$

$$\textit{Feedback} \quad W_{ijk} = \left(C + \log \frac{p_{ij}(1 - q_{ij})}{(1 - p_{ij})\, q_{ij}} \right) * f_{ik}$$

where

W_{ijk} = the term weight for term i in query j and document k
IDF_i = the IDF weight for term i in the entire collection
p_{ij} = the probability that term i is assigned within the set of relevant documents for query j

$$p_{ij} = \frac{r + 0.5}{R + 1.0} \quad \textit{when } r > 0$$

$$= 0.01 \quad \textit{when } r = 0$$

q_{ij} = the probability that term i is assigned within the set of nonrelevant documents for query j

$$q_{ij} = \frac{n - r + 0.5}{N - R + 1.0}$$

r = the number of relevant documents for query j having term i
R = the total number of relevant documents for query j
n = the number of documents in the collection having term i
N = the number of documents in the collection

$$f_{ik} = K + (1 - K) \frac{freq_{ik}}{maxfreq_k}$$

where

$freq_{ik}$ = the frequency of term i in document k
$maxfreq_k$ = the maximum frequency of any term in document k

Two adjustable constants, C and K, provide methods for adjusting the weighting scheme for different types of data. Based on the experiments previously reported, a reasonable estimate for C would be 0 for automatically indexed collections or for feedback searching. This allows the IDF or the relevance weighting to be the dominant factor. Only for manually indexed collections should C be set higher to allow the mere existence of a term within a document to carry more weight. The setting of the constant K should be around 0.3 for the initial search of regular length documents (i.e., documents having many multiple occurrences of a term), rising to around 0.5 for feedback searches. This allows the within-document frequency to play a large role in the initial search, and a somewhat diminished role in subsequent searches, where it is assumed that the relevance weighting becomes more and more important. For short documents, the within-document frequency plays a minimal role and should be either removed from the scheme (such as suggested by Salton and Buckley [1990]) or downweighted by setting K from 0.5 to 0.7.

If other weighting schemes based on criteria such as document structure have been used, then it is likely that the overall importance of these schemes in the total weighting needs to be modified in a manner similar to the downweighting of document frequency weights using the constant K. This will depend on the relative importance of these additional weighting schemes with respect to the importance of matching a given keyword, and will require some experimentation in order to properly introduce relevance feedback to these schemes.

The weighting scheme above only affects the ranks of documents containing terms originally in the query. To be truly effective, some type of query expansion needs to be done. Two alternative sources exist for new query terms. First, the query could be expanded by maximal spanning tree or nearest neighbor techniques (or other automatic thesaurus methods), offering users a selection of terms that are the terms most closely related to the individual query terms. These terms should be in a single list, grouped by expanded terms for each query term, with users selecting appropriate terms for addition to the query.

Although this expansion method works even in situations with no relevant documents retrieved, it has been shown that query expansion by related terms is not as effective as expansion by terms from relevant documents. The second alternative method is therefore to present users with a sorted list of terms from the relevant documents, with the list sorted on the total frequency of the given term within the entire set of retrieved relevant documents (possibly modified by the IDF or normalized noise measure of the term), with users selecting appropriate terms for addition to the query.

Whereas user selection is strongly recommended, it would be possible to use either of these query expansion techniques automatically, adding either the top 20 or so terms from a sorted list of terms from the relevant documents, or adding the closest related term using the automatic thesaurus method for each input query term (see Harman 1992).

A somewhat different approach to user term selection is to get more initial input from the user, such as possible related terms, relative importance of query terms, and important grouping of those terms (phrases). Croft and Das (1990) showed that using this technique in combination with relevance feedback with user selected terms improved results even more than feedback alone, with only a 35 percent overlap in terms found in relevant documents with those suggested by the users initially.

Care should be taken when using either of the two query expansion methods on collections of short documents such as ones with less than 25 index terms. User selection becomes even more critical in this situation, as it has been shown in the past that these expansion methods are unreliable for short documents, such as titles or very short abstracts.

11.5 SOME THOUGHTS ON THE EFFICIENT IMPLEMENTATION OF RELEVANCE FEEDBACK OR QUERY MODIFICATION

Because of the lack of use of relevance feedback in operational systems in general, little work has been done in achieving efficient implementations for large data sets of the recommended feedback algorithms discussed in section 11.4. This section therefore contains only guidelines for efficient implementations, rather than descriptions of actual implementations that have been fully tested. The first part of the section lists the data and data structure needs for relevance feedback, with discussions of alternative methods of meeting these needs, and the second part of the section contains a proposal expanding the basic ranking system described in section 14.6 of Chapter 14 to include relevance feedback and other query modification.

11.5.1 Data and Structure Requirements for Relevance Feedback and Query Modification

The major data needed by relevance feedback and other query modification techniques is a list of the terms contained in each retrieved document. These terms become input to structures designed for reweighting of query terms and for collecting lists of terms for query expansion. Unfortunately, most of the retrieval systems described in this chapter and Chapter 14 involve the use of inverted files for fast response time. This means that the index lists the documents containing each term, but not the terms contained in each document. For large data sets, this inverted file is the only supplemental file stored because of space issues. The input text is kept for display purposes only, with no lists being kept of all the significant words in each document.

For small collections, lists of the terms within each document can be kept (see Porter [1988] for a description of the necessary structures used in the MUSCAT system). For larger data sets, an alternative method would be to parse the retrieved documents in the background while users are looking at the document titles. Although this may be time consuming, the prototype experience of Harman and Candela (1990) using a background secondary string search on retrieved records indicates that this additional work can be accomplished with minimal effect on response time. Even a slight response time delay for feedback may be preferable to the high overhead of storage needed for the lists of terms in a per document order.

Assuming that these term lists are available, either through past storage or through on-line parsing, a structure needs to be built to merge a list of all terms in relevant documents, keeping track of the total number of postings (documents containing one or more occurrences of the term), and the total frequency of terms within all relevant documents. If negative feedback is used such as in Rocchio's algorithm, then an additional list needs to be kept for nonrelevant documents. These lists could be implemented as sets of sorted lists using some type of binary search and insert algorithm, or using an efficient binary tree method such as the right-threaded tree used in the indexing method described in Chapter 3 on Inverted Files. This structure is the major data structure needed for query term reweighting and for production of lists of sorted terms for query expansion. Suggestions for the use of this structure are given in section 11.5.2.

If some type of automatic thesaurus method is to be used in query expansion, then additional storage may be needed. This storage could be minimized by attaching the closest related term to each term in the dictionary portion of the inverted file (or the closest two or three terms). Alternatively, there could be extensive structures needed for more sophisticated methods using complex interrelationships.

11.5.2 A Proposal for an Efficient Implementation of Relevance Feedback

This proposal is based on the implementation of the ranking system as described in section 14.6 of Chapter 14. It should be made clear that the modifications for feedback suggested in this section have not been implemented and therefore should be used only as an illustration of implementations rather than as thoroughly tested techniques. Nevertheless, the issues discussed in this section apply to any efficient implementation of relevance feedback.

The inverted file as shown in Figure 11.1 is the same as that shown in Figure 14.3 in Chapter 14, with two modifications: the terms are complete words rather than stems, and there are two additional fields holding closely related terms. These

term	number of postings	IDF	term1	term2	offset
abstract	1	2.3	summary	paper	
being	1	2.3	human	existence	
character	1	2.3	ASCII	letter	
human	1	2.3	person	animal	
index	1	2.3	term	book	
literate	1	2.3	learning	school	
novel	1	2.3	author	book	
paper	1	2.3	journal	sheets	
report	2	1.6	technical	paper	
technique	1	2.3	method	retrieval	

Figure 11.1 Dictionary and Postings File with Related Terms

modifications allow query expansion using some type of automatic thesaurus such as a nearest neighbor algorithm.

The use of the full terms (as compared to stems only) is necessary because of the addition of the related terms. Stems could be used if some extension to the basic retrieval system to permit the use of both stems and full terms were in effect. See section 14.7.1 of Chapter 14 for an example of such a system and form a natural extension of Figure 14.5 of that chapter to include related terms. The inverted file would be constructed exactly as described in section 14.6 of that chapter, with the two related terms being added using some type of term-term relating algorithm (see Chapter 16 on clustering for details of these algorithms).

The searching itself would proceed as described in the basic retrieval system. After a ranked list of documents are retrieved, users would have an option of doing relevance feedback rather than submitting a new query. If the user selects to start relevance feedback, he or she would be asked to mark retrieved documents that are relevant and to indicate to the system the last document scanned during retrieval. The system would start building the merged list of terms previously described in the background as soon as the marking starts. After the user indicates that all relevant documents have been marked, the system recomputes the weights of the original query terms based on the reweighting schemes recommended in section 11.4. Additionally, the query is expanded by this merged term list, either by automatically adding the terms with the highest "rank" in the list (again see section 11.4 for recommended methods of sorting the list) or preferably by showing the user the sorted list and adding only those terms selected by the user. If no relevant documents are indicated, no reweighting is done, and the term list shown to the user is the list of related terms based on those previously stored in the inverted file. The expanded and reweighted query is run as if it were an initial query, but all documents marked as scanned by the user do not appear in the revised retrieved list.

Two further modifications are necessary to the basic searching routine to allow feedback. First, the weights stored in the postings must be only the normalized document frequency weights (option 2 in section 14.6.1 of Chapter 14) rather than the combined weighting using the normalized document frequency weights and the IDF. This permits the IDF to be pulled from the inverted file on the initial search and combined with the normalized document frequency weight, but allows the new relevance weights to be combined with the normalized document frequency weights on subsequent searches.

The second modification is not strictly necessary but probably would ensure adequate response time. The basic retrieval algorithm is time-dependent on the number of query terms. As the number of query terms grows large, the number of retrieved documents also grows large and the final sort for the list of documents becomes very time-consuming. The pruning modifications described in section 14.7.5 of Chapter 14 become critical to good performance for long queries. Some of the more elaborate pruning methods described in that section may be even more appropriate as they eliminate even the need to retrieve some documents.

11.6 SUMMARY

This chapter has presented a survey of relevance feedback techniques both for reweighting query terms and for adding new query terms. Recommendations and guidelines for building relevance feedback components have been given. More experimentation in the use of relevance feedback in operational systems is needed to verify the guidelines in this proposal. Relevance feedback has clearly proven itself in the laboratory and now needs only efficient implementations to hasten its use in operational systems.

REFERENCES

ATTAR, R., and A. S. FRAENKEL. 1981. "Experiments in Local Metrical Feedback in Full-Text Retrieval Systems." *Information Processing and Management*, 17(3), 115–26.

BLAIR, D. C., and M. E. MARON. 1985. "An Evaluation of the Retrieval Effectiveness of a Full-Text Document-Retrieval System." *Communications of the ACM,* 28(3), 289–311.

BELEW, R. K. 1989. "Adaptive Information Retrieval: Using a Connectionist Representation to Retrieve and Learn About Documents." Paper presented at ACM Conference on Research and Development in Information Retrieval, Boston, Mass.

BOVEY, J. D., and S. E. ROBERTSON. 1984. "An Algorithm for Weighted Searching on a Boolean System." *Information Technology: Research and Development*, 3(1), 84–87.

CROFT, W. B. 1983. "Experiments with Representation in a Document Retrieval System." *Information Technology: Research and Development*, 2(1), 1–21.

CROFT, W. B., and R. DAS. 1990. "Experiments in Query Acquistion and Use in Document Retrieval Systems." Paper presented at 13th International Conference on Research and Development in Information Retrieval, Brussels, Belgium.

CROFT, W. B., and D. J. HARPER. 1979. Using Probabilistic Models of Document Retrieval Without Relevance Information. *Journal of Documentation,* 35(4), 285–95.

CROUCH, C. J. 1988. "A Cluster-Based Approach to Thesaurus Construction." Paper presented at ACM Conference on Research and Development in Information Retrieval, Grenoble, France.

DILLON, M., J. ULMSCHNEIDER, and J. DESPER. 1983. "A Prevalence Formula for Automatic Relevance Feedback in Boolean Systems." *Information Processing and Management*, 19(1), 27–36.

DOSZKOCS, T. E. 1978. "AID, an Associative Interactive Dictionary for Online Searching." *Online Review* 2(2), 163–74.

DOSZKOCS, T. E. 1982. "From Research to Application: The CITE Natural Language Information Retrieval System," in *Research and Development in Information Retrieval,* eds. G. Salton and H. J. Schneider, pp. 251–62. Berlin: Springer.

DUMAIS, S. T. 1990. "Enhancing Performance in Latent Semantic Indexing (LSI) Retrieval." Unpublished manuscript.

FOX, E. A. 1987. "Testing the Applicability of Intelligent Methods for Information Retrieval." *Information Services & Use* 7, 119–38.

FUHR, N. 1989. "Models for Retrieval with Probabilistic Indexing." *Information Processing and Management*, 25(1), 55–72.

GUNTZER, U., G. JUTTNER, G. SEEGMULLER, and F. SARRE. 1989. "Automatic Thesaurus Construction by Machine Learning from Retrieval Sessions." *Information Processing and Management*, 25(3), 265–73.

HALL, H., and N. WEIDERMAN. 1967. "The Evaluation Problem in Relevance Feedback." Report No. ISR–12 to the National Science Foundation from Department of Computer Science, Cornell University, June.

HARMAN, D. 1986. "An Experimental Study of Factors Important in Document Ranking." Paper presented at ACM Conference on Research and Development in Information Retrieval, Pisa, Italy.

HARMAN, D. 1988. "Towards Interactive Query Expansion." Paper presented at ACM Conference on Research and Development in Information Retrieval, Grenoble, France.

HARMAN, D., and G. CANDELA. 1990. "Retrieving Records from a Gigabyte of Text on a Minicomputer Using Statistical Ranking." *Journal of the American Society for Information Science,* 41(8), 581–89.

HARMAN, D. 1992. "Relevance Feedback Revisited." Paper presented at ACM Conference on Research and Development in Information Retrieval, Copenhagen, Denmark.

HARPER, D. J. 1980. *Relevance Feedback in Document Retrieval Systems: An Evaluation of Probabilistic Strategies.* Doctoral dissertation, Jesus College, Cambridge, England.

HARPER, D. J., and C. J. VAN RIJSBERGEN. 1978. "An Evaluation of Feedback in Document Retrieval Using Co-Occurrence Data." *Journal of Documentation,* 34(3), 189–216.

IDE, E. 1969. "Relevance Feedback in an Automatic Document Retrieval System." Report No. ISR–15 to National Science Foundation from Department of Computer Science, Cornell University, January.

IDE, E. 1971. "New Experiments in Relevance Feedback," in *The SMART Retrieval System,* ed. G. Salton, pp. 337–54. Englewood Cliffs, N.J.: Prentice Hall.

INGWERSEN, P. 1984. "A Cognitive View of Three Selected Online Search Facilities." *Online Review* 8(5), 465–92.

LANCASTER, F. W. 1969. "MEDLARS: Report on the Evaluation of Its Operating Efficiency." *American Documentation,* 20(2) 119–48.

LESK, M. E. 1969. "Word-Word Associations in Document Retrieval Systems." *American Documentation,* 20(1), 8–36.

MARON, M. E., and J. L. KUHNS. 1960. "On Relevance, Probabilistic Indexing and Information Retrieval." *Association for Computing Machinery,* 7(3), 216–44.

MINKER, J., G. A. WILSON, and B. H. ZIMMERMAN. 1972. "An Evaluation of Query Expansion by the Addition of Clustered Terms for a Document Retrieval System." *Information Storage and Retrieval,* 8(6), 329–48.

NOREAULT, T. 1979. *User Directed Relevance Feedback.* Doctoral dissertation, School of Information Studies, Syracuse University.

ODDY, R. N. 1977. "Information Retrieval Through Man-Machine Dialogue." *Documentation,* 33(1), 1–14.

PORTER, M. F. 1982. "Implementing a Probabilistic Information Retrieval System." *Information Technology: Research and Development,* 1(2), 131–156.

PORTER, M. F., and V. GALPIN. 1988. "Relevance Feedback in a Public Access Catalogue for a Research Library: Muscat at the Scott Polar Research Institute." *Program,* 22(1), 1–20.

RADECKI, T. 1988. "Improvements to Conventional Boolean Retrieval Systems." *Information Processing and Management,* 24(3), 513–23.

ROCCHIO, J. J. 1971. "Relevance Feedback in Information Retrieval." In Salton G. (Ed.), *The SMART Retrieval System* (pp. 313–23). Englewood Cliffs, N.J.: Prentice Hall, Inc.

ROBERTSON, S. E., and K. SPARCK JONES 1976. "Relevance Weighting of Search Terms." *J. of the American Society for Information Science,* 27(3), 129–46.

ROBERTSON, S. E., C. L. THOMPSON, M. J. MACASKILL, and J. D. BOVEY, 1986. "Weighting, Ranking and Relevance Feedback in a Front-end System." *Journal of Information Science,* 12, 71–5.

SALTON, G. 1970. "Evaluation Problems in Interactive Information Retrieval." *Information Storage and Retrieval,* 6(1), 29–44.

SALTON, G. 1971. *The SMART Retrieval System.* Englewood Cliffs, N.J.: Prentice Hall, Inc.

SALTON, G., and C. BUCKLEY 1990. "Improving Retrieval Performance by Relevance Feedback." *Journal of the American Society for Information Science,* 41(4), 288–97.

SALTON, G., and M. MCGILL 1983. *Introduction to Modern Information Retrieval.* New York: McGraw-Hill.

SMEATON, A. F., and C. J. VAN RIJSBERGEN 1983. "The Retrieval Effects of Query Expansion on a Feedback Document Retrieval System." *The Computer Journal,* 26(3), 239–46.

SPARCK JONES, K. 1972. "A Statistical Interpretation of Term Specificity and Its Application in Retrieval." *Documentation,* 28(1), 11–21.

SPARCK JONES, K. 1979a. "Experiments in Relevance Weighting of Search Terms." *Information Processing and Management,* 15(3), 133–44.

SPARCK JONES, K. 1979b. "Search Term Relevance Weighting Given Little Relevance Information." *Documentation,* 35(1), 30–48.

SPARCK JONES, K., and E. O. BARBER. 1971. "What Makes an Automatic Keyword Classification Effective." *J. American Society for Information Science,* 22(3), 166–75.

STANFILL, C., and B. KAHLE. 1986. "Parallel Free-Text Search on the Connection Machine System." *Communications of the ACM,* 29(12), 1229–39.

VAN RIJSBERGEN, C. J. 1986. "A New Theoretical Framework For Information Retrieval." Paper presented at ACM Conference on Research and Development in Information Retrieval, Pisa, Italy.

VERNIMB, C. 1977. "Automatic Query Adjustment in Document Retrieval." *Information Processing and Management,* 13(6), 339–53.

WONG, S. K. M., and Y. Y. YAO. 1990. "Query Formulation in Linear Retrieval Models." *J. American Society for Information Science,* 41(5), 324–29.

WU, H., and G. SALTON. 1981. "The Estimation of Term Relevance Weights using Relevance Feedback." *Documentation,* 37(4), 194–214.

12

Boolean Operations

Steven Wartik

Software Productivity Consortium

Abstract

This chapter presents an overview of Boolean operations, which are one means of expressing queries in information retrieval systems. The concepts of Boolean operations are introduced, and two implementations based on sets are given. One implementation uses bit vectors; the other, hashing. The relative performance characteristics of the approaches are shown.

12.1 INTRODUCTION

This chapter explores one aspect of how information retrieval systems efficiently process user requests. Most systems rely heavily on the ability to perform *Boolean operations*. User requests are typically phrased in terms of Boolean operations. Hence, the ability to translate them into a form that may be speedily evaluated is of paramount importance. Techniques for doing so form the subject of this chapter.

Information retrieval systems manage documents. These differ from the data stored in traditional database management systems in that they have much less structure. The data are not organized into neat little units with uniform content, where an integer may be expected at a particular location or a string at another. Little may be reliably determined beyond the existence of a document and its boundaries. Of course, information may be derived from a document (such as inverted indices—see Chapter 3). However, such information is invisible to the user of an information retrieval system. He or she sees only a document, with no particular structure save units derived from natural languages, such as words, sentences, or paragraphs.

This creates a problem for information retrieval systems: queries tend to be vague, especially when compared to database management systems. The latter, with their precise characterization of data, permit a broad range of queries that can exploit known properties of the data. Thus, while a database management system user might issue a query such as:

```
select Name, Age from Person where Age > 25
```

the user of an information retrieval system has far less flexibility. The information retrieval system cannot hope to determine what sequence of characters in the documents under consideration represent age. It has no knowledge of document structure and therefore cannot make inferences about portions of a document.

Queries on documents in information retrieval systems, then, are limited to operations involving character strings, at best with some knowledge of sentence structure. A typical query might be, "Give me the names of all documents containing sentences with the words 'computer' and 'science'." Despite its seeming simplicity, such a query can be very costly. In a database management system, one might optimize this query by working from sorted data, and using search algorithms that capitalize on such order. An information retrieval system, however, cannot re-order a document's text. A search for a word within a document may therefore take time linearly proportional to the size of the document. As mentioned, the situation can be improved through the use of indices, but the use of a partial index can limit the flexibility of an information retrieval system, and a full index is often prohibitively expensive.

In any case, the size of the data is often enormous. Information retrieval systems manipulate huge amounts of information, often orders of magnitude more than is found in database management systems. Even if indexing is used, the data sets will be prohibitively large. Simple-minded algorithms to process queries will take unacceptable amounts of time and space.

Boolean operations are the key to describing queries, and their efficient implementation is essential. The typical technique is to use sets. This chapter covers how to implement Boolean operations as sets, and also how to efficiently implement set operations. It emphasizes sets that are expected to contain large numbers of elements. Section 12.2 discussess Boolean operations in more detail, describing precisely their relationship to sets. Section 12.3 presents an abstraction of sets. Sections 12.5 and 12.6 present various implementations of this abstraction. The final section analyzes the run-time properties of the implementation approaches.

12.2 BOOLEAN EXPRESSIONS AND THEIR REPRESENTATION AS SETS

Boolean expressions are formed from user queries. In some information retrieval systems, the user enters them directly. In more sophisticated systems, the user enters natural language, which the system converts into Boolean expressions. In any event, they are then evaluated to determine the results of the query. This section will show how Boolean expressions are built from queries, and how those expressions are translated into sets.

An information retrieval system accesses some set of documents. The system must be able to uniquely identify each document. In this chapter, it will suffice to have documents named $doc_1, doc_2, \ldots, doc_n$. It is assumed that the name "doc_i" provides enough information to locate the information associated with document i. In reality, an addressing table would probably be associated with the names of documents, linking each name to some disk location, but this detail can be safely ignored for now.

Boolean expressions are formed from queries. They represent a request to determine what documents contain (or do not contain) a given set of keywords. For example

```
Find all documents containing "information".
```

is a query that, when evaluated, should yield a (possibly empty) set of documents, each of which contains the word "information" somewhere within its body. Most of the words in the sentence are noise, however. By definition, a query searches a set of documents to determine their content. The above is therefore usually represented as the Boolean expression:

```
information
```

which means, "A set whose elements are the names of all documents containing the pattern 'information'."

Some queries attempt to find documents that do *not* contain a particular pattern, a fact that the corresponding Boolean expression must indicate. This is done using a "not" operator, prefixed to the expression. For example, the query:

```
Find all documents that do not contain "information".
```

is represented as the Boolean expression:

```
not information
```

Most queries involve searching more than one term. For example, a user might say any of the following:

```
Find all documents containing "information" and "retrieval".

Find all documents containing "information"
or "retrieval" (or both).

Find all documents containing "information" or
"retrieval", but not both.
```

Only documents containing both "information" and "retrieval" will satisfy the first query, whereas the second will be satisfied by a document that contains either of the two words. Documents satisfying the third query are a subset of those that satisfy the second. In fact, those documents in the second query are the union of the documents in the first and third.

Each of the above queries illustrates a particular concept that may form a Boolean expression. These concepts are, respectively, conjunction, disjunction, and exclusive disjunction. They are represented in Boolean expressions using the operators and, or, and xor. The queries above would therefore be:

```
information and retrieval
information or retrieval
information xor retrieval
```

Boolean expressions may be formed from other Boolean expressions to yield rather complex structures. Consider the following query:

```
Find all documents containing "information", "retrieval",
or not containing both "retrieval" and "science".
```

This translates into the following Boolean expression:

```
(information and retrieval) or not (retrieval and science)
```

Parentheses are often helpful to avoid ambiguity.

Each portion of a Boolean expression yields a set of documents. These portions are evaluated separately, then simplified using techniques that will be discussed in this chapter. That is, "all documents containing 'information'" yields a set of documents D_1, and "all documents containing 'retrieval'" yields some set D_2. The information retrieval system must combine these two sets to yield the set D_3 that contains only documents with both "information" and "retrieval."

The reader may be wondering how certain complex queries are handled. For instance, how is "all documents containing 'information' and 'retrieval' in the same sentence" represented as a Boolean expression? This question will be answered in other chapters. The concern of this chapter is not to study techniques for determining if a document contains a pattern. Rather, given a set of documents known to contain a pattern, the issue at hand is how to combine those patterns efficiently to answer a larger query. In other words, other chapters will discuss how to determine which documents contain "information," and which contain "retrieval." Here, the assumption is that the respective sets are known; the issue is how to combine those sets to determine what documents might contain both, either, or neither.

Combining the terms of Boolean expressions is conceptually quite simple. It involves sequences of familiar set operations. Let U represent the names of all documents stored. Let D_1 and D_2 represent the names of those documents that contain patterns P_1 and P_2, respectively. The following list defines how to evaluate Boolean expression operators in terms of the sets:

1. $U - D_1$ is the set of all documents not containing P_1 (not).
2. $D_1 \cap D_2$ is the set of all documents containing both P_1 and P_2 (and).
3. $D_1 \cup D_2$ is the set of all documents containing either P_1 or P_2 (or).
4. $D_1 \cup D_2 - D_1 \cap D_2$ is the set of all documents containing either P_1 or P_2, but not both (xor).

The following example illustrates these expressions. Consider a set of five documents, and suppose that they contain the terms shown in Figure 12.1. The expressions given above will now be evaluated using the data in Figure 12.1. For instance, the Boolean expression "information" is the names of all documents containing the term "information":

$$\{doc_1, doc_3\}$$

The expression "information and retrieval" is:

$$\{doc_1, doc_3\} \cap \{doc_1, doc_2, doc_4\} = \{doc_1\}$$

whereas "information or retrieval" is:

$$\{doc_1, doc_3\} \cup \{doc_1, doc_2, doc_4\} = \{doc_1, doc_2, doc_3, doc_4\}$$

As a more complex example:

{information and retrieval} or not {retrieval and science}

is:

$$(\{doc_1, doc_3\} \cap \{doc_1, doc_2, doc_4\}) \cup \{doc_1, doc_2, doc_3, doc_4, doc_5\}$$
$$- (\{doc_1, doc_2\} \cap \{doc_2, doc_4, doc_5\})$$
$$= \{doc_2\} \cup \{doc_1, doc_3, doc_4, doc_5\}$$
$$= \{doc_1, doc_2, doc_3, doc_4, doc_5\}$$

Document	Terms
doc_1	algorithm, information, retrieval
doc_2	retrieval, science
doc_3	algorithm, information, science
doc_4	pattern, retrieval, science
doc_5	science, algorithm

Figure 12.1 Example documents and their terms

12.3 OPERATIONS ON SETS

Before discussing how to implement sets, it is necessary to define them more precisely. Sets are a familiar concept, and implementations for them may be found in many data structures textbooks. However, no two textbooks seem to have precisely the same operations, and the semantics of the operations vary from book to book (Does an operation modify its inputs? Is it a procedure or a function?). A little time spent discussing the meaning of a set as used in this chapter will avoid confusion.

12.3.1 Set Interface

A set is a homogeneous, unordered collection of elements. In programming language terms, a set has an associated "element data type," and all elements of the set must be of this type. Each element data type has a *key*. For a given set, no two elements ever simultaneously possess the same key. An element data type may also specify other data that will be included along with the element. These data values need not be unique among all elements of a set. If the key constitutes the entire value of a set element, however, then by definition all values in a set differ.

From the discussion in the previous section, it should be no surprise that the familiar set operations of union, intersection, and difference will be required. However, certain supporting operations will be necessary to provide a satsifactory algorithmic implementation of sets. The presentation will be done using the information hiding principle advanced by Parnas (1972), wherein a set is presented in two parts—a collection of access programs that define the operations a program may legally perform on a set, and an implementation for those programs.

To specify a set, one must provide an element data type *E*. This specifies the types of elements that may populate a given instance of a set. Some programming languages, such as Ada, permit programmers to enforce the constraint that a set contain homogeneous data. In C, the programming language used here, this constraint is unenforceable. However, only a little care is required to ensure that sets are in fact homogeneous.

The first order of business is to declare a data type for a set, and for elements of the set:

```
typedef <...>  set;
typedef <...>  elementType;
```

The structure of a set will be defined later, when the implementation is given. For now, it suffices to know that such a type is available. The definition for element types will depend on the type of data to be stored in the set. In C, it is generally possible to use the type "char*" to store data of any type. However, creating type-specific operations is usually better practice. Moreover, one implementation for sets given here cannot easily represent pointer data; in fact, short would be the best choice. This point will be discussed in more detail in each implementation.

Figure 12.2 shows the operations that constitute the interface to a set. A few conventions will be used that should be noted now:

1. All operations use pointers to values of type set. In C, pointer-valued parameters are generally used for parameters that a routine is to modify, or for efficiency. Here, the reason is usually efficiency. An operation does not modify its parameter unless so noted.

2. The existence of a Boolean data type is assumed. This type may be easily declared using the facilities of the C preprocessor:

```
#define TRUE 1
#define FALSE 0
typedef int boolean;
```

3. The system using the sets will not modify element values once they have been inserted into a set. This problem might arise in C if a set contained strings. Consider the following:

```
v = "abc";
Insert(s, v);
v[1] = 'x';
```

Unless Insert has stored a copy of the string, the value of v will change inside s, since s will contain a pointer to the string rather than a unique value. This problem can be solved easily in two ways:

a. The application will agree not to modify values that are used in sets.
b. The specification of a set can include a function that creates a copy of a datum.

Case a turns out to suffice for information retrieval. Since it is simpler, it will be used in this chapter.

4. Unless explicitly stated otherwise, a set variable may not appear twice in a parameter list. That is, neither of the following are legal:

```
Copy(s, s);
Unite(a, b, b);
```

This restriction is actually not necessary for all routines, but occurs frequently enough to warrant its inclusion.

```
void Clear(set *s);             /* Make s contain zero elements. */

void Insert(set *s,             /* Modify s to contain e, if  */
            elementType e);     /* it does not already.       */

void Delete(set *s,             /* Remove e from s.           */
            elementType e);

void Unite(set *s1, set *s2,    /* Make s3 the union of sets  */
           set *s3);            /* s1 and s2.                 */


void Intersect(set *s1, set *s2, /* Make s3 the intersection  */
               set *s3);         /* of sets s1 and s2.        */
```

Figure 12.2 Set interface operations

```
void Subtract(set *s1, set *s2,      /* Make s3 the difference  */
              set *s3);              /* of sets s1 and s2.       */

boolean Empty(set *s);               /* Return TRUE iff s has    */
                                     /* zero elements.           */

boolean Member(set *s,               /* Return TRUE iff e is a   */
               elementType e);       /* member of s.             */

void Copy(set *source,               /* Make "destination" the   */
          set *destination);         /* same set as "source".    */

void Iterate(set *s,                 /* Call f(e) once for every */
             boolean (*f)());        /* element e in set s.      */

boolean Error_Occurred();            /* Return TRUE iff the last */
                                     /* operation caused an error. */
```

Figure 12.2 (*cont.*)

Most of the operations are self-explanatory, as they implement familiar set functions. The Iterate operation may require some explanation. Once a Boolean expression has been evaluated, the information retrieval system will need to determine all elements in the set. The system should not depend on a particular implementation of sets, so it must have some other means to access all elements. This is exactly what Iterate provides. The system will call it, supplying as a parameter a C routine that accomplishes some desired function. Iterate will execute this function once for every element in the set, supplying the element to the routine as a parameter. For example, suppose a developer writes the following C procedure:

```
boolean PrintElement(i)
    elementType    i;
{
    printf("The value is %d\n", i);
    return TRUE;
}
```

The following statement would then print all elements of a set S of integers:

```
Iterate(S, PrintElement);
```

No qualifications are made about the order of the elements in the iteration; it is completely random so far as the routine calling Iterate is concerned. The only guarantee is that each element in the set is passed to f() exactly once.

It will be possible to pass parameters to the operations that would, if accepted, result in an erroneous set. Some error-handling mechanism is therefore needed. This mechanism must allow an information retrieval system to detect when an `error` has occurred. The `Error_Occurred()` routine, which can be used to check the status of an operation, achieves this. Its value is TRUE if an error occurred during the last executed set operation, and FALSE if no error occurred. A system that wished to check the validity of each operation might contain code such as the following:

```
Intersect(s1, s2, s3);
if ( Error_Occurred() ) {
    . . .
}
```

The error handling will be accomplished such that a set will always be valid according to the rules of its implementation, even if an error occurred. Applications may therefore attempt corrective action and try again.

12.3.2 Packaging

The interface given in Figure 12.2 can provide an information retrieval system with operations on sets of various types. These operations may be used by many parts of the system. Their packaging must make this expedient. Information retrieval systems are large and consist of many subsystems. The code for a typical information retrieval system will probably be spread throughout many files. The set operations must be packaged such that each subsystem—that is, set of files—needing access to sets may have them in the simplest possible way, involving no duplication of code.

The usual C technique for doing this is to package the interface in an "include file" (see Kernighan and Ritchie [1988]). This file contains specifications of the types, constants, and procedures that make up the set package, but omits any executable code. (The one exception is routines implemented as macros, rather than procedures. Their expansion, which includes executable code, appears in the include file.)

An implementation of a set would therefore be packaged as follows:

1. An include file, which might be named "set.h". It would contain all of Figure 12.2, plus the type definition and accompanying constants for the set data type. (Ideally the definition of the type would not be in the interface, but C discourages this.)

2. A file containing implementations of the routines, which might be named "set.c". Since set.h contains certain type definitions needed in the implementation, it begins with the line:

```
#include "set.h"
```

12.3.3 Example

The routines' use will be illustrated by using them to solve the query given at the end of section 12.2. Doing so requires the use of six sets—three for each of the patterns, plus three to hold intermediate values and the results. Figure 12.3 gives the code. The issue of how the sets are initialized is ignored here; it is the subject of Chapter 3. That would involve calls to the Insert routine, one for each document to be inserted in a set.

Note that the code has been given independently from the implementation. While this is possible, subsequent analysis will demonstrate that complete independence is not desirable. The implementations include routines that improve run-time performance by supplying implementation-specific details.

```
#include "set.h"

SolveQuery()
{
    set info_docs, retr_docs, sci_docs;
    set t1, t2, t3;

    Clear(&info_docs);
    Clear(&retr_docs);
    Clear(&sci_docs);

    Clear(&t1);
    Clear(&t2);
    Clear(&t3);

    ... Find the documents containing "information",
        "retrieval" and "science", and put their names
        into info_docs, retr_docs, and sci_docs,
        respectively ...

    Intersect(&info_docs, &retr_docs, &t1);
    Intersect(&retr_docs, &sci_docs, &t2);
    Unite(&t1, &retr_docs, &t3);
    Subtract(&t3, &t2, &t1);
    /* Set t1 contains the result of the query. */
}
```

Figure 12.3 Solving a simple set query

12.4 GENERAL CONSIDERATIONS FOR IMPLEMENTING SETS

Before considering specific techniques for implementing sets, it is worth mentioning the trade-offs one may encounter. Space and time considerations are as applicable in set algorithms as in any other area. However, the sets used in information retrieval can vary greatly in size, indeed by many orders of magnitude. Small documents, or ones being queried in the context of a particular domain, may have only a few terms. Then again, some documents will have tens of thousands of unique index terms on which users may wish to search. Sets for the former may easily be kept in memory and manipulated using fixed-space algorithms. Sets for the latter may require secondary memory implementation strategies. The same information retrieval system may well access both types of documents. One implementation approach to sets might not be enough.

In any case, large rather than small sets are likely to be the exception rather than the rule. Furthermore, the amount of information on one's system seldom shrinks. The ever-increasing amount of knowledge has made gigabyte information bases commonplace. Terabyte systems are not uncommon. Indeed, they will probably be the rule as global networks proliferate. Planning for a small, stable information base is unwise, then, and will lead to unacceptable performance. Every ounce of computing power must therefore be squeezed out of the algorithms that implement Boolean operations. The ones given here attempt to do so. They sometimes sacrifice clarity for speed, but a reader familiar with the C programming language should be able to figure them out without undue effort.

Two implementation strategies are given. This only scratches the surface of possibilities. The two approaches are sufficiently diverse as to be representative of most major trade-offs, however, and therefore will help the reader understand the benefits of other approaches he or she may come across. The technique of *balanced trees* is worthy of consideration; its performance is, in most respects, intermediate with respect to the approaches in this chapter. See Sedgewick (1990) for an excellent treatment of the topic.

The implementor of an information retrieval system should carefully consider the relationship of the two approaches. Certain external factors may drive which ones are practical. For instance, one technique (bit vectors) is very fast but relies on representing document names as unique integers. Doing so is certainly feasible, but—unless one's documents really are named doc_1, doc_2, . . . —potentially time-consuming. Whether performing the mapping for each set will result in time savings depends on the document names and the hardware available.

The desire to use this approach may also drive other design decisions in an information retrieval system. Document names are maintained in inverted indices; if the indices are sorted, the names can be mapped much more rapidly than if they are unsorted. Of course, sorting the names is an expensive operation, and practical only for precomputed indices.

This discussion illustrates the complexity that arises from a seemingly simple choice. Such decisions may influence the architecture of the entire system.

12.5 BIT VECTORS

Bit vectors are a simple approach to implementing sets. They provide an extremely fast implementation that is particularly suited to sets where the element type has a small domain of possible values. The representation is not compact, as will be seen, but may be appropriate if the number of documents is small.

The approach using bit vectors is to represent a set as a sequence of bits, with one bit for each possible element in the domain of the element type. It is assumed that each value in the element's domain maps to a unique bit. If a bit's value is 1, then the element represented by that bit is in the set; if 0, the element is not in the set. These values map to the TRUE and FALSE constants of the Boolean data type, which provides a clearer understanding of the bit's purpose (TRUE means an element is in a set, FALSE means it is not) than do the digits.

Most computers do not understand bit strings of arbitrary lengths. A program must reference a minimum or maximum number of bits in a given operation—usually corresponding to a byte, word, or the like. It is therefore necessary to arrange the bit string such that it can be treated as a whole, or referenced bit-by-bit, as appropriate. The usual approach is to declare a bit string as a sequence of contiguous storage. Access to individual bits is achieved by first accessing the byte containing the desired bit(s), and then applying a "mask-and-shift" sequence (illustrated below) to recover specific bits.

The technique takes full advantage of computer hardware to achieve efficiency of operations. Most computers have instructions to perform and, or, xor, and not operations on bit strings. The C programming language, which provides access to bit-level operations, is well suited to bit vector implementations.

Consider an example. Suppose there are 20 documents, and suppose further that they may be uniquely identified by numbering them from 1 to 20, inclusive. A string of 20 bits will be used to represent sets of these documents. The first task is to determine the mapping between the numbers and bits. A logical approach is to have document i map to bit i. However, in C the first bit has index 0, not 1. Therefore, document i actually maps to bit $i - 1$.

Suppose a search reveals that, of the 20 documents, only documents 3, 8, 11, and 12 contain patterns of interest. The bit vector set to represent this consists of 0's at all elements except those four positions:

$$001000010011000000000000$$

The alert reader will notice that this string actually consists of 24 bits, not 20. The reason is that computers are not usually capable of storing exactly 20 bits. Most store information in multiples of 8 bits, an assumption made here. Padding the string with zeros is therefore necessary.

Suppose the system now needs to know whether document i is in the set. There is no C operation that allows bit $i - 1$ to be retrieved directly. However, it can be done by extracting the byte containing bit $i - 1$ and then setting all other bits in that byte to zero. If the resulting byte is nonzero, then bit $i - 1$ must have been 1; if it is zero, bit $i - 1$ must have been 0. The first step, then, is to compute the byte containing bit $i - 1$. Since there are 8 bits in a byte, each byte stores information on up to 8 elements of a set. Therefore, bit $i - 1$ is in byte $(i - 1)/8$ (as with bits, the first byte is indexed by 0, not 1).

The next step is to isolate the individual bit. Modulo arithmetic is used to do so: the bit is at location $(i - 1) \bmod 8$ within the byte, since the mapping scheme sequences bits in order. Shifting the bit to the first position of the byte, and then and'ing the byte with 1, yields a byte that contains 1 if the bit is 1, and 0 if the bit is 0. The complete C expression to access the bit is therefore:

```
( vector[(i-1)/8] >> (i-1)%8 ) & 01
```

The inverse operation—setting a particular bit, that is, adding an element to a set—is performed in essentially the reverse manner.

An understanding of bit-manipulation concepts makes the implementation of the remaining operations straightforward. For instance, the intersection of two sets as bit vectors is just a loop that uses C's & operation:

```
for ( i = 0; i < length(s1); i++ )
    s3[i] = s1[i]&s2[i];
```

assuming that length(s) returns the number of bytes needed to represent set s.

The drawback of using bit vectors arises when the domain of the element type is large. Representing a set of integers on a 32-bit computer requires bit vectors of length $2^{31}/8 = 268,435,456$ bytes, an amount beyond most computers' capacities. Knowing that the set will only contain a few of these elements at any time does not help. A set implemented using the above mapping still requires the full amount of space to store the two-element set containing -2^{31} and $2^{31} - 1$. Indeed, many compilers that use bit vectors to implement sets restrict the domain to that of the maximum number of bits in a single word—typically 60 or 64. This usually limits their utility to sets of single characters.

The situation is even worse if the element type is character strings, such as might be used to hold document names. A 10-element character string restricted to upper- and lowercase letters has 52^{10} possible values. Clearly, bit strings will be impractical for such situations. However, there are enough small domains to warrant the consideration of bit vectors as a set implementation technique.

If large bit vectors are impractical, there must be a way to specify the domain of elements of a set. This will require adding a new function to the interface given in Figure 12.2. The function will create a new set capable of storing elements from a given range of values.

```
void Create(int lower, int upper, set *s);
```

In other words, all sets will be treated as sets of integers between lower and upper, inclusive. The set operations will return sets of the same domain as their parameters, and will refuse to operate on sets of two different domains.

Since set operations need to know the domain of elements, a set will need to include information on elements. The implementation for sets, then, will contain three pieces of information: the lower and upper bounds of the set, and the bit string defining the set's elements at any time. The following structure presents this information:

```
#define MAX_ELEMENTS 256
#define WORDSIZE 8
typedef struct {
    int     lower;
    int     upper;
    char    bits[MAX_ELEMENTS\WORDSIZE];
} set;
```

This implementation rather arbitrarily restricts the maximum number of elements that a set may contain to 256. It is possible to provide more flexibility, by making bits a pointer and allocating space for it at run time, but doing so defeats the point of using bit strings for fast access—the system must worry about garbage collection issues. Such flexibility is better achieved using other representations. The implementation also defines the word size—that is, the number of bits per word in a value of type char — at 8. It is worth noting that using an int array might prove faster. Most C implementations have 8 bits in a datum of type char, and 16 or 32 in an int; using an int might make the operations that manipulate entire bytes more efficient. The decision will depend on the underlying hardware, and the types of accesses to sets that occur most frequently. Empirical analysis is the best way to resolve the question.

The implementation for Create is:

```
void Create(lower, upper, s)
    int     lower, upper;
    set     *s;
{
    if ( lower > upper
       || (upper − lower) >= MAX_ELEMENTS ) {
        error_occurred = TRUE;
        return;
    }
    s->lower = lower;
    s->upper = upper;
    error_occurred = FALSE;
}
```

The routine simply initializes the bounds of the set. The first few lines, which deal with errors, bear explanation. As mentioned above, errors will be flagged through the use of a function `Error_Occurred`. This routine will be implemented as a reference to a "hidden" variable:

```
static boolean error_occurred;
```

which would appear in the set's implementation file. Each set operation has the responsibility to set this variable to either TRUE or FALSE. The implementation of `Error_Occurred` is then:

```
boolean Error_Occurred()
{
    return error_occurred;
}
```

Note that `Create` does not initialize the set's contents; that is, the set is not guaranteed empty.

```
void Clear(s)
    set     *s;
{
    register int    i, Number_Of_Bytes;
    Number_Of_Bytes = (s->upper - s-lower)/WORDSIZE + 1;
    for ( i = 0; i < Number_Of_Bytes; i++ )
        s->bits[i] = 0;
    error_occurred = FALSE;
}
```

Since a zero indicates that an element is not in a set, and since s's bits are all zeros, set s contains no elements.

Insertion and deletion of elements are handled by setting the appropriate bit to 1 and 0, respectively. Figure 12.4 shows the code to do so. The routines mask the byte containing the appropriate bit with a bit string that turns the bit on or off, respectively. The bit string for `Insert` consists of a string of 0's, with a 1 at the appropriate bit; or'ing this string with a byte with result in a byte unchanged except for (possibly) the bit at the location of the 1 in the bit string. The bit string for `Delete` consists of a string of 1's, with a 0 at the appropriate bit; and'ing this string with a byte will result in a byte unchanged except for (possibly) the bit at the location of the 0. C's bit-oriented operators make this simple.

The code for routines that test properties of a set was given above, in simplified form. Figure 12.5 shows the complete C routines. Note that `Member` is defined to be erroneous if e is not of the correct domain, that is, if it is outside the lower and upper bounds. It still returns FALSE since, as a function, it must return some value. An alternate approach would be to indicate that it is not in the set, without also flagging an error. However, this weakens the abstraction.

```
void Insert(s, e)
    set             *s;
    elementType     e;
{
    if ( e < s->lower || e > s->upper ) {
        error_occurred = TRUE;
        return;
    }
    s->bits[(e-s->lower)/WORDSIZE] |= 01 << ((e-s->lower)%WORDSIZE);
    error_occurred = FALSE;
}


void Delete(s, e)
    set             *s;
    elementType     e;
{

    if ( e < s->lower || e > s->upper ) {
        error_occurred = TRUE;
        return;
    }
    s->bits[(e-s->lower)/WORDSIZE] &= ˉ(01 << ((e-s->lower)%WORDSIZE));
    error_occurred = FALSE;
}
```

Figure 12.4 Inserting and deleting elements in a bit-vector set

```
boolean Empty(s)
    set     *s;
{
    register int  i, Number_Of_Bytes;
    error_occurred = FALSE;
    Number_Of_Bytes = (s->upper - s->lower)/WORDSIZE + 1;
    for ( i = 0; i < Number_Of_Bytes; i++ )
        if ( s->bits[i] )
            return FALSE;
    return TRUE;
}


boolean Member(s, e)
    set    *s;
    elementType    e;
{
    if ( error_occurred = (e < s->lower || e < s->upper) )
        return FALSE;
    return (s->bits[(e - s->lower)/WORDSIZE] >>
        (e - s->lower)%WORDSIZE) & 01;
}
```

Figure 12.5 Empty and Member bit-vector routines

The Intersect, Unite, and Subtract routines are next. The operations will be restricted such that all three parameters must have the same bounds. This makes the bit-vector approach simple. (Extending the operations to accommodate sets with other bounds is not difficult, but is somewhat harder for systems to use. It is left as an exercise.) Two sets thus constrained will have the same mapping function, so bit i of one set will represent the same element as bit i of another. This means that entire bytes can be combined using C's bit operators. The equivalence of two sets is tested using the macro:

```
#define equivalent(s1, s2) \
    ((s1)->lower==(s2)->lower && (s1)->upper==(s2)->upper)
```

Figures 12.6–12.8 show the code.

```
void Unite(s1, s2, s3)
    set    *s1, *s2;
    set    *s3;
{

    register int  i, Number_Of_Bytes;

    if ( ! (equivalent(s1, s2) && equivalent(s2, s3)) ) {
        error_occurred = TRUE;
        return;
    }

    Number_Of_Bytes = (s1->upper - s1->lower)/WORDSIZE + 1;
    for ( i = 0 ; i Number_Of_Bytes; i++ )
        s3->bits[i] = (s1->bits[i] | s2->bits[i]);
    error_occurred = FALSE;
}
```

Figure 12.6 Unite bit-vector routine

Applications sometimes need to copy sets. Using bit vectors, this is straightforward. The bits array must be copied byte by byte, since C does not permit assignment of entire arrays:

```
void Copy(source, destination)
    set *source, *destination;
{

    register int      i;

        if ( ! equivalent(source, destination) ) {
            error_occurred = TRUE;
            return;
        }
    for ( i = 0; i < MAX_ELEMENTS/WORDSIZE; i++ )
        destination-bits[i] = source->bits[i];
    error_occurred = FALSE;
    }
```

```
void Intersect(s1, s2, s3)
    set     *s1, *s2;
    set     *s3;
{

    register int  i, Number_Of_Bytes;


    if ( ! (equivalent(s1, s2) && equivalent(s2, s3)) ) {
        error_occurred = TRUE;
        return;
    }

    Number_Of_Bytes = ( s1->upper - s1->lower)/WORDSIZE + 1;
    for ( i = 0 ; i < Number_Of_Bytes; i++ )
        s3->bits[i] = (s1->bits[i] & s2->bits[i]);
    error_occurred = FALSE;
}
```

Figure 12.7 Intersect bit-vector routine

```
void Subtract(s1, s2, s3)
    set     *s1, *s2;
    set     *s3;
{

    register int  i, Number_Of_Bytes;

    if ( ! (equivalent(s1, s2) && equivalent(s2, s3)) ) {
        error_occurred = TRUE;
        return;
    }

    Number_Of_Bytes = (s1->upper - s1->lower)/WORDSIZE + 1;
    for ( i = 0 ; i < Number_Of_Bytes; i++ )
        s3->bits[i] = s1->bits[i] & ˜(s2->bits[i]);
    error_occurred = FALSE;
}
```

Figure 12.8 Subtract bit-vector routine

The final operation is iteration. This operation uses C's dereferencing features to execute an application-specified function. Figure 12.9 shows the code. The function f receives each element—not the bit, but the actual value. This requires converting the bit position into the value, the inverse mapping from that required for

```
void Iterate(s, f)
    set     *s;
    boolean (*f)();
{
    register int    i, j, Number_Of_Bytes;
    Number_Of_Bytes = (s->upper - s->lower)/WORDSIZE + 1;

    error_occurred = FALSE;

    for ( i = 0; i < Number_Of_Bytes; i++ )
        for ( j = 0; j < WORDSIZE; j++ )
            if ( (s->bits[i] >> j) % 2 )
                if ( ! (*f)(j + i*WORDSIZE + s->lower) )
                    return;
}
```

Figure 12.9 Bit-vector iterator routine

other operations. The function is expected to return a Boolean value. If this value is TRUE, another element will be passed to f; if FALSE, the iteration will cease. This lets applications exert some control over the iteration.

12.6 HASHING

If a large number of documents must be searched, or if representing their names using integers is not convenient, then bit vectors are unacceptable. This section will show how to use *hashing,* another common set implementation technique. The approach is not as fast as bit vectors, but it makes far more efficient use of space. In fact, whereas bit vectors explicitly restrict the maximum number of elements, hashing permits sets of arbitrary size. The trade-off is in speed: performance is inversely proportional to a set's cardinality. However, good performance characteristics can be achieved if one has some idea in advance of the average size of the sets that will be manipulated, a quantity that is usually available.

Hashing is actually useful in implementing many important IR operations. Chapter 13 gives an in-depth presentation of hashing. Readers not familiar with hashing may wish to study that chapter before reading any more of this section.

The implementation will use chaining, not open addressing. It is possible, but risky, to use open addressing. A hash table must be resized when full, which is a difficult operation, as explained later.

The concepts underlying the hashing-based implementation are straightforward. Each set is implemented using a single hash table. An element is inserted in a set by inserting it into the set's hash table. Its presence is verified by examining the appropriate bucket.

This implementation will be less restrictive about typing than the implementation given for bit vectors. No assumptions will be made about the type of data; the application using the hash table will be responsible for assuring that the elements are all homogeneously typed. The results will be unpredictable if this requirement is violated. In return, it will be possible to store any type of data—not just integers. The application must provide some hints to the set operation routines about the nature of the data, however. It will supply the number of buckets and a hashing function $f(v)$, mapping from the domain of the set elements to integers. This lets applications achieve much better performance. The information will be passed as part of the process of creating a set. There will be some enforcement of set types, however, and it will be based on this information.

The implementation of the set, then, will need to maintain this information. A plausible implementation of the set type is:

```
typedef char        element_Type;

typedef struct be_str {
    elementType   datum;
    struct be_str *next_datum;
} bucket_element;

typedef struct {
    int           Number_Of_Buckets;
    bucket_element **buckets;
    int           (*hashing_function) ();
    boolean       (*comparator) ();
} set;
```

The first type definition gives the data type for set elements. Each datum is of type "char *", a C convention for a variable to contain information of any type. The second definition is used to construct the linked lists that form the buckets. The third definition contains the information needed for a set. Note that the buckets are not preallocated; only a pointer is included in the definition. The array of buckets is allocated when the set is created.

The restrictions on set equivalence can be greatly relaxed for hash sets. There are no bounds that need to be identical, as in bit vectors. The appropriate hashing function must be applied—that is, the hashing function from one table should not be used on another—but adhering to this rule is simple, since the function is included in the structure.

The creation routine is given in Figure 12.10. Note that its interface is different from the bit-vector approach, reflecting the different information needed to maintain and manipulate the sets. A "Comparator" routine must also be provided. This routine, given two values of type elementType, should return TRUE if they are

```
void Create(Number_Of_Buckets, Hashing_Function, Comparator, s)
    int      Number_Of_Buckets;
    int      (*Hashing_Function)();
    boolean  (*Comparator)();
    set      *s;
{
    register unsigned int  Bucket_Array_Size;
    register int           i;

    if ( Number_Of_Buckets <= 0 ) {
        error_occurred = TRUE;
        return;
    }
    s->Number_Of_Buckets = Number_Of_Buckets;
    s->hashing_function = Hashing_Function;
    s->comparator = Comparator;
    Bucket_Array_Size = sizeof(bucket_element) * Number_Of_Buckets;
    s->buckets = (bucket_element **)malloc(Bucket_Array_Size);
    if ( error_occurred = (s->buckets == NULL) )
        return;
    for ( i = 0; i < Number_Of_Buckets; i++ )
        s->buckets[i] = (bucket_element *)NULL;

}
```

Figure 12.10 Hashing version of Create

equal, and FALSE if they are not. Such a routine is needed for hash tables containing strings or dynamically allocated data, since C's "==" operator does not understand such structures.

C's global memory allocation routine, malloc, is used to provide space for the buckets. The use of dynamic memory requires some care. It must be freed when no longer needed, lest the application eventually run out of space. This will require the introduction of a "Destroy" operation, whose purpose is opposite of Create. Its implementation is left as an exercise to the reader.

In the bit-vector implementation, Create leaves the set in an uninitialized state, needing to be cleared before use. This is not feasible in hashing. The reason is that clearing the set involves freeing dynamically allocated space. In C, the presence of such storage is indicated by a non-null pointer. Therefore, Clear might become confused if Create did not set all buckets to NULL. That, however, leaves the set "cleared." This does leave Clear able to de-allocate space:

```
void Clear(s)
    set    *s;
{
```

```
              register int        i;
              register bucket_element *b, *next_b;

              for ( i = 0; i < s->Number_Of_Buckets; i++ )
                  if ( s->buckets[i] != NULL ) {
                      b = s->buckets[i];
                      while ( b != NULL ) {
                          next_b = b->next_datum;
                              free( (char *)b );
                              b = next_b;
                      }
                          s->buckets[i] = NULL;
                  }
                  error_occurred = FALSE;
          }
```

Almost all the operations on sets will use the hashing function. Rather than repeat it in each routine, the following C macro will be used:

```
#define hash(s,e)  (abs((*((s)->hashing_function))(e)) %
                           (s)->Number_Of_Buckets)
```

Insertion and deletion into a hash table involve linked-list operations. Figures 12.11 and 12.12 contain one implementation. This version of `Insert()` inserts an element by traversing the list associated with the bucket to which it maps. If the element is not already in the list, it is inserted at the list's head. Insertion at the head is common because, in practice, elements added recently tend to be accessed most often. Data sets for which this does not hold could use an implementation where the element is added at the end of the list. Note that application-supplied hashing function is equivalent to $f(v)$, not $h(v)$, that is, its range is all integers rather than all integers between a certain bucket size. This simplifies dynamic resizing of hash tables (an improvement discussed in Chapter 13).

Deleting an element is done using a standard linked-list technique: the list is searched for the element while a pointer is kept to the previous node. If the element is found, the pointer to the previous node is used to make that node point to the one following the element to be deleted. The storage for the deleted node is then freed. Note that if the `datum` component of the node points to dynamically allocated memory, that memory will be lost unless some other node points to it. This situation may be rectified by adding a `Free_datum` function parameter to `Create`, an extension left to the reader.

Testing whether the set is empty involves testing if there are any pointers to elements. Figure 12.13 contains the code for this. It also contains the implementation of `Member`, done using linked-list traversal.

Constructing the union of two sets implemented using hashing is somewhat more involved than is the operation with bit vectors. No one-to-one correspondence can be established between elements. All elements that hash to the same bucket will

```
void Insert(s, e)
    set            *s;
    elementType    e;
{
    register bucket_element *b, *New_Element;
    register int            bucket;

    error_occurred = FALSE;

    bucket = hash(s,e);
    for ( b = s->buckets[bucket]; b != NULL ; b = b->next_datum )
        if ( (*(s->comparator))(b->datum, e) )
            return;

    New_Element = (bucket_element *)malloc(sizeof (bucket_element));
    if ( New_Element == NULL ) {
        error_occurred = TRUE;
        return;
    }
    New_Element->datum = e;
    New_Element->next_datum = s->buckets[bucket];
    s->buckets[bucket] = New_Element;
}
```

Figure 12.11 Inserting elements in a hash table set

```
void Delete(s, e)
        set            *s;
        elementType    e;
{
    register bucket_element *b, *previous;
    register int            bucket;

    error_occurred = FALSE;

    bucket = hash(s, e);
    if ( (b = s->buckets[bucket]) == NULL )
        return;
    if ( (*(s->comparator))(b->datum, e) )
        s->buckets[bucket] = b->next_datum;
    else {
        while ( b->next_datum != NULL ) {
            if ( (*(s->comparator))(b->datum, e) )
                break;
            previous = b;
            b = b->next_datum;
        }
```

Figure 12.12 Deleting elements from a hash table set

```
                            if ( b == NULL )
                                return;
                            previous->next_datum = b->next_datum;
                }
                free( (char *)b );
        }
```

Figure 12.12 (*cont.*)

```
boolean Empty(s)
    set    *s;
{
    register int i;

    error_occurred = FALSE;
    for ( i = 0; i < s->Number_Of_Buckets; i++ )
        if ( s->buckets[i] != NULL )
            return FALSE;
    return TRUE;
}

boolean Member(s, e)
        set                *s;
        elementType        e;
{
    register bucket_element *b;
    register int            bucket;

    error_occurred = FALSE;

    bucket = hash(s, e);
    for ( b = s->buckets[bucket]; b != NULL ; b = b->next_datum )
        if ( (*(s->comparator))(b->datum, e) )
            return TRUE;
    return FALSE;
}
```

Figure 12.13 Empty and Member hashing routines

be in the same list, but the respective lists may be ordered differently—a list's order depends on the order in which elements were inserted. The approach used is to add each element of set s1 to s3, then scan through each element of s2, adding the element to s3 if it is not already there. Figure 12.14 shows the implementation.

The concepts behind the implementations of intersection and subtraction are similar. They are shown in Figures 12.15 and 12.16. Intersecting involves traversing through s1 and adding to s3 those elements that are also in s2; subtracting works by adding to s3 those elements that are in s1 but not s2.

```
void Unite(s1, s2, s3)
    set    *s1, *s2;
    set    *s3;
{
    register int            i;
    register bucket_element *b;

    Copy(s1, s3);
    if ( Error_Occurred() )
        return;

    for ( i = 0; i < s2->Number_Of_Buckets; i++ ) {
        if ( s2->buckets[i] == NULL )
            continue;
        for ( b = s2->buckets[i]; b != NULL; b = b->next_datum )
            if ( ! Member(s3, b->datum) ) {
                Insert(s3, b->datum);
                if ( Error_Occurred() )
                    return;
            }
    }
    error_occurred = FALSE;
}
```

Figure 12.14 Unite hashing routine

```
void Intersect(s1, s2, s3)
    set    *s1, *s2;
    set    *s3;
{
    register int            i;
    register bucket_element *b;

    Clear(s3);

    for ( i = 0; i < s1->Number_Of_Buckets; i++ ) {
        if ( s1->buckets[i] == NULL )
            continue;
        for ( b = s1->buckets[i]; b != NULL; b = b->next_datum )
            if ( Member(s2, b->datum) ) {
                Insert(s3, b->datum);
                if ( Error_Occurred() )
                    return;
            }
    }
    error_occurred = FALSE;
}
```

Figure 12.15 Intersect hashing routine

```
void Subtract(s1, s2, s3)
    set    *s1, *s2;
    set    *s3;
{
    register int            i;
    register bucket_element *b;

    Clear(s3);

    for ( i = 0; i < s1->Number_Of_Buckets; i++ ) {
        if ( s1->buckets[i] == NULL )
            continue;
        for ( b = s1->buckets[i]; b != NULL; b = b->next_datum )
            if ( ! Member(s2, b->datum) ) {
                Insert(s3, b->datum);
                if ( Error_Occurred() )
                    return;
            }
    }
    error_occurred = FALSE;
}
```

Figure 12.16 Subtract hashing routine

Copying a hash table involves copying the bucket array, plus all lists in the buckets. The code to do so is in Figure 12.17. The routine does *not* simply copy the lists; the data from one must be rehashed into the other, since the two may not have identical bucket array lengths or hash functions. Even if the tables are equivalent in these respects, they will not be identical after the copying operation: the order of elements within the buckets is reversed. This will only show up during iteration. Since the order of elements during iteration is not defined, the difference is irrelevant.

The final operation is iteration. It is shown in Figure 12.18. The technique to be used is similar to that of Copy: traverse through each list in each bucket, passing each datum to the function provided to Iterate. Unlike bit vectors, this traversal will almost certainly not yield the elements in any particular oder. The order will depend on both the hashing function and the order of insertion.

12.7 ANALYSIS

To aid the reader in understanding the relative merits of the two implementations, this section presents an analysis of the time and space required for the two set implementation techniques. The analysis for each is straightforward. The operations of most concern are Insert, Unite, Intersect, and Subtract, since it is presumed that most applications will spend the majority of their time manipulating sets

```
void Copy(source, destination)
    set *source, *destination;
{
    register int              i, h;
    register bucket_element   *e, *b;

    Clear(destination);
    for ( i = 0; i < source->Number_Of_Buckets; i++ ) {
        if ( source->buckets[i] == NULL )
            continue;
        for ( b = source->buckets[i]; b != NULL; b = b->next_datum ) {
            h = hash(destination, b->datum);
            e = (bucket_element *)malloc(sizeof (bucket_element));
            if ( e == NULL ) {
                error_occurred = TRUE;
                return;
            }
            e->datum = b->datum;
            e->next_datum = destination->buckets[h];
            destination->buckets[h] = e;
        }
    }
    error_occurred = FALSE;
}
```

Figure 12.17   Copying a hash table set

```
void Iterate(s, f)
    set     *s;
    boolean (*f)();
{
    register int            i;
    register bucket_element *b;

    error_occurred = FALSE;

    for ( i = 0; i < s->Number_Of_Buckets; i++ )
        for ( b = s->buckets[i]; b != NULL; b = b->next_datum )
            if ( ! (*f)(b->datum) )
                return;
}
```

Figure 12.18   Hashing iterator routine

rather than creating them. For the sake of completeness, however, all routines will be analyzed.

For bit vectors, the insertion and deletion operations are $O(C)$, that is, their running time is constant. The exact time will depend on the speed of the division operation on the underlying hardware, the fundamental bottleneck in the implementation (bit operations such as &= and ˜ are usually much quicker). The other operations, which iterate across the set, have running time that depends on the set domain. Assuming this quantity to be N, they require $O(N)$ steps. The actual value will be closer to N/WORDSIZE, since the operations are able to access entire words rather than individual bits. The exception is Iterate(), which must scan every bit, making it closer to $O(N)$.

The space requirements for bit vectors are somewhat worse. They are also constant, but potentially quite large. In the implementation given here, MAX_ELEMENTS/WORDSIZE+2 × sizeof(int) bytes will be needed to store any bit-vector set. As noted previously, this can easily be rather large.

The behavior of hashing algorithms is not quite so predictable. It depends on the randomness of the hashing function on the data being stored. Assuming that the hashing function is "reasonably" random, worst-case and expected behavior are not difficult to derive. Worst-case will be presented first. The hashing function is usually chosen to be $O(C)$ (nonlinear functions defeat the advantages of hashing). The time required once the hashing function is computed will be proportional to the number of elements in the bucket. At worst, all elements will be in a single bucket. If so, then insertion, deletion, and membership tests all require $O(N)$, where N is the number of elements in the set. The union, intersection, and difference routines have significantly poorer worst-case behavior. Consider the Unite operation on two sets that each have all elements in a single bucket. The Member() test requires $O(N)$ steps for a single invocation. Since the inner for-loop iterates through N elements, the complexity of the loop is $O(N^2)$. This logic also applies to Intersect and Subtract.

The expected running time is significantly better. If the elements are distributed randomly, and if the number of elements N is less than the number of buckets B, then the expected number of elements in any bucket is less than one. Thus, the expected time for insertion, deletion, and membership testing would be constant, and the expected time for uniting, intersecting, or subtracting two sets would be $O(N)$. This is likely to be a great improvement over bit vectors, since the number of elements in a set is usually very small compared to the number of elements in a domain. Of course, N cannot easily be predicted in advance, so N may very well exceed B. Even so, N must reach B^2 before the performance degrades to $O(N^2)$ for union, intersection, and difference. Moreover, the number of buckets can also be increased at any time to exceed N, lowering the expected complexity to $O(C)$. Table 12.1 summarizes this data for both approaches.

Hash tables require considerably less space than bit vectors. The size is determined more by the number of elements than the size of the domain. The exact formula for the space depends on the number of buckets as well. Assuming that P is the

Table 12.1: Relative Algorithmic Complexity for Different Set Implementations

	Hashing		Bit Vectors	
	Worst-Case	**Average**	**Worst-Case**	**Average**
`Insert/Delete/Member`	$O(N)$	$O(C)$	$O(C)$	$O(C)$
`Unite/Intersect/Subtract`	$O(N^2)$	$O(N)$	$O(W)$	$O(W)$
`Create/Empty`	$O(B)$	$O(B)$	$O(W)$	$O(W)$
`Copy`	$O(N)$	$O(N)$	$O(W)$	$O(W)$

N = number of elements
C = constant
B = number of buckets in hash table
W = number of words in bit string

space required to store a pointer, and that each element requires E units of space, a hash table of N element requires

$$BP + NP + NE$$

units. Table 12.2 contrasts the space requirements for bit vectors and hash tables. Bytes are assumed to contain 8 bits, pointers 16. The sets are representing integers; it is assumed that the minimum possible size will be used (i.e., short, int, or long). The hash table has 503 buckets, implying that any hash table requires at least 1,006 bytes. The tables show how the advantages of bit vectors rapidly diminish in proportion to the size of the number of elements in the domain.

Table 12.2: Relative Space Requirements for Different Set Implementations

Bit Vectors			
Domain Size	**Number of Elements**		
	64	**1024**	**2^{15}**
256	32	—	—
2^{15}	4096	4096	4096
2^{31}	2^{28}	2^{28}	2^{28}

Hash Tables			
Domain Size	**Number of Elements**		
	64	**1024**	**2^{15}**
256	1198	4078	99,310
2^{15}	1262	5102	132,078
2^{31}	1390	7100	197,614

REFERENCES

KERNIGHAN, B. W., and D. M. RITCHIE. 1988. *The C Programming Language*, 2nd ed. Englewood Cliffs, N.J.: Prentice Hall.

PARNAS, D. L. 1972. On the Criteria to be Used in Decomposing Systems into Modules. *Communications of the ACM*, 15(12), 1053–58.

SEDGEWICK, R. 1990. *Algorithms in C*. Reading, Mass: Addison-Wesley.

13

Hashing Algorithms

Steven Wartik **Edward Fox** **Lenwood Heath** **Qi-Fan Chen**

Software Productivity Consortium
Virginia Polytechnic Institute and State University

Abstract

This chapter discusses hashing, an information storage and retrieval technique useful for implementing many of the other structures in this book. The concepts underlying hashing are presented, along with two implementation strategies. The chapter also contains an extensive discussion of perfect hashing, an important optimization in information retrieval, and an $O(n)$ algorithm to find minimal perfect hash functions for a set of keys.

13.1 INTRODUCTION

Accessing information based on a key is a central operation in information retrieval. An information retrieval system must determine, given a particular value, the location (or locations) of information that have been decided to be relevant to that value. Other chapters in this book have addressed the issue; in particular, Chapters 3–6 have dealt with useful techniques for organizing files for efficient access. However, these chapters have been concerned with file-level concerns. They have not covered the fundamental underlying algorithms for organizing the indices to these files.

This chapter discusses *hashing*, a ubiquitous information retrieval strategy for providing efficient access to information based on a key. Under many conditions, hashing is effective both in time and space. Information can usually be accessed in constant time (although the worst-case performance can be quite poor). Space use is not optimal but is at least acceptable for most circumstances.

The material in this chapter stresses the most important concepts of hashing, and how it can be implemented. Some important theory for hashing is presented, but without derivation. Knuth (1973) provides a fuller treatment, and also gives a history and bibliography of many of the concepts in this chapter.

Hashing does have some drawbacks. As this chapter will demonstrate, they can be summarized by mentioning that it pays to know something about the data being stored; lack of such knowledge can lead to large performance fluctuations. Relevant factors include some knowledge of the domain (English prose vs. technical text, for instance), information regarding the number of keys that will be stored, and stability

of data. If these factors can be predicted with some reliability—and in an information retrieval system, they usually can—then hashing can be used to advantage over
most other types of retrieval algorithms.

13.2 CONCEPTS OF HASHING

The problem at hand is to define and implement a mapping from a domain of keys to
a domain of locations. The domain of keys can be any data type—strings, integers,
and so on. The domain of locations is usually the m integers between 0 and $m - 1$,
inclusive. The mapping between these two domains should be both quick to compute
and compact to represent.

Consider the problem first from the performance standpoint. The goal is to
avoid *collisions*. A collision occurs when two or more keys map to the same location. If no keys collide, then locating the information associated with a key is simply
the process of determining the key's location. Whenever a collision occurs, some extra computation is necessary to further determine a unique location for a key. Collisions therefore degrade performance.

Assume the domain of keys has N possible values. Collisions are always possible whenever $N > m$, that is, when the number of values exceeds the number of locations in which they can be stored. The best performance is therefore achieved by
having $N = m$, and using a 1 : 1 mapping between keys and locations. Defining
such a mapping is easy. It requires only a little knowledge of the representation of
the key domain. For example, if keys are consecutive integers in the range (N_1, N_2),
then $m = N_2 - N_1 + 1$ and the mapping on a key k is $k - N_1$. If keys are two-
character strings of lowercase letters, then $m = 26 \times 26$, and the mapping (using C
character manipulation for ASCII) is $(k[0] - 'a') * (k[1] - 'a')$. These two
mappings can be computed in constant time, and are therefore ideal from a performance standpoint.

Now consider compactness. If keys are drawn from the set of strings of letters
up to 10 characters long—too short to be of use in information retrieval systems—
then $N = \Sigma_{i=1}^{10} 52^i \approx 10^{17}$. An implementation of a mapping with $m = N$ is impossible: no existing computer contains enough memory. The mapping that is best suited
to performance is wasteful of space.

The problem is that the mapping is defined over all N values, that is, over all
possible keys in a very large domain. In practice, no application ever stores all keys
in a domain simultaneously unless the size of the domain is small. Let n be the number of keys actually stored. In most applications, $n \ll N$, so only a few of the many
possible keys are in use at any time. From the standpoint of compactness, the ideal
representation would have $m = 1$; that is, all locations would be in use, no matter
how many keys are in the table. All keys collide, and a strategy must exist to resolve
collisions. As discussed above, any such strategy will require extra computation.

The mapping involved in hashing thus has two facets of performance: number
of collisions and amount of unused storage. Optimization of one occurs at the ex-

Hashing Algorithms   Chap. 13

pense of the other. The approach behind hashing is to optimize both; that is, to tune both simultaneously so as to achieve a reasonably low number of collisions together with a reasonably small amount of unused space.

The concept underlying hashing is to choose m to be approximately the maximum expected value of n. (The exact value depends on the implementation technique.) Since $n \ll N$, in theory many collisions are possible, and indeed are expected in practice. However, n is usually sufficiently small that memory consumption is not excessive; also, an attempt is made to choose a mapping that randomly spreads keys throughout the locations, lowering the probability of collision.

The information to be retrieved is stored in a *hash table*. A hash table is best thought of as an array of m locations, called *buckets*. Each bucket is indexed by an integer between 0 and $m - 1$. A bucket can be empty, meaning that it corresponds to no key in use, or not empty, meaning that it does correspond to a key in use, that information has been placed in it, and that subsequent attempts to place information in it based on another key will result in a collision. (Whether "not empty" is equivalent to "full" depends on the implementation, as sections 13.4.1 and 13.4.2 show.)

The mapping between a key and a bucket is called the *hash function*. This is a function whose domain is that of the keys, and whose range is between 0 and $m - 1$, inclusive. Storing a value in a hash table involves using the hash function to compute the bucket to which a key corresponds, and placing the information in that bucket. Retrieving information requires using the hash function to compute the bucket that contains it.

For example, suppose a hash table is to be implemented with 5 buckets, and a hash function $h(k) = k \bmod 5$, where k is an integer, is used to map keys into the table. Figure 13.1 shows the hash table after the keys 1, 2, and 64 have been inserted. 1 is stored in bucket 1 because 1 mod 5 = 1, 2 is stored in bucket 2 because 2 mod 5 = 2, and so on.

This scheme works well as long as there are no collisions. The time to store and retrieve data is proportional to the time to compute the hash function. Typically, this function is very simple, and can be calculated in constant time. The space required to store the elements is that required for an array of m elements. Unless m is very large, this should not be a problem.

In practice, however, collisions should be expected. Indeed, storing more than m distinct keys into a hash table with m will always cause collisions. Even with fewer than m keys, choosing a hash function that distributes keys uniformly is sufficiently difficult that collisions can be expected to start occurring long before the hash table fills up.

This suggests two areas for further study: first, how to choose a hash function, and second, what to do when a collision occurs. Section 13.3 discusses hash func-

Buckets

0	1	2	3	4
	1	2		64

$h(k) = k \bmod 5$
Table contains 1, 2, 64

Figure 13.1 Visual illustration of a hash table

tions. Section 13.4 presents two implementation techniques and the collision resolution strategies they employ. Section 13.5 explains perfect hash functions, a technique for avoiding, rather than resolving, collisions.

13.3 HASHING FUNCTIONS

The choice of hash function is extremely important. The ideal function, termed a *perfect* hash function, would distribute all elements across the buckets such that no collisions ever occurred. As discussed in the previous section, this is desirable for performance reasons. Mapping a key to a bucket is quick, but all collision-resolution strategies take extra time—as much as $\theta(m + n)$. Retrieval times become nonuniform, making performance hard to predict. A perfect hash function guarantees uniform performance.

Perfect hash functions are extremely hard to achieve, however, and are generally only possible in specialized circumstances, such as when the set of elements to hash is known in advance. Another such circumstance was illustrated in Chapter 12: the bit-vector implementation of a set illustrates a perfect hash function. Every possible value has a unique bucket. This illustrates an important point: the more buckets a hash table contains, the better the performance is likely to be. Bucket quantity must be considered carefully. Even with a large number of buckets, though, a hash table is still only as good as its hash function.

The most important consideration in choosing a hash function is the type of data to be hashed. Data sets are often biased in some way, and a failure to account for this bias can ruin the effectiveness of the hash table. For example, the hash table in Figure 13.1 is storing integers that are all powers of two. If all keys are to be powers of two, then $h(k) = k \mod 5$ is a poor choice: no key will ever map to bucket 0. As another example, suppose a hash table is be used to store last names. A 26-bucket hash table using a hash function that maps the first letter of the last name to the buckets would be a poor choice: names are much more likely to begin with certain letters than others (very few last names begin with "X").

A hash function's range must be an integer between 0 and $m - 1$, where m is the number of buckets. This suggests that the hash function should be of the form:

$$h(v) = f(v) \mod m$$

since modulo arithmetic yields a value in the desired range. Knuth (1973) suggests using as the value for m a prime number such that $r^k \mod m = a \mod m$, where r is the radix of v, and a and k are small. Empirical evidence has found that this choice gives good performance in many situations. (However, Figure 13.1 shows that making m a prime number is not always desirable.)

The function $f(v)$ should account for nuances in the data, if any are known. If v is not an integer, then the internal integer representation of its bits is used, or the first portion thereof. For example, $f(v)$ for a nonempty charcter string might be the

Hashing Algorithms   Chap. 13

ASCII character-code value of the last character of the string. For a four-byte floating-point number, $f(v)$ might be the integer value of the first byte.

Such simple-minded schemes are usually not acceptable. The problems of using the first character of a string have already been discussed; the last character is better, but not much so. In many computers, the first type of a floating-point word is the exponent, so all numbers of the same magnitude will hash to the same bucket. It is usually better to treat v as a sequence of bytes and do one of the following for $f(v)$:

1. Sum or multiply all the bytes. Overflow can be ignored.
2. Use the last (or middle) byte instead of the first.
3. Use the square of a few of the middle bytes.

The last method, called the "mid-square" method, can be computed quickly and generally produces satisfactory results.

13.4 IMPLEMENTING HASHING

Once the hash function and table size have been determined, it remains to choose the scheme by which they shall be realized. All techniques use the same general approach: the hash table is implemented as an array of m buckets, numbered from 0 to $m - 1$. The following operations are usually provided by an implementation of hashing:

1. Initialization: indicate that the hash table contains no elements.
2. Insertion: insert information, indexed by a key k, into a hash table. If the hash table already contains k, then it cannot be inserted. (Some implementations do allow such insertion, to permit replacing existing information.)
3. Retrieval: given a key k, retrieve the information associated with it.
4. Deletion: remove the information associated with key k from a hash table, if any exists. New information indexed by k may subsequently be placed in the table.

Compare this definition with the one given in Chapter 12. There, the "information" associated with a key is simply the presence or absence of that key. This chapter considers the more general case, where other information (e.g., document names) is associated with a key.

Figure 13.2 shows a C-language interface that realizes the above operations. The routines all operate on three data types: hashTable, key, and information. The definition of the hashTable type will be left to the following sections, since particular implementation techniques require different structures. The

```
void Initialize(hashTable *h);  /* Make h empty.                */

void Insert(hashTable *h,       /* Insert i into h, keyed       */
            key k,              /* by k.                        */
            information i);

void Delete(hashTable *h,       /* Delete from h the            */
            key k);             /* information associated       */
                                /* with k.                      */

information                     /* Retrieve from h the          */
    Retrieve(hashTable *h,      /* information associated       */
             key k);            /* with k.                      */

#define OKAY          0         /* These values are returned    */
#define DUPLICATE_KEY 1         /* by op_status(), indicating   */
#define NO_SUCH_KEY   2         /* the result of the operation  */
#define TABLE_FULL    3         /* last executed.               */
int op_status();
```

Figure 13.2 Interface to a hashing implementation

data types of the key and the information are application-dependent; of course, the
hash function must be targeted toward the key's data type.

13.4.1 Chained Hashing

The first implementation strategy is called chained hashing. It is so named because each bucket stores a linked list—that is, a chain—of key-information pairs,
rather than a single one. The solution to a collision, then, is straightforward. If a key
maps to a bucket containing no information, it is placed at the head of the list for
that bucket. If a key maps to a bucket that already has information, it is placed in the
list associated with that bucket. (Usually it is placed at the head of the list, on the
assumption that information recently stored is likely to be accessed sooner than
older information; this is also simplest to implement.) Figure 13.3 shows how the

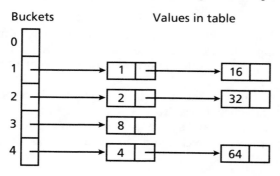

Figure 13.3 Visual illustration of a chained hash table

Hashing Algorithms   Chap. 13

hash table from Figure 13.1 would appear if it was a chained table and all powers of two from 1 to 64 had been stored in it.

In this scheme, a bucket may have any number of elements. A hash table with m buckets may therefore store more than m keys. However, performance will degrade as the number of keys increases. Computing the bucket in which a key resides is still fast—a matter of evaluating the hash function—but locating it within that bucket (or simply determining its presence, which is necessary in all operations) requires traversing the linked list. In the worst case (where all n keys map to a single location), the average time to locate an element will be proportional to $n/2$. In the best case (where all chains are of equal length), the time will be proportional to n/m. It is best not to use hashing when n is expected to greatly exceed m, so n/m can be expected to remain linearly proportional to m. Usually, most chains' lengths will be close to this ratio, so the expected time is still constant.

The hashing-based implementation of Boolean operations in Chapter 12 uses chains. Most of the code from the routines Insert, Delete, Clear (for Initialize), and Member (for Retrieve) can be used directly. Chapter 12 also discussed the need for a routine to create the table. This routine had as parameters the hash function and an element-comparison routine, which shows how this information may be associated with the table.

Since the code is so similar, it will not be repeated here. Instead, a sketch is given of the differences. This is easily illustrated by considering the new data types needed. The hash table is declared as follows:

```
typedef ... information;
typedef ... key;

typedef struct be_str {
    key            k;
    information    i;
    struct be_str *next_datum;
};

typedef struct {
    int             Number_Of_Buckets;
    bucket_element  *buckets;
    int             (*hashing_function) ();
    boolean         (*comparator) ();
} hashTable;
```

As in Chapter 12, the specifics of information and key are application-dependent, and so are not given here. The main difference from the routines in Chapter 12 lies in the need to associate the information with its key in a bucket. Hence, each bucket has a field for information. The line in Insert:

```
New_Element->datum = e;
```

is replaced with:

```
New_Element->k = k;
New_Element->i = i;
```

The other routines differ analogously.

13.4.2 Open Addressing

Sometimes, the likelihood that the number of keys will exceed the number of buckets is quite low. This might happen, for instance, when a collection of data is expected to remain static for a long period of time (as is often true in information retrieval). In such a circumstance, the keys associated with the data can be determined at the time the data is stored. As another example, sometimes the maximum number of keys is known, and the average number is expected to hover around that value. In these cases, the flexibility offered by chained hashing is wasted. A technique tailored to the amount of storage expected to be used is preferable.

This is the philosophy behind open addressing. Each bucket in the hash table can contain a single key-information pair. (That is, a bucket that is not empty is "full.") Information is stored in the table by computing the hash function value of its key. If the bucket indexed by that value is empty, the key and information are stored there. If the bucket is not empty, another bucket is (deterministically) selected. This process, called *probing,* repeats until an empty bucket is found.

Many strategies to select another bucket exist. The simplest is *linear probing.* The hash table is implemented as an array of buckets, each being a structure holding a key, associated information, and an indication of whether the bucket is empty. When a collision is detected at bucket b, bucket $b + 1$ is "probed" to see if it is empty. If $b + 1 = m$, then bucket 0 is tried. In other words, buckets are sequentially searched until an empty bucket is found.

For example, consider Figure 13.4(a), which shows a 10-bucket hashing table containing powers of two between 1 and 16, where $h(v) = v \bmod 10$. Suppose the keys 32, 64, 128, 256, and 512 are now inserted. Key 32 collides with key 2, so it is inserted in bucket 3. Key 64 collides with key 4, so it is inserted in bucket 5. By the time key 512 is inserted, the table is as in Figure 13.4(b), with all buckets except 0 full. Inserting key 512 necessitates the sequence of probes shown in Figure 13.4(c). Worse, this sequence is duplicated each time 512 is retrieved. Retrieving all other elements will take little time requiring at most one extra probe, but retrieving 512 will be expensive.

This illustrates a characteristic of linear probing known as *clustering*: the tendency of keys to cluster around a single location. Clustering greatly increases the average time to locate keys in a hash table. It has been shown (see Sedgewick [1990], for instance) that, for a table less than two-thirds full, linear probing uses an average of less than five probes, but for tables that are nearly full, the average number of probes becomes proportional to m.

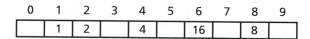

(a) After inserting 1, 2, 4, 8, and 16

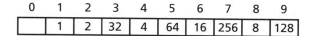

(b) After inserting 32, 64, 128, and 256

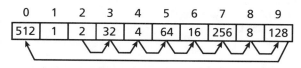

(c) Inserting 512

Figure 13.4 Clustering in a hash table

The problem is that hashing is based on the assumption that most keys won't map to the same address. Linear probing, however, avoids collisions by clustering keys around the address to which they map, ruining the suitability of nearby buckets. What is desirable is a more random redistribution. A better scheme than linear probing is to redistribute colliding keys randomly. This will not prevent collisions, but it will lessen the number of collisions due to clustering.

The redistribution can be done using some function $h_2(b)$ that, when applied to a bucket index b, yields another bucket index. In other words, the original hash function having failed, a second one is applied to the bucket. As with linear probing, another probe will be tried if the new bucket is also full. This introduces some constraints on h_2. $h_2 = b + m$ would be a poor choice: it would always try the same bucket. $h_2 = b + m/i$ where m is a multiple of i would also be bad: it can only try m/i of the buckets in the table. Ideally, successive applications of h_2 should examine every bucket. (Note that linear probing does this: it is simply $h_2(b) = (b + 1)$ mod m). This will happen if $h_2(b) = (b + i)$ mod m, where i is not a divisor of m. A commonly used scheme employs a formula called *quadratic probing*. This uses a sequence of probes of the form $h + i$, where $i = 1, 4, 9, \ldots$. This is not guaranteed to probe every bucket, but the results are usually quite satisfactory.

In open addressing, it is possible to fill a hash table—that is, to place it in a state where no more information can be stored in it. As mentioned above, open addressing is best when the maximum number of keys to be stored does not exceed m. There are, however, strategies for coping when this situation arises unexpectedly. The hash table may be redefined to contain more buckets, for instance. This extension is straightforward. It can degrade performance, however, since the hash function might have been tuned to the original bucket size.

The data structures for implementing open addressing are simpler than for chained hashing, because all that is needed is an array. A suitable definition for a hash table is:

```
typedef struct {
    key         k;
    information i;

    bool    empty;
} bucket;

typedef struct {
    int     number_of_buckets;
    bucket *buckets;
    int     (*hashing_function) ();
    int     (*comparator) ();
} hashTable;
```

Each element of the table is a structure, not a pointer, so using a null pointer to indicate if a bucket is empty or full no longer works. Hence, a field empty has been added to each bucket. If the key is itself a pointer type, then the key field can be used to store this information. The implementation here considers the more general case.

Except for probing, the algorithms are also simpler, since no linked list manipulation is needed. Figures 13.5–13.8 show how it is done. As before, the macro:

```
#define hash(h, k)  ((*((h)->hashing_function))(k) % (h)->number_of_buckets)
```

is defined to abstract the computation of a bucket for a key.

```
void Initialize(h)
    hashTable *h;
{
    register int i;

    status = OKAY;
    for ( i = 0; i < h->number_of_buckets; i++ )
        h->buckets[i].empty = TRUE;
}
```

Figure 13.5 Initializing an open-addressed hash table

These routines all behave similarly. They attempt to locate either an empty bucket (for Insert) or a bucket with a key of interest. This is done through some probing sequence. The basic operations of probing are initialization (setting up to begin the probe), determining if all spots have been probed, and determining the next bucket to probe. Figure 13.9 shows how quadratic probing could be implemented. The probe is considered to have failed when $(m + 1)/2$ buckets have been tried. In practice, this value has been shown to give good results.

```
void Insert(h, k, i)
    hashTable   *h;
    key         k;
    information i;
{
    register int b;
    b = hash(h, k);

    status = OKAY;
    Initialize_Probe(h);
    while ( ! h->buckets[b].empty && ! Probe_Exhausted(h) ) {
        if ( (*h->comparator)(k, h->buckets[b].k) ) {
            status = DUPLICATE_KEY;
            return;
        }
        b = probe(h);
    }
    if ( h->buckets[b].empty ) {
        h->buckets[b].i = i;
        h->buckets[b].k = k;
        h->buckets[b].empty = FALSE;
    }
    else
        status = TABLE_FULL;
}
```

Figure 13.6 Inserting into an open-addressed hash table

```
void Delete(h, k)
    hashTable   *h;
    key         k;
{
    register int b;

    status = OKAY;
    b = hash(h, k);
    Initialize_Probe(h);
    while ( ! h->buckets[b].empty && ! Probe_Exhausted(h) ) {
        if ( (*h->comparator)(k, h->buckets[b].k) ) {
            h->buckets[b].empty = TRUE;
            return;
        }
        b = probe(h);
    }
    status = NO_SUCH_KEY;
}
```

Figure 13.7 Deleting from an open-addressed hash table

```
information Retrieve(h, k)
    hashTable    *h;
    key           k;
{
    register int b;

    status = OKAY;
    b = hash(h, k);
    Initialize_Probe(h, b);
    while ( ! h->buckets[b].empty && ! Probe_Exhausted(h) ) {
        if ( (*h->comparator)(k, h->buckets[b].k) )
            return h->buckets[b].i;
        b = probe(h);
    }
    status = NO_SUCH_KEY;
    return h->buckets[0].i;    /* Return a dummy value. */
}
```

Figure 13.8 Retrieving from an open-addressed hash table

```
static int      number_of_probes;
static int      last_bucket;

void Initialize_Probe(h, starting_bucket)
    hashTable   *h;
    int          starting_bucket;
{
    number_of_probes = 1;
    last_bucket = starting_bucket;
}


int probe(h)
    hashTable    *h;
{
    number_of_probes++;
    last_bucket = (last_bucket + number_of_probes*number_of_probes)
                      % h->number_of_buckets;
    return last_bucket;
}


bool Probe_Exhausted(h)
    hashTable *h;
{
    return (number_of_probes >= (h->number_of_buckets+1)/2);
}
```

Figure 13.9 Quadratic probing implementation

13.5 MINIMAL PERFECT HASH FUNCTIONS

Section 13.3 mentioned that the ideal hash function would avoid collisions by mapping all keys to distinct locations. This is termed a *perfect hash function*. A perfect hash function is ideal from a performance standpoint in that the time to locate the bucket corresponding to a particular key is always the time needed to compute the hash function. This predictability improves the ability to precisely infer performance characteristics.

Perfect hash functions are possible, but generally only when the set of keys to be hashed is known at the time the function is derived. Best of all under this condition is a *minimal perfect hash function*, a perfect hash function with the property that it hashes m keys to m buckets with no collisions. Not only is performance optimized, but no space is wasted in the hash table.

In general, it is difficult to find a MPHF. Knuth (1973) observes that only one in 10 million functions is a perfect hash function for mapping the 31 most frequently used English words into 41 addresses. Minimal perfect hash functions are rarer still.

This section presents an algorithm for finding minimal perfect hash functions for a given set of keys. The algorithm is not guaranteed to work, but is almost always successful. Before explaining the algorithm, it will be helpful to give some background on the topic.

13.5.1 Existence Proof

One might ask whether a minimal perfect hash function (hereafter abbreviated MPHF) h exists for a set of keys. Jaeschke (1981) proves that the answer is yes. Consider the problem of mapping a set of m positive integers, bounded above by N without collisions into a hash table T with m buckets. The following algorithm defines a suitable MPHF:

```
Store the keys in an array k of length m.
Allocate an array A of length N, and initialize all values to ERROR.
for ( i = 1; i < m; i++ )
    A[k[i]] = i
```

The array A defines h: allowable keys map into addresses $\{0, ..., m - 1\}$ and other keys map into ERROR.

This defines a MPHF, but the array A is mostly empty; since usually $m \ll N$, the hash function occupies too much space to be useful. In other words, efficient use of storage in hashing encompasses the representation of the hash function as well as optimal use of buckets. Both must be acceptably small if minimal perfect hashing is to be practical.

13.5.2 An Algorithm to Compute a MPHF: Concepts

The scarcity of suitable functions suggests that it is best to search function spaces for them using computer programs. There are several strategies for doing so. The simplest is to select a class of functions that is likely to include a number of minimal perfect hash functions, and then search for a MPHF in that class by assigning different values to each of the parameters characterizing the class.

Carter and Wegman (1979) introduced the idea of a class H of functions that are *universal*$_2$, that is, where no pair of distinct keys collides very often. By random selection from H, one can select candidate functions and expect that a hash function having a small number of collisions can be found quickly. This technique has been applied to dynamic hashing by Ramakrishna and Larson (1989).

Sprugnoli (1978) proposes two classes of functions, one with two and the other with four parameters, that each may yield a MPHF, but searching for usable parameter values is feasible only for very small key sets. Jaeschke (1981) suggests a reciprocal hashing scheme with three parameters, guaranteed to find a MPHF, but only practical when $m \leq 20$. Chang (1986) proposes a method with only one parameter. Its value is likely to be very large, and a function is required that assigns a distinct prime to each key. However, he gives no algorithm for that function. A practical algorithm finding perfect hash functions for fairly large key sets is described by Cormack et al. (1985). They illustrate trade-offs between time and size of the hash function, but do not give tight bounds on total time to find PHFs or experimental details for very large key sets.

The above-mentioned "search-only" methods may (if general enough, and if enough time is allotted) directly yield a perfect hash function, with the right assignment of parameters. However, analysis of the lower bound on the size of a suitable MPHF suggests that if parameter values are not to be virtually unbounded, then there must be a moderate number of parameters to assign. In the algorithms of Cichelli (1980) and of Cercone et al. (1983) are two important concepts: using tables of values as the parameters, and using a mapping, ordering, and searching (MOS) approach (see Figure 13.10). While their tables seem too small to handle very large key sets, the MOS approach is an important contribution to the field of perfect hashing.

In the MOS approach, construction of a MPHF is accomplished in three steps. First, the **mapping** step transforms the key set from an original to a new universe. Second, the **ordering** step places the keys in a sequence that determines the order in which hash values are assigned to keys. The ordering step may partition the order into subsequences of consecutive keys. A subsequence may be thought of as a *level*, with the keys of each level assigned their hash values at the same time. Third, the **searching** step assigns hash values to the keys of each level. If the Searching step encounters a level it is unable to accommodate, it backtracks, sometimes to an ear-

$$\boxed{\textit{MAPPING} \longrightarrow \textit{ORDERING} \longrightarrow \textit{SEARCHING}}$$

Figure 13.10 MOS method to find perfect hash functions

lier level, assigns new hash values to the keys of that level, and tries again to assign hash values to later levels.

13.5.3 Sager's Method and Improvement

Sager (1984, 1985) formalizes and extends Cichelli's approach. Like Cichelli, he assumes that a key is given as a character string. In the mapping step, three auxiliary (hash) functions are defined on the original universe of keys U:

$$h_0: \quad U \to \{0, \ldots, m - 1\}$$

$$h_1: \quad U \to \{0, \ldots, r - 1\}$$

$$h_2: \quad U \to \{r, \ldots, 2r - 1\}$$

where r is a parameter (typically $\leq m/2$) that determines the space to store the perfect hash function (i.e., $|h| = 2r$). The auxiliary functions compress each key k into a unique identifier

$$(h_0(k), h_1(k), h_2(k))$$

which is a triple of integers in a new universe of size mr^2. The class of functions searched is

$$h(k) = \left(h_0(k) + g(h_1(k)) + g(h_2(k)) \right) \quad (\text{mod } m) \tag{1}$$

where g is a function whose values are selected during the search.

Sager uses a graph that represents the constraints among keys. The mapping step goes from keys to triples to a special bipartite graph, the *dependency graph*, whose vertices are the $h_1(k)$ and $h_2(k)$ values and whose edges represent the words. The two vertex sets of the dependency graph are $\{0, \ldots, r - 1\}$ and $\{r, \ldots, 2r - 1\}$. For each key k, there is an edge connecting $h_1(k)$ and $h_2(k)$, labeled by k. See Figure 13.11. Note that it is quite possible that some vertices will have no associated arcs (keys), and that some arcs may have the same pairs of vertices as their endpoints.

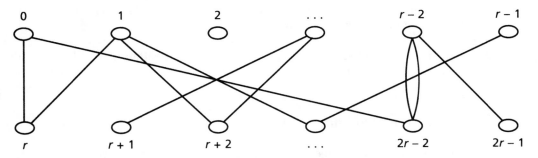

Figure 13.11 Dependency graph

In the ordering step, Sager employs a heuristic called *mincycle* that is based on finding short cycles in the graph. Each iteration of the ordering step identifies a set of unselected edges in the dependency graph in as many small cycles as possible. The set of keys corresponding to that set of edges constitutes the next level in the ordering.

There is no proof given that a minimum perfect hash function can be found, but mincycle is very successful on sets of a few hundred keys. Mincycle takes $O(m^4)$ time and $O(m^3)$ space, while the subsequent Searching step usually takes only $O(m)$ time.

Sager chooses values for r that are proportional to m. A typical value is $r = m/2$. In the case of minimal perfect hashing ($m = n$), it requires $2r = n$ computer words of lg n bits each to represent g. Fox et al. (1989a) have shown, using an argument due to Mehlhorn (1982), that a lower bound on the number of bits per key needed to represent a MPHF is approximately 1.4427. Sager's value is therefore somewhat higher than the optimal. To save space, the ratio ($2r/n$) must be reduced as low as possible, certainly below 1. Early work to explore and improve Sager's technique led to an implementation, with some slight improvements and with extensive instrumentation added on, described by Datta (1988). Further investigation by Fox et al. (1989a) yielded a modified algorithm requiring $O(m^3)$ time. This algorithm has been used to find MPHFs for sets of over a thousand words.

One thousand word key sets is good but still impractical for many information retrieval applications. As described in Fox et al. (1989b), Heath subsequently devised an $O(m \log m)$ algorithm, which is practical for large sets of keys. It is based on three crucial observations of previous work:

1. Randomness must be exploited whenever possible. The functions suggested by Sager do not yield distinct triples in the mapping stage with large key sets. Randomness can help improve this property.
2. The vertex degree distribution in the dependency graph is highly skewed. This can be exploited to make the ordering step much more efficient. Previously, it required up to $O(m^3)$ time; this observation reduces it to $O(m \log m)$.
3. Assigning g values to a set of related words can be viewed as trying to fit a pattern into a partially filled disk, where it is important to enter large patterns while the disk is only partially full.

Since the mapping and searching steps are $O(m)$, the algorithm is $O(m \log m)$ with the improved ordering step.

13.5.4 The Algorithm

This section presents the algorithm. It is described in terms of its three steps, plus the main program that fits these steps together. A complete implementation is too large to fit comfortably into this chapter, but it is included as an appendix.

The main program

The main program takes four parameters: the name of a file containing a list of *m* keys, *m*, a ratio for determining the size of the hash table, and the name of a file in which the output is to be written. It executes each of the three steps and, if they all succeed, creates a file containing a MPHF for the keys. Figure 13.12 outlines the main routine.

The main program is responsible for allocating enough arcs and vertices to form the dependency graph for the algorithm. "arcs" is an array of the arcs, and "vertices" an array of the vertices. Each arc corresponds to exactly one key. The data structures associated with arcs are as follows:

```
typedef struct arc {                 typedef struct {
    int h0, h12[2];                      int no_arcs;
    struct arc *next_edge[2];            arcType *arcArray;
} arcType;                           } arcsType;


main(argc, argv)
    int     argc;
    char    *argv[];
{
    arcsType        arcs;
    verticesType vertices;
    int             seed;

    allocate_arcs( &arcs, atoi(argv[2]) );
    allocate_vertices( &vertices, atoi(argv[2]) * atof(argv[3]) );

    if ( mapping( arcs, vertices, &seed, argv[1] ) == NORM ) {
        ordering( arcs, vertices );
        if ( searching ( arcs, vertices ) == NORM )
            write_gfun ( vertices, seed, argv[4] );
    }
}
```

Figure 13.12 Main program for MPHF algorithm

The arcType structure stores the h_0, h_1 and h_2 values for an arc, plus two singly linked lists that store the vertices arcs incident to the vertices h_1 and h_2. The arcsType structure is an array of all arcs, with a record of how many exist.

The data structures for vertices have the form:

```
typedef struct {                     typedef struct {
    int g, pred, succ;                   int no_vertices,
    struct arc  *first_edge;                 maxDegree,
} vertexType;                                vsHead,
                                             vsTail,
                                             rlistHead;
                                     vertexType* vertexArray;
                                     } verticesType;
```

In vertexType, the first_edge field is the header of a linked list of arcs incident to the vertex (the next_edge values of arcType continue the list). The pred and succ fields are a doubly linked vertex list whose purpose is explained in the ordering stage. The g field ultimately stores the g function, computed during the searching stage. To save space, however, it is used for different purposes during each of the three stages.

The dependency graph created by the mapping step has 2r vertices. (The value of r is the product of m and the ratio supplied as the third parameter to the main routine. It is therefore possible to exert some control over the size of the hash function. A large value of r increases the probability of finding a MPHF at the expense of memory.) The variable vertices, of type verticesType, holds all vertices. The fields of vertices will be explained as they are used in the various steps.

The mapping step

The code for the mapping step is shown in Figure 13.13. The step is responsible for constructing the dependency graph from the keys. This is done as follows. Three random number tables, one for each of h_0, h_1, h_2, are initialized. The number of columns in the table determines the greatest possible key length. The number of rows is currently 128: one for each possible ASCII character. (This is not strictly necessary but helps exploit randomness.) Next, the routine map_to_triples maps each key k to a triple (h_0, h_1, h_2) using the formulas:

```
int mapping( key_file, arcs, vertices, seed )
    char         *key_file;       /* in: name of file containing keys.     */
    arcsType     *arcs;           /* out: arcs in bipartite graph.         */
    verticesType *vertices;       /* out: vertices in bipartite graph.     */
    int          *seed;           /* out: seed selected to initialize the  */
                                  /* random tables.                        */
{
    int mapping_tries = 0;
    randomTablesType randomTables; /* Three random number tables.          */

    while ( mapping_tries++ < MAPPINGS ) {
        initialize_arcs( arcs );
        initialize_vertices( vertices );
        initialize_randomTable( randomTables, seed );
        map_to_triples( key_file, arcs, vertices->no_vertices/2, randomTables );
        if ( construct_graph(arcs, vertices) == NORM )
            return(NORM);
    }
    return(ABNORM);
}
```

Figure 13.13 The mapping routine

```
int construct_graph( arcs, vertices )
    arcsType      *arcs;          /* in out: arcs.                              */
    verticesType *vertices;       /* in out: vertices.                          */
{
    int i,                        /* Iterator over all arcs.                    */
        j,                        /* j = 0 and 1 for h1 and h2 side, respectively. */
        status = NORM,
        vertex;

    for ( j = 0; j < 2; j++ ) {
        for ( i = 0; i < arcs->no_arcs; i++ ) {
            vertex = arcs->arcArray[i].h12[j];    /* Update vertex degree */
            vertices->vertexArray[vertex].g++;    /* count and adjacency  */
            arcs->arcArray[i].next_edge[j] =      /* list.                */
                    vertices->vertexArray[vertex].first_edge;
            vertices->vertexArray[vertex].first_edge = &arcs ->arcArray[i];

            if ( (j == 0) && check_dup( &arcs->arcArray[i] ) == ABNORM ) {
                status = ABNORM;          /* Duplicate found. */
                break;
            }
                        /* Figure out the maximal degree of the graph. */
            if ( vertices->vertexArray[vertex].g > vertices->maxDegree )
                vertices->maxDegree = vertices->vertexArray[vertex].g;
        }
    }
    return(status);
}
```

Figure 13.14 The `construct_graph` routine

$$h_0(k) = \sum_{i=1}^{\text{len } k} table_{0i}(k_i) \tag{2}$$

$$h_1(k) = \left(\sum_{i=1}^{\text{len } k} table_{1i}(k_i) \right) \bmod r \tag{3}$$

$$h_2(k) = \left(\sum_{i=1}^{\text{len } k} table_{2i}(k_i) \right) \bmod r + r \tag{4}$$

That is, each function h_1 is computed as the sum of the random numbers indexed by the ASCII values of the key's characters. The triple for the ith key in the input file is saved in the ith entry in the `arcs` array.

The mapping step then builds the dependency graph. Half of the vertices in the dependency graph correspond to the h_1 values and are labeled $0, \ldots, r - 1$. The other half correspond to the h_2 values and are labeled $r, \ldots, 2r - 1$. There is one edge in the dependency graph for each key. A key k corresponds to an edge k, between the vertex labeled $h_1(k)$ and $h_2(k)$. There may be other edges between $h_1(k)$ and $h_2(k)$, but they are labeled with keys other than k.

Figure 13.14 shows the routine `construct_graph()`, which builds the dependency graph. The arcs have already been built (in `map_to_triples()`); what remains is to build the vertex array. Each arc is searched; the vertices associated with it are the values stored in h12[0] and h12[1]. The degree counts of these vertices are incremented, and the incidence lists associated with each vertex are updated.

Because the triples are generated using random numbers, it is possible for two triples to be identical. If this happens, a new set of random number tables must be generated, and the mapping step repeated. There is never a guarantee that all triples will be unique, although duplicates are fairly rare in practice—it can be demonstrated to be approximately $r^2/2m^3$. This value rapidly approaches 1 as m grows. To prevent infinite loops, the mapping step is never attempted more than a fixed number of times.

The ordering step

The goal of the ordering step is to partition the keys into a sequence of levels. The step produces an ordering of the vertices of the dependency graph (excluding those of degree 0, which do not correspond to any key). From this ordering, the partition is easily derived. If the vertex ordering is $v_1, \ldots, v_t$, then the level of keys $K(v_i)$ corresponding to a vertex v_i, $1 \le i \le t$, is the set of edges incident to both v_i and a vertex earlier in the ordering. More formally, if $0 \le v_i < r$, then

$$K(v_i) = \{k_j \mid h_1(k_j) = v_i, h_2(k_j) = v_s, s < i\} \tag{5}$$

Similarly, if $r \le v_i < 2r$, then

$$K(v_i) = \{k_j \mid h_2(k_j) = v_i, h_1(k_j) = v_s, s < i\} \tag{6}$$

The rationale for this ordering comes from the observation that the vertex degree distribution is skewed toward vertices of low degree. For reasons discussed in the section on the searching step, it is desirable to have levels that are as small as possible, and to have any large levels early in the ordering.

The heuristic used to order the vertices is analogous to the algorithm by Prim (1957) for constructing a minimum spanning tree. At each iteration of Prim's algorithm, an arc is added to the minimum spanning tree that is lowest in cost such that one vertex of the arc is in the partially formed spanning tree and the other vertex is not. In the ordering step, the arc selected is the one that has maximal degree at the vertex not adjacent to any selected arcs. If several arcs are equivalent, one is chosen randomly. Since the dependency graph may consist of several disconnected graphs, the selection process will not stop after the vertices in the first component graph are ordered. Rather, it will continue to process components until all vertices of nonzero degree have been put into the ordering. Figure 13.15 shows the ordering step's implementation.

The vertex sequence is maintained in a list termed the "VS list," the head of which is the vsHead field of the vertices variable. Ordering the vertices efficiently requires quickly finding the next vertex to be added into the VS list. There are two types of vertices to consider. The first are those that start a new component graph to be explored. To handle these, the ordering step first builds (in the

```
void ordering( arcs, vertices )
    arcsType            *arcs;      /* in out: the arcs.        */
    verticesType        *vertices; /* in out: the vertices.    */
{
    int            degree, side;
    vertexType *vertex;
    arcType        *arc;

    vertices->vsHead = vertices->vsTail = NP;   /* Initialize the VS list. */
    initialize_rList( vertices );
    allocate_vheap( arcs->no_arcs, vertices->no_vertices );

    while ( vertices->rlistHead != -1 ) { /* Process each component graph. */
        initialize_vheap();
        vertex = &vertices->vertexArray[vertices->rlistHead];
        do {
            vertex->g = 0;                          /* Mark node "visited".   */
            delete_from_rList( vertex, vertices );
            append_to_VS( vertex, vertices );
            if ( vertex->first_edge != 0 ) {
                /* Add adjacent nodes that are not visited and   */
                /* not in virtual heap to the virtual heap.      */

                side = vertex - vertices->vertexArray >= vertices->no_vertices/2;
                arc = vertex->first_edge;
                while ( arc != 0 ) {
                    int        adj_node = arc->h12[(side+1)%2];

                    if ( (degree = vertices->vertexArray[adj_node].g) > 0 ) {
                        add_to_vheap( &vertices->vertexArray[adj_node], degree );
                        vertices->vertexArray[adj_node].g *= -1;
                    }
                    arc = arc->next_edge[side];
                }
            }
        } while ( max_degree_vertex( &vertex ) == NORM );
    }
    free_vheap();
}
```

Figure 13.15 The ordering step

initialize_rList() routine) a doubly linked list of all vertices in descending order of degree. This list, whose head is in the rlistHead field of the vertices variable, and whose elements are linked via the succ and prec fields of a vertexType,
can be built in linear time because of the distribution of the degrees. Since the first
vertex is most likely to be within the largest component of the graph, the routine almost always correctly orders the vertices in the largest component first, rather than

in the smaller components (which would produce a degraded ordering). The starting vertices for other components are easily decided from the rList.

The second type of vertices to be added to the VS list are those adjacent to others already ordered. These are handled by keeping track of all vertices not yet ordered, but adjacent to vertices in the ordering. A heap is used to do this. The algorithm is as follows. Each component of the graph is considered in a separate iteration of the main loop of ordering: The heap is first emptied, and a vertex of maximal degree is extracted from the rList. It is marked visited (the g field is used to do so), and added to the heap.

All vertices adjacent to it are then added to the heap if they have not already been visited and are not already in the heap. Next, max_degree_vertex() removes from the heap a vertex of maximal degree with respect to others in the heap. This becomes the next "visited" vertex; it is deleted from the rList, added to the VS list, and its adjacent vertices added to the heap, as above. This process repeats until the heap is empty, at which time the next component in the graph is selected. When all components have been processed, and the heap is empty, the vertex sequence has been created.

The time to perform this step is bounded by the time to perform operations on the heap, normally $O(\log n)$. However, the skewed vertex distribution facilitates an optimization. A vertex of degree i, $1 \leq i \leq 5$, is not stored on the heap. Instead, five stacks are used, stack i containing only vertices of degree i. The heap therefore contains only vertices of degree greater than 5, a small fraction of the total number. Vertices can be pushed onto and popped from a stack in constant time; the expected time of the ordering step becomes $O(n)$ as a result.

This optimization detail is hidden by the vheap (virtual heap) module. It is not shown here but can be described quite simply. The add_to_vheap() routine takes both a vertex and its degree as parameters and can therefore determine whether to place the vertex on the heap or in a stack. The max_degree_vertex() routine obtains a vertex of maximum degree by first searching the heap; if the heap is empty, it searches stacks 5, 4, 3, 2, and 1, in that order. The implementations of these two routines are based on well-known algorithms for implementing stacks and heaps; see Sedgewick (1990), for instance.

The searching step

The search step scans the VS list produced by the ordering step and tries to assign hash values to the keys, one level at a time. The hash function ultimately used has the form given in equation (1). Since h_0, h_1 and h_2 have already been computed, what remains is to determine g.

The algorithm to compute g is again based on the insight into vertex degree distribution. The VS list contains vertices with higher degrees first; the partition into levels therefore contains larger groups of interrelated words early on. If these are processed first, the cases most likely to be troublesome are eliminated first. Note that the ordering step does not actually yield a data structure of physically distinct levels;

```
int searching( arcs, vertices )
    arcsType            *arcs;
    verticesType        *vertices;
{
    int         i,                  /* Each vertex in the VS list.       */
                searching_tries = 0, /* Running count of searching tries. */
                status = ABNORM;    /* Condition variable.               */
    char        *disk;              /* Simulated hash table.             */
    intSetType  primes,             /* Table of primes for pattern shifts. */
                slotSet;            /* Set of hash addresses.            */

    disk = (char*) owncalloc( arcs->no_arcs, sizeof(char) );
    slotSet.intSetRep = (int*) owncalloc( vertices->maxDegree, sizeof(int) );
    initialize_primes( arcs->no_arcs, &primes );

    while ( (searching_tries++ < SEARCHINGS) && (status == ABNORM) ) {
        status = NORM;
        i = vertices->vsHead;               /* Get the highest-level vertex. */
        initialize_search( arcs, vertices, disk );

        while ( i != NP ) { /* Fit keys of level of vertex i onto the disk. */
            vertices->vertexArray[i].prec = VISIT;

            if ( fit_pattern(arcs, vertices, i,
                        disk, &primes, &slotSet) == ABNORM ) {
                status = ABNORM;            /* Search failed at vertex i.  Try */
                break;                      /* a new pattern.                  */
            }
            else        /* Search succeeded.  Proceed to next node. */
                i = vertices->vertexArray[i].succ;
        }
    }

    free( disk );
    free( (char *)slotSet.intSetRep );
    free( (char *)primes.intSetRep );
    return(status);
}
```

Figure 13.16 The searching step

this is simply a concept that is useful in understanding the algorithm. The levels are easily determined from the ordering in the VS list using equations (5) and (6).

The simplest way to assure that the keys are correctly fit into a hash table is to actually build a hash table. The disk variable in searching() is used for this purpose. The initialize_search() routine initializes it to an array of m slots (since the hash function is to be minimal as well as perfect), each of which is set to EMPTY. As the g function is computed for a key, the hash address h for the key is determined, and slot h in disk is marked FULL.

The implementation of the searching step is shown in Figure 13.16. Because a searching step is not guaranteed to find a suitable set of values for g, the step is repeated up to a constant number of times. Each repetition works as follows. An empty disk is allocated, all vertices are marked as not visited (in this step, the prec field holds this information), and the g field of each vertex is set to a random value. Using a random value for g often contributes to a high probability of fitting all keys.

The next vertex i in the VS list is then selected. All keys at the level of i must be fit onto the disk. This is the task of fit_pattern(), which behaves as follows. Given vertex i and disk, it examines each arc in $K(v_i)$ to see if the arc's key is at the current level (this is indicated by whether or not the vertex adjacent to i had already been visited). If so, it determines if the current values of g for vertex i and the vertices adjacent to i make any keys hash to an already-filled spot. If all keys fit, then fit-pattern() has succeeded for this level. It marks each hash address for the examined keys as FULL in disk, and terminates.

The g value determines what might be considered a "pattern." Because all keys of a particular level are associated with some vertex v_i, the hash function's value for all $k \in K(v_i)$ is determined in part by the value of g for v_i. Any change to g will shift the hash addresses of all keys associated with a given level.

This observation provides the motivation for the action to take when a collision is detected. If fit_pattern() detects a collision for some $k \in K(v_i)$, it computes a new pattern—that is, a new value for g for vertex i. All keys on the level will therefore be shifted to new addresses. The formula used to compute the new value for g is:

$$g \leftarrow (g + s) \bmod m$$

where s is a prime number. This means that all possible values for g can be tested in at most m tries. The searching() routine computes a table of prime numbers before computing hash addresses. It passes this table to fit-pattern(), which randomly chooses one value for the table to be used as the shift. Ideally, each vertex should have a different prime. Computing m primes is expensive, however, so a fixed number are generated. Twenty small primes have been shown, empirically, to give satisfactory results.

Using the MPHF

When the searching step is through, the main routine writes the MPHF to a file. All that is necessary is to write the size of the graph, the seed used to start random number generation, and the values of g for each vertex. Another program can then use the MPHF by:

1. Regenerating the three random number tables, which are needed to recompute h_0, h_1, and h_2.
2. Rereading the values of g.

Recall that the mapping step included a call to the routine map_to_triples(),
whose purpose was to compute the triples for all keys. This routine calls on
compute_h012() to actually compute the triples for a given key; compute_h012()
is simply an implementation of equations (2)–(4). Given a key, then, all that is
needed to compute its hash address is the code:

```
arcType arc;
compute_h012( no_arcs, r, tables, key, &arc );
hash = abs(arc.h0 +
           mphf->gArray[arc.h12[0]] +
           mphf->gArray[arc.h12[1]]
           ) % mphf->no_arcs;
```

where tables contains the three tables, mphf the g values, and r the number of
vertices on one side of the dependency graph. This is the approach used by the retrieval routine in the appendix.

Discussion

The algorithm presented in this section provides a practical means to compute
minimal perfect hash functions for small to extremely large sets of keys. Indeed, the
algorithm has been verified on key set sizes of over one million; previous approaches could not have computed an MPHF for a set that large in reasonable time.
One of its more interesting applications has been to compute the keys for an optical
disk of information; see Fox (1990).

The resulting hash function is much more complex than the approaches suggested in section 13.3. Somewhat more time is necessary to use the MPHF, both to
initialize it and to compute a key's value. For very small data sets, the overhead
may not be justified, but for large data sets the algorithm in this section will be, on
the average, much quicker. In any case, it is a constant-time algorithm, and there
are always advantages to being able to predict the time needed to locate a key.

The MPHF uses a large amount of space. Ostensibly, its size is proportional to
the number of vertices in the dependency graph, that is, $O(r)$. Actually, except for
very large key sets, most space is consumed by the three random number tables,
which must be present at both the computation and regeneration of the MPHF. Each
table has 128 rows and 150 columns, which requires over 1/4 megabyte of storage;
this suggests that for small key sets, the approach suggested in section 13.5.1 might
be more practical! However, an examination of the equations that access the tables
(see the Mapping section step) shows that the actual number of columns used is no
more than the length of the longest key. Moreover, while having 128 rows helps exploit randomness, a MPHF can be found with fewer. The implementation could
therefore be rewritten to use much less space. This is left as an exercise to the
reader.

REFERENCES

CARTER, J. L., and M. N. WEGMAN. 1979. "Universal Classes of Hash Functions." *J. Computer and System Sciences*, 18, 143–54.

CERCONE, N., M. KRAUSE, and J. BOATES. 1983. "Minimal and Almost Minimal Perfect Hash Function Search with Application to Natural Language Lexicon Design." *Computers and Mathematics with Applications 9*, 215–31.

CHANG, C. C. 1986. "Letter Oriented Reciprocal Hashing Scheme." *Information Sciences 38*, 243–55.

CICHELLI, R. J. 1980. "Minimal Perfect Hash Functions Made Simple." *Communications of the ACM*, *23*, 17–19.

CORMACK, G. V., R. N. S. HORSPOOL, and M. KAISERSWERTH. 1985. "Practical Perfect Hashing." *The Computer Journal 28*, 54–58.

DATTA, S. 1988. "Implementation of a Perfect Hash Function Scheme." Blacksburg, Va.: Technical Report TR-89-9 (Master's Report), Department of Computer Science, Virginia Polytechnic Institute and State University.

FOX, E. A., Q. CHEN, L. HEATH, and S. DATTA. 1989a. "A More Cost Effective Algorithm for Finding Perfect Hash Functions." Paper presented at the Seventeenth Annual ACM Computer Science Conference, Louisville, KY.

FOX, E. A., Q. CHEN, and L. HEATH. 1989b. "An $O(n \log n)$ Algorithm for Finding Minimal Perfect Hash Functions." Blacksburg, Va.: TR 89-10, Department of Computer Science, Virginia Polytechnic Institute and State University.

FOX, E. A. 1990. Virginia Disc One. CD-ROM published by Virginia Polytechnic Institute and State University. Ruckersville, Va.: Nimbus Records.

JAESCHKE, G. 1981. "Reciprocal Hashing—a Method for Generating Minimal Perfect Hash Functions." *Communications of the ACM*, *24*, 829–33.

KNUTH, D. E. 1973. *The Art of Computer Programming, Vol. 3: Sorting and Searching*. Reading, Mass.: Addison-Wesley.

MEHLHORN, K. 1982. "On the Program Size of Perfect and Universal Hash Functions." Paper presented at the 23rd IEEE Symposium on Foundations of Computer Science.

PRIM, R. C. 1957. "Shortest Connection Networks and Some Generalizations." *Bell System Technical Journal 36*.

RAMAKRISHNA, M. V., and P. LARSON. 1989. "File Organization Using Composite Perfect Hashing." *ACM Transactions on Database Systems*, *14*, 231–63.

SAGER, T. J. 1984. "A New Method for Generating Minimal Perfect Hashing Functions." Rolla, Mo.: Technical Report CSc-84-15, Department of Computer Science, University of Missouri-Rolla.

SAGER, T. J. 1985. "A Polynomial Time Generator for Minimal Perfect Hash Functions." *Communications of the ACM*, *28*, 523–32.

SEDGEWICK, R. 1990. *Algorithms in C*. Reading, Mass.: Addison-Wesley.

SPRUGNOLI, R. 1978. "Perfect Hashing Functions: a Single Probe Retrieving Method for Static Sets." *Communications of the ACM*, *20*, 841–50.

APPENDIX: MPHF IMPLEMENTATION

What follows is a complete implementation of the minimal perfect hashing function algorithm. It consists of nineteen files of source code, plus a makefile (for the Unix utility **make**) containing compilation instructions. The beginning of each file (except the makefile, which come first) is marked by a comment consisting of a line of asterisks, with the file's name embedded in it.

```
#
# Makefile for the minimal perfect hash algorithm.
#
# Directives:
#       phf                      Make phf, a program to generate a MPHF.
#
#       regen_mphf.a             Make an object code library capable of
#                                regenerating an MPHF from the specification
#                                file generated by phf.
#
#       regen_driver             Make regen_driver, a program to test
#                                the code in regen_mphf.a
#
#       all      (default)       Make the three above items.
#
#       regression               Execute a regression test.  The phf program
#                                should terminate indicating success.  The
#                                regen_driver program silently checks its
#                                results; no news is good news.
#
#       lint                     Various flavors of consistency checking.
#       lint_phf
#       lint_regen
#
#

COMMON_OBJS=    compute_hfns.o randomTables.o pmrandom.o support.o
COMMON_SRCS=    compute_hfns.c randomTables.c pmrandom.c support.c
COMMON_HDRS=    compute_hfns.h randomTables.h pmrandom.h support.h \
                   const.h types.h

MPHF_OBJS=      main.o mapping.o ordering.o searching.o vheap.o
MPHF_SRCS=      main.c mapping.c ordering.c searching.c vheap.c
MPHF_HDRS=      vheap.h

REGEN_OBJS=     regen_mphf.o
REGEN_SRCS=     regen_mphf.c
REGEN_HDRS=     regen_mphf.h

RD_OBJS=        regen_driver.o
RD_SRCS=        regen_driver.c
```

```
PHFLIB= regen_mphf.a

CFLAGS= -O
LDFLAGS=
LIBS=    -lm

all: phf regen_driver

phf: $(PHFLIB) $(MPHF_OBJS)
        $(CC) -o phf $(LDFLAGS) $(MPHF_OBJS) $(PHFLIB) -lm

$(PHFLIB):      $(REGEN_OBJS) $(COMMON_OBJS)
        ar r $(PHFLIB) $?
        ranlib $(PHFLIB)

regen_driver:   $(RD_OBJS) $(PHFLIB)
        $(CC) $(LDFLAGS) -o regen_driver $(RD_OBJS) $(PHFLIB) $(LIBS)

regression: phf regen_driver
        ./phf keywords 'wc -l < keywords' 0.8 /tmp/hashing-output
        ./regen_driver /tmp/hashing-output keywords > /tmp/hashed-words
        rm /tmp/hashing-output /tmp/hashed-words

lint: lint_phf lint_regen

lint_phf:
        lint $(MPHF_SRCS) $(COMMON_SRCS) $(LIBS)

lint_regen:
        lint $(RD_SRCS) $(REGEN_SRCS) $(COMMON_SRCS) $(LIBS)

compute_hfns.o: const.h randomTables.h types.h
main.o:         const.h types.h support.h
mapping.o:      const.h pmrandom.h compute_hfns.h types.h support.h
ordering.o:     const.h types.h vheap.h support.h
randomTables.o: const.h pmrandom.h randomTables.h types.h
searching.o:    const.h pmrandom.h support.h types.h
support.o:      const.h types.h support.h
pmrandom.o:     pmrandom.h
vheap.o:        const.h support.h types.h vheap.h


/***************************** compute_hfns.h *************************
```

Purpose: External declarations for computing the three h functions
                associated with a key.

Provenance: Written and tested by Q. Chen and E. Fox, March 1991.
                Edited and tested by S. Wartik, April 1991.

```
    Notes:        None.

**/

#ifdef __STDC__

extern void      compute_h012( int n, int r, randomTablesType tables,
                               char *key, arcType *arc );
#else

extern void      compute_h012();
#endif
/*************************** const.h *********************************

   Purpose:      Define globally-useful constant values.

   Provenance:   Written and tested by Q. Chen and E. Fox, March 1991.
                 Edited and tested by S. Wartik, April 1991.

   Notes:        None.
**/

#define MAX_INT  ((unsigned)(~0)) >> 1    /* Maximum integer.     */
#define NP -1             /* Null pointer for array-based linked lists. */

#define NORM     0        /* Normal return.                    */
#define ABNORM  -1        /* Abnormal return.                  */

#define MAPPINGS    4     /* Total number of mapping runs.     */
#define SEARCHINGS 10     /* Total number of searching runs.   */

#define MAX_KEY_LENG COLUMNS    /* Maximum length of a key.      */
#define PRIMES 20               /* Number of primes, used in searching stage. */

#define NOTVISIT  0       /* Indication of an un-visited node.        */
#define VISIT     1       /* Indication of a visited node.            */
#define EMPTY    '0'      /* Indication of an empty slot in the disk. */
#define FULL     '1'      /* Indication of a filled slot in the disk. */


/*************************** pmrandom.h *************************

   Purpose:      External declarations for random-number generator
                 package used by this program.

   Provenance:   Written and tested by Q. Chen and E. Fox, March 1991.
                 Edited by S. Wartik, April 1991.
```

Notes: The implementation is better than the random number
                    generator from the C library. It is taken from Park and
                    Miller's paper, "Random Number Generators: Good Ones are
                    Hard to Find," in CACM 31 (1988), pp. 1192-1201.
**/

```
#ifdef __STDC__
extern void      setseed(int);    /* Set the seed to a specified value.      */
extern int       pmrandom();      /* Get next random number in the sequence. */
extern int       getseed();       /* Get the current value of the seed.      */
#else
extern void      setseed();
extern int       pmrandom();
extern int       getseed();
#endif

#define DEFAULT_SEED    23
```
/*************************** randomTables.h *****************************

  Purpose: External definitions for the three random number tables.

  Provenance: Written and tested by Q. Chen and E. Fox, March 1991.
                   Edited and tested by S. Wartik, April 1991.

**/

```
#define NO_TABLES 3     /* Number of random number tables.          */
#define ROWS 128        /* Rows of the random table (suitable for char). */
#define COLUMNS 150     /* Columns of the random table.             */

typedef int randomTablesType[NO_TABLES][ROWS][COLUMNS]; /* random number table */

#ifdef __STDC__

extern void      initialize_randomTable( randomTablesType tables, int *seed );

#else

extern void      initialize_randomTable();

#endif
```

/***************************** regen_mphf.h ********************

  Purpose: External declarations for regenerating and using
                   an already-computed minimal perfect hashing function.

```
    Provenance:    Written and tested by Q. Chen and E. Fox, March 1991.
                   Edited and tested by S. Wartik, April 1991.

    Notes:         None.
**/

typedef struct {
    int            no_arcs;         /* Number of keys (arcs) in the key set.    */
    int            no_vertices;     /* Number of vertices used to compute MPHF. */
    int            seed;            /* The seed used for the random number tables. */
    randomTablesType    tables;     /* The random number tables.                */
    int            *gArray;         /* The array to hold g values.              */
} mphfType;

#ifdef __STDC__

extern int     regen_mphf ( mphfType *mphf, char *spec_file );
extern void    release_mphf ( mphfType *mphf );
extern int     retrieve ( mphfType *mphf, char *key );

#else

extern int     regen_mphf ();
extern void    release_mphf ();

extern int     retrieve ();

#endif

/*************************** support.h ********************************

    Purpose:       External interface for support routines.

    Provenance:    Written and tested by Q. Chen and E. Fox, March 1991.
                   Edited and tested by S. Wartik, April 1991.

    Notes:         None.
**/

#ifdef __STDC__

extern char    *owncalloc(int n, int size);
extern char    *ownrealloc(char *area, int new_size);

extern void    write_gfun(arcsType *arcs, verticesType *vertices,
                          int tbl_seed, char *spec_file);

extern int     verify_mphf(arcsType *arcs, verticesType *vertices);
```

```
#else

extern char      *owncalloc();
extern char      *ownrealloc();

extern void      write_gfun();

extern int       verify_mphf();

#endif


/*************************  types.h  ********************************

    Purpose:     Define globally-useful data types.

    Provenance:  Written and tested by Q. Chen and E. Fox, March 1991.
                 Edited and tested by S. Wartik, April 1991.

    Notes:       None.
**/

#include "const.h"

typedef struct arc {           /* arc data structure              */
    int  h0,                   /* h0 value                        */
         h12[2];               /* h1 and h2 values                */
    struct arc *next_edge[2];  /* pointer to arc sharing same h1 or */
}  arcType;                    /* h2 values                       */

typedef struct {               /* vertex data structure           */
    struct arc *first_edge;    /* pointer to the first adjacent edge */
    int  g,                    /* g value.                        */
         prec,                 /* backward pointer of the vertex-list */
         succ;                 /* forward pointer of the vertex-list  */
}  vertexType;

typedef struct {               /* arcs data structure      */
    int no_arcs;               /* number of arcs in the graph */
    arcType* arcArray;         /* arc array                */
}  arcsType;

typedef struct {               /* vertices data structure       */
    int no_vertices,           /* number of vertices in the graph */
        maxDegree,             /* max degree of the graph       */
        vsHead,                /* VS list head                  */
        vsTail,                /* VS list tail                  */
        rlistHead;             /* remaining vertex list head    */
    vertexType* vertexArray;   /* vertex array                  */
}  verticesType;
```

```
typedef struct {          /* integer set data structure    */
   int count,             /* number of elements in the set  */
      *intSetRep;         /* set representation             */
} intSetType;
```

/************************** vheap.h ********************************

   Purpose: Define a "virtual heap" module.

   Provenance: Written and tested by Q. Chen and E. Fox, March 1991.
                  Edited and tested by S. Wartik, April 1991.

   Notes: This isn't intended as a general-purpose stack/heap
                  implementation. It's tailored toward stacks and heaps
                  of vertices and their degrees, using a representation suitable
                  for accessing them (in this case, an integer index into
                  the vertices->verex array identifies the vertex).
**/

```
#ifdef __STDC__

extern void      allocate_vheap( int no_arcs, int no_vertices );

extern void      initialize_vheap();

extern void      add_to_vheap ( vertexType *vertex, int degree );
extern int       max_degree_vertex ( vertexType **vertex );

extern void      free_vheap();

#else

extern void      allocate_vheap();

extern void      initialize_vheap();

extern void      add_to_vheap ();
extern int       max_degree_vertex ();

extern void      free_vheap();

#endif
```

/************************** compute_hfns.c ************************

   Purpose: Computation of the three h functions associated with
               a key.

Provenance: Written and tested by Q. Chen and E. Fox, March 1991.
                Edited and tested by S. Wartik, April 1991.

Notes: None.

**/

```
#include <stdio.h>
#include <string.h>

#include "types.h"
#include "randomTables.h"


/**************************************************************************

        compute_h012( int, int, randomTablesType, char*, arcType* )

   Return:      void

   Purpose:     Compute the triple for a key.  On return, the h0 and h12
                fields of "arc" have the triple's values.
**/

void compute_h012(n, r, tables, key, arc)
    int             n,          /* in: number of arcs.                   */
                    r;          /* in: size of h1 or h2 side of the graph. */
    randomTablesType tables;    /* in: pointer to the random tables.     */
    char            *key;       /* in: key string.                       */
    arcType         *arc;       /* out: the key's arc entry.             */
{
    int i,              /* Iterator over each table.                    */
        j,              /* Iterator over each character in "key".       */
        sum[NO_TABLES], /* Running sum of h0, h1 and h2 values.         */
        length;         /* The length of "key".                         */

    length = strlen(key) ;
    sum[0] = sum[1] = sum[2] = 0 ;

    for ( i = 0; i < NO_TABLES; i++ )         /* Sum over all the characters */
        for ( j = 0; j < length; j++ )        /* in the key.                */
            sum[i] += table[i][(key[j]%ROWS)][j];

    arc->h0      = abs( sum[0] ) % n;          /* Assign mappings for each   */
    arc->h12[0]  = abs( sum[1] ) % r;          /* of h0, h1, and h2 according */
    arc->h12[1]  = abs( sum[2] ) % r + r;      /* to the sums computed.      */
}
```

/****************************** main.c ******************************

Purpose: Main routine, driving the MPHF creation.

Provenance: Written and tested by Q. Chen and E. Fox, March 1991.
                Edited and tested by S. Wartik, April 1991.

Notes: When compiled, the resulting program is used as follows:

                        phf I L R O

        where:

                I   Name of the file to be used as input. It should contain
                    one or more newline-terminated strings.

                L   The number of lines in I.

                R   A real number, giving a ratio between L and the size of
                    the hashing function generated. 1.0 is usually a viable
                    value.   In general, L*R should be an integer.

                O   Name of a file to be used as output. It will contain
                    the MPHF if one is found.
**/

#include <stdio.h>
#include <math.h>
#include <string.h>

#include "types.h"
#include "support.h"

#ifdef __STDC__

extern void   ordering(arcsType *arcs, verticesType *vertices);

extern void   allocate_arcs(arcsType* arcs, int n);
extern void   allocate_vertices(verticesType* vertices, int n);
extern void   free_arcs(arcsType* arcs);
extern void   free_vertices(verticesType* vertices);

extern void   exit();

#else

extern void   ordering();
```
```

```
extern void      allocate_arcs();
extern void      allocate_vertices();
extern void      free_arcs();
extern void      free_vertices();

extern void      exit();

#endif

/*************************************************************************
          main(argc, argv)

   Returns:       int — zero on success, non-zero on failure.

   Purpose:       Take the inputs and call three routines to carry out mapping,
                  ordering and searching three tasks. If they all succeed,
                  write the MPHF to the spec file.
**/

main( argc, argv )
          int      argc;
          char     *argv[];          /* arg1: key file;     arg2: key set size;  */
                                     /* arg3: ratio;        arg4: spec file       */
{
    int          status,           /* Return status variable.                   */
                 seed;             /* Seed used to initialize the three random  */
                                   /* tables.                                    */
    char         *key_file_name,
                 *specification_file_name;

    int          lines_in_keyword_file;
    double       ratio;

    arcsType          arcs;        /* These variables hold all the arcs         */
    verticesType      vertices;    /* and vertices generated.                   */

    if ( argc != 5 ) {
        fprintf(stderr, "Usage: %s keywords kw-lines ratio output-file\n",
                argv[0]);
        exit(1);
    }

    key_file_name = argv[1];
    if ( (lines_in_keyword_file = atoi(argv[2])) <= 0 ) {
        fputs("The 2nd parameter must be a positive integer.\n", stderr);
        exit(1);
    }
```

```
    else if ( (ratio = atof(argv[3])) <= 0.0 ) {
        fputs("The 3rd parameter must be a positive floating-point value.\n",
                stderr);
        exit(1);
    }

    allocate_arcs( &arcs, lines_in_keyword_file );
    allocate_vertices( &vertices, (int)(lines_in_keyword_file * ratio) );
    specification_file_name = argv[4];

    if ( (status = mapping( key_file_name, &arcs, &vertices, &seed )) == NORM ) {
        ordering( &arcs, &vertices );
        if ( (status = searching( &arcs, &vertices )) == NORM &&
                (status = verify_mphf( &arcs, &vertices )) == NORM )
            write_gfun( &arcs, &vertices, seed, specification_file_name );
    }

    free_arcs( &arcs );
    free_vertices( &vertices );
    fprintf(stderr, "MPHF creation %s.\n",
                    (status == NORM ? "succeeded" : "failed"));

    return(status);
}

/***********************************************************************

        allocate_arcs( arcsType*, int )

  Returns:      void

  Purpose:      Given an expected number of arcs, allocate space for an arc data
                structure containing that many arcs, and place the number of
                arcs in the "no_arcs" field of the arc data structure.
**/

void allocate_arcs( arcs, n )
    arcsType    *arcs;          /* out: Receives allocated storage.    */
    int         n;             /* in: Expected number of arcs.         */
{
    arcs->no_arcs = n;
    arcs->arcArray = (arcType*) owncalloc( sizeof(arcType), n );
}


/***********************************************************************

        allocate_vertices( verticesType* , int )
```

Purpose: Given an expected number of vertices, allocate space for a vertex
                data structure containing that many vertices, and place the
                number of vertices in the "no_vertices" field of the vertex
                data structure.
**/

```
void allocate_vertices( vertices, n )
    verticesType        *vertices;        /* out: Receives allocated storage. */
    int                 n;                /* in: Expected number of vertices. */
{
    if (n % 2 != 0) n++;
    vertices->no_vertices = n;
    vertices->vertexArray = (vertexType*) owncalloc(sizeof(vertexType), n );
}
```

/***

        free_arcs(arcsType*)

  Purpose: Deallocate space for an arc data structure.
**/

```
void free_arcs( arcs )
    arcsType  *arcs;                          /* in out: Space to de-allocate.   */
{
    free( (char *)arcs->arcArray );
}
```

/***

        free_vertices(verticesType*)

  Purpose: Deallocate space for a vertex data structure.
**/

```
void free_vertices( vertices )
    verticesType        *vertices;        /* in out: Space to de-allocate.  */
{
    free( (char *)vertices->vertexArray );
}
```

/*************************** mapping.c ****************************

  Purpose: Implement the mapping stage of the MPHF algorithm.

  Provenance: Written and tested by Q. Chen and E. Fox, March 1991.
                  Edited and tested by S. Wartik, April 1991.

```
**/

#include <stdio.h>

#include "types.h"
#include "pmrandom.h"
#include "randomTables.h"
#include "compute_hfns.h"

#ifdef __STDC__

extern void     initialize_arcs( arcsType *arcs );
extern void     initialize_vertices( verticesType *vertices );
extern int      check_dup( arcType *firstArc );
extern int      construct_graph( arcsType *arcs, verticesType *vertices );
extern void     map_to_triples( char *key_file, arcsType *arcs,
                                int r, randomTablesType tables );

extern void     exit( int status );

#else

extern void     initialize_arcs();
extern void     initialize_vertices();
extern int      check_dup();
extern int      construct_graph();
extern void     map_to_triples();

extern void     exit();

#endif

/***********************************************************************

        mapping( char*, arcsType*, verticesType*, int )
```

Return: int — NORM if a mapping can be found, ABNORM if not.

Purpose: Perform the mapping stage: Map all keys to triples and construct
                the bipartite graph. This involves:

                — Allocating the arcs and vertices structures.
                — Generating the h0, h1, and h2 functions.
                — Building the lists of edges, ordered by degree.

```
**/
```

Appendix: MPHF Implementation   **331**

```
int mapping( key_file, arcs, vertices, seed )
    char        *key_file;       /* in: name of file containing keys.   */
    arcsType    *arcs;           /* out: arcs in bipartite graph.        */
    verticesType *vertices;      /* out: vertices in bipartite graph.    */
    int         *seed;           /* out: seed selected to initialize the */
                                 /* random tables.                       */
{

    int mapping_tries = 0;
    randomTablesType randomTables;         /* Three random number tables.        */

    while ( mapping_tries++< MAPPINGS ) {
        initialize_arcs( arcs );
        initialize_vertices( vertices );
        initialize_randomTable( randomTables, seed );
        map_to_triples( key_file, arcs, vertices->no_vertices/2, randomTables );
        if ( construct_graph(arcs, vertices) == NORM )
            return(NORM);
        fputs((mapping_tries < MAPPINGS ? "Trying again.\n" : "Giving up.\n"),
            stderr);
    }
    return(ABNORM);
}

/***********************************************************************

        map_to_triples( char*, arcsType*, int, randomTablesType )

  Return:     void

  Purpose:    Compute triples of (h0, h1, h2) for all keys and store
              them in the arc data structure.
**/

void map_to_triples(key_file, arcs, r, tables)
    char        *key_file;       /* in: key file name             */
    arcsType    *arcs;           /* out: the arcs data structure  */
    int         r;               /* in: size of h1 or h2 side     */
    randomTablesType tables;     /* in: random number tables      */
{
    FILE        *fp;                     /* Input file pointer.   */
    int         i = 0;                   /* Iterator over arcs.   */
    char        string[MAX_KEY_LENG];    /* Key string holder.    */

    if ( (fp = fopen(key_file, "r")) == NULL ) {
        fprintf(stderr, "Can't read \"%s\".\n", key_file);
        exit(1);
    }
```

```
    while ( fgets( string, MAX_KEY_LENG, fp ) != NULL &&
           i <arcs->no_arcs ) {
        string[strlen(string)-1] = '\0';        /* Exclude the '\n'. */
        compute_h012( arcs->no_arcs, r, tables, string, &arcs->arcArray[i++] );
    }

    if ( i != arcs->no_arcs ) {
        fprintf(stderr, "File \"%s\" contains %d keys, not %d. ",
                key_file, i, arcs->no_arcs);
        fputs("Re-execute with correct value.\n", stderr);
        exit(1);
    }
    else if ( ! feof(fp ) ) {
        fprintf(stderr, "File \"%s\" contains more than %d keys. ",
                key_file, arcs->no_arcs);
        fputs("Re-execute with correct value.\n", stderr);
        exit(1);
    }

    fclose(fp);
}


/***************************************************************************


        construct_graph( arcsType*, verticesType* )

    Return:       int — NORM if a graph can be built without duplicate arcs,
                  ABNORM if it can't.

    Purpose:      Construct the bipartite graph out of triples.  On successful
                  return,

                      — Each vertex's degree has been determined, and placed
                        in its "g" field.
                      — The maximal degree of the graph has been determined.
                      — The "first_edge" field of vertices is a linked list
                        of adjacent edges.
**/

int construct_graph( arcs, vertices )
    arcsType     *arcs;          /* in out: arcs.                          */
    verticesType *vertices;      /* in out: vertices.                      */
{
    int i,              /* Iterator over all arcs.                         */
        j,              /* j = 0 and 1 for h1 and h2 side, respectively. */
        status = NORM,
        vertex;
```

```
    for ( j = 0; j < 2; j++ ) {
        for ( i = 0; i < arcs->no_arcs; i++ ) {
            vertex = arcs->arcArray[i].h12[j];   /* Update vertex degree */
            vertices->vertexArray[vertex].g++;   /* count and vertex      */
            arcs->arcArray[i].next_edge[j] =     /* adjacency list.       */
                    vertices->vertexArray[vertex].first_edge;
            vertices->vertexArray[vertex].first_edge = &arcs ->arcArray[i];

            if ( (j == 0) && check_dup( &arcs->arcArray[i] ) == ABNORM ) {
                fputs("Duplicate found.\n", stderr);
                status = ABNORM;
                break;
            }

                        /* Figure out the maximal degree of the graph. */
            if ( vertices->vertexArray[vertex].g > vertices->maxDegree )
                vertices->maxDegree = vertices->vertexArray[vertex].g;
        }
    }
    return(status);
}

/*************************************************************************

        check_dup( arcType )

  Return:       int -- NORM if no duplicate triple exists, ABNORM if one does.

  Purpose:      Test if some arc on the arc list has an identical triple to
                the first arc on the list.
**/

int check_dup(firstArc)
    arcType *firstArc; /* in: arc at the head of a list.          */
{
    arcType *arc = firstArc->next_edge[0];
    while ( arc != 0 ) {
        if ( ( firstArc->h0 == arc->h0 ) &&
            ( firstArc->h12[1] == arc->h12[1] ) )
            return(ABNORM);                                   /* Duplication found. */
        arc = arc->next_edge[0];
    }
    return(NORM);                                             /* No duplication.    */
}

/*************************************************************************

        initialize_arcs( arcsType* )
```

```
    Return:        void

    Purpose:       Make the edge pointers of each arc nil.
**/

void initialize_arcs( arcs )
    arcsType *arcs;         /* out: arcs structure.              */
{
    int i;

    for ( i = 0; i < arcs->no_arcs; i++ ) {
        arcs->arcArray[i].next_edge[0] = 0;
        arcs->arcArray[i].next_edge[1] = 0;
    }
}


/**********************************************************************

        initialize_vertices( verticesType* )

    Return:        void

    Purpose:       For each vertex, set the degree to 0 and make the
                   edge list empty.
**/

void initialize_vertices( vertices )
    verticesType *vertices;        /* out: vertex structure.      */
{
    int i;

    vertices->maxDegree = 0;
    for ( i = 0; i < vertices->no_vertices; i++ ) {
        vertices->vertexArray[i].first_edge = 0;
        vertices->vertexArray[i].g = 0;
    }
}


/************************** ordering.c ********************************

    Purpose:     Implement the ordering stage of the MPHF algorithm.

    Provenance:  Written and tested by Q. Chen and E. Fox, March 1991.
                 Edited and tested by S. Wartik, April 1991.

    Notes:       None.
**/
```

```
#include <stdio.h>

#include "types.h"
#include "support.h"
#include "vheap.h"

#ifdef __STDC__

extern void      delete_from_rList( vertexType *vertex, verticesType *vertices );
extern void      append_to_VS( vertexType *vertex, verticesType *vertices );
extern void      initialize_rList( verticesType *vertices );

#else

extern void      delete_from_rList();
extern void      append_to_VS();
extern void      initialize_rList();

#endif

/*************************************************************************

        ordering( arcs, vertices )

  Return:       void

  Purpose:      Generate an ordering of the vertices.

  Notes:        The ordering of the vertices is a linked list, the head
                of which is in vertices->vsList.  The "next element"
                pointer for each node is in the "succ" field of each
                vertex component. Note that the "succ" field has two
                purposes in this step. One is that just mentioned.  The
                other is to be part of the rList used in this step.
**/

void ordering( arcs, vertices )
    arcsType              *arcs;      /* in out: the arcs data structure.     */
    verticesType          *vertices; /* in out: the vertices data structure. */
{
    int        degree,
               side;                    /* Indicates side of graph.       */

    vertexType *vertex;
    arcType    *arc;

    vertices->vsHead = vertices->vsTail = NP;    /* Initialize the VS list. */
```

```
      initialize_rList( vertices );
      allocate_vheap( arcs->no_arcs, vertices->no_vertices );

      while ( vertices->rlistHead != -1 ) {          /* Process each component graph. */
          initialize_vheap();
          vertex = &vertices->vertexArray[vertices->rlistHead];
      do {
          vertex->g = 0;                              /* Mark node "visited".  */
          delete_from_rList( vertex, vertices );
          append_to_VS( vertex, vertices );
          if ( vertex->first_edge != 0 ) {
              /* Add adjacent nodes that are not visited and */
              /* not in virtual heap to the virtual heap.    */

              side = vertex - vertices->vertexArray >= vertices->no_vertices/2;

              arc = vertex->first_edge;
              while ( arc != 0 ) {
                  int      adj_node;    /* Node adjacent to vertex. */

                  adj_node = arc->h12[(side+1)%2];
                  degree = vertices->vertexArray[adj_node].g;

                  if ( degree > 0 ) {              /* One such node is found. */
                      add_to_vheap( &vertices->vertexArray[adj_node], degree );
                      vertices->vertexArray[adj_node].g *= -1;
                  }
                  arc = arc->next_edge[side];
              }
          }
      } while ( max_degree_vertex( &vertex ) == NORM );
      }
      free_vheap();
}




      delete_from_rList( vertex, vertices )

  Return:      void

  Purpose:     Delete a vertex pointing at by vertex from the rList stored
               in the vertices data structure.
**/
```

```
void delete_from_rList( vertex, vertices )
    vertexType   *vertex;          /* in: vertex to delete.        */
    verticesType *vertices;        /* out: vertices data structure. */
{
    if ( vertex->prec != NP )
        vertices->vertexArray[vertex-prec].succ = vertex->succ;
    else
        vertices->rlistHead = vertex->succ;

    if ( vertex->succ != NP )
        vertices->vertexArray[vertex->succ].prec = vertex->pre>c;
}


/***************************************************************************

         append_to_VS( vertex, vertices )

   Return:       void

   Purpose:      Append the vertex to the vertex ordering VS.
   **/

   void append_to_VS( vertex, vertices )
       vertexType   *vertex;          /* in: the vertex to be added.     */
       verticesType *vertices;        /* out: the vertices data structure. */
   {
       int newTail = vertex - vertices->vertexArray;

       vertex->succ = vertex->prec = NP;
       if ( vertices->vsHead == NP )
           vertices->vsHead = newTail;
       else
         vertices->vertexArray[vertices->vsTail].succ = newTail;
       vertices->vsTail = newTail;
   }


/***************************************************************************

         initialize_rList( vertices )

   Return:       void

   Purpose:      Set up an rList from the vertices. An rList is a
                 doubly-linked list of vertices in decending order of
                 degree.

   Notes:        pred and succ are used to store the list.
   **/
```

```
void initialize_rList( vertices )
    verticesType *vertices;        /* in out: vertices to be ordered.   */
{


int         i, j, previous;
intSetType  heads,    /* Two sets of pointers. Element i of "heads" points at */
            tails;    /* the head of a list about degree i, 0<=i<=maxDegree. */
                      /* The elements of "tails" are the corresponding tails. */

heads.count = vertices->maxDegree + 1;
heads.intSetRep = (int*)owncalloc( heads.count, sizeof(int) );
for ( i = 0; i < heads.count; i++ )
    heads.intSetRep[i] = NP;

tails.count = vertices->maxDegree + 1;
tails.intSetRep = (int*)owncalloc( tails.count, sizeof(int) );
for ( i = 0; i < tails.count; i++ )
    tails.intSetRep[i] = NP;

                    /* Construct lists for vertices being of */
                    /* degree 0, 1, ... maxDegree.           */
for ( i = 0; i < vertices->no_vertices; i++ ) {
    previous = heads.intSetRep[vertices->vertexArray[i].g];
    vertices->vertexArray[i].succ = previous;
    if ( previous != NP )
        vertices->vertexArray[previous].prec = i;
    else
        tails.intSetRep[vertices->vertexArray[i].g] = i;
    heads.intSetRep[vertices->vertexArray[i].g] = i;
    vertices->vertexArray[i].prec = NP;
}


    /* Construct the rList by linking lists for vertices being of */
    /* degree 0, 1, ... maxDegree.                                */
for ( i = heads.count - 1; i > 1; i-- )
    if ( tails.intSetRep[i] != NP ) {
        for ( j = i - 1; j >= 1; j-- )
            if ( heads.intSetRep[j] != NP )
                break;
        if ( j >= 1 ) {
            vertices->vertexArray[tails.intSetRep[i]].succ =
                    heads.intSetRep[j];
            vertices->vertexArray[heads.intSetRep[j]].prec =
                    tails.intSetRep[i];
        }
    }

    }
vertices->rlistHead = heads.intSetRep[vertices-> maxDegree];
```

```
    free(  (char *)heads.intSetRep  );
    free(  (char *)tails.intSetRep  );
}
```

/*************************** pmrandom.c **************************

Purpose: Implement a random—number generator package for this program.

Provenance: Written and tested by Q. Chen and E. Fox, March 1991.
             Edited by S. Wartik, April 1991.

Notes: It is assumed that the C data type "int" can store
             32-bit quantities.
**/

```
#include "pmrandom.h"

static int seed = DEFAULT_SEED;    /* The seed of the random number generator. */
```

/***
       setseed(int)

  Returns: int

  Purpose: Set the seed for the random number generator.

  Plan: Uses a formula suggested by Park and Miller. See above.

  Notes: None.
**/

```
void setseed( new_seed )
    int new_seed;
{
        int     low, high, test;

    if ( (new_seed < 1) || (new_seed > 2147483646) )
        new_seed = DEFAULT_SEED;
    high = new_seed / 127773;              /* 127773 = 2147483647 div 16807   */
    low  = new_seed % 127773;
    test = 16807 * low − 2836 * high;   /* 2836 = 2147483647 mod 16807   */
    seed = ( test > 0 ) ? test : test + 2147483647;
}
```

/***

         pmrandom()

```
Returns:     void

Purpose:     Return the next random number in the sequence.

Plan:        Uses the formula:

                 f () = ( 16807 * seed ) mod 2147483647.

             The value of "seed" must be within [1, ..., 2147483646].

Notes:       None.
**/

int pmrandom()
{
    int tmp = seed;

    setseed(seed);
    return(tmp);
}


/*********************************************************************

        getseed()

Returns:        int

Purpose:        Get the current value of the seed.

Notes:          None.
**/

int getseed()
{
    return (seed);
}

/*********************** randomTables.c ***************************

Purpose:     Routines for handling the random number tables.

Provenance:  Written and tested by Q. Chen and E. Fox, March 1991.
             Edited and tested by S. Wartik, April 1991.

Notes:       None.

**/
```

```
#include "types.h"
#include "pmrandom.h"
#include "randomTables.h"

/**************************************************************************

         initialize_randomTable(randomTablesType, int)

  Return:        void

  Purpose:       Initialize the three random number tables and return the
                 seed used.
**/

void initialize_randomTable(tables, seed)
     randomTablesType tables;    /*out: Tables of random numbers.        */
     int              *seed;     /*out: seed used to initialize tables. */
{
     int i, j, k;                /*Iterators over the tables.           */

     *seed = getseed();
     setseed(*seed);

     for (i=0; i < NO_TABLES; i++)    /*Initialize the tables.          */
     for (j=0; j < ROWS; j++)
        for (k = 0; k < COLUMNS; k++)
            tables[i][j][k] = pmrandom();
}

/*************************** regen_driver.c **************************

  Purpose:      A program to test regenerating and using a precomputed hashing
                function.

  Provenance:   Written and tested by Q. Chen and E. Fox, April 1991.
                Edited and tested by S. Wartik, April 1991.

  Notes:        The program is used as follows:

                       regen_driver mphf-file keyword-file

                The result is a set of lines, written to stdout, indicating
                the bucket of each keyword in the keyword file.
**/

#include  < stdio.h >
#include  < string.h >
#include  < math.h >
```

```
#include  "types.h"
#include  "randomTables.h"
#include  "regen_mphf.h"

#ifdef __STDC__

extern void      retrieveAll ( mphfType *mphf, char *key_file );

extern void      exit( int status );

#else

extern void      retrieveAll ();

extern void      exit();

#endif

/*********************************************************************

            main( int, char** )

   Return:       Nothing.

   Purpose:      See the header for this file.
**/

main( argc, argv )
   int argc;
   char *argv[];        /* arg1: mphf file; arg2: key file */

   mphfType mphf;

   if ( argc != 3 ) {
       fprintf(stderr, "Usage: %s mphf-file key-file\n", argv[0]);
       exit(1);
   }

   if ( regen_mphf ( &mphf, argv[1] ) == NORM )
       retrieveAll ( &mphf, argv[2] );
   else {
       fprintf(stderr, "Can't regenerate hashing function from \"%s\".\n",
               argv[1]);
       exit(1);
   }
```

```
    release_mphf ( &mphf );
    exit(0);
}


/**************************************************************************

            retrieveAll ( mphfType*, char* )

    Return:        void

    Purpose:       Given a file of keys and a structure describing a
                   MPHF previously computed for those keys, print
                   each key's location on the standard output stream.
**/

void retrieveAll ( mphf, key_file )
    mphfType        *mphf;                       /* in: mphf specification.     */
    char            *key_file;                   /* in: the key file.           */
{
    FILE            *fp;                          /* Handle for specification file. */
    char            string[MAX_KEY_LENG];        /* Key string.                 */
    int             hash;                         /* Computed hash value.        */
    int             max_bucket_length;           /* The maximum number of chars */
                                                 /* needed to represent a bucket */
                                                 /* index as a string.          */

    if ( (fp = fopen(key_file, "r")) == 0 ) {
        fprintf(stderr, "Can't read file \"%s\".\n", key_file);
        exit(1);
    }

    max_bucket_length = (int)log10((double)mphf->no_arcs) + 1;
    while ( fgets( string, MAX_KEY_LENG, fp ) != 0 ) {
        string[strlen(string)-1] = '\0';
        hash = retrieve( mphf, string );
        printf("Bucket %*d: %s\n", max_bucket_length, hash, string);
    }

    fclose(fp);
}


/*************************** regen_mphf.c ************************

    Purpose:       Routines to regenerate and use a previously-computed
                   minimal perfect hashing function.
```

```
           Provenance:  Written and tested by Q. Chen and E. Fox, March 1991.
                        Edited and tested by S. Wartik, April 1991.

     Notes:       None.
**/

#include  < stdio.h >

#include "types.h"
#include "randomTables.h"
#include "regen_mphf.h"
#include "compute_hfns.h"

/**************************************************************************

          regen_mphf ( mphfType*, char* )

     Return:       int -- NORM if the MPHF could be reconstructed,
                   ABNORM if it couldn't.

     Purpose:      Regenerate a MPHF from a specification file.

     Notes:        What is regenerated is the table of random numbers. The
                   retrieve() procedure can use these numbers to re-create
                   the h0, h1 and h2 values, and from that, the hash value.

                   If the specification file doesn't seem to correspond
                   to the expected format, ABNORM is returned. However,
                   there is no way to tell what caused the error.
**/

int regen_mphf ( mphf, spec_file_name )
    mphfType    *mphf;             /* out: the regenerated MPHF structure. */
    char        *spec_file_name;   /* in: MPHF specification file.       */
{
    int         i;                 /* Iterator through vertices.          */
    FILE        *spec_file;

    if ( (spec_file = fopen(spec_file_name, "r")) == NULL ) return ABNORM;

    if ( fscanf(spec_file, "%d\n%d\n%d\n",
            &mphf->no_arcs, &mphf->no_vertices, &mphf->seed) != 3 ) {
        fclose(spec_file);
        return ABNORM;             /* File is improperly formatted. */
    }

    mphf->gArray = (int*) owncalloc( mphf->no_vertices, sizeof(int) );
```

```
        for ( i = 0; i < mphf->no_vertices; i++ )
            if ( fscanf(spec_file, "%d\n", &mphf->gArray[i] ) != 1 ) {
                fclose(spec_file);
                return ABNORM;     /* File is improperly formatted. */
            }

        if ( ! feof(spec_file) ) {
            fclose(spec_file);
            return ABNORM;         /* File is improperly formatted.  */
        }

        initialize_randomTable( mphf->tables, &mphf->seed );

        fclose(spec_file);

        return NORM;
}

/**************************************************************************

        release_mphf ( mphfType*, char* )

    Return:        void

    Purpose:       Release the dynamically-allocated storage associated with
                   an MPHF.

**/

void release_mphf ( mphf )
    mphfType *mphf;                 /* in out: pointer to the MPHF structure.  */

{
    free( (char *)mphf->gArray );
}


/**************************************************************************

        retrieve ( mphfType*, char* )
    Return:        int — a value in the range 0..mphf-no_arcs-1.

    Purpose:       Given an MPHF and a key, return the key's hash value.

**/
```

```
int retrieve ( mphf, key )
    mphfType    *mphf;      /* in: the mphf specification.             */
    char        *key;       /* in: the key, terminated by a null character.  */
{
    int         hash;       /* The computed hash value.                */
    arcType     arc;        /* Storage used to hold the h0, h1 and h2 values. */

    compute_h012 (mphf->no_arcs, (mphf->no_vertices) / 2,
                  mphf->tables, key, &arc);
    hash = abs (arc.h0 +
                mphf->gArray[arc.h12[0]] +
                mphf->gArray[arc.h12[1]]
                ) % mphf->no_arcs;
    return hash;
}


/***************************** searching.c *****************************

  Purpose:        Implement the searching stage of the MPHF algorithm.

  Provenance:     Written and tested by Q. Chen and E. Fox, March 1991.
                  Edited and tested by S. Wartik, April 1991.

  Notes:          The other two stages must have been performed already.
**/

#include < stdio.h >

#include "types.h"
#include "pmrandom.h"
#include "support.h"

#ifdef __STDC__

extern int      fit_pattern ( arcsType* arcs, verticesType* vertices, int i,
                              char* disk, intSetType *primes, intSetType* slotSet );
extern void     initialize_search ( arcsType* arcs, verticesType* vertices, char* disk );
extern void     initialize_primes ( int n, intSetType* primes );

#else

extern int      fit_pattern ();
extern void     initialize_search ();
extern void     initialize_primes ();

#endif
```

```
/***************************************************************************

            searching( arcsType*, verticesType* )

    Return:         int — NORM on success, ABNORM on failure.

    Purpose:        Search a MPHF for the key set.

    Notes:          The "prec" field is used as the "vertex visited" marker.

                    The slotSet variable actually is only used in fit_pattern().
                    However, since storage for it must be dynamically allocated,
                    and since this routine calls fit_pattern() repeatedly,
                    it's declared here, where storage can be allocated just once.
**/

int searching( arcs, vertices )
    arcsType            *arcs;
    verticesType        *vertices;
{
    int         i,                      /* Each vertex in the VS list.      */
                searching_tries = 0,    /* Running count of searching tries.  */
                status = ABNORM;        /* Condition variable.              */
    char        *disk;                  /* Simulated hash table.            */
    intSetType  primes,                 /* Table of primes for pattern shifts. */
                slotSet;                /* Set of hash addresses.           */

    disk = (char*) owncalloc( arcs->no_arcs, sizeof(char) );
    slotSet.intSetRep = (int*) owncalloc( vertices->maxDegree, sizeof(int) );
    initialize_primes( arcs->no_arcs, &primes );
    while ( (searching_tries++ < SEARCHINGS) && (status == ABNORM) ) {
        status = NORM;
        i = vertices->vsHead;               /* Get the highest-level vertex. */
        initialize_search( arcs, vertices, disk );

        while ( i != NP ) {     /* Fit keys of level of vertex i onto the disk. */
            vertices->vertexArray[i].prec = VISIT;

            if ( fit_pattern(arcs, vertices, i, disk, &primes, &slotSet) == ABNORM )
                status = ABNORM;        /* Search failed at vertex i. Try */
                break;                  /* a new pattern.                 */
            }
            else                /* Search succeeded. Proceed to next node. */
                i = vertices->vertexArray[i].succ;
        }
    }
```

```
            free( disk );
            free( (char *)slotSet.intSetRep );
            free( (char *)primes.intSetRep );
            return(status);
        }


/**************************************************************************

            fit_pattern( arcsType*, verticesType*, int, char*,
                         intSetType*, intSetType* )

    Return:         int — NORM if a fit is found, ABNORM if not.

    Purpose:        Compute a pattern for a level and fit it onto the hash table.
                    If a pattern is found, then the g values for vertices on that
                    level are set appropriately, and the slots on the disk for
                    the vertices are filled.
**/

int fit_pattern( arcs, vertices, i, disk, primes, slotSet )
    arcsType        *arcs;      /* in: The arcs in the graph.                  */
    verticesType    *vertices; /* in out: The vertices in the graph.           */
    int             i;          /* in: Vertex's location in vertex-selected list. */
    char            *disk;      /* in out: The hash table (disk).              */
    intSetType      *primes,    /* in: Prime number table                      */
                    *slotSet;   /* Set of slots taken by keys in this pattern. */

{
    arcType *arc;               /* Current arc.                       */
    int     shift,              /* Shift value for the pattern.       */
            side,               /* Side indicator (0 or 1).           */
            hashAddress         /* Hash address being tried.          */
            fitOK = ABNORM,     /* Fit condition variable.            */
            no_fits = 0;        /* Running count of attempts to fit.  */

    side = (i >= vertices->no_vertices/2);
    shift = primes->intSetRep[pmrandom() % primes->count];

    while ((no_fits++ < arcs->no_arcs) && (fitOK == ABNORM) ) {

        fitOK = NORM;
        slotSet->count = 0;              /* Initialize slot set to empty.    */

        arc = vertices->vertexArray[i].first_edge;
        while ( arc != 0 ) { /* Iterate over all arcs in this level. */
```

```
        /* If the key for arc is at this level, */
        /* get its hash address.               */
        if ( vertices->vertexArray[arc->h12[(side+1)%2]].prec == VISIT ) {

            hashAddress = abs(arc-h0 +
                vertices->vertexArray[arc->h12[0]].g +
                vertices->vertexArray[arc->h12[1]].g
                ) % arcs->no_arcs;

                    /* See if this key can be put at hashAddress. */
            if ( disk[hashAddress] != EMPTY ) {       /* Collision. Clear  */
                int k;                                 /* marked slots in disk.*/
                for ( k = 0; k < slotSet->count; k++ )
                    disk[slotSet->intSetRep[k]] = EMPTY;

                    /* Try a new shift. */
                vertices->vertexArray[i].g =
                    ( vertices->vertexArray[i].g + shift ) % arcs->no_arcs;
                fitOK = ABNORM;
                break;
            }
            else {      /* Success. Remember the address, */
                    /* and mark the table.           */
                slotSet->intSetRep[slotSet->count++] = hashAddress;
                disk[hashAddress] = FULL;

            }
        } /* end of if */
        arc = arc->next_edge[side];       /* Hash next arc. */
    } /* end of inner while */
} /* end of outer while */
return(fitOK);
}


/**************************************************************************


        initialize_search( arcsType*, verticesType*, char* )

  Return:       void

  Purpose:      Prepare for the search stage: Put random values in all
                the g fields, mark all vertices un-visited, and empty the disk.

**/
```

```
void
initialize_search( arcs, vertices, disk )
   arcsType      *arcs;           /* in: arcs.            */
   verticesType *vertices;        /* out: vertices.       */
   char          *disk;           /* out: the hash table. */
{

   int i;

   setseed( pmrandom() );                            /* Set the seed.     */

   for ( i = 0; i < vertices->no_vertices; i++ ) {
     vertices->vertexArray[i].g = pmrandom() % arcs->no_arcs;
     vertices->vertexArray[i].prec = NOTVISIT;
   }
                                                     /* Reset the hash table.*/
   for ( i = 0; i < arcs->no_arcs; disk[i++] = EMPTY );
}

/*************************************************************************

         initialize_primes( int, intSetType* )

   Return:    void

   Purpose:   Set up the prime number table.
**/

void
initialize_primes( n, primes )
   int n;                     /* in: the size of the hash table. */
   intSetType *primes;        /* out: the prime number table.    */
{
   int i,
       testingNumber = 2;        /* Testing number for possible prime numbers. */

   primes->intSetRep = (int*) owncalloc( PRIMES, sizeof(int) );

   primes->intSetRep[0] = 1;        /* 1 is added to the table, although it */

   primes->count = 1;               /* is not a prime.                      */
   while ( (testingNumber++ < n) && (primes->count < PRIMES) ) {
     if ( n % testingNumber != 0 ) {                 /* Get first PRIMES-1     */
       for ( i = testingNumber - 1; i> 0; i-- )          /* prime numbers.    */
       if ( testingNumber % i == 0 )
          break;
```

```
      if ( i == 1 ) primes->intSetRep[primes->count++] = testingNumber;
   } /* end of if */
 } /* end of while */
}
```

/*************************** support.c *********************************

    Purpose: Provide some useful support routines:

                  — Storage allocators that exit on error (since this
                    isn't a subroutine library, there's no need for
                    fancy error-handling).

                  — A routine to write the MPHF to a file.

                  — A routine to verify the correctness of a MPHF.

    Provenance: Written and tested by Q. Chen and E. Fox, March 1991.
                Edited and tested by S. Wartik, April 1991.

    Notes: None.
**/

```
#include  < stdio.h >

#include "types.h"

#ifdef __STDC__

extern char     *malloc( unsigned int size );
extern char     *realloc ( char *area, unsigned int size );

extern void     exit();

#else

extern char     *malloc(),
                *realloc();

extern void     exit();

#endif
```

/**
        owncalloc(n, size)

    Return: char * — Pointer to a chunk of memory.

```
Purpose:        Allocate a chunk of memory of 'n' elements each of size 'size'.
                Return the pointer to the chunk. Abort if no space is available.
**/


char *owncalloc( n, size )
    int         n,      /* in: number of elements.   */
                size;   /* in: size of each element. */
{
    char        *temp;

    if ( (temp = malloc( (unsigned int)(n*size) )) == 0 ) {
        fputs("Panic: cannot allocate memory.\n", stderr);
        exit(1);
    }
    return(temp);
}


/***********************************************************************
        ownrealloc( n, size )

  Return:       char * -- Pointer to a chunk of memory.

  Purpose:      Re-allocate a chunk of memory pointed to by area -- make it
                new_size bytes. Abort if no space is available.
**/


char *ownrealloc( area, new_size )
    char        *area;          /* in: area to re-allocate. */
    int         new_size;       /* in: new size.            */
{
    char        *temp;

    if ( (temp = realloc( area, (unsigned)new_size )) == 0 ) {
        fputs("Panic: cannot reallocate memory.\n", stderr);
        exit(1);
    }
    return(temp);
}


/***********************************************************************
        write_gfun( arcs, vertices, tbl_seed, spec_file )

  Return:       void

  Purpose:      Write the MPHF specification to a file
**/
```

```
void
write_gfun( arcs, vertices, tbl_seed, spec_file )
    arcsType        *arcs;        /* in: the arcs.                          */
    verticesType    *vertices;    /* in: the vertices.                      */
    int             tbl_seed;     /* in: seed used to set up random number tables. */
    char            *spec_file;   /* in: name of the specification file.    */
{
    int             i;            /* Iterator through vertices.             */
    FILE            *fp;          /* Handle for specification file.         */

    if ( (fp = fopen(spec_file, "w")) == NULL ) {
        fprintf(stderr, "Can't create hashing specification file \"%s\".\n",
                    spec_file);
        exit(1);
    }

    fprintf(fp, "%d\n%d\n%d\n",
                arcs->no_arcs, vertices->no_vertices, tbl_seed);
    for ( i = 0; i < vertices->no_vertices; i++ )
        fprintf(fp, "%d\n", vertices->vertexArray[i].g);

    fclose(fp);
}


/**************************************************************************

        verify_mphf( arcs, vertices )

 Return:        int -- NORM if MPHF is correct, ABNORM if not.

 Purpose:       Verify the computed MPHF is indeed minimal and perfect
**/

int verify_mphf( arcs, vertices )
    arcsType    *arcs;            /* in: the arcs.     */
    verticesType *vertices;       /* in: the vertices. */
{
    int         i,
                status = NORM,
                hash;             /* Hash value of a key. */
    char        *disk;            /* Hash table.          */

    disk = owncalloc( arcs->no_arcs, sizeof(char) );

    for( i = 0; i < arcs->no_arcs; disk[i++] = EMPTY );
```

```
    for ( i = 0; i < arcs->no_arcs; i++ ) {
        hash = abs ( arcs->arcArray[i].h0 +
                     vertices->vertexArray[arcs->arcArray[i].h12[0]].g +
                     vertices->vertexArray[arcs->arcArray[i].h12[1]].g
                     ) % arcs->no_arcs ;

        if ( hash < 0 ) {
          fprintf(stderr, "Panic: negative hash value.\n");
          status = ABNORM;
          break;
        }

        if ( disk[hash] == FULL ) {
            fprintf(stderr, "Panic: hash entry collided at");
            fprintf(stderr, " position %d by the %dth word!\n", hash, i);
            status = ABNORM;
            break;
        }
        else
        disk[hash] = FULL;
    }

  free( (char *)disk );

  return(status);
}


/*********************** vheap.c *********************************

   Purpose:      Implement a "virtual heap": a combination of stacks and
                 a heap.

   Provenance:   Written and tested by Q. Chen and E. Fox, March 1991.
                 Edited and tested by S. Wartik, April 1991.

   Notes:        The point of the combination is that a stack is a more
                 efficient data structure. Vertices of low degree
                 (specifically, those <= NO_STACKS) are stored in stacks,
                 since they are more common. Vertices of high degree are
                 stored in the heap.

**/

#include <math.h>
#include <stdio.h>
```

```c
#include "types.h"
#include "support.h"
#include "vheap.h"

#define NO_STACKS 6    /* The number of stacks in use.          */
#define DEF_SIZE 10    /* The default size of a heap or a stack. */

typedef struct {              /* Stack data structure.            */
    int stackTop,             /* Stack top.                       */
        stackSize;            /* Allocated stack area size.       */
    vertexType **stackRep;    /* Stack area.                      */
} stackType;

typedef struct {              /* Heap cell data structure.             */
    int degree;               /* Key field, containing vertex's degree. */
    vertexType *vertex:       /* Info field, holding vertex's address. */
} heapCell;

typedef struct {              /* Heap data structure.            */
    int heapTop,              /* Heap top.                       */
        heapSize;             /* Allocated heap area size.       */
    heapCell *heapRep;        /* Heap area.                      */
} heapType;

stackType        stacks[NO_STACKS];    /* The stacks of the virtual heap. */
heapType         heap;                 /* The heap portion.               */

#ifdef __STDC__

extern void      push( stackType *stack, vertexType *vertex );
extern int       pop( stackType *stack, vertexType **vertex );
extern void      enter_heap( int degree, vertexType *vertex );
extern int       remove_from_heap( vertexType **vertex );

#else

extern void      push();
extern int       pop();
extern void      enter_heap();
extern int       remove_from_heap();

#endif

/***********************************************************************/

        add_to_vheap( vertex, degree )

  Return:        void
```

```
    Purpose:        Add a vertex of a specified degree to the virtual heap.

**/

void add_to_vheap( vertex, degree )
    vertexType        *vertex;        /* in: a vertex to be added.        */
    int               degree;         /* in: the vertex's degree.         */
{
    if ( degree > NO_STACKS )
        enter_heap( degree, vertex );
    else
        push( &stacks[degree-1], vertex );
}

/*********************************************************************

        max_degree_vertex( vertex )

  Return:        int -- NORM if a vertex could be found, ABNORM if the
                 virtual heap (stacks and heap) is empty.

  Purpose:       Find the unvisited vertex with maximal degree from the
                 virtual heap.  Place it in "vertex".

  Plan:          First check the heap; remove_from_heap() automatically
                 removes a vertex of maximal degree.  If the heap is
                 empty, try the stacks, one at a time.
**/

int max_degree_vertex( vertex )
    vertexType    **vertex;                     /* out: the vertex found. */
{
    int i;

    if ( remove_from_heap( vertex ) == NORM ) /* heap empty? */
        return(NORM);

    for( i = NO_STACKS - 1; i >= 0; i-- )                /* stacks empty? */
        if ( pop( &stacks[i], vertex ) == NORM )
            return (NORM);

    return(ABNORM);    /* No node at all. The component has been processed. */
}

/*********************************************************************

        push(stack, vertex )
```

```
    Return:         void

    Purpose:        Push a vertex pointer onto a stack.
**/

static void push(stack, vertex)
        stackType       *stack;      /* in out: the stack.   */
        vertexType      *vertex;     /* in: the vertex.      */
{
    stack->stackTop++;

        /* Expand stack if it doesn't have enough space. */
    if ( stack->stackTop >= stack->stackSize ) {
        fprintf(stderr, "Warning: stack overflow. Re-allocating.\n");
        stack->stackSize *= 2;
        stack->stackRep =
                (vertexType**)ownrealloc( (char *)stack->stackRep,
                                    sizeof(vertexType*) * stack-stackSize );

    }

    stack->stackRep[stack->stackTop] = vertex;
}


/***********************************************************************
        pop( stack, vertex )

    Return:         int — Index of a vertex.

    Purpose:        Pop up a vertex pointer from the stack. Return -1 if the stack
                    was empty, 0 if it wasn't.
**/

static int pop( stack, vertex )
    stackType   *stack;
    vertexType  **vertex;
{
    if ( stack->stackTop == -1 )
        return(-1);      /* stack empty */

    *vertex = stack->stackRep[stack->stackTop--];
    return(0);      /* stack not empty */
}


/***********************************************************************
        enter_heap( degree, vertex )
```

```
    Return:     void

    Purpose:    Insert a vertex pointer and its degree into the heap.

**/

static void enter_heap( degree, vertex )
    int         degree;         /* in: the degree of the node.   */
    vertexType *vertex;         /* in: the vertex pointer.       */
{

    int k = heap.heapTop++ ;

    if ( k >= heap.heapSize ) {
        heap.heapSize = 2 * heap.heapSize;
        heap.heapRep =
                (heapCell*)ownrealloc( (char *)heap.heapRep,
                                    sizeof(heapCell) * heap.heapSize );
    }

    heap.heapRep[k].degree = degree;
    heap.heapRep[k].vertex = vertex;

    while ( heap.heapRep[k/2].degree <= degree ) {
        heap.heapRep[k].degree = heap.heapRep[k/2].degree;
        heap.heapRep[k].vertex = heap.heapRep[k/2].vertex;
        k /= 2;
    }

    heap.heapRep[k].degree = degree;
    heap.heapRep[k].vertex = vertex;
}

/***************************************************************************

        remove_from_heap( vertex )

  Return:       int — -1 if the heap is empty when the routine is called,
                0 if it isn't.

  Purpose:      Remove a vertex of maximal degree from the heap, and
                return it.
**/

static int remove_from_heap( vertex )
        vertexType      **vertex;   /* out: the vertex selected.   */
{
```

```
    int         k, j;              /* Iterators through the heap.          */
    heapCell    tempCell;          /* Heap element currently being examined.   */

    if ( heap.heapTop == 1 ) return(-1);

    *vertex = heap.heapRep[1].vertex;
    heap.heapTop--;

    tempCell.degree =
        heap.heapRep[1].degree= heap.heapRep[heap.heapTop].degree;
    tempCell.vertex = heap.heapRep[1].vertex =
        heap.heapRep[heap.heapTop].vertex;

    k = 1;                                          /* Go down the heap. */
    while ( k <= heap.heapTop / 2 ) {
        j = 2 * k;
        if ( (j < heap.heapTop ) &&
            (heap.heapRep[j].degree< heap.heapRep[j+1].degree) )
            j++;
        if ( tempCell.degree > heap.heapRep[j].degree )
            break;
        heap.heapRep[k].degree = heap.heapRep[j].degree;
        heap.heapRep[k].vertex = heap.heapRep[j].vertex;
        k = j;
    } /* end of while */

    heap.heapRep[k].degree = tempCell.degree;
    heap.heapRep[k].vertex = tempCell.vertex;
    return(0);
}


/***************************************************************************

        initialize_vheap()

  Return:       void

  Purpose:      Set the heap and stacks to their empty states.
**/

void initialize_vheap()
{
    int i;

    heap.heapRep[0].degree = MAX_INT;
    heap.heapTop = 1;
```

```
    for ( i = 1;  i < heap.heapSize;  i++ ) {
        heap.heapRep[i].degree = 0;

    heap.heapRep[i].vertex = 0;
  }
  for ( i = 0;  i NO_STACKS;  stacks[i++].stackTop = -1 );
}

/************************************************************************
    free_vheap()
 Return:     void
 Purpose:    Deallocate space for stacks and heap.
**/
void free_vheap()
{
  int i;
  for ( i = 0;  i NO_STACKS;  free((char *)stacks[i++].stackRep) );
  free( (char *)heap.heapRep );
}

/************************************************************************
    allocate_vheap( no_arcs, no_vertices )
 Return:     void
 Purpose:    Estimate and allocate space for the heap and the stacks.
**/

void allocate_vheap( no_arcs, no_vertices )
  int      no_arcs,          /* in: number of arcs.        */
           no_vertices;      /* in: number of vertices.     */
{
  int   i,                 /* iteration variable.        */
        sum = 0;           /* partial sum of degree.       */
  double lambda,             /* lambda = |E| / ( |V| / 2 )      */
         Pr0,              /* Pr0 = Pr(X = 0)        */
         Pri;              /* Pri = Pr(X = i)        */

  lambda = (double)(2*no_arcs) / (double)no_vertices;
  Pr0 = Pri = exp(-lambda);          /* Compute Pr(x = 0). */

  for ( i = 1;  i = NO_STACKS;  i++ ) {   /* Compute the expected number  */
    Pri *= lambda/(double)(i);      /* of nodes of degree 1, 2, ..., */
                        /* NO_STACKS.         */
    stacks[i-1].stackSize = (int) 2 * no_vertices * Pri;
    sum += stacks[i-1].stackSize ;
  }
```

```
   for ( i = 0; i NO_STACKS; i++ ) {   /* Allocate stack space. */
     if ( stacks[i].stackSize = 0 ) stacks[i].stackSize = DEF_SIZE;
       stacks[i].stackRep =
         (vertexType**) owncalloc( stacks[i].stackSize, sizeof(vertexType*)
);
   }

   heap.heapSize = no_vertices - sum - (int) 2 * no_vertices * Pr0;
   if ( heap.heapSize = 0 ) heap.heapSize = DEF_SIZE;
   heap.heapRep =                    /* Allocate heap space. */
       (heapCell*) owncalloc( heap.heapSize, sizeof(heapCell) );
}
```

14

Ranking Algorithms

Donna Harman

National Institute of Standards and Technology

Abstract

This chapter presents both a summary of past research done in the development of ranking algorithms and detailed instructions on implementing a ranking type of retrieval system. This type of retrieval system takes as input a natural language query without Boolean syntax and produces a list of records that "answer" the query, with the records ranked in order of likely relevance. Ranking retrieval systems are particularly appropriate for end-users.

14.1 INTRODUCTION

Boolean systems were first developed and marketed over 30 years ago at a time when computing power was minimal compared with today. Because of this, these systems require the user to provide sufficient syntactical restrictions in their query to limit the number of documents retrieved, and those retrieved documents are not ranked in order of any relationship to the user's query. Although the Boolean systems offer very powerful on-line search capabilities to librarians and other trained intermediaries, they tend to provide very poor service to end-users, particularly those who use the system on an infrequent basis (Cleverdon 1983). These end-users are likely to be familiar with the terminology of the data set they are searching, but lack the training and practice necessary to get consistently good results from a Boolean system because of the complex query syntax required by these systems. The ranking approach to retrieval seems to be more oriented toward these end-users. This approach allows the user to input a simple query such as a sentence or a phrase (no Boolean connectors) and retrieve a list of documents ranked in order of likely relevance.

The main reason the natural language/ranking approach is more effective for end-users is that all the terms in the query are used for retrieval, with the results being ranked based on co-occurrence of query terms, as modified by statistical term-weighting (to be explained later in the chapter). This method eliminates the often-wrong Boolean syntax used by end-users, and provides some results even if a query term is incorrect, that is, it is not the term used in the data, it is misspelled, and so on. The ranking methodology also works well for the complex queries that may be difficult for end-users to express in Boolean logic. For example, "human factors and/or system performance in medical databases" is difficult for end-users to express in Boolean logic because it contains many high- or medium-frequency words without any clear necessary Boolean syntax. The ranking method would do well with this query.

This chapter describes the implementation of a ranking system and is organized in the following manner. Section 14.2 shows a conceptual illustration of how ranking is done. Section 14.3 presents various theoretical models used in ranking and reviews past experiments using these models. Section 14.4 describes results from several experiments directly comparing various ranking schemes, along with brief discussions of the type of ranking methods found in the few operational systems that have used this retrieval technique. Section 14.5 summarizes the results from sections 14.3 and 14.4, presenting a series of recommended ranking schemes for various situations. Section 14.6 describes the implementation of a basic ranking retrieval system, with section 14.7 showing possible variations to this scheme based on retrieval environments. Section 14.8 discusses some topics closely related to ranking and provides some suggestions for further reading in these areas, and section 14.9 summarizes the chapter.

The terms "record" and "document" are used interchangeably throughout this chapter, as are the terms "data set," "database," and "collection," depending on the retrieval environment being discussed.

14.2 HOW RANKING IS DONE

Assume that a given textual data set uses i unique terms. A document can then be represented by a vector $(t_1, t_2, t_3, \ldots, t_n)$, where t_i has a value of 1 if term i is present, and 0 if term i is absent in the document. A query can be represented in the same manner. Figure 14.1 shows this representation for a data set with seven unique terms.

The top section of Figure 14.1 shows the seven terms in this data set. The second section shows a natural language query and its translation into a conceptual vector, with 1's in vector positions of words included in the query, and 0's to indicate a lack of those words. For example, the first "1" indicates the presence of the word "factor," the second "1" indicates the presence of the word "information," the first "0" indicates the absence of the word "help." The third section of Figure 14.1 shows a similar conceptual representation of three documents in this data set. To determine which document best matches the query, a simple dot product of the query vector and each document vector is made (left side of the fourth section) and the results used to rank the documents.

It is possible to perform the same operation using weighted vectors as shown in the right side of the bottom section of Figure 14.1. In the example, each term is weighted by the total number of times it appears in the record, for example, "factors" appears twice in document 1, "information" appears three times in docu-

CONCEPTUAL TERM WEIGHTING

factors information help human operation retrieval systems

Query human factors in information retrieval systems
VECTOR (1 1 0 1 0 1 1)

Record 1 containing human, factors, information, retrieval
VECTOR (1 1 0 1 0 1 0)

Record 2 containing human, factors, help, systems
VECTOR (1 0 1 1 0 0 1)

Record 3 containing factors, operation, systems
VECTOR (1 0 0 0 1 0 1)

SIMPLE MATCH		WEIGHTED MATCH	
Query	(1 1 0 1 0 1 1)	Query	(1 1 0 1 0 1 1)
Rec 1	(1 1 0 1 0 1 0)	Rec 1	(2 3 0 5 0 3 0)
	(1 1 0 1 0 1 0) = 4		(2 3 0 5 0 3 0) = 13
Query	(1 1 0 1 0 1 1)	Query	(1 1 0 1 0 1 1)
Rec 2	(1 0 1 1 0 0 1)	Rec 2	(2 0 4 5 0 0 1)
	(1 0 0 1 0 0 1) = 3		(2 0 0 5 0 0 1) = 8
Query	(1 1 0 1 0 1 1)	Query	(1 1 0 1 0 1 1)
Rec 3	(1 0 0 0 1 0 1)	Rec 3	(2 0 0 0 2 0 1)
	(1 0 0 0 0 0 1) = 2		(2 0 0 0 0 0 1) = 3

Figure 14.1 A simple illustration of statistical ranking

ment 1, and so on. These term-weights could reflect different measures, such as the scarcity of a term in the data set (i.e., "human" probably occurs less frequently than "systems" in a computer science data set), the frequency of a term in the given document (as shown in the example), or some user-specified term-weight. This term-weighting usually provides substantial improvement in the ranking.

14.3 RANKING MODELS AND EXPERIMENTS WITH THESE MODELS

In 1957 Luhn published a paper proposing a statistical approach to searching literary information. He suggested that "the more two representations agreed in given elements and their distribution, the higher would be the probability of their representing similar information." Maron and Kuhns (1960) went much further by suggesting how to actually weight terms, including some small-scale experiments in term-weighting. The information retrieval research community has continued to develop many models for the ranking technique over the last 30 years (for an overview, see Belkin and Croft [1987]). Although it is not necessary to understand the theoretical models involved in ranking in detail in order to implement a ranking retrieval system, it is helpful to know about them as they have provided a framework for the vast majority of retrieval experiments that contributed to the development of the ranking techniques used today.

All the experimental results presented in the models are based on using standard test collections and using standard recall and precision measures for evaluation. Results are presented in a roughly chronological order to provide some sense of the development of knowledge about ranking through these experiments.

Ranking models can be divided into two types: those that rank the query against individual documents and those that rank the query against entire sets of related documents. The first type of ranking model, those that rank individual documents against the query, covers several theoretical models, but the principle ones are the vector space model and the probabilistic model.

14.3.1 The Vector Space Model

The sample document and query vectors described in section 14.2 can be envisioned as an n-dimensional vector space, where n corresponds to the number of unique terms in the data set. A vector matching operation, based on the cosine correlation used to measure the cosine of the angle between vectors, can then be used to compute the similarity between a document and a query, and documents can be ranked based on that similarity.

$$similarity\ (d_j, q_k) = \frac{\sum_{i=1}^{n} (td_{ij} \times tq_{ik})}{\sqrt{\sum_{i=1}^{n} td_{ij}^2 \times \sum_{i=1}^{n} tq_{ik}^2}}$$

where

td_{ij} = the ith term in the vector for document j
tq_{ik} = the ith term in the vector for query k
n = the number of unique terms in the data set

This model has been used as the basis for many ranking retrieval experiments, in particular the SMART system experiments under Salton and his associates (1968, 1971, 1973, 1981, 1983, 1988). These ranking experiments started in 1964 at Harvard University, moved to Cornell University in 1968, and form a large part of the research in information retrieval. The SMART experiments cover many areas of information retrieval such as relevance feedback, clustering, and experiments with suffixing, synonyms, and phrases. Only those experiments dealing directly with term-weighting and ranking will be discussed here.

Early experiments (Salton and Lesk 1968; Salton 1971, p. 143) using the SMART system tested an overlap similarity function against the cosine correlation measure and tried simple term-weighting using the frequency of terms within the documents. These experiments showed that within-document frequency weighting improved performance over no term-weighting (in varying amounts depending on the test collection used). Further, they showed that use of the cosine correlation with frequency term-weighting provided better performance than the overlap similarity because of the automatic inclusion of document length normalization by the cosine similarity function (again, the results varied somewhat depending on the test collection used).

A second major set of experiments was done by Salton and Yang (1973) to further develop the term-weighting schemes. Of particular interest in these experiments were the term-weighting schemes relying on term importance within an entire collection rather than only within a given document. Clearly more weight should be given to query terms matching document terms that are rare within a collection. Salton and Yang were able to show significant performance improvement using a term-weighting scheme that combined the within-document frequency weighting with a new term-weighting scheme, the inverted document frequency (IDF; Sparck Jones 1972) that is based on the Zipf distribution of a term within the entire collection (see page 373 for the definition of IDF).

A recent paper by Salton and Buckley (1988) summarizes 20 years of SMART experiments in automatic term-weighting by trying 287 distinct combinations of term-weighting assignments, with or without cosine normalization, on six standard collections. Besides confirming that the best document term-weighting is provided by a product of the within-document term frequency and the IDF, normalized by the cosine measure, they show performance improvements using enhanced query term-weighting measures for queries with term frequencies greater than one. These weighting schemes are further discussed in section 14.5.

14.3.2 Probabilistic Models

Although a model of probabilistic indexing was proposed and tested by Maron and Kuhns (1960), the major probabilistic model in use today was developed by Robertson and Sparck Jones (1976). This model is based on the premise that terms that appear in previously retrieved relevant documents for a given query should be given a higher weight than if they had not appeared in those relevant documents. In particular, they presented the following table showing the distribution of term t in relevant and nonrelevant documents for query q.

		Document Relevance		
		+	−	
Document Indexing	+	r	$n - r$	n
	−	$R - r$	$N - n - R + r$	$N - n$
		R	$N - R$	N

N = the number of documents in the collection

R = the number of relevant documents for query q

n = the number of documents having term t

r = the number of relevant documents having term t

$$w^1 = \log \frac{\left(\dfrac{r}{R}\right)}{\left(\dfrac{n}{N}\right)} \qquad w^2 = \log \frac{\left(\dfrac{r}{R}\right)}{\left(\dfrac{n-r}{N-R}\right)}$$

$$w^3 = \log \frac{\left(\dfrac{r}{R-r}\right)}{\left(\dfrac{n}{N-n}\right)} \qquad w^4 = \log \frac{\left(\dfrac{r}{R-r}\right)}{\left(\dfrac{n-r}{N-n-R+r}\right)}$$

They then use this table to derive four formulas that reflect the relative distribution of terms in the relevant and nonrelevant documents, and propose that these formulas be used for term-weighting (the logs are related to actual use of the formulas in term-weighting).

Robertson and Sparck Jones also formally derive these formulas, and show that theoretical preference is for F4.

Formula F1 had been used by Barkla (1969) for relevance feedback in a SDI service and by Miller (1971) in devising a probabilistic search strategy for Medlars. It was also used by Sparck Jones (1975) in devising optimal performance yardsticks for test collections. Formula F4 (minus the log) is the term precision weighting measure proposed by Yu and Salton (1976).

Robertson and Sparck Jones used these four formulas in a series of experiments with the manually indexed Cranfield collection. They did experiments using all the relevance judgments to weight the terms to see what the optimal performance would be, and also used relevance judgments from half the collection to weight the terms for retrieval from the second half of the collection. In both cases, formula F4 was superior (closely followed by F3), with a large drop in performance between the optimal performance and the "predictive" performance, as would be expected. The experimental verification of the theoretical superiority of F4 provided additional weight to the importance of this new model.

The use of this theory as a predictive device was further investigated by Sparck Jones (1979a) who used a slightly modified version of F1 and F4 and again got much better results for F4 than for F1, even on a large test collection. Sparck Jones (1979b) tried using this measure (F4 only) in a manner that would mimic a typical on-line session using relevance feedback and found that adding the relevance weighting from only the first couple of relevant documents retrieved by a ranking system still produced performance improvements.

Work up to this point using probabilistic indexing required the use of at least a few relevant documents, making this model more closely related to relevance feedback than to term-weighting schemes of other models. In 1979 Croft and Harper published a paper detailing a series of experiments using probabilistic indexing without out any relevance information. Starting with a probabilistic restatement of F4, they assume that all query terms have equal probability of occurring in relevant documents and derive a term-weighting formula that combines a weight based on the number of matching terms and on a term-weighting similar to the IDF measure.

$$similarity_{jk} = \sum_{i=1}^{Q} (C + \log \frac{(N-n_i)}{n_i})$$

where

Q = the number of matching terms between document j and query k
C = a constant for tuning the similarity function
n_i = the number of documents having term i in the data set
N = the number of documents in the data set

Experimental results showed that this term-weighting produced somewhat better results than the use of the IDF measure alone. Being able to provide different values to C allows this weighting measure to be tailored to various collections. Setting C to 1 ranks the documents by IDF weighting within number of matches, a method that was suitable for the manually indexed Cranfield collection used in this study (because it can be assumed that each matching query term was very significant). C was set much lower in tests with the UKCIS2 collection (Harper 1980) because the terms were assumed to be less accurate, and the documents were very short (consisting of titles only).

Croft (1983) expanded his combination weighting scheme to incorporate within-document frequency weights, again using a tuning factor K on these weights to allow tailoring to particular collections. The results show significant improvement over both the IDF weighting alone and the combination weighting, with the scaling factor K playing a large part in tuning the weighting to different collections.

$$similarity_{jk} = \sum_{i=1}^{Q} (C + IDF_i) * f_{ij})$$

where

Q = the number of matching terms between document j and query k

IDF_i = the IDF weight for term i in the entire collection (see page 373 for the definition of IDF)

$$f_{ij} = K + (1 - K) \frac{freq_{ij}}{maxfreq_j}$$

where

$freq_{ij}$ = the frequency of term i in document j

K = a constant for adjusting the relative importance of the two weighting schemes

$maxfreq_j$ = the maximum frequency of any term in document j

The best value for K proved to be 0.3 for the automatically indexed Cranfield collection, and 0.5 for the NPL collection, confirming that within-document term frequency plays a much smaller role in the NPL collection with its short documents having few repeating terms.

14.3.3 Other Models for Ranking Individual Documents

Several other models have been used in developing term-weighting measures. The inverted document frequency measure heavily used in implementing both the vector space model and the probabilistic model was derived by Sparck Jones (1972) from observing the Zipf distribution curve for collection vocabulary. Others have tried more complex term distributions, most notably the 2-Poisson model proposed by Bookstein and Swanson (1974) and implemented and tested by Harter (1975) and

Raghavan et al. (1983). This distribution model proved much less successful because of the difficulty in estimating the many parameters needed for implementation.

14.3.4 Set-Oriented Ranking Models

The most well known of the set-oriented models are the clustering models where a query is ranked against a hierarchically grouped set of related documents. This model is the subject of Chapter 16 and will not be further discussed here.

Models based on fuzzy set theory have been proposed (for a summary, see Bookstein [1985]) but have not received enough experimental implementations to be used in practice (except when combined with Boolean queries such as in the P-Norm discussed in Chapter 15).

The theory of rough sets has been applied to information retrieval (Srinivasan 1989) but similarly has not been developed far enough to be used in practice.

14.4 OTHER EXPERIMENTS INVOLVING RANKING

14.4.1 Direct Comparison of Similarity Measures and Term-Weighting Schemes

There have been several studies examining the various factors involved in ranking that have not been based on any particular model but have instead used some method of comparing directly various similarity measures and term-weighting schemes.

Sparck Jones (1973) explored different types of term frequency weightings involving term frequency within a document, term frequency within a collection, term postings within a document (a binary measure), and term postings within a collection, along with normalizing these measures for document length. She used four collections, with indexing generally taken from manually extracted keywords instead of using full-text indexing, and with all queries based on manual keywords. Her results showed that using the term frequency (or postings) within a collection always improved performance, but that using term frequency (or postings) within a document improved performance only for some collections. The various term-weighting schemes were not combined in this experiment.

McGill et al. (1979) examined the literature from different fields to select 67 similarity measures and 39 term-weighting schemes. He used these to rank results from Boolean retrievals using both controlled (manually indexed) and uncontrolled (full-text) indexing. For both controlled and uncontrolled vocabulary he found a significant difference in the performance of similarity measures, with a group of about 15 different similarity measures all performing significantly better than the rest. This group included both the cosine correlation and the inner product function used in the probabilistic models. The term-weighting results were more mixed, with no significant difference found when using controlled vocabulary (i.e., term-weighting made no difference) and an overall significant difference found for uncontrolled vocabulary. There was a lack of significant difference between pairs of term-weighting measures for uncontrolled vocabulary, however, which could indicate that the difference between linear combinations of term-weighting schemes is significant but that individual pairs of term-weighting schemes are not significantly different.

A different approach was taken by Harman (1986). She selected four term-weighting factors proven important in past research and tried different combinations in order to arrive at an "optimum" term-weighting scheme. Full-text indexing was used on various standard test collections, with full-text indexing also done on the queries. The four factors investigated were: the number of matches between a document and a query, the distribution of a term within a document collection, the frequency of a term within a document, and the length of the document. Two different measures for the distribution of a term within a document collection were used, the IDF measure by Sparck Jones and a revised implementation of the "noise" measure (Dennis 1964; Salton and McGill 1983). Note that the use of noise here refers to how much a term can be considered useful for retrieval versus being simply a "noisy" term, and examines the concentration of terms within documents rather than just the number of postings or occurrences. She found that when using the single measures alone, the distribution of the term within the collection improved performance almost twice as much for the Cranfield collection as using only within-document frequency. Combining the within-document frequency with either the IDF or noise measure, and normalizing for document length improved results more than twice as much as using the IDF or noise alone in the Cranfield collection. Other collections showed less improvement, but the same relative merit of the term-weighting schemes was found. The noise measure consistently slightly outperformed the IDF (however with no significant difference).

14.4.2 Ranking Based on Document Structure

Some ranking experiments have relied more on document or intradocument structure than on the term-weighting described earlier. Bernstein and Williamson (1984) built a ranking retrieval system for a highly structured knowledge base, the Hepatitis Knowledge Base. Their ranking algorithms used not only weights based on term importance both within an entire collection and within a given document, but also on the structural position of the term, such as within summary paragraphs versus within text paragraphs. A very elaborate weighting scheme was devised for this experiment, tailored to the particular structure of the knowledge base. In SIBRIS, an operational information retrieval system (Wade et al. 1989), document and query structures are also used to influence the ranking, increasing term-weights for terms in titles of documents and decreasing term weights for terms added to a query from a thesaurus.

A very different approach based on complex intradocument structure was used in the experiments involving latent semantic indexing (Lochbaum and Streeter

1989). The indexing and retrieval were based on the singular value decomposition (related to factor analysis) of a term-document matrix from the entire document collection. This was combined with weighting using both a function of term frequency within a document (the root mean square normalization), and a function of term frequency within the entire collection (the noise or entropy measure, or alternatively the IDF measure). The results were generally superior to those using term-weighting alone, although further development is necessary before this approach is fast enough for use in large retrieval systems.

14.4.3 Ranking Techniques Used in Operational Systems

Several operational retrieval systems have implemented ranking algorithms as central to their search mechanism. The SIRE system, as implemented at Syracuse University (Noreault et al. 1977) built a hybrid system using Boolean searching and a vector-model-based ranking scheme, weighting by the use of raw term frequency within documents (for more on the hybrid aspects of this system, see section 14.7.3). A commercial outgrowth of this system, marketed as Personal Librarian, uses ranking based on different factors, including the IDF and the frequency of a term within a document. This system assigns higher ranks to documents matching greater numbers of query terms than would normally be done in the ranking schemes discussed experimentally.

The CITE system, designed as an interface to MEDLINE (Doszkocs 1982), ranked documents based solely on the IDF weighting, as no within-document frequencies were available from the MEDLINE files. For details on the search system associated with CITE, see section 14.7.2. The OPAKI project (Walker and Jones 1987) worked with on-line catalogs and also used the IDF measure alone. Although other small-scale operational systems using ranking exist, often their ranking algorithms are not clear from publications, and so these are not listed here.

14.5 A GUIDE TO SELECTING RANKING TECHNIQUES

In looking at results from all the experiments, some trends clearly emerge.

1. The use of term-weighting based on the distribution of a term within a collection always improves performance (or at minimum does not hurt performance). The IDF measure has been commonly used, either in its form as originally used, or in a form somewhat normalized.

$$IDF_i = \log_2 \frac{N}{n_i} + 1 \qquad (Sparck\ Jones\ 1972)$$

$$IDF_i = \log_2 \frac{maxn}{n_i} + 1 \qquad (Sparck\ Jones\ 1979)$$

$$IDF_i = \log_2 \frac{N - n_i}{n_i} \qquad (Croft\ and\ Harper\ 1979)$$

where

N = the number of documents in the collection
n_i = the total number of occurrences of term i in the collection
$maxn$ = the maximum frequency of any term in the collection

A possible alternative is the noise or entropy measure tried in several experiments.

$$normalized\ noise_i = maxnoise - noise_i,$$

$$noise_i = \sum_{k=1}^{N} \frac{Freq_{ik}}{TFreq_i} \log_2 \frac{TFreq_i}{Freq_{ik}} \qquad (Harman\ 1986)$$

$$entropy_i = 1 - \frac{\sum_{k=1}^{N} \dfrac{Freq_{ik}}{TFreq_i} \log_2 \dfrac{TFreq_i}{Freq_{ik}}}{\log_2 N} \qquad (Lochbaum\ \&\ Streeter\ 1989)$$

where

N = the number of documents in the collection
$maxnoise$ = the highest noise of any term in the collection
$Freq_{ik}$ = the frequency of term i in document k
$TFreq_i$ = the total frequency of term i in the collection

2. The combination of the within-document frequency with the IDF weight often provides even more improvement. There are several reasons why this improvement is inconsistent across collections. First, it is very important to normalize the within-document frequency in some manner, both to moderate the effect of high-frequency terms in a document (i.e., a term appearing 20 times is not 20 times as important as one appearing only once) and to compensate for document length. This normalization has taken various forms in different experiments, but the lack of proper normalization techniques in some experiments has likely hidden possible improvements. A second reason for the inconsistent improvements found for within-document frequencies is the fact that some collections have very short documents (such as titles only) and therefore within-document frequencies play no role in these collections. Finally, the effects of within-document frequency may need to be tailored to collections, such as was done by Croft (1983) in using a sliding importance factor K, and by Salton and Buckley (1988) in providing different combination schemes for term-weighting. This tailoring seems to be particularly critical for manually indexed or controlled vocabulary data where use of within-document frequencies may even hurt performance. Either of the following normalized within-document frequency measures can be safely used.

$$cfreq_{ij} = K + (1 - K) \frac{freq_{ij}}{maxfreq_j} \qquad (Croft\ 1983)$$

$$nfreq_{ij} = \frac{\log_2 (freq_{ij} + 1)}{\log_2 length_j} \qquad (Harman\ 1986)$$

where

$freq_{ij}$ = the frequency of term i in document j
$maxfreq_j$ = the maximum frequency of any term in document j
$length_j$ = the number of unique terms in document j

3. Assuming within-document term frequencies are to be used, several methods can be used for combining these with the IDF measure. The combination recommended for most situations by Salton and Buckley is given below (a complete set of weighting schemes is presented in their 1988 paper).

$$similarity\ (Q,D) = \frac{\sum_{i=1}^{t} (w_{iq} \times w_{ij})}{\sqrt{\sum_{i=1}^{t} (w_{iq})^2 \times \sum_{i=1}^{t} (w_{ij})^2}}$$

where

$$w_{iq} = \left(0.5 + \frac{0.5\ freq_{iq}}{maxfreq_q} \right) \times IDF_i$$

and

$w_{ij} = freq_{ij} \times IDF_i$
$freq_{iq}$ = the frequency of term i in query q
$maxfreq_j$ = the maximum frequency of any term in query $maxfreq_q$
IDF_i = the IDF of term i in the entire collection
$freq_{ij}$ = the frequency of term i in document j

Salton and Buckley suggest reducing the query weighting w_{iq} to only the within-document frequency ($freq_{iq}$) for long queries containing multiple occurrences of terms, and to use only binary weighting of documents ($w_{ij} = 1$ or 0) for collections with short documents or collections using controlled vocabulary.

Many combinations of term-weighting can be done using the inner product. Whereas there is more flexibility available here than in the cosine measure, the need for providing normalization of within-document frequencies is more critical. Two possible combinations are given below that calculate the matching strength of a query to document j, with symbol definitions the same as those previously given.

$$similarity_j = \sum_{i=1}^{Q} ((C + IDF_i) \times cfreq_{ij}) \qquad (Croft\ 1983)$$

where

$$cfreq_{ij} = K + (1 - K)\frac{freq_{ij}}{maxfreq_j}$$

C should be set to low values (near 0) for automatically indexed collections, and to higher values such as 1 for manually indexed collections. K should be set to low values (0.3 was used by Croft) for collections with long (35 or more terms) documents, and to higher values (0.5 or higher) for collections with short documents, reducing the role of within-document frequency.

One alternative ranking using the inner product (but without adjustable constants) is given below.

$$similarity_j = \sum_{i=1}^{Q} \frac{\log_2 (freq_{ij} + 1) \times IDF_i}{\log_2 length_j} \qquad (Harman\ 1986)$$

4. It can be very useful to add additional weight for document structure, such as higher weightings for terms appearing in the title or abstract versus those appearing only in the text. This additional weighting needs to be considered with respect to the particular data set being used for searching. User weighting can also be considered as additional weighting, although this type of weighting has generally proven unsatisfactory in the past.

5. The use of relevance weighting after some initial retrieval is very effective. Relevance weighting is discussed further in Chapter 11 on relevance feedback.

14.6 DATA STRUCTURES AND ALGORITHMS FOR RANKING

This section will describe a simple but complete implementation of the ranking part of a retrieval system. Modifications of this implementation that enhance its efficiency or are necessary for other retrieval environments are given in section 14.7, with cross-references made to these enhancements throughout this section.

The implementation will be described as two interlocking pieces: the indexing of the text and the using (searching) of that index to return a ranked list of record identification numbers (ids). The index shown is a straightforward inverted file, created once per major update (thus only once for a static data set), and is used to provide the necessary speed for searching. Although it is possible to build a ranking retrieval system without some type of index (either by storing and searching all terms in a document or by using signature files in ranking such as described in section 14.8.5), the use of these indices improves efficiency by several orders of magnitude. The penalty paid for this efficiency is the need to update the index as the data set changes. Except for data sets with critical hourly updates (such as stock quotes), this is generally not a problem. An enhancement to the indexing program to allow easier updating is given in section 14.7.4.

The description of the search process does not include the interface issues or the actual data retrieval issues. It is assumed that a natural language query is passed to the search process in some manner, and that the list of ranked record id numbers that is returned by the search process is used as input to some routine which maps these ids onto data locations and displays a list of titles or short data descriptors for user selection.

14.6.1 The Creation of an Inverted File

The inverted file described here is a modification to the inverted files described in Chapter 3 on that subject. It would be feasible to use structures other than simple inverted files, such as the more complex structures mentioned in that chapter, as long as the elements needed for ranking are provided. The use of a ranking system instead of a Boolean retrieval system has several important implications for supporting inverted file structures.

1. The use of ranking means that there is little need for the adjacency operations or field restrictions necessary in Boolean. Therefore, only the record id has to be stored as the location for each word, creating a much smaller index than for Boolean systems (in the order of 10% to 15% of the text size). If it is determined that the ranking system must also handle adjacency or field restrictions, then either the index must record the additional location information (field location, word position within record, and so on) as described for Boolean inverted files, or an alternative method (see section 14.8.4) can be used that does not increase storage but increases response time when using these particular operations. The inverted file presented here will assume that only record location is necessary.

2. The use of ranking means that strategies needed in Boolean systems to increase precision are not only unnecessary but should be discarded in favor of strategies that increase recall at the expense of precision. In the area of parsing, this may mean relaxing the rules about hyphenation to create indexing both in hyphenated and nonhyphenated form. In the area of stoplists, it may mean a less restrictive stoplist. For example, in a data set about computers, the ultra-high frequency term "computer" may be in a stoplist for Boolean systems but would not need to be considered a common word for ranking systems. In the area of stemming, a ranking system seems to work better by automatically expanding the query using stemming (Frakes 1984; Harman and Candela 1990) rather than by forcing the user to ask for expansion by wild-cards. A more appropri-

ate stemming strategy for ranking therefore is to use stemming in creation of the inverted file. An enhancement of this stemming option would be to allow the user to specify a "don't stem" character, and the modifications necessary to handle this are given in section 14.7.1.

Although an inverted file with frequency information (Figure 14.2) could be used directly by the search routine, it is usually processed into an improved final format.

term	recno	freq
ab	2	1
being	2	1
charact	2	1
human	2	1
index	1	1
literat	1	1
novel	1	1
pap	1	1
report	1	1
report	2	1
technique	1	2

Figure 14.2 Inverted file with frequency information

This format is based on the search methods and the weighting methods used, but a common search technique (and the one discussed here) is to use a binary search routine on the file to locate the query words. This implies that the file to be searched should be as short as possible, and for this reason the single file shown containing the terms, record ids, and frequencies is usually split into two pieces for searching: the dictionary containing the term, along with statistics about that term such as number of postings and IDF, and then a pointer to the location of the postings file for that term. The postings file contains the record ids and the weights for all occurrences of the term. In this manner the dictionary used in the binary search has only one "line" per unique term.

The above illustration is a conceptual form of the necessary files; the actual form depends on the details of the search routine and on the hardware being used. Work using large data sets (Harman and Candela 1990) showed that for a file of 2,653 records, there were 5,123 unique terms with an average of 14 postings/term and a maximum of over 2,000 postings for a term. A larger data set of 38,304 records had dictionaries on the order of 250,000 lines (250,000 unique terms, including some numerals) and an average of 88 postings per record. From these statistics it is clear that efficient storage structures for both the binary search and the reading of the postings are critical. Ideally, both files could be read into memory when a data set is opened. Somewhat less ideally, only the dictionary could be stored in memory, with disk access for the postings file. Usually, however, both parts of the index must be processed from disk. More details of the storage and use of these files is given in the description of the search process. Recent work on the effective use of inverted files suggests better ways of storing and searching these files (Burkowski 1990; Cutting and Pedersen 1990).

The dictionary and postings file shown (Figure 14.3) stores a term-weight of simply the raw frequency of a term in a record. If this is the actual weight stored, then all the calculations of term-weights must be done in the search routine itself, providing a heavy overhead per posting. There are four major options for storing weights in the postings file, each having advantages and disadvantages.

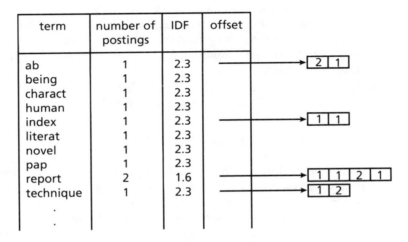

Figure 14.3 A dictionary and postings file

1. Store the raw frequency. This produces the slowest search (likely much too slow for large data sets), but the most flexible system in that term-weighting algorithms can be changed without changing the index.

2. Store a normalized frequency. Any of the normalized frequencies shown in section 14.5 can be used to translate the raw frequency to a normalized frequency. Using Harman's normalized frequency as an example, the raw frequency for each term from the final table of the inversion process would be transformed into a log function and then divided by the log of the length of the corresponding record (the lengths of the records were collected and saved in the parsing step). This operation would be done during the creation of the final dictionary and postings file, and this normalized frequency would be inserted in the postings file in place of the raw frequency shown. The same procedure could be done for Croft's normalized frequency or any other normalized frequency used in an inner product similarity function, assuming appropriate

record statistics have been stored during parsing. However, this option is not suitable for use with the cosine similarity function using Salton's method as the normalization for length includes the IDF factor. The advantage of this term-weighting option is that updating (assuming only the addition of new records and not modification of old ones) would not require the postings to be changed. This option would improve response time considerably over option 1, although option 3 may be somewhat faster (depending on search hardware).

3. Store the completely weighted term. Again, any of the combination weighting schemes shown in section 14.5 are suitable, including those using the cosine similarity function. This option allows a simple addition of each weight during the search process, rather than first multiplying by the IDF of the term, and provides very fast response time. This was the option taken by Harman and Candela (1990) in searching on 806 megabytes of data. The disadvantage of this option is that updating requires changing all postings because the IDF is an integral part of the posting (and the IDF measure changes as any additions are made to the data set). Additionally, relevance feedback reweighting is difficult using this option.

4. If no within-record weighting is used, then the postings records do not have to store weights. All processing would be done in the search routines.

14.6.2 Searching the Inverted File

One way of using an inverted file to produce statistically ranked output is to first retrieve all records containing the search terms, then use the weighting information for each term in those records to compute the total weight for each of those retrieved records, and finally sort those records. The search time for this method is heavily dependent on the number of retrieved records and becomes prohibitive when used on large data sets.

This process can be made much less dependent on the number of records retrieved by using a method developed by Doszkocs for CITE (Doszkocs 1982). In this method, a block of storage was used as a hash table to accumulate the total record weights by hashing on the record id into unique "accumulator" addresses (for more details, see Doszkocs [1982]). This makes the searching process relatively independent of the number of retrieved records—only the sort for the final set of ranks is affected by the number of records being sorted.

This was the method chosen for the basic search process (see Figure 14.4). A block of storage containing an "accumulator" for every unique record id is reserved, usually on the order of 300 Kbytes for large data sets. The query is parsed using the same parser that was used for the index creation, with each term then checked against the stoplist for removal of common terms. If the query term is not common, it is then passed through the stemming routine and a binary search for that stem is executed against the dictionary. (For algorithms to do efficient binary searches, see

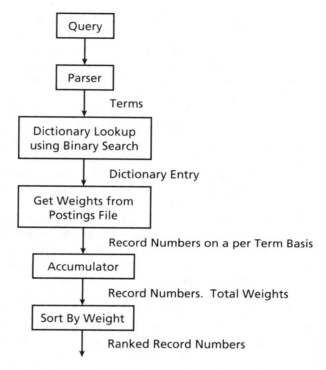

Figure 14.4 Flowchart of search engine

Knuth [1973], and for an alternative to binary searching see section 14.7.4.) If the stem is found in the dictionary, the address of the postings list for that stem is returned, along with the corresponding IDF and the number of postings.

The next step is to use the address of the postings and the number of postings to read the record ids, with the total term-weight for each record id being added to the contents of its unique accumulator. If option 3 was used for weighting, then this total is immediately available and only a simple addition is needed. If option 2 was used for weighting, then the weight stored in the postings is the normalized frequency of the stem in that record, and this needs to be multiplied by the IDF of that stem before the addition. If option 1 was used for weighting, then the full term-weight must be calculated, as the weight stored in the posting is the raw frequency of the stem in that record. Loading the necessary record statistics, such as record length, into memory before searching is essential to maintain any reasonable response time for this weighting option. As each query term is processed, its postings cause further additions to the accumulators. When all the query terms have been handled, accumulators with nonzero weights are sorted to produce the final ranked record list.

There are several major inefficiencies of this technique. First, the I/O needs to be minimized. A read of one byte essentially takes the same time as a read of many bytes (a buffer full) and this factor can be utilized by doing a single read for all the postings of a given term, and then separating the buffer into record ids and weights. This requires a sequential storage of the postings in the index, with the postings pointer in the dictionary being used to control the location of the read operation, and the number of postings (also stored in the dictionary) being used to control the length of the read (and the separation of the buffer). As some terms have thousands of postings for large data sets, doing a separate read for each posting can be very time-consuming. This same logic could be applied to the binary search of the dictionary, which takes about 14 reads per search for the larger data sets. The time saved may be considerably less, however. A final time savings on I/O could be done by loading the dictionary into memory when opening a data set.

A second time savings can be gained at the expense of some memory space. Whereas the storage for the "accumulators" can be hashed to avoid having to hold one storage area for each data set record, this is definitely not necessary for smaller data sets, and may not be useful except for extremely large data sets such as those used in CITE (which need even more modification; see section 14.7.2). Some time is saved by direct access to memory rather than through hashing, and as many unique postings are involved in most queries, the total time savings may be considerable. Harman and Candela (1990) found that almost every user query had at least one term that had postings in half the data set, and usually at least three quarters of the data set was involved in most queries.

A final major bottleneck can be the sort step of the "accumulators" for large data sets. Even a fast sort of thousands of records is very time consuming. An enhancement can be made to reduce the number of records sorted (see section 14.7.5).

14.7 MODIFICATIONS AND ENHANCEMENTS TO THE BASIC INDEXING AND SEARCH PROCESSES

There are many possible modifications and enhancements to the basic indexing and search processes, some of which are necessary because of special retrieval environments (those involving large and very large data sets are discussed), and some of which are techniques for enhancing response time or improving ease of updating. Each of the following topics deals with a specific set of changes that need to be made in the basic indexing and/or search routines to allow the particular enhancement being discussed. The level of detail is somewhat less than in section 14.6, either because less detail is available or because the implementation of the technique is complex and details are left out in the interest of space. It should be noted that, unlike section 14.6, some of the implementations discussed here should be used with caution as they are usually more experimental, and may have unknown problems or side effects.

Ranking Algorithms   Chap. 14

14.7.1 Handling Both Stemmed and Unstemmed Query Terms

It was observed by Frakes (1984) and confirmed by Harman and Candela (1990) that if query terms were automatically stemmed in a ranking system, users generally got better results. In some cases, however, a stem is produced that leads to improper results, causing query failure. The basic indexing and search processes described in section 14.6 suggest no manner of coping with this problem, as the original record terms are not stored in the inverted file; only their stems are used. The following technique was developed for the prototype retrieval system described in Harman and Candela (1990) to handle this problem, but it is not thought to be an optimal method.

Clearly two separate inverted files could be created and stored, one for stems and one for the unstemmed terms. Query terms would normally use the stemmed version, but query terms marked with a "don't stem" character would be routed to the unstemmed version. Whereas this would solve the problem for smaller data sets, it creates a storage problem for the large data sets. A hybrid inverted file was devised to merge these files, saving no space in the dictionary part, but saving considerable storage over that needed to store two versions of the postings. This storage savings is at the expense of some additional search time and therefore may not be the optimal solution. An example of the merged inverted file is shown in Figure 14.5.

This hybrid dictionary is in alphabetic stem order, with the terms sorted within the stem, and contains the stem, the number of postings and IDF of the stem, the term, the number of postings and IDF of the term, a bit to indicate if the term is stemmed or not stemmed, and the offset of the postings for this stem/term combina-

Stem	number of postings	IDF	term	number of postings	IDF	indexbit	offset
absorb	15	7.5	absorbed	8	8.5	1	→
absorb	15	7.5	absorbing	1	11.5	1	→
absorb	15	7.5	absorbtion	6	8.9	1	→
abstract	4	9.5	abstract	4	9.5	0	
abund	1	11.5	abundantly	1	11.5	1	
academ	3	9.9	academic	3	9.9	1	
accel	20	7.1	acceleration	16	7.5	1	
accel	20	7.1	accelerations	2	10.5	1	
accel	20	7.1	accelerator	2	10.5	1	

Figure 14.5 Merged dictionary and postings file

tion. Note that the merged dictionary takes one line per unstemmed term, making it considerably larger than the stemmed dictionary, and resulting in longer binary searches for most terms (which will be stemmed). The hybrid postings list saves the storage necessary for one copy of the record id by merging the stemmed and unstemmed weight (creating a postings element of 3 positions for stemmed terms). Terms that have no stem for a given data set only have the basic 2-element postings record.

As can be expected, the search process needs major modifications to handle these hybrid inverted files. Each query term that is stemmed must now map to multiple dictionary entries, and postings lists must be handled more carefully as some terms have three elements in their postings list and some have only two.

Clearly, for data sets that are relatively small it is best to use the two separate inverted files because the storage savings are not large enough to justify the additional complexity in indexing and searching. Possibly the use of two separate dictionaries, both mapping to the same hybrid posting file, would improve search time without the loss of storage efficiency, but this has not been tried.

14.7.2 Searching in Very Large Data Sets

In 1982, MEDLINE had approximately 600,000 on-line records, with records being added at a rate of approximately 21,000 per month (Doszkocs 1982). The use of the fixed block of storage to accumulate record weights that is described in the basic search process (section 14.6) becomes impossible for this huge data set. Doszkocs solved the problem in his experimental front-end to MEDLINE (the CITE system) by segmenting the inverted file into 8K segments, each holding about 48,000 records, and then hashing these record addresses into the fixed block of accumulators. The basic search process is therefore unchanged except that instead of each record of the data set having a unique accumulator, the accumulators hold only a subset of the records and each subset is processed as if it were the entire data set, with each set of results shown to the user. The subsetting or segmenting is done in reverse chronological order. Because users are often most concerned with recent records, they seldom request to search many segments. For more details see Doszkocs (1982).

14.7.3 A Boolean System with Ranking

There are many ways to combine Boolean searches and ranking. A simple extension of the basic search process in section 14.6 can be made that allows noncomplex Boolean statements to be handled (see section 14.8.4). This extension, however, limits the Boolean capability and increases response time when using Boolean operators. Very elaborate schemes have been devised that combine Boolean with ranking, and references are made to these in section 14.8.3. However, none of these schemes involve extensions to the basic search process in section 14.6.

The SIRE system (Noreault, Koll, and McGill 1977) incorporates a full Boolean capability with a variation of the basic search process. The system accepts queries that are either Boolean logic strings (similar to many commercial on-line systems) or natural language queries (processed as Boolean queries with implicit OR connectors between all query terms). The user may request ranked output.

A Boolean query is processed in two steps. After stemming, each term in the query is checked against the inverted file (this could be done by using the binary search described in section 14.6). The record ids and raw frequencies for the term being processed are combined with those of the previous set of terms according to the appropriate Boolean logic. A running sum containing the numerator of the cosine similarity is updated by adding the new record frequencies, and this is continued until the entire Boolean query is processed. Note that this combining of sets for complex Boolean queries can be a complicated operation. If ranked output is wanted, the denominator of the cosine is computed from previously stored document lengths and the query length, and the records are sorted based on their similarity to the query.

Whereas the cosine similarity is used here with raw frequency term-weighting only (at least in the experiment described in Noreault, Koll and McGill [1977]), any of the term-weighting functions described in section 14.5 could be used. There are no modifications to the basic inverted file needed unless adjacency, field restrictions, and other such types of Boolean operations are desired. The major modification to the basic search process is to correctly merge postings from the query terms based on the Boolean logic in the query before ranking is done. As the final computations of the similarity measure and the sorting of the ranks are done only for those records that are selected by the Boolean logic, this enhancement probably has a faster response time for Boolean queries, and no increase in response time for natural language queries compared to the basic search process described in section 14.6.

14.7.4 Hashing into the Dictionary and Other Enhancements for Ease of Updating

The basic inverted file creation and search process described in section 14.6 assumes a fairly static data set or a willingness to do frequent updates to the entire inverted file. For smaller data sets, or for environments where ease of update and flexibility are more important than query response time, the inverted file could have a structure more conducive to updating. This was done in Croft's experimental retrieval system (Croft and Ruggles 1984). Their inverted file consists of the dictionary containing the terms and pointers to the postings file, but the dictionary is not alphabetically sorted. Instead it is a bucketed (10 slots/bucket) hash table that is accessed by hashing the query terms to find matching entries. Not only is this likely to be a faster access method than the binary search, but it also creates an extendable dictionary, with no reordering for updates. This necessity for ease of update also changes the postings structure, which becomes a series of linked variable length lists capable of infinite update expansion. The term-weighting is done in the search process using the raw frequencies stored in the postings lists.

This system therefore is much more flexible and much easier to update than the basic inverted file and search process described in section 14.6. Although the hash access method is likely faster than a binary search, the processing of the linked postings records and the search-time term-weighting will hurt response time considerably. This is not a major factor for small data sets and for some retrieval environments, especially those involved in research into new retrieval mechanisms.

Note that the binary search described in the basic search process could be replaced with the hashing method to further decrease response time for searching using the basic search process. This would require a different organization of the final inverted index file that contains the dictionary, but would not affect the postings lists (which would be sequentially stored for search time improvements).

14.7.5 Pruning

A major time bottleneck in the basic search process is the sort of the accumulators for large data sets. Various methods have been developed for dealing with this problem. Buckley and Lewit (1985) presented an elaborate "stopping condition" for reducing the number of accumulators to be sorted without significantly affecting performance. Perry and Willett (1983) and Lucarella (1983) also described methods of reducing the number of cells involved in this final sort. The following method serves only as an illustration of a very simple pruning procedure, with an example of the time savings that can be expected using a pruning technique on a large data set. This method is based on the fact that most records for queries are retrieved based on matching only query terms of high data set frequency. These records are still sorted, but serve only to increase sort time, as they are seldom, if ever, useful. These records can be retrieved in the normal manner, but pruned before addition to the retrieved record list (and therefore not sorted). Harman and Candela (1990) experimented with various pruning algorithms using this method, looking for an algorithm that not only improved response time, but did not significantly hurt retrieval results. Their changed search algorithm with pruning is as follows:

1. Sort all query terms (stems) by decreasing IDF value.
2. Do a binary search for the first term (i.e., the highest IDF) and get the address of the postings list for that term.
3. Read the entire postings file for that term into a buffer and add the term weights for each record id into the contents of the unique accumulator for the record id.
4. Check the IDF of the next query term. If the IDF is greater than or equal to one third the maximum IDF of any term in the data set, then repeat steps 2, 3, and 4. Otherwise repeat steps 2, 3, and 4, but do not add weights to zero

weight accumulators, that is, high-frequency (low IDF) terms are allowed to only increment the weights of already selected record ids, not select a new record.

5. Sort the accumulators with nonzero weights to produce the final ranked record list. Note that records containing only high-frequency terms will not have any weight added to their accumulator and therefore are not sorted.

6. If a query has only high-frequency terms (several user queries had this problem), then pruning cannot be done (or a fancier algorithm needs to be created). A check needs to be made after step 1 for this.

Table 14.1 shows some timing results of this pruning algorithm. The test queries are those brought in by users during testing of a prototype ranking retrieval system.

Table 14.1: Response Time

Size of Data Set	1.6 Meg	50 Meg	268 Meg	806 Meg
Number of queries	13	38	17	17
Average number of terms per query	4.1	3.5	3.5	3.5
Average number of records retrieved	797	2843	5869	22654
Average response time per query (no pruning)	0.38	1.2	2.6	4.1
Average response time per query (pruning)	0.28	0.58	1.1	1.6

The response time for the 806 megabyte data set assumes parallel processing of the three parts of the data set, and would be longer if the data set could not be processed in parallel.

As can be seen, the response times are greatly affected by pruning. The other pruning techniques mentioned earlier should result in the same magnitude of time savings, making pruning techniques an important issue for ranking retrieval systems needing fast response times.

14.8 TOPICS RELATED TO RANKING

14.8.1 Ranking and Relevance Feedback

Ranking retrieval systems and relevance feedback have been closely connected throughout the past 25 years of research. Relevance feedback was one of the first features to be added to the basic SMART system (Salton 1971), and is the foundation for the probabilistic indexing model (Robertson and Sparck Jones 1976). Whereas ranking can be done without the use of relevance feedback, retrieval will be further improved by the addition of this query modification technique. For further details, see Chapter 11.

14.8.2 Ranking and Clustering

Ranking retrieval systems have also been closely associated with clustering. Early efforts to improve the efficiency of ranking systems for use in large data sets proposed the use of clustering techniques to avoid dealing with ranking the entire collection (Salton 1971). It was also suggested that clustering could improve the performance of retrieval by pregrouping like documents (Jardine and van Rijsbergen 1971). For further details on clustering and its use in ranking systems, see Chapter 16.

14.8.3 Ranking and Boolean Systems

Because of the predominance of Boolean retrieval systems, several attempts have been made to integrate the ranking model and the Boolean model (for a summary, see Bookstein [1985]). The only methodology for this that has received widespread testing using the standard collections is the P-Norm method allowing the use of soft Boolean operators. This method is well described in Salton and Voorhees (1985) and in Chapter 15.

14.8.4 Use of Ranking in Two-level Search Schemes

The basic ranking search methodology described in the chapter is so fast that it is effective to use in situations requiring simple restrictions on natural language queries. Examples of these types of restrictions would be requirements involving Boolean operators, proximity operators, special publication dates, specific authors, or the use of phrases instead of simple terms. These situations can be accommodated by the basic ranking search system using a two-level search. The input query is processed similarly to a natural language query, except that the system notes the presence of special syntax denoting phrase limits or other field or proximity limitations. Using the following examples

```
clustering using "nearest neighbor" techniques
efficient clustering techniques [Author Willett]
```

the queries would be parsed into single terms and the documents ranked as if there were no special syntax. An efficient file structure is used to record which query term appears in which given retrieved document. The list of ranked documents is returned as before, but only documents passing the added restriction are given to the user. This usually requires a second pass over the actual document, that is, each document marked as containing "nearest" and "neighbor" is passed through a fast string search algorithm looking for the phrase "nearest neighbor," or all documents containing "Willett" have their author field checked for "Willett." Although this seems a tedious method of handling phrases or field restrictions, it can be done in parallel with user browsing operations so that users are often unaware that a second processing step is occurring. This method was used in the prototype built by Harman and Candela (1990) and provided a very effective way of handling phrases and other limitations without increasing indexing overhead.

14.8.5 Ranking and Signature Files

It is possible to provide ranking using signature files (for details on signature files, see Chapter 4 on that subject). Croft and Savino (1988) provide a ranking technique that combines the IDF measure with an estimated normalized within-document frequency, using simple modifications of the standard signature file technique (see the chapter on signature files). That study also suggests that the ability of a ranking system to use the smaller inverted files discussed in this chapter makes storage and efficiency of ranking techniques competitive with that of signature files.

Signature files have also been used in SIBRIS, an operational information retrieval system (Wade et al. 1989), which is based on a two-stage search using signature files for a first cut and then ranking retrieved documents by term-weighting.

14.9 SUMMARY

This chapter has presented a survey of statistical ranking models and experiments, and detailed the actual implementation of a basic ranking retrieval system. Extensions to this basic system have been shown that modify the basic system to efficiently handle different retrieval environments.

REFERENCES

BELKIN, N. J. and W. B. CROFT. 1987. "Retrieval Techniques," in Williams, M. (Ed.), *Annual Review of Information Science and Technology,* ed. M. Williams, pp. 109–45. New York: Elsevier Science Publishers.

BARKLA, J. K. 1969. "Construction of Weighted Term Profiles by Measuring Frequency and Specificity in Relevant Items." Paper presented at the Second International Cranfield Conference on Mechanized Information Storage and Retrieval Systems, Cranfield, Bedford, England.

BERNSTEIN, L. M., and R. E. WILLIAMSON. 1984. "Testing of a Natural Language Retrieval System for a Full Text Knowledge Base." *J. American Society for Information Science,* 35(4), 235–47.

BOOKSTEIN, A. 1985. "Probability and Fuzzy-Set Applications to Information Retrieval," in *Annual Review of Information Science and Technology,* ed. M. Williams, pp. 117–51. New York: Knowledge Industry Publications, Inc.

BOOKSTEIN, A., and D. KRAFT. 1977. "Operations Research Applied to Document Indexing and Retrieval Decisions." *J. Association for Computing Machinery,* 24(3), 418–27.

BOOKSTEIN, A., and D. R. SWANSON. 1974. "Probabilistic Models for Automatic Indexing." *J. American Society for Information Science,* 25, 312–19.

BUCKLEY, C., and A. LEWIT. 1985. "Optimization of Inverted Vector Searches." Paper presented at the Eighth International Conference on Research and Development in Information Retrieval, Montreal, Canada.

BURKOWSKI, F. J. 1990. "Surrogate Subsets: A Free Space Management Strategy for the Index of a Text Retrieval System." Paper presented at ACM Conference on Research and Development in Information Retrieval, Brussels, Belgium.

CLEVERDON, C. 1983. "Optimizing Convenient Online Access to Bibliographic Databases." *Information Services and Use,* 4(1/2), 37–47.

COOPER, W. S., and M. E. MARON. 1978. "Foundations of Probabilistic and Utility-Theoretic Indexing." *J. Association for Computing Machinery,* 25(1), 67–80.

CROFT, W. B. 1983. "Experiments with Representation in a Document Retrieval System." *Information Technology: Research and Development,* 2(1), 1–21.

CROFT, W. B., and D. J. HARPER. 1979. "Using Probabilistic Models of Document Retrieval Without Relevance Information." *Documentation,* 35(4), 285–95.

CROFT, W. B., and L. RUGGLES. 1984. "The Implementation of a Document Retrieval System," in *Research and Development in Information Retrieval,* eds. G. Salton and H. J. Schneider, pp. 28–37. Berlin: Springer-Verlag.

CROFT, W. B., and P. SAVINO. 1988. "Implementing Ranking Strategies Using Text Signatures." *ACM Transactions on Office Information Systems,* 6(1), 42–62.

CUTTING, D., and J. PEDERSEN. 1990. "Optimizations for Dynamic Inverted Index Maintenance." Paper presented at ACM Conference on Research and Development in Information Retrieval, Brussels, Belgium.

DENNIS, S. F. 1964. "The Construction of a Thesaurus Automatically from a Sample of Text." Paper presented at the Statistical Association Methods for Mechanized Documentation. (National Bureau of Standards Miscellaneous Publication 269).

DOSZKOCS, T. E. 1982. "From Research to Application: The CITE Natural Language Information Retrieval System," in *Research and Development in Information Retrieval,* eds. G. Salton and H. J. Schneider, pp. 251–62. Berlin: Springer-Verlag.

FRAKES, W. B. 1984. "Term Conflation for Information Retrieval." Paper presented at the Third Joint BCS and ACM symposium on Research and Development in Information Retrieval, Cambridge, England.

HARMAN, D. 1986. "An Experimental Study of Factors Important in Document Ranking." Paper presented at ACM Conference on Research and Development in Information Retrieval, Pisa, Italy.

HARMAN, D., and G. CANDELA. 1990. "Retrieving Records from a Gigabyte of Text on a Minicomputer using Statistical Ranking." *J. American Society for Information Science,* in press.

HARPER, D. J. 1980. *Relevance Feedback in Document Retrieval Systems: An Evaluation of Probabilistic Strategies.* Doctoral dissertation, Jesus College, Cambridge, England.

HARTER, S. P. 1975. "A Probabilistic Approach to Automatic Keyword Indexing." *J. American Society for Information Science,* 26(5), 280–89.

JARDINE, N., and C. J. VAN RIJSBERGEN. 1971. "The Use of Hierarchic Clustering in Information Retrieval." *Information Storage and Retrieval,* 7(5), 217–40.

KNUTH, D. E. 1973. *The Art of Computer Programming,* Reading, Mass.: Addison-Wesley.

LOCHBAUM, K. E., and L. A. STREETER. 1989. "Comparing and Combining the Effectiveness of Latent Semantic Indexing and the Ordinary Vector Space Model for Information Retrieval." *Information Processing and Management,* 25(6), 665–76.

LUCARELLA, D. 1983. "A Document Retrieval System Based on Nearest Neighbor Searching." *J. of Information Science,* 6, 25–33.

LUHN, H. P. 1957. "A Statistical Approach to Mechanized Encoding and Searching of Literary Information." *IBM J. Research and Development,* 1(4), 309–17.

MARON, M. E., and J. L. KUHNS. 1960. "On Relevance, Probabilistic Indexing and Information Retrieval." *J. Association for Computing Machinery,* 7(3), 216–44.

MCGILL, M., M. KOLL, and T. NOREAULT. 1979. *An Evaluation of Factors Affecting Document Ranking by Information Retrieval Systems.* Report from the School of Information Studies, Syracuse University, Syracuse, New York.

MILLER, W. L. 1971. "A Probabilistic Search Strategy for Medlars." *J. Documentation,* 27(4), 254–66.

NOREAULT, T., M. KOLL, and M. MCGILL. 1977. "Automatic Ranked Output from Boolean Searches in SIRE." *J. American Society for Information Science,* 28(6), 333–39.

PERRY, S. A., and P. WILLETT. 1983. "A Review of the Use of Inverted Files for Best Match Searching in Information Retrieval Systems." *J. Information Science,* 6, 59–66.

RAGHAVAN, V. V., H. P. SHI, and C. T. YU. 1983. "Evaluation of the 2–Poisson Model as a Basis for Using Term Frequency Data in Searching." Paper presented at the Sixth International Conference on Research and Development in Information Retrieval, Bethesda, Maryland.

ROBERTSON, S. E., and K. SPARCK JONES. 1976. "Relevance Weighting of Search Terms." *J. American Society for Information Science,* 27(3), 129–46.

SALTON, G. 1971. *The SMART Retrieval System—Experiments in Automatic Document Processing.* Englewood Cliffs, N.J.: Prentice Hall.

SALTON, G., and C. BUCKLEY. 1988. "Term-Weighting Approaches in Automatic Text Retrieval," *Information Processing and Management,* 24(5), 513–23.

SALTON, G., and M. E. LESK. 1968. "Computer Evaluation of Indexing and Text Processing." *J. Association for Computing Machinery,* 15(1), 8–36.

SALTON, G., and M. MCGILL. 1983. *Introduction to Modern Information Retrieval.* New York: McGraw-Hill.

SALTON, G., H. WU, and C. T. YU. 1981. "The Measurement of Term Importance in Automatic Indexing." *J. American Society for Information Science,* 32(3), 175–86.

SALTON, G., and C. S. YANG. 1973. "On the Specification of Term Values in Automatic Indexing." *J. Documentation,* 29(4), 351–72.

SPARCK JONES, K. 1972. "A Statistical Interpretation of Term Specificity and Its Application in Retrieval." *J. Documentation,* 28(1), 11–20.

SPARCK JONES, K. 1973. "Index Term Weighting." *Information Storage and Retrieval,* 9(11), 619–33.

SPARCK JONES, K. 1975. "A Performance Yardstick for Test Collections." *J. Documentation,* 31(4), 266–72.

SPARCK JONES, K. 1979a. "Experiments in Relevance Weighting of Search Terms." *Information Processing and Management,* 15(3), 133–44.

SPARCK JONES, K. 1979b. "Search Term Relevance Weighting Given Little Relevance Information." *J. Documentation,* 35(1), 30–48.

SPARCK JONES, K. 1981. *Information Retrieval Experiment.* London: Butterworths.

SRINIVASAN, P. 1989. "Intelligent Information Retrieval Using Rough Set Approximations." *Information Processing and Management,* 25(4), 347–61.

VAN RIJSBERGEN, C. J. 1976. "File Organization in Library Automation and Information Retrieval." *J. Documentation,* 32(4), 294–317.

WADE, S. J., P. WILLETT, and D. BAWDEN. 1989. "SIBRIS: the Sandwich Interactive Browsing and Ranking Information System." *J. Information Science,* 15, 249–60.

WALKER, S., and R. M. JONES. 1987. *Improving Subject Retrieval in Online Catalogues,* British Library Research Paper 24.

YU, C. T., and G. SALTON. 1976. "Precision Weighting—An Effective Automatic Indexing Method." *J. Association for Computing Machinery,* 23(1), 76–88.

15

Extended Boolean Models

E. Fox, S. Betrabet, M. Koushik

Department of Computer Science
Virginia Tech (Virginia Polytechnic Institute & State University)
Blacksburg, VA 24061-0106

W. Lee

Systems Analyst
Acumenics Research and Technology
9990 Lee Highway
Suite 580
Fairfax, VA 22030

Abstract

The classical interpretation of the Boolean operators in an information retrieval system is in general too strict. A standard Boolean query rarely comes close to retrieving all and only those documents which are relevant to a query. Many models have been proposed with the aim of softening the interpretation of the Boolean operators in order to improve the precision and recall of the search results. This chapter discusses three such models: the Mixed Min and Max (MMM), the Paice, and the P-norm models. The MMM and Paice models are essentially variations of the classical fuzzy-set model, while the P-norm scheme is a distance-based approach. Our experimental results indicate that each of the above models provides better performance than the classical Boolean model in terms of retrieval effectiveness.

15.1 INTRODUCTION

In the standard Boolean retrieval model, each document is associated with a set of keywords or index terms, and each query is in the form of a Boolean expression. The Boolean expression consists of a set of index terms connected by the Boolean operators *and, or,* and *not*. The documents retrieved for a given query are those that contain index terms in the combination specified by the query. As can be seen from the discussion in Chapter 10, the Boolean model is popular in operational environments because it is easy to implement and is very efficient in terms of the time required to process a query. Boolean retrieval systems are also capable of giving high performance in terms of recall and precision if the query is well formulated. However, the model has the following limitations, as discussed by a number of authors: Bookstein (1985), Cater & Kraft (1987), Cooper (1988), Wong et al. (1988), Paice (1984), Salton, Fox & Wu (1983).

- The Boolean model gives counterintuitive results for certain types of queries. For example, consider a query of the form *A and B and C and D and E*. A document indexed by all but one of the above terms will not be retrieved in response to this query. Intuitively, it appears that the user would be interested in such a document, and that it should be retrieved. Similarly, for a query of the form *A or B or C or D or E,* a document indexed by any of these terms is considered just as important as a document indexed by some or all of them. This limitation of the Boolean model is due to its strict interpretation of the Boolean operators. Our experimental studies have shown that such a strict interpretation is not compatible with the user's interpretation; for example, results of the retrieval based on a strict interpretation have lower precision than results from a P-norm interpretation as shown by Salton, Fox & Wu (1983). Hence, we need to *soften* the Boolean operators, and account for the uncertainties that are present in choosing them. We can do this by making the *and* query behave a bit like the *or* query and the *or* query behave somewhat like the *and* query.
- The standard Boolean model has no provision for ranking documents. However, systems combining features of both the Boolean and the vector models have been built to allow for ranking the result of a Boolean query, for example, the SIRE system (1977) Noreault, Koll & McGill. Ranking the documents in the order of decreasing relevance allows the user to see the most relevant document first. Also, the user would be able to sequentially scan the documents, and stop at a certain point if he/she finds that many of the documents are no longer relevant to the query.
- During the indexing process for the Boolean model, it is necessary to decide whether a particular document is either relevant or nonrelevant with respect to a given index term. In the Boolean model, there is no provision for capturing the uncertainty that is present in making indexing decisions. Assigning weights to index terms adds information during the indexing process.
- The Boolean model has no provision for assigning importance factors or weights to query terms. Yet, searchers often can rate or rank index terms in queries based on how indicative they are of desired content. It would be useful to allow weights to be assigned to (some) query terms, to indicate that the presence or absence of a particular query term is more important than that of another term.

Many retrieval models have been proposed as alternatives to the Boolean model. This chapter discusses three such models:

- MMM
- Paice
- P-norm

These models avoid the strict interpretation of the Boolean operators, and attempt to provide a ranking of the retrieved documents in order of decreasing relevance to the query. They attempt to take into account the uncertainty involved in the indexing process. In addition, the P-norm model has the ability to consider weighted query terms. Experimental results have shown that these models can given an improvement of more than 100 percent in precision, at fixed recall levels, over the standard Boolean model as reported in Lee (1988).

We begin with a description of each model, and then discuss the data structures and algorithms that implement them. A few examples of the similarity computation in each model are also provided. We conclude with a short discussion of the relative merits of these models.

15.2 EXTENDED BOOLEAN MODELS

In the three models discussed below, a document has a weight associated with each index term. This document weight is a measure of the degree to which the document is characterized by that term. Without loss of generality, we assume that document weights for all index terms lie in the range $[0,1]$. This is less restrictive than in the standard Boolean model, which limits the values to the extremes of the range, namely 0 and 1.

To retrieve documents relevant to a given query, we need to calculate the query-document similarity for documents in the collection. The query-document similarity is an attempt to predict the relevance of a document to the query. In the following subsections, we consider each model and its method for calculating similarity.

15.2.1 The MMM model

This model is based on the concept of fuzzy sets proposed by Zadeh (1965). In fuzzy-set theory, an element has a varying degree of membership, say d_A, to a given set A instead of the traditional membership choice (is an element/is not an element).

In the Mixed Min and Max (MMM) model developed by Fox and Sharat (1986), each index term has a fuzzy set associated with it. The document weight of a document with respect to an index term A is considered to be the degree of membership of the document in the fuzzy set associated with A. The degree of membership for union and intersection are defined as follows in Fuzzy set theory:

$$d_{A \cap B} = \min(d_A, d_b)$$

$$d_{A \cup B} = \max(d_A, d_b)$$

According to fuzzy set theory, documents that should be retrieved for a query of the form *A or B*, should be in the fuzzy set associated with the union of the two sets *A* and *B*. Similarly, the documents that should be retrieved for a query of the form *A and B*, should be in the fuzzy set associated with the intersection of the two sets. Hence, it is possible to define the similarity of a document to the *or* query to be $\max(d_A, d_B)$, and the similarity of the document to the *and* query to be $\min(d_A, d_B)$. The MMM model attempts to soften the Boolean operators by considering the query-document similarity to be a linear combination of the *min* and *max* document weights.

Thus, given a document D with index-term weights $d_{A1}, d_{A2}, \ldots, d_{An}$ for terms $A_1, A_2, \ldots, A_n$, and the queries

$$Q_{or} = (A_1 \ or \ A_2 \ or \ \ldots \ or \ A_n) \ \text{and}$$

$$Q_{and} = (A_1 \ and \ A_2 \ and \ \ldots \ and \ A_n),$$

the query-document similarity in the MMM model is computed as follows:

$$SIM(Q_{or}, D) = C_{or1} * \max(d_{A1}, d_{A2}, \ldots, d_{An}) + C_{or2} * \min(d_{A1}, d_{A2}, \ldots, d_{An})$$

$$SIM(Q_{and}, D) = C_{and1} * \min(d_{A1}, d_{A2}, \ldots, d_{An}) + C_{and2} * \max(d_{A1}, d_{A2} \ldots, d_{An})$$

where C_{or1}, C_{or2} are "softness" coefficients for the *or* operator, and C_{and1}, C_{and2} are softness coefficients for the *and* operator. Since we would like to give the maximum of the document weights more importance while considering an *or* query and the minimum more importance while considering an *and* query, generally we have $C_{or1} > C_{or2}$ and $C_{and1} > C_{and2}$. For simplicity it is generally assumed that $C_{or1} = 1 - C_{or2}$ and $C_{and1} = 1 - C_{and2}$.

Our experiments (Lee & Fox 1988) indicate that the best performance usually occurs with C_{and1} in the range [0.5, 0.8] and with $C_{or1} > 0.2$. In general, the computational cost is low, and retrieval effectiveness is good, much better than with the standard Boolean model, as can be seen from Table 1 in section 15.4 below.

15.2.2 The Paice Model

The model proposed by Paice (1984) is also based on fuzzy-set theory. It is similar to the MMM model in that it assumes that there is a fuzzy set associated with each index term, and the document weight of a document with respect to an index term represents the degree of membership of the document with respect to the fuzzy set associated with that index term. However, while the MMM model considers only the maximum and the minimum document weights for the index terms while calculating the similarity, the Paice model takes into account all of the document weights.

Thus, given a document D with index-term weights $d_{A1}, d_{A2}, \ldots, d_{An}$ for terms $A_1, A_2, \ldots, A_n$, and the queries

$$Q_{or} = (A_1 \text{ or } A_2 \text{ or } \ldots \text{ or } A_n) \text{ and}$$

$$Q_{and} = (A_1 \text{ and } A_2 \text{ and } \ldots \text{ and } A_n)$$

the query-document similarity in the Paice model is computed as follows:

$$SIM(Q, D) = \sum_{i=1}^{n} r^{i-1} d_i \bigg/ \sum_{i=1}^{n} r^{i-1}$$

where the d_i's are considered in descending order for *or* queries and in ascending order for *and* queries. Note that when $n = 2$, the Paice model behaves like the MMM model.

The experiments conducted by Lee & Fox (1988) have shown that setting the value of r to 1.0 for *and* queries, and to 0.7 for *or* queries, gives good retrieval effectiveness. The computational cost for this model is higher than that for the MMM model. This is because the MMM model only requires the determination of *min* or *max* of a set of term weights each time an *and* or *or* clause is considered, which can be done with an O(n) algorithm as described in Aho and Ullman (1974). The Paice model requires the term weights to be sorted in ascending or descending order, depending on whether an *and* clause or an *or* clause is being considered. This requires at least an 0(n log n) sorting algorithm. A good deal of floating point calculation is needed also.

15.2.3 The P-norm Model

Besides allowing document weights for index terms, the P-norm model also allows query terms to have weights. In the P-norm model, a document D with weights $d_{A_1}, d_{A_2}, \ldots, d_{A_n}$ with respect to index terms $A_1, A_2, \ldots, A_n$ is considered to be a point with coordinates $(d_{A_1}, d_{A_2}, \ldots, d_{A_n})$ in an n-dimensional space. These document weights are generally obtained using term frequency and inverse document frequency statistics, with proper normalization as described by Fox (1983).

Consider an *or* query of the form $d_{A_1} \text{ or } d_{A_2} \ldots \text{ or } d_{A_n}$. It is clear that the point having all the n coordinates equal to 0 (indicating that all the index terms are absent) is to be avoided for this query, whereas for an *and* query of the form $d_{A_1} \text{ and } d_{A_2} \ldots \text{ and } d_{A_n}$, the point with all the n coordinates equal to 1 (indicating that all the index terms have weight 1) is the most desirable point. Thus, it is possible to rank the documents (i.e., from those with highest similarity to those with lowest similarity) in order of decreasing distance from the point $(0, 0, \ldots, 0)$ for an *or* query, and in order of increasing distance from the point $(1, 1, \ldots, 1)$ for an *and* query.

In the P-norm model, the generalized queries are of the form:

$$Q_{orp} = (A_1, a_1) \; or_P \; (A_2, a_2) \; or_P \; \ldots \; or_P \; (A_n, a_n), \text{ and}$$

$$Q_{andp} = (A_1, a_1) \; and_P \; (A_2, a_2) \; and_P \; \ldots \; and_P \; (A_n, a_n).$$

We note that the operators have coefficients P which indicate the degree of strictness (from 1 for least strict to ∞ for most strict, i.e., the Boolean case) of the operator. Also, the query terms have weights (i.e., a_i) which indicate their relative importance. Sophisticated users may wish to assign the P-values and query weights. Extensive experimentation demonstrated that system-assigned p-values (e.g., $p = 2$ throughout a query) can give good results, and that uniform query weighting of 1 or based on inverse document frequency will lead to effective retrieval as described by Fox (1983).

The query-document similarity for the P-norm model is calculated using the following formulae:

$$\text{SIM}(Q_{orp}, D) = \sqrt[P]{\frac{a_1^P d_{A1}^P + a_2^P d_{A2}^P + \cdots + a_n^P d_{An}^P}{a_1^P + a_2^P + \cdots + a_n^P}},$$

$$\text{SIM}(Q_{andp}, D) = 1 - \sqrt[P]{\frac{a_1^P(1 - d_{A1})^P + a_2^P(1 - d_{A2})^P + \cdots a_n^P(1 - d_{An})^P}{a_1^P + a_2^P + \cdots + a_n^P}}, \text{ and}$$

$$\text{SIM}(Q_{not}, D) = 1 - SIM(Q, D).$$

Numerous experiments have shown the P-norm model to be very effective as reported in Salton, Fox & Wu (1983), Fox & Sharat (1986), Lee & Fox (1988), Fox (1983). However, when the P-value is greater than one, the computational expense can be high. This is because of the need for expensive exponentiation computations.

15.3 IMPLEMENTATION

As in any other information retrieval system, we need to convert the given set of documents and queries into a standard format. We first discuss the data structures used in our implementation, and then follow up with a discussion of the actual algorithms.

15.3.1 Data Structures

There are several important data structures for both the document and query representations.

Document structure

Given a set of documents, the goal is to index them, that is, find the index terms in the collection, and assign document weights for each document with respect to each index term. To calculate the document weight for an index term, a weighting technique such as normalized $(tf * idf)_{ik}$ can be used. A more detailed discussion of weighting techniques is provided in Chapter 10. The data structure for a document consists of an array *doc_wts* that stores the document weights as shown below. The element $doc\_wt[i]$ is the document weight for the *i*th index term.

```
typedef struct
{
    float doc_wts[NUM_ITERM];   /*document weight vector*/

} DOC_STRUCT
```

Query Structure

We assume that each query has an id associated with it, and is in the form of a tree with the operators as internal nodes and index terms as the leaves (see Figure 15.1). The data structure used to store a query is as follows:

```
typedef struct
{   long         query_id;          /* query id */
    TREE_NODE    *beg_node_array;    /* array of query nodes */
    ITERM_TUPLE  *beg_iterm_array;   /* array of index terms */
    OP_TUPLE     *beg_op_array;      /* array of operators */

} QUERY_STRUCT
```

We see from the query structure that there are three arrays associated with each query (see Figure 15.2):

- an array of the nodes in the query tree
- an array of index terms
- an array of operators

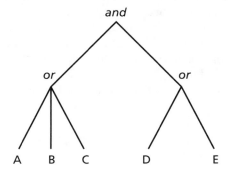

Figure 15.1 Structure of query *(A or B or C) and (D or E)*

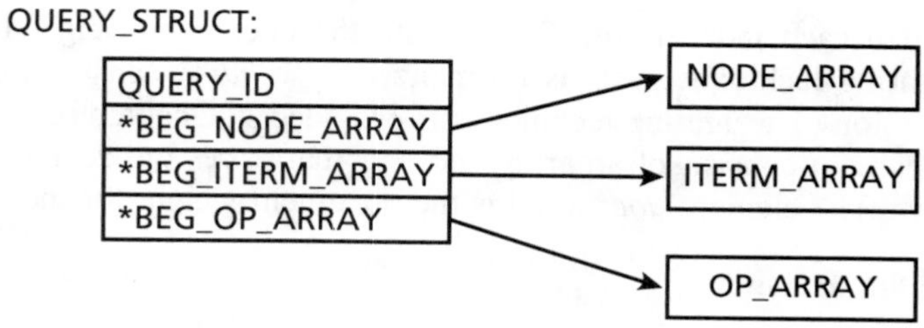

QUERY_STRUCT:

Figure 15.2 Structure of QUERY–STRUCT

In the query structure we store the address of the first element of each array. In our implementation we assume that the first element of the node array is the root of the query tree.

The tree-node structure is as follows:

```
typedef struct
{
    int         iterm_op_index;    /* index of index-term/operator for
                                      leaf/non-leaf node resp. */
    short       child_index;       /*index of the left child of the
                                      current node */
    short       sibling_index;     /* index of right sibling of the
                                      current node */

} TREE_NODE       /* structure of a node in the query tree */
```

In this structure, the child_index is the index of the leftmost child of the current node within the array of nodes. Similarly, sibling_index is the index of the next node to the right of the current node within the array of nodes. If a node does not have any children / siblings to its right, the value of its child_index / sibling_index will be equal to UNDEF (−1).

It is possible to determine whether the current node is an operator node or an index-term node by examining the value of child_index (see Figure 15.3). Since index terms can only be leaves of the tree, they cannot have any children, whereas operators will have at least one child. Hence, if child_index has value UNDEF, then it implies that the current node is an index-term node; otherwise it implies that the node is an operator node. The iterm_op_index in the TREE_NODE structure is the index number of the index-term/operator associated with the current node within the array of index-term/operators.

The data structure that stores information about an index term is as follows:

```
typedef struct
{
    long      iterm_num;    /* unique ID given to index-term */
    float     iterm_wt;     /* weight of the index-term */

} ITERM_TUPLE   /* structure of an index term */
```

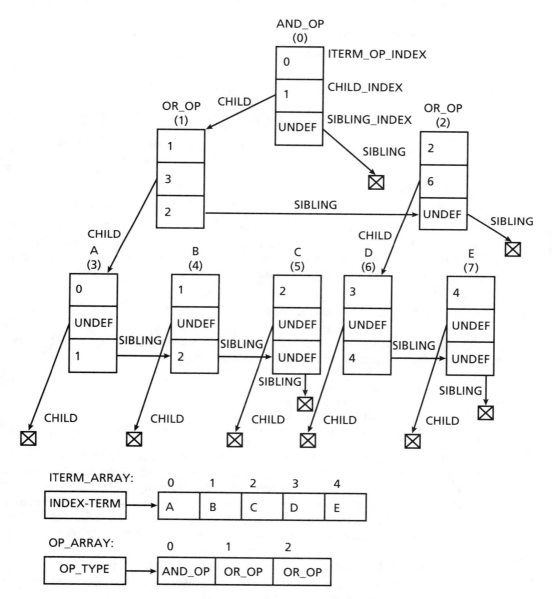

Figure 15.3 Data structures generated for query *((A or B or C) and (D or E))*

Here, iterm_num is the unique number given to an index term. Note that iterm_wt, which is the weight of the index term in the query, is used only for P-norm queries.

The data structure for an operator is as follows:

```
typedef struct
{
    int             op_type;    /* type of operator -
                                   AND_OP / OR_OP / NOT_OP */
    long            op_coeff;   /* coefficient of the operator -
                                   = 0.0 for NOT_OP
                                   = C_or1 / C _and1 for MMM model,
                                   = r value for Paice model, and
                                   = P value for P-norm model */
    float           op_wt;      /* wt. of the operator */
} OP_TUPLE                       /* structure of an operator */
```

If the MMM model is being used, then op_coeff is the C_{or1} / C_{and1} value. (Note: We assume that $C_{or2} = 1 - C_{or1}$ and $C_{and2} = 1 - C_{and1}$.) If on the other hand the Paice model is being used, then the op_coeff is the r value. If the P-norm model is being used, then op_coeff is the P-value.

15.3.2 Algorithms and Examples

Given a query and a set of documents in the standard form, we use the following algorithm to retrieve and rank documents:

```
For each document
        Find similarity;
Sort similarities;
Display document / similarity data in descending order.
```

In order to calculate the query-document similarity, we start from the root of the query tree, and find the similarity for each child. (Refer to the appendix for the C program.) If the child is an index term, then the similarity is the document weight for that index term. If it is an operator, then we recursively calculate the similarity for each child of that node. Once the similarity value is determined for a child, further processing is different for the various models and is described below:

• For the MMM model:

We update the values of two variables, *maximum* and *minimum* (both of type double), where

$$maximum = \max(d_{A1}\ d_{A2}, \ldots, d_{An}), \text{ and}$$

$$minimum = \min(d_{A1}, d_{A2}, \ldots, d_{An}).$$

- For the Paice model:

  We store the similarity in an array (of type double), *child_sims*, which will contain the similarities of the children of the current node.

- For the P-norm model:

  We update the values of two variables, *numerator* and *denominator* (both of type double), where

  $$numerator = a_1^P d_{A1}^P + a_2^P d_{A2}^P + \cdots + a_n^P d_{An}^P \text{ for } or_P \text{ queries,}$$

  $$numerator = a_1^P(1 - d_{A1})^P + a_2^P(1 - d_{A2})^P + \cdots + a_n^P(1 - d_{An})^P$$
  $$\text{for } and_P \text{ queries, and}$$

  $$denominator = a_1^P + a_2^P + \cdots + a_n^P \text{ for both types of queries.}$$

Once all the children of the node have been considered, we use the appropriate formula to find the actual similarity.

- For the MMM model, we can calculate the similarity for the node by using the following formula:

  $$SIM(Q, D) = C_{op} * maximum + (1 - C_{op}) * minimum,$$

For example, if the document weights for the index terms A, B, and C in a query Q of the form A *or* B *or* C and for a particular document D are 0.5, 0.8, and 0.6, respectively, then the maximum of the three is 0.8, and the minimum 0.5. If the coefficient of the *or* operator is 0.7, then, using the above formula, the MMM similarity between the given document and query is

$$SIM(Q, D) = 0.7 * 0.8 + (1 - 0.7) * 0.5 = 0.71$$

If the Paice similarity is being calculated, we begin by sorting the array *child_sims* in descending order for an *OR* node, and in ascending order for an *AND* node. We then use the following formula to calculate the Paice query-document similarity.

$$SIM(Q, D) = \sum_{i=1}^{n} r^{i-1} \, child\_sims[i] \Big/ \sum_{i=1}^{n} r^{i-1}$$

For the query Q given above, since the operator is *OR_OP* we sort the similarities in descending order. We will therefore have the similarities in the order: $0.8, 0.6, 0.5$. Hence, using the formula given above, with the assumption that $r = 0.7$, the Paice similarity between the given document and query will then be

$$SIM(Q, D) = 0.7^0 * 0.8 + 0.7^1 * 0.6 + 0.7^2 * 0.5 / 0.7^0 + 0.7^1 + 0.7^2$$
$$= 1.465/2.19 = 0.6689$$

- If the P-norm similarity is being calculated, then we use the values of the *numerator* and *denominator* in the following formula to calculate the P-norm query-document similarity:

$$SIM(Q_{or}, D) = (numerator/denominator)^{1/p\_value}$$

$$SIM(Q_{and}, D) = 1 - (numerator/denominator)^{1/p\_value}$$

If for the query Q given above, the query term weights are 0.5 and the operator coefficient or the *P or* operator has the coefficient value is 2, then the value of the numerator and denominator after considering the three index terms will be

Index	Term	Numerator	Denominator
1	A	$0 + 0.5^2 * 0.5^2$ $= 0.0625$	$0 + 0.5^2$ $= 0.25$
2	B	$0.0625 + 0.5^2 * 0.8^2$ $= 0.2225$	$0.25 + 0.5^2$ $= 0.50$
3	C	$0.225 + 0.5^2 * 0.6^2$ $= 0.3125$	$0.50 + 0.5^2$ $= 0.75.$

Using the final values of the numerator and denominator and the formula given above, the query-document similarity $SIM(Q_{or}, D)$ will be

$$SIM(Q_{or}, D) = (0.3125/0.75)^{1/2} = 0.6455$$

The C programs that implement these algorithms are given in the appendix. The routine *cal_sim( )* is called with the array containing the document weights which are of type float as the first parameter, the query vector which is of type QUERY_STRUCT as the second parameter, and the third argument sim_type which determines the type of similarity being computed, that is, MMM, Paice, or P-norm. Based on the value of the third parameter, one of the following sets of routines is called for further computations:

- *mmm_sim( )*: MMM model
- *paice_sim( )*: Paice model
- *update_*numer_denom( ) & *p_norm_sim( )*: P-norm model

15.4 CONCLUSION

Numerous experiments performed with the extended Boolean models have shown that they give much better performance than the standard Boolean model as reported by Lee & Fox (1988). Table 15.1 gives the percentage improvement in the average precision that these models showed over the standard Boolean model for three test

Table 15.1: Percentage Improvements Over Standard Boolean Model Test Collection

Scheme	CISI		CACM		INSPEC	
	Best Average Precision	Rank	Best Average Precision	Rank	Best Average Precision	Rank
P-norm	79	1	106	2	210	1
Paice	77	2	104	3	206	2
MMM	68	3	109	1	195	3

collections: the CISI, CACM, and the INSPEC collections. As can be seen in the table, all three models show substantial improvement over the standard Boolean model. In fact, for the CACM and the INSPEC collections, all three models show more than 100 percent improvement.

The P-norm model is computationally expensive because of the number of exponentiation operations that it requires. The Paice model requires one to sort the similarities of the children. This adds to its computational overhead. The MMM model clearly has the least computational overhead of the three models.

The standard Boolean model is still the most efficient model. But by using any one of the extended Boolean models, it is possible to get much better performance. Based on experimental studies, the MMM model appears to be the least expensive, while the P-norm model gives the best results in terms of average precision.

REFERENCES

AHO, A. J., and J. ULLMAN. 1974. "The Design and Analysis of Computer Algorithms." Reading, Mass.: Addison-Wesley.

BOOKSTEIN, A. 1985. "Probability and Fuzzy-Set Applications to Information Retrieval," in M. E. Williams, ed., *Annual Review of Information Science and Technology (ARIST),* 20, 117–51.

CATER, S. C., and D. H. KRAFT. 1987, June. "TIRS: A Topological Information Retrieval System Satisfying the Requirements of the Waller-Kraft Wish List." Presented at the 10th Annual Int'l ACM-SIGIR Conference on R&D in Information Retrieval, 171–80.

COOPER, W. S. 1988. "Getting Beyond Boole." *Information Processing & Management* 24(3), 243–48.

FOX, E. A. 1983. "Extending the Boolean and Vector Space Models of Information Retrieval with P-Norm Queries and Multiple Concept Types." Cornell University, August.

FOX, E. A., and S. SHARAT. 1986. "A Comparison of Two Methods for Soft Boolean Interpretation in Information Retrieval." Technical Report TR-86-1, Virginia Tech, Department of Computer Science.

LEE, W. C., and E. A. FOX. 1988. "Experimental Comparison of Schemes for Interpreting Boolean Queries." Virginia Tech M.S. Thesis, Technical Report TR-88-27 Department of Computer Science.

NOREAULT, T., M. KOLL, and M. J. McGILL. 1977. "Automatic Ranked Output from Boolean Searches in SIRE." *J. American Society for Information Science*, 28(6), 333–39.

PAICE, C. P. 1984. "Soft Evaluation of Boolean Search Queries in Information Retrieval Systems." *Information Technology, Res. Dev. Applications,* 3(1), 33–42.

SALTON, G., E. A. FOX, and H. WU. 1983. "Extended Boolean Information Retrieval." *Communications of the ACM,* 26(12), 1022–36.

WONG, S. K. M., W. ZIARKO, V. V. RAGHAVAN, and P. C. N. WONG. 1988. "Extended Boolean Query Processing in the Generalized Vector Space Model." *Information Systems* 14(1), 47–63.

ZADEH, L. A. 1965. "Fuzzy Sets," *Information and Control*, 8, 338–53.

Appendix

```
/**
** Compute query–document similarity using MMM, Paice and P–norm
** formulas
**/

#include <stdio.h>
#include <math.h>

#define UNDEF-1

#define NOT_OP  -2
#define AND_OP  -3
#define OR_OP   -4

#define MMM_SIM    1
#define PAICE_SIM  2
#define P_NORM_SIM 3

#define P_INFINITY 0.0    /* Used only for P–norm model */


typedef struct
    {
    long iterm_num;         /* Unique ID given to the index–term */
    float iterm_wt;         /* Weight of index–term (P–norm queries only) */

    } ITERM_TUPLE;          /* Structure of an index–term in a query */


typedef struct
    {
    int   op_type;          /* operator type – AND_OP, OP_OP, NOT_OP */
```

```
        float op_coeff;              /* Coefficient of the operator
                                        = 0.0 for NOT_OP,
                                        = C_or1/C_and1 for MMM model,
                                        = r value for Paice model, and
                                        = P value for P-norm model */
        float op_wt;                 /* Wt. of operator - (P-norm queries only) */

        } OP_TUPLE;                  /* Structure of an operator in a query */



    typedef struct
        {
        long iterm_op_index;         /* If child_index = UNDEF then concept
                                        index, else operator index */
        short child_index;           /* Current node's left child index */
        short sibling_index;         /* Current node's right sibling index */

        } TREE_NODE;                 /* Structure of a node in the query tree */

    typedef struct
        {
        long    query_id;                    /* Query id */
        TREE_NODE  *beg_node_array;          /* Array of query nodes */
        ITERM_TUPLE *beg_iterm_array;        /* Array of index terms */
        OP-TUPLE    *beg_op_array;           /* Array of operators */

        } QUERY-STRUCT;                      /* Structure of a query */



    #define NUM_ITERMS 1000                  /* Max. no. of index-terms
                                                allowed in a document */


    /*****************************************************************
            double
            calc_sim ( doc_wts, query_vec, sim_type )


    Returns: The MMM / Paice / P-norm similarity between the given
        document and query.


    Purpose: To compute:
        MMM_SIM (Doc, Query ) if sim_type = MMM_SIM, or
        PAICE_SIM (Doc, Query ) if sim_type = PAICE_SIM, or
        P_NORM_SIM (Doc, Query ) if sim_type = P_NORM_SIM,
```

Plan: Call the routine to calculate the similarity by passing
        to it the index of the root of the query tree (= zero).

***/

```
double
calc_sim ( doc_wts, query_vec, sim_type )

  float   doc_wts[NUM_ITERMS];              /* In: doc. weights vector  */
  register QUERY_STRUCT *query_vec;         /* In: Given Query vector   */
  short   sim_type;                         /* In: Similarity type flag */

    {

    double calc_tree_sim ();

    if ( ( sim_type != MMM_SIM ) && ( sim_type != PAICE-SIM ) &&
         ( sim_type != P_NORM_SIM ) )
         fprintf ( stderr, "calc_sim: illegal similarity\
                               type %d, query %d\n", sim_type,
                               query_vec- > query_id );

    return ( calc_tree_sim (doc_wts, query_vec, 0, sim_type ) );

    }
```

/***

```
        static double
        calc_tree_sim ( doc_wts, query_vec, root_index, sim_type )
```

Returns: The similarity between the given document and the
         subtree of the query tree with its root at ROOT_INDEX

Purpose: To compute: SIM (Doc, Query-subtree)

Plan: If the root of the subtree is an index-term then
             similarity is the document wt. for that index-term
           else, if it is an operator then,
             if the operator == NOT_OP then
                     (1) Calculate the similarity of the child of
                         the current node (CHILD_VALUE)
                     (2) Return (1.0 - CHILD_VALUE)
             else if the operator == AND_OP or OR_OP then
                     (1) Calculate the similarity considering
                         each child of the current node

```
          (2) If (SIM_TYPE == MMM_SIM) then
                   Find the maximum and the minimum of
                   these similarities,
              else if (SIM_TYPE == PAICE_SIM) then
                   Store this similarity in the array
                   child_sims,
              else if (SIM_TYPE == P_NORM_SIM) then
                   Find the numerator and denominator
                   to be used in the formula
              else
                   Print "invalid sim_type".
          (3) Use the appropriate similarity computation
                   formula to compute the similarity for
                   the current node.


*********************************************************************/


static double
calc_tree_sim ( doc_wts, query_vec, root_index, sim_type)

  float    doc_wts [NUM_ITERMS];            /* In: Document weights */
  register QUERY_STRUCT *query_vec;         /* In: Query vector */
  short    root_index;                      /* In: Index of the root of the
                                               subtree to be evaluated */
  short    sim_type;                        /* In: Similarity type flag */


  {

  register TREE_NODE *root_ptr;             /* Addr. of the root of the
                                               subtree being considered */
  register TREE_NODE *child_ptr;            /* Addr. of a child of the root
                                               of subtree being considered */
  register OP_TUPLE *op_ptr;                /* Addr. of current operator */
  register ITERM_TUPLE *iterm_ptr;          /* Addr. of current index-term */
  long            doc_index;                /* Index of the weight of the
                                               current index-term within
                                               DOC-WTS array */
  short           child_index;              /* Index of the child of the root
                                               within the set of tree nodes */
  double          child_value;              /* Sim. of child's subtree */

  /* Declarations for MMM model */

  double          maximum;                  /* Maximum (children's sim.) */
  double          minimum;                  /* Minimum (children's sim.) */
  double          mmm_sim ();               /* Func. computing MMM sim. */
```

```
/* Declarations for Paice model */

    double    child_sims[NUM_ITERMS];        /* Array to store sim. of all
                                                the children of the root */
    int       curr_i;                        /* Number of sim. stored in
                                                child_sims */
    double    paice_sim ();              /* Func. computing Paice sim. */

/* Declarations for P-norm model */

    double          child_wt;                /* Wt. of the child */
    double          numerator;               /* Numerator in sim. formula */
    double          denominator;             /* Denominator in sim. formula */
    void            update_numer_denom();    /* Func. updating value of */
                                             /* numerator & denominator */
    double          p_norm_sim ();           /* Func. computing P-norm sim. */

    double calc_tree_sim();                  /* Recursive call for each subtree */


/* Addr. of first node of the tree + index of the current node
   = the addr. of the root of the subtree under consideration */

root_ptr = query_vec->beg_node_array + root_index;

if (UNDEF == root_ptr->child_index)
    {

/* If node is an index-term, then return its doc-wt. Index in */
/* the doc_wts array is the ITERM_NUM of current index-term */

        iterm_ptr = query_vec->beg_iterm_array + root_ptr->iterm_op_index;
        doc-index = iterm_ptr->iterm_num;

        return ( (double) doc_wts [doc_index] );

    }
else
    { /* If current node is an operator, then compute its sim. */

        op_ptr = query_vec->beg_op_array + root_ptr->iterm_op_index;

        if ( ( op_ptr->op_type != NOT_OP ) &&
            ( op_ptr->op_type != OR_OP ) &&
            ( op_ptr->op_type != AND_OP ) )
            {               /* if neither NOT, OR or AND */
            fprintf ( stderr, "calc_tree_sim:\
```

```
                           illegal operator type %d, query %d.\n",
                 op_ptr->op_type, query_vec->query_id);

      return ( (double) UNDEF );
      }

switch (op_ptr->op_type)
  {
  case (NOT_OP):   /* If the operator is NOT_OP */

        if (UNDEF != (query_vec->beg_node_array +
                root_ptr->child_index)->sibling_index)
            {   /* NOT_OP operator can have only one child */
            fprintf(stderr,
            "calc_tree_sim: NOT operator has more\
            than one child.\n');
            return ( (double) UNDEF);
            }

        /* if only child, return (1.0 - similarity of child) */

        if ((double) UNDEF == (child_value =
                calc_tree_sim ( doc_wts, query_vec,
                      root_ptr->child_index, sim_type)))
          return ( (double) UNDEF );

        return ( 1.0-child_value );
    break;

    case (OR_OP):
    case (AND_OP):   /* If the operator is OR_OP or AND_OP */

            maximum = -99999.0;
            minimum = 99999.0;              /* Init. for MMM model */

            curr_i = -1;                    /* Init. for Paice model */

            numerator = 0.0;
            denominator = 0.0;             /* Init. for P-norm model */

            /* Start with the first child of the current node, *
             * consider each of its siblings, until none left */

        for (child_index = root_ptr->child_index;
            UNDEF != child_index;
            child_index = (query_vec->beg_node_array +
                                    child_index)->sibling_index )
                {
```

```
                    if ((double)UNDEF == (child_value =
                              calc_tree_sim ( doc_wts, query_vec, child_index,
                                        sim_type)))
                         return ((double UNDEF);

        switch (sim_type)
        {
        case (MMM_SIM):   /* update max and mim */
                maximum = (child_value > maximum) ? child_value
                              : maximum;
                minimum = (child_value < minimum) ? child_value
                              : minimum;
                break;

        case (PAICE_SIM):
                curr_i = curr_i + 1;
                child_sims [curr_i] = child_value;
        break;

        case (P_NORM_SIM): /* Find the wt. of the child */

                child_ptr = query_vec->beg_node_array +
                              root_ptr->child_index;
                if (UNDEF == child_ptr->child_index)
                    child_wt = (query_vec->beg_iterm_array +
                         child_ptr->iterm_op_index)->iterm_wt;
                else
                    child_wt = (query_vec->beg_op_array +
                              child_ptr->iterm_op_index)->op_wt;
                    update_numer_denom ( child_value, child_wt,
                              op_ptr->op_type, op_ptr->op_coeff,
                              &numerator, &denominator );
                break;
        }   /* switch - sim_type */
    }     /* for */

                /* After considering all the children, compute the *
                 * sim. of current subtree with appropriate formula */

if ( sim_type == MMM_SIM )
   return ( mmm_sim ( op_ptr->op_coeff,
                         op_ptr->op_type, maximum, minimum));
else
if ( sim_type == PAICE_SIM )
   return (paice_sim (op_ptr->op_coeff,
                         op_ptr->op_type, child_sims, curr_i ));
else
if ( sim_type == P_NORM_SIM )
```

```
                       return ( p_norm_sim (op_ptr->op_coeff,
                                op_ptr->op_type, numerator, denominator ) );

       }         /* switch - op_ptr->op_type */
   }            /* else */

}


/*******************************************************************
          double
          mmm_sim (coeff, type, maximum, minimum)

Returns: The MMM similarity

Purpose: To calculate the MMM similarity using
          MAXIMUM and MINIMUM.

          SIM(Qor, D) = coeff * MAXIMUM + (1-coeff) * MINIMUM
          SIM(Qand, D) = coeff * MINIMUM + (1-coeff) * MAXIMUM

Plan:    Depending on the type of the operator use the
          appropriate formula

*******************************************************************/

double
mmm_sim ( op_coeff, op_type, maximum, minimum )

  register float op_coeff;   /* In: Value of the coefficient */
  int op_type;                    /* In: Type of operator */
  double maximum;                      /* In: Maximum of the similarities */
  double minimum;                      /* In: Minimum of the similarities */

  {


  if ( op_type == OR_OP )
     return ( (op_coeff * maximum + (1 - op_coeff) * minimum));
  else
  if ( op_type == AND_OP )
     return ( (op_coeff * minimum + (1 - op_coeff) * maximum));

}

/*******************************************************************
          double
          paice_sim (op_coeff, op_type, child_sims, num_i)
```

Returns: The Paice similarity

Purpose: To calculate the Paice similarity using the
Paice similarity computation formula

Plan: Sort the array in ascending order
         If the operator is OR_OP then:
             numerator = SUM (child_sims[i] * op_coeff$\wedge$(num_i − i));
                                 for i = 0 to num_i
             denominator = SUM (op_coeff$\wedge$(num_i−i));
                                 for i = 0 to num_i

         else if the operator is AND_OP then:
             numerator = SUM (child_sims[i] *op_coeff$\wedge$(i));
                                 for i = 0 to num_i
             denominator = SUM (op_coeff$\wedge$(i));
                                 for i = 0 to num_i

**/
```
double
paice_sim ( op_coeff, op_type, child_sims, num_i )

  register float op_coeff;              /* In: Coefficient r */
  int     op_type;                      /* In: Type of operator */
  double  child_sims[NUM_ITERMS];    /* In: Array containing sim. */
  int     num_i;                        /* In: No. of elements in
                                               child_sim */


  {

  int     i;
  double  numerator;
  double  denominator;
  double  power;

  void   qsort ();              /* Quick Sort Func. in C lib. */
  int    comp_double ();              /* Func. used by qsort */

  qsort ( (char *) child_sims, num_i,
            sizeof (double), comp_double );
  numerator = 0;
  denominator = 0;

  if ( op_type == OR_OP )
     {
```

```
            for (i = 0;  i <=num_i;  i++)
              {
              power = pow((double) op_coeff, (double)num_i-i);
              numerator = numerator + power*child_sims[i];
              denominator = denominator + power;
              }
            return (numerator/denominator);
}
else
if(op_type == AND_OP)
  {
  for (i = 0;  i <= num_i;  i++)
              {
              power = pow((double) op_coeff,  (double)i);
              numerator = numerator + power * child_sims[i];
              denominator = denominator + power;
              }
            return ( numerator / denominator );
      }

}


/********************************************************************
        int
        comp_double ( d1,  d2 );

Returns:  int

Purpose:  Compares d1 and d2 and returns -1, 0, or 1.

********************************************************************/

int
comp_double (d1,  d2)

double *d1,  *d2;

{

  if (*d1 < *d2)
          return (-1);
  else
  if (*d1 == *d2)
          return (0);
  else
          return (1);

}
```

```
/************************************************************************
            void
            update_numer_denom (value, weight, op_type, p_value,
                                     numerator, denominator)

Returns: Void

Purpose: Update the values of NUMERATOR and DENOMINATOR

Plan:   If  P_value  ==  P_INFINITY then
                if VALUE > NUMERATOR then
                        NUMERATOR = VALUE
         DENOMINATOR = 1

            else
             if  OP_TYPE  ==  OR_OP then
                    NUMERATOR   = NUMERATOR + weight/\P_value * value/\P_value
                    DENOMINATOR = DENOMINATOR + weight/\P_value

             if  OP_TYPE  ==  AND_OP then
                    NUMERATOR   = NUMERATOR + weight/\P_value *
                                        (1 - value)/\P_value
                    DENOMINATOR = DENOMINATOR + weight/\P_value


**************************************************************************/
void
update_numer_denom ( value, weight, op_type, p_value,
                     numerator, denominator )

  double  value;                      /* In: The sim. of the child */
  double  weight;                     /* In: The query weight */
  register float    p_value;          /* In: The p_value */
  int    op_type;                     /* In: The type of the operator */

  register double *numerator;   /* Out: Numerator in p-norm sim.
                                          calculation formula */
  register double *denominator; /* Out: Denominator in p-norm sim.
                                          calculation formula */

  {

  double  power
  double  pow()
```

```
    if (p_value == P_INFINITY)
        {
            *denominator = 1;
        if (value > *numerator)
          *numerator = value;
        }
    else
    switch (op_type)
          {
    case (OR_OP):
            power = pow (weight, p_value);

            *numerator = *numerator + power * pow(value, p_value);
            *denominator = *denominator + power;
          break;
    case (AND_OP):
            power = pow (weight, p_value );
            *numerator = *numerator + power * pow(1-value, p_value);
            *denominator = *denominator + power;
          break;
          }
}


/**********************************************************************
          double
          p_norm_sim (p_value, op_type, numerator, denominator)

Returns: The P-norm similarity

Purpose: To calculate the P-norm similarity using the
          P-norm similarity computation formula

Plan:     Depending on the type of the operator use the
          appropriate formula

          SIM(Q(P_INFINITY), D) = NUMERATOR

          SIM(Qor_P, D)  = (NUMERATOR / DENOMINATOR) ∧ (1/P)
          SIM(Qand_P, D) = 1 - (NUMERATOR / DENOMINATOR) ∧ (1/P)

**********************************************************************/

double
p_norm_sim ( p_value, op_type numerator, denominator)
```

```
register float p_value;         /* In: P value */
int op_type;                    /* In: Type of operator */
double numerator;               /* In: Numerator */
double denominator;             /* In: Denominator */

{

double pow();


if  (p_value == P_INFINITY)
    return (numerator);

else
if  (op_type == OR_OP)
    return (pow (numerator / denominator, 1/p_value));
else
if  (op_type == AND_OP)
    return (1 - pow (numerator / denominator, 1/p_value));

}
```

16

Clustering Algorithms

Edie Rasmussen
University of Pittsburgh

Abstract

Cluster analysis is a technique for multivariate analysis that assigns items to automatically created groups based on a calculation of the degree of association between items and groups. In the information retrieval (IR) field, cluster analysis has been used to create groups of documents with the goal of improving the efficiency and effectiveness of retrieval, or to determine the structure of the literature of a field. The terms in a document collection can also be clustered to show their relationships. The two main types of cluster analysis methods are the nonhierarchical, which divide a data set of N items into M clusters, and the hierarchical, which produce a nested data set in which pairs of items or clusters are successively linked. The nonhierarchical methods such as the single pass and reallocation methods are heuristic in nature and require less computation than the hierarchical methods. However, the hierarchical methods have usually been preferred for cluster-based document retrieval. The commonly used hierarchical methods, such as single link, complete link, group average link, and Ward's method, have high space and time requirements. In order to cluster the large data sets with high dimensionality that are typically found in IR applications, good algorithms (ideally $O(N^2)$ time, $O(N)$ space) must be found. Examples are the SLINK and minimal spanning tree algorithms for the single link method, the Voorhees algorithm for group average link, and the reciprocal nearest neighbor algorithm for Ward's method.

16.1 CLUSTER ANALYSIS

16.1.1 Introduction

Cluster analysis is a statistical technique used to generate a category structure which fits a set of observations. The groups which are formed should have a high degree of association between members of the same group and a low degree between members of different groups (Anderberg 1973). While cluster analysis is sometimes referred to as automatic classification, this is not strictly accurate since the classes formed are not known prior to processing, as classification implies, but are defined by the items assigned to them.

Because there is no need for the classes to be identified prior to processing, cluster analysis is useful to provide structure in large multivariate data sets. It has been described as a tool of discovery because it has the potential to reveal previously undetected relationships based on complex data (Anderberg 1973). An early application of cluster analysis was to determine taxonomic relationships among species. Psychiatric profiles, medical and clinical data, census and survey data, images, and chemical structures and properties have all been studied using cluster analytic methods, and there is an extensive and widely scattered journal literature on the subject.

Basic texts include those by Anderberg (1973), Hartigan (1975), Everitt (1980), Aldenderfer and Blashfield (1984), Romesburg (1984), Spath (1985), Jain and Dubes (1988) and Kaufman (1990). Taxonomic applications have been described by Sneath and Sokal (1973), and social science applications by Lorr (1983) and Hudson and Associates (1982). Comprehensive reviews by Lee (1981), Dubes and Jain (1980) and Gordon (1987) are also recommended.

Because cluster analysis is a technique for multivariate analysis that has application in many fields, it is supported by a number of software packages which are often available in academic and other computing environments. Most of the methods and some of the algorithms described in this chapter are found in statistical analysis packages such as SAS, SPSSX, and BMDP and cluster analysis packages such as CLUSTAN and CLUSTAR/CLUSTID. Brief descriptions and sources for these and other packages are provided by Romesburg (1984).

16.1.2 Applications in Information Retrieval

The ability of cluster analysis to categorize by assigning items to automatically created groups gives it a natural affinity with the aims of information storage and retrieval. Cluster analysis can be performed on documents in several ways:

- Documents may be clustered on the basis of the terms that they contain. The aim of this approach has usually been to provide more efficient or more effective retrieval, though it has also been used after retrieval to provide structure to large sets of retrieved documents. In distributed systems, clustering can be used to allocate documents for storage. A recent review (Willett 1988) provides a comprehensive summary of research on term-based document clustering.

- Documents may be clustered based on co-occurring citations in order to provide insights into the nature of the literature of a field (e.g., Small and Sweeney [1985]).

- Terms may be clustered on the basis of the documents in which they co-occur, in order to aid in the construction of a thesaurus or in the enhancement of queries (e.g., Crouch [1988]).

Although cluster analysis can be easily implemented with available software packages, it is not without problems. These include:

- Selecting the attributes on which items are to be clustered and their representation.

- Selecting an appropriate clustering method and similarity measure from those available.
- Creating the clusters or cluster hierarchies, which can be expensive in terms of computational resources.
- Assessing the validity of the result obtained.
- If the collection to be clustered is a dynamic one, the requirements for update must be considered.
- If the aim is to use the clustered collection as the basis for information retrieval, a method for searching the clusters or cluster hierarchy must be selected.

The emphasis in this chapter will be on the range of clustering methods available and algorithms for their implementation, with discussion of the applications and evaluation that have been carried out in an information retrieval environment. The following notation will be used: N for the number of items D_i in a data set, L for its dimensionality, and M for the number of clusters C_i created. It will be assumed that the items to be clustered are documents, and each document D_i (or cluster representative C_i) is represented by $(weight_{i1}, \ldots, weight_{iL})$, where $weight_{ik}$ is the weight assigned to $term_k$ in D_i or C_i. The choice of an appropriate document representation is discussed elsewhere in this text; a summary of research on term-weighting approaches is provided by Salton and Buckley (1988).

16.2 MEASURES OF ASSOCIATION

16.2.1 Introduction

In order to cluster the items in a data set, some means of quantifying the degree of association between them is required. This may be a distance measure, or a measure of similarity or dissimilarity. Some clustering methods have a theoretical requirement for use of a specific measure (Euclidean distance for Ward's method, for example), but more commonly the choice of measure is at the discretion of the researcher.

While there are a number of similarity measures available, and the choice of similarity measure can have an effect on the clustering results obtained, there have been only a few comparative studies (summarized by Willett [1988]). In cluster-based retrieval, the determination of interdocument similarity depends on both the document representation, in terms of the weights assigned to the indexing terms characterizing each document, and the similarity coefficient that is chosen. The results of tests by Willett (1983) of similarity coefficients in cluster-based retrieval suggest that it is important to use a measure that is normalized by the length of the document vectors. The results of tests on weighting schemes were less definitive but suggested that weighting of document terms is not as significant in improving performance in cluster-based retrieval as it is in other types of retrieval. Sneath and

Sokal (1973) point out that simple similarity coefficients are often monotonic with more complex ones, and argue against the use of weighting schemes. The measures described below are commonly used in information retrieval applications. They are appropriate for binary or real-valued weighting scheme.

16.2.2 Similarity Measures

A variety of distance and similarity measures is given by Anderberg (1973), while those most suitable for comparing document vectors are discussed by Salton (1989). The Dice, Jaccard and cosine coefficients have the attractions of simplicity and normalization and have often been used for document clustering.

Dice coefficient:

$$S_{D_i, D_j} = \frac{2 \sum_{k=1}^{L} (weight_{ik} weight_{jk})}{\sum_{k=1}^{L} weight_{ik}^2 + \sum_{k=1}^{L} weight_{jk}^2}$$

If binary term weights are used, the Dice Coefficient reduces to:

$$S_{D_i, D_j} = \frac{2C}{A + B}$$

where C is the number of terms that D_i and D_j have in common, and A and B are the number of terms in D_i and D_j.

Jaccard coefficient:

$$S_{D_i, D_j} = \frac{\sum_{k=1}^{L} (weight_{ij} weight_{jk})}{\sum_{k=1}^{L} weight_{ik}^2 + \sum_{k=1}^{L} weight_{jk}^2 - \sum_{k=1}^{L} (weight_{ik} weight_{jk})}$$

Cosine coefficient:

$$S_{D_i, D_j} = \frac{\sum_{k=1}^{L} (weight_{ij} weight_{jk})}{\sqrt{\sum_{k=1}^{L} weight_{ik}^2 \sum_{k=1}^{L} weight_{jk}^2}}$$

16.2.3 The Similarity Matrix

Many clustering methods are based on a pairwise coupling of the most similar documents or clusters, so that the similarity between every pair of points must be known. This necessitates the calculation of the *similarity matrix*; when the similarity measure is symmetric ($S_{ij} = S_{ji}$), the lower triangular matrix is sufficient (Figure 16.1).

The inverted file algorithm is particularly useful in limiting the amount of computation required to calculate a similarity matrix, if the similarity measure used is one that results in a 0 value whenever a document-document or document-cluster

$$S = \begin{vmatrix} S_{21} & & & \\ S_{31} & S_{32} & & \\ S_{41} & S_{42} & S_{43} & \\ \vdots & \vdots & \vdots & \ddots \\ S_{N1} & S_{N2} & S_{N3} & \cdots & S_{N(N-1)} \end{vmatrix}$$

Figure 16.1 Similarity matrix

pair have no terms in common (Willett 1980; Perry and Willett 1983). The document term list is used as an index to the inverted index lists that are needed for the similarity calculation. Only those document/cluster pairs that share at least one common term will have their similarity calculated; the remaining values in the similarity matrix are set to 0. The inverted file algorithm is as follows:

```
for ( docno = 0; docno < n; docno++ )
  {
    for ( i = 0; i < doclength; i++ )
      {
        retrieve_inverted_list ( term[i] );
        for ( j = 0; j < invlength; j++ ) counter[doc[j]]++;
      }
    for ( doc2 = 0; doc2 < n; doc2++ )
      {
        if (counter[doc2]) calc_similarity( docno, doc2 );
      }
  }
```

The inverted file algorithm can be effectively incorporated in the clustering algorithms described in this chapter when the calculation of the similarity matrix, or a single row of it, is required for a document collection.

It should be noted that the similarity matrix can be the basis for identifying a nearest neighbor (NN), that is, finding the closest vector to a given vector from a set of N multidimensional vectors. The identification of an NN arises in many clustering algorithms, and for large data sets makes a significant contribution to the computational requirement. Calculating and storing the similarity matrix, or recalculating it when needed, provides a brute force approach to nearest neighbor identification. Therefore, if an efficient NN-finding algorithm can be incorporated into the clustering algorithm, considerable savings of processing time may be achieved. However, although there are a number of techniques available for introducing efficiency into the NN-finding process (Bentley et al. 1980; Murtagh 1985), these techniques are generally inappropriate for data sets with the high dimensionality typical of information retrieval applications. Use of the inverted file algorithm to calculate the similarity matrix or a row of it seems to be the best optimization technique available in these circumstances.

16.3 CLUSTERING METHODS

16.3.1 Methods and Associated Algorithms

There are a very large number of ways of sorting N objects into M groups, a problem compounded by the fact that M is usually unknown. Most of the possible arrangements are of no interest; it is the role of a clustering method to identify a set of groups or cluster that reflects some underlying structure in the data. Moreover, there are many clustering methods available, which have differing theoretical or empirical bases and therefore produce different cluster structures. For a given clustering *method*, there may be a choice of clustering *algorithm* or means to implement the method. The choice of clustering method will determine the outcome, the choice of algorithm will determine the efficiency with which it is achieved. In this section, an overview of the clustering methods most used in information retrieval will be provided. The associated algorithms that are best suited to the processing of the large data sets found in information retrieval applications are discussed in sections 16.4 and 16.5.

16.3.2 Computational and Storage Requirements

In cases where the data set to be processed is very large, the resources required for cluster analysis may be considerable. A major component of the computation required is the calculation of the document-document or document-cluster similarity. The time requirement will be minimally $O(NM)$, where M is the number of clusters, for the simpler reallocation methods; where the similarity matrix must be constructed, the proportionality is at least N^2. Most of the preferred clustering methods have time requirements of at least $O(N^2)$. The storage requirement will be $O(N)$ if the data set is stored, or $O(N^2)$ if the similarity matrix is stored. For large N this may be unacceptable, and disk accesses may make processing time too large if the similarity matrix is stored on disk. An alternative is to recalculate the similarity matrix from the stored data whenever it is needed to identify the current most similar pair, but this increases the time requirement by a factor of N^2.

Because of the heavy demands of processing and storage requirements, much of the early work on cluster analysis for information retrieval was limited to small data sets, often only a few hundred items. However, improvements in processing and storage capacity and the introduction of efficient algorithms for implementing some clustering methods and finding nearest neighbors have it feasible to cluster increasingly large data sets. Salton and Bergmark (1981) have pointed out that there is a high degree of parallelism in the calculation of a set of similarity values, and parallel hardware also offers the potential for increased processing efficiency (Willett and Rasmussen 1990).

16.3.3 Survey of Clustering Methods

Clustering methods are usually categorized according to the type of cluster structure they produce. The simple *nonhierarchical* methods divide the data set of N objects into M clusters; where no overlap is allowed, these are known as partitioning methods. Each item has membership in the cluster with which it is most similar, and the cluster may be represented by a centroid or cluster representative that is indicative of the characteristics of the items it contains. The more complex *hierarchical* methods produce a nested data set in which pairs of items or clusters are successively linked until every item in the data set is connected. The hierarchical methods can be either *agglomerative*, with $N - 1$ pairwise joins beginning from an unclustered data set, or *divisive*, beginning with all objects in a single cluster and progressing through $N - 1$ divisions of some cluster into a smaller cluster. The divisive methods are less commonly used and few algorithms are available; only agglomerative methods will be discussed in this chapter.

Nonhierarchical methods

The nonhierarchical methods are heuristic in nature, since a priori decisions about the number of clusters, cluster size, criterion for cluster membership, and form of cluster representation are required. Since the large number of possible divisions of N items into M clusters make an optimal solution impossible, the nonhierarchical methods attempt to find an approximation, usually by partitioning the data set in some way and then reallocating items until some criterion is optimized. The computational requirement $O(NM)$ is much lower than for the hierarchical methods if $M << N$, so that large data sets can be partitioned. The nonhierarchical methods were used for most of the early work in document clustering when computational resources were limited; see for example work on the SMART project, described by Salton (1971).

Hierarchical methods

Most of the early published work on cluster analysis employed hierarchical methods (Blashfield and Aldenderfer 1978), though this was not so in the IR field. With improvements in computer resources, the easy availability of software packages for cluster analysis, and improved algorithms, the last decade of work on clustering in IR retrieval has concentrated on the hierarchical agglomerative clustering methods (HACM, Willett [1988]).

The cluster structure resulting from a hierarchical agglomerative clustering method is often displayed as a *dendrogram* like that shown in Figure 16.2. The order of pairwise coupling of the objects in the data set is shown, and the value of the similarity function (level) at which each fusion occurred. The dendrogram is a useful

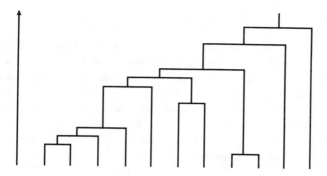

Figure 16.2 Dendrogram of
a hierarchical classification

representation when considering retrieval from a clustered set of documents, since it
indicates the paths that the retrieval process may follow.

The most commonly used hierarchical agglomerative clustering methods and
their characteristics are:

- **single link:** The single link method joins, at each step, the most similar pair of
  objects that are not yet in the same cluster. It has some attractive theoretical
  properties (Jardine and Sibson 1971) and can be implemented relatively efficiently, so it has been widely used. However, it has a tendency toward formation of long straggly clusters, or chaining, which makes it suitable for delineat-
  ing ellipsoidal clusters but unsuitable for isolating spherical or poorly separated
  clusters.

- **complete link:** The complete link method uses the least similar pair between
  each of two clusters to determine the intercluster similarity; it is called complete link because all entities in a cluster are linked to one another within some
  minimum similarity. Small, tightly bound clusters are characteristic of this
  method.

- **group average link:** As the name implies, the group average link method uses
  the average values of the pairwise links within a cluster to determine similarity. All objects contribute to intercluster similarity, resulting in a structure intermediate between the loosely bound single link clusters and tightly bound
  complete link clusters. The group average method has ranked well in evaluative studies of clustering methods (Lorr 1983).

- **Ward's method:** Ward's method is also known as the minimum variance
  method because it joins at each stage the cluster pair whose merger minimizes
  the increase in the total within-group error sum of squares, based on the Euclidean distance between centroids. It tends to produce homogeneous clusters
  and a symmetric hierarchy, and its definition of a cluster center of gravity provides a useful way of representing a cluster. Tests have shown it to be good at
  recovering cluster structure, though it is sensitive to outliers and poor at recovering elongated clusters (Lorr 1983).

Two other HACM are sometimes used, the *centroid* and *median* methods. In the centroid method, each cluster as it is formed is represented by the coordinates of a group centroid, and at each stage in the clustering the pair of clusters with the most similar mean centroid is merged. The median method is similar but the centroids of the two merging clusters are not weighted proportionally to the size of the clusters. A disadvantage of these two methods is that a newly formed cluster may be more like some point than were its constituent points, resulting in reversals or inversions in the cluster hierarchy.

16.4 ALGORITHMS FOR NONHIERARCHICAL METHODS

16.4.1 Single Pass Methods

The single pass method is particularly simple since it requires that the data set be processed only once. The general algorithm is as follows:

1. Assign the first document D_1 as the representative for C_1.
2. For D_i, calculate the similarity S with the representative for each existing cluster.
3. If S_{max} is greater than a threshold value S_T, add the item to the corresponding cluster and recalculate the cluster representative; otherwise, use D_i to initiate a new cluster.
4. If an item D_i remains to be clustered, return to step 2.

Though the single pass method has the advantage of simplicity, it is often criticized for its tendency to produce large clusters early in the clustering pass, and because the clusters formed are not independent of the order in which the data set is processed. It is sometimes used to form the groups that are used to initiate reallocation clustering. An example of a single pass algorithm developed for document clustering is the cover coefficient algorithm (Can and Ozkarahan 1984). In this algorithm, a set of documents is selected as cluster seeds, and then each document is assigned to the cluster seed that maximally covers it. For D_i, the cover coefficient is a measure that incorporates the extent to which it is covered by D_j and the uniqueness of D_i, that is, the extent to which it is covered by itself.

16.4.2 Reallocation Methods

The reallocation methods operate by selecting some initial partition of the data set and then moving items from cluster to cluster to obtain an improved partition. Anderberg (1973) discusses some of the criteria that have been suggested to establish an initial partition and to monitor the improvement achieved by reallocation. A general algorithm is:

1. Select M cluster representatives or centroids.
2. For $i = 1$ to N, assign D_i to the most similar centroid.
3. For $j = 1$ to M, recalculate the cluster centroid C_j.
4. Repeat steps 2 and 3 until there is little or no change in cluster membership during a pass through the file.

The single pass and reallocation methods were used in early work in cluster analysis in IR, such as the clustering experiments carried out in the SMART project (Salton 1971). Their time and storage requirements are much lower than those of the HACM and much larger data sets could be processed. With improved processing capability and more efficient hierarchical algorithms, the HACMs are now usually preferred in practice, and the nonhierarchical methods will not be considered further in this chapter.

16.5 ALGORITHMS FOR HIERARCHICAL METHODS

16.5.1 General Algorithm for the HACM

All of the hierarchical agglomerative clustering methods can be described by a general algorithm:

1. Identify the two closest points and combine them in a cluster.
2. Identify and combine the next two closest points (treating existing clusters as points).
3. If more than one cluster remains, return to step 1.

Individual HACM differ in the way in which the most similar pair is defined, and in the means used to represent a cluster. Lance and Williams (1966) proposed a general combinatorial formula, the Lance-Williams dissimilarity update formula, for calculating dissimilarities between new clusters and existing points, based on the dissimilarities prior to formation of the new cluster. If objects C_i and C_j have just been merged to form cluster $C_{i,j}$, the dissimilarity d between the new cluster and any existing cluster C_k is given by:

$$d_{C_{i,j}C_k} = \alpha_i d_{C_i C_k} + \alpha_j d_{C_j C_k} + \beta d_{C_i C_j} + \gamma \left| d_{C_i C_k} - d_{C_j C_k} \right|$$

This formula can be modified to accomodate a variety of HACM by choice of the values of α, β, and γ. The hierarchical clustering methods previously discussed are presented in Table 16.1 in the context of their Lance-Williams parameters and cluster centers.

Table 16.1 Characteristics of HACM

HACM	Lance-Williams parameters	Cluster centers
Single link	$\alpha_i = \dfrac{1}{2}$ $\beta = 0$ $\gamma = -\dfrac{1}{2}$	—
Complete link	$\alpha_i = \dfrac{1}{2}$ $\beta = 0$ $\gamma = \dfrac{1}{2}$	—
Group average	$\alpha_i = \dfrac{m_i}{m_i + m_j}$ $\beta = 0$ $\gamma = 0$	—
Median	$\alpha_i = \dfrac{1}{2}$ $\beta = -\dfrac{1}{4}$ $\gamma = 0$	$C_{i,j} = \dfrac{C_i + C_j}{2}$
Centroid	$\alpha_i = \dfrac{m_i}{m_i + m_j}$ $\beta = -\dfrac{m_i m_j}{(m_i + m_j)^2}$ $\gamma = 0$	$C_{i,j} = \dfrac{m_i C_i + m_j C_j}{m_i + m_j}$
Ward's method	$\alpha_i = \dfrac{m_i + m_k}{m_i + m_j + m_k}$ $\beta = -\dfrac{m_k}{m_i + m_j + m_k}$ $\gamma = 0$	$C_{i,j} = \dfrac{m_i C_i + m_j C_j}{m_i + m_j}$

Notes: m_i is the number of items in C_i; the dissimilarity measure used for Ward's method must be the increase in variance (section 16.5.5).

There are three approaches to implementation of the general HACM (Anderberg 1973), each of which has implications for the time and storage requirements for processing. In the *stored matrix* approach, an $N \times N$ matrix containing all pairwise dissimilarity values is stored, and the Lance-Williams update formula makes it possible to recalculate the dissimilarity between cluster centers using only the stored values. The time requirement is $O(N^2)$, rising to $O(N^3)$ if a simple serial scan of the similarity matrix is used; the storage requirement is $O(N^2)$. A *stored data* approach has only an $O(N)$ storage requirement but the need to recalculate the pairwise dissimilarity values for each fusion leads to an $O(N^3)$ time requirement. In the *sorted matrix* approach, the dissimilarity matrix is calculated $(O(N^2))$ and then sorted $(O(N^2 \log N^2))$ prior to the construction of the hierarchy $(O(N^2))$. The data set need not be stored and the similarity matrix is processed serially, which minimizes disk accesses. However, this approach is suitable only for the single link and complete link methods, which do not require the recalculation of similarities during clustering.

In addition to the general algorithm, there are also algorithms specific to individual HACM. For some methods, algorithms have been developed that are the optimal $O(N^2)$ in time and $O(N)$ in space (Murtagh 1984). These include several algorithms for the single link method, Defay's algorithm for complete link, and a nearest-neighbor algorithm for Ward's method, all of which are discussed below.

16.5.2 Single Link Method

The single link method merges at each stage the closest previously unlinked pair of points in the data set. Since the distance between two clusters is defined as the distance between the closest pair of points each of which is in one of the two clusters, no cluster centroid or representative is required, and there is no need to recalculate the similarity matrix during processing. This makes the method attractive both from a computational and a storage perspective, and it also has desirable mathematical properties (Jardine and Sibson 1971), so that it is one of the most widely used of the HACM.

A number of algorithms for the single link method have been reviewed by Rohlf (1982), including related minimal spanning tree algorithms. The computational requirements range from $O(N \log N)$ to $O(N^5)$. Many of these algorithms are not suitable for information retrieval applications where the data sets have large N and high dimensionality. The single link algorithms discussed below are those that have been found most useful for information retrieval.

Van Rijsbergen algorithm

Van Rijsbergen (1971) developed an algorithm to generate the single link hierarchy that allowed the similarity values to be presented in any order and therefore did not require the storage of the similarity matrix. It is $O(N^2)$ in time and $O(N)$ in storage requirements. It generates the hierarchy in the form of a data structure that both facilitates searching and is easily updated, and was the first to be applied to a relatively large collection of 11,613 documents (Croft 1977). However, most later work with large collections has used either the SLINK or Prim-Dijkstra algorithm, which are quite simple to implement.

SLINK algorithm

The SLINK algorithm (Sibson 1973) is optimally efficient, $O(N^2)$ for computation and $O(N)$ for time, and therefore suitable for large data sets. It is simply a sequence of operations by which a representation of the single link hierarchy can be recursively updated; the dendrogram is built by inserting one point at a time into the representation.

The hierarchy is generated in a form known as the *pointer representation*, which consists of two functions π and λ for a data set numbered $1..N$, with the following conditions:

- $\pi(N) = N$
- $\pi(i) > i$
- $\lambda(N) = \infty$
- $\lambda(\pi(i)) > \lambda(i)$ for $i < N$

In simple terms, $\lambda(i)$ is the lowest level (distance or dissimilarity) at which i is no longer the last (i.e., the highest numbered) object in its cluster, and $\pi(i)$ is the last object in the cluster it joins at this level; a mathematical definition for these parameters is provided by Sibson (1973).

Fortran code for SLINK is provided in the original paper (Sibson 1973). In the pseudocode below, three arrays of dimension N are used: *pi* (to hold the pointer representation), *lambda* (to hold the distance value associated with each pointer), and *distance* (to process the current row of the distance matrix); *next* indicates the current pointer for a point being examined.

```
/* initialize pi and lambda for a single point representation */
pi[0] = 0;
lambda[0] = MAXINT;
/*iteratively add the remaining N-1 points to the hierarchy */
for (i = 1; i < N; i++)
  {
    pi[i] = i;
    lambda[i] = MAXINT;
    /* calculate and store a row of the distance matrix for i */
    for (j = 0; j < i-1; j++) distance[j] =calc_distance(i,j);
    for (j = 0; j < i-1; j++)
      {
        next = pi[j];
        if (lambda[j] < distance[j])
          distance[next] = min(distance[next],distance[j]);
        else
          {
            distance[next] = min(lambda[j],distance[next]);
            pi[j] = i;
            lambda[j] = distance[j];
          }
      }
    /* relabel clusters if necessary */
    for (j = 0; j < i-1; j++)
```

```
        {
            next = pi[j];
            if (lambda[next] < lambda[j])
                pi[j] = i;
        }
    }
```

For output in the form of a dendrogram, the pointer representation can be converted into the *packed representation*. This can be accomplished in $O(N^2)$ time (with a small coefficient for N^2) and $O(N)$ space. A FORTRAN subroutine to effect the transformation is provided in Sibson's original paper.

Minimal spanning tree algorithms

A minimal spanning tree (MST) is a tree linking N objects with $N - 1$ connections so that there are no loops and the sum of the $N - 1$ dissimilarities is minimized. It can be shown that all the information required to generate a single link hierarchy for a set of points is contained in their MST (Gower and Ross 1969). Once an MST has been constructed, the corresponding single link hierarchy can be generated in $O(N^2)$ operations; or the data structures for the MST can be modified so that the hierarchy can be built simultaneously (Rohlf 1982).

Two fundamental construction principles for MSTs are:

1. Any isolated point can be connected to a nearest neighbor.
2. Any isolated fragment (subset of an MST) can be connected to a nearest neighbor by a shortest available link.

The Prim-Dijkstra algorithm (Dijkstra 1976) consists of a single application of principle 1, followed by $N - 1$ iterations of principle 2, so that the MST is grown by enlarging a single fragment:

1. Place an arbitrary point in the MST and connect its nearest neighbor to it.
2. Find the point not in the MST closest to any point in the MST and add it to the fragment.
3. If a point remains that is not in the fragment, return to step 2.

The algorithm requires $O(N^2)$ time if, for each point not in the fragment, the identity and distance to its nearest neighbor in the fragment is stored. As each new point is added to the fragment, the distance from that point to each point not in the fragment is calculated, and the NN information is updated if necessary. Since the dissimilarity matrix need not be stored, the storage requirement is $O(N)$.

A FORTRAN version of the Prim-Dijkstra algorithm is provided by Whitney (1972). The algorithm here uses arrays *npoint* and *ndistance* to hold information on the nearest in-tree neighbor for each point, and *notintree* is a list of the *nt* unconnected points. *Lastpoint* is the latest point added to the tree.

```
/* initialize lists */
for (i = 0;  i < n;  i++)
  {
    ndistance[i] = MAXINT;
    notintree[i] = i;
  }
/* arbitrarily place the Nth point in the MST */
lastpoint = n;
nt = n-1;
/* grow the tree an object at a time */
for ( i = 0;  i < n-1; i++)
  {
    /*consider the lastpoint in the tree for the NN list */
    for (j = 0;  j < nt;  j++)
      {
        D = calculate_distance(lastpoint, notintree[j]);
        if (D < ndistance[j]
          {
            npoint[j] =lastpoint;
            ndistance[j] = D;
          }
      }
    /* find the unconnected point closest to a point in the  */
    /* tree                                                  */
    nj = index_of_min(ndistance);
    /* add this point to the MST; store this point and their */
    /* clustering level                                      */
    lastpoint = notintree[nj];
    store_in_MST ( lastpoint, npoint[nj], ndistance[nj]);
    /* remove lastpoint from notintree list; */
    /* close up npoint and ndistance lists    */
    notintree[nj] = nt;
    npoint[nj] = npoint[nt];
    ndistance[nj] =ndistance[nt];
    nt = nt - 1;
  }

}
```

16.5.3 Complete Link Method

The small, tightly bound clusters typical of the complete link method have performed well in comparative studies of document retrieval (Voorhees 1986a). Unfortunately, it is difficult to apply to large data sets since there does not seem to be an algorithm more effective than the stored data or stored matrix approach to the general HACM algorithm.

Defays' CLINK algorithm

The best-known algorithm for implementing the complete link method is the CLINK algorithm developed by Defays (1977). It is presented in a form analogous to the SLINK algorithm, uses the same three arrays (*pi*, *lambda*, and *distance*), and like SLINK, produces output in the form of the pointer representation. Defays presents a CLINK subroutine which allows his algorithm to be incorporated into Sibson's original FORTRAN program for SLINK. CLINK is efficient, requiring $O(N^2)$ time, $O(N)$ space, but it does not seem to generate an exact hierarchy and has given unsatisfactory results in some information retrieval experiments (El-Hamdouchi and Willett 1989).

Voorhees algorithm

The Voorhees algorithm (1986b) for the complete link method has been used to cluster relatively large document collections with better retrieval results than the CLINK algorithm (El-Hamdouchi and Willett 1989). It is a variation on the sorted matrix approach, and is based on the fact that if the similarities between all pairs of documents are processed in descending order, two clusters of size m_i and m_j can be merged as soon as the $m_i \times m_j$th similarity of documents in the respective clusters is reached. This requires a sorted list of document-document similarities, and a means of counting the number of similarities seen between any two active clusters. The large number of zero-valued similarities in a typical document collection make it more efficient than its worst case $O(N^3)$ time, $O(N^2)$ storage requirement would suggest; however it is still very demanding of resources, and El-Hamdouchi and Willett found it impractical to apply it to the largest of the collections they studied.

16.5.4 Group Average Link Method

Because the similarity between two clusters is determined by the average value of all the pairwise links between points for which each is in one of the two clusters, no general $O(N^2)$ time, $O(N)$ space algorithm is known. The general HACM algorithm can be used, but with $O(N^3)$ time for the stored data approach and $O(N^2)$ storage for the stored matrix approach, implementation may be impractical for a large collection. However, a more efficient special case algorithm is available.

Voorhees algorithm

Voorhees (1986b) has pointed out that the group average link hierarchy can be constructed in $O(N^2)$ time, $O(N)$ space if the similarity between documents chosen is the inner product of two vectors using appropriately weighted vectors. In this case, the similarity between a cluster centroid and any document is equal to the mean similarity between the document and all the documents in the cluster. Since the centroid of the cluster is the mean of all the document vectors, the centroids can be used to compute the similarities between the clusters while requiring only $O(N)$ space. Voorhees was able to cluster a document collection of 12,684 items using this algorithm, for which she provides pseudocode.

Using Voorhees' weighting scheme and intercentroid similarity, El-Hamdouchi (1987) was able to implement the group average link method using the reciprocal nearest neighbor algorithm described below for Ward's method.

16.5.5 Ward's Method

Ward's method (Ward 1963; Ward and Hook 1963) follows the general algorithm for the HACM, where the object/cluster pair joined at each stage is the one whose merger minimizes the increase in the total within-group squared deviation about the means, or variance. When two points D_i and D_j are clustered, the increase in variance I_{ij} is given by:

$$I_{ij} = \frac{m_i m_j}{m_i + m_j} \, d_{ij}^2$$

where m_i is the number of objects in D_i and d_{ij}^2 is the squared Euclidean distance, given by:

$$d_{ij}^2 = \sum_{K=1}^{L} (x_{ik} - x_{jk})^2$$

where D_i is represented by a vector $(x_{i1}, x_{i2}, \ldots, x_{iL})$ in L-dimensional space. The cluster center for a pair of points D_i and D_j is given by:

$$\frac{m_i D_i + m_j D_j}{m_i + m_j}$$

Reciprocal nearest neighbor algorithm

The mathematical properties of Ward's method make it a suitable candidate for a reciprocal nearest neighbor (RNN) algorithm (Murtaugh 1983, 1985). For any point or cluster, there exists a chain of nearest neighbors (NNs) so that

$$NN(i) = j; \ NN(j) = k; \ \ldots; \ NN(p) = q; \ NN(q) = p$$

The chain must end in some pair of objects that are RNNs, since the interobject distances are monotonically decreasing along the chain (ties must be arbitrarily resolved).

An efficient clustering algorithm can be based on the process of following a chain of nearest neighbors:

1. Select an arbitrary point.
2. Follow the NN chain from this point till an RNN pair is found.
3. Merge these two points and replace them with a single point.
4. If there is a point in the NN chain preceding the merged points, return to step 2; otherwise return to step 1. Stop when only one point remains.

This algorithm requires $O(N^2)$ computation but only $O(N)$ storage. It carries out agglomerations in restricted spatial regions, rather than in strict order of increasing dissimilarity, but still results (for Ward's method) in a hierarchy that is unique and exact. This is designated the Single Cluster Algorithm since it carries out one agglomeration per iteration; a Multiple Cluster Algorithm, suitable for parallel processing, has also been proposed (Murtagh 1985).

16.6 EVALUATION AND VALIDATION

As Dubes and Jain (1980, p. 179) point out:

> The thoughtful user of a clustering method or algorithm must answer two questions: (i) Which clustering method is appropriate for a particular data set? (ii) How does one determine whether the results of a clustering method truly characterize the data?

These are important questions because any clustering method will produce a set of clusters, and results are sought which reflect some "natural" grouping rather than one that arises as an artifact of the method. The answer to the first question can be found in evaluative studies of clustering methods, and to the second question, in validation techniques for clustering solutions.

16.6.1 Evaluation

Many evaluative studies have attempted to determine the "best" clustering method (Lorr 1983) by applying a range of clustering methods to test data sets and comparing the quality of the results, for example by using artificially created data structures, or comparing the cluster results to a classification established by experts in the field. Even under laboratory conditions it is difficult to evaluate clustering methods, since each method has different properties and strengths. The results of these studies do not suggest a single best method, though Ward's method, and in more recent studies, the group average method, have performed well. It is usually advisable to apply more than one clustering method and use some validation method to check the reliability of the resulting cluster structure.

For retrieval purposes, the "best" method for clustering a document collection is that which provides the most effective retrieval in response to a query. Several evaluative studies have taken this approach, using standard test collections of documents and queries. Most of the early work used approximate clustering methods, or the least demanding of the HACM, the single link method, a restriction imposed by limited processing resources. However, two recent studies are noteworthy for their use of relatively large document collections for the evaluation of a variety of HACM (El-Hamdouchi and Willett 1989; Voorhees 1986a). Voorhees compared single link, complete link, and group average methods, using document collections of up to 12,684 items, while El-Hamdouchi and Willett compared these three methods plus Ward's method on document collections of up to 27,361 items. Voorhees found complete link most effective for larger collections, with complete and group average link comparable for smaller collections; single link hierarchies provided the worst retrieval performance. El-Hamdouchi and Willett found group average most suitable for document clustering. Complete link was not as effective as in the Voorhees study, though this may be attributed to use of Defays' CLINK algorithm. As noted in section 16.8.1, there are several ways in which retrieval from a clustered document collection can be performed, making comparisons difficult when using retrieval as an evaluative tool for clustering methods.

16.6.2 Validation

Cluster validity procedures are used to verify whether the data structure produced by the clustering method can be used to provide statistical evidence of the phenomenon under study. Dubes and Jain (1980) survey the approaches that have been used, categorizing them on their ability to answer four questions: is the data matrix random? how well does a hierarchy fit a proximity matrix? is a partition valid? and which individual clusters appearing in a hierarchy are valid? Willett (1988) has reviewed the application of validation methods to clustering of document collections, primarily the application of the random graph hypothesis and the use of distortion measures.

An approach that is carried out prior to clustering is also potentially useful. Tests for *clustering tendency* attempt to determine whether worthwhile retrieval performance would be achieved by clustering a data set, before investing the computational resources which clustering the data set would entail. El-Hamdouchi and Willett (1987) describe three such tests. The *overlap test* is applied to a set of documents for which query-relevance judgments are available. All the relevant-relevant (RR) and relevant-nonrelevant (RNR) interdocument similarities are calculated for a given query, and the overlap (the fraction of the RR and RNR distributions that is common to both) is calculated. Collections with a low overlap value are expected to be better suited to clustering than those with high overlap values. Voorhees' *nearest neighbor test* considers, for each relevant document for a query, how many of its *n* nearest neighbors are also relevant; by averaging over all relevant documents for all queries in a test colleciton, a single indicator for a collection can be obtained. The *density test* is defined as the total number of postings in the document collection divided by the product of the number of documents and the number of terms that have been used for the indexing of those documents. It is particularly useful because it does not require any predetermined query-relevance data or any calculation of inter-document similarities. Of the three tests, the density test provided the best indication of actual retrieval performance from a clustered data set.

The goal of a hierarchical clustering process may be to partition the data set into some unknown number of clusters M (which may be visualized as drawing a horizontal line across the dendrogram at some clustering level). This requires the application of a *stopping rule,* a statistical test to predict the clustering level that will determine M. Milligan and Cooper (1985) evaluated and ranked 30 such rules, one or more of which is usually present in a software package for cluster analysis (though not necessarily those ranked highest by Milligan and Cooper).

16.7 UPDATING THE CLUSTER STRUCTURE

In many information retrieval environments, the collection is dynamic, with new items being added on a regular basis, and, less frequently, old items withdrawn. Since clustering a large data set is resource-intensive, some mechanism for updating the cluster structure without the need to recluster the entire collection is desirable. Relatively little work has been done on methods for cluster maintenance (Can and Ozkarahan 1989), particularly for the hierarchical methods. In certain cases, update of the cluster structure is implicit in the clustering algorithm. This is true of both the van Rijsbergen and SLINK algorithms for the single link method, and the CLINK algorithm for the complete link method, all of which operate by iteratively inserting a document into an existing hierarchy.

Where the application uses a partitioned data set (from a nonhierarchical or hierarchical method), new items may simply be added to the most similar partition until the cluster structure becomes distorted and it is necessary to regenerate it. For a few methods, cluster update has been specifically incorporated. Crouch's reallocation algorithm includes a mechanism for cluster maintenance (Crouch 1975). Can and Ozkarahan (1989) review the approaches that have been taken for cluster maintenance and propose a strategy for dynamic cluster maintenance based on their cover coefficient concept.

16.8 DOCUMENT RETRIEVAL FROM A CLUSTERED DATA SET

Document clustering has been studied because of its potential for improving the efficiency of retrieval, for improving the effectiveness of retrieval, and because it provides an alternative to Boolean or best match retrieval. Initially the emphasis was on efficiency: document collections were partitioned, using nonhierarchical methods, and queries were matched against cluster centroids, which reduced the number of query-document comparisons that were necessary in a serial search. Studies of retrieval from partitioned document collections showed that though retrieval efficiency was achieved, there was a decrease in retrieval effectiveness (Salton 1971). Subsequent study has concentrated on the effectiveness of retrieval from hierarchically clustered document collections, based on the *cluster hypothesis,* which states that associations between documents convey information about the relevance of documents to requests (van Rijsbergen 1979).

16.8.1 Approaches to Retrieval

There are several ways in which a query can be matched against the documents in a hierarchy (Willett 1988). A *top-down search* involves entering the tree at the root and matching the query against the cluster at each node, moving down the tree following the path of greater similarity. The search is terminated according to some criterion, for instance when the cluster size drops below the number of documents desired, or when the query-cluster similarity begins to decrease. A single cluster is retrieved when the search is terminated. Since it is difficult to adequately represent the clusters in the very large top-level clusters, a useful modification is to eliminate the top-level clusters by applying a threshold clustering level to the hierarchy to obtain a partition, and using the best of these mid-level clusters as the starting point for the top-down search. The top-down strategy has been shown to work well with the complete link method (Voorhees 1986a).

A *bottom-up search* begins with some document or cluster at the base of the tree and moves up until the retrieval criterion is satisfied; the beginning document may be an item known to be relevant prior to the search, or it can be obtained by a best match search of documents or lowest-level clusters. Comparative studies suggest that the bottom-up search gives the best results (apart from the complete link method), particularly when the search is limited to the bottom-level clusters (Willett 1988). Output may be based on retrieval of a single cluster, or the top-ranking clusters may be retrieved to produce a predetermined number of either documents or clusters; in the latter case, the documents retrieved may themselves be ranked against the query.

A simple retrieval mechanism is based on *nearest neighbor clusters,* that is, retrieving a document and that document most similar to it. Griffiths et al. (1984) determined that for a variety of test collections, search performance comparable to or better than that obtainable from nonclustered collections could be obtained using this method.

16.8.2 Cluster Representatives

A centroid or cluster representative is a record that is used to represent the characteristics of the documents in a cluster. It is required in retrieval so that the degree of similarity between a query and a cluster can be determined; it is also needed in the nonhierarchical methods where document-cluster similarity must be determined in order to add documents to the most similar cluster. Ranks or frequencies have been used to weight terms in the representative; usually a threshold is applied to eliminate less significant terms and shorten the cluster representative. A binary representative may also be used, for example including a term if it occurs in more than $log_2 m$ documents in the cluster (Jardine and van Rijsbergen 1971).

16.9 CONCLUSION

Cluster analysis is an effective technique for structuring a data set, and a wide choice of methods and algorithms exists. It is important to consider the questions raised in section 16.1.2 regarding the potential application, selection of methods and algorithm and the parameters associated with it, and evaluation and validation of the results. Much of the work to date in cluster analysis has been limited by the considerable resources required by clustering, and only recently have results from relatively large-scale clustering become available.

REFERENCES

ALDENDERFER, M. S., and R. K. BLASHFIELD. 1984. *Cluster Analysis*. Beverly Hills: Sage.

ANDERBERG, M. R. 1973. *Cluster Analysis for Applications*. New York: Academic.

BENTLEY, J. L., B. W. WEIDE, and A. C. YAO. 1980. "Optimal Expected-Time Algorithms for Closest Point Problems." *ACM Transactions on Mathematical Software*, 6, 563–80.

BLASHFIELD, R. K., and M. S. ALDENDERFER. 1978. "The Literature on Cluster Analysis." *Multivariate Behavioral Research*, 13, 271–95.

CAN, F., and E. A. OZKARAHAN. 1984. "Two Partitioning Type Clustering Algorithms." *J. American Society for Information Science*, 35, 268–76.

CAN, F., and E. A. OZKARAHAN. 1989. "Dynamic Cluster Maintenance." *Information Processing & Management*, 25, 275–91.

CROFT, W. B. 1977. "Clustering Large Files of Documents Using the Single-Link Method." *J. American Society for Information Science*, 28, 341–44.

CROUCH, C. J. 1988. "A Cluster-Based Approach to Thesaurus Construction" in *11th International Conference on Research and Development in Information Retrieval*, New York: ACM, 309–20.

CROUCH, D. B. 1975. "A File Organization and Maintenance Procedure for Dynamic Document Collections." *Information Processing & Management*, 11, 11–21.

DEFAYS, D. 1977. "An Efficient Algorithm for a Complete Link Method." *Computer Journal*, 20, 364–66.

DIJKSTRA, E. W. 1976. "The Problem of the Shortest Subspanning Tree." *A Discipline of Programming*. Englewood Cliffs, N.J.: Prentice Hall, 154–60.

DUBES, R., and A. K. JAIN. 1980. "Clustering Methodologies in Exploratory Data Analysis." *Advances in Computers*, 19, 113–227.

EL-HAMDOUCHI, A. 1987. *The Use of Inter-Document Relationships in Information Retrieval.* Ph.D. thesis, University of Sheffield.

EL-HAMDOUCHI, A., and P. WILLETT. 1987. "Techniques for the Measurement of Clustering Tendency in Document Retrieval Systems." *Information Science,* 13, 361–65.

EL-HAMDOUCHI, A., and P. WILLETT. 1987. "Techniques for the Measurement of Clustering Tendency in Document Retrieval Systems." *J. Information Science,* 13, 361–65.

EVERITT, B. 1980. *Cluster Analysis,* 2nd ed. New York: Halsted.

GORDON, A. D. 1987. "A Review of Hierarchical Classification." *J. Royal Statistical Society, Series A,* 150(2), 119–37.

GOWER, J. C., and G. J. S. ROSS. 1969. "Minimum Spanning Trees and Single Linkage Cluster Analysis." *Applied Statistics,* 18, 54–64.

GRIFFITHS, A., L. A. ROBINSON, and P. WILLETT. 1984. "Hierarchic Agglomerative Clustering Methods for Automatic Document Classification." *J. Documentation,* 40, 175–205.

HARTIGAN, J. A. 1975. *Clustering Algorithms.* New York: Wiley.

HUDSON, H. C., and ASSOCIATES. 1983. *Classifying Social Data: New Applications of Analytical Methods for Social Science Research.* San Francisco: Jossey-Bass.

JAIN, A. K., and R. C. DUBES. 1988. *Algorithms for Clustering Data.* Englewood Cliffs, N.J.: Prentice Hall.

JARDINE, N., and R. SIBSON. 1971. *Mathematical Taxonomy.* London: Wiley.

JARDINE, N., and C. J. VAN RIJSBERGEN. 1971. "The Use of Hierarchic Clustering in Information Retrieval." *Information Storage and Retrieval,* 7, 217–40.

KAUFMAN, L. 1990. *Finding Groups in Data: An Introduction to Cluster Analysis.* New York: Wiley.

LANCE, G. N., and W. T. WILLIAMS. 1966. "A General Theory of Classificatory Sorting Strategies. 1. Hierarchical systems." *Computer Journal,* 9, 373–80.

LEE, R. C. T. 1981. "Clustering Analysis and Its Applications." *Advances in Information Systems Science,* 8, 169–292.

LORR, M. 1983. *Cluster Analysis for Social Scientists: Techniques for Analyzing and Simplifying Complex Blocks of Data.* San Francisco: Jossey-Bass.

MILLIGAN, G. W., and M. C. COOPER. 1985. "An Examination of Procedures for Determining the Number of Clusters in a Data Set." *Psychometrika,* 50, 159–79.

MURTAGH, F. 1983. "A Survey of Recent Advances in Hierarchical Clustering Algorithms." *Computer Journal,* 26, 354–59.

MURTAGH, F. 1984. "Complexities of Hierarchic Clustering Algorithms: State of the Art." *Computational Statistics Quarterly,* 1, 101–13.

MURTAGH, F. 1985. *Multidimensional Clustering Algorithms.* Vienna: Physica-Verlag (COMPSTAT Lectures 4).

PERRY, S. A., and P. WILLETT. 1983. "A Review of the Use of Inverted Files for Best Match Searching in Information Retrieval Systems." *J. Information Science,* 6, 59–66.

ROHLF, F. J. 1982. "Single-Link Clustering Algorithms," *Classification, Pattern Recognition, and Reduction of Dimensionality,* eds. P. R. Krishnaiah and J. N. Kanal, pp. 267–84. Amsterdam: North-Holland (Handbook of Statistics, Vol. 2).

ROMESBURG, H. C. 1984. *Cluster Analysis for Researchers.* Belmont, Calif.: Lifetime Learning.

SALTON, G., ed. 1971. *The SMART Retrieval System.* Englewood Cliffs, N.J.: Prentice Hall.

SALTON, G. 1989. *Automatic Text Processing*. Reading, Mass.: Addison-Wesley.

SALTON, G., and D. BERGMARK. 1981. "Parallel Computations in Information Retrieval." *Lecture Notes in Computer Science*, 111, 328–42.

SALTON, G., and C. BUCKLEY. 1988. "Term-Weighting Approaches in Automatic Text Retrieval." *Information Processing & Management*, 24, 513–23.

SIBSON, R. 1973. "SLINK: an Optimally Efficient Algorithm for the Single-Link Cluster Method." *Computer Journal*, 16, 30–34.

SMALL, H., and E. SWEENEY. 1985. "Clustering the Science Citation Index Using Cocitations. I. A Comparison of Methods." *Scientometrics*, 7, 391–409.

SNEATH, P. H. A., and R. R. Sokal. 1973. *Numerical Taxonomy; the Principles and Practice of Numerical Classification*. San Francisco: W. H. Freeman.

SPATH, H. 1985. *Cluster Dissection and Analysis*. Chichester: Ellis Horwood.

VAN RIJSBERGEN, C. J. 1971. "An Algorithm for Information Structuring and Retrieval." *Computer Journal*, 14, 407–12.

VAN RIJSBERGEN, C. J. 1979. *Information Retrieval*. London: Butterworths.

VOORHEES, E. M. 1986a. *The Effectiveness and Efficiency of Agglomerative Hierarchic Clustering in Document Retrieval*. Ph.D. thesis, Cornell University.

VOORHEES, E. M. 1986b. "Implementing Agglomerative Hierarchic Clustering Algorithms for Use in Document Retrieval. *Information Processing & Management*, 22, 465–76.

WARD, J. H., JR. 1963. "Hierarchical Grouping to Optimize an Objective Function. *J. American Statistical Association*, 58(301), 235–44.

WARD, J. H., JR. and M. E. HOOK. 1963. "Application of an Hierarchical Grouping Procedure to a Problem of Grouping Profiles." *Educational and Psychological Measurement*, 23, 69–81.

WHITNEY, V. K. M. 1972. "Algorithm 422: Minimal Spanning Tree." *Communications of the ACM*, 15, 273–74.

WILLETT, P. 1980. "Document Clustering Using an Inverted File Approach." *J. Information Science*, 2, 223–31.

WILLETT, P. 1983. "Similarity Coefficients and Weighting Functions for Automatic Document Classification: an Empirical Comparison." *International Classification*, 10, 138–42.

WILLETT, P. 1988. "Recent Trends in Hierarchic Document Clustering: A Critical Review." *Information Processing & Management*, 24(5), 577–97.

WILLETT, P., and E. M. RASMUSSEN. 1990. *Parallel Database Processing*. London: Pitman (Research Monographs in Parallel and Distributed Computing).

17

Special-Purpose Hardware for Information Retrieval

Lee A. Hollaar

Department of Computer Science
University of Utah

Abstract

Many approaches for using special purpose hardware to enhance the performance of an information retrieval have been proposed or implemented. Rather than using conventional digital computers or parallel processors developed for general applications, these special purpose processors have been designed specifically for particular facets of information retrieval, such as the rapid searching of unstructured data or manipulating surrogates or indices for the information in the database. After discussing the reasons why a special purpose processor may be desirable, three different techniques for implementing a text scanner are presented—associative memories, finite state machines, and cellular arrays. The problems of using a conventional microprocessor are discussed, along with possible hardware enhancements to improve its performance. System performance considerations, especially when the use of an index or other surrogate shift the performance from text scanning to a "seek and search" mode, are covered. Finally, special purpose processors for handling surrogates and the use of optical processing are presented.

17.1 INTRODUCTION

The previous chapters have described techniques for implementing information retrieval systems on general purpose computing systems, including parallel machines designed to handle a variety of applications. However, there are times when an information retrieval system implemented using general purpose hardware may not be cost-effective or provide adequate performance. For example, to achieve satisfactory performance most information retrieval systems use some form of index. However, for a database consisting of messages that must be available as soon as they are received, there is no time available to construct, update, and maintain an index. Instead, special purpose searhcing hardware can provide the desired solution.

Special purpose hardware development for information retrieval has generally fallen into two areas—systems for rapidly searching unstructured data and systems for manipulating surrogates or indices for the information in the database. While most special purpose systems have been implemented using conventional digital logic, recently the use of optical processing has been suggested. The availability of fast microprocessors may also lead to special purpose systems that resemble a conventional workstation, but have additional logic to enhance their processing of information, more efficient connection and use of peripheral devices such as disk drives, or operating system software optimized for the particular application.

17.1.1 Search Patterns

The design of a special purpose processor is heavily influenced by the types of operations that will be performed. In the case of text searching, these are the patterns and operators that are allowed when specifying a query. The most basic operation is performing an exact match search for a specified string of characters, which may represent either a single word or phrase. Proper handling of phrases may be more complex than simply searching for the words of the phrase each separated by a blank. Unless the text in the database has been carefully edited so that it fits a standard form, the words of the desired phrase may not be separated only by a single blank, but could be separated by a newline sequence (if the phrase started on one line and ended on another), more than one blank or some other space character (like a horizontal tab), typographic markup (such as changing from roman to italic type), a footnote reference, or other complications. Most special purpose text searchers can only handle the most basic phrase structures.

In addition to exactly matching a string of characters, it is often desirable to specify a more complex match pattern. A regular expression can specify not only a specific character to match at a pattern location, but can indicate a set of characters (such as an upper- or lowercase A, any vowel, the start of a line, or a word delimiter). It also can indicate that a pattern element can optionally occur or can occur more than once, or indicate two or more alternative patterns that are acceptable in a location.

While regular expressions could be used to specify the search pattern, often an information retrieval system will allow only a specific set of operations based on the nature of searching text. The most common of these operations is the *don't care* or *wildcard,* which specifies that any character is acceptable in a particular location in the search pattern (single-character or fixed-length don't care, FLDC) or an arbitrary number of characters are acceptable at the location (variable-length don't care, VLDC). The VLDC can either come at the start of a word (an initial VLDC, matching a pattern with any prefix), end of a word (a terminal VLDC, matching a pattern with any suffix), at both the start or end of a word (matching a specified stem), embedded within a word (an embedded VLDC), or any combination of these. Some text searchers cannot handle VLDCs, or can handle only initial or terminal VLDCs.

One other special pattern may specify that a numeric string should occur at the pattern location, and its value should be within a given range. Another pattern may specify an error tolerance, where the pattern is matched if there are fewer than n

characters that don't match. These options are not commonly available on hardware-based text searchers (Yu et al. 1986).

Search expression often contain two or more patterns combined with Boolean operators, the most common being *and, or*, and *and not*. Word proximity, an extended form of *and*, indicates that two search terms need to be located within a specified number of words in the database for a match to occur. Proximity can be either *directed* (X must be followed within *n* words by Y) or *undirected* (R and S must be within *n* words of each other, but in any order). Like phrases, word proximity is complicated by markup or other information embedded in the text.

A search expression also can specify that a term, phrase, or Boolean combination must occur in particular contexts for a match to occur. For example, a search may look for "hardware and text retrieval in abstract" or "patent and software within 2 sentences." Other operators may expand the number of terms in a query. A macro facility allows the user to include a predefined subexpression into a query, while a thesaurus can automatically form the or of all synonyms of a word. For example, "airplane" might expand to "airplane or plane or 747 or DC-10 . . . ."

17.1.2 Hardware Implementations

Many people have proposed implementations of information retrieval functions using custom hardware. Many of these consider only one aspect of information retrieval, without considering its effect on the overall retrieval system and its performance. Simple searchers, capable of exact matching against a small number of patterns (possibly containing don't cares) have been particularly popular as a VLSI design project. However, only a small number of these have been incorporated into complete information retrieval systems.

The algorithms implemented in hardware differ from the algorithms described in the previous chapters in two fundamental ways. They are much simpler but do many things in parallel or inherently in the logic. The reason for the simplicity is that each alternative in an algorithm often requires its own logic or increases the complexity of the other hardware. This not only complicates the design, but can result in slower performance because of longer data paths and increased loading of output drivers. It is also easier to design a simple function that is then replicated many times than a large single unit incorporating a variety of functions.

Many operations that would be cumbersome on a conventional processor are very simple to perform in custom hardware. As an example, the program to reverse the order of the bits of a word takes a number of steps of isolating, aligning, and replacing each bit of the word. In hardware, it simply takes the changing of the connections from straight-through to reversed. No active logic is required and the operation is done in zero time. If operations do not have to share hardware, they can be done simultaneously (for example, the shift-and-add being done in parallel with the decrementing of a counter during a multiplication). Because of this, most hardware solutions are not simply faster implementations of standard information retrieval algorithms.

17.2 TEXT SEARCHERS

The most commonly proposed special purpose hardware system for text information retrieval is a searcher. The rationale for needing a special search engine is that a conventional processor cannot search rapidly enough to give reasonable response time. For example, egrep on a 12 MIPS RISC processor (Sun SPARCstation-1) can search at about 250 KBytes per second. The searching of a 10 GByte database would take 40,000 seconds (over 11 hours). If a large database resides on a number of disk drives, it will be faster and more efficient not to bring the raw information from the disk into a central processor, but instead search it with a processor closer to the disk. Because each search processor is operating only on the data on its disk, the search time will remain the same as the database size increases and the additional disks (each with a searcher) necessary to hold the database increases the parallelism of the search.

However, because of the slow searching speeds for a central processor, most commercial information retrieval systems use some sort of inverted file index rather than actually searching the documents. The argument in the past against inverted files was that they substantially increase the storage requirements of a database. The index may take more disks than the database itself (Bird et al. 1978), but this may be less of a concern with lower-cost disk drives. This means that to be competitive, the cost of searching must be comparable to the cost of a disk drive.

However, there are a number of problems associated with inverted files or other document surrogates besides their storage requirements. In many cases, information is discarded to reduce the size of the surrogate. For inverted files, commonly occurring words are generally not included in the index. This means that a search for a phrase like "changing of the guard" really finds anything that has "changing," any two words, and "guard." The phrase "To be or not to be, that is the question" matches any document containing the word "question," since all other words in the phrase are discarded. A similar problem exists for superimposed code words, where the combining of the codes for two words makes it seem like another word is present when it is not.

These artifacts caused by the use of a surrogate tend to confuse a user because it is not clear why a document that doesn't match the query was retrieved. Time is spent trying to understand an irrelevant document, perhaps more time than would be spent reviewing a relevant one. But even if this were not the case, there are other problems associated with the use of a surrogate for locating documents. Time must be spent building and maintaining the surrogate, a nontrivial amount of time for very large databases. Also, a document is not retrievable until it has been entered into the surrogate data structure. This may not be acceptable for a message retrieval system, where incoming documents must be available as soon as they have arrived.

17.2.1 Searcher Structure

Most proposed text searchers divide the work into three activities: search control, term matching, and query resolution. Search control includes taking a request from the processor running the retrieval system, configuring the search hardware (typically by loading appropriate tables and registers), managing the reading of the data from the disks, and reporting back the results to the retrieval system. This search control is best performed by a conventional microprocessor (or, in the past, a minicomputer).

Searching for particular terms or patterns is performed by the special hardware, with the results passed to a query resolver that handles operations such as Booleans, contexts, and proximities. This considerably simplifies the search patterns. A good example of this is a query that specifies that five different terms must occur in the same paragraph, in any order. The regular expression for handling this is very complex, consisting of looking for the start of paragraph pattern, then all possible orderings of the five terms (120 sequences), then the end of the paragraph pattern. A better way is for the term matcher to look for the individual terms of the pattern. The query resolver then combines the term matcher results, which indicate that particular terms have been detected to determine if the pattern has been matched. Because this latter processing is required only when a term has been found, its realtime requirements are considerably less than that of comparing characters from the disk, and it can be handled by a conventional processor.

In effect, the term matcher converts a document into a list of entries that are a shorthand description of the document as it pertains to the query. The query resolution program can then process this greatly reduced information according to whatever scheme is desired. This could be a Boolean query language enhanced with contexts and word location proximity, weighted term document scoring, or any other technique.

Three different techniques have been proposed for implementing the term matcher: associative memories, finite state machines, and cellular arrays (Hollaar 1979). As their performance improves, standard microprocessors, perhaps augmented with simple hardware assists, can also be used for the term matcher.

If commodity disk drives are used to keep costs low, rather than special drives like those with parallel reads, the disk transfer and seek rates will determine the speed of the searcher. There are two possible options: match the term comparator to the nominal transfer rate of the disk (raw read bit rate), or match it to the effective transfer rate (average bit rate when seeks and rotational latency are considered). In either case, the same performance will result, since it is based on how many characters come from the disk in a unit of time. Matching to the effective transfer rate permits a lower comparator speed at the expense of buffer memory. How much lower depends on the seek characteristics for the typical or worst-case queries. Matching to the nominal transfer rate was used for many searcher implementations, because of the high cost of memory for buffers at the time they were proposed.

Associative Memories

In an associative memory, each memory word has a comparator. The bit pattern in the comparand register is sent to each of these comparators, which indicate whether it matches their memory word. The comparison can be done in one cycle regardless of the size of the memory, but the cost per bit is considerably higher than for conventional memory because of the logic required. (A dynamic RAM memory cell may need only a single transistor, while an associative memory cell has tens or hundreds of transistors, depending on whether features such as masking to selectively compare bits in a word are implemented.)

If the cost were ignored, an associative memory would seem ideal for finding the locations of a pattern within a database. It is not. First of all, the data must be broken down into fixed-length groups to match the width of the associative memory. This could be done on word delimiters, in which case the width of the associative memory would have to be the length of the longest word and much space would be wasted, or it would have to be every n characters, packing the associative memory. In the latter case, however, words start in arbitrary positions within the width of the associative memory and will not always line up with the pattern. This can be solved by cycling the pattern through the width of the associative memory, but this is complicated by words that start in one memory location and end in another. Handling of VLDCs, especially embedded ones, is also difficult.

A more cost-effective approach is to store the search terms in the associative memory and shift the data through the comparand register. Essentially, this uses the associative memory as a set of comparators, each programmed with one of the search terms. This approach works well for fully specified terms, ones with fixed-length don't cares, or for initial or terminal VLDCs. Embedded VLDCs cannot be easily handled.

Besides the obvious parallel-comparator implementation for an associative memory, two schemes based on hardware hashing of the comparand have been suggested. Bird et al. (1979) proposed a hashing based on the length of the comparand word and its initial characters, while Burkowski (1982) used a small mapping RAM based on subsets of the search terms selected so that each has a unique bit pattern. While these approaches substantially reduce the cost of implementing the associative memory, they both suffer from the inability to handle embedded VLDCs or classes of chracters (any delimiter, a number, any letter) in a pattern.

Finite State Machines

Finite state automata are capable of recognizing any regular expression. An FSA can be described as a 5-tuple $\{A, S, M, B, F\}$ where A is the input alphabet, S is a set of elements called states, M is a mapping from AxS into S, B is a member of S called the beginning state, and F is a nonempty subset of S called the final states. The operation of the FSA is simple. At the start, it is in state B. Whenever a character arrives, the mapping M is used to determine the next state of the FSA. This process continues until a final state is reached, indicating the term that has been matched. Implementation is equally simple. A memory holds the mapping function M as an array of states. Each state contains an array with one entry for each character in the input alphabet, indicating the next state. A register holds the memory base address for the current state, and is concatenated with the input character to give the memory address to read to find the next state, which is then loaded into the register.

There is a problem with the straightforward FSA implementation—the size of memory required for the mapping function. For a query with 250 terms (as might occur when a thesaurus is used), about 2000 states would be necessary. For seven-bit input characters, this would require over 3 million bits of memory. Although that does not seem high today, 15 years ago that was the same order of magnitude for the memory found on a mainframe computer, and would cost hundreds of thousands of dollars.

Two ways of reducing the memory requirements of the FSA, at the expense of additional logic, have been proposed. Bird observed that there are two different state transition types in the mapping memory: sequential and index (Mayper et al. 1980). Sequential states are used for matching single characters, and are stored sequentially in memory. Matching the character causes the state register to be advanced by one and a mismatch causes it to go to a specified failure address. For a seven-bit input character, only eight bits are necessary for each sequential state—seven for the match character and one to indicate it is a sequential state.

In those places where there is more than one character of interest, the index state is used. It consists of a code indicating it is an index state and a bit vector indicating the interesting characters in the mapping. A seven-bit input character requires a 128-bit vector. When an index state is processed, the first action is to determine whether the bit corresponding to the input character is set. If not, a transition is made to a default state. If the bit is set, the number of bits set for characters with a lower value is determined and used as an index added to the current state address to give the location of a word that contains the address of the next state. Since there are far more sequential states than index states, the bit requirements are reduced. Extrapolating from the figures in Haskin et al. (1983), approximately 250 Kbits would be necessary for the 250-term query.

There are a number of difficulties with the Bird approach. The first is the dramatic size difference between the sequential and index states (8 bits vs. over 128 bits). This is mitigated by having more than one sequential state in each memory word, although some parts of the word might end up unused, and by operating on nibbles (half bytes) rather than the full character for index states. This reduces the vector to 16 bits and simplifies the hardware necessary to compute the index, at the expense of two index operations per character and a more complex state table.

Another difficulty is that when any search term has an initial VLDC, all states must be index states, substantially increasing the memory requirements. To solve this problem, Bird suggested having two matchers, one for terms that don't have initial VLDCs and a smaller one for those that have them. He also suggested a third FSA to handle phrases, rather than as part of the query resolver.

The other way of reducing the FSA memory requirements was proposed by Haskin (1980) (further described in Haskin et al. [1983] and Hollaar et al. [1984]). It consists of dividing the FSA state table into a number of partitions that can then be processed in parallel. The partitions are made so that each state must check only a single character, like the Bird sequential state, to determine whether to go to a specified address or a mismatch state. If there is more than one character that could occur simultaneously, each must be in a different partition. This can be easily determined by an examination of all the terms when the state tables are being constructed. A successful match not only specifies the next state in a partition, but can force another partition into a specified state.

For example, if the terms DOG and DOT were specified, the first state would look for a D and transition to state 2 when it is found. That state would look for an O. However, since the next state needs to look for both a G and a T, a successful match of the O would cause a transition to state 3, which would look for a G, and would force another partition into a state looking for a T. This fork operation consists of forcing the address of a neighbor matcher, since the partitioning technique assures that the neighbor is in an idle state.

A state can be programmed for an exact match, a match ignoring the bit that differentiates between upper- and lowercase characters, or a match if the input character is of a particular class (numeric, alphabetic, delimiter). A startup mechanism is used to simplify the partitioning of the state table, and to reduce the matcher requirements eliminating starts that would terminate after the initial character of the word. All forms of fixed- and variable-length don't cares can be handled. For the set of 250 terms, approximately 20 character matchers of less than 5 Kbits each are necessary, for a total memory requirement of under 100 Kbits, less than half the bits of the Bird FSA and a thirtieth of the conventional FSA requirements. Moreover, the matchers are cycled only once for each input character, allowing the use of slower memories than would be possible with the Bird FSA.

Cellular Arrays

A cellular array uses a large number of very simple matchers connected in a string or as a more complex structure (Hollaar 1979). In its most basic form, the cell is programmed with a single match character. The cell has an input enable line and an output match line, as well as an input that is connected to a bus containing the current input character. Whenever the enable line is true, the cell compares the character on the bus to its match character, and if they are equal, sets its output match line true. FLDCs can be handled by a dummy cell that repeats its enable line delayed by one character time, and VLDCs by a cell that sets its match output whenever its enable line is set and clears it when a word delimiter is found (assuming that VLDCs should not extend across a word). The cells can also be extended to handle matching of classes of characters, like delimiters. Of course, any addition to a cell beyond an exact character match complicates its design and means fewer cells can be placed on an integrated circuit.

One of the first cellular matchers was General Electric's GESCAN, developed in the mid-1960s (Crew et al. 1967). It was capable of searching data stored on special magnetic tape drives at 120,000 characters per second, based on a query programmed into 80 cells. Copeland (1978) proposed a similar cellular system as an extension to a database machine; it was capable of handling a single bounded-length pattern string. Mukhopadhyay (1979) proposed a complex cell and a variety of ways to interconnect the cells to handle regular expressions and much of the pattern matching capabilities of SNOBOL4. However, the number of gates needed for a general interconnection network for n cells is $O(n^2)$, so for a reasonable number of cells the cost of the interconnections will exceed the cost of the cells. Lee (1985) (also Lee and Lochovsky [1990]) proposed a cellular system as part of a larger hardware-implemented information retrieval system that placed blocks of the data into the cellular array and broadcast programming instructions based on the search pattern to all the cells. Foster and Kung (1980) proposed a systolic pattern matcher, where both the pattern and the data being searched are moved through the cellular array. This eliminates the need to broadcast the data to every cell, eliminating a heavily loaded data bus.

Cellular arrays are used in two currently marketed search machines. A spin-off of General Electric, GESCAN International, has developed a new implementation of GESCAN that can be attached to a minicomputer or workstation. Rather than use a special tape drive, data is read from the host disk system and transferred to the search logic. The host also acts as the query resolver. Each integrated circuit contains 16 cells, and can operate at 5 MBytes per second. The Fast Data Finder from TRW (Yu et al. 1986) uses a cell that can perform not only single character comparisons, but also includes support for ignoring misspellings and numeric comparisons. Each integrated circuit holds 8 cells, and up to 9,216 cells can be included in a system. It can search at 12.5 MBytes per second, although the disk storing the data often limits its speed.

Standard Microprocessors

It was clear a decade ago that available microprocessors could not keep up with the disk for a multiterm match, but the latest RISC-based processors are substantially faster than mainframe computers were only a few years ago, at a fraction of the cost. While their performance depends on the particular algorithm used for searching, looking at the inner loop for the various grep programs, egrep appears to have the tightest loop for complex multiterm searches. On a Sun SPARC, an optimized version takes 10 instructions and 13 cycles. This means that the inner loop searching rate for a 25 MHz SPARCstation-1 is about 1.92 MBytes per second, approximately the nominal disk rate of 1.875 MBytes per second for a 15 MHz drive. A 40 MHz SPARC will run at over 3 MBytes per second.

But even as microprocessors become faster, they still may not be a good choice for handling the basic term matching operation. To achieve a high MIPS rate, the program for the microprocessor must be stored in a high-speed memory. For a

25 MHz machine, it must have a cycle time of less than 40 ns. This means the use of a cache memory to achieve better performance than would be available with dynamic RAM, increasing the cost and complexity of the microprocessor system.

If we look at the inner loop for egrep, we find that it implements a finite state recognizer, using two arrays. The first one is indexed by the current state and the input character and gives the next state. The second indicates whether a match has been found. For a system handling 250 terms, to accommodate large searches generated by a thesaurus, about 2,000 states would be necessary. An FSA for handling 2,000 states and 7-bit characters would take 12 256K RAMs and an 11-bit holding register, costing well under $50.

Of course, it is not necessary for the line between the microprocessor and the special search hardware to be drawn between term matching and query resolution as an alternative to performing the entire search in the microprocessor. Hardware augmentation can be used to improve the search performance of the microprocessor. For example, a simple startup mechanism such as was used in the PFSA could be used to initially examine the input characters, with the processor only having to work when the start of a possible match has been found (Hollaar 1991). As microprocessor cost performance continues to improve, they will play a larger role in the implementation of special purpose text searchers. These systems will differ from general purpose systems using the same microprocessor by having low-overhead control programs rather than general operating systems like UNIX, simplified interfaces connecting their peripheral devices, file systems optimized for text searching, and some custom logic to assist in the matching process.

17.2.2 Search Performance

Text searchers were proposed as a means of improving the response time over a conventional computer doing the search, without the problems associated with using a surrogate such as an inverted file. Using a special purpose searcher that operates at disk speed, the time necessary to complete a user's query is the time it takes to read all the data from a disk drive. While this obviously varies with the type of disk, for most low-cost, high-capacity disks it is about five minutes. This is far too long for an interactive system, and complicates the search control by requiring that a number of different user queries must be combined in a batch to give reasonable performance.

One solution to this problem is to make the search go faster by using higher performance disks, but this substantially increases the system cost because of the low production volumes and resulting higher costs for such disks. Furthermore, the speedup is on the order of 10, while a factor of 100 or more is desirable for an interactive system.

A more reasonable solution is to combine the attributes of searching and using a surrogate to overcome the difficulties with each approach. An inexact surrogate can be used to eliminate documents that have no hope of matching a query. Superimposed codewords will provide a list of documents that is a superset of the documents containing the search terms; if the term doesn't really occur in the document, but is an artifact of the superimposed codeword scheme, it will be eliminated by the search. A fully inverted file, where every term is indexed with its location within a document is not necessary; phrases, contexts, and word location proximities can be handled by the following search.

Rather than the 50 percent to 300 percent overhead for a fully inverted file (Bird et al. 1978), a partially inverted file could have an overhead of less that 5% (Hollaar 1991). This is because only one entry is necessary in the list of documents containing a word no matter how many times a word occurs in the document, and information regarding the location of the word within the document is not stored. The partially inverted surrogate also provides a quick feedback to the user on whether the follow-up search should even be started. It may indicate that too few documents (and possibly no documents, if a term that is not in the database is used) or too many documents would be searched, based on the user's intuition of what is in the database. The search could then be canceled and the query refined, based on information from the index.

It is not necessary to index a document before it is available. As long as the number of unindexed documents remains low relative to an average search, they can simply be added to the list of documents for every search, making them available as soon as the text is loaded.

Seek and search mode

When a surrogate is used to reduce the number of documents to be searched, the search goes from a scan to a seek and search mode. This changes the critical disk parameter from its transfer rate to its seek time relative to document transfer time. To see why this is so, consider an ESDI drive like the Maxtor XT-8760, where the seek time and rotational latency to position to the start of a document is about 20 milliseconds. It takes another 25 msec to read 35,000 characters (the size of the average U. S. Patent, for example) off two tracks, for a total of 45 msec. The effective transfer rate is about 750 KBytes per second, 40 percent of the nominal transfer rate of 1,875 KBytes per second. The effective transfer rate will be less for smaller documents, since the seek time will remain the same but the amount of data read will be less. A disk drive with the same seek characteristics, but which could read the data in zero time, would be only 2.25 times faster.

Just as parallel transfer drives are not particularly effective in a seek and search mode, optical drives with their high seek times are even more devastating to search performance. If the seek time in the small document example above were changed to a 150 ms positioning time (typical of today's optical disks), the effective transfer rate is only 148 KBytes per second, less than 8 percent of the nominal transfer rate.

Substantial improvements can be made by using an appropriate file system. A randomly organized file system, where blocks are placed in any convenient free location on the disk and a pointer (either in the previous block or in a master block) is used to locate the next data block(such as used in most file systems) is convenient for a time sharing system, where files come and go. However, using our example ESDI disk drive, if we have to do an average seek before reading a 512 byte block, we will have an effective transfer rate of under 50 KBytes per second. The use of a large block size improves this, at the expense of higher unusable disk capacity due to internal fragmentation.

The use of a contiguous file system, where each document is stored in consecutive disk blocks, substantially improves disk performance. In one disk revolution after positioning, almost 50 blocks can be read, rather than just one. Since the documents are seldom removed (or expanded) after they are loaded into a archival text database, the problems of file reorganization and lost disk space are minimal.

17.3 SURROGATE PROCESSORS

While text searching has been the most commonly proposed information retrieval operating to be implemented using special purpose hardware, a number of people have examined manipulating document surrogates using custom processors. These have included processors for the merging of the sorted lists of documents in an inverted file index and for searching the document signatures to find specified patterns.

17.3.1 List Merging

The index for an inverted file contains pointers to items within the database. These pointers are generally stored in sorted order to ease their combining to determine those documents that match a particular query. The basic merging operation produces a list of pointers that is the union (for an OR operation), intersection (for an AND), or Boolean difference (for an AND NOT). While this is a simple operation to program on a general purpose computer, the overhead associated with aligning data, processing auxiliary fields, and flow of control such as loop counters mean that the mainframe computers of the 1970s were saturated keeping up with disk reads.

Stellhorn (1977) proposed a system that took blocks of the sorted lists and merged them in a block-parallel, bit-serial fashion. Logic following the merge operation removed either duplicate (for an OR) or duplicate and single entries (for an AND). Hollaar (1978) developed a system based on a simple merge element (both serial and parallel versions were designed) connected by a network or arranged as a binary tree, which was programmed to match the merge operation specified by the query. Both of these systems were 10 to 100 times faster than a conventional computer of the time. However, as processors have become less expensive and much faster, special purpose hardware for list merging is does not seem cost-effective today.

17.3.2 Signature Processors

A signature file, as discussed in a previous chapter, provides an alternative to storing a list of document pointers for each word in the database. A signature is developed for each document that attempts to capture the contents of the document. These signatures, which are considerably smaller than the actual documents, are then searched for potential matches. These matches can be directly presented to the user, or can be searched to eliminate false matches caused by information dropped when the signatures were created.

The most common signature is based on superimposed codewords. Keywords or word stems are selected from the document and hashed to produce an n-bit vector that has m bits set. These vectors are then ORed together to form the signature. Determining whether a document contains a particular word simply requires checking to see if the bits corresponding to the hash of that word are set in the signature. Note that superimposed codewords do not readily allow don't cares or context and proximity operations, and may produce "false drops" when the bit vectors representing two words are ORed, and the result has all the bits of another word, not present in the document, set.

Ahuja and Roberts (1980) proposed storing the superimposed codeword signatures in an associative memory. To reduce the cost, rather than have comparators for every bit in the associative memory, they divided the signatures into blocks and stored each block in a memory module. During the associative search, a codeword is read from the memory, compared against the desired pattern, whether there was a match is saved, and the next codeword from the memory is examined. This word-serial, bit-parallel approach reduces the hardware requirements to one comparator (for as many bits as are in the codeword) per memory module, plus the associated control logic.

Lee (1985) (also Lee and Lochovsky [1990]) observed that it is not necessary to check every bit position of the signatures, but only those that are set in the hash of the word of interest. Since the number of bits set in a hash is small compared to the number of bits in the codeword, this can substantially improve the search performance. Since the same bits in each codeword are being skipped, a word-parallel, bit-serial architecture is best.

17.4 OPTICAL PROCESSORS

The previously discussed special purpose systems were all based on conventional digital electronics. Spurred by work on laser-based compact disk technology and the use of fiber optics for high-speed data transmission, there has been renewed interest in employing optically based approaches in information retrieval. This has included improving the bandwidth of optical mass storage and optical searching of information.

17.4.1 Improved Optical Storage

As we previously mentioned, most optical storage systems now in use do not have either the data rate or access speed of magnetic disk memories. This is particularly true for compact disks, which were originally designed to handle the relatively low data rates needed for reproducing audio information. However, there are ways of substantially increasing the data rates of optical disks beyond the standard techniques of increasing the bit density or rotational speed of the disk.

It is difficult to build a magnetic read head that can read data from many adjacent, closely spaced tracks at the same time. However, it is possible to have a laser beam that illuminates many adjacent tracks, with the information from each track falling on a different position of a photodetector array. This allows a byte or word of data to be read out with only minimal problems of alignment or skewed data. In the case of a parallel-head magnetic drive, the relative timing of the bits of the word depends on the mechanical alignment of the different heads, which can change with temperature or movement during seeks.

Even more interesting is the use of a holographic memory, rather than a rotating optical disk. This offers the potential of not only improved data rates, but also better storage densities and access times. Berra et al. (1989) discusses a page hologram memory capable of holding 725 MBytes on a 6-inch square card, and volume holograms capable of holding up to 10^{12} bits. Since access to information in the holographic memory does not require moving a read head assembly and waiting for a disk to rotate to the start of the data, access times are reduced and rotational latency is eliminated. Instead, the laser beam can be deflected to the proper position in under 100 msec and all the information on the page will be immediately available.

17.4.2 Optical Data Processing

Although it is possible to convert the optical signals from a laser disk or holographic memory to electrical signals and process them using conventional digital electronics, one also can use optical means for comparing the information against a pattern without the need for conversion. Berra et al. (1989) discuss a number of these techniques, and present an optical full text search design (Mitkas et al. 1989).

Optical comparisons are performed by using an exclusive-OR operation on dual rail logic (both true and complement of each bit is available). A 1 bit is stored as a TF pattern, and a 0 bit as FT. A spatial light modulator (SLM), which is a one- or two-dimensional array that can alter some parameter of the optical signals passing through the array, such as intensity or phase, is placed in the light path. In its simplest form, the SLM is programmed to form a mask in which individual bits are either passed (P) or blocked (X). XP is used for comparing against a 1, PX for comparing against a 0, and XX can be used for a don't care in a particular bit position. If all pattern bits match the data bits, no light will be passed. It only takes a lens and a single detector to determine if there is a match.

For example, if the pattern is 10d1, where d is a don't care, the mask will be XPPXXXXP. For data of 1011 (dual rail form of TFFTTFTF) or 1001 (TFFTFTTF), no light will be passed, while for data 0011 (FTFTTFTF), the resulting light pattern will be FTFFFFFF, so light is passed and a mismatch is indicated.

The optical text search machine contains a page composer, which generates optical patterns to be fed to the optical comparator. Its main element is a fast optical scanner that converts the sequential (and possibly byte-parallel) input from the optical disk to two-dimensional patterns consisting of shifting sequences of the bytes of text. The optical comparator masks these patterns with an array programmed with all the search terms. Photodetectors sense whether no light passes, indicating a match of a particular term. It is possible to do 100,000 parallel comparisons using an SLM in a single step. Other optical techniques can be employed to allow the multiple input streams to be handled through the same SLM, further increasing its performance.

17.5 SUMMARY

A number of special-purpose hardware systems have been proposed to provide most cost-effective or faster performance for information retrieval systems. Most of these have been text scanners, and several of these have been used in special applications.

While high-speed microprocessors and general purpose parallel machines can now provide much of the performance that previously required special purpose logic (such as for index merging), it still appears that hardware augmentation to those processors can improve the performance of a large system at a small cost. Special purpose hardware for information retrieval will continue to be an interesting research and development area.

REFERENCES

AHUJA, S. R., & C. S. ROBERTS. 1980, "An Associative/Parallel Processor for Partial Match Retrieval Using Superimposed Codes." *Proceedings of the 7th Annual Symposium on Computer Architecture,* May 6–8, 1980 (published as *SIGARCH Newsletter,* vol. 8, no. 3) pp. 218–27.

BERRA, P. B., A. GHAFOOR, P. A. MITKAS, S. J. MARCINKOWSKI, & M. GUIZANI. 1989. *IEEE Transactions on Knowledge and Data Engineering,* (1), 111–32.

BIRD, R. M., J. B. NEWSBAUM, & J. L. TREFFTZS. 1978, "Text File Inversion: An Evaluation." *Fourth Workshop on Computer Architecture for Non-Numeric Processing,* Syracuse University, August 1978 (published as SIGIR vol. 13, no. 2; SIGARCH vol. 7, no. 2; and SIGMOD vol. 10, no. 1), pp. 42–50.

BIRD, R. M., & J. C. TU. 1979, "Associative Crosspoint Processor System." U. S. Patent 4,152, 762, May 1, 1979.

BURKOWSKI, F. J. 1982, "A Hardware Hashing Scheme in the Design of a Multiterm String Comparator." *IEEE Transactions on Computers,* C-31, (9), 825–34.

COPELAND, G. P. 1978, "String Storage and Searching for Data Base Applications: Implementation of the INDY Backend Kernel." *Fourth Workshop on Computer Architecture for Non-Numeric Processing,* Syracuse University, August 1978 (published as SIGIR vol. 13, no. 2; SIGARCH vol 7, no. 2; and SIGMOD vol. 10, no. 1), pp. 8–17.

CREW, B. L., & M. N. GUNZBURG. 1967, "Information Storage and Retrieval System." U. S. Patent 3,358,270, December 12, 1967.

FOSTER, M. J., & H. T. KUNG. 1980. "Design of Special-Purpose VLSI Chips: Examples and Opinions." *Proceedings of the 7th Annual Symposium on Computer Architecture,* May 6–8, 1980 (published as SIGARCH Newsletter, vol. 8, no. 3) pp. 300–07.

HASKIN, R. L. 1980. "Hardware for Searching Very Large Text Databases." Ph.D. Thesis, University of Illinois at Urbana-Champaign, August.

HASKIN, R. L., & L. A. HOLLAAR. 1983, "Operational Characteristics of a Hardware-based Pattern Matcher." *ACM Transactions on Database Systems,* 8(1).

HOLLAAR, L. A. 1978. "Specialized Merge Processor Networks for Combining Sorted Lists." *ACM Transactions on Database Systems,* 3(3), 272–84.

HOLLAAR, L. A. 1979. "Text Retrieval Computers." *Computer,* 12(3), 40–52.

HOLLAAR, L. A., & R. L. HASKIN. 1984, "Method and System for Matching Encoded Characters." U. S. Patent 4,450,520, May 22, 1984.

HOLLAAR, L. A. 1991. "Special-Purpose Hardware For Text Searching: Past Experience, Future Potential." *Information Processing & Management,* Vol. 27, No. 4, pp. 371–78.

LEE, D. L. 1985. "The Design and Evaluation of a Text-Retrieval Machine for Large Databases." Ph.D. Thesis, University of Toronto, September.

LEE, D. L., & F. H. Lochovsky. 1990, "HYTREM—A Hybrid Text-Retrieval Machine for Large Databases." *IEEE Transactions on Computers,* 39(1), 111–23.

MAYPER, V. Jr., A. L. NAGY, R. M. BIRD, J. C. TU, & L. S. MICHAELS. 1980. "Finite State Automaton with Multiple State Types." U. S. Patent 4,241,402, December 23, 1980.

MITKAS, P. A., P. B. BERRA, & P. S. GUILFOYLE. 1989, "An Optical System for Full Text Search." *Proceedings of SIGIR 89.*

MUKHOPADHYAY, A. 1979, "Hardware Algorithms for Nonnumeric Computation." *IEEE Transactions on Computers,* C-28(6), 384–89.

ROBERTS, D. C. 1978. "A Specialized Computer Architecture for Text Retrieval." *Fourth Workshop on Computer Architecture for Non-Numeric Processing,* Syracuse University, August 1978 (published as SIGIR vol. 13, no. 2; SIGARCH vol. 7, no. 2; and SIGMOD vol. 10, no. 1), pp. 51–59.

STELLHORN, W. H. 1977. "An Inverted File Processor for Information Retrieval." *IEEE Transactions on Computers,* C-26(12), 1258–67.

YU, K.-I, S.-P. HSU, R. E. HEISS, Jr., & L. Z. HASIUK. 1986. "Pipelined for Speed: The Fast Data Finder System." *Quest, Technology at TRW,* 9(2), Winter 1986/1987, 4–19.

18

Parallel Information Retrieval Algorithms

Craig Stanfill

Thinking Machines Corporation
245 First Street
Cambridge, Massachusetts

Abstract

Data Parallel computers, such as the Connection Machine CM-2, can provide interactive access to text databases containing tens, hundreds, or even thousands of Gigabytes of data. This chapter starts by presenting a brief overview of data parallel computing, a performance model of the CM-2, and a model of the workload involved in searching text databases. The remainder of the chapter discusses various algorithms used in information retrieval and gives performance estimates based on the data and processing models just presented. First, three algorithms are introduced for determining the N highest scores in a list of M scored documents. Next, the parallel signature file representation is described. Two document scoring algorithms are fully described; a sketch of a boolean query algorithm are also presented. The discussion of signatures concludes with consideration of false hit rates, data compression, secondary/tertiary storage, and the circumstances under which signatures should be considered. The final major section discusses inverted file methods. Two methods, parallel inverted files and partitioned posting files, are considered in detail. Finally, issues relating to secondary storage are briefly considered.

18.1 INTRODUCTION

The time required to search a text database is, in the limit, proportional to the size of the database. It stands to reason, then, that as databases grow they will eventually become so large that interactive response is no longer possible using conventional (serial) machines. At this point, we must either accept longer response times or employ a faster form of computer. Parallel computers are attractive in this respect: parallel machines exist which are up to four orders of magnitude faster than typical serial machines. In this chapter we will examine the data structure and algorithmic issues involved in harnessing this power.

In this chapter we are concerned with vector-model document ranking systems. In such systems, both documents and queries are modeled as vectors. At a superficial level, retrieval consists of (1) computing the dot-product of the query vector with every document vector; and (2) determining which documents have the highest scores. In practice, of course, both document and query vectors are extremely sparse; coping with this sparseness lies at the heart of the design of practical scoring algorithms.

The organization of the chapter is as follows. First, we will describe the notation used to describe parallel algorithms, and present a timing model for one parallel computer, the Connection Machine® System model CM-2™.[1] Second, we will define a model of the retrieval task that will allow us to derive performance estimates. Third, we will look at algorithms for ranking documents once they have been scored.[2] Fourth, we will consider one database representation, called *parallel signature files,* which represents the database as a set of signatures. Fifth, we will consider two different file structures based on inverted indexes. Sixth, we will briefly look at issues relating to secondary storage and I/O. Finally, we will summarize the results and delineate areas for continued research.

18.2 DATA PARALLEL COMPUTING

The algorithms presented in this chapter utilize the *data parallel* computing model proposed by Hillis and Steele (1986). In this model, there is a single program that controls a large number of processing elements, each of which will be performing the same operation at any moment. Parallelism is expressed by the creation of parallel data structures and the invocation of parallel operators. The model is made manifest in *data parallel programming languages,* such as the C* language developed by Thinking Machines Corporation (1990). The body of this section presents some basic data structures, operators, and notations which will be required to understand the algorithms presented in the remainder of the chapter. The section will conclude with a concise performance model for one implementation of the data parallel model (the Connection Machine model CM-2). More details on the architecture of this machine are provided by Hillis (1985) and Thinking Machines Corporation (1987).

Data types are implicit in the algorithmic notation presented below. In general, scalar variables are lowercase, for example, i. Scalar constants are all uppercase, for example, N_PROCS. Parallel integer-valued variables are prefixed with P_, e.g. P_x. Parallel Boolean-valued variables are prefixed with B_. Other aspects of data type, such as underlying structure and array declarations, will be left implicit and may be deduced by reading the accompanying text.

18.2.1 Shapes and Local Computation

C* includes all the usual C data structures and operations. These are called *scalar variables* and *scalar operations.*

A *shape* may be thought of as an array of processors. Each element of a shape is referred to as a *position.* A *parallel variable* is defined by a base type and a shape. It can be thought of as a vector having one element per position in the shape. A parallel variable can store one value at each of its positions. For example, if P is defined in a shape with 8 positions, it will have storage for 8 different values. When we display the contents of memory in the course of describing data structures and algorithms, variables will run from top to bottom and positions will run from left to right.

---

[1] Connection Machine® is a registered trademark of Thinking Machines Corporation. C*® is a registered trademark of Thinking Machines Corporation. CM-2™, CM™, and DataVault™ are trademarks of Thinking Machines Corporation.

[2] This topic is presented first because certain aspects of document scoring will be difficult to understand if the data arrangements convenient to document ranking have not yet been presented.

Thus, if we have two variables, P_1 and P_2, we might display them as follows:

P_1	8	6	3	4	9	1	2	0
P_2	7	14	8	29	17	34	1	9

Individual values of a parallel variable are obtained by *left indexing:* element 4 of P_1 is referenced as [4]P_1, and has a value of 9. All indexing is zero-based.

There is a globally defined parallel variable, P_position, which contains 0 in position 0, 1 in position 1, and so on.

It is also possible to have parallel arrays. For example, P_array might be a parallel variable of length 3:

P_array[0]	4	38	17	87	30	38	90	81
P_array[1]	37	3	56	39	89	10	10	38
P_array[2]	01	83	79	85	13	87	38	61

Array subscripting (*right indexing*) is done as usual; element 1 of P_array would be referred to as P_array[1], and would be a parallel integer having 8 positions. Left and right indexing may be combined, so that the 4'th position of the 0'th element of P_array would be referred to as [4]P_array[0], and have the value of 30.

Each scalar arithmetic operator (+, *, etc.) has a vector counterpart that is applied elementwise to its operands. For example, the following line of code multiplies each element of P_x by the corresponding element of P_y, then the stores the result in P_z:

```
P_z = P_x * P_y;
```

This might result in the following data store:

P_x	1	1	1	2	2	2	3	3
P_y	1	2	3	1	2	3	1	2
P_z	1	2	3	2	4	6	3	6

At any moment, a given shape has a set of *active positions*. All positions are initially active. Parallel operations, such as arithmetic and assignment, take effect only at active positions. The set of active positions may be altered by using the where statement, which is a parallel analogue to the scalar if statement. The where statement first evaluates a test. The body will then be executed with the active set restricted to those positions where the test returned nonzero results. The else clause, if present, will then be executed wherever the test returned 0. For example, the following computes the smaller of two numbers:

```
where (P_1 P_2)
    P_min = P_1;
else
    P_min = P_2;
```

18.2.2 Nonlocal Operations

Everything mentioned up to this point involves the simple extension of scalar data structures and operations to vector data structures and element-wise vector operations. We will now consider some basic operations that involve operating on data spread across multiple positions; these are collectively referred to as *nonlocal operations*.

The simplest of these operations are the *global reduction* operations. These operations compute cumulative sums, cumulative minima/maxima, and cumulative bitwise AND/ORs across all active positions in a shape. The following unary operators are used to stand for the global reduction operators:

$$+= \quad \text{Cumulative sum}$$
$$\&= \quad \text{Cumulative bitwise AND}$$
$$|= \quad \text{Cumulative bitwise OR}$$
$$>?= \quad \text{Cumulative maximum}$$
$$<?= \quad \text{Cumulative minimum}$$

Suppose, for example, we wish to compute the arithmetic mean of P_x. This may be done by computing the cumulative sum of P_x and dividing it by the number of active positions. This second quantity can be computed by finding the cumulative sum (over all active positions) of 1:

$$\text{mean} = (+= \text{ P\_x}) / (+= 1);$$

Parallel left-indexing may be used to *send* data from one position to another. In this operation, it is useful to think of each position in a shape as corresponding to a processor. When it sees an expression such as [P_i]P_y = P_x, it will send its value of P_x to position P_i, and store it in P_y. For example, one might see the following:

P_x	5	0	6	4	1	7	3	2
P_i	7	4	1	2	5	0	6	3
P_y	7	6	4	2	0	1	3	5

In the event that multiple positions are sending data to the same destination, conflicts may be resolved by arbitrarily choosing one value, by choosing the largest/smallest value, by adding the values, or by taking the bitwise AND/OR of the values. These different methods of resolving collisions are specified by using one of the following binary operatores:[3]

$$= \quad \text{Send with overwrite (arbitrary choice)}$$
$$+= \quad \text{Send with add}$$

---

[3] These are referred to as the *send-reduce* operators.

&=   Send with bitwise AND

|=   Send with bitwise OR

<?=   Send with minimum

>?=   Send with maximum

These are binary forms of the global reduce operations introduced above.

The final group of nonlocal operations to be considered here are called scan operations, and are used to compute running sums, running maxima/minima, and running bitwise AND/OR's. In it simplest form, scan_with_add will take a parallel variable and return a value which, at a given position, is the cumulative sum of all positions to its left, including itself. For example:

P_x	2	0	1	2	4	3	2	1
scan_with_add(P_x)	2	2	3	5	9	12	14	15

Optionally, a Boolean flag (called a *segment flag*) may be supplied. Wherever this flag is equal to 1, it causes the running total to be reset to 0. For example:

P_x	2	0	1	2	4	3	2	1
B_s	1	0	0	0	1	0	1	0
add_scan(P_x, B_s)	2	2	3	5	4	7	2	3

18.2.3 Performance Model

We will now consider the performance of one parallel computer, the Connection Machine model CM-2. In scalar C, the various primitive operators such as + and = have fairly uniform time requirements. On parallel computers, however, different operators may have vastly differing time requirements. For example, adding two parallel variables is a purely local operation, and is very fast. Parallel left-indexing, on the other hand, involves moving data from one processor to another, and is two orders of magnitude slower.

In addition, any realization of this model must take into account the fact that a given machine has a finite number of processing elements and, if a shape becomes large enough, several positions will map to the same physical processor. We call the ratio of the number of positions in a shape to the number of physical processors the *virtual processing ratio* (VP ratio). As the VP ratio increases, each processor must do the work of several and, as a first approximation, a linear increase in running time will be observed.

The following symbols will be used:

N_{procs} The number of physical processors

τ The VP ratio

We express the time required for each operator by an equation of the form $c_1 + c_2r$. For example, if an operator takes time $2 + 10r$, then it will take 12 microseconds at a VP ratio of 1, 22 microseconds at a VP ratio of 2, and so forth. For convenience, we will also include the time required for an operator at a VP ratio of 1. On the CM-2, the time required for scalar operations is generally insignificant and will be ignored.

To arrive at a time estimate for an algorithm, we first create an algorithm skeleton in which all purely scalar operations except for looping are eliminated, and all identifiers are replaced with P for parallel integers, B for parallel Booleans, and S for scalars. Loop constructs will be replaced by a simple notation of the form loop(count). All return statements will be deleted. Assignment statements which might reasonably be eliminated by a compiler will be suppressed. Finally, because the cost of scalar right-indexing is zero, all instances of P[S] will be replaced with P. From this skeleton, the number of times each parallel operator is called may be determined. The time requirements are then looked up in a table provided at the end of this section, and an estimate constructed.

For example, suppose we have a parallel array of length N and wish to find the sum of its elements across all positions. The algorithm for this is as follows:

```
sum_array(P_array)
  {
  P_result = 0;
  for (i = 0; i< N; i++)
     P_result += P_array;
  return (+= P_result);
  }
```

This has the skeleton:

```
P = S
loop(N)
    P += P
(+= P)
```

It requires time:

Operation	Calls	Time per Call
P = S	1	$3 + 15r$
P += P	n	$3 + 28r$
(+= P)	1	$137 + 70r$
Total		$(140 + 3n) + (85 + 28n)r$

The following timing equations characterize the performance of the CM-2.[4]

[4] Throughout this chapter, all times are in microseconds unless noted otherwise.

Operator	Time	r = 1	Comments
B = S	3 + 3r	6	
B \$= B	3 + 3r	6	
B \$\$ B	3 + 3r	6	
where (B)	8 + 2r	10	
S = [S]P	16	16	
[S]P = S	16	16	
P = S	3 + 15r	18	
P += S	3 + 28r	31	
P += P	3 + 28r	31	
P[P] = P	11 + 60r	71	
P = P[P]	11 + 60r	71	
P == S	18 + 67r	85	Same time for <= etc.
(>?= P)	137 + 70r	207	Same time for += etc.
scan_with_or	632 + 56r	688	
scan_with_add	740 + 170r	910	
[P]P = P	2159r	2159	Same time for += etc.
[P]P[P] = P	2159r	2159	Same time for += etc.

18.3 A MODEL OF THE RETRIEVAL TASK

Evaluating the performance of various retrieval algorithms requires constructing a model of the retrieval task. This model will capture several aspects of text databases that are of importance in performance estimates, such as the distribution of query terms and the distribution of word-frequencies.

A *database* consists of a set of documents, each of which is indexed to produce a set of *terms* (usually words or word stems) which, in some cases, will be assigned *weights*. A *query* consists of a set of weighted terms. Retrieval consists of (1) scoring each document in the database, and (2) ranking the documents so as to present the user with those documents having the highest scores. Implementing this process requires a data structure to represent the database, an algorithm for scoring the documents, and an algorithm for ranking the documents once they have been scored. Important considerations in evaluating an implementation include storage requirements, the compute- and I/O- times for the scoring process, and the compute time for the ranking process.

Estimating these performance characteristics requires a model of the database and queries. The model proposed by Stanfill (1988, 1991) will be used. The most important parameters are the size of the database, the number of documents, the number of terms in the database, and the distributions of term frequencies in the database and in the queries. To this end, some specific values for various numerical parameters must be used. The parameters that have been chosen are typical of full text newspaper databases. For actual applications, the prudent engineer will duplicate the simulations using measurements derived from the actual database at hand.

The following definitions are used:

$|D|$			Size of the database in megabytes
R_{docs}			Number of documents per megabyte
N_{docs}	$=$	$|D|R_{docs}$	Total documents in the database
T_i			The i'th term in the lexicon
$f(T_i)$			Frequency of T_i, in occurrences per megabyte
Q			Random variable modeling query-term selection
Z	$=$	$f(Q)$	Distribution of query-term frequencies
$\bar{Z}$	#		Average query-term frequency
N_{terms}			Number of terms per query
N_{ret}			Number of documents returned to the user
L			Number of terms in a randomly chosen document
$\bar{L}$	#		Average number of terms per document

The majority of these parameters can be measured directly. The greatest difficulty comes with f and Q which model, respectively, the frequency of terms in the database and the frequency of terms in queries. Ideally, one would measure f and Q directly from a working database. In practice, these measurements can be difficult to obtain. Fortunately, it is possible to derive a reasonable model of f and Q from first principles plus a set of more easily made measurements (Stanfill [1989] provides the details of the derivation).

For full-text newspaper databases, the following parameters seem reasonable and satisfy all the above constraints. They will be used in the remainder of this chapter, and will be referred to as the *standard variables* of the retrieval parameters.

R_{docs}	200
$\bar{L}$	288
$\bar{Z}$	3
N_{terms}	10
N_{ret}	20

18.4 RANKING

Retrieval consists of (1) scoring documents, and (2) determining which documents received the highest scores. This second step—ranking—will be considered first. Any of the ranking algorithms discussed below may be used in combination with any of the scoring algorithms which will be discussed later. It should be noted that, while scoring is probably the more interesting part of the retrieval process, ranking may be a large portion of the overall compute cost, and ranking algorithms are as deserving of careful design as are scoring algorithms.

The problem may be stated as follows: given a set of N_{docs} integers (scores), identify the N_{ret} highest-ranking examples. The scores may be stored in one of two formats: with either one score per position, or with an array of N_{rows} scores per position. The former case involves a VP ratio

$$r = \left\lceil \frac{N_{docs}}{N_{procs}} \right\rceil$$

The second case, assuming a VP ratio of one is used, requires an array of size

$$N_{rows} = \left\lceil \frac{N_{docs}}{N_{procs}} \right\rceil$$

We will assume there is a fast method for converting a parallel variable at a VP ratio of r to a parallel array having N_{rows} cells per processor. Such a function is, in fact, provided on the Connection Machine; it requires essentially zero time.

18.4.1 System-Supplied Rank Functions

Many parallel computing systems provide a parallel ranking routine which, given a parallel integer, returns 0 for the largest integer, 1 for the next largest, and so forth.[5] This may be used to solve the problem quite directly: one finds the rank of every score, then sends the score and document identifier to the position indexed by its rank. The first N_{ret} values are then read out.

For example:

P_score	83	98	1	38	78	37	17	55
rank	1	0	7	4	2	5	6	3
After send	98	83	78	55	38	37	17	1

The algorithm is as follows:

```
rank_system(dest, P_doc_score, P_doc_id)
    {
    P_rank = rank(P_doc_score);
    [P_rank]P_doc_score = P_doc_score;
    [P_rank]P_doc_id    = P_doc_id;

    for (i = 0; i < N_RET; i++)
        {
        dest[i].score = [i]P_doc_score;
        dest[i].id    = [i]P_doc_id;
        }
    }
```

[5] On the CM-2 this routine takes time 30004r.

This has the skeleton:

```
P = rank()
[P]P = P
[P]P = P
loop(N_RET)
    {
        S = [S]P
        S = [S]P
    }
```

Its timing characteristics are:

Operation	Calls	Time per Call
rank( )	1	$30004r$
[P]P = P	2	$2159r$
S = [S]P	$2N_{ret}$	16
Total		$32N_{ret} + 34322r$

Substituting the VP ratio $r = \left\lceil \dfrac{N_{docs}}{N_{procs}} \right\rceil$ gives a time of:

$$T = 32N_{ret} + 34322 \left\lceil \frac{N_{docs}}{N_{procs}} \right\rceil$$

18.4.2 Iterative Extraction

The system-supplied ranking function does much more work than is really required: it ranks all N_{docs} scores, rather than the N_{ret} which are ultimately used. Since we usually have $N_{ret} \ll N_{docs}$, we may look for an algorithm that avoids this unnecessary work. The algorithm that follows, called *iterative extraction,* accomplishes this by use of the global-maximum (>?=P) operation.

The insight is as follows: if we were only interested in the higest-ranking document, we could determine it by direct application of the global maximum operation. Having done this, we could remove that document from further consideration and repeat the operation. For example, we might start with:

P_score	83	98	1	38	78	37	17	55

We find that the largest score is 98, located at position 1. That score can be eliminated from further consideration by setting it to -1:

P_score	83	−1	1	38	78	37	17	55

On the next iteration, 83 will be the highest-ranking score. The algorithm is as follows:

```
rank_iterative(dest, P_doc_score, P_doc_id)
    {
    for (i = 0; i < N_RET; i++)
        {
        best_score = ( >?= P_doc_score);
        where (P_doc_score == best_score)
                {
                position = ( <?= P_position);
                dest[i].score = [position]P_doc_score;
                dest[i].id    = [position]P_doc_id;
                [position]P_doc_score = −1;
                }
        }
    }
```

This has the skeleton:

```
loop (N_RET)
    {
    S = ( >?= P)
    where (P == S)
        {
        S = ( <?= P)
        S = [S]P
        S = [S]P
        [S]P = S
        }
    }
```

And the timing:

Operation	Calls	Time per Call
(>?= P)	$2N_{ret}$	$137 + 70r$
P == S	N_{ret}	$18 + 67r$
where	N_{ret}	$8 + 2r$
S = [S]P	$2N_{ret}$	16
[S]P = S	N_{ret}	16
Total		$348N_{ret} + 209N_{ret}r$

Substituting the VP ratio $r = \left\lceil \dfrac{N_{docs}}{N_{procs}} \right\rceil$ gives a time of:

$$348N_{ret} + 209N_{ret}\left\lceil \frac{N_{docs}}{N_{procs}} \right\rceil$$

18.4.3 Hutchinson's Algorithm

The following algorithm, due to Jim Hutchinson (1988), improves on iterative extraction. Hutchinson's algorithm starts with an array of

$$N_{rows} = \left\lceil \frac{N_{docs}}{N_{procs}} \right\rceil$$

scores stored in each position, at a VP ratio of 1. For example, with 32 documents, 8 processors, and 4 rows we might have the following data:

P_scores [0]	88	16	87	10	94	04	21	11
P_scores [1]	90	17	83	30	37	39	42	17
P_scores [2]	48	43	10	62	4	12	10	9
P_scores [3]	83	98	1	38	78	37	17	55

We start by extracting the largest score in each row, placing the results in a parallel variable called P_best:

P_scores [0]	88	16	87	10	−1	4	21	11
P_scores [1]	−1	17	83	30	37	39	42	17
P_scores [2]	48	43	10	−1	4	12	10	9
P_scores [3]	83	−1	1	38	78	37	17	55
P_best	94	90	62	98	−1	−1	−1	−1

We then extract the best of the best (in this case 98):

P_scores [0]	88	16	87	10	94	4	21	11
P_scores [1]	−1	17	83	30	37	39	42	17
P_scores [2]	48	43	10	−1	4	12	10	9
P_scores [3]	83	−1	1	38	78	37	17	55
P_best	94	90	62	−1	−1	−1	−1	−1

and replenish it from the appropriate row (3 in this case).

P_scores [0]	88	16	87	10	94	4	21	11
P_scores [1]	−1	17	83	30	37	39	42	17
P_scores [2]	48	43	10	−1	4	12	10	9
P_scores [3]	−1	−1	1	38	78	37	17	55
P_best	94	90	62	83	−1	−1	−1	−1

This is repeated N_{ret} times. The algorithm involves two pieces. First is the basic extraction step:

```
extract_step(P_best_score, P_best_id, P_scores, P_ids, row)
    {
    max_score = (>?= P_scores[row]);
    where (P_scores[row] == max_score)
        {
        position = (<?= P_position);
        [row]P_best_score = [position]P_scores[row];
        [row]P_best_id    = [position]P_scores[row];
        [position]P_scores[row] = −1;
        }
    }
```

This has the skeleton:

```
S = (>?= P)
where (P == S)
    {
    S = (<?= P)
    [S]P = [S]P
    [S]P = [S]P
    [S]P = S
    }
```

We do not have a separate timing figure for [S]P = [S]P, but we note that this could be rewritten as S = [S]P; [S]P = S. The timing is thus as follows:

Operation	Calls	Time per Call
(>?= P)	2	207
where	1	10
S == P	1	85
[S]P = S	3	16
S = [S]P	2	16
Total		589

Given this extraction step subroutine, one can easily implement Hutchinson's algorithm:

```
rank_hutchinson(dest, P_scores, P_ids)
    {
    P_best_score = -1;
    P_best_id    = 0;
    for (row = 0; row < N_ROWS; row++)
        extract_step(P_best_score,  P_best_id,
                       P_scores, P_ids, row);

    for (i = 0; i < N_RET; i++)
        {
        best_of_best = (>?= P_best_score);
        where (P_best_score == best_of_best)
            {
            position       = (<?= P_position);
            dest[i].score = [position]P_scores;
            dest[i].id    = [position]P_ids;
            [positions]P_best_score = -1;
            }
        extract_step(P_best_score,  P_best_id,
                       P_scores, P_ids, row);
        }
    }
```

This has the skeleton:

```
P = S
P = S
loop(N_ROWS)
    extract_step()
loop(N_RET)
    {
    S = (>?= P)
    where(P == S)
        {
        S = (<?= P)
        S = [S]P
        S = [S]P
        [S]P = S
        }
    extract_step()
    }
```

Its timing is as follows:

Operation	Calls	Time per Call
(>?= P)	$2N_{ret}$	207
S==P	N_{ret}	85
where	N_{ret}	10
S=[S]P	$2N_{ret}$	16
[S]P = S	N_{ret}	16
extract_step	$(N_{rows} + N_{ret})$	589
Total		$1149N_{ret} + 589N_{rows}$

Substituting in the value of N_{rows} we arrive at:

$$1149N_{ret} + 589 \left\lceil \frac{N_{docs}}{N_{procs}} \right\rceil$$

18.4.4 Summary

We have examined three ranking algorithms in this section: the system-defined ranking algorithm, iterative extraction, and Hutchinson's algorithm. Their times are as follows:

System Ranking Algorithm $\qquad 32N_{ret} + 34322 \left\lceil \frac{N_{docs}}{N_{procs}} \right\rceil$

Iterative Extraction $\qquad 348N_{ret} + 209N_{ret} \left\lceil \frac{N_{docs}}{N_{procs}} \right\rceil$

Hutchinson's Algorithm $\qquad 1149N_{ret} + 589 \left\lceil \frac{N_{docs}}{N_{procs}} \right\rceil$

For very small versions of N_{ret}, iterative extraction is prefered; for very large values of N_{ret}, the system ranking function is preferred, but in most cases Hutchinson's algorithm will be preferred. Considering various sizes of database, with a 65,536 processor Connection Machine, and our standard database parameters, the following rank times should be observed:

$|D|$	N_{docs}	System	Iterative	Hutchinson
1 GB	200×10^3	138 ms	24 ms	25 ms
10 GB	2×10^6	1064 ms	137 ms	41 ms
100 GB	20×10^6	10503 ms	1286 ms	203 ms
1000 GB	200×10^6	104751 ms	12764 ms	1821 ms

The time required to rank documents is clearly not an obstacle to the implementation of very large IR systems. The remainder of the chapter will be concerned with several methods for representing and scoring documents; these methods will then use one of the algorithms described above (presumably Hutchinson's) for ranking.

18.5 PARALLEL SIGNATURE FILES

The first scoring method to be considered here is based on *parallel signature files*. This file structure has been described by Stanfill and Kahle (1986, 1988, 1990a) and by Pogue and Willet (1987). This method is an adaptation of the overlap encoding techniques discussed in this book.

Overlap encoded signatures are a data structure that may be quickly probed for the presence of a word. A difficulty associated with this data structure is that the probe will sometimes return *present* when it should not. This is variously referred to as a *false hit* or a *false drop*. Adjusting the encoding parameters can reduce, but never eliminate, this possibility. Depending on the probability of such a false hit, signatures may be used in two manners. First, it is possible to use signatures as a filtering mechanism, requiring a two-phase search in which phase 1 probes a signature file for possible matches and phase 2 re-evaluates the query against the full text of documents accepted by phase 1. Second, if the false hit rate is sufficiently low, it is possible to use signatures in a single phase system. We will choose our signature parameters in anticipation of the second case but, if the former is desired, the results shown below may still be applied.

18.5.1 Overlap Encoding

An overlap encoding scheme is defined by the following parameters:

S_{bits}	Size of signature in bits
S_{weight}	Weight of word signatures
S_{words}	Number of words to be inserted in each signature
$H_j(T_i)$	A set of S_{weight} hash functions

Unless otherwise specified, the following values will be used:

S_{bits}	4096
S_{weight}	10
S_{words}	120

A signature is created by allocating S_{bits} bits of memory and initializing them to 0. To insert a word into a signature, each of the hash functions is applied to the word and the corresponding bits set in the signature. The algorithm for doing this is as follows:

```
create_signature(B_signature, words)
    {
    for (i = 0; i < S_BITS; i++)
        B_signature[i] = 0;
    for (i = 0; i < S_WORDS; i++)
        for (j = 0; j < S_WEIGHT; j++)
            B_signature[hash(j, words[i])] = 1;
    }
```

The timing characteristics of this algorithm will not be presented.

18.5.2 Probing a Signature

To test a signature for the presence of a word, all S_{weight} hash functions are applied to it and the corresponding bits of the signature are ANDed together. A result of 0 is interpreted as *absent* and a result of 1 is interpreted as *present*.

```
probe_signature(B_signature, word)
    {
    B_result = 1;
    for (i = 0; i < S_WEIGHT; i++)
        B_result &= B_signature[i];
    return B_result;
    }
```

This has the skeleton:

```
B = S
loop(S_WEIGHT)
    B &= B
```

Its timing is:

Operation	Calls	Time per Call
B = S B &= B	1 S_{weight}	$3 + 3r$ $3 + 3r$
Total Total for $S_{weight} = 10$		$3(1 + S_{weight})(1 + r)$ $33 + 33r$

The VP ratio will be determined by total number of signatures in the database. This, in turn, depends on the number of signatures per document. A randomly chosen document will have the length L, and require

$$\left\lceil \frac{L}{S_{words}} \right\rceil$$

signatures. If the distribution of L is reasonably smooth, then a good approximation for the average number of signatures per document is:

$$\frac{1}{2} + \frac{\bar{L}}{S_{words}}$$

The number of signatures in a database is then

$$\left(\frac{1}{2} + \frac{\bar{L}}{S_{words}} \right) N_{docs}$$

and the VP ratio is

$$\left\lceil \left(\frac{1}{2} + \frac{\bar{L}}{S_{words}} \right) \frac{N_{docs}}{N_{procs}} \right\rceil$$

We can now compute the average time per query term:

$$T = 33 + 33 \left\lceil \left(\frac{1}{2} + \frac{\bar{L}}{S_{words}} \right) \frac{N_{docs}}{N_{procs}} \right\rceil$$

18.5.3 Scoring Algorithms

Documents having more than S_{words} must be split into multiple signatures. These signatures can then be placed in consecutive positions, and flag bits used to indicate the first and last positions for each document. For example, given the following set of documents:

This is the initial document	This is yet another document	Still another document taking yet more space than the others

we might arrive at signatures divided as follows:

B_signature	This is the	initial docu- ment	This is yet	another docu- ment	Still another docu- ment	taking yet more	space than the	others
B_first	1	0	1	0	1	0	0	0
B_last	0	1	0	1	0	0	0	1

We can then determine which documents contain a given word by (1) probing the signatures for that word, and (2) using a `scan_with_or` operation to combine the results across multiple positions. For example, probing for "yet" we obtain the following results:

B_signature	This is the	initial docu-ment	This is yet	another docu-ment	Still another docu-ment	taking yet more	space than the	others
B_first	1	0	1	0	1	0	0	0
B_last	0	1	0	1	0	0	0	1
probe ("yet")	0	0	1	0	0	1	0	0
scan_with_or	0	0	1	1	0	1	1	1

This routine returns either 1 or 0 in the last position of each document, according to whether any of its signatures contained the word. The value at other positions is not meaningful.

The algorithm for this is as follows:

```
probe_document(B_signature, B_first, word)
    {
    B_local = probe_signature(B_signature, word);
    B_result = scan_with_or(B_local, B_first);
    }
```

This is the skeleton:

```
B = probe_signature()
B = scan_with_or()
```

Its timing is:

Operation	Calls	Time per Call
probe_signature	1	$33 + 33r$
scan_with_or	1	$632 + 56r$
Total		$665 + 89r$

Using the above building blocks, it is fairly simple to construct a scoring algorithm. In this algorithm a query consists of an array of *terms*. Each term consists of a word and a weight. The score for a document is the sum of the weights of the words it contains. It may be implemented thus:

```
score_document(B_signature, B_first, terms)
   {
   P_score = 0;
   for (i = 0; i < N_TERMS; i++)
      {
      B_probe = probe_document(B_signature, terms[i].word, B_first)
      where (B_probe)
           P_score += terms[i].weight;
      }
   return P_score;
   }
```

This has the skeleton:

```
P = S
loop (N_TERMS)
   {
   B = probe_document()
   where (B)
      P += S
   }
```

Its timing characteristics are as follows:

Operation	Calls	Time per Call
P = S	1	$3 + 15r$
probe_document	N_{terms}	$665 + 89r$
where	N_{terms}	$8 + 2r$
P += S	N_{terms}	$3 + 28r$
Total		$3 + 676N_{terms} + (15 + 119N_{terms})r$

It is straightforward to implement Boolean queries with the *probe_document* operation outlined above. Times for Boolean queries will be slightly less than times for document scoring. As a simplification, each query term may be: (1) a binary AND operation, (2) a binary OR operation, (3) a NOT operation, or (4) a word. Here is a complete Boolean query engine:

```
query(B_signature, B_first, term)
   {
   arg0 = term-args[0];
   arg1 = term-args[1];
   switch (term-connective)
      {
```

```
case AND:  return    query(B_signature, B_first, arg0) &&
                     query(B_signature, B_first, arg1);
case OR:   return    query(B_signature, B_first, arg0) ||
                     query(B_signature, B_first, arg1);
case NOT:  return  ! query(B_signature, B_first, arg0);
case WORD: return probe_document(B_signature, B_first, arg0);
  }
}
```

The timing characteristics of this routine will not be considered in detail; it should suffice to state that one call to probe_document is required for each word in the query, and that probe_document accounts for essentially all the time consumed by this routine.

18.5.4 An Optimization

The bulk of the time in the signature scoring algorithm is taken up by the probe_document operation. The bulk of the time for that operation, in turn, is taken up by the scan_with_or operation. This operation is performed once per query term. We should then seek to pull the operation outside the query-term loop. This may be done by (1) computing the score for each signature independently, then (2) summing the scores at the end. This is accomlished by the following routine:

```
score_document(B_signature, B_first, terms)
    {
    P_score = 0;
    for (i = 0; i < N_TERMS; i++)
        {
        B_probe = probe_signature(B_signature, term[i].word);
        where (B_probe)
            P_score += term[i].weight;
        }
    P_score = scan_with_add(P_score, B_first);
    return P_score;
    }
```

This has the skeleton:

```
P = S;
loop(N_TERMS)
    {
    B = probe_signature();
    where (B)
        P += S;
    }
P = scan_with_add();
```

The timing characteristics are as follows:

Operation	Calls	Time per Call
P = S	1	$3 + 15r$
probe_signature	N_{terms}	$33 + 33r$
where	N_{terms}	$8 + 2r$
P += S	N_{terms}	$3 + 28r$
scan_with_add	1	$740 + 170r$
Total		$(743 + 44N_{terms}) + (185 + 63N_{terms})r$

Comparing the two scoring algorithms, we see:

Basic Algorithm $(3 + 676N_{terms}) + (15 + 119N_{terms})r$

Improved Algorithm $(743 + 44N_{terms}) + (185 + 63N_{terms})r$

The dominant term in the timing formula, $N_{terms}r$, has been reduced from 119 to 63 so, in the limit, the new algorithm is 1.9 times faster. The question arises, however, as to what this second algorithm is computing. If each query term occurs no more than once per document, then the two algorithms compute the same result. If, however, a query term occurs in more than one signature per document, it will be counted double or even treble, and the score of that document will, as a consequence, be elevated. This might, in fact, be beneficial in that it yields an approximation to document-term weighting. Properly controlled, then, this feature of the algorithm might be beneficial. In any event, it is a simple matter to delete duplicate word occurances before creating the signatures.

18.5.5 Combining Scoring and Ranking

The final step in executing a query is to rank the documents using one of the algorithms noted in the previous section. Those algorithms assumed, however, that every position contained a document score. The signature algorithm leaves us with only the last position of each document containing a score. Use of the previously explained algorithms thus requires some slight adaptation. The simplest such adaptation is to pad the scores out with -1. In addition, if Hutchinson's ranking algorithm is to be used, it will be necessary to force the system to view a parallel score variable at a high VP ratio as an array of scores at a VP ratio of 1; the details are beyond the scope of this discussion.

Taking into account the VP ratio used in signature scoring, the ranking time will be:

$$1149N_{ret} + 589\left[\left(\frac{1}{2} + \frac{\bar{L}}{S_{words}}\right)\frac{N_{docs}}{N_{procs}}\right]$$

Substituting the standard values for N_{terms}, N_{ret}, $\bar{L}$, and S_{words} gives us a scoring time of:

$$1183 + 815\left[2.9\frac{N_{docs}}{N_{procs}}\right]$$

and a ranking time of:

$$22980 + 589\left[2.9\frac{N_{docs}}{N_{procs}}\right]$$

The times for various sizes of database, on a machine with 65,536 processors, are as follows:

$|D|$	N_{docs}	Score	Rank	Total
1 GB	200×10^3	9 ms	28 ms	37 ms
10 GB	2×10^6	74 ms	75 ms	149 ms
100 GB	20×10^6	723 ms	545 ms	1268 ms
1000 GB	200×10^6	7215 ms	5236 ms	12451 ms

18.5.6 Extension to Secondary/Tertiary Storage

It is possible that a signature file will not fit in primary storage, either because it is not possible to configure a machine with sufficient memory or because the expense of doing so is unjustified. In such cases it is necessary that the signature file reside on either secondary or tertiary storage. Such a file can then be searched by repetitively (1) transferring signatures from secondary storage to memory, (2) using the above signature-based algorithms to score the documents, and (3) storing the scores in a parallel array. When the full database has been passed through memory, any of the above ranking algorithms may be invoked to find the best matches. The algorithms described above need to be modified, but the compute time should be unchanged. There will, however, be the added expense of reading the signature file into primary memory. If R_{IO} is the I/O rate in megabytes per second, and c is the signature file compression factor (q.v. below), then the time to read a signature file through memory will be: $\frac{c|D|}{R_{IO}}$ For a fully configured CM-2, $R_{IO} = 200$. The signature parameters we have assumed yield a compression factor $c = 30$ percent (q.v. below). This leads to the following I/O times:

$|D|$	I/O Time
1 GB	2 sec
10 GB	15 sec
100 GB	150 sec
1000 GB	1500 sec

Comparing the I/O time with the compute time, it is clear that this method is I/O bound. As a result, it is necessary to execute multiple queries in one batch in order ot make good use of the compute hardware. This is done by repeatedly (1) transferring signatures from secondary storage to memory; (2) calling the signature-based scoring routine once for each query; and (3) saving the scores produced for each query in a separate array. When all signatures have been read, the ranking algorithm is called once for each query. Again, the algorithms described above need modification, but the basic principles remain unchanged. Given the above parameters, executing batches of 100 queries seems reasonable, yielding the following times:

$|D|$	I/O Time	Search Time (100 queries)	Total
1 GB	2 sec	4 sec	6 sec
10 GB	15 sec	15 sec	30 sec
100 GB	150 sec	127 sec	277 sec
1000 GB	1500 sec	1245 sec	2745 sec

This has not, in practice, proved an attractive search method.

18.5.7 Effects of Signature Parameters

It is guaranteed that, if a word is inserted into a signature, probing for it will return *present*. It is possible, however, for a probe to return *present* for a word that was never inserted. This is referred to variously as a *false drop* or a *false hit*. The probability of a false hit depends on the size of the signature, the number of hash codes, and the number of bits set in the table. The number of bits actually set depends, in turn, on the number of words inserted into the table. The following approximation has proved useful:

$$P_{false} = \left(1 - \left(\frac{S_{bits} - 1}{S_{bits}} \right)^{S_{words} S_{weight}} \right)^{S_{weight}}$$

There is a trade-off between the false hit probability and the amount of space required for the signatures. As more words are put into each signature (i.e., as S_{words} increases), the total number of signatures decreases while the probability of a false hit increases. We will now evaluate the effects of signature parameters on storage requirements and the number of false hits.

A megabyte of text contains, on the average, R_{docs} documents, each of which requires an average of $\frac{1}{2} + \frac{L}{S_{words}}$ signatures. Each signature, in turn, requires $\frac{S_{bits}}{8}$ bytes of storage. Multiplying the two quantities yields the number of bytes of signature space required to represent 1 megabyte of input text. This gives us a compression factor[6] of:

$$\text{compression} = R_{docs}\left(\frac{1}{2} + \frac{\bar{L}}{S_{words}}\right)\frac{S_{bits}}{8} \times 10^{-6}$$

If we multiply the number of signatures per megabyte by P_{false}, we get the expected number of false hits per megabyte:

$$P_{false}R_{docs}\left(\frac{1}{2} + \frac{\bar{L}}{S_{words}}\right)$$

We can now examine how varying S_{words} alters the false hit probability and the compression factor:

S_{words}	Signatures/MB	Compression	P_{false}	False hits/GB
40	1540	77%	4.87×10^{-11}	7.50×10^{-5}
80	820	42%	3.09×10^{-8}	2.50×10^{-2}
120	580	30%	1.12×10^{-6}	6.48×10^{-1}
160	460	24%	1.25×10^{-5}	5.75×10^{0}
200	388	20%	7.41×10^{-5}	2.88×10^{1}
240	340	17%	2.94×10^{-4}	1.00×10^{2}
280	306	16%	8.88×10^{-4}	2.72×10^{2}
320	280	14%	2.20×10^{-3}	6.15×10^{2}

Signature representations may also be tuned by varying S_{bits} and S_{words} in concert. As long as $S_{bits} = kS_{words}$ for some constant k, the false hit rate will remain approximately constant. For example, assuming $S_{weight} = 10$ and $S_{bits} = 34.133S_{words}$, we get the following values for P_{false}:

S_{words}	S_{bits}	P_{false}
80	2731	1.1163×10^{-6}
120	4096	1.1169×10^{-6}
160	5461	1.1172×10^{-6}

Since the computation required to probe a signature is constant regardless of the size of the signature, doubling the signature size will (ideally) halve the number of signatures and consequently halve the amount of computation. The degree to which computational load may be reduced by increasing signature size is limited by its effect on storage requirements. Keeping $S_{bits} = 34.133S_{words}$, $S_{weight} = 10$ and

---

[6] The compression factor is defined as the ratio of the signature file size to the full text.

varying S_{words}, we get the following compression rates:

S_{words}	S_{bits}	c
60	2048	27%
120	4096	30%
240	8192	35%

Clearly, for a fixed k (hence, as described above, a fixed false hit rate), storage costs increase as S_{bits} increases, and it is not feasible to increase S_{bits} indefinitely.

For the database parameters assumed above, it appears that a signature size of 4096 bits is reasonable.

18.5.8 Discussion

The signature-based algorithms described above have a number of advantages and disadvantages. There are two main disadvantages. First, as noted by Salton and Buckley (1988) and by Croft (1988), signatures do not support general document-term weighting, a problem that may produce results inferior to those available with full document-term weighting and normalization. Second, as pointed out by Stone (1987), the I/O time will, for single queries, overwhelm the query time. This limits the practical use of parallel signature files to relatively small databases which fit in memory. Parallel signature files do, however, have several strengths that make them worthy of consideration for some applications. First, constructing and updating a signature file is both fast and simple: to add a document, we simply generate new signatures and append them to the file. This makes them attractive for databases which are frequently modified. Second, the signature algorithms described above make very simple demands on the hardware; all local operations can be easily and efficiently implemented using bit-serial SIMD hardware, and the only nonlocal operation scan_with_add can be efficiently implemented with very simple inter-processor communication methods which scale to very large numbers of processors. Third, signature representations work well with serial storage media such as tape. Given recent progress in the development of high-capacity, high-transfer rate, low-cost tape media, this ability to efficiently utilize serial media may become quite important. In any event, as the cost of random access memory continues to fall, the restriction that the database fit in primary memory may become less important.

18.6 PARALLEL INVERTED FILES

An inverted file is a data structure that, for every word in the source file, contains a list of the documents in which it occurs. For example, the following source file:

This is the initial document	This is yet another document	Still another document taking yet more space than the others

has the following inverted index:

```
another    1   2
document   0   1   2
initial    0
is         0   1
more       2
others     2
space      2
still      2
taking     2
than       2
the        0   2
this       0   1
yet        1   2
```

Each element of an inverted index is called a *posting*, and minimally consists of a document identifier. Postings may contain additional information needed to support the search method being implemented. For example, if document-term weighting is used, each posting must contain a weight. In the event that a term occurs multiple times in a document, the implementer must decided whether to generate a single posting or multiple postings. For IR schemes based on document-term weighting, the former is preferred; for schemes based on proximity operations, the latter is most useful.

The two inverted file algorithms described in this chapter differ in (1) how they store and represent postings, and (2) how they process postings.

18.6.1 Data Structure

The parallel inverted file structure proposed by Stanfill, Thau, and Waltz (1989) is a straightforward adaptation of the conventional serial inverted file structure. A parallel inverted file is a parallel array of postings such that the postings for a given word occupy contiguous positions within a contiguous series of rows, plus an index structure indicating the start row, end row, start position, and end position of the block of postings for each word. For example, given the database and inverted file shown above, the following parallel inverted file would result:

Postings			
1	2	0	1
2	0	0	1
2	2	2	2
2	2	0	2
0	1	1	2

Index				
Word	**First Row**	**First Position**	**Last Row**	**Last Position**
another	0	0	0	1
document	0	2	1	0
initial	1	1	1	1
is	1	2	1	3
more	2	0	2	0
others	2	1	2	1
space	2	2	2	2
still	2	3	2	3
taking	3	0	3	0
than	3	1	3	1
the	3	2	3	3
this	4	0	4	1
yet	4	2	4	3

In order to estimate the performance of algorithms using this representation, it is necessary to know how many rows of postings need to be processed. The following discussion uses these symbols:

P_i The number of postings for term T_i

R_i The number of rows in which postings for T_i occur

$\overline{R}$ The average number of rows per query term

(r, p) A row-position pair

Assume the first posting for term T_i is stored starting at (r, p). The last posting for T_i will then be stored at

$$\left(r + \left[\frac{p + P_i - 1}{N_{procs}}\right], (p + P_i - 1) \bmod N_{procs}\right)$$

and the number of rows occupied by T_i will be

$$\left[\frac{p + P_i - 1}{N_{procs}}\right] + 1$$

Assuming p is uniformly distributed between 0 and $N_{procs}-1$, the expected value of this expression is

$$\frac{P_i}{N_{procs}} + 1$$

From our frequency distribution model we know T_i occurs $f(T_i)$ times per megabyte, so $P_i = |D| f(T_i)$. This gives us:

$$R_i = \frac{|D| f(T_i)}{N_{procs}} + 1$$

Taking into account the random selection of query terms (the random variable Q), we get a formula for the average number of rows per query-term:

$$\bar{R} = E\left(\frac{|D| f(Q)}{N_{procs}} + 1\right)$$

Also from the distribution model, $f(Q) = Z$, and $E(f(Q)) = \bar{Z}$. This gives us:

$$\bar{R} = \frac{|D| \bar{Z}}{N_{procs}} + 1$$

18.6.2 The Scoring Algorithm

The scoring algorithm for parallel inverted files involves using both left- and right-indexing to increment a score accumulator. We start by creating an array of score registers, such as is used by Hutchinson's ranking algorithm. Each document is assigned a row and a position within that row. For example, document i might be mapped to row $i \bmod N_{procs}$, position $\left[\frac{i}{N_{procs}}\right]$. Each posting is then modified so that, rather than containing a document identifier, it contains the row and position to which it will be sent. The Send with add operation is then used to add a weight to the score accumulator. The algorithm is as follows:

```
score_term(P_scores, P_postings, term)
  {
  for (row = term.start_row; row <= term.end_row; row++)
    {
    if (row == term.start_row)
       start_position = term.start_position;
    else
       start_position = 0;
    if (row == term.end_row)
       end_position = term.end_position;
    else
       end_position = N_PROCS-1;
```

```
where ((start_position <= P_position) &&
        (P_position <= end_position))
    {
    P_dest_pos = P_postings[row].dest_pos;
    P_dest_row = P_postings[row].dest_row;
    [P_dest_pos]P_scores[P_dest_row] += term.weight;
    }
  }
}
```

The inner loop of this algorithm will be executed, on the average, $\bar{R}$ times. This yields the following skeleton:

```
loop (R_BAR)
   where ((S = P) && (P = S)) /* Also 1 B && B operation */
      [P]P[P] += S
```

This has the following timing characteristics:

Operation	Calls	Time per Call
S <= P	$2\bar{R}$	85
B && B	$\bar{R}$	6
where	$\bar{R}$	10
[P]P[P] += S	$\bar{R}$	2159
Total		$2345\bar{R}$

Taking into account the value of $\bar{R}$ yields the following time per query term:

$$2345\left(1 + \frac{|D|\bar{Z}}{N_{procs}}\right)$$

Substituting our standard value for $\bar{Z}$, we get times for a 65,536 processor CM-2. Times for scoring 10 terms and for ranking are also included. Finally, the total retrieval time for a 10-term query is shown.

$|D|$	Time	10 Terms	Rank	Total
1 GB	2 ms	25 ms	25 ms	50 ms
10 GB	3 ms	34 ms	41 ms	75 ms
100 GB	13 ms	131 ms	203 ms	334 ms
1000 GB	110 ms	1097 ms	1821 ms	2918 ms

18.6.3 Document Term Weighting

Up to now, the algorithms we have discussed support only binary document models, in which the only information encoded in the database is whether a given term appears in a document or not. The parallel inverted file structure can also support document term weighting, in which each posting incorporates a weighting factor; this weighting factor measures the strength of usage of a term within the document. The following variant on the query execution algorithm is then used:

```
score_weighted_term(P_scores, P_postings, term)
  {
  for (row = term.start_row; row = term.end_row; row++)
    {
    if (row == term.start_row)
       start_position = term.start_position;
    else
       start_position = 0;
    if (row == term.end_row)
       end_position = term.end_position;
    else
       end_position = N_PROCS-1;
    where ((start_position = P_position) &&
           (P_position = end_position))
       {
       P_dest_pos = P_postings[row].dest_pos;
       P_dest_row = P_postings[row].dest_row;
       P_weight = term.weight * P_postings[row].weight;
       [P_dest_pos]P_scores[P_dest_row] += P_weight;
       }
    }
  }
```

This algorithm requires only slightly more time than the unweighted version.

18.7 PARTITIONED POSTING FILES

The parallel posting file algorithm contains a [P]P[P] += S operation in the inner loop. This operation is rather slow, and we would like to find a method which eliminates it. The following algorithm, based on a data structure called a *partitioned posting file* proposed by Stanfill (1990b, 1991), uses a P[P] += S operation instead. The basic idea is to put the postings in the same position as the mailbox to which they will ultimately be sent.

This section will use the following new symbols:

$$F \qquad \text{Partitioning factor, in rows per partition}$$
$$NP_i \qquad \text{The number of partitions for term } T_i$$
$$\overline{NP} \qquad \text{The average number of partitions per query term}$$

For example, we might have the following set of documents (repeated from the section just above):

This is the initial document	This is yet another document than the others	Still another document taking yet more space

Suppose, on a 2-processor machine, we assign documents 0 and 1 to position 0, and document 2 to position 1. Postings would be assigned as follows:

another	1	another	2
document	0	document	2
document	1	more	2
initial	0	others	2
is	0	space	2
is	1	still	2
the	0	taking	2
this	0	than	2
this	1	the	2
yet	1	yet	2

In the example above, note that the two postings of *another* occur in a single row, whereas the two postings of *the* occur in two rows that are not even adjacent. As one progresses through the lexicon one will discover that this *skewing* effect increases without bound. We control skewing by dividing the rows of the posting file into fixed-size *partitions*, and requiring that all words in one partition are $\leq$ the words in the next partition. We will use the symbol F to stand for the partitioning factor, in rows per partition. In the example just above, if we blindly divide the postings into four-row partitions, the following will result:

another	1	another	2
document	0	document	2
document	1	more	2
initial	0	others	2
is	0	space	2
is	1	still	2
the	0	taking	2
this	0	than	2
this	1	the	2
yet	1	yet	2

This partitioning is illegal because partition 0 contains a word (*others*) which comes lexically after a word from partition 1 (*is*). To produce a legal partitioning, some of the postings must be moved to different rows. For example:

another	1	another	2
document	0	document	2
document	1		
initial	0		
is	0	more	2
is	1	others	2
		space	2
		still	2
the	0	taking	2
this	0	than	2
this	1	the	2
yet	1	yet	2

The partitioning constraint forces us to periodically introduce empty space into the file in order to keep skewing within bounds. Analytic results are not available, but results reported by Stanfill (1990b) suggest that this approach is successful. In the remainder of this section we will assume that, for "reasonable" values of F, the postings for term T_i may be found in an average of

$$NP_i = 1 + \frac{P_i}{FN_{procs}}$$

partitions. Using the same reasoning as in the previous section, we find that the average number of partitions per query term will be:

$$\overline{NP} = 1 + \frac{|D|\overline{Z}}{FN_{procs}}$$

In the examples that follow, we will use $F = 4$.[7]

We now compress the posting file by the following method. First, we note that we do not need to store the full document identifier; we only need a row number which will allow us to address a score accumulator. In this example, document 0 maps to row 0, position 0; document 1 maps to row 1, position 0; and document 2 maps to row 0, position 1. This gives us:

another	1	another	0
document	0	document	0
document	1		
initial	0		
is	0	more	0
is	1	others	0
		space	0
		still	0
the	0	taking	0
this	0	than	0
this	1	the	0
yet	1	yet	0

Next, we assign a unique *tag* to each word within a partition. For example, partition 0 contains the words "another," "document," and "initial"; these are assigned tags 0, 1, and 2 respectively. This second compression yields:

[7] The actual CM-2 implementation employs a processing model in which the machine is viewed as 2048 32-bit processors. In this context, $F = 128$, $N_{procs} = 2048$, and all operations are 32 times faster. We have described the implementation as if $F = 4$ and $N_{procs} = 65536$ in order to avoid complicating the presentation.

0	1	0	0
1	0	1	0
1	1		
2	0		
0	0	1	0
0	1	2	0
		3	0
		4	0
2	0	0	0
3	0	1	0
3	1	2	0
4	1	4	0

Once we have partitioned the posting file, we construct an index file which gives the first and last partition for each word, plus its tag. In the example above, this index file is as follows:

Word	First Partition	Last Partition	Tag
another	0	0	0
document	0	0	1
initial	0	0	2
is	1	1	0
more	1	1	1
others	1	1	2
space	1	1	3
still	1	1	4
taking	2	2	0
than	2	2	1
the	2	2	2
this	2	2	3
yet	2	2	4

18.7.1 Scoring Algorithm

Processing the postings for a single query term involves scanning the partitions containing that term and, when instances of that term are found, incrementing a score accumulator.

```
score_term(P_score_array, P_partitions, term)
   {
   for(i = term.first; i = term.last; i++)
      for (j = 0; j < F; j++)
```

```
where (P_partitions[i][j].tag == term.word)
    {
    P_dest_row = P_partitions[i][j].dest_row;
    P_score_array[dest_row] += term.score;
    }
}
```

The average number of partitions to be processed is, by definition, $\overline{NP}$. This gives us the number of iterations for the outer loop. We do not have a distinct timing figure for the P[P] += S operation, but we do have timings for the equivalent sequence P = P[P]; P += S; P[P] = P.

We thus end up with the following skeleton:

```
loop (NP_BAR)
    loop (V)
        where (P == S)
            {
            P = P[P]
            P += S
            P[P] = P
            }
```

Its timing characteristics are:

Operation	Calls	Time per Call
where	$F\overline{NP}$	10
P = P[P]	$F\overline{NP}$	71
P += S	$F\overline{NP}$	31
P[P] = P	$F\overline{NP}$	71
Total		183 $F\overline{NP}$

Taking into account the formula presented above for $\overline{NP}$ yields the following time estimate:

$$183F\left(1 + \frac{|D|\overline{Z}}{FN_{procs}}\right)$$

Substituting our standard values for $\overline{Z}$ and F, we get the times for a 65,536 processor CM-2. Times to score 10 terms and to rank the document are also included. Finally, the total time is given.

$\lvert D \rvert$	Time	10 terms	Rank	Total
1 GB	1 ms	7 ms	25 ms	32 ms
10 GB	1 ms	8 ms	203 ms	219 ms
100 GB	2 ms	16 ms	203 ms	219 ms
1000 GB	9 ms	91 ms	1821 ms	1921 ms

As was the case with the parallel inverted file representation, document term weighting can be supported by this representation; the modification to the data structures and scoring algorithm is similar.

18.8 SECONDARY STORAGE

One major advantage of inverted files is that it is possible to query them without loading the entire file into memory. The algorithms shown above have assumed that the section of the file required to process a given query are already in memory. While a full discussion of the evolving field of I/O systems for parallel computing is beyond the scope of this paper, a brief presentation is in order. In the final analysis, most of what is known about I/O systems with large numbers of disks (e.g. mainframe computers) will probably hold true for parallel systems.

This discussion is oriented towards the partitioned posting file representation. For this algorithm, the disk system is called on to simply read partitions into memory.

18.8.1 Single-Transfer I/O on Disk Arrays

I/O systems for parallel computers are typically built from large arrays of simple disks. For example, the CM-2 supports a disk array called the Data Vault™ which contains 32 data disk plus 8 ECC disks.[8] It may be thought of as a single disk drive with an average latency of 200 milliseconds and a transfer rate of 25 MB/second. Up to 8 Data Vaults may be simultaneously active, yielding a transfer rate of up to 200 MB/second. This access method achieves very high transfer rates, but does not yield many I/O's per second; this can be crippling for all but the very largest databases. Consider, for example, a 64K processor Connection Machine with 8 disk arrays operating in single transfer mode. Assume we are using the partitioned posting file representation, and that each posting requires 4 bytes of storage. The storage required by each partition is then $4FN_{procs}$.

The average query-term requires $\overline{NP}$ partitions to be loaded. These partitions may be contiguously stored on disk, so the entire group of partitions may be trans-

---

[8] Data Vault is a trademark of Thinking Machines Corporation

ferred in a single operation. The time is then:

$$N_{terms}\left(T_{seek} + \frac{4FN_{procs}\left(1 + \frac{|D|\bar{Z}}{FN_{procs}}\right)}{R_{IO}}\right)$$

Given a seek time of 200 milliseconds and a transfer rate of 200 M-B/second, plus our other standard assumptions, the following per-term times will result:

$|D|$	Seek	Transfer	Score
1 GB	200 ms	5 ms	1 ms
10 GB	200 ms	5 ms	1 ms
100 GB	200 ms	11 ms	2 ms
1000 GB	200 ms	65 ms	9 ms

Under these circumstances, the system is severely seek-bound for all but the very largest databases.

18.8.2 Independent Disk Access

Fortunately, the disk arrays contain buried in them the possibility of solving the problem. Each Data Vault has 32 disks embedded in it; a system with 8 disk arrays thus has a total of 256 disks. It is possible to access these disks independently. Under this I/O model, each disk transfers a block of data into the memories of all processors. The latency is stil 200 milliseconds, but 256 blocks of data will be transferred rather than 1. This has the capability of greatly reducing the impact of seek times on system performance.

At this point in time, independent disk access methods for parallel computers are still in development; considerable work is required to determine their likely performance in the context of information retrieval. Stanfill and Thau (1991) have arrived at some preliminary results.

18.9 SUMMARY

The basic algorithmic issues associated with implementing information retrieval systems on databases of up to 1000 GB may be considered solved at this point in time.

The largest difficulty remaining in the implementation of parallel inverted file algorithms remains the I/O system. Disk arrays, operating in single-transfer mode, do not provide a sufficiently large number of I/O's per second to match available processing speeds until database sizes approach a thousand Gigabytes or more. Multi-transfer I/O systems have the potential to solve this problem, but are not yet available for data parallel computers. At this point, parallel inverted file algorithms are restricted to databases which either fit in primary memory or are large enough that the high latency time is less of an issue. However, these problems are very likely to find solution in the next few years.

It should be clear at this point that the engineering and algorithmic issues involved in building large-scale Information Retrieval systems are well on their way to solution and, over the next decade, we can reasonably look forward to interactive access to text databases, no matter how large they may be.

REFERENCES

CROFT, B. (1988). Implementing Ranking Strategies Using Text Signatures. *ACM Transactions on Office Information Systems, 6*(1), 42–62.

HILLIS, D. (1985) *The Connection Machine,* Cambridge, MA: MIT Press.

HILLIS, D. & and STEELE, G. (1986). Data Parallel Algorithms. *Communications of the ACM, 29*(12), 1170-1183.

HUTCHINSON, J. (1988). Personal Communications.

POGUE, C. & WILLETT, P. (1987). Use of Text Signatures for Document Retrieval in a Highly Parallel Environment. *Parallel Computing, 4,* 259–268.

SALTON, G. & BUCKLEY, C. (1988). Parallel Text Search Methods. *Communications of the ACM, 31*(2), 202–215.

STANFILL, C. & KAHLE, B. (1986). Parallel Free-Text Search on the Connection Machine System. *Communications of the ACM, 29*(12), 1229–1239.

STANFILL, C. (1988a). Parallel Computing for Information Retrieval: Recent Developments. Technical Report DR88-1. Cambridge, MA: Thinking Machines Corporationl

STANFILL, C., THAU, R. & WALTZ, D. (1989). A Parallel Indexed Algorithm for Information Retrieval. Paper Presented at the International Conference on Research and Development in Information Retrieval. Cambridge, MA.

STANFILL, C. (1990a). Information Retrieval Using Parallel Signature Files. *IEEE Data Engineering Bulletin, 13*(1), 33–40.

STANFILL, C. (1990b). Partitioned Posting Files: a Parallel Inverted File Structure for Information Retrieval. Paper presented at the International Conference on Research and Development in Information Retrieval. Brussels, Belgium.

STANFILL, C. & THAU, R. (1991). Information Retrieval on the Connection Machine: 1 to 8192 Gigabytes. *Information Processing and Management, 27*(4), 285–310.

STONE, H. (1987). Parallel Querying of Large Databases: a Case Study. *Computer, 20*(10), 11–21.

Thinking Machines Corporation. (1987). Connection Machine model CM-2 technical specifications. Cambridge, MA: Thinking Machines Corporation.

Thinking Machines Corporation. (1990). C* Programming Guide. Cambridge, MA: Thinking Machines Corporation.

Index

498